D0812612

LIBRARY
STAMFORD BRANCH
UNIVERSITY OF CONNECTICUT

PUERTO RICO

*Freedom
and Power
in the
Caribbean*

PUERTO RICO

Freedom
and Power
in the
Caribbean

Gordon K. Lewis

1963

New York

LIBRARY
STAMFORD BRANCH
UNIVERSITY OF CONNECTICUT

F
1958
L4

All Rights Reserved
Copyright © 1963 by
GORDON K. LEWIS

Published by MR Press
333 Sixth Avenue
New York 14, N. Y.

Manufactured in the United States of America
Library of Congress catalog card number 63-20065

For

PILAR BARBOSA DE ROSARIO

to
whose affectionate
hospitality
and
vivacious political
enthusiasm
I owe my
apprenticeship in the
understanding of
Puerto Rican life
and politics

5/75

Preface

THIS book seeks basically to do a number of things, all of them necessarily related inextricably to each other. First, it is an extensive examination of the general experience of Puerto Rican life and thought in all of its manifold and rich variety. Secondly, it seeks to place that experience within the larger framework of the Pan-Caribbean world, a peculiarly neeeded task in the light of the notorious fact that most books published on the island society, having been composed in the main by Americans, have been too easily tempted to see it as a tropical terminus of the American way of life rather than as a threshold to the wider Caribbean and Middle American worlds.* Thirdly, the volume, by the very nature of the ideological presuppositions on which it is based, is an essay on Puerto Rico as a continuing neo-colonial society, and therefore on the particular character of the United States as a continuing neo-colonial power within the Caribbean region. Fourthly, and finally, Puerto Rico is here viewed as a prototype, in one way, of the imposing array of the new problems stemming from the mutual confrontation of the developed and the underdeveloped societies in the modern world.

None of these varied aspects, of course, can in any proper sense be treated separately, for they hang together as integral components of the total Puerto Rican socio-cultural picture. It is indeed one of the purposes of the book to counteract, as best it may, the academic specialization which has hitherto confined the scholastic analysis of the island to the grievous limitations of the specialist academic mind coming out of the "research" industry of American universities. One consequence of that fact has been that the society and its people only too frequently have been seen from the perspective of absentee scholarship, as evil in its own way as absentee economic and political control, and not from the perspective of the Creole culture. The *risorgi-*

---

* In order to avoid any confusion the terms *America* and *Americans* are used throughout this book as meaning, respectively, the United States and citizens of the United States.

mento of radical nationalism in the Caribbean, as elsewhere, promises finally to redress that imbalance. Dr. Eric Williams' recent volume on the *History of the People of Trinidad and Tobago* is a pioneer work in this new task of Creole scholarship, while recent books like Daniel Guérin's *The West Indies and Their Future* and Katrin Norris' *Jamaica: The Search for an Identity* are welcome evidence that the European socialist tradition is beginning to look at the Caribbean culture with refreshingly perceptive and sympathetic vision. It is hoped that this volume will help further that movement with particular reference to Puerto Rico as the meeting ground of the Hispano-American colonial civilization.

It must of course always seem an essay in intellectual impertinence for any outsider, however personally sympathetic to local pride and prejudice, to set himself such a task as this, even perhaps merely to compose a book at all on his host society. I must therefore crave pardon of all those friends and acquaintances, both Puerto Ricans and "continentals," who over the years have helped me, sometimes consciously, sometimes only indirectly, toward an understanding of the island life and manners. They are far too numerous to list fully. Yet it would be ingratitude not to mention at least some of them: Robert Anderson, John Augelli, Chancellor Jaime Benítez, Severo Colberg, Héctor Estades, Eugenio Fernández-Méndez, Antonio González, Manuel Maldonado Denis, Robert Manners, Herbert Marty, Thomas Mathews, Richard Morse, Pedro Muñoz-Amato, Milton Pabon, Lewis Richardson, Charles Rosario, Beate Salz, William Sinz, Howard Stanton, Alfred Thorne, José Arsenio Torres, Charles Toth, José Vega, Arthur Vidich, Alvin Wartel, and Henry Wells. Few of them, I imagine, will agree altogether with the nature of my argument. Some of them will be alarmed. All of them, I hope, will be excited.

There are two persons who merit special mention. They are the Governor himself, *don* Luis Muñoz Marín, and *doña* Pilar Barbosa de Rosario. Of the first it is enough to say that no one can have come into close touch with him without feeling the remarkable quality of his personality, his essential humanism, his quick humor, his sure grasp of both the American and Puerto Rican folkways, not least of all his statesmanship deserving, perhaps, of a wider stage than that of a tiny Antillean society. Any book that seeks to say something worthwhile about Puerto Rico, even if it disagrees with the Governor's public policy, must owe a special meed of praise to him; and I offer it here with pleasure. To *doña* Pilar Barbosa de Rosario I owe so much that I have taken the liberty of dedicating the book to her. It goes without saying that both of these Puerto Ricans, embodying as they do in their names the twin leading political family traditions of the island, will disagree in many fundamental senses with what I have to say. But they will disagree, one may be sure, with mannered pleasure, for both are lively spirits for whom intellectual controversy, and not its vulgar substitute, political disputatiousness, is the very lifeblood of their existence.

To the University of Puerto Rico I owe a large debt for its willingness to relieve me, in substantial measure, of teaching duties in order to concentrate more fully upon research and writing. Ever since, indeed, Pedro Muñoz-Amato, as the then Dean of the College of Social Sciences, generously invited me to come to the island in the long ago summer of 1949 and later, in 1954, to join the faculty permanently, the University administrative officialdom has been far more understanding of the sort of practical help that intellectual production requires than that of most of the continental American universities I have been associated with since coming to the United States. I am grateful to the Fund for Social Analysis, now defunct, for generous financial aid during the research and writing stages. A number of Puerto Rican friends and patrons have been of great help in recruiting assistance to meet the financial costs of publishing the book, among them being Raúl Serrano-Geyls, Enrique Campos del Toro, and Euladio Rodriguez Otero; and in this matter a special vote of thanks must go to Eugenio Fernández-Méndez for his untiring efforts at a critical moment. John Rackliffe has been of incalculable help in the editing work. Connie Sutton and Sam Hurwitz have acted throughout as kind and encouraging friends. Leo Huberman and Paul Sweezy, as publishers, have all along been liberal in every full sense of that now jaded adjective of American life. Finally, I owe more than I can say to my wife Sybil for the tremendous patience and devotion with which she has helped me throughout this long task.

Gordon K. Lewis

Trujillo Alto,
Puerto Rico.
May 22, 1963.

Contents

The Nature of the Problem

WHEN in 1898 the Puerto Rican people passed to the suzerainty of the United States of America, they were confronted with almost unrelieved ignorance on the part of their new masters concerning the island territory and its history; the open contempt of Mr. Dooley's remark that no American had ever heard of the island unless a friend got a job there was not unrepresentative of United States national opinion at the close of the Spanish-American War. The remark would be impossible today, for during the intervening years the island and its people have made a tremendous impact upon the American imagination.

The incorporation of the new territorial acquisition into the federal political scheme, dating from 1900, has created a vast complex of relationships. On the one side, Americans have become aware of a Puerto Rican "problem" as they have experienced, especially since the end of World War II, a new wave of mass immigration, this time not of European aliens but of fellow citizens from the island ward in the Caribbean. The phenomenon has been all the more poignant because America had almost forgotten, since Congress in 1924 had put an end to unrestricted immigration, the characteristic problems involved in acculturating the stranger at the gate which had figured so largely in national debate before that time. The Puerto Rican migrant has, moreover, brought with him his own peculiar brand of drama, for he has come to the continent not by way of the old mid-Atlantic passage, but by way of the cheap nonstop flights between his island home and New York that began after 1943 as a result of his own local government's struggle with the Civil Aeronautics Board to secure for him and his family adequate and reliable air transport at rates that he could afford to pay.

On the other side, Puerto Ricans have seen their migration pattern as the latest illustration of America's great historic reputation as refuge for the oppressed and land of promise for the ambitious. Like imperial Spain before the transfer of power, America may have exhibited features of colonialist rule; but for the average Puerto Rican she has offered advantages, including full freedom of movement to the metropolitan society, that Spain never offered. It is at least symptomatic that since 1900 there has been in the island no political movement for a return to Spanish rule which can compare, for example, with the preoccupation elsewhere in the Caribbean of British Guianese with the dream of a "continental destiny" linking them to the Southern American republics, or of certain sections of the population of British Honduras with the dream of uniting with the Middle American ethnic stream by means of incorporation with the neighboring state of Guatemala. There has been nothing to equal the readiness of the military reactionary groups of Santo Domingo in 1861 to take the opportunity of American preoccupation with the Civil War to hand back that newly emancipated colony to Spain. United States rule may have meant at times that Puerto Ricans could be scourged with whips; but Spanish rule had meant, far worse, that they could be driven with scorpions.

Even so, for Puerto Ricans as for other migrant groups before them, the exodus to the United States has brought them face to face with the massive gulf that separates the American dream from the American reality. As they have settled down to create their own "little America" in the slum ghettos of Harlem and elsewhere, they have been faced with gathering hostility. That they are responsible for the grim housing shortage in New York has taken on since 1945 almost the status of a popular belief. It is argued against them that they will never become fully Americanized because of their different cultural background, their language, their tendency to congregate into ghetto districts. Their living habits, shaped inevitably by the public style of life in an overcrowded tropical economy, are "different" and therefore considered somehow inferior. They are blamed by the more irresponsible city press for the growth of juvenile gangsterism—so much so that, as the leading San Juan newspaper has noted, they have been blamed for all the ills of the metropolis with the single exception of the prevalence of rats.[1] * They are subjected to the ugly pressures of race prejudice, for only too often the Puerto Rican who regards himself at home as "white" rapidly discovers to his horror that the American scheme of ethnic identification classifies him as Negro; and his own fatal ambiguity in relation to the color problem receives a new emphasis by the shame and degradation that he experiences. It is true that so far there is little evidence of a return on the part of majority America to the organized anti-immigrant propaganda of an earlier period; nor has any one voice of national stature emerged

---

* The Notes follow the text, at pages 575-613.

to repeat the vigorous Anglo-Saxon Americanism of Thomas Bailey Aldrich and Henry Pratt Fairchild. At the same time there has been, not merely since the postwar influx of islanders but from the very moment of American occupation, a strong fear among many Americans of Puerto Rican "penetration" and a powerful effort, correspondingly, to keep the islander "in his place" as a second-class citizen.

One aspect of this effort has been the prolonged rearguard struggle, successful for so long, to deny full internal self-government to Puerto Rico; it took Congress some nineteen years to grant citizenship to the island population (1917) and some forty-nine years to institute a local administration based on the popular election of the chief executive (1947). Even when such concessions have been made, they have been not so much the willing grants of imperial imagination (like the retreat of the British Raj from India in 1947) as reluctant acts of a Congressional conservatism; it is significant, for example, that the Jones Act, granting American citizenship to the islanders, was enacted at a time (1917) when America felt obliged to prove her liberalism as against imperial Germany—just as it took the pressure of Axis propaganda against British imperialism to convert Britain's policy towards her Caribbean colonies, as evidenced in the West Indies Royal Commission Report of 1940, into the more liberal policies following 1945. Again, there have been few appointed governors in the Puerto Rican record who have not shared the anti-*criollo* prejudice secreted in the remarks of Governor Arthur Yager before the House Committee on Insular Affairs in 1916 that Puerto Ricans were a "tropical" people lacking the "stamina" and "initiative" to adjust to conditions of American life.[2]

It is not surprising, then, that every so often the Congress is stirred by the demand—the Tydings Bills of 1936 and 1943, for example, and the 1959 resolution of Congressman Moulder—that the Puerto Rican "problem" be solved by granting outright independence to the island. The demand exemplifies both the continuing view among certain sections of American opinion of Puerto Ricans as inferior "Latins" who do not really "belong" in the American family (the most intransigent opponent of the commonwealth status granted to the island in 1952 was a powerful senator from the Deep South) and the essential instability, even now, of the formal constitutional relationship between the territory and the United States. Puerto Ricans, altogether, still await full and complete incorporation into the greater society of the American union.

There is, in real truth, a Puerto Rican problem. But it is a problem originally created not by Puerto Ricans but by Americans. Puerto Ricans were annexed, unasked, by American forces in 1898, in one

of the most grossly incompetently organized naval-military campaigns
in the national history. Until 1917 they were entitled to, but did not
receive, the treatment in terms of colonial trusteeship due them as
wards of the American power; after 1917 they were entitled to, but
similarly did not receive, rights they were justified in claiming as
American citizens. Like all migrant minorities, they have been considered, once they have settled in New York, as the cause of metropolitan ills instead of merely the occasion for the full revelation of
those ills; for after all, the social defects of New York life are the
result not of Puerto Rican immigration but of the dismal failure of
metropolitan municipal government over the last twenty years or so
to plan imaginatively for the proper provision of housing, schooling,
and recreation facilities for its labor force. In part, of course, the
problem is one of political status, for there is a large body of insular
opinion not satisfied that the commonwealth status established by
Congress in 1952 can be a permanent solution; the next statehood
struggle in Congress will certainly be over Puerto Rico. In part it is
one of ethnic and cultural attitudes, for there are many Puerto Ricans
who resent the pose of liberal condescension with which even many
well-meaning Americans view them. There has always been a temptation on the part of the American Protestant mind to look distrustingly
at an island population overwhelmingly Catholic. A leading Puerto
Rican politician in the early days of American occupation who was
otherwise sympathetic to the United States could point to the danger
of "religious carpetbaggers" from the North and cite the case of the
Puerto Rican student who, in passing through Valparaiso, Indiana,
heard a Protestant minister castigating Catholic Puerto Rico on the
fragile basis of a book entitled *Down in Porto Rico*;[3] and American
reaction to the intrusion of the Puerto Rican Catholic hierarchy
into local island politics in 1960 suggests that the hostility is by no
means dead. Nor are many Puerto Ricans yet satisfied that the American conviction of national superiority, however attenuated it may be
by the persuasive atmosphere of the democratic ethic, is still not the
underlying assumption of most Americans to the island and its people.
The uproar unleashed by Alfred Kazin's article in a national liberal
magazine was suggestive on that score; and the San Juan English-
speaking press is full of angry correspondence chiding Puerto Ricans
for being "ungrateful" for the benefits of American rule and of the
American presence.

Although it may be arguable whether the present political status of
the island has or has not terminated territorial imperialism, there can
be little doubt that there remains a very real cultural imperialism in
the relationship, if only because cultural satellization remains long

in colonial societies even when political satellization has disappeared. From the very beginning, the leading ideas of the insular politics have been copied from America, when they have not been imposed. That is perhaps why no island political leader since 1898 has managed to create a genuinely new, indigenous theory. In each case—Muñoz Rivera, Barbosa, Barceló, Santiago Iglesias, Governor Luis Muñoz Marín today—the "theory" has rarely been more than a selection of those elements of American thought that seem to fit the insular condition. Even the most comic elements of that thought have been taken over by the Puerto Rican admirer; it is enough to read José Benítez's *The United States and the Political Destiny of Puerto Rico* published in 1958 (much of it simply a bald reprinting of official documents, including the Puerto Rican Constitution) to appreciate how the rodomontade of Manifest Destiny can be borrowed for the sake of identifying the island with the notion of the twentieth-century American power as a new Rome conquering an adoring world.

This cultural confusion, in turn, is part of the relentless "Americanization" of almost all facets of the society. The process—as elsewhere in Latin America; for example, the concern of the Mexican intelligentsia with the *pocho* culture of Mexican life—has aroused much resentment and excited discussion among the elite on the island. So, it is possible to find in San Juan, as in Mexico City or Lima or Rio de Janeiro, intellectual circles whose sentiments towards the United States are not unlike those that a cultivated Hellene must have felt for the conquering Roman—sentiments perhaps even more bitter in the Puerto Ricans because they do not have, to compensate for their subjection, the consoling knowledge that their own culture has at least Hellenized the new power. Modern America has not discovered, any more than did classical Rome, the art of reconciling subordinate nations to its rule; nor has it found a way to reconcile the subordination with the democratic content of the American creed. The inescapable moral ambiguity created by all this afflicts not only the sensitive Puerto Rican but also the liberal American; for American imperialism, unlike the British variety, has never really succeeded in developing an abiding sense of national mission overseas. Despite the massive benefits, then, that United States rule has brought to the island, and which the local English language newspapers are never tired of eulogizing, the American resident in Puerto Rico who cherishes the liberal ideal must at times feel, deep in his heart, that he has no right to be there.

This tension, of course, is not as acute as it was in French Algeria or Dutch Indonesia, since for more than half a century the connection with the United States has acquainted the mass of Puerto Rican people with some of the best realities, as well as the worst, of American life. It is true that there has been, and continues to be, a real cultural colonialism, an ideological imperialism, tying Puerto Ricans by chains of silk to the American power. Yet at the same time it would be idle to deny the intellectual emancipation that has come to many Puerto Ricans as a consequence of the American national passion for education. Entire generations of island students have graduated from American universities; indeed, the first Puerto Rican Negro to obtain such a university education was the political leader José Celso Barbosa, who attended the University of Michigan in the 1870's. Since then the trek northward has become an entrenched habit, and all the leading American universities can count strong local chapters in the island; although it is a pity that so far no Puerto Rican has sat down to compose a record of the experience in the manner, from elsewhere in the Caribbean, of Dr. Eric Williams' *A Colonial at Oxford*. No educated Puerto Rican, therefore, is likely to view the United States, in the fashion of the Latin-American intellectual whose training has been in the Hispanic tradition, as no more than an alliance of technical genius and cultural illiteracy. He will know his United States too well for that. In its own turn, the University of Puerto Rico (founded, suggestively enough, in 1903 at the beginning of the American regime, although the demand for a local university goes back as far as the local instructions given to Ramón Power, the first elected deputy from the island to the national Cortes, in 1810) has benefited vastly from the United States scholar and teacher: in 1960, for example, there was a total of at least 95 American continental teachers in a combined faculty of 1116 at the Rio Piedras campus of the main university. The island working classes have also had their share of direct American experience, some of which is returned to the total sum of local knowledge by way of returning migrants. Dr. John Augelli discovered a large percentage of returns among people emigrating to New York from a small *municipio* in the eastern mountain interior of the island in the years following World War II; while a more recent study shows that for the island as a whole there is an astonishing percentage of return: in 1958 some 59,000 persons returned to the island, while a total of 85,000 left it for the mainland. For the first time in the long history of American immigration there is a two-way movement: the working class migrant may decide, after an almost casual decision to make the trip north, to return home instead of remaining permanently. Since the cost of the northward trip today represents about two weeks' pay for the average working islander as against some three months' earnings in the prewar period, it is evident that this is a new phenomenon in the historic migration movement to the promised land.[4] It would be difficult, as a result, to find any small town in the island that does not possess its quota of younger people with stateside experience, or of veterans of American armed services.

The result of this two-way migration, of course, is that while it would be a palpable exaggeration to say that there is no anti-Americanism on the island, at the same time there is little if any widespread hatred of the *norteamericano*. A generation ago, perhaps, the hatred was there, before the local industrial revolution and American economic expansionism began to alleviate mass poverty on the island; certainly the sort of raucous public baiting of individual Americans described in Wenzell Brown's *Dynamite on Our Doorstep*, a novel of the '40s concerned with a period when the virulently anti-Yankee Nationalist Party was in its heyday, suggests that poverty and despair could finally goad into embittered violence even the Puerto Ricans, trained by four centuries of Spanish rule into a habit of uncomplaining submissiveness. The local patriot feels a real pride in the fact that San Juan was a flourishing imperial city a century before Jamestown was founded. But he now no longer wishes to drive the Americans into the sea on that account.

Yet not even the largest optimism could pretend that United States–Puerto Rican relationships have reached their ultimate felicity. The Puerto Rican countryman, the *jíbaro*, goes to the stateside cities; there he rapidly becomes part of the *lumpenproletariat* of the American economic system, successively exploited by the sweatshop employer, the racketeering union using devices like the "sweetheart" contract, the aspiring Tammany politician, the tough police, the organized narcotics syndicate, the city bureaucrat. The entire literature on this topic—from C. Wright Mills's *The Puerto Rican Journey* through such sociological studies as Dr. Elena Padilla's *Up from Puerto Rico* to angry journalistic exposés like Dan Wakefield's *Island in the City*, and culminating in Oscar Handlin's *The Newcomers*—provides exhaustive and depressing documentation of the economic and social enslavement of the latest migrant body in American history. If instead of to a city job the migrant goes to work in the sugar beet areas of Michigan or the truck farms of New Jersey or Florida, he goes into industries still notorious, after a generation of the New Deal, for their brutalized working conditions and their freedom from any effective legislative control. His sole advantage as a Puerto Rican is that he is likely to be better off than, say, his counterpart from the British West Indian islands, since the Office of Migration of his Commonwealth Government, centered in New York, enjoys an enviable record of eager investigation of conditions, and indeed protects the migrant worker in a way that no foreign government in the history of Atlantic migration has ever protected its nationals once they reach American soil.

Even so, that protective action—like individual state action within the federal system—is seriously hampered by the absence of Congressional control. It also has its own internal limitations, for so vital is the migration flow to the north as a safety valve for the low-standard island economy that it is not difficult to believe the charges sometimes made (by Representative Adam Clayton Powell in 1959, for instance) that the Commonwealth Government does not fully advise its citizens of the conditions awaiting them in New York and other cities. Any effort by Washington to curb the flow, by putting Puerto Ricans on the restrictive quota system for example, could have only disastrous consequences, possibly the outbreak of social revolution in the island. That kind of consideration is clearly behind the resistance of Caribbean leadership in the English-speaking islands to the growing demand in Great Britain for parliamentary restrictions upon immigration from British Commonwealth countries into the United Kingdom. Wherever the blame lies, it is at least true, as the Federal Commission on Civil Rights has pointed out, that there are some hundred thousand Puerto Ricans in New York City who cannot speak or understand English, and the statistic certainly casts doubt upon the adequacy of the Commonwealth Government's program of teaching English to prospective migrants. The island worker truly benefits from his freedom of movement within the American economy, but he remains its hewer of wood and drawer of water. He may not hate America as a result, yet he has little reason to love it.

A great deal of lyrical praise has been devoted to a fabulously inexpensive communications system between San Juan and the States that enables continentals (including the tourists) and islanders to "know each other better." But it is hard not to feel that much of the praise rests upon the naive assumption of much American liberalism that "people to people relationships," as the phrase goes, lead to better mutual understandings. The history of islander-continental intercourse hardly bears out the assumption. To begin with, Americans came to the island not as colonizers (it is difficult to colonize in the classic sense an already overcrowded and poverty-stricken land), but as adventuresome individuals, and they retained the missionary complex of the resident outsider, as distinct from the assimilationism of the genuine colonist. At the start there may have been plans for full-scale settlement, rather like Cromwell's plan for the settlement of Jamaica with English yeomen-farmers. But, as in seventeenth-century Jamaica, any such plans were frustrated by the rapid development of a plantation economy of large holdings worked by absentee capitalists; and Americans never came to the island *en masse.*

Nor has the more recent upsurge of tourism brought deeper mutual understanding. For the tourist anywhere is rarely interested in enlarging his mental boundaries; he wants to be entertained, not instructed. Also, the American tourist in Puerto Rico comes from a selective social background not representative of the American people as a whole: in 1957, 54 percent of the flow of tourists into San Juan came from families with incomes of $10,000 or more; only 12 percent had incomes below $5000.[5] Once in Puerto Rico, the tourist rarely strays beyond the ken of the tourist hotels and their organized trips; the night clubs offer him mostly stateside fare; and he has no need to speak anything but English. If he is tempted to read a book about the island he is likely to choose something like Ruth Gruber's *Puerto Rico: Island of Promise,* a journalistic account of change and progress in the island, enhanced by charming illustrations and written in a style of breathless and uncritical enthusiasm.

The paradox speaks for itself: the island middle classes (with the exception of certain professional groups like doctors) rarely seek professional advancement in the States, while people from the American working classes rarely come to the island, so that travelers in both cases come mainly from the opposite poles of their respective social systems. The America that Puerto Rico sees is thus the America of the affluent classes on vacation and of the managerial, professional, and bureaucratic groups represented by resident Americans on the island. The Puerto Rico that America sees is that of the transplanted lower rural and urban groups, distorted and deformed in their collective portrait as they seek to adjust themselves to the terrifying pressures of the American urban jungle. It is small wonder that the two worlds do not as yet fully understand each other.

So far, all this concerns the problem, basically domestic, of America's character as a colonial power. In that sense, the United States record in Puerto Rico falls into a common pattern that includes the Philippines (until 1946), Hawaii (until 1959), the Panama Canal Zone, the United States Virgin Islands, and, since 1945, American Micronesia. But there is a larger, more global perspective in the case of Puerto Rico. Within the last generation the island has been advertised internationally as a model for underdeveloped countries moving from stagnation to growth. The industrialization program of the Commonwealth Government, its now famous Operation Bootstrap, has received international attention as a prime example of the industrial revolution making its way in the hitherto "backward" areas of the

world. It can hardly be regarded, of course, as an example of a positive American colonial policy, since in one way it has been made
possible by the absence of such a policy—the characteristic pattern
in the governance of the American dependencies has been a mixture
of formal political liberty and *laissez-faire* economic drift which leaves
a wide leeway for local experimentation in economic policy. Even so,
the Puerto Rican achievement of transforming a predominantly agricultural economy into a predominantly industrial one, catalogued in
volumes like Harvey Perloff's *Economic Future of Puerto Rico* and
Earl Parker Hanson's *Transformation*, has been remarkable. The factory has replaced the sugar *central* as the basic unit of the economy;
agriculture has yielded to industry its place as the leading income-
earner of the society. The very pace of industrialization has been
impressive; it is doubtful if the annual growth rate has been equaled
anywhere within the general category of underdeveloped economies.
It is clear why the island has become, through the Caribbean Training
Program sponsored jointly by the local government and the United
States International Cooperation Administration, a center for Point
Four students throughout the world, and a visit to the island has
become almost mandatory for planners in all underdeveloped economies from Ghana to Trinidad.

The significance of these economic triumphs for relations between
the United States and the rest of the world is self-evident. While the
central issue of the nineteenth century was the internal distribution
of wealth within the leading Western industrial nations, the central
issue of the twentieth century undoubtedly centers upon the question
of the international distribution of wealth between the rich nations
and the poor emergent nations of Asia, Africa, and Latin America. If
the Puerto Rican experiment can be viewed legitimately as a model
in the solution of that global problem, American leadership may
indeed claim that the experiment is an exportable commodity and
that it does indeed possess, as its more enthusiastic champions assert,
a world significance.

It would be idle to deny the tremendous import, in world affairs, of
such a claim. For, with her tremendous wealth and prodigality, modern America more than any other single power symbolizes the grotesque imbalance of the wealth of nations in the twentieth century.
With 6.5 percent of the total world population within her borders,
she enjoys over 40 percent of the total world income. Her average per
capita income is $2,223, while that of Asia is $27 and that of Africa
$33. The income inequalities are part cause, part result of other
inequalities between the rich and poor nations in every other aspect
of life. There is the malnutrition which prejudices the health of at

least 85 percent of the world's population. There are the killer diseases such as the malaria that presently affects some 300 million people throughout the world. In every vital statistic—infant mortality, life expectancy, diet, the geography of hunger—the "backward" societies live at a still primitive level. The moral quality of life is, in its own turn, stunted for the peoples of those societies, and in many cases the small economic growth that they can achieve is wiped out by an appalling rate of population increase; even in Puerto Rico, where modern methods and attitudes concerning birth control find a receptive audience, there is a real possibility that the population will increase by 50 percent within the next two decades. Nor should sight be lost of the effect of mass poverty and illiteracy upon the political life of such societies, for such conditions rapidly breed political dictatorships; in the Caribbean region itself it is at least suggestive that a comparatively low illiteracy rate (13.4 percent in Puerto Rico) goes hand in hand with democratic stability in government, and a high rate (85 percent in Haiti, 74 percent in the Dominican Republic) has been accompanied by the typical Creole despotisms. The health, wealth, and happiness of the world, clearly enough, are still pretty much the monopoly of the privileged welfare societies of the "Atlantic world."

Such polarizations of wealth and poverty, which would not now be tolerated within the boundaries of the wealthy nations, have been tolerated at the international level chiefly for two reasons: (1) Until only yesterday, the underprivileged peoples lacked both the political machinery and the driving ambition to rid themselves of their discontents; and (2) they have generally received little aid from the progressive forces within the colonial powers. The first handicap is rapidly vanishing as the postwar march towards freedom and nationalism gathers new strength and the new nations increasingly challenge the leadership of the older powers within the United Nations and other international governmental bodies. But the second handicap remains still a massive obstacle. British progressive ideologies like Fabianism, for example, have rarely been excited by international or racial questions; in the original *Fabian Essays* of 1889 there was only a brief mention even of the United States, and Graham Wallas once pointed out that up to 1920 the only Fabian Society publication on international problems was Leonard Woolf's early volume on *International Government*. Moreover, the Fabians' belief in the expert inhibited their developing innovations in colonial policy; that is why Sidney Webb, who was Colonial Secretary in the second Labour Government of 1929, left no mark of his own upon the Colonial Office. It was, again, accident and not policy that made out of Lord Olivier, one of the founding members of the Society, perhaps the most enlightened

Governor that the Crown Colony of Jamaica ever enjoyed. It is true
that in recent years the British Labour Party has made up for that
earlier neglect; but there is little evidence to suggest that the British
electorate is even now willing to make the sacrifices in its living standards that would be demanded if the Labour Party's present plan to
allocate one percent of the national income to colonial and post-
colonial development were to become government policy. Colonial
Development and Welfare schemes, like the Colombo Plan, have
tended to assume that the agricultural raw-materials character of the
colonial and former colonial economies would continue and to concentrate on the modernization of "social overheads" rather than on a
radical transformation of the production relations of these economies
—which would then probably threaten Great Britain's position within
world commercial markets. The Labour Party's imaginative World
Plan for Mutual Aid is still only an aspiration, although its insistence
upon concerted intergovernmental action to fill the gap between rich
and poor lands left by the failure, so far, of international private
interests to invest sufficient funds in any except a few more lucrative
sectors of the underdeveloped countries remains, surely, the proper
insistence for future national policy.

Nor has liberalism in the United States been much more successful.
The New Deal, in its foreign policy, was little more than a continuance of John Hay's "Open Door," and the architects of the New Deal
never rose, any more than American leaders before them, to the
supreme challenge of organizing the development of world resources
as part of an international war on world poverty. The Marshall Plan
was not followed by a similar plan for the non-Western societies, and
non-Western leaders have not been slow to note the undertones of
ethnic discrimination secreted in that failure. The announcement in
1961 of President Kennedy's far-reaching Alliance for Progress as
the first step in implementing the Act of Bogotá promises to give
American leadership a new start, on a hemispheric scale, in this whole
field of endeavor, for in its leading concepts—the relation of economic development to social progress, the need for long-range commitments as distinct from the piecemeal projects of the old technical
assistance programs, the recognition that international economic
institutions appropriate to a Latin-American program must get away
from the fiscal and administrative orthodoxies characteristic of bodies
like the World Bank and the International Monetary Fund, the sentiment, above all else, for an international technical civil service that
will transcend merely national loyalties—it seeks to break new ground
and create new precedents.

It remains to be seen, however, whether the enterprise will be sufficient to meet successfully all the ills of Latin-American society. Its primary emphasis is upon programs—land reform, mass housing developments, extended educational and health services, organization of food reserves, rational control of commodity prices—which, as public works items, may do little to change the basic production patterns of the South American economies and therefore to challenge the extensive grip of United States investment capital throughout the hemisphere. The administrative machinery it proposes, in particular the device of an American single-mission chief within each recipient country who will be accountable to the United States ambassador accredited to the country, raises the possibility that the same tragic involvement of economic aid with the furtherance of United States political goals may be repeated once more on a larger canvas; and the possibility is gravely enhanced by the program's requirement that aid will depend on the readiness of the recipient government to undertake measures of domestic reform—land reform, tax reform, and improved educational facilities—thereby committing the United States to direct intervention in Latin-American domestic affairs. It will be difficult to persuade Latin-American governments, traditionally sensitive to United States penetration, to accept the requirement with any alacrity. It seems clear that a program which contemplates such severe modifications of internal policies and structures could only become palatable to the Latin-American public mind by being made the exclusive property of a genuinely representative hemispheric organization enjoying the full confidence of the region's governments. The failure of the Kennedy "New Frontier" to consult the Organization of American States in the development of its Cuban policy hardly encourages optimism concerning the emergence of such an inter-American system.

For the burgeoning patterns of new relationships between the technologically matured and the technologically backward societies are as much a matter of mutual consultation as of mutual aid. The frame of reference of modern world politics is no longer the "Atlantic community"—that phrase in itself is indeed nothing much more than a Churchillian euphemism for the doctrine of racial superiority in international relations. Fifty years of Europe are no longer better than a cycle of Cathay. That is evident enough from the changing character of the British Commonwealth, for the entry of the Asian members after 1947, followed by the African, symbolized the gradual transformation of the Commonwealth from an empire of power into an area of culture. The entry of the racially pluralist society of Hawaii into the family of American states, in its turn, gave a new fillip to the cause of Puerto Rican statehood within the Union. This changing climate of opinion demands not merely the acceptance of the non-

Western societies into world politics but also—and far more difficult
for the Western educated mind to concede—their acceptance into
world culture as carriers of religious and philosophical systems that
can match, and even historically predate, the accumulated body of
Western thought.

There is much evidence to suggest that this radical readjustment of
attitudes will turn out to be especially painful for the American liberal
mind. Not even Franklin Roosevelt was free of the characteristically
American conviction that revolutions in the "backward" continents
must be seen through and ought perhaps to be modeled on the neo-
democratic prism of the American Revolution. That is why, as President, he could suggest in 1942 that the Indian problem might be
solved if the subcontinent were to federate itself along the lines of the
American Articles of Confederation of 1783. That explains, too,
why, a generation later, the liberal advisers of President Kennedy
have so grievously misread the inner meaning of the Cuban Revolution; they impose upon the Latin-American social scene liberal pre-
sumptions about social change that have their roots in the narrow and
peculiar experience of colonial America. It is perhaps only because
Rooseveltian liberalism in these matters has always been seen against
the convenient foil of Mr. Churchill's archaic romantic imperialism
that its own serious limitations have not been fully perceived. But it is
no more statesmanlike, and certainly no more anthropologically correct, to imagine that the non-Western peoples should reshape themselves as liberal Americans than it is to insist that they should
reconstruct themselves as English gentlemen.

It is within this global framework that the Puerto Rican problem
must be viewed. Obviously, the new nations of Africa and Asia and
Latin America must be called in to redress the balance of the old. It
is the argument of the new Puerto Rico that has been ushered in since
1940 by Governor Muñoz and his Popular Democratic Party that its
own experience constitutes a model of such readjustment, in this case
between the United States and one of its dependent territories. The
argument, as expounded in the immense literature on the claim origi-
nating in San Juan and Washington, consists of three elements. The
first is economic: the experience of Operation Bootstrap shows that
industrialization can be effectively promoted in a "backward" colonial
economy largely bereft of native raw material—promoted, moreover,
by the planned use of the latent energy of its own indigenous population. The second is political–constitutional: American colonialism
has been successfully replaced with a new contractual relationship
which grants the island internal self-government and a new status of

commonwealth "association" with the federal union. This argument is usually accompanied by the assertion that the status sets up a new form of state, a fresh application, as it were, of traditional federalism to new conditions. "What Puerto Rico also suggests," in the words of Governor Muñoz to a Harvard audience, "is that the federalist principle is very much alive, that it is dynamic and not a fixed pattern, and can constantly create new ways of relationships between diverse peoples, quite distinct from the known constitutional forms."[6] The third is cultural: the problem of understanding between peoples of varying socio-cultural patterns is on the way to being solved through cultural intermixing, a kind of culture grafting between Puerto Ricans and Americans. In this argument, Puerto Rico is conceived as a bridgehead wherein may be seen, in the phrase of the Commonwealth Constitution of 1952, the coexistence of the two great cultures of the American hemisphere.

It is altogether a persuasive argument; but it must be said, by way of preliminary statement, that it can only be accepted by the student of the Puerto Rican condition with serious reservations. The breakthrough to an industrializing economy has resulted not so much from bold federal planning as from limited local planning, largely dependent for its fiscal sources upon federal largesse to the island. The official literature emphasizes the postwar rehabilitation programs, but those programs might have failed if accumulated federal expenditures before that period had not established all those costly public services—schools, highways, water and sewage facilities, the basic fabric, indeed of urban life itself—so essential to the establishment of factories in new locations. The largesse has been on a scale—it has been estimated that between 1898 and 1945 the United States Government contributed over five hundred million dollars to the island[7]—that dwarfs the financial aid received during the same period either by the neighboring British islands from Great Britain or by the United States Virgin Islands from Washington; what is more, the largesse has been distributed with an almost careless generosity compared with the cheeseparing "Treasury control" that has accompanied monies received from London by the grant-aided units of the British islands. Indeed, the political genius with which Puerto Rico has managed to become, since 1900, a skilled "lobbyist" in the federal capital, despite the handicaps involved in the denial of direct representation in Congress, has in itself been a major factor in the island's economic growth; one need only compare that record with, say, the federal neglect of a Pacific dependency like American Samoa[8] to be made aware of Puerto Rico's advantageous position.

Yet the use of the term "revolution"—so frequently used in the apologetic literature—to describe the consequences of all this is questionable. For in any sense of Marxist sociology the term implies a radical change, usually undertaken by a progressive social class, in the ownership and direction of the production-means of a society. What has taken place in Puerto Rico is rather an addition to the production-means without any change in the principle of either their private ownership or their use in the service of the profit motive. There is a "new order," patently enough, but in contrast to the "old order" it is new in degree only, not in kind. The official thesis here suffers from the same deficiency as the official dogma of the Democratic Party in the United States—enshrined in the volumes written on the theme by Professor Arthur Schlesinger Jr.—that the New Deal in 1933 ushered in a "new order" to replace the "old order" of Republican America. Under this "new order" there has been a larger social control of business enterprise and possibly the growth of a new sense of public responsibility on the part of the nation's business leadership. But the control, as the record of the independent regulatory commissions shows, has become nominal only, while the spate of recent writing on the psychopathology of the "organization man" in American industry forcibly suggests that a new social consciousness, if it is present, has not so much altered the inborn nature of the business world as merely added an unnatural burden of guilt to the corporate power struggle. Similarly, in Puerto Rico there is little evidence to suggest that the new business groups thrown up by industrialization can offer anything new, either of behavior or philosophy, to that struggle, of which, indeed, they are an integral part.

A similar *caveat* must be entered against the theory of a Puerto Rican cultural and constitutional "revolution." The unsatisfactory character of the cultural relationships between the island and the United States has already been noted; Puerto Ricans are, as it were, still at school in the American classroom. As far as the constitutional relationships are concerned, there has been a real enlargement of internal self-government since 1947, real enough if compared with the earlier near-absolute rule of the United States Navy in Guam and American Samoa and of the United States Army Engineers in the Panama Canal Zone. But the sizeable segments of Puerto Rican opinion that challenge any braver claim about the abolition of colonial status, and the continuing argument on the island as to what its status is and should be, raging as it does as unabated as ever, both suggest the dangers of optimism on this score. The government party of the *Populares* appeals to the "revolution of 1940," the year of its remarkable accession to power in the territorial politics. But, again, this is a party and not a national slogan. To many Puerto Ricans

1940 fails to be a date of national liberation, comparable to 1911 in Mexico or 1947 in India or 1960 in Nigeria. There is no coherent philosophy of the "revolution"; it is worth noting that Governor Muñoz has not felt tempted to indite, as Colonel Nasser has done in the Egyptian case, any such philosophical statement. For both the independence and statehood movements in the island, then, the present constitutional status remains colonialist in character. If, indeed, the present Speaker of the local House of Representatives could bring himself to speak out to American officialdom in the same independent manner as did the separatist Speaker of the old House of Delegates, fifty years ago, in the latter's proud letter to Senator Poindexter in 1913, the *Popular* leader would find himself obliged to repeat the basic argument of that earlier statement on status, that is, that American citizenship for Puerto Ricans could not be worth the having if it did not mean full statehood, for without that guarantee it would convert the islanders into second-class citizens. That, indeed, is how matters have subsequently turned out, and how they remain. That could be seen, plainly enough, in the spirited debate centering around the plebiscite movement of 1962. For the correspondence, preceding the plebiscite, between Governor Muñoz and President Kennedy, was an implicit confession of the failure of the Commonwealth device to assuage the status debate; while the *Popular* sponsorship of various devices calculated to "perfect" the Commonwealth arrangement, some of them requiring amendments of the federal constitution—the right of Puerto Ricans to vote in presidential elections, Puerto Rican veto power over congressional legislation applicable to the island, and so on—seemed to many critics to be red herrings designed to take attention away from the basic issue of sovereignty. It is for all these reasons, and more, that it is Cuba, not Puerto Rico, that has excited the Latin-American world and that promises to become, so to speak, the guiding star of the hitherto repressed Latin-American renaissance.

These reservations, of course, are not aimed at denying credit where credit is due. The record of American munificence in Puerto Rico has not been lost upon the Creole populations of the neighboring islands under European rule. As far back as 1920 an American traveler in the region could report that the working classes of those islands appeared to favor the idea of American annexation in the belief that the American system considered working-class aspirations more generously than did the British, with only a single doubt concerning the "color bar" to qualify the attitude.[9] That sentiment would be less uncritical today, especially since the Caribbean peoples have now been directly exposed to that color bar as Americans have taken it with them to their leased bases throughout the region; but the economic benefits of American expenditures in Puerto Rico are regarded still with much envy and admiration, and the new nationalist reform governments in Trinidad and Jamaica have even copied administrative devices from Puerto Rico—the idea, for example, of an independent corporation, free from civil service restrictions, which concentrates upon finding outside capital investment for incorporation into economic development programs. As far as constitutional development is concerned, however, there is a growing conviction among West Indians in the former British Caribbean islands that when they attained Dominion status in 1962 they finally surpassed Puerto Rico in the struggle for political independence. For despite the curious attempt of Puerto Rican leadership to write off the idea of national independence as an archaic Victorian ideology, the central, cardinal political fact in the Caribbean is, as it is in Asia and Africa, the tremendous resurgence of the nationalist ideology. It is no longer possible to say of the peoples of the region, as did an American liberal observer in 1947, that political independence is quite undesirable for them and that they do not want it.[10] The new nationalism is there in the West Indies political movements led by men like Dr. Cheddi Jagan and Dr. Eric Williams; in the growing public disaffection to the now completely discredited French policy of assimilation, political and cultural, in the French West Indies; in, above all, the Cuban Revolution. The continuation of the American connection may well mean that Puerto Rico will become more and more isolated from that main current of Caribbean life.

Understanding of the Puerto Rican problem has been steadily hampered by the varying and often distorted images of the island and its people presented to the American public. There was, to start with, the romantic image of a rustic, unspoiled paradise, summed up in the observation of one of the first writers (1898) on the newly acquired Caribbean possession that "poverty is almost unknown in Porto Rico, for almost every man owns his own horse and every woman is the possessor of chickens."[11] Conversely, there was the image of a dirty, backward island now come happily into American care; generations of American readers have been regaled with descriptions of the waterfront slums of San Juan composed by visiting newsmen eager to seize upon the sensational and dramatic in the island life. With the growth of the tourist trade in the last decade or so the powerful media of American mass advertising have been recruited to portray the island, in the manner of the bland *New Yorker* magazine advertisements, as an idyllic spot for investment or retirement. Finally, as the tensions of the Cold War have grown, the island society, with its peculiar constitutional status and economic advance, has been set forth as the American answer to world Communism, the "showcase of democratic government, international cooperation and fraternal countenance in the free world."[12]

In addition, sociologists and cultural anthropologists have contributed their share to the world-image of the island, for in spite of its small size, no "underdeveloped" society in the modern world has been so thoroughly examined by the professional academic mind as this one. The examination has spawned a prodigious literature, for which any student of the Puerto Rican condition must be grateful. It collates fact, attitude, opinion in a way quite unknown to nonsociological work; and it provides a happy contrast to the literature of lyrical acclamation, of which, perhaps, Hanson's volume is the outstanding example, for it is not unfair to say of that volume that its author's irrepressible egotism—like some other Cortes on a peak in Puerto Rico—surveys the Puerto Rican "revolution" and acclaims it as his own magnificent discovery.[13]

Valuable as it is, however, the sociological literature is the fruit of the American sociological imagination, and with some notable exceptions, suffers from its characteristic defects: the confusion of profundity with obscurity, a dehumanizing jargon, the effort to explain simple phenomena by complex "explanations," the construction of over-elaborate theoretical structures (mostly owing their inspiration to the work of Talcott Parsons), the depersonalization of the individual (who is viewed as a respondent for questionnaires or as a statistic in tables), the proving of the obvious through the media of formidable instruments of analysis. Thus, to take one example only, it is open to some doubt as to whether the authors of the study of *Social Class and Social Change in Puerto Rico* needed over four hundred pages to prove that most Puerto Ricans view their educational system as the most effective point of leverage and occupational promotion in the total social system or that, again, most of them set over against the new class stratification a traditional conviction of individual moral worth that has little to do with material or social privilege.[14] It would be astonishing, indeed, if that were not so in a society which, somewhat like early Victorian England or twentieth-century France, possesses a set of pre-industrial social values with which it meets the onslaught of rapid industrialization; and, just as in those two larger European societies, the transition in Puerto Rico has been better portrayed in the novel and the play, those, for example, of René Marqués and Enrique Laguerre. The paramount importance of parental aspirations in the later achievement of the child is no more graphically expressed than in the figure of "*Doña*

Gabriela" in René Marqués's play *La Carreta*; while there is no better
discussion on the cultural implications of social modernization in
Puerto Rican society than the agitated conversation between the small-
town doctor and priest described in perhaps Puerto Rico's most
famous novel, Zeno Gandía's *La Charca*, a conversation all the more
illuminating because it was composed by its author some four years
before the transfer to American rule accelerated the process of change.

One corollary of the island's role as an experimental laboratory of
social change is that it perennially suffers from the ubiquitous visiting
consultant, whose reports in turn help to perpetuate some of the misleading images of the insular realities. The consultant comes clothed
with the authority of the expert. He is usually American, composing
an American report; the 1959 report on insular educational problems
by three eminent European educators indeed represented almost the
first attempt on the part of the local leadership to diversify the origin
of its advice. Generally speaking, he has to spend the first three
months of his visit learning, *di grado in grado*, the elementary facts of
local life and the last three months in writing up a report within his
"field," the recommendations of which, if accepted, will shape the
lives of thousands of people. The internal marketing expert who
believes in the absolute virtue of the huge food market; the educa-
tionist who passionately subscribes to the articles of faith of Columbia
University Teachers College; the family planner advocating a more
"democratic" family group which means, in effect, the characteristically American female-dominated household in which the husband
plays the role of the eldest child; the eminent constitutionalist visiting
Puerto Rico, like a modern Plato arriving to aid a latter-day Syracuse
colony in drafting an ideal constitution: they all contribute, with their
respective nostrums, to the social and political indigestion that comes
from an excess of advice, and all suffer from the assumption that the
American Way, in its various applied forms, is the first principle of
civilization. Nor, indeed, do they always do Puerto Rico the courtesy
of careful study: it was possible, in 1962, for a staff member of the
federal House Education and Labor Committee to compose a report
on the teaching of social studies in the local school system after only
four days of discussion with local school officials. This general disease
has been noted by the Middle States Association of Colleges in its
1959 report on the leading insular university. "The University,"
it observed tartly, "has looked up too long or too much to the
norteamericano. There has been a constant flow of advice to the
University. Too, the magnetic draw of the exotic, irenical Caribbean
makes it easy for the University to secure skilled advice and consultation from the Continent. Many people would volunteer—the Uni-

versity pays them." . . . "What is thus recommended," the report concludes of the end-result of this condition, "sometimes reflects the prejudices of an outlook and purpose wholly incompatible with a different humanistic inspiration and philosophical persuasion. Whole anwers do not emerge nor are some of them even appropriate."[15] The field of education itself offers some of the most grievous examples of this phenomenon. But there is hardly a segment of Puerto Rican experience as a whole that could not yield its own further examples.

The society has thus rarely been seen as a composite whole. The specialist monograph, the intensive report on a special problem, are legion. But there is missing the comprehensive work that puts all of the interrelated parts together in the larger picture of the island's life and work. The Brookings Institution attempted the task in its 1930 report *Porto Rico and Its Problems,* but with limited success because of its primary concern with the concept of administrative efficiency within the continuing framework of colonialism. The Columbia University 1949 study *The People of Puerto Rico* was limited by its primary concern with the analysis of cultural subsections of the national experience from an anthropological viewpoint. In addition, too many of the writers on Puerto Rico make value-laden judgments about the political connection with the United States or the economic philosophy of a social-welfare capitalism that possess little logical relationship to the facts they excavate and analyze; so, when the authors of the most comprehensive analysis of class in Puerto Rican society opine that for future policy-making "no major ideological turns are required; no new basic features of the social system need to be developed; no new tricky devices for launching a developmental program need to be contrived," it is clear that they are making a value judgment about both the political status of Puerto Rico and the ideological direction of Puerto Rican public policy-making which is in no way supported by the quantitative mass of material that precedes it and which in any case is hardly consistent with the claim that a scientific methodology is being applied to the problem.[16] Just as in the case of British Africa the work of the British cultural anthropologists, in its ideological presuppositions, has given aid and comfort to the Colonial Office regime, so in the case of Puerto Rico the work of the American sociologist pre-empts the very future of the society by its assumption that the island is to remain within the United States political and economic system. Instead of becoming concerned with how Puerto Ricans might live in the future, sociological investigation passes only too readily to the task, more congenial to the academic mind, of annotating how Puerto Ricans live now. At its worst it becomes an *apologia* for the status quo, at its best a "scientism" based upon the spurious assumption that objectivity about method must involve neutrality about ultimate issues. It is urgent to emphasize all this because unfortunately too much of the literature on Puerto Rico— by Puerto Ricans as well as others—bears the stamp of the half-baked card-index mind that avoids hard thought about the problematical future in a fierce preoccupation with the obvious present.

The Puerto Rican experience, clearly enough, raises problems of some urgency in the modern world. Can "backward" societies indus- trialize without necessarily committing the mistakes of nineteenth- century industrial change—the gross neglect of the countryside, for instance, and the growth of ugly urbanized wastelands? Is the welfare- state ideology (all contemporary nationalist movements espouse it) in itself sufficient to withstand the emergence of a Westernized class society, especially as the traditional criteria of caste, kinship, and religious custom give way to those of income and occupation as modernization proceeds apace? Will the new colonial nationalisms repeat the errors of Western nationalisms? Can "democracy" emerge and survive in situations profoundly different from those surrounding its original rise in England, France, and the United States? Or must "democracy" itself be seen not as a moral absolute but as a social phenomenon that does not necessarily have to follow the Western pattern? What fresh relationships between politics and culture will arise?

The answer to some of these questions in regard to Puerto Rico will have to be shaped in conscious awareness of the fact that for some sixty years the island society has been exposed to American modern- izing influence, so that it is not a "new" society in the sense that countries like Ghana or Lebanon or Burma are "new" societies break- ing for the first time through the crust of custom. Yet even if it can- not be viewed as a "model"—the concept of the model is perhaps a questionable application of a term of mathematical economics to social processes—it may still be seen as a not unrepresentative exam- ple of what happens to a poorly endowed society once its people are exposed to the forces of modern science and technology.

Whatever answers Puerto Rico might provide to this catalogue of questions, it is at least certain that the early contemptuous dismissal of the island summed up in Mr. Dooley's remark is rapidly being replaced by knowledge and, less certainly perhaps, understanding on the part of the American people. For one thing, San Juan has become one of the leading convention cities of America within the last decade. During 1959 the city was host to the annual AFL-CIO conference, the conference of United States state governors, and a conference on the interchange of persons between North and South America sponsored by the Organization of American States. The reorganization of the Caribbean Commission has resulted in the transfer of the headquarters of the successor body, the Caribbean Organization, from Port of Spain, Trinidad, to San Juan. It may be only a matter of time before one or both of the major American political parties can be persuaded to carry their nominating conventions to the Caribbean capital. For another thing, the modern revolution in aviation technology has finally broken down the age-old isolation of the island. The introduction of the "pure-jet" airliner into the New York–San Juan run by Pan-American Airways in 1959 puts the island only four hours away from Manhattan. When a jet airliner can fly from St. Louis to Caracas in the time a train takes to go from St. Louis to Chicago, it is evident that the traditional attitudes of American isolationism belong to the trash heap of discredited ideas. Puerto Rico, like the rest of the world, can only benefit from that truth and from its increasing acceptance by the American people.

Even more. Puerto Rico must benefit from the fact that the entire Caribbean area, like Latin America in general, has become front-page news within the last few years. The status of the area as little more than a geographical expression—the outcome of the historic decline of the Caribbean sugar industry in the second half of the nineteenth century—is almost surely drawing to a close. Caribbean leaders like Governor Muñoz, Mr. Norman Manley, Dr. Cheddi Jagan, and Dr. Eric Williams already enjoy international reputations, and they are anxious to put the reputations into the service of a Caribbean transformation through which their societies will be considered as Caribbean communities in their own right rather than as nothing more than the vague West Indian background of migration "problems" in the metropolitan countries. The Cuban Revolution especially has brought the Latin-American social problem to the forefront of international politics and diplomacy, for it seems likely that *fidelismo* will become a hemispheric idea which—like the idea of equality in Europe after 1789—will create an entirely new world in the area. It will no longer be possible for Latin-American revolutions to be written off as Gilbertian jokes, for increasingly they are certain to take on the *fidelista* garb. All over the continent, the same types of groups which created Nasserism in the Middle East—landless peasants, disinherited Indians, university students, young army officers, the unemployed of the sprawling cities—are on the move. Simultaneously, the groups that have traditionally composed the Latin American ruling class—feudal and *comprador* elements, oil plutocrats, Hispanic "old families"—are on the defensive as they become aware of the contagious quality of the Cuban 26th of July movement. In the face of this accentuation of social conflict in the hemisphere, the rest of the world has been compelled to revise drastically its operating assumptions about Latin America and the Caribbean. The United States power has been compelled to recognize the obsolescence of the theory of American exceptionalism, for it is now apparent that there is fertile ground in the area for the European radical social doctrines. The Soviet Russian power, correspondingly, has been driven to revise its catalogue of world priorities, among which Latin America has always occupied a low position. Neither Washington nor Moscow, that is to say, can take the hemisphere for granted. Its citizens therefore, it is safe to prophesy, can anticipate for the 1960's a politics of big-power courtesy as both sides vie for their allegiance.

Puerto Rico is certain to figure more and more in that politics and in its development. In terms of military strategy it is already the nerve center of the Caribbean Sea frontier, a not unimportant function when it is remembered that German submarine raiders were able to penetrate the area's defenses during World War II with astonishing ease. In terms of political strategy its very geographical location will give it enhanced importance in the policy-making rooms of Washington; the presence of the Dominican exile front in San Juan, especially in the aftermath of the assassination of the Dominican dictator Rafael Trujillo in 1961, emphasized the delicacy of the problems facing the American power in an area literally overcrowded with explosive situations. These considerations explain, perhaps, the readiness of President Kennedy to select two Puerto Ricans for important positions in his new administration, Dr. Arturo Morales-Carrión as Deputy Assistant Secretary of State for Inter-American Affairs and Mr. Teodoro Moscoso as ambassador to Venezuela (later as Director of the Alliance for Progress), thus finally heeding the long-standing plea from San Juan that Puerto Rican talent be used in the Latin-American field. The appointments, of course, must be viewed in proper perspective. They do not as yet mean a Puerto Rican influence of any importance in the shaping of Latin-American policy, for many Puerto Rican liberals have been bitterly disappointed at the failure of the administration to consult them before it undertook what they regard as the appalling error of the United States-sponsored counter-revolutionary invasion of Cuba. Nor should the fact be overlooked that much of Latin-American opinion sees the attention being paid Puerto Rico as the attention of the chess-master who seeks to use his pawn to the best advantage, and Puerto Rican emissaries abroad face a task of formidable proportions as they seek to clear away that suspicion. Puerto Rico, all in all, is on the move. But no one, as yet, can be certain about her final destination.

PART I

THE PAST

The Caribbean Background

THE history of Puerto Rico is of course intimately related to the history of the Caribbean region. The sweep of historical forces that have been since the Discovery the dominant agents of change in the archipelago—European colonization, slavery, the *encomienda* and plantation systems, the sugar economy, Emancipation—has also shaped Puerto Rican society. Each force has not, of course, had an identical impact in each island, because the controlling external relations of each have been with its imperial owner and not with its Caribbean neighbors. The resulting anomalous decentralization of the region has worked to isolate island from island, island group from island group, and explains the absence, still, of any real pan-Caribbean consciousness in the region as a whole, as well as its continuing political Balkanization. Nevertheless, the massive forces sweeping over the area have left at least a common historical experience and a common imprint upon its peoples. In that sense Puerto Rico, even though it may now be the most Americanized society in the Caribbean Sea, belongs by historical fiat to the West Indies.

The Caribbean is a region, to begin with, of a great antiquity and a rich and brilliant cultural variety. Its historical span stretches over four centuries. The first three great voyages of Columbus had ended by the close of the fifteenth century; Cortés entered Aztec Mexico in 1519, the year of Charles V's accession to the Spanish imperial throne; and by 1700, when the Atlantic seaboard colonies of Massachusetts and Virginia were hardly beyond the first stages of settlement, the four great powers of economic and military aggression in the Caribbean—the French, Dutch, Spanish, and English—had established flourishing island and mainland colonies there. The consequent Europeanization of the islands and of the South American littoral produced, in its wake, large cities rivaling those of Europe in size and magnificence; the loot that Morgan and other Caribbean buccaneers were able to take in the capture of such cities as Puerto Bello and Panama easily equaled the booty of contemporary European warfare.

The enormous racial and cultural variety of the region, still its ultimate fascination, stems from the fact that at one time or another practically every European nation has joined in the scramble for its control. Besides the major powers—including the Portuguese in Brazil—the lesser European kingdoms also left their mark. Denmark ruled the Virgin Islands group for more than two centuries before their sale to the United States in 1917. The Dukes of Courland once occupied Tobago. Sweden ruled the island of St. Barthélemy from 1784 to 1877. The Order of St. John of Jerusalem, under its Grand Masters in Malta, ruled St. Croix for a brief period in the eighteenth century.

Some of the Caribbean atmosphere, again, owes its origin to the European refugee. Barbados welcomed the English Royalist fleeing from the Protectorate after 1649. Jamaica in the same period was partly colonized, under Cromwell's Great Western Design, by both Puritan and Jewish emigrants. Portuguese Jewish refugees from the Spanish Inquisition became active colonists in Spanish America. During the nineteenth century British Trinidad and Spanish Puerto Rico, in their turn, became centers for conservative refugees fleeing the national liberation movements in the Spanish imperial mainland colonies.

In addition, there came, from the very beginning, every type of European adventurer, eager to obtain a share of the legendary spoils of the New World and, in the case of the non-Spaniard, to despoil the hated Spaniard of his Catholic empire overseas. The Welsh Royalist, the Dutch Jew, Cromwell's transported Irish prisoner, the obscure Spanish soldier, the Puritan merchant-adventurer, the Catholic friar—all crowded into a society of brutal vigor and tropical brilliance in which personal ambition and greed could assert themselves free from the caste and class restrictions of Europe. John Esquemeling's famous account of the organized pirate society in the small island of Tortuga —*The Buccaneers and Marooners of America*—is actually a perfect description of Hobbes's "masterless man" in a social order that had hardly begun to control his instinct for anarchy. Most of the descendants of these early adventurers, of course, have been absorbed into the racial melting-pot of the island life; but the "Redlegs" of Barbados and St. Vincent, white descendants of transported Royalists, and the "white zombies" of French Guiana, descendants of liberated prisoners of the evil fortress of Cayenne, survive into the twentieth century as bizarre relics of the chaotic and brutal history of the region. And all of this, finally, has taken place in an arc of islands so overwhelmingly beautiful in its gifts of tropical nature that from Columbus on, its discoverers have been tempted, like the Lotus Eaters, to yield up the rest of their lives to its allure. The record of its magical enchantment, what Eugène Revert has called *la magie antillaise*, already manifest in the remarkable autobiography of Père Labat, *Nouveau Voyage aux Iles de l'Amérique* (1722), has produced its own unique literature: Lafcadio Hearn's appealing *Two Years in the French West Indies*, for example, or, more latterly, fictional reconstructions of the Caribbean Golden Age in such novels as Patrick Leigh Fermor's *The Violins of St. Jacques.*

It would be easy enough to make of all this a romantic story of "islands in the sun," a historical canvas of sex, piracy, and slave revolt in the fashion of books like German Arciniegas's *Caribbean: Sea of the New World.* A large literature of that sort caters to the tourist mentality—in fact, the sentimental novel of an earlier literature similarly did much to romanticize the Caribbean for the eighteenth-century European liberal. Saint-Pierre's *Paul et Virginie* is perhaps the most famous example; while another novel, Michael Scott's *Tom Cringle's Log*, preserved a genial and romantic vision of a splendid English Jamaica for whole generations of English schoolboys. The reality behind the romance could hardly have been more different. For Caribbean history since the Discovery has been first the history of European imperialism and second the history of slavery. With variations from island to island, the Caribbean economy has been based on the extensive sugar plantation worked by forced colored labor under European supervision for the ultimate benefit of absentee owners. The introduction of sugar superseded earlier efforts to create a small settler economy (the transition is fully described in Richard Ligon's early *History of Barbados* [1673]), and sugar immediately required a large and cheap labor force capable of heavy, unremitting work under tropical conditions. For two hundred years the demand was met by the slave trade.

During that period, some ten million Africans were transplanted, via the horror of the Atlantic passage transports, to the American and West Indian colonies. The supreme offense of that crime could be matched only, perhaps, by the cruelty with which earlier the Spanish and Portuguese settlers and soldiers had, through forced labor in the mines, systematically exterminated the original Arawak Indians of the islands. The social organization of slavery, in its own turn, meant in effect the complete militarization of the plantation economy to avert the ever-present danger of slave rebellion. One has only to read such a document as the *Diary* of Lady Nugent, who was in Jamaica during the Napoleonic wars with her husband Sir George Nugent, the governor, to be made aware of how the fear of revolt was a brooding omnipresence in the daily lives of the planter class, requiring the almost continuous presence of a friendly naval squadron or of reliable "home" regiments to allay its terrible pressure. Nor did the formal abolition of slavery in the nineteenth century release the Caribbean Negro masses from servitude; it merely replaced the whip of slavery with the prison of low-cost agricultural "free" labor. Even at his most fortunate, the ex-slave could be no more than a *petit propriétaire* growing tropical agricultural commodities—cotton, rice, coffee, tobacco—which prices were determined in the world markets by economic forces beyond his control. European capital was withdrawn, to be redirected to the more profitable fields of Africa and Asia. The Caribbean plantocracy, sacrificed by its European protectors as free trade destroyed the privileged status of West Indian sugar on the world market, either sold out or stayed on to symbolize the decayed gentility of a depressed economy, dreaming of a "Golden Age" that would never return.

Certain leading characteristics of the area help to explain its historic and tragic decline and its present condition. In the first place, the society that grew up after 1700 was a society of slaves and masters. The relationship was frankly one of open exploitation of the slave as a chattel by the combined forces of the local planter and merchant, the estate overseer, and the overseas "West India interest." Inevitably, the relationship brutalized both sides. It made impossible, as slavery always has, any mutual trust or devotion between the two sides. For a slave society is, in the words of a West Indian apologist concerned on the whole to defend the institution, one based on fear, and fear supersedes right.[1] The dictum of an old Antiguan planter that "the worse you behave to a Negro, the better he behaves to you"[2] was only one of the more crude rationalizations invented to justify the system; the rest of the well-known directory of myths about the "Negro character," which survived even Emancipation, followed easily.

In such a world there was little room on either side for cultivation of intellectual or social arts; indeed, the art of combining slavery with the arts is a Greco-Roman achievement the Caribbean planter never learned. Every observer—Père Labat, Lady Nugent, Bryan Edwards, "Monk" Lewis, Sir Robert Schomburgk, Baron von Humboldt— agrees in testimony as to the character of the West Indian "great house": the lives of the master class centered around drinking, dancing, sexual excess, and insipid conversation. The master who attempted, like "Monk" Lewis in his north Jamaican estate in the period after the Napoleonic wars, to be humane to his slaves rapidly discovered that he would be vilified by his fellow planters as a dangerous revolutionary and that his society would be shunned. Cultural development was sacrificed to the search for big profits in what were, more often than not, hazardous and speculative enterprises. That is why, to take a British example, Schomburgk could observe of official society in the Georgetown of the 1840's that spendthrift and ostentatious luxury had become the rule and that it retained as a consequence an extraordinarily large amount of unnaturalness and ceremonial stiffness. And that is why, again, to take a Spanish example from an earlier period of the Caribbean slave society, the Golden Age of Cervantes and Calderón and Lope de Vega found little reflection in the Spanish overseas empire and why, as a Puerto Rican historian has noted, the sole relic of that age in Spanish Puerto Rico was the great library of Bishop Balbuena that was destroyed by the Dutch marauders early in the seventeenth century.

The Caribbean plantocracy in general, indeed, constituted one of the most backward classes known to modern history. It entertained a profound contempt for education and all its works to the point where this scandalized even the unexacting commentators of the Augustan Age. Not only did the Spanish refuse to grant the Puerto Rican request for a university; it took the British more than a century to adopt the proposal for a University College put forward by the white minister James Phillips in Jamaica in 1845, with the formation of the University College of the West Indies in 1948. Even as late as 1920 the sugar owners of Jamaica could oppose the mildest forms of education for children on the grounds that such training would spoil them as juvenile workers on the estates. Nor was the governmental side of the dominant class much better, for the liberal-minded civil servant who came out to the colonies from his home office rapidly succumbed to the moral poison of becoming overnight a member of a ruling class in a Victorian type of society; untrained to be an aristocrat, he was placed in the position of being one in a slaveowning society. The judgments passed upon government official and planter did not vary, as a consequence, for more than two centuries in their basic critique. One of the British Colonial Office abolitionists of the 1830's could observe that no civilized society on earth was so entirely destitute as that of the West Indies, being completely devoid of leisure, literary and scientific intercourse, and liberal recreations; and fifty years later Sir Henry Alcazar could tell the visiting British Royal Commission of 1897 that the introduction of indentured Indian contract labor into the colony had resulted in keeping the ruling class of Trinidad at the moral level of slaveowners.

The slave, on the other hand, was likewise compelled to live in a world of his own, a world despised and feared by others, half Westernized, half African, all the more threatening to the members of the master class because they were so ignorant of its real character. The forces of official society—law, religion, government—were organized in such a way as to prevent dissatisfaction from erupting into revolt. Home governments, it is true, attempted to enforce humane legislation to protect the slave; in the Spanish case the comparative liberalism of the legislation, culminating in the great Code of 1789, had its roots in the medieval legal precepts on slavery. But the combination of local interest and geographical distance made evasion on the part of the Creole plantocracies relatively easy, and resistance was powerful. In the case of Cuba, Madrid was virtually obliged in 1791 to withdraw the code; while in Puerto Rico legislation against the slave was always more effectively enforced than legislation against the master, so much so that the officials designated by law to protect the interests of the slaves became in fact defenders of the slaveowners.[3] And indeed, the various codes passed by the home governments were protective only in a comparative sense; all of them permitted various forms of mutilation as appropriate punishment for disobedience. As Peytraud has noted, moreover, in regard to his monumental study, the motives of the home governments in protecting the slave were commercial rather than humane in their character. Nor was the slave much aided by the development throughout the seventeenth and eighteenth centuries of ideas of constitutional liberty, for these ideas were largely the vehicle of the planter class and its professional and mercantile allies in their own struggle against the metropolitan executive and legislative bodies. The fight, indeed, of local governmental assemblies against the imperial parliaments in the pre-Emancipation Caribbean societies, as in contemporary Kenya and Rhodesia, conspired to serve the interests of the master classes rather than those of the depressed groups. There is an interesting passage in Adam Smith's *The Wealth of Nations* in which he points out, as one illustration of that truth, that the condition of the slave was generally better under an arbitrary government, as in the French West Indian islands, than it was under a free government, as in the British islands, since in the latter case the state power was in large part, through the means of the colonial legislative assemblies based upon an extremely limited suffrage, in the hands of the slave owners themselves.[4] Altogether, the slave lived under a despotic system tempered only by the individual master's sense of humanity or by the willingness and power of the home government to interfere on his behalf. His sole hope lay in servile revolt; he could not withdraw and create a "state within the state," as did the Maroons of Jamaica, since only in the cockpit country of that island was such a move physically possible. Hence, then, the long record of Caribbean slave revolt and the fierce countermeasures of the master class. Captain Stedman's account (1796) of the savage Dutch repression of the revolt of runaway slaves and "bush" Negroes in the Surinam interior of the 1770's provides appalling evidence of the fate that awaited the recaptured slave who had deserted his master.

But revolt, nevertheless, was always around the corner; and the Abbé Raynal, in a famous and prophetic passage in his great history, wrote of the terrible retribution that would overtake the Caribbean slaveowning society if the Negroes should ever find a leader sufficiently courageous to lead them into a racial civil war of vengeance and slaughter.[5] The passage was originally penned in 1770. It was fulfilled a generation later with the emergence of the black Spartacus Toussaint l'Ouverture and the explosion of the great Haitian war of black liberation.

The second characteristic of Caribbean society, deriving from this fact that it was a house divided against itself, was the steady resistance that it evinced, both before and after Emancipation, to outside liberal influence; in other words, the unyielding parochialism of its governing climate of opinion. Outside influence made some mark, of course, most notably in the prolonged campaign for abolition, in which local liberal forces developed to help that influence; the abolition of slavery in Puerto Rico, for example, stemmed in large part from a remarkable report presented to the Spanish Crown in 1867 by a local commission of eminent Creole liberals. But on the whole, liberal influences were resisted fiercely by Caribbean reaction. Every voice seeking to defend the Indian or the slave or the emancipated Negro has been systematically vilified by that reaction's representatives. The great work of Bartolomé de Las Casas in defending the original Indian populations of the islands against Spanish brutality was traduced by later Spanish writers as a "black legend" purveyed by a traitor to the Spanish cause. So successful were they, indeed, that it is even today possible for Puerto Rican newspaper readers to be entertained with amusing accounts of how New Englanders still retain a curious image of the Spanish "character" based upon that "legend."[6] The attack upon slavery launched by the French *philosophes* after 1750, summed up in the Abbé Raynal's *Histoire philosophique et politique des établissements et du commerce des Européens dans les deux Indes* (1770), earned for its protagonists bitter hatred among the white societies of the French Antilles. Similarly, the plantocracy of the British islands saw in the efforts of the Baptist and Methodist clergy to offer a rudimentary education to the Negroes nothing less than an attempt to encourage a black Haitian revolution. The most that could be expected from any supporter of the local vested interests surrounding the institution of slavery was a recognition of its evil when it involved a rival nation; thus, Bryan Edwards, the "moderate" voice of the English planters in the late eighteenth century, could find no language sufficiently violent to denounce the Spanish extermination of the Arawaks in Hispaniola and Puerto Rico, while he could conveniently forget his humanitarianism when he came to discuss the slave institution in his contemporary British island society.

This record is not of merely historical interest, for the post-Emancipation society was as hostile, in different ways, to outside liberalizing influences as was its slavery predecessor. Lord Olivier, the enlightened administrator in Jamaica at the turn of the century, was not too kindly accepted by the conservative elements, either English or Creole. And to realize how much of the historical exclusivism of the area has been able to survive into the middle of the twentieth century, it is only necessary to read Governor Rexford G. Tugwell's sensitive account of the hate campaign launched against him by the "better elements" of Puerto Rican society after 1941 because he refused, unlike his gubernatorial predecessors, to fit into the mold of a pliable and "noncontroversial" governor.[7]

One corollary of that general resistance to liberal influence was that both under slavery and Emancipation the world of the Caribbean masses remained dark and unknown to the rest of the society. Transplanted forcibly from his African tribal culture into the new conditions of Caribbean life, the slave became a deculturated individual. Losing one world, he was driven to create a new one. The work of the cultural anthropologists has by now amply demonstrated that the survivals of the African culture patterns, despite the well-known thesis of Herskovits, were extremely small and scattered in the Caribbean and that in their place the slave society produced its own cultural amalgam of African and Caribbean: the Voodoo world of rural Haiti, Jamaican Obeahism, the great religious Myal movement, of which present-day cults like the Shouters of Trinidad are probable survivors. But it is symptomatic that both the folklore and the linguistics of this Afro-Antillean "new world" were in large part ignored by the region's historians, with the exceptions, in the English islands, of writers like Edward Long and "Monk" Lewis. There was a temptation to see that world either as a new multiracial community moving, under the wise guidance of the slaveowners, to a fuller civilization (the theme of works like the *Annals* of the cleric-historian G. W. Bridges) or as, once the distorting element of slavery had gone, a Victorian class society tempered by the civilizing influence of Christianity (the theme of such works as W. J. Gardner's *History of Jamaica*). And if, as in these two cases, the local historian knew little at first hand of the world of the masses, even less was known by the local planter class

and the European humanitarian. The planter rationalized his ignorance by embracing the myth of the Negro saved from the hell of
neomedieval Africa, the humanitarian by developing the myth of the
"noble savage." Neither myth came anywhere near to recognizing the
anthropological realities. The truth is that even today very little is
known of the thought patterns of the Caribbean Negro during his
centuries of bondage, with the exception of the hints contained in the
Anancy stories and the Maroon legends.

This lack of knowledge of the world of the Caribbean masses exemplifies the third leading characteristic of Caribbean history: that
not only the dominant institutions but also the leading attitudes of the
society have been shaped by and large by the European white influence. The ethnic composition of the society has been basically
Negro. But its social and political directions have been European—
and moreover, selectively European. For whatever the great European
achievements in the arts, in science, and in technology may have been
since the century of genius after 1600, it must be remembered that in
the Caribbean, as in most other colonial areas, there has been little
opportunity of access to their enjoyment. European control has meant,
rather, exposure to the less attractive attributes of Europe—its lust
for adventure, its drive for expansion, its search for overseas profits,
and not least its racial arrogance and the pride of the European man
as he has made himself, since 1500, the conqueror of the universe.
From the moment of European discovery, the Caribbean was carved
up among the rival European imperialisms with scant regard for its
own permanent interests; the Papal Donation of 1493 set the pattern
for deciding Caribbean destinies by the power politics of European
chancelleries.

The consequences have been deep and far-reaching. Aside from the
obvious political and economic consequences, there was the fact that
the European mind as a whole failed to apply the idea of equality—
so much at the center of European liberalism—to the Caribbean
peoples. There is hardly a single spokesman for that liberalism who
felt able to accept the Negro as the equal of the white person. Victorian England thus received its impressions of the Caribbean Negro
from writers generally hostile to him. Carlyle's venom on the "nigger
question," Trollope's ingenuous paternalism mixed with undertones
of anti-semitism, James Anthony Froude's bitter negrophobia (the
latter serving the additional purpose, as one West Indian critic pointed
out, of attacking the extension of democratic self-government in
Britain itself)[8]—all identified the Victorian moral ethic with white
supremacy; all, too, contributed to the popular image of "Quashie,"
the freed slave whose habits of laziness and irresponsibility were sup-

posed to have been the major cause of the decline of the sugar industry in the British islands after 1834.

The attitude even pervaded the mental atmosphere of the white friends of the Negro. It would be idle to deny or belittle the nobility of purpose that activated great humanitarians like Clarkson and Wilberforce or American liberal statesmen like Jefferson and Lincoln. But of the Englishmen it must be said and especially of Wilberforce, that their concept of the Negro hardly went beyond that of a child who must be protected against the power of his masters. Wilberforce's liberalism was tarnished, too, by his hostility to the cause of the new industrial workingclass in England, by his opposition to the movement for parliamentary reform, and by his support of Pitt's repressive measures against domestic liberalism during the French wars. And of the American statesmen it must be admitted that they had very little insight into the cultural or anthropological roots of the "race question." Both Jefferson and Lincoln, of course, rejected the white master–black servant concept. But Jefferson, following David Hume, believed in the racial inferiority of Negroes and penned, in his *Notes on the State of Virginia,* one of the most objectionable passages in the written record of racial animosity. Lincoln, in turn, was only slowly and reluctantly driven, under the pressure of events, to replace his earlier emphasis upon the salvation of the Union, even at the price of compromising with the slave states on the issue of slavery, with his later emphasis upon the concept of full political equality between Negro and white; and even then his apprehensions about the prospect of adjusting the white American society to the free Negro led him, at one point during the war, to seek a solution through resettlement of all American Negroes on a Caribbean island. Whether, indeed, the prejudice has had racial or cultural roots, the white man, in the history of his relations with the Negro, has rarely been able to divest himself of an inborn assurance of his own superiority. Nor, again, is this fact of merely historical interest. It remains, still, a living belief. It continues to exist in many of the English in the contemporary West Indies, for while their attitude to the colored person is less crude than that of the South African Boer, it is still something far short of a consciously accepted idea of democratic equality. Prejudice can still peer out, too, from the chinks in the armor of the contemporary American liberal, as is evident from Tugwell's expressed opinion on a visit to Puerto Rico in 1934 as a Washington official, that the Puerto Rican people were not of sufficiently good material to be capable of programs of democratic collectivist planning.[9]

Even before efforts to clothe prejudice in the protective aura of a philosophical system had helped develop the American philosophy of

Manifest Destiny, Europeans had established the popularity of such efforts. Christian writers on the subject, both Catholic and Protestant, uncritically accepted the classical view that slavery, as a condition, was the consequence of either natural inequality or of conquest in war. In this the deists agreed with their orthodox opponents; so that Locke, in justifying slavery by right of conquest, was able to bypass the moral challenge to the institution implicit in the Lockeian natural law theories, and influenced later writers like William Paley. Other British apologists, like William Robertson in his once famous work on the *History of America,* adopted the view promulgated by Montesquieu that slavery was a system made necessary not so much by racial as by climatic reasons. Clerical apologists were fond of invoking the obscurantist argument of a divine will that imposes slavery upon the world for purposes inscrutable to man. For those who could not accept supernatural reasons (increasingly the case after 1750) there was the semi-sociological argument of a "dark Africa" from whose heathenism the Negro had been saved, although the argument was precariously founded upon dubious accounts by travelers in the eighteenth-century African kingdoms of Dahomey and Abyssinia. Others, again, who could not accept the argument of innate nature managed to defend slavery on the ground that its workings could be ameliorated by legislation and goodwill, although they failed to face up to the problem of how to persuade a recalcitrant planter class to accept amelioration; the argument received a well-known expression in the *Account of the European Settlements in America* published at the time of the American Revolution and popularly supposed to have been partly written by Edmund Burke in a moment of financial embarrassment.

The nineteenth century saw the rise of new and more sophisticated rationalizations for inequality. An entire offshoot of social Darwinism came into being to justify "race" attitudes in the name of eugenics and social evolution. The idea of unequal social evolution was particularly appealing, for it was able to dispense with arguments about individual merit and bypass the compulsive logic of natural law. There was something of this argument in James Froude's *The English in the West Indies.* One of its most polished statements appeared in Benjamin Kidd's essay on *The Control of the Tropics,* published, by a curious coincidence, in 1898, the same year in which the United States started out on her career as a modern world power with the outbreak of the Spanish-American war. The rule of the white man in the tropics Kidd justified not by innate racial superiority but by the cultural fact that only the higher "social efficiency" of the European and North American states could guarantee the rational exploitation of the tropical economies. "The first step to the solution of the problem before us," he wrote confidently, "is simply to acquire the principle that in dealing with the *natural* inhabitants of the tropics we are dealing with peoples who represent the same stage in the history of the development of the race that the child does in the development of the individual. . . . If we look," he continued, "to the native social systems of the tropical East, to the primitive savagery of Central Africa, to the West Indian islands in the past in process of being assisted into the position of modern states by Great Britain, to the Black Republic of Haiti in the present, or to modern Liberia in the future, the lesson seems everywhere the same; it is that there will be no development of the resources of the tropics under native government."[10] The argument is not very different from the pseudoscientific paraphernalia of the German Nazi "philosophers" as they sought, forty years later, to justify the European hegemony of the Third Reich.

Two footnotes should be appended to this account of European social theory on the matter of "race." The first is that with the exception of the Quakers, the organized churches of the period rarely challenged, in their official capacity, the basic lower status of the Negro. They undertook no root and branch onslaught upon slavery; the British Society for the Propagation of the Gospel even owned slaves in the West Indies. Both the Methodist and Baptist churches, of course, had an honorable record in attempting the humanitarian reform of slavery. The Catholic Church also sought amelioration, but as to abolition, Rome was at best prepared to applaud it once it was achieved by other forces, as a reading of the letter of Pope Leo XIII to the bishops of Brazil on the occasion of Brazilian abolition makes clear.[11] It was not any Christian parliament, however, but the deist Assembly of the French Revolution that first abolished slavery—in 1791, forty-three years before England and eighty-two years before Spain.

The second footnote is that the alignments of European attitudes during this prolonged debate were not always what might have been expected. The prevaricating attitude of the Enlightenment has already been noted and one more example may suffice: in the fifteenth chapter of his great work Montesquieu could pen a celebrated passage in which he sought to justify slavery by denying common sense or moral sentiment to the Negro. On the other hand, thinkers usually conservative in their views were sometimes surprisingly liberal on this issue; thus, Dr. Johnson could oppose the system of slavery on grounds of natural liberty, and could even utter, while on a visit to Oxford, a toast to "the next insurrection of the Negroes in the West Indies" which Bryan Edwards reported in tones of scandalized horror.

The apologetic literature was thus lengthy and formidable. Much of it, of course, was concerned merely to rationalize the status quo. Some of it, however, dreamed of an imperial regeneration of the colonies. The dream failed, largely because by 1850 most of the European "mother" countries had decided that West Indian enterprise was a losing concern. So, while writers like Froude played with the idea, Carlylean-wise, of a new and benevolent imperial paternalism coaching the "lesser" peoples of the colonies into fuller maturity, protecting them at once against both their own weaknesses and the shortcomings of the merely utilitarian system of commercial empire (the idea received a West Indian expression in W. P. Livingstone's *Black Jamaica* of 1899 and there is still something of its tone in the work of contemporary Catholic sociologists and anthropologists in the Caribbean), the realities were far different; and Tory Democracy succeeded no more in the colonies than it did at home. As the twin gospels of free trade and anticolonialist free enterprise came to dominate European policies, the Caribbean planter and the Caribbean peasant were both compelled to shift for themselves. That abolition and the withdrawal of protectionism should have been merely the beginning and not the end of a positive philosophy setting out to reconstruct the Caribbean society on new developmental principles, was an insight unappreciated by economic liberalism. "The gift of freedom," a recent student has concluded, "could not by itself transform the recipients or endow them with a nineteenth century European conception of utility as the proper test of progress."[12] Despite real differences in the colonial policies of the various powers, the remark applied to all of them as they faced the need for reorienting the colonial economies on a nonslave basis. Emancipation in the French colonies in 1848, one of the first acts of the Second Republic, was followed by the assumption among both liberals and socialists in France that the only future for the liberated Creole lay in his cultural development as a "black Frenchman": an outlook so bankrupt that by the time of the Third Republic the Caribbean was known to the average Frenchman only as the point of origin of the vast Panama Canal scandals and the site of the infamous tropical prison of Devil's Island. Indeed, it was not until the very last days of the Republic that the bestiality of that penal colony was exposed to the world through the books of René Belbénoit. In the Spanish case, where a somewhat different process was at work, the success of the national liberationist movements after 1820, resulting in the development of the great Latin American imperial viceroyalties into the new independent republics, served only to tighten more than ever the Spanish grip on the remaining Caribbean colonies and to inhibit any reform movement there that might have grown out of the reforms of Carlos III in the latter part of the eighteenth century. And in the British case, finally, the chance of an enlightened imperialism—the dream, for example, of the "theorists of 1830," whose Bible was Edward Wakefield's *The Art of Colonization*—lost out to the belief, shared by the major political parties, of the mid-century period that colonies were at once economically wasteful and morally indefensible.

In all these cases, the abolitionist mentality blandly assumed that emancipation was enough, so that, in the phrase of Lord Harris with reference to the British islands, a race had been freed but a society had not been formed. The consequences for social harmony were fatal. On the one side, the freed slave, in natural reaction against his former condition, relapsed into habits it was only too easy for his former masters to denounce as "negroid laziness." On the other, the employer class used the "laziness" to justify its own failure to adopt more efficient methods of sugar production under changed conditions or, more important yet, to turn experimentally to other crops. That class, indeed, used its still potent power (in the British case) to sabotage the social elevation of the free Negro by the introduction of the East Indian indentured laborer, with disastrous consequences for the social patterns of later West Indian life; just as later, in the twentieth century, the American sugar companies dominating the economy of the Dominican Republic helped to create a serious social problem by their large-scale importation of black Haitian seasonal labor into a society traditionally hostile to its neighbor of the same island.

By the end of the nineteenth century, then, the Caribbean had become, in place of its once splendid tradition, a forgotten and derelict corner of the world, occasionally visited by the more adventuresome traveler. Its economy was a precarious "windfall economy," dependent upon intermittent bursts of activity like the construction of the Panama Canal. As the metropolitan mercantile houses withdrew their capital, the islands declined into a state of somnolent stagnation. Nevis, in its eighteenth-century heyday the Saratoga of the West India gentry, degenerated into a forgotten outpost, as it remains still today. Froude described in two angry chapters the scandalous neglect of Dominica, and his description is almost a portrait of the island eighty years later, while natural disasters added their own quota of ruin, like the Kingston earthquake of 1907 and the Mont Pelée eruption that destroyed the charming French Antillean town of Saint-Pierre in Martinique in 1902. Technological changes also accelerated the decay; the growth of the steamship and the replacement of coal with oil dealt a sharp blow to those ports like St. Thomas that had been the great *termini* of the transatlantic passage to the West Indies, and to those like Castries in St. Lucia that had been prosperous maritime coaling stations. Spasmodic aid under an occasional energetic colonial secretary—for example, Joseph Chamberlain in the British Colonial Office—only emphasized the general indifference of the home governments. The Caribbean slipped away altogether from the notice of the European world. It is almost not too much to say that by 1900 the sociological discovery of the region was at pretty much the same stage as its geographical discovery had been four centuries earlier.

Since the time of Columbus, the Caribbean Sea has thus been the pawn of European dynastic and commercial rivalries. It has provided a theater for the display of European sea power; indeed, it has been very much a nursery of European naval genius, and whether or not the battle of Waterloo was won on the playing fields of Eton, it is certain that the victory at Trafalgar was guaranteed in the waters of the Antilles. The kaleidoscopic fortunes of the islands have been made and unmade by the treaty arrangements of European congresses. Just as the commercial revolution of Europe after 1600 made these fortunes, so, after 1800, the industrial revolution of Europe unmade them. The progressive elements of European thought had devoted great idealism to the native Caribbean cause, as Wordsworth's noble *Sonnet to Toussaint l'Ouverture* testifies. But the decline of revolutionary fervor in Europe after 1848 meant a corresponding decline in European concern with the colonial peoples. Later in the century, the concern degenerated into the sort of loose romanticization of the tropical New World associated with the stylistic poetry of Heredia and the French Parnassian school, and hardly of sufficient intellectual power to stand up against the onslaught of the new sociological racialism, warning against the black and yellow "perils," of writers like C. H. Pearson. As with all societies in decline, the genius and talent of Antillean life were driven abroad in search of opportunity and recognition: Alexander Hamilton in the eighteenth century, the Dumas family in the nineteenth, the young artists and writers of the present period. The modern revolutionary movements of nationalism and democracy have touched the area only recently. The society has rarely been seen in its own light and on its own terms. Only too often it has been seen by friend and foe alike through the naturally distorted perspective of the imperial governing class or the hurried traveler or the friends of the local liberal causes in metropolitan capitals. The early Spanish and French writers saw it through the perspective of Catholic Christianity, and not even the medieval humanism of Las Casas or the fine sociological sense of Père du Têrtre went much beyond the framework of the perspective. An entire library of European histories and travel tales retailed the region to the new European reading public as a *locus* of fantastic legends and heroic adventures: the New World sections of Rabelais' great picaresque novel, Sir Walter Raleigh's dream of the fabulous Guianas, *Robinson Crusoe* and *Treasure Island*. Even the more responsible academic histories of the region have been written, in the main, from the outside viewpoint, seeing developments within the Caribbean as merely appendices to the histories of the respective "homelands." That sort of book is still written, as Mrs. Mary Proudfoot's volume on *The United States and Britain in the Caribbean Islands* (1954) illustrates. Much even of the new work done on Puerto Rico by Puerto Rican sociologists tends to follow the lines of research laid down by the work of continental sociologists. The economic dependency of the countries of the region on absentee-owned business enterprise has thus been reflected in, and accompanied by, their intellectual dependency on absentee-sponsored academic enterprise.

What all this has meant, finally, for the *homo caribiensis*, in terms of both social oppression and psychological deprivation, it would, even now, be difficult to estimate. Emphasis on the fact that so much of the political and economic history of the region has mirrored the struggles between rival overseas powers for the profits of sugar and slavery has tended to obscure the graver social and psychological consequences of the slave-based sugar economy. Yet those consequences are in large measure the key to the present nature of the society. Forcibly uprooted from his African culture, the Negro was compelled to adjust to an utterly alien culture. His descendants, both black and colored, have inherited the tortured ambivalence of his position. They have lived in a world controlled by groups—whether the Spanish in Puerto Rico or the British in Jamaica or the Dutch in the Guiana lowlands—who have regarded themselves as outsiders residing in the tropics only so long as they could reap a profit. The Creole concept of "home" has thus suffered from a snobbish attachment to the "mother" country, thereby gravely inhibiting the growth of an effective sentiment of indigenous citizenship. Little effort has been exerted to help the native masses believe in the institutions of government and society as instruments of their own civic advancement. The classic heritage of slavery—identification of manual labor with social degradation—still survives, so that the region's agricultural industries are handicapped by occupational preferences for white-collar jobs. The luxuries of existence—fine houses, good food, travel—have been reserved first for a white governing class and second for a colored middle-class *élite* in the civil service and in commercial enterprise.

The average laborer of the society, as the Moyne Commissioners of 1945 noted in the case of the British islands, has been confined to his own island even more strictly than the English laborer was tied to his parish in the most rigid phase of the Settlement Laws. Nor has the educated West Indian been any more successful in identifying himself with Caribbean value patterns, for he has grown up and been educated in a school of values that has identified progress with things European and backwardness with things West Indian. His final ambition has been to associate himself as much as possible with the respectable and prestige-carrying metropolitan tradition, so that Caribbean society is well acquainted with his psyche of maladjustment, whether he be a West Indian student returned from Oxford or a Haitian middle-class gentleman emulating the manner of the *boulevardier parisien* or a Puerto Rican upper-class individual acting out the life-style of the Castilian *caballero* or remodeling himself, later, as a *pitiyanqui*. He has been taught to despise his own society and to adore an alien society that accepts him only with reluctance; so he has been trapped, homeless and alienated, between two worlds that do not want him. It is not then inapt to compare the experience of the Afro-Caribbean Negro with that of the European Jew, for they have both been shaped by the seminal force of uprootedness. "Like the Jews," a Jamaican wrote in 1899 of the Negro classes of the region, "they have had un-forgettable experiences. They have come through the wilderness, through a land of drought and of the shadow of death, through a land that no white man has passed through, and where no white man has dwelt, and the misery and loneliness of it all is still with them. The more they evolve and the more they know, the more the heritage of the race becomes a mystery, strange alike in its origin and in its intolerable pressure upon every moment of their lives."[13]

As the Caribbean thus entered the twentieth century, it was a society characterized by poverty, neglect, despair, and an almost complete absence of any community consciousness. There was little of a Caribbean sense to hold social classes or racial groups together. The mutual distrust of uprooted black and expatriate white, as Mr. Philip Curtin's *Two Jamaicas* has shown in the case of Victorian Jamaica, perpetuated disharmony in a society where except for the intermediate group of mixed colored, no group felt in any real sense at home; and even among the colored, the sense of belonging was strained with the feeling that their patrimony was a sort of Naboth's vineyard of which they had been unjustly dispossessed. The sole type of social alliance was that of convenience; thus Schomburgk drew attention to the shameful ill-treatment of the Guiana Indian aborigines by the Dutch

European ruling class despite the fact that every Negro rebellion in the colony, including the great Coromantyn rebellion of 1793-1794, had been put down with their help. Colonial government, as a matter of fact, placed a calculated premium upon that sort of disharmony, since it divided local opinion by attaching to itself local elements whose advancement lay in the art of pleasing the imperial government and its local representatives. That helps to explain why the Caribbean planter class had no principle of loyalty except to its own interests. The Jamaican planter class was even prepared in 1865 to give up the old representative assembly and submit to the iniquity of Crown Colony government in order to block constitutional reform that would have granted the vote to emancipated slaves. Before them, the Haitian planters had secretly negotiated with the British Government to take over the island with a view to preventing the abolition of slavery by the French Government under the Revolution. Similarly, certain sections of the Cuban and Puerto Rican slaveowning classes were prepared, seditiously, to countenance annexation to the slave states of the American South once the Spanish Cortes commenced its debate on abolition. And even when colonialism was finally replaced with national independence, as in Haiti and the Dominican Republic and the Central American states, it turned out to be a half empty victory only, inasmuch as the external struggle against the European governments merely gave way to an internal class and color struggle between the mulatto middle class and the black rural peasant masses. For although 1789 ended the aristocracy of white economic power in the politically free islands, it did nothing to prevent its supersession by the aristocracy of color.

Indeed, it would be a more than Herculean task to estimate fully the ravages worked by color psychology in Caribbean life, both past and present. It is true that the barriers between the white and the other groups did not grow, as in other colonial areas, into rigid caste lines. At the same time the disease of racialism appeared in other and more subtle forms. A complex system of values grew up emphasizing skin color and ethnic affiliation as the badges of social respectability; complex because the racial vagaries of Caribbean existence, as the painstaking classifications of Moreau de Saint-Méry in the French islands at the end of the eighteenth century dramatized, had produced at least some sixty different combinations of black and white in the Creole populations. Thus there came into being the characteristic multilayered pigmentocracy of Caribbean life, much of it based upon marriage habits designed, as the saying goes, to add some cream to the coffee, and compelling a vast and disproportionate volume of individual anxiety and effort into the search for social acceptance by the white and light-skinned groups. Energy and talent that should have gone into creative social activities got wasted in the personal struggles of men and women who had been taught by everything in their society to be secretly ashamed of their color. Bitterness, frustration, chauvinism became, all in all, too much a part of many private lives. Social pressures produced either, on the one side, an art of evasive deference to superiors or, on the other, an aggressive individualism, the sort of defiant attitude to social authority that has been delightfully catalogued in much of the Trinidadian calypso. Those defense mechanisms have then been invoked by the dominant class as evidence to justify the image of the Caribbean native as shiftless and morally untrustworthy. Altogether, it is not too much to say that by 1900 the European liberal spirit had succeeded in releasing the Caribbean peoples from the more onerous of their objective institutional burdens, but had done little to relieve them of the more subtle yet equally oppressive subjective burdens laid upon them by colonialism and slavery. That remained, still, a task for the future.

The Spanish Legacy

THROUGHOUT the four centuries from the Spanish Conquest to the American occupation of 1898, Puerto Rico was at once representative of the Caribbean and unique: representative because its history was shaped by the same concatenation of forces—war, conquest, slavery, commercial mercantilism—that were at work in the whole area; unique because the Council of the Indies treated the island not so much as a territory to be colonized as a strategic outpost of empire —the cockpit, indeed, of the Hispanic Caribbean defense system—so that its civilian aspect was altogether subordinated to its military significance. Just as the port of Acapulco on the Pacific side of the Central American isthmus was the axis of the Spanish China trade, so San Juan developed as the nerve center of the Spanish defense system on the Caribbean side. It is suggestive that the massive masonry of the outer San Juan fortifications failed only once—on the occasion of Lord Cumberland's short-lived occupation of 1597—to repel the foreign invader, until in 1898 Admiral William T. Sampson's great ironclads demonstrated their final obsolescence. They remain, like English Harbour in Antigua, as impressive memorials of an age when dynastic conflicts in Europe were frequently settled by decisive naval engagements in Caribbean waters.

The main genius of Hispanic colonization tended to bypass Borinquen. Wealth-hungry adventurers from Spain found little attraction in an island that could not satisfy their lust for gold, and official attempts to maintain the island's Spanish population by prohibiting emigration to the burgeoning societies of the Central and South American mainland were ineffective in the face of the exotic legends that rapidly developed about Mexico and Peru. For two centuries after its publication in 1609, famous books such as the *Comentarios Reales* of the Inca Garcilaso de la Vega, with their romantic invocation of the pre-Columbian civilizations, captured the Spanish mind; and Puerto Rico had few counterattractions to offer. Even the interest of the Spanish Crown in the island was limited (certainly until the middle of the eighteenth century, when the growing commerce with Spain and the expanding slave trade between Africa and Venezuela brought with them an economic revival) to the construction of the insular fortifications, which were mainly financed by enormous subsidies from the royal treasury in Mexico City.

In the seventeenth and eighteenth centuries, the Crown considered the island a main link in the chain of ports defending the passage of the great treasure fleets between the New World and Spain. After 1800, and especially after the revolt of the mainland colonies in the 1820's, it was viewed as a center of operations against the revolutionary movements. Thus the apparent concessions granted to the island by the *Cédula de Gracias* of 1815 were really prompted by a desire, first, to use the island as a steppingstone toward reconquest of the revolting colonies and, second, to obtain from its residents the financial tribute that could no longer come from the latter.[1] The same policy was adopted toward Cuba; Baron von Humboldt's monumental account of his travels in the equinoctial regions of America has much to say about the complete absorption of Cuba's revenues into the maintenance of a huge military and naval establishment out of all proportion to the ability of its citizens to sustain.[2]

Just so was San Juan, from its early days, a military society, with its tone set by the Spanish soldiery. Almost without exception, the governors appointed from Madrid were military officers whose main interest remained the care of their personal fortunes in the permutations of court and army politics at home. Hardly a single governor in the entire roster up to 1898 can begin to compare with such first-class governors as Gravesande in the Dutch Caribbean and Lord Elgin in the British. Professional armies are rarely the school of statesmen, and in the golden age of the sixteenth century a Spanish leader who rose from the ranks, like Balboa, or from the poor gentry, like Cortes, was hardly the type to be usually appointed to the office of colonial governor by the metropolitan ministries in Madrid. The occupant of the gubernatorial palace in San Juan tended to be a military aristocrat, used to the habit of autocratic command: at his best, he could be a Marshal Baldrich; at his worst, he could be a General Sanz. There was no local participation in his appointment and no significant local influence upon the duration or the direction of his policy. His political instinct, generally speaking, was conservative, if not reactionary. His attitude to the Puerto Rican colonist was summed up, perhaps, in the remark of one governor that a people that was entertained would not indulge in conspiracy, and of another that the island population could be adequately governed with a whip and a violin.

The essence of Spain's policy toward Cuba and Puerto Rico was one of calculated exclusivism. The tragedy of both possessions, in one sense, lay in the fact that as Spain was driven out of the mainland the insult that their rulers felt to their pride expressed itself in a fierce determination to maintain some remnant of a once great empire as proof that the Spanish spirit had not entirely lost its colonizing vocation. After Spain's defeat on the continent, more and more of its energy was diverted to the islands, with disastrous results for the liberal movements in Havana and San Juan. The policy of the home government was, as much as circumstances would permit, to seal off both islands from the evil contagion of the liberal spirit, especially as it emanated from the young North American democracy, and the influx of royalist refugees into the islands after the great victory of Bolívar at Ayacucho (1824) contributed to the success of the antiliberal forces (as did the influx of American Tories into Canada after 1776). The policy was reflected in both an economic and a political fashion. Economically, it entailed a neomercantilist protectionism designed to restrict commercial relationships with the non-Hispanic Caribbean, and especially with the important North American market, and to tie the insular economy unilaterally to the Spanish system. The policy was designed primarily to serve the narrow interests of the Castilian mercantile houses whose members controlled the San Juan trade; and it had the additional consequence of crippling the capitalist expansion of the local sugar and coffee industries, whose owners relied upon the good will of the San Juan merchants and bankers. Puerto Rico sugar was denied free entry to the home market, controlled by the Andalusian sugar interests; other products were similarly restricted. At the same time island producers were denied the benefit of a free-trade treaty arrangement with Washington, which would have opened up the North American market. An enlightened policy—in the words of a Puerto Rican deputy to the national Cortes—could have made of Puerto Rico, with its strategic position between the Pacific and Atlantic oceans, a great mercantile emporium, especially since Columbus's dream of an isthmus canal was to become a reality within a century. As it was, the opportunity was lost to the more enlightened Danish government, so that neighboring St. Thomas, with its free port, rather than San Juan became the flourishing center of the Caribbean commercial system.[3] The reforms of 1815, true enough, witnessed the tentative abandonment of economic exclusivism and commercial monopoly by permitting legal trading between the island and foreign countries; a final recognition, as a Puerto Rican economic historian has pointed out, of the economic reality of the island as an exposed location in the middle of a rich trading area, graphically illustrated in the enormous extent to which clandestine trade had grown

by the end of the eighteenth century.[4] But the reforms did little beyond conceding the practical impossibility of keeping the island a
closed society in the midst of an open regional economy. They were
not followed up, through the rest of the century, with either the administrative reforms or the official encouragement of local economic
enterprise needed to give them flesh and blood—yet those reforms had
long been requested by the Crown's own advisers, as far back as the
important report rendered by Marshal O'Reylly in 1785. The economic potential of the island remained virtually untouched. Raynal's
acid indictment of Spanish rule—"This island, the possession of which
would have made the fortune of an active nation, is scarcely known
in the world"—applied even until 1898.

The Bourbon exclusivist policy also had its political side. The system of government used for the New World colonies was derived from
the *Leyes de Indias* promulgated by the Council of the Indies during
the sixteenth century. Originally devised to protect the interests of
the Spanish monarchical state, the system remained substantially unaltered even throughout the century of European liberalism after
1789. Its governing body of laws, in the words of Calixto Bernal, did
not recognize political rights, the head and center of all other rights,
and inculcated nothing but the habit of passive obedience and a
philosophy knowing nothing save the omnipotent will of the monarch.[5]
As far as the colonies were concerned, this meant that they were governed by an utterly arbitrary system. It involved three principles:
absence of *criollo* participation in government; denial to the native
population of any influence, formal or informal, upon official policy;
and concentration of legal and political powers in the military authority of the governor. The governor was accountable only to the
Ministerio del Ultramar in Madrid; he alone appointed the members
of his council; and in his fourfold capacity as captain-general of the
local military and naval forces, as *Intendente,* as superior judge in the
judicial system, and as *Vicepatrono* in all religious matters, he exercised complete local authority over all aspects of the national life;
and remained, in effect, the unilateral source of all official authority.
The distance separating the colony from Madrid enhanced the governor's power, since all Madrid demanded was that the island military
defense be in good order. So long as that end was ensured and so
long as no open rebellion—as the ill-prepared and ill-fated *Grito de
Lares* in 1868—occurred to embarrass the home authorities, the governor was left pretty much to his own devices. The natural result was
the almost complete absence of permanent and known principle in the
local government of the colony. Each governor chose the direction
that pleased him. The price that Puerto Rico paid for the system, or

absence of system, was bitterly noted by the local patriot Salvador Brau in his *Cartas al Ministerio de Ultramar*. "Does Méndez de Vigo come," he asked satirically, "and found a *casa de beneficiencia* for orphans and mental defectives? So Méndez de Vigo is applauded. Does Venezuela come and condemn the *fiestas sanjuaneras* and set up the system of individual identification cards? Then the identification card is accepted and the *fiestas* are suppressed. Does Norzagaray come and reinstate the horse races? Then everybody rides like cowboys again. The Puerto Rican masses are a people very easily influenced, they adapt themselves to every circumstance and take their ups and downs with resignation, reserving their approval for every separate occasion, almost as if to offer proof of the unalterable character of their legendary Hispanic sentiment."[6]

The system, in brief, was absolute. In the sharp phrase of Castelar with reference to its operation in Cuba, kings who were constitutional in Spain were absolute in Cuba, and ministers who were responsible in Spain could proceed as they pleased in matters affecting Cuba. Its liberalization could come only from Spain, too, saving a root and branch destruction by colony revolt. Spanish economic policy concentrated almost exclusively upon garnering the massive profits of the continuing slave trade, and the island governors rarely possessed ambitions beyond the assurance of their own private share of the profits: Gurney described in 1840, in his book on the West Indies, how the trade, a generation after its formal abolition, continued as a highly organized operation by an alliance of American shipbuilding capitalism, Cuban trading houses and corrupt colonial officials, with even the possible connivance of the American consular officials in Havana.[7]

Nor only that. Colonialism, as a system, has invariably carried with it not only the moral subserviency of the governed but also the moral seduction of the governing administrative class. The great lesson which Burke established in his indictment of Warren Hastings—that liberalism and empire cannot go together in a society with any lasting moral success—had its own illustration in nineteenth-century Cuba and Puerto Rico. The possibility of reform by liberal-minded governors (a real possibility in the British Caribbean) was sterilized by the rapidity with which appointees noted for their liberalism at home identified themselves with the local conservative elements once they assumed their posts. At home General Prim had been a leader of the revolution of 1868 against the monarchy; as governor of Puerto Rico he was a brutal reactionary, responsible for the passage of one of the harshest penal codes (1849) directed against the Negro slave in the history of Spanish rule. Similarly, General Messina, regarded at home as an unreliable man deserving of prolonged incarceration in the prisons of Spanish Africa, became, in San Juan after 1862, one of the most repressive of the island's governors. Nor could reform be expected of the general Spanish administrative class, for its personnel were drawn from a closed caste of upper-class Spaniards favored by successive governors; and the nepotism that infected the entire machinery of colonial government was encouraged, not challenged, by the fact that, as Labra pointed out in his study of the system, Madrid used overseas appointments to rid itself of socially disgraced or politically undesirable individuals, while the Colonial Minister was surrounded by a veritable court of aspirants for the more lucrative overseas positions.[8]

Thus, none of the projects for political and administrative reform advanced by the Puerto Rican liberal movement and its leaders after 1815—the Quiñones-Varela project of 1823, the report of the Belvis-Quiñones-Acosta Commission of 1867, the Ponce Plan of 1886—were ever fulfilled to any serious extent. The great moments of promise for the Creole liberals were those provided by the spasmodic victories of the liberal-constitutionalist forces in Spain; in every case, reform in San Juan had to wait upon liberal advance in Madrid. Just as the key to progress in Victorian India lay in London, so in the Puerto Rican case the key to San Juan was in Madrid.

This was the case all the way. It was the case with the first steps toward reform of the autocratic centralist system embodied in the reforming measures of 1809 and reaffirmed by the liberal constitution of 1812, which gave the island its first elected delegate, Dr. Ramón Power, to the *Junta Suprema* in Madrid. It was the case with the promise in 1837 of special legislation aimed at recognizing the peculiar problems of the overseas provinces; with the reform stemming from the establishment of the constitutional regime after the 1868 revolution, including restoration of the right to nominate local deputies to the national parliament; and with the subsequent promise of a self-governing and federated Puerto Rico within the new national constitution thrown up by the establishment of the Republic in 1873. It was the case, finally, and at the eleventh hour and the fifty-ninth minute, with the grant of the charter of autonomy in 1897, prompted as that act was by the desire of the liberal Sagasta ministry in Madrid to prevent Puerto Rico becoming another Cuba in open rebellion. In all these cases the reforms were never more than short-lived, and the transitory victory of the overseas liberal movement reflected faithfully the transitory victory of the liberal movement at home. So, the liberal surge of the 1820's and 1830's did not prevent the dictatorship within the island of General Nervaez and the *década intranquila* of the

1850's. The candle lit in 1837 soon flickered out; in the bitter phrase of Salvador Brau, they promised us special laws and then proceeded to wait in silence for thirty-one years. But the spirit of 1868 did little more and in its last days of life meant nothing much more for the Caribbean dependency than a sad transition from the Republican farce of 1873 to the Conservative tragicomedy of 1874. The ineffectiveness of the local liberalism was dramatically emphasized by the fact that as late as 1887 a Spanish captain-general in San Juan could impose upon the island the repression of the *componte,* including illegal arrest of the more famous of liberal leaders and their subsequent torture, of various kinds, and thus create for Puerto Rican history the lasting commemoration of the *año terrible.* The supineness of the same liberalism, as distinct from its ineffectiveness, found expression in the curious fact that the leadership of the leading liberal party, the *Partido Autonomista,* expressed their loyalist support of the government measures in a private interview with the governor, despite the fact that those measures had been motivated in the main by a desire to crush that party. That episode, indeed, was typical, for it showed how much the defense of the liberal idea was taken over, not by the local colonial elements, but by the liberal elements at home. For it was the liberal forces in the Spanish national capital that protested most actively against the *componte*; in much the same way as in the not dissimilar case of the Morant Bay rebellion in neighboring Jamaica in 1865 it had been English liberal opinion, led by the younger Mill, that had immediately sensed the horror of the pogrom unleashed by Governor Eyre, rather than any liberal force in Jamaica itself.

In the end-result, the reformist record in Puerto Rico justified Acosta's observation that what Fray Iñigo Abbad had said about the island in his great *History* of 1788 had continued to apply, with more or less severity, throughout the nineteenth century, for the government of the island remained substantially as he had then described it.[9] In 1898, Puerto Ricans were in reality not much nearer to governing themselves than they had been a century earlier, except for the promise of the charter of autonomy. It was still true, as a Puerto Rican liberal had said earlier in the century, that the plums of Puerto Rico were plucked in the island and eaten in Spain. As things turned out subsequently, the issue was only finally resolved by the war of 1898 and the subsequent transfer of sovereignty to the United States.

The nature of the society thus shaped by Hispanic conservatism could be easily foreseen. Exclusion from foreign trade and commerce, though only imperfectly enforced after 1815, involved exclusion from foreign cultural and intellectual influence. Similarly, denial of commercial reciprocity between homeland and colony drew in its wake denial of intellectual and cultural reciprocity. The island leadership's century-long demand for a local university was never granted; and even the mild proposal for a *colegio central* put forward by the San Juan Creole respectable elements was crushed by the hostile reception of a governor who insisted that those who wanted to study could go to Spain, and that if they could not afford to do so it was just as well, since all the poor required was the ability to read and write and imbibe some Christian doctrine.[10] Every effort was made, in addition, to discourage local youth from attending the schools of the North American democracy, on the Catholic ground that they would there become familiar with the corrupting elements of secularist thought. The influence of the Church, indeed, in shaping the Puerto Rican society during this period cannot be overestimated. The liberal intentions of the Crown were not strong enough to keep out of the *Cédula de Gracias* of 1815 a strict prohibition upon the entry of non-Catholic immigrants into the island, a prohibition based partly upon the fear that religious diversity could only mean stimulating the heresy of political independence. As a result, it was left to the neighboring island of St. Thomas, as its main port of Charlotte Amalie flourished, to demonstrate the close relationship between religious toleration and economic prosperity. The same ecclesiastical conservatism stifled the insular press, and the authorities, by the use of the censorship, prohibited the entry of most of the outstanding liberal literature of the century. The prohibition included, in 1862, Hugo's *Les Misérables* and Renan's influential *Vie de Jésus* among other titles; and one of the leading writers of nineteenth-century Puerto Rico, Alejandro Tapia y Rivera, has described how publication of his great work on the historical bibliography of the island, *Biblioteca Histórica de Puerto Rico,* was delayed on the curious ground that it included, among other items, some lines extracted from the eulogy in verse written by the sixteenth-century soldier Juan de Castellanos and supposed, by the censor, to be injurious to the reputation of the *conquistadores.*[11] Much of the nature of insular culture and society, even today, is only explicable in the light of the general fact that for some four centuries the Catholic Church was enabled, without any real competition from other forces, to mold both social institutions and popular attitudes. Even as late in the century of the Enlightenment as 1775, a Spanish official could compose a monograph on the state of the island of which the longest and most detailed chapters were devoted, without a breath of criticism, to a description of the military and ecclesiastical institutions of the society.[12]

Nor was the economic and social character of the island any happier. Since defense considerations were paramount, Puerto Rico never became economically the sort of sugar colony, like Barbados or Santo Domingo, characteristic of the Caribbean economies of England and France, with a slave system based upon large-scale migration of home capital and the inefficient but nevertheless profitable utilization of an incompetent labor force. Official policy, the nature of the laws governing the inheritance of land and property, the difficulties of obtaining credit from the closed circle of San Juan Castilian merchants whose commercial preferences meant at once the signal neglect of local agriculture and the discouragement of local capital accumulation, the widespread habit of smuggling that involved practically all of the interior population in its machinations: all of these factors help to explain why it was that in 1898 only 21 percent of the total area of the island was under cultivation. State expenditure went for ornamental institutions of the society rather than productive ones: in the last year of the Spanish regime the insular budget appropriated nearly three times as much revenue for the purpose of the state church as for those of the entire educational system, while the expenses of the army, navy, and church together totaled nearly one-half of the budget. The total amount of money spent on public education, indeed, some twenty thousand dollars, was just equal to the salary of the Spanish governor.[13] The interests of the burgeoning *criollo* bourgeoisie were subordinated at every point to those of the metropolitan mercantile and commercial classes, so that, among other things, there was a conspicuous absence of all of the services which a local capitalism would have required for its success: after four centuries of Spanish rule the island possessed no banks, no effective circulation of money, only two or three roads, and a bare twenty kilometers of railroad track. It is symptomatic that the first serious attempt to discover and appraise reliable statistical data about population, employment and general living standards in the island was undertaken and completed immediately after the American conquest, in the form of the remarkable *Report on the Island of Porto Rico* composed in 1899 by the United States Resident Commissioner.[14] Civilian life, generally speaking, remained the instrument of military life. As a result, Puerto Rico possessed neither, on the one hand, a rich commercial tradition giving birth to a pleasing domestic architecture comparable to that so splendidly embodied in the great manor houses of Barbados and Jamaica nor, on the other, the sort of urban culture that would have grown up out of a flourishing indigenous capitalism; it is revealing that in 1898 the capital city had a population of less than thirty-five thousand and that there were only eighteen other towns with populations in excess of twenty-five hundred. The separation between town and countryside was exacerbated by an almost medieval communications system, for, typically, Spain restricted her construction activities in the island to the building of a road system by her military engineers—the impressive *carretera militar* linking the north and south coasts of the island across the central mountain range, and built by convict and imported Chinese labor—with an eye to ready control over any movement of revolt. Even journeying from hamlet to hamlet was a hazardous enterprise, and this, combined with the difficult mountainous terrain of the interior highlands, added its own contribution to the endemic parochialism and cultural philistinism of rural life.

The social structure of the island was comparatively simple. At the top was the military-administrative-ecclesiastical leadership of what was basically a clerico-military state, for all the efforts to separate the civil and military branches of the government, as in the proposed reforms of 1869–1870, had turned out to be stillborn. Usually in alliance with that group of the politically privileged class of bureaucratic officials, there was the class of powerful merchants and their employees; then below them the group of professional men—doctors, lawyers, teachers, and journalists—who contributed so extensively to the intellectual life of the capital and to the liberal-reformist movement. In the countryside, social structure was primarily determined by the character of the sugar and the coffee *haciendas,* owned by the social class of *hacendados* and worked, in the case of coffee, by the white or mestizo *agregado* and, in the case of sugar, by the Negro slave and the free day laborer. In the case of sugar, there was a sizable number of owners who had been rich refugees from Haiti and South America; and that fact, combined with postwar prosperity in the sugar markets after 1815, encouraged technological concentration and *latifundia* in sugar while the economy of the coffee highlands remained characterized by the small productive unit. The island proletariat was divided into the class of propertyless sugar workers, concentrated in the coastal sugar plains, and the class of mountain *jíbaros,* of whom many clung to a small property or lived on the margins of the coffee industry.

Two things, in particular, must be noted about the Puerto Rican laborer during this period. In the first place, the Spanish conspiracy laws remained throughout an effective deterrent to independent labor or trade union activity. The individual worker was tied to his local district by custom and, equally important, by the infamous *libreta* or pass system, introduced in 1849, whereby his freedom of movement was severely limited and his failure to obtain work, inevitable in an economy plagued by a superabundance of labor, was in effect penalized as a criminal offense. It is suggestive that throughout the last century of the Spanish period no voice save that of Salvador Brau in his public-spirited address on *Las Clases Jornaleras* in 1882 was lifted to recommend community action for the amelioration of the poverty of the laborer and of the social degradation that accompanied it—for example, the introduction of the cooperative principle (what Brau wanted) on the basis of the Rochdale system.

In the second place, the Puerto Rican proletarian, and especially the *campesino* of the mountain and country districts, developed into a unique pre-industrial character type. Because he, as that type, constituted the beginnings of the peasant class so typical of Puerto Rican society even today, it is of some importance to notice the unique style of his social development. He inherited, to begin with, the anti-social individualism of the early Spanish settlers, many of whom had been common soldiers and sailors eager to try their own luck in the Caribbean game of cutting loose from official authority and, in this particular case, of setting themselves up as entrepreneurs in the remote highlands. Both Marshal O'Reylly in 1785 and Colonel Flinter in 1833 noted in their respective reports the cultural consequences of that behavior. Noting the preference of the original settler for smuggling over agriculture, O'Reylly saw with some sympathy the roots of the preference: "These lazy and unsuitable men," he asked, "without tools and lacking any knowledge of agriculture, and without anyone to help in the levelling of the forest, how else could they better themselves? The habits of indolence were encouraged by a sweet climate that required very little clothing by way of protection, so that one could be content with an ordinary striped shirt and a pair of loose trousers, and since everybody lived thus there were no reasons for competing one against the other; and the sentiment was reinforced by the fertility of the land and the luxuriance of its wild fruits."[15] Flinter noted the same reasons for the decadent seminatural economy of the descendants of those earlier occupants: "a few coffee trees and plantains," he wrote, "a cow and a horse, an acre of land in corn and sweet potatoes, constitute the property of what would be denominated a comfortable *jíbaro*. This individual mounted on his emaciated horse, dressed in a broad-brimmed straw hat, cotton jacket, clean shirt and checkered pantaloons, sallies forth from his cabin to mass, to a cockfight or to a dance, thinking himself the most independent and happy being in existence."[16] The portrait, in sum, is one of an almost utopian rustic simplicity. It disguised, of course, a poverty of terrible dimensions: at the turn of the century the surgeon of the American Army of Occupation was driven to report that although Puerto Ricans lived an almost completely outdoor life, the island was the filthiest area known. At the same time, the portrait helps to explain the massive psychological power of *insularismo* in the island

tradition and the comparative absence of any sense of unity or
identity between the various groups of a community thus so much
physically separated from each other.

Like all Caribbean countries, Spanish Puerto Rico was naturally
affected by the phenomenon of slavery. The Spanish crown had suppressed its misgivings about the institution in the very first century of
colonization, especially when its theological advisers had taken the
position that the Church had never outright condemned it. The Negro
population of the island, consequently, like that of Hispaniola, increased rapidly during the early years of settlement, especially once
the original Indian population had disappeared as a source of forced
labor. But two factors intervened to prevent the Negro ascendancy
characteristic of the wealthy sugar islands. The first was that, after
1815, the heavy influx of Spaniards began to shift the ratio between
the two races, so much so that by 1830 (as far as it is possible to
judge) the balance had changed in favor of a white majority. The
white peasantry was not expelled from the island, as it was in Barbados, for example, nor did African slaves and their descendants
overwhelm the Caucasian population, as in Haiti. The second factor
was that from the beginning the Spanish settlers had had no prejudice
against intermarriage with either Indians or mulattoes, despite the
fact that the racial admixture was looked upon with disapproval by the
outsider, like the visiting Benedictine monk Fray Iñigo Abbad, who
saw in it the original cause of the defects of the Puerto Rican national
character as a whole.[17] The mixed society thus created, although
scornful of the Negro, at the same time became more and more
tolerant of the social advance of the colored man with talent, as the
well-known case of Ramón Emeterio Betances—born, on his own
admission, of an irregular relationship between his parents—amply
proved, for his enforced European exile was the outcome not so much
of his color or parentage as of his radical political opinions. It is
possible, too, that religious prejudice was throughout sharper than
that of race. For although slavery was finally abolished, tardily enough,
in 1873, the society remained to the very end of the Spanish regime
an Iberian clerical state maintaining its barriers against the heretic
and non-Catholic. Not the least intriguing example of that bias was
the fact that for some time throughout the eighteenth century, Puerto
Rico became a haven for slaves escaping from the neighboring slave
islands, who were welcomed by the Spanish authorities with the
single proviso that they accept the Catholic religion and swear loyalty
to the Spanish Crown.

This is not to say, of course, that Spanish Puerto Rico was a racial
democracy, for it was far from being that. Fray Iñigo Abbad noted, in

his discussion of race in the society, that the worst affront in it was to be a Negro or the descendant of a Negro.[18] The island, it is true, never suffered from a general slave uprising. But Dr. Díaz Soler's authoritative study of the history of island slavery, *Historia de la Esclavitud Negra en Puerto Rico 1493–1890,* documented a not insignificant incidence of sporadic revolts and attempted revolts up to the middle of the nineteenth century.[19] The severe *Bando contra la Raza Africana* promulgated by General Prim in 1848, in direct response to the St. Croix and Martinique slave rebellions of that year, indicated how deep the fear of servile revolt lay even in the consciousness of a society in which the institution of slavery was relatively underdeveloped. Despite, too, the comparatively small percentage of the population that was directly enslaved—there were nine times the number in neighboring Cuba—the social repercussions of the institution were extensive enough. Nominally free labor was to some degree assimilated to the status of its slave competitor, as not infrequently occurs when it co-exists with slavery forms. Because, indeed, of the insufficiency of labor supplies recruited from the clandestine slave trade, an extensive "free" labor force had to be coerced into work; and the system of compulsory registration—the "work book" regime—imposed upon the "free" laborer in 1849 had the effect of forcing upon him what was to all intents and purposes a status of peonage. The attempt of Spanish historians to portray Spanish Antillean slaveowners as more humane than others must be seen within the light of all this. For an allegedly "humane" policy was made possible—if indeed it did exist as a fact— by the existence, at least in Puerto Rico, of a large and free but legally defenseless labor population that the ruling class could use at will. The atmosphere of slavery thus impregnated social organization even when its legal basis had disappeared, as had been the case earlier with the apprenticeship system in Jamaica in the decade after emancipation. It was doubtless for that reason that the Puerto Rican Commissioners of 1867, in their report on the proposed abolition of slavery, emphatically insisted that there could be no halfway station between slavery and freedom, and that any attempt to initiate the proposed abolition as a gradualist instead of an immediate measure would be doomed to failure.[20]

The territorial society, in brief, was a composite of various factors —military government, slavery, however ameliorated, economic *patronalismo,* religious pride—that combined to make of it a fundamentally authoritarian society. That could be seen in a number of ways. It was there in the Spanish social religion of *hidalguismo;* never far from the official mind was the superb snobbishness enshrined in the observation of an early writer on the island that the landing, for a brief moment, of the Castilian grandee the Duke of Escalona at the small town of Aguada in 1640 *en route* to New Spain was the most splendid event that the island had witnessed since the original Discovery of the Indies.[21] It was there in the morbid security complex of the insular government, always fearful of the invasion from Santo Domingo or Venezuela that somehow never materialized. One of the leading island intellectuals of the nineteenth century could point with scorn to the curious fact that the San Juan government could devote a wonderfully detailed *reglamento* in 1825 to the supervision of cock-fighting, while on the other hand it was another forty years before the same government could be persuaded to undertake, through the establishment of the first rural schools, the education of the country labourer.[22] It was there in the widespread corruption of an expatriate clergy; by 1898, certainly, the gulf between populace and church was complete, and the Puerto Rican layman who remarked at that time that "we dare not send our daughters to confession" was giving vent to an almost universal distrust of official spiritual leadership.[23] There might have been some connection, there, with the fact that San Juan, on the urgent request of its very first bishop, had been the first bishopric in the New World to receive into its hands the authority of the Catholic Inquisition.[24]

Above all, there was the massive demoralization of social and individual values worked by the whole spirit and practice of colonialism. The best elements of men declined under a system that denied them any full expression, even to the point of the loss of self-respect. The moral passivity of the masses, the absence of a community sense, the general indifference to every consideration save that of personal protection and personal advancement, all were noted with an almost obsessive exhaustiveness by Puerto Rican writers throughout the century. The separation between classes was reflected even in the dualism of popular entertainment, for there was nothing to bridge the chasm between the Europeanized dances and balls of San Juan society and the Afro-Antillean dances of the popular folk culture.[25] The chasm, indeed, was widened by the temptation of the middle and upper classes, Puerto Rican and Spanish alike, to see the "vices" of the proletariat as the cause, instead of the consequence, of its social degradation. They refused to see that, first, the "vices" were not so much the result of ingrained personal indolence or even of a tropical climate as they were the result of the social failure to cultivate the moral and intellectual faculties of the masses; and that, second, even when it was legitimate to designate a cultural habit, like gambling, as a "vice," it was also urgent to remember that it was a behavior pattern that characterized all social classes in a social system that cramped and confined individual talent and ability.[26] Nor was the chasm of class bridged by the growth of racial unity on the part of the nonwhite elements, for the freed colored class, in Puerto Rico as elsewhere, preferred to seek the approbation of their white superiors rather than risk social opprobrium by identifying themselves with the Negro population.

A society of despair produced, finally, a literature of despair. The note of despair, indeed, was the common feature of all the nativist writing, save as some of its authors sought an escape in a colonial emulation of European Romanticism. It was there in the detailed annotation of the moral and mental poverty of the Puerto Rican proletariat in volumes like the *El Campesino Puertorriqueño* of Del Valle Atiles and the *Costumbres y Tradiciones* of Manuel Fernández Juncos. It was there in the device of the public subscription to all sorts of charities whereby the Puerto Rican bourgeois matron sought to salve her guilt complex, and which was pilloried in the verse of José Gualberto Padilla. Something of it, again, was in the semiautobiographical novel *La Peregrinación de Bayoán,* composed hurriedly in Madrid by the young Puerto Rican philosopher Eugenio María de Hostos and conceived, in his own words, as at once a book on the aspirations of the Antilles and on the duties of Spain in the region. There was, finally, the testimony of the unfinished autobiography of Alejandro Tapia y Rivera in which there is drawn the portrait of a young and eager spirit, influenced by liberalism and Christian humanism, gradually learning how to survive in a colonial society full of routine, lethargy, and moral corruption, and governed by men who deported themselves, in the Puerto Rican's phrase, not as mere officials but as ancient viceroys living still in the period of the Conquest. "Without schools," wrote Salvador Brau in a *cri de coeur* that serves as a fine summing up of the argument, "without books, whose importation is banned by the Customs, without metropolitan newspapers whose circulation is suppressed, without political representation, without municipal self-government, lacking either thought or conscience, the physical and mental energies of our people are exclusively absorbed in the production of sugar to sell to England and the United States; Puerto Rico is simply a factory openly exploited. It offers lucrative returns to the big planters, whose sugar wealth is employed to send their sons abroad in search of academic degrees they cannot obtain in the island; many of the latter returning to their native land after a prolonged residence in free and civilized societies in order to run after quarrelsome cockfights regulated by Captains-General, when they are not wasting their time in other games such as roulette, cards and rowdy theatricals; all of which constitutes some sort of burnt offering for a people whose national well-being has been founded upon the shame of slave-labor, whose will has been sterilized by the atrophy of the national spirit and whose customs have been corrupted by objectionable festivals in which the rhythm of the zamba and the crack of the driving whip join together in a single echo; and all of this set within the calm of a serene atmosphere and amid the perfumes of an exuberant vegetation."[27]

Puerto Rican liberalism came to fruition within this environment between 1815 and 1898. The nature of the movement, in terms of both its political theory and its political strategy, is worth noting because it helps to explain to some degree local political attitudes under the subsequent American regime. It is perhaps not too much to claim, indeed, that after 1898 the nature of the play remained essentially unaltered, with the single exception that the leading part was transferred from Madrid to Washington. Just as Ireland, after 1800, remained irrepressibly Irish despite its incorporation into the British political system, so Puerto Rico retained the Latin style of its politics despite its inclusion, by the accident of war, in the American political system.

The outstanding feature, without doubt, of the local liberal movement was its intractable Hispanophilism. For nothing else can explain the odd fact, frequently remarked upon by Puerto Ricans themselves, that, apart from the amateur-like effort of the "revolt of the sergeants" in 1835 and the Lares skirmish in 1868, the island did not throw up, as did Cuba, a serious insurrectionary movement against the Spanish power. It had its individual equivalents of the great Cuban revolutionary leaders like Céspedes and Figueredo and Martí, but they somehow never managed to get beyond playing with romantic fantasies about revolution. It had, too, its own romantic exiles in foreign capitals, but they failed to foment anything comparable to the great drama of the Cuban War. At each moment of liberal upsurge—1809, 1823, 1836, 1868, 1896—the Puerto Rican leadership preferred to rely upon the strategy of extracting concessions from Madrid rather than to challenge openly the Spanish jurisdiction. That was the case both in the unorganized period of political agitation before 1866 and in the period after that date when the right conceded to the island to elect local deputies to the national parliament compelled the local factions to organize themselves more explicitly into liberal and conservative party groups. The last thirty years of Spanish suzerainty witnessed a whole cycle of various permutations in the liberal camp, from the *Partido Liberal Reformista* of 1869, through the *Partido Asimilista* of 1883, to the *Partido Autonomista* of 1887 and the final

split of that latter group into *liberales* and *puros*, constituting through
its bifurcation the genesis of the new party alignments of the American period. But throughout all of the rivalries and regroupings, the
assumption that Puerto Rico could get what she desired by means of
reforms conceded by the national parties in Madrid remained the
major premise shaping the strategy of freedom. The fraternal call
from the Cuban revolutionists to join in overthrowing Spanish rule
fell on unresponsive ears, with the exception of the tiny separatist
minority. The occasional suggestion by a Puerto Rican intellectual
like de Hostos, for example, that all the verbiage of Spanish promises
meant really nothing and that only a decisive separation from a "barbarous patriotism" in which the interests of Spain and the interests of
humanity were conceived to be coincidental could satisfy the demands
of freedom,[28] was brushed aside lest it feed the Spanish suspicion that
the liberal demands were simply a cloak for the sedition of independence. The occasional insight which perceived that it was meaningless
to speak about limited reforms in a colonial system so utterly centralized that, in effect, there were no institutions to reform[29] was put
aside for the same reason.

The upshot of this attitude, naturally enough, was that the local
parties were placed in a position where every play they made was
called from Spain. Their activities were limited to responding as energetically as possible to every opportunity provided by the changing
circumstances of Spanish internal politics. The terms of the argument
were throughout set by the national center. That is why the history of
the insular liberal leadership after 1870 or so is a history of visiting
commissions to Spain, of pacts arranged with friendly Spanish parties,
of memoranda forwarded to the Overseas Ministry of the national
government. From Baldorioty de Castro to Luis Muñoz Rivera, every
political leader spent his genius in elaborate attempts to gain friends
and influence people in the *politica madrileña*. Each sought to organize a fusion with the political faction in Madrid likely to obtain power,
even to the point of disregarding the dangers present in the possible
organizational assimilation of the local parties into the metropolitan
groups, of which they would then become merely the overseas
branches.[30] To be made aware of the profound weakness inherent in
the Puerto Rican liberal strategy, it is only necessary to read the story
of the Autonomist Commission and its efforts in 1896 to arrange a
fusion, first with Cánovas and then with Sagasta—with its vacilla-
tions, the efforts of its members to anticipate the turn of the wheel in
a political crisis brought on by the Cuban War, the struggles against
the general indifference of national leaders to the Puerto Rican matter
so long as the island did not erupt into violence, the readiness to com-

promise with any group likely to be able to form the next ministry when, as a matter of principle, negotiations should have been restricted to the Spanish republicans. The strategy sacrificed principle to maneuver; that is evident enough in the gradual acceptance by Muñoz Rivera, between 1890 and 1898, of a policy of opportunism dressed up as a wise empiricism, as a *practicismo político frente al platonismo*. It placed too heavy a premium upon alliance with the winning side in the lottery of Spanish politics, and thus exposed its architects to the charge that they were only concerned with gaining office in San Juan and enjoying the sweet fruits of power and patronage. The charge can be read between the lines, to take a single example only, of the private correspondence of the makers of the Sagasta Pact of 1897.[31]

All this is evident, in another way, in the gross incongruousness of Puerto Rican liberal hopes when they are compared with the Spanish realities. The *autonomista* ideology dreamed of a self-governing Puerto Rico as an equal partner in a Spanish federated union, combining national unity with cultural diversity; as had been prescribed, indeed, by the Spanish revolutionary assembly in the republican constitutional project of 1873. The idea, at bottom, was one of federal autonomy rooted in the federal principle, although interminable debate raged between those, like Pi y Margall, who thought along the lines of a close federal association on the American model and those, like Rafael María de Labra, who advocated a loose federal structure on the model of the then emerging British Commonwealth. There is little doubt, in any case, of the tremendous influence of the British imperial system upon Spanish constitutional thinkers and Puerto Rican liberal politicians alike. The difficulty was, to put it bluntly, that Spain was not England. There was no long tradition of constitutional government, as in London, to guarantee a liberal imperial outlook. There was never any real chance at any moment of a retreat from the official policy of treating the Antillean islands as colonial provinces. If, indeed, there had been change, everything pointed to change in the direction of full assimilation into the peninsular society rather than of provincial autonomy. Nor must the crucial fact be overlooked that, from the Conquest onwards, official directives from the center of power in Madrid government departments had had a way of losing their liberal content as they crossed the Atlantic. That had been the case with the royal effort in the early period to protect the interests of the aboriginal Indians and, later, of the enslaved Negroes.[32] It was the case, later still, with the attempt of statesmen like Macanaz and Jovellanos to introduce the political and philosophic thought of the Enlightenment into Spain and the Spanish empire under Charles III, supported by the political theory of the Spanish

regalists; one of the very few permanent fruits of that ill-fated enterprise being the revelation to Europe, through the tremendous journeys
of von Humboldt, of the wealth and society of the New World.

It was the case, finally, with the failure of Spanish republicanism
during the nineteenth century to reshape its home society and, after
that, the colonial societies overseas. For no home party outside of the
republican persuasion ever seriously considered provincial autonomy
as a feasible policy. Spanish leading opinion far too often thought in
terms of a supposed "Latin" incapacity for self-government, even if,
logically, the generalization applied as much to Spaniards as to
Puerto Ricans or Cubans. The republican groups had little popular
support, and the gibe that Spain could produce a republic that had
no republicans was not without some truth. Yet all this never seems
to have been sufficiently persuasive to encourage Puerto Rico to break
the umbilical cord binding it to the metropolis. A break, in many
ways, would have been justified, for Spanish diplomacy was not above
using the island as a pawn on the chessboard of European national
rivalries. A Puerto Rican historian has rendered a fascinating account
of a curious episode in 1837 involving the proposal of the Spanish
regent doña María Cristina de Borbón to sell Cuba, Puerto Rico and
the Philippine Islands to the French government, the sale to be facilitated by the payment of a handsome bribe to the aging and cynical
Prince Talleyrand, and only frustrated, at the very last moment, by
the sense of national honor of one of the Spanish emissaries.[33]

Reforms, of course, came eventually. But when they did come they
were invariably the outcome not of a spontaneous and coherent policy
but of the momentary need to retain Puerto Rican good will in crisis.
The reforms of 1812 were thus dictated by the need, first, to prevent
open separation from a Spain weakened by the Peninsular War and,
second, to use the island as a base for counterrevolutionary operations
against Venezuela. Similarly, at the other end of the century, the
concession of autonomy was wrested from the Madrid government
in the midst of its embarrassing difficulties with Maceo's successes
against General Weyler's butchery in Cuba and with the increasing
hostility of American public opinion to its Cuban policy. That is why
there is a pathetic unreality about the thesis, still frequently heard in
Puerto Rican anti-American circles, that the Charter of 1897 was
never given a proper chance to prove itself and fulfill its promise. For
the thesis is only valid if one can assume a continuing readiness on
the part of Spain to maintain and extend that promise, had the island
remained under Spanish control. Nothing in Spanish national history
during the twentieth century, however, justifies such an expectation.
The Republic could not save itself against either the Rivera dictator-

ship or the Franco rebellion of 1936, and could certainly not guarantee the maintenance of the liberal principle in the colonial territories of either Africa or the Antilles. Nor did the transition from monarchy to republic to military dictatorship promise any real change, for under both of the regimes lasting any time, the Spanish people have been governed by the same forces—army, church, rural grandees, professional elites—that had been responsible for converting the nation, after the seventeenth century, into a mere geographical expression. There is nothing in that record to suggest that even without a war in 1898 the promise of reform exacted in crisis would have been honored with the return to normal times, or that Spanish indifference would have been replaced with an alert concern. The disillusioned remark of a Cuban intellectual upon the moral quality of the Cuban Creole Tory ruling class—"We were born and grew up in a house of ruined grandees"—merely reflected, after all, the colonial reproduction of the Spanish tradition at home. It could not have been any different in Puerto Rico. There was something, altogether, about Spanish autocracy that poisoned liberal dreams; it was certainly behind the fate, to take one of the more famous of these dreams, of the great design of Las Casas to establish, on behalf of the Latin-American Indian, a vast Indian commonwealth stretching from the Caribbean Sea to Peru. The Puerto Rican liberal dream could not have turned out more successfully.

The Puerto Rican liberal thus permitted himself to remain a *leal español* against all the evidence that his loyalty was rarely appreciated at its true worth. The only groups that did not do this were those exiles who constituted the Puerto Rican section of the Cuban Revolutionary Party in New York after 1895, or isolated individuals at home like Eduardo Baselge and Damián Castillo, who sponsored a brief and hopeless insurrection against the San Juan regime in 1898. The Creole loyalist was expected to be satisfied with a blind faith in the possibility of future reform, never the guarantee of immediate action. He could not escape, if he were honest, the psychological torture of such a condition. "Two ideas," wrote Gómez Brioso, one of the members of the 1896 Commission to Madrid, to his *confrères* at home, "struggle for supremacy in my mind: concern for the present and concern for the future. As for the first, I do not consider myself confident, while for the second I carry sufficient faith. Can I accept, without damaging that faith, the responsibility of subordinating the first to the second, without any guarantee of a solution, simply for the glory of the moment, and without taking into account the possible unhappy contingency of a future that may almost be upon us?"[34] The Puerto Rican liberal never really answered that hard question. In the long run, as a consequence, he sacrificed both present and future to his chronic indecisiveness. He had to endure the final humiliation of being rescued by the expeditious action of others, in this case the American action of 1898. His struggle against Spanish injustice thus ended not with a bang but a whimper. He thus made it possible for events, as they overwhelmed him, to fulfill the prophecy of those of his countrymen who had earlier observed that Spain would either save Puerto Rico from American penetration, or the United States would save Puerto Rico from the injustices of Spain.

The Rise of the American Mediterranean

THE roots of American interest in the Caribbean go back, historically, to the very foundation of the Republic. Modern scholarship has amply documented the important role of the West Indian trade in the commercial life of the American colonies, and the economic importance of the region was emphasized more than a century later by the status of the Panama Canal as the key to the commercial expansion of the Pacific. This economic basis of American interest was reinforced, of course, by strategic considerations. From the infancy of the American experiment, its leading statesmen lived in constant apprehension of the encroachments of the European powers in the hemisphere. The apprehension was not unfounded when it is remembered that for the best part of a century after 1787 the Republic had to face the icy hostility of most of the European chancelleries, and as late as the Civil War period it was possible for a British political leader as liberal as Gladstone to be making speeches in support of the cause of the Confederacy. British policies in Canada, the Oregon controversy, the bizarre adventure of the Second Empire in Mexico, the fear of European diplomatic influence in the independent state of Texas after 1836, all contributed to buttress the American qualms about the dangers of European expansionism. There was no particular fear about Spanish aggression designed to regain the lost American colonies, for Spain was clearly on the decline and, indeed, many of the later American attitudes to Puerto Rico can only be properly understood if they are seen as offshoots of an earlier contempt for Spanish decadence in the region; it was not too difficult to extend Mr. Dooley's Chicago-Irish lampooning of the Spaniard to the Cuban and the Puerto Rican. The real fear of every American Secretary of State, from Jefferson to Bryan, was that the hemispheric territories in the vicinity of the United States would be torn from Spain and fall into the more aggressive clutch of Britain or France or, later, of Germany. The fear received its definitive theoretical expression in the Monroe Doctrine of 1823, based in turn, as that Doctrine was, upon the New World isolationism of Washington and Jefferson. Its practical application was mapped out in the form of American policies within the field of Caribbean international relationships, beginning with the audacious Louisiana procurement of 1803 and ending with what essentially became, after the war of 1898, the organization of an American sphere of influence more and more insulated against European penetration and controlled by a Caribbean application of the dogma of Manifest Destiny.

The details of that development are well known. Before 1898 they were part of a larger American national expansionism on the immediate national frontiers—the acquisition of Florida, the Texan War, the control of the Pacific coast. After 1898 they came to constitute a more aggressive policy in the more immediate Caribbean area— the seizure of Cuba and Puerto Rico, the establishment of the Panama Republic as an instrument for American control of the isthmian canal, the growth of "dollar diplomacy" in Haiti and Santo Domingo, military intervention in the Central American states, strategic imperialism in the form of acquired naval bases and an effort, somewhat less successful, to set up American influence in the states of the South American continental littoral. It should be noted that there has been, throughout, a remarkable consistency of policy on the part of successive American national administrations. Both of the major political parties have espoused the Caribbean expansionist program. The Grant Administration, it is true, failed to obtain Congressional consent to its proposal to annex Santo Domingo by treaty, but a generation later no influential voice was raised against the annexation of the Spanish islands. Seward and Blaine, as Republican Secretaries of State, were matched in their zeal for annexation as a policy by Democratic Secretaries like Olney. And once popular disapprobation of overseas expansion began to decline after 1893 every President from McKinley to Coolidge, and every Secretary of State from Hay to Kellogg, whatever his party affiliation and whatever the tone of his utterances on United States relations with the Latin American-Caribbean world, was impelled to much the same sort of decision when confronted with the responsibility of solving one of the perennial Caribbean crises. A record of anti-imperialist sentiment did not prevent Bryan, in his brief occupancy of the State Department, from propagating a scheme for obtaining a controlling influence in the affairs of the Central American republics by means of an American insurance of their bond issues on the world financial market. Both of the liberal Presidents Cleveland and Wilson entertained high ideals of international morality with indisputable sincerity. But the one approved the Olney dispatch of 1895 on the Venezuelan dispute which became one of the best-known statements of the new expansionism in its assertion that "the United States is practically sovereign on this continent, and its fiat is law upon the subjects to which it confines its interposition"; while the other's real sense of shame over the first Mexican War of 1845-1846 as a ruthless predatory enterprise did not prevent him from adopting a policy of active, albeit reluctant, interference in the affairs of revolutionary Mexico after 1913; nor did it deter him from a policy of paternal despotism in the Central America and Caribbean areas that included the Crowder mission of "preventative intervention" in Cuba and the military occupation of Haiti and Santo Domingo by the United States Marines.

The sole distinction between Republican and Democratic actions was, at best, one of degree rather than one of kind. Both agreed with the new nationalism. Both supported the type of sentiment contained in the observation of the Assistant Secretary of State in 1904 that "it seems plain that no picture of our future is complete which does not contemplate and comprehend the United States as the dominant power in the Caribbean." The power of the isolationist tradition in the national life, of course, had not forever disappeared under the bewitching influence of such sentiments on the larger world canvas, as the withdrawal from the League of Nations experiment decisively showed. But withdrawal from Europe was never coupled with any idea of withdrawal from the Caribbean. Even an isolationist America, like the concept of a "fortress America" a generation later, subsumed an exclusive American sovereignty within the region. By the end of the First World War this had become a settled element of national foreign policy, both Democratic and Republican. The earlier dream of a virtuous farmers' Republic abjuring imperialist habits—described, for example, in the statement of Representative Rhea in 1811 that he would not be in favor of annexing West Indian territory unless "it would please the Almighty Maker of worlds to move the foundations of the West Indian islands and place them alongside of the United States"[1]—had by that time become irrevocably lost with the departed springtime innocence of the American people.

The factors that went into the making of this American imperialism were naturally miscellaneous. There was the growing popularity, in the '90s, of the cult of sea power made fashionable by the writings of Captain Mahan. There was the occasional influence of the American filibuster like Walker in his Nicaraguan escapade and General Cazneau in Santo Domingo; as well as their European counterparts, like the quixotic figure of the Danish Captain Christmas who played a sort of Rafael Sabatini hero role in the extended negotiations that led up to the sale of the Danish West Indies to the United States in 1917. There was even, at times, the temptation to use external adventure as a means of assuaging domestic discontents, as evidenced in Seward's "Thoughts for the Consideration of the President," composed at a moment of Union difficulties during the Civil War. There was the influence, always formidable in American life, of the popular press, and American historical scholarship has fully demonstrated the contribution of the Hearst and Pulitzer "yellow press" towards generating a popular war sentiment in the period immediately preceding the outbreak of war in 1898.[2] Along with this there went the feeling, semi-militaristic as it was, that outside adventure was "healthy" for a nation, a feeling publicized not only by American conservative writers but also hinted at by liberals like Herbert Croly.

All of these elements, however, were ancillary causes only, not to be compared in their importance with the twin major factors of economic interest and continental defense strategy. With regard to the first factor, the relationship between the state power and organized business interests in the growth of overseas expansionism in the American case has not always been easy to decipher, for there was present no separate class, like the "nabobs" of British India or the "West India interest" in the eighteenth century English House of Commons, whose sole interest lay in overseas economic imperialism, nor were the interests of American capitalism so sharply divided between the groups operating in the domestic field and those specializing in the foreign field. Nor is it intellectually a sound enterprise to portray the nationalist expansionist program as a self-conscious and evil manipulation of the political process by "big business," for so to do— as is the tendency in a book like *Dollar Diplomacy* written by Scott Nearing and Joseph Freeman in 1925—is to undertake the thoroughly un-Marxist procedure of attributing motives to the imperialists instead of recognizing their behavior as a simple and logical consequence of the system they in part represent. Yet however passive a role American business played in the initial impetus towards expansion, it did not long delay in seizing firm hold of the commercial opportunities opened up by the military men and the politicians. Within less than a generation after the Treaty of Paris (1898), the large American sugar corporations had taken over the bulk of cane production in Cuba, Santo Domingo and Puerto Rico, replacing the *colono* system of cultivation with the bureaucratized impersonality of the huge and heavily capitalized *central*. By 1925, with the exception of a few Italian-owned concerns, the principal sugar estates in Santo Domingo were American-owned;[3] by 1933, the year of the first Batista *coup d'état*, American sugar investment had become the basis of the Cuban economy, supported by incorporation into the United States import quota system; while by 1935, on the eve of the local agrarian reform movement, nearly fifty percent of all lands operated by sugar companies in Puerto Rico were under the control of the big four American-owned concerns.[4] A similar process occurred in the world of oil. The fabulously rich Maracaibo oilfields of Venezuela, opened up in 1918, were taken over by the international oil cartels, with a predominant American interest, with the result that by 1955 American companies occupied a commanding position in the industry's gross investment, to the extent of some 61 percent, as compared with the figure of 47 percent in the Middle East and 54 percent in Canada. By this time, too, Venezuela had become, in Rómulo Betancourt's book title, a "petroleum factory" controlled by an alliance of American oil men and native militarists.[5]

The semi-feudal empires of sugar and oil, in their turn, were reinforced by the financial and mercantile Americanization of the Caribbean and Central American countries. With the aid of the State Department the New York banking houses became the guarantors of the bonded indebtedness of one country after another. The favorite device to procure this end was that of a compulsory American customs receivership, frequently guaranteed by treaty arrangement, as, for example, in the 1907 convention forced upon Santo Domingo. The device had the double effect of, first, directing the flotation of loans to the New York financial market and, second, creating a practically airtight monopoly for the intrusion of a variety of American business concessions in the fields of public works, mining, fruit cultivation, electricity and railroad services, steamship communications and lumber exploitation. The outcome, for most of the small countries concerned, was a system in which government, politics, economic activity, the very texture of social life itself, were shaped by the *Diktat* of the major foreign trading concerns. "His country," wrote the well-known American journalist Richard Harding Davis at the turn of the century describing the average Caribbean citizen, "no matter what her name may be, is ruled by a firm of coffee merchants in New York City, or by a German railroad corporation, or by a line of coasting steamers, or by a great trading house, with headquarters in Berlin, or London, or Bordeaux. . . . You find this condition of affairs all through Central America, and you are not long in a Republic before you learn which merchant or which bank or which railroad corporation controls it, and you soon grow to look upon a mule loaded with boxes bearing the trademark of a certain business house with more respect than upon a soldier who wears the linen ribbon of the Government."[6] The only change that had taken place, a generation later, was that American enterprise had become relatively more powerful as the economic meaning of the Monroe Doctrine conferred upon the American

banker, in alliance with the American government, the exclusive prerogative of enforcing the terms of the commercial relationship upon
the Caribbean consumer. A series of case studies by American scholars—Leland H. Jenks's *Our Cuban Colony*, Melvin M. Knight's *The
Americans in Santo Domingo,* Fred Rippy's *The Capitalists and
Colombia*—has described what this process fully involved. By 1930
the region had indeed become the American Mediterranean.

The second leading factor in the process, apart from economic
aggrandizement, was that of American national defense. From the
very start, when Balboa forced his way across the Darien isthmus to
reach the Pacific, the international existence of the Caribbean Sea has
whirled around the weighty strategic importance of the Panama-
Nicaragua canal project. It engaged the attention of the early Spanish
historians of the New World like Herrera, of Humboldt, of Franklin,
of Goethe. The most famous of all Latin American emancipators saw
the vast political implications of its geography: "If the world," Bolívar
wrote, "were to select a spot for its capital, it would seem that the
Isthmus of Panama must needs be chosen for this august destiny,
situated as it is at the center of the world, looking in one direction
towards Asia, and in the other towards Africa and Europe, and equidistant from America's two extremities."[7] Characteristically, however,
as its Canal diplomacy unfolded, the American leviathan power was
concerned less with the cultural than with the commercial, and even
more the strategic, promise of the isthmian passage; and Panama City
today is hardly a Paris or a Rio de Janeiro. Control of the passage
would mean a connecting link between the American east and west
coasts; it would facilitate hemispheric defense, a need graphically
illustrated by the naval dispositions of the 1898 war; and it would
finally establish American paramount interest in the whole area. All
this came to require, from the viewpoint of the American nationalist,
both a unilateral American regulation of the Canal region and a right
to fortify the immediate environment; and these demands were slowly
advanced to abrogate, finally, the promise of a neutralized and non-
militarized Canal written into the clauses of the early Clayton-Bulwer
Treaty of 1850. This meant, too, the final sacrifice of both the commercial interests of Great Britain in the Canal—surely as real as
American interests—and of the collective interest of the international
community to the single interest of the American nation. Senator
Morgan's extravagant claim that the construction of the canal should
be seen as "the proud mission of our Government and people, under
a providence that is as peculiar to them as the founding of the kingdom of the Messiah was to the seed of Abraham"[8] has been the sort
of braggadocio, as much as any real defense needs, that has driven

Washington increasingly into a policy of going beyond the Canal area to construct naval and air bases throughout the land screen that faces it: Roosevelt Roads, Guantánamo, Chaguaramas.

Perhaps, indeed, the argument of defense has been exaggerated. At least one American authority noted as far back as 1929 that an elaborate system of Caribbean naval stations east of the Canal did not seem necessary as a defense against Japanese attack from the west of it, and that the progress of aviation was rapidly bringing nearer the day when Japanese aviators would be able to reach the American continent without going near the Canal or its Caribbean defenses;[9] and the Pearl Harbor attack twelve years later vindicated the accuracy of the analysis. The chief motive behind the purchase of the Danish West Indies in 1917, again, was the desire to prevent Germany from securing a naval base at St. Thomas or St. John. But, as later events turned out, the only threat of an enemy beachhead being established in the archipelago came from the possibility that Britain or France, in their efforts to appease the Axis powers after 1935, might have been willing to hand over the territories of either Trinidad or Martinique and Guadeloupe to Hitlerite Germany. But this contingency was met by President Roosevelt's readiness to have the United States fleet seize the islands in case the threat were to materialize.[10] The secret power exercised by military cliques on the foreign policies of European nations is an old story. What is surprising is that the anti-militarist bias of the democartic creed did not prevent a similar secret power from growing up in Washington after the 1890's. Indeed, it is not without some significance that some of the most industrious architects in the shaping of the Caribbean as an American lake were naval men like Captain Mahan and military men like General Leonard Wood; and they were in fact members of the neo-Hamiltonian movement centered around an important group of men—Henry Cabot Lodge, Elihu Root, Herbert Croly, Albert J. Beveridge, and the two Adams brothers—who attempted between 1890 and 1920 to reinstate the ethic of military professionalism in the estimation of a society given over too much, as they saw it, to the corroding values of a business pacifism. Their effort failed with the return to "normalcy" in 1920. But it did not fail before they had succeeded in persuading national opinion that the Caribbean, at least, was henceforth to be regarded and retained as an American sphere of influence.

Two elements in the pattern of "Manifest Destiny" deserve some extended annotation. The first is the armory of methods utilized by the United States in its practical application of the theory. It has been one of the myths of the American democracy that it was above employing the methods that had been used by a quasi-feudal Europe in the search for world power. Yet the history of American enterprise in the Caribbean reveals not merely a readiness to emulate those methods but also a genius in improving upon them. There was the method of armed intervention to protect American propertied interests, as in Cuba in 1906 and Haiti in 1915. There was the method of the "financial protectorate" imposed, as in Haiti and Santo Domingo, by formal treaty and, in Cuba, by measures such as the famous Platt Amendment of 1902 which conferred a right of continuous American intervention in the local fiscal sovereignty. There was the tactic of forcing an "undesirable" political leader out of office by withdrawing or withholding diplomatic recognition, as was the case with the Huerta regime in Mexico in 1913; although the fact that a Latin American *político* had used terrorist methods as evil as those of General Huerta in order to gain power did not elsewhere deter Washington from recognition. Nor was there any real aversion to the method of military intervention for the purpose of promoting revolutions favorable to the American interest; the most famous and the least excusable of such adventures was President Theodore Roosevelt's provocative encouragement of the "revolution" in the province of Panama in 1903 engineered by the French international adventurer Bunau-Varilla as the occasion for the final capitulation of the helpless Colombian government and Congress to the American scheme for obtaining a unilaterally controlled zone in the Panama district. Outright occupation of a country of course was repugnant, genuinely so, to American governments. But the sentiment did not prevent the transformation of a Central American nation like Nicaragua into what was, bluntly, a "client state" run by American-appointed officials, nor did it deter the McKinley administration from the brutal suppression of the patriotic Aguinaldo insurrection against the American occupants of Luzon in the Philippine Islands after 1898.

Patently the Achilles heel of all imperialist enterprise—it is founded, in the last resort, upon naked force—appeared in the American case just as in the British and the French. Certainly, it was nothing less than a gesture of poetic justice that, in 1897, the Spanish Minister of State replied to American protests against Spanish brutality in Cuba with the pertinent reminder that the Spanish army in that island had done nothing more than what Sheridan had done in his wartime invasion of the Shenandoah Valley or what Sherman had done in his terrible march through Georgia or what, finally, the Confederate government had perpetrated in its huge prison camp at Andersonville.[11] The brutality of Marines in Haiti and Santo Domingo, if less spectacular, was equally real. The general situation was further compromised by the fact that in the absence of any tradition of American colonial administration the men who were appointed by Washington to be ministers or special executive agents or financial receivers in the Caribbean countries were hardly of the best caliber. They were appointed, in the main, on the basis of the spoils system, not on that of merit or of record. Secretary of State Bryan's letter of 1913 addressed to the General Receiver of Customs in Santo Domingo, requesting knowledge of any likely appointments that might be put to use as rewards for "deserving Democrats," is well known. The unhappy result, only too often, was the appointment of men like Charles Magoon in Cuba and James Mark Sullivan in Santo Domingo.

The second aspect of "Manifest Destiny" to be noted is the impressive catalogue of intellectual rationalizations to which it gave birth as Americans sought to square their new-found imperialism with their democratic and egalitarian tradition. In this respect the United States did not differ from other nations, although it is possible that the Puritan background of the tradition, as in England, made the search for a moral foundation more urgent than was true of other nations. In any case, the collection of theories whereby Americans have justified to themselves the pursuit of empire is at once varied and astonishing. Dr. Albert Weinberg's definitive analysis has listed them with a remarkable anthropological exhaustiveness.[12] The justification has at times taken the form that it is a "law of nature" for a people to expand, sometimes the form that if expansion ceases death supervenes. Or it has been the argument of natural right, which then justifies claims to expansion by geographical propinquity, the argument of national security, or the claim that action is necessary to prevent the possible accession of a dangerous neighbor. Or outward growth may be justified by a theory of predestined geographical use, so that the superior ability of the American to "use" the territory he has coveted becomes, as in the case of the American Indian, a sufficient rationalization of forced expropriation. The doctrine of the "white man's burden" is likewise invoked, so that it becomes the moral duty of America to civilize the "backward" peoples, to spread Christianity, to prevent (a special glossary on the text) the sacrifice of native peoples to Catholic "barbarism" such as that of Spain in the Philippines. The religious argument was a powerful one with the American Protestant missionaries who used their Calvinist economic virtues to found the first dynasty of wealthy expatriate clans in the Hawaiian Islands after 1820. The decline of Christian faith has made it obsolete and old-fashioned in a later century, but the universe of reference of the "quiet American" in the contemporary world overseas is really much the same sort of thing stripped of its religious verbiage.

In the Caribbean, two other ingenious systematizations of policy
were invoked. One was the thesis that the American nation is justified
in territorial seizure where the present occupying country hinders the
interests of "collective civilization" by its refusal or tardiness in cultivating the potential of the region under its jurisdiction. This was the
official justification for President Theodore Roosevelt's actions in relation to the Panama Canal. According to this thesis the United States
held a vague mandate from world civilization to coerce a nation
which, by its "selfish" actions (in the Canal issue, Colombia), stood
in the way of measures that would benefit the world as a whole. It was
a position anticipated as early as 1826 in Representative Cambreling's
observation, with reference to Cuba, that "The right of Spain once
extinguished, from the nature of our position, and our peculiar and
various associations with that Island, our right becomes supreme; it
resists the European right of purchase; it is even paramount to the
Mexican and Colombian right of war."[13] The doctrine here defended
applied apparently not only to the exploitation of virgin lands but also
to the economic and technical development of already established
economies. Thus President Taft could speak of the necessity of re-
membering, when thinking of the Caribbean, that "it is essential that
the countries within that sphere shall be removed from the jeopardy
involved by heavy foreign debt, and chaotic national finances, and
from the ever-present danger of international complications due to
disorder at home. Hence, the United States has been glad to encourage
and support American bankers who were willing to lend a hand to the
financial rehabilitation of such countries."[14]

The other argument particularly used with reference to Caribbean
action, apart from this one of America as the trustee of international
interests, concerned the self-image that Americans have always tended
to have of themselves as the greatest exponents of "democracy" the
world has seen. Whatever the historical and ideological roots of the
idea—the "New World" ideology, the impact of the frontier on
American thought, natural law theories—it has seen democracy not
merely as a system of government but also as a moral condition; and
it has seen its exportation to other nations as the peculiar duty of
American leadership. The truth does not seem to have made itself
evident to that leadership that representative institutions of the Western liberal type have been the outcome of a special collection of social
and cultural conditions in the advanced industrializing societies of the
nineteenth century and not of a universal and absolute law of social
nature. Even as sophisticated a mind as Woodrow Wilson's was able
to combine a theoretical recognition of this truth with a passionate
belief in the obligation of America to push "good" government upon

less fortunate peoples. His remark to Sir William Tyrrell, that "I propose to teach the South American Republics to elect good men,"[15]
meant, in effect, American intervention in the affairs of these countries
and American sponsorship of local candidates who measured up to
American standards of "goodness." This was the case, at least, with
President Guerrero in Panama in 1904 and with President Jiménez in
Santo Domingo in 1914. Sponsorship could not avoid a more or less
permanent intervention in order to keep the favored candidate in
office. For the entire theory of "democracy," in its American sense,
required the presence of far too many factors that were conspicuously
absent in the societies to the south. Politics, in Mexico or Nicaragua,
or Cuba or Haiti, careered around the representative type of politician
who combined strong personal ability with a complete absence of
scruple with respect to the methods he pursued in satisfying his ambition. The idea of popular consent was thus even more of an antiquated
fiction than it was in the United States. For it was certain that a
politician who owed his office to the good will of the American State
Department, often backed by a show of open force, could not hope to
play any genuinely "democratic" role in the governing of his society.
For his main obligation was to the foreign authority; and the main
purpose desired of him was the effective maintenance of "order" so
that the outside propertied and strategic interests might not be placed
in peril. Finally, the spirit no less than the method of compulsory
democracy was illiberal, being accompanied by an attitude of self-
righteous condescension to those supposed to benefit from it. The
worst example of course was the spectacle of the opprobrious epithets
hurled by President Roosevelt against the Bogotá politicians who,
naturally enough, were reluctant to yield to the "big stick" tactics of
Washington during the Canal crisis of 1902-1903. Yet even when a
cultured mind, such as Root's, was in charge at the State Department,
this sort of arrogant contempt was replaced, not by a sense of equality,
but by a pervasive patronizing tone. The Secretary's statement that
the people of Central America "are perfectly willing to sit at the feet
of Gamaliel if Gamaliel won't kick them or bat them on the head"[16]
was, after all, hardly a complimentary remark. Franklin Roosevelt,
it is true, repudiated the idea behind all of this that the United States
had a right, by means of the doctrine of paramount interest, to act
alone as the policeman of the hemisphere. He insisted that "when the
failure of orderly processes affects the other nations of the continent . . . it becomes the joint concern of a whole continent in which
we are all neighbors."[17] But this was in 1933, before the new President had had a chance to invent institutional methods that would be
appropriate to a foreign policy of friendly collaboration.

The ideology of "democracy for export" accounts for much of the apologetic literature on the United States in the Caribbean. The American citizen has been told that American rule or influence has brought enormous benefits to the Caribbean peoples by way of stamping out diseases, improving sanitation and communications, building schoolhouses and establishing honest and efficient methods of public administration. Much of all this is true, for it would demand a complete absence of any sense of proportion not to admit that there are areas of Caribbean life, in education, in irrigation, in medicine, in which the devoted zeal of American officials has been worthy of all honor, within the limits that conditions have permitted. As a surgeon of the United States Army, General Wood's interest in health improvement and sanitation in Cuba after 1898 became a famous chapter in the history of the world's fight against tropical diseases. It required a quite obsessional hatred of Americans to believe—as did the Puerto Rican Nationalist Party in an unfortunate episode in 1932 —that American doctors could undertake a deliberate scheme of exterminating native populations under the guise of treating them for tropical illnesses. Apart, however, from the consideration as to whether even genuine progress that is imposed upon a politically subordinate society can be regarded as "democratic" in any real sense of the word, there is the distinct consideration that the details of the progress have been incidental effects rather than central purposes of American action. They were not elements of a deliberately conceived imperial policy, nor did they correspond in any way to grand outlines of imperial intent worked out by officials with care and foresight, as had been the case, for example, with British officials ever since Macaulay in India. American officials never anticipated a permanent stay for their rule in occupied countries, because the national administrations preferred, if possible, to seek their ends by indirect rather than direct rule. Thus no administration in Washington ever considered, as some American private citizens interested in the Caribbean at times suggested, the issuance of a proclamation establishing a fifty-year tenure in an occupied country for the purpose of helping to replace the habit of *caudillismo* in politics with that of parliamentary responsibility after the Western fashion.[18]

And once the period of direct military intervention was replaced, after 1930 or so, with a period of indirect political and diplomatic influence, the general result was that the improvement measures introduced by American officials were of a transient character only, lacking a base in the form of any long-term planning for social and economic rehabilitation. Even more important, they lacked the base of a popular support in the countries concerned, an absolute necessity were they to become anything permanent. Indeed, the measures carried through often had the consequence, if not the planned purpose, of streamlining political and administrative machinery for the better exploitation by outside interests of the Caribbean resources; the new road system developed in Puerto Rico after 1900, for example, primarily catered to the transportation needs of the new American sugar companies. Individual American officials often managed to create a sense of genuine partnership with their local counterparts. But this was the exception, not the rule. It was extremely rare for Washington, when it made its diplomatic appointments in the region, deliberately to set out to court Caribbean approval by the appointment of a Negro ambassador or minister. A notable exception was the appointment of Frederick Douglass to the Port-au-Prince post in 1889, and it is worth recording that during his two years' stay in the island he completed the writing of an introduction to the first English version of the life of Toussaint l'Ouverture written by the great French Senator, Victor Schoelcher, who had been mainly responsible for the French slavery emanciaption measure of 1848. Nor, indeed, was the record of the American administrative official always an impeccable one. Perhaps the best-known example of his irresponsibility was that of the United States Commissioner in Santo Domingo, J. H. Hollander, one-time President of Johns Hopkins University, whose acceptance of a handsome private fee from the Dominican government was unearthed by a House of Representatives subcommittee in 1911 and subsequently aired for the Caribbean audience by the prominent Dominican intellectual Fabio Fiallo, whose imprisonment a decade later by the American military government became one of the *causes célèbres* of Latin American freedom.[19]

In sum, American activity in the Caribbean, like all colonial activity anywhere, must be finally judged by its essences and not by its accidents. Democratic altruism and its offshoots were throughout subordinated to strategic and commercial considerations. This can be seen in the gradual transformation of the Monroe Doctrine, during the century after its promulgation, from a limited doctrine of non-intervention into a doctrine justifying open intervention on the part of the United States into the internal affairs of the hemisphere as a whole. The change was justified on the ground that the United States, by virtue of its geographical position and political power, enjoyed a natural right as the special guardian of hemispheric liberties. The presumed guarantee against the possible abuse of that right was seen in America's eminent moral distinction as a free society. The guarantee assumed a sort of neo-Grecian theory of "civilization" versus "barbarity." As the constitutional theorist John W. Burgess phrased it, it was "the manifest mission of the Teutonic nations, that interference in the affairs of populations not wholly barbaric, which have made some progress in state organization, but which manifest incapacity to solve the problem of political civilization with any degree of completeness, is a justifiable policy."[20] The guarantee, obviously enough, was a nebulous one. By the time that the first Roosevelt issued his famous corollary to the Monroe Doctrine in 1904 the theory of guardianship had in truth become a wide-ranging theory of a hemispheric police power which could be used whenever the United States decided that its vague criteria had been violated. What had been in its origin a prohibition of European imperialist adventure in the hemisphere became transformed, in fact, into a mandate for American imperialism. The Doctrine had become, in Alberdi's phrase, a doctrine of intervention against intervention. It is hardly a matter for surprise, then, that whereas President Monroe's original declaration had been received with almost unanimous approval, even relief, by the newly formed Latin American republics, its later metamorphosis into a neo-imperialist idea naturally led to disillusionment and hostility.

Bolívar's early fears are of course well known. Such fears became more widespread as the young American power took on more and more the habits of European power politics. For even although Washington administrations were usually reluctant to countenance the ideas of the annexationists—of which one of the best known enterprises was the effort of pro-Confederacy groups to annex Haiti as an addition to the column of the "slave states" of the American South— the idea of an indirect American guardianship was never far from their mind. From a Caribbean point of view there was little difference between annexationism and the view, embodied in the outlook of John Quincy Adams, that the best policy for the United States was to permit an ailing Spain to retain Cuba until it could be wrested from her without the risk of later losing it—an outlook which explains why the American delegates to the abortive 1826 Panama Congress carried instructions to oppose the separation of the Antillean colony from Spain. Increasingly after that Congress, accordingly, there emerged a search for Pan-American institutions that could serve as resistants to the growth of United States tutelage over the region. The search was accompanied by political concepts, such as Pan-Hispanism and Pan-Caribbeanism, designed to offset the cultural penetration of the region by American ideas. Hence, therefore, a growing literature on the part of the Latin American intelligentsia to emphasize the historical dignity of their cultural heritage as against the strident tones of the "Yankee" democracy. The institutional search led ultimately to the creation of bodies like the Pan-American Union, for example, always with the confederationist bias initially given to the search by Bolivarian political thought. For its grand purpose throughout was to clothe with some institutional apparatus the proud boast of the 1826 Congress that "A hundred centuries hence, posterity, searching for the origin of our public law and recalling the compacts that solidified its destiny, will finger with respect the protocols of the Isthmus."

The intellectual counterpart to this growth of institutions based on the needs, social, economic and strategic, of the Latin American and Caribbean peoples also became more assertive, especially after the turn of the century. It is to be seen in the work of José Enrique Rodó, in the poetry of Rubén Darío, in the scholarship of García Calderón, in the famous essay of Manuel Ugarte on *The Destiny of a Continent*. It is true that the note of much of the literature was that of a shrill and shallow vituperation, often curiously ill informed about the realities of American life. The observation of the Colombian novelist Vargas Vila that "wherever the Englishman goes, a village is born; wherever the Yankee goes, a race dies" indicated that, only too often, the Latin American publicist frequently went beyond a spirit of anger, warranted by the facts, to a spirit of ugly hatred. It thus became only too easy for Americans to discount the entire criticism as the fruit of spleen or envy. It could be dismissed as just another expression of the clamorous and exaggerated rhetoric of the "Latin temperament." But the original sin, nevertheless, lay with the Americans. Nor were Americans, as a people, helped towards a more understanding attitude by their leaders. As late in the day as 1928—to take examples from the Caribbean only—President Coolidge could blandly notify Puerto Ricans that "the United States has made no promise to the people of Porto Rico that has not been more than fulfilled"; and, following him, President Hoover could leave a lasting wound with the people of the American Virgin Islands by his inopportune remark that these American possessions were "an effective poorhouse." The "Open Door" policy, on a larger scale, made it plain after 1899 that the full weight of American officialdom would be thrown behind the economic expansion of American business overseas; and the "Good Neighbor" policy of the New Deal, a generation later, did not fundamentally alter this end.

The general upshot of all this was a disastrous neglect of any sustained effort to consider Latin susceptibilities, to meet Latin prides and prejudices halfway. In one way, possibly, the unpopularity of the United States was unavoidable. For there is no record in history of an empire that in the long run has not had to pay the price of the general dislike of its subjects. The unpopularity nevertheless was needlessly

exacerbated by the general American character traits: the almost
boyish passion of the American to be liked, the general American
contempt for the past, the tendency of the American people to reduce
the culturally strange to the status of the "backward" or the "picturesque," their conviction that other people can solve their problems
only by copying the American Way. With Latin America, too, all this
was immeasurably strengthened by the general fact that alien to each
other in language, race, habitual practices and thought patterns, each
civilization, North American and South American, entertained an
abiding assurance of its own innate superiority and a tendency to
boastfulness so deeply imbedded as almost to seem, in both cases, a
dominant national trait. There had been no real clash between the
two opposites for the best part of their respective histories, with the
exception of the Mexican War; for while the North American drive
had been towards the virgin west the South American drive had been
towards the consolidation of a national independence in the southern
hemisphere frequently applauded and supported by liberal and democratic sentiment within the United States. After the Spanish American
War that ceased to be so. The hitherto divergent paths crossed as the
American democracy embraced the ambitions of a hemispheric leader.
This involved overseas territorial acquisition, what Professor Bemis
has styled the "great national aberration." It was the peculiar fate of
Puerto Rico to become, thereafter, a testing ground of the conflicts
that were thereby unleashed.

The Imperialism of Neglect: 1898-1932

THE transfer of Puerto Rico from Spain to the United States owed its astonishing smoothness to the fact that a war between the two nations was certain to be a naval war rather than a destructive land campaign and equally certain, as Calixto Bernal had noted as early as 1865, to end in an American victory since the American forces would restrict themselves to the Caribbean theater where they held the strategic advantage.[1] The easy transition was accelerated by the absence of any real regret on the part of Puerto Ricans for the passing of the Spanish overlordship. Few of them, it is safe to say, would have cared for the sort of Spanish Quixotism which suggested to the Governor-General in charge of the island at the time of the American military landings the appalling idea of exposing the defenseless seaport of Ponce to the possible bombardment of the American naval guns, a possibility that was in fact only forestalled by the hurried intervention of the British Vice-Consul in that southern metropolis.[2] Nor did there appear, in the sixty years following the transfer of sovereignty, any sort of patriotic literature cultivating the myth of a Spanish Puerto Rico flowing with milk and honey. The romantic regret for Spain was purveyed not so much by the Puerto Rican intellectuals as by the visiting European writer like Luis Araquistain in his book of 1928, *L'Agonie Antillaise*. The thesis of that book was to portray a Caribbean "decadence" charged against the unfortunate "Africanization" of the region that had allegedly been undertaken by all the colonizing powers in the region with, it was urged, the signal exception of Spain. In refutation of the thesis it was only necessary to point out, as did the French writer Paul Morand a little later, that if there had in fact occurred any "decadence" in the area it was as much due to Spanish colonial policy as to any other; for, once enriched, the *grand seigneurs* of the reign of Philip II had no more bothered to attend in person to their New World holdings than the court nobility of Louis XVI had visited their Haitian plantations.[3] A Spanish colony, of course, remained in Puerto Rico after 1898 and attempted through institutions like the *Casa de España* to perpetuate a tradition of devotion to the past ideals of the peninsular kingdom. But its members remained too aloof from local affairs really to matter. Their program, if any, centered around the feeling that, with the coming of the Americans, a feudal domain over which they had once ruled had been unceremoniously snatched away from them. And, in any case, the Spanish Civil War of 1936 finally shattered their dream of a serene and united Spain to which Puerto Rico might one day have peacefully returned. The portrait of a happy Spanish Caribbean, in brief, was no closer to the realities than, to take another hemispheric myth, the romantic dream of *indianismo* that was employed by anti-Spanish writers, even as late as the nineteenth century, as a weapon with which to exaggerate the black record of the Spanish conquerors of the sixteenth century.

From the beginning, then, the society was generously receptive to American penetration and American guidance. Indeed, it was only by a stroke of luck that Puerto Ricans had had the opportunity of release from Spain at all, and there had been fears among the Puerto Rican revolutionary groups in New York that the island would be by-passed by the war activities. The expedition to the island, as a military movement, had been hardly more than a casual by-product of the major concentration on Cuba; and even then it occurred, in part, because General Miles had been anxious to emulate in Puerto Rico the achievements of General Shafter in Cuba. The conquest completed, however, Puerto Ricans settled down to what was to become a process of Americanization in all corners of their national life, economic, technological, cultural, political, educational. Actively or passively, all sections of opinion initially accepted the process. It was not until the economic depression of the 1930's that the process had to confront, in the Nationalist Party, the first concerted anti-colonial movement predicated upon the theory that, legally as well as morally, the American authority had no right to be in the island except by the fiat of conquest.

The Puerto Rican response to the process, as a matter of fact, was not always a simple one. For an anti-Spanish sentiment did not always necessarily imply a pro-American one. A Puerto Rican scholar, Dr. Eugenio Fernández-Méndez, has pointed out, on the contrary, that the years after 1898 witnessed at least three different stages in the anthropology of Creole attitudes to the character of the Americanizing process. First, between 1898 and 1900, there was a period of hospitable and hopeful reception. Second, between 1900 and 1929, this first response was followed by a growing sentiment, essentially colonialist, of resentment and opposition. To this, third, after 1929, there succeeded a more positive search, on the part of the insular intelligentsia, for a cultural autonomy and a sense of national selfhood, epitomized most famously of all in Antonio Pedreira's essay on *Insularismo*. In each stage, of course, the cultural question was tied to the political question; and still is. During the third stage, in particular, the political groups that have sought a Creole cultural affirmation have been divided into those, like the Nationalist and the Independence Parties, wanting a complete rupture, gradual or immediate, of the political ties to the United States, and those, like the Liberal Party and, later on, the Popular Democratic Party, desiring some sort of autonomous political status which would retain those ties at the same time as they permitted recognition of the unique cultural identity of the island community. The debate, throughout all three stages, has been spirited. It has given vent to a legion of answers to the problem. Its tone has ranged from black pessimism to disarming optimism. Throughout it all, however, every participant in it has known that he has been dealing with a theme of truly tragic dimensions.[4]

The real American rule, from the outset, was not so much the new form of government introduced by the American Congress as the massive economic penetration that followed hard on its heels. Americans looked at the new territory, characteristically, in terms of its business opportunities. One of the first books written on the island for the American reading public, William Dinwiddie's *Porto Rico: Conditions and Possibilities*, was a frank attempt to appraise business opportunities for imaginative entrepreneurs. Another volume, Albert Gardner Robinson's *The Porto Rico of Today*, published in 1899, sought, as its main purpose, to "throw light upon the commercial possibilities in our new possession that lie within the reach of American business men."[5] The new American officialdom also campaigned assiduously for more private capital to "develop" the island. Commissioner Henry Carroll, in his important Report to President McKinley in 1899, insisted that the prosperity of the island "cannot be accomplished without the influx of new capital."[6] The Committee appointed by the Secretary of War in the same year to investigate civil affairs recommended that "the most favorable conditions should be made to encourage the investment of capital" in the island.[7] The United States Consul in San Juan spoke of the several thousand letters he had received from continental business men seeking information about investment opportunities, in part because they had heard of the island people that ". . . they are not a class of people acquainted with strikes. . . ." The annual Report, finally, of the first civilian Governor, Charles H. Allen, attained almost lyrical proportions when it addressed itself to the same question of investment: ". . . when the American capitalist realizes that there is a surplus of *labor accustomed to the Tropics*, and that the return of capital is exceedingly profitable, it is my feeling that he will come here . . . to make at least five spears of grass to grow where one had grown before, *to the immense and permanent prosperity* of the Island."[8] The salesmanlike language was perhaps hardly necessary, for within two weeks of the military occupation of the island the first advance guard of business representatives arrived, many of them impecunious young men who hoped to benefit rapidly from speculative possibilities; while, more importantly, the House of Representatives was told as early as April 1900 that syndicates to buy up practically all of the rich sugar, tobacco, and coffee lands of the island were already being organized, and that representatives of the great railroad, telegraph, and other corporations had been besieging Congress for months for the purpose of obtaining lucrative concessions.[9]

The economic history of the island for the next forty years was, in a sense, the remarkable success of those efforts. By 1930 the twin developments of economic concentration and of absentee ownership in insular enterprise had been carried almost to the limit. In the field of public utilities and banking the degree of absentee ownership by American corporations was some 60 percent; in the tobacco industry, 80 percent; in the sugar industry 60 percent; and in the steamship lines operating between the island ports and the mainland ports, almost 100 percent, the latter by reason of the fact that after 1900 the insular economy lost its free bargaining power in that field as a consequence of being placed under the coastwise shipping legislation of the United States, and to the detriment, incidentally, of the island's export costs in comparison with those of her Caribbean neighbors. In the case of sugar, by 1930 the "big four" of the American companies and allied interests operated, all told, some 46 percent of all lands worked for sugar; in the case of shipping, the system served to give four American shipping lines a virtual monopoly apiece over the transportation of passengers and commodities between the island and the mainland. The phenomenon of absenteeism, of course, was not introduced by the American investor, for the richer of the "sugar barons" in Spanish Puerto Rico had themselves been absentee landlords, Spanish from the start, and it was a change of detail rather than of underlying circumstance that, at this time, the corporate stockholder in the United States succeeded to the status of absentee owner. Nor, moreover, was it something new that, coming under the American tariff system, the Puerto Rican consumer was henceforth obliged to buy his basic necessities, including his indispensable foodstuffs, in the American market at tariff-inflated prices, for under the previous regime he had been equally the victim of Spanish mercantilist practice.

What was new, in both cases, was that a decadent and inefficient capitalism was replaced by a dynamic and efficient capitalism; but the new efficiency worked for the interests of the colonial producer and not for those of the consumer. The exploitation of the island's resources became at once more systematic and more routinized. The groups that resisted the technological and organizational changes involved in that fact were few indeed; and Dr. Thomas Cochran's study of the older Hispanic-oriented San Juan merchant class houses has shown that even where the members of that commercial class resisted the introduction of impersonal bureaucratic methods in their business arrangements—except for the introduction of business machines no technological or administrative changes of any importance had taken place in many of their mercantile establishments even as late as the 1940's—they were happy enough to garner the fruits of the new prosperity.[10]

The *locus classicus* of economic change was, of course, the sugar industry. Nothing could better illustrate, indeed, how the basic folkways of life are set by the demands of economic enterprise. For in 1898 the controlling factor in the island's foreign trade had been the famous coffee product, protected by the Spanish tariff, whereas sugar had played a secondary role. With the change of sovereignty, however, the American investor found that he could obtain a larger profit in the resuscitation of the sugar industry, since the American consumer was already addicted to other, non-Puerto Rican, coffees. The result was that a traditional industry that had long been the natural cash crop of the independent Puerto Rican highland farmer was allowed to languish, not even being permitted the protection—which sugar immediately received—of the American tariff; and at the same time it was cut off from its old European markets. The results were calamitous; and at least one Puerto Rican writer has insisted that the industry was destroyed not, as one myth would have it, by the grievous San Ciriaco hurricane of 1899 but by the deliberate economic policy of the new American regime.[11] Its place was rapidly taken over by a tariff-protected sugar empire. By 1930 sugar was responsible for some 78 percent of all capital invested in manufacturing; its exports constituted some 65 percent of all products exported; and in capital invested the industry accounted for five times the amounts invested in the coffee and tobacco industries combined.

The decline of the "small man" in agriculture was inevitable. The structure of the sugar industry, as it yielded to large-scale production changes, both technological and managerial, facilitated the dependence of the small planter, the *colono* class, upon the centralized sugar factory. The *colono* contract, which determined the whole range of relationships between the two, was heavily weighted in favor of the latter, for the *colono* incurred all the expenses of cultivation, including the grim hazard of hurricane, paid interest at an exorbitant rate on the money he invariably had to borrow, in most cases from the *central* management, and generally bore the high costs inevitably attached to a system in which field and factory were under separate and therefore uncoordinated supervision. The smaller type of *colono,* who operated less than fifty acres, found himself working against impossible odds. In the long run he was obliged to yield to one of two courses: either to continue borrowing until his capital expired or to sell his property outright to the larger concerns. The statistics of land sales indicate that he was driven, more often than not, to do the latter. This meant the gradual absorption of the small into the large holding, with all the social and cultural effects that land concentration always brings with it. It was not for nothing that this agrarian lower middle class became one of the most activist of political groups during the 1930's.

There were other consequences equally unfortunate. There ensued a grave and dangerous distortion in both the utilization and the returns of the resources of the island, human and natural. There was distortion in resource utilization by reason of the fact that the aggressive promotion of commercial crops and the tendency of the latifundia to alienate land hitherto devoted to subsistence food growing resulted in a steady decline in the production of crops that could be used for local trade or immediate domestic consumption. The Puerto Rican consumer was thus obliged to buy high-priced imported foods from the American market or, as was the case with the poverty-stricken majority, be driven back to, virtually, a starvation diet of the very simplest of ground provisions.[12] The profitability of sugar in reality stifled the continuing growth of production of rice and of corn, both of which had been industries of considerable importance before 1898. That the island was capable of raising far more produce for home consumption without materially endangering the major export crops was in fact demonstrated by the success of the official program, under a government food commission, of local food production during the First World War. But the end of hostilities meant the relaxation of organized public effort and a return to judging economic effort in terms of private profit. "Apparently," concluded the Brookings Institution study, *Porto Rico and Its Problems* in 1930, "a development that was socially desirable proved to be economically unprofitable."[13] Here as elsewhere the island had to pay the price exacted by an exaggerated emphasis upon a monoculture capitalist economy. And this meant, in addition, a distortion of economic reward, for sugar was characterized by high profits and low wages. The most famous of all

Puerto Rican trade union leaders, Santiago Iglesias, estimated in 1920 (when the war-induced sugar "dance of the millions" was at its height) that 70 percent of the total profits of the industry in Puerto Rico went to foreigners, and that of the remaining 30 percent a large amount was spent abroad by wealthy Puerto Rican shareholders.[14] The consequences of this draining off of the national wealth were incalculable.

"I do not know," wrote Bernardin de Saint-Pierre during the eighteenth-century golden age of sugar capitalism, "if coffee and sugar are necessary to the happiness of Europe, but I do know that those two crops have been the scourge of two parts of the world."[15] American Puerto Rico, as far as sugar was concerned, bore out the truth of the observation. No single fact illustrated it so graphically, perhaps, as the dismal story of the concerted efforts of the sugar corporations and their allies, after 1900, to repeal the so-called 500-Acre Law which the Congress had written into the first Organic Act of Puerto Rico in 1900, and which it repeated (as if to reassert its original intentions) in the second Organic Act of 1917. The belief which underlay the prohibition against land holdings above that figure—that the best solution to the agrarian problem was the fractionalization of corporate-owned latifundia—went back, of course, to the neo-Jeffersonian ideas of the trust-busting legislation of the United States Congress after 1889. Puerto Rico became American territory in the very middle of that legislative period and could not escape its touch. The federal Congressional attitude coincided too with the belief, almost an *ideé fixe,* of Latin American and Caribbean politicians that the ideal economy was that of a healthy agriculture founded upon the social type of the *petit propriétaire,* rather like the Haitian homestead pattern of small growers in a closed economy. That the belief looked to the past rather than to the future, however, provided no justification for the combined efforts, in Puerto Rico, of governors, sugar corporation attorneys and insular officials to seek the repeal of the federal legislation over a period of more than thirty-five years. Up to 1917 the campaign took the form of open attempts at repeal directed to Washington; after that date it became more of an underground propaganda, usually by "respectable" sources aided or subsidized by the sugar interests. It is a matter of record that Dr. Clark, the editor of the Brookings Institution study in 1930, subsequently admitted to having recommended the repeal of "this futile act" on the basis of the advice solely of legal counsel and that, in addition, the volume written by Gayer, Homan, and James in 1938 on *The Sugar Economy of Puerto Rico,* in which Dr. Clark's recommendation was endorsed, was composed at the instigation of American-financed land-owning interests in the island.[16]

As events turned out, the failure of the repeal movement was academic only. For the same period witnessed a persistent and successful evasion of the legislation by means of a series of consolidations in sugar ownership. No attempt was made either by the federal or local government to enforce its terms. There were, in fact, neither enforcement nor penalty clauses of consequence to put teeth into the law. Though the federal Congress, wedded to the economic philosophy of trust busting, was adamant against the sugar pressure groups in their repeal campaign, it failed, at the same time, as much in Puerto Rico as on the mainland, to discover the administrative methods and the administrative zeal appropriate to a rigorous enforcement of its legislation. That the task nevertheless was not an impossible one was made evident by the swift success of American official policy, in the contemporary case of the Philippines, in putting an end to the agrarian monopoly of the "Friars' Lands" which had been in large part responsible for the local insurrection against Spain before the war. Here the success was in the main part due to the genius of William H. Taft as administrator in the Pacific dependency, and the failure to solve a not dissimilar problem in Puerto Rico was due to the absence, in part, of such genius in the American officialdom in the island. "Looking at things in retrospect," a Puerto Rican authority on the matter has concluded, "it is not difficult to discern that whereas the vision of enlightened administrators had solved a grave problem for the Filipinos, an utter lack of vision, orientation and courage had created a grave problem for Puerto Ricans."[17] By 1935 the tragedy of the thing had finally become apparent to Washington. "Puerto Rico," wrote Secretary Ickes to Senator Duncan Fletcher in that year, "has been the victim of the *laissez faire* economy which has developed the rapid growth of great absentee owned sugar corporations, which have absorbed much land formerly belonging to small independent growers and who in consequence have been reduced to virtual economic serfdom. While the inclusion of Puerto Rico within our tariff walls has been highly beneficial to the stockholders of those corporations, the benefits have not been passed down to the mass of Puerto Ricans. These on the contrary have seen the lands on which they formerly raised subsistence crops given over to sugar production while they have been gradually driven to import all their food staples, paying for them the high prices brought about by the tariff. There is today more widespread misery and destitution and far more unemployment in Puerto Rico than at any previous time in its history."[18]

By 1930 Puerto Rico had thus become a typical sugar island. The socio-cultural superstructure erected on top of this economic base centered, accordingly, around the value patterns traditionally associated with the "King Sugar" ideology. Society, politics, culture, all were touched by these patterns. The spectrum of political attitudes was delicately adjusted to the patterns, so that it was altogether fitting that the towns of the high country in the center and west of the island should have become a stronghold of pro-independence sentiment since they were in the heart of the coffee region destroyed, in part, by the new prestige of sugar. Thus the town of Lares gave its name to the most famous of local revolts against Spain, and the town of Jayuya its name to a brief stand, in 1950, against the American power. The game of politics came to make its central concern the question of the next year's sugar quota to be agreed upon by the American Congress; and it became one sure way to embarrass seriously any politician to accuse him of wishing to liquidate the sugar industry. Much, perhaps, of the ferocity of the game in Puerto Rico might be traced to the fact that the natural instability of a raw commodity product in an uncertain world market was intensified by the extra-natural instability that stemmed from the latent hostility always present in the Congress to the claims of offshore producing areas that might at any moment result in quota or preference changes detrimental to the interests of competing continental districts.

The change in the production base entailed changes, inevitably, in the insular social structure. What took place in the island after 1898 was the replacement of a rudimentary rural capitalism by an industrial, high-finance capitalism. The characteristic social type of the former economy—the individual and independent *hacendado* working his family farm—gave way to the managerial hierarchy of the corporate sugar factory. Statistics showed the change. In 1894, 205 sugar haciendas had marketed the island crop; by 1948, they had been reduced to 35 central stations, twelve of which were in the hands of the four leading corporations and concentrating, in their production, some 39 percent of the total output. The statistics dramatized the decline—as in eighteenth century England—of an entire social class, for as the *criollo* estate owner was forced to sell out to the expatriate corporations he either became the raw material of a decaying gentility or that of a new *rentier* class, becoming, in the latter case, a land agent or a company manager for the new owners. Like all dispossessed classes, its members looked upon their successors with small affection and it was from this source, as much as from any other, that there emerged the feeling that 1898 had merely inaugurated the rule of "Yankee carpetbaggers" from the North. Even when the change entailed merely loss of prestige and not of landed wealth, the reaction was not dissimilar; and the figure of Don Pedro in Wenzell Brown's novel, *Dynamite on Our Doorstep,* accurately embodied the violent anti-Americanism of the type, recruiting its terrible strength from the deep feudalistic sentiment of Spanish days.

The decline of this class was naturally accompanied by the decline of the way of life it had constructed. The charm and sweetness of the old style were undoubtedly real; and they have been lovingly described in Antonio Oliver Frau's volume of short stories, *Cuentos y leyendas del cafetal,* published in 1938 when, as features of the social landscape, they had already practically disappeared for ever. They exist today only in the form of somewhat idealized reminiscences by "old hands" who remember them before they passed away as part of the old plantation life. As the family-type hacienda was supplanted by the corporate *central* organization there went hand in hand with the change a quiet revolution in an entire category of folkways. A semi-feudal paternalism, protecting the worker from the worst of the onslaughts of rural life, gave way to an impersonal wage system. The local resident landowner who cared for his employees and who gained, in many cases, the reward of their affectionate respect was replaced by the American manager whose attitude, on the contrary, was shaped by the fact that he was an outsider likely in the future to be posted elsewhere by his distant head office in the States. The old face-to-face relationship with the *padre de agrego* or *señor de ingenio,* both in the sugar and the coffee regions, yielded to a more formalized and bureaucratized dependency upon the manager, the store boss and the labor foreman; while the system of company credit and piecework incentive combined together to place the worker at the mercy of unscrupulous company town practices and equally unscrupulous labor contractors. The older social types of the Puerto Rican small town and countryside—gathered together in the gently satirical portraits of the *Galería Puertorriqueña* of Manuel Fernández Juncos—were followed by types more adjusted to the new production relations; and although the figure of *el tigre* in that collection, the type of the sharpster who gets ahead in life by taking sly advantage of the human weaknesses of his fellow men, predated the American occupation by some two decades it described nonetheless accurately the sort of antisocial attitudes encouraged by the acquisitive instinct of American business life. Dr. Sidney Mintz has described in detail what the transition meant for a typical sugar plantation on the south coast in the period following its sale to one of the new American corporations.[19] The human cost involved in it all is muted in that account, perhaps, by the prudent language of the anthropologist. But Puerto Ricans themselves were fully aware of the cost; and said so. In the words of the 1927 statement of the Puerto Rican Socialist Party, the

only visible heads of the enormous gorgon that sucked the blood of the
Puerto Rican people were the unimportant figures of its managers and
agents. The economic government that ruled over the island citizen
had in fact become an invisible force as foreign power replaced local
power.[20]

The déclassé bourgeois thus had company in the shape of the
proletarianized worker. The highland *jíbaro* and the sugar worker of
the coastal plains were subjected, even more brutally, to the process
of technological rationalization. They became daily wage earners—
those who could obtain work at all—in the classical sense, with the
difference that employment in primary-producing economies is seasonal only and therefore more hazardous in its fundamental character. They became propertyless, too, in the classical sense, for it is
general experience, to which Puerto Rico proved to be no exception,
that large corporate farms in a densely populated economy are invariably detrimental to the community welfare; thus in Puerto Rico
by 1930 some 150,000 workers, with 600,000 dependents, owned no
land at all. The employee was dependent upon the corporation for
credit, employment, and housing; and if the plantation house that
he inhabited was frequently superior to the wretched hut that the
jíbaro built for himself from rudimentary resources, this was mainly
because it was more convenient for the management to have an ever-
ready supply of labor resident on its property. The dissolution, especially, of the mountain region enterprises converted the highland
farmer and the sharecropper more and more into migrants seeking
work on the coast, and the process, already under way before 1898,
was accelerated by the rapid decline of coffee production after that
date. And while the process had its compensating features—it facilitated, for example, the growth of social fraternization between the
white highland peasant and the Negro coastal plantation employee—
its main effect, sociologically, was to stimulate a rapid disorganization
in the life of the communities it visited. Even by 1930, long before
the mass migrant exodus to the United States and before the advent
of the worst period of the economic depression of the 1930's, the
island was struggling with the aggravating problem of excessive urbanization as country people flocked to the coastal cities; an early study
of conditions in one of the poorest quarters of San Juan indicated that
90 percent of the residents came from other parts of the island.[21] The
rural squatter, who could be ejected from his mountain hut at will by
the landowner, was thus matched by the urban squatter who crowded
into the slums of the coastal towns. The process of proletarianization
thus fostered was not counterbalanced, either, by the rise of a large
and prosperous middle class of well-to-do farmers, on the European

model, which might have acted as a cushion between the few and the many. At best, the economic changes created no more than a new subgroup of middling professional people, in the main directly or indirectly associated with the new ruling class of managers, agents, attorneys, and salesmen, and therefore quite removed, either in contact or in sympathies, from the rural masses.

The individual Puerto Rican was thus exposed to the full blast of a socio-economic revolution that was allowed to run its course with little effort on the part of the federal political power to channel it into more desirable social directions or to shield the more defenseless local groups from its consequences. This was evident enough in the particular case of the *jíbaro,* at once the largest group of the society and the most neglected. The tragedy of this rural Puerto Rican is that he has been, under both of the historic regimes, at once the object of a romantic idealization on the part of the more vocal and more prosperous groups in the island and the victim of a persistent exploitation, often on the part of the same groups. Spain, it is true, was originally responsible for his moral and social degradation and for his banishment to the more remote hill areas as a forgotten and submerged person. But the American regime did little to raise him from that level, as is indeed made sufficiently evident by the striking similarities between reports on his condition at the beginning of the regime and those of a generation later. "The *jíbaro,* mountain bred," wrote Drs. Bailey Ashford and Gutiérrez Igaravídez in their outstanding medical report of 1900, "avoids the town whenever possible, avoids the genteel life of a civilization higher than that of his own. He instinctively tucks his little hut away in the most inaccessible spots; he shrinks from the stranger and lapses into stolid silence when brought face to face with things that are foreign to his life. He does this because he has been made to feel that he must do all that he is told by established authority, and he knows that this authority never takes the trouble to look for him unless it expects to get something out of him; because he is suspicious of outsiders, having been too often led astray by false prophets and disappointed by broken promises; because he realises that he is not a free agent anywhere save in the mountain fastnesses." Added to this there was the fear bred of the social and mental gulf between him and his "betters," who regarded him with condescending and half-affectionate contempt: "this lack of mental contact, of a common ground of interest between the *jíbaro* and the better class of Puerto Ricans drives the former to charlatans for his medical advice, to the wild fruits and vegetables of the interior for his food, and to weird creeds for his religious comfort."[22] The monograph that Professor José Rosario penned for the Clark Report some thirty years later on *The Porto Rican Peasant and His Historical Antecedents* corroborated most of this earlier evidence and showed that, at the very best, conditions had changed in degree only and not in substance. There was the same dismal and ugly housing: two thirds of peasant homes had no latrines. Despite an active public health program, disease was still rampant: 90 percent of the country people still suffered from hookworm. To start a conversation with a *jíbaro* family about health, in Rosario's sentence, was like opening a catalogue of diseases. Trained medical attention was still scanty and the promiscuous use of patent medicines still widespread. Malnutrition was rife, verging on real starvation in the slack employment season. The same discrimination in the educational advantages available to the town child and the country child that had prevailed under the Spanish flag still persisted under the American. The enormous increase in productivity in the insular economy due to American investment and American technical improvements, especially in the sugar industry, was heartening, but its benefits were largely nullified by the tremendous population increase during the same period. In 1930 as in 1900, all told, the effective growth of community consciousness was inhibited by the isolation and the ignorance of the countryman. What leisure time was available, finally, was consumed in anti-cultural amusements such as petty gambling and cockfighting. With the exception of the Protestant churches which had arrived after the American occupation, there were few groups undertaking any serious work in either the social or the moral rehabilitation of the masses. It remained one of the tasks of the future to mobilize the social mind of the island in favor of maintaining and continuing that work.[23]

It would be a gross libel on the real virtues of the American character, of course, to say that all this went unnoticed. The American people have rarely ignored an open appeal to their generosity and they have given of it willingly, even to the point of wasteful prodigality. The Puerto Rican plight, as it was brought to their attention by journalists and publicists after 1898, did not fail of response on their part. The work of voluntary associations during the thirty years after 1900 was of real and lasting value. The Protestant churches made the island a vital mission field. The San Juan Presbyterian Hospital became a byword in the Puerto Rican household, and its professional standards were rewarded with the honor of being the first hospital in the West Indies to win accreditation from the American College of Surgeons. The Board of Presbyterian Missions introduced, in the form of the San Germán Polytechnic Institute, the characteristically American phenomenon of the privately endowed college. The major activity of the American Red Cross inaugurated, and especially through its Public Health Nursing program, the use of the trained nurse in insular medical organization. The Rockefeller Foundation spent a small fortune in combatting such diseases as hookworm and malaria. And Columbia University undertook, in collaboration with the University of Puerto Rico, the planned rehabilitation of the island's educational system. These efforts were backed up by the activities of the insular government, once authority had been transferred from military officials to civilian officials in 1900. Departments like those of Education and of Agriculture and Labor achieved quite remarkable results in their respective fields; the reduction in the rate of illiteracy by roughly one half of its appalling 1900 level within one generation, to take one example only, was evidence of the new concepts of public health and public administration propagated by the new regime. Altogether something like fifty million dollars in loan funds, in addition to tax revenues amounting to about one tenth of that sum, had been spent in the island by the federal government by the time the Brookings Institution Report of 1930 was published.

But at least three things must be said of all this. In the first place, official expenditures concentrated most heavily upon appropriations for public works projects—roads, public buildings, municipal utilities, and power plants—and therefore did little more than touch the surface of the deeper social and economic ills. Such projects are, at best, limited in their power to generate full employment (a condition the Puerto Rican economy has never enjoyed) while they cease to possess even that limited power once an economy reaches the level of public works saturation. The main emphasis of government enterprise was in fact placed upon the maintenance of law and order rather than upon the promotion of any kind of long-range social planning; an emphasis suggested in the fact that of the nine principal administrative departments comprising the governmental structure only three— Health, Education, and Agriculture and Labor—could conceivably be thought of as coming under that category of planning; while the remaining six—Justice, Finance, Interior, Police, the Auditor's Office, and the Office of the Executive Secretary—came under the category of public order. Second, the tax system instituted by the government after 1900 failed, on the whole, to challenge the enormous export of wealth taken from the island in the form of foreign-owned company dividends and profits. It was estimated in 1930 that of the four principal industries coffee alone was primarily Puerto Rican in its management and ownership and that the remaining three—sugar, tobacco, and fruit—held absentee properties amounting in their sum total to some 52 million dollars.[24] Yet the rate of public taxation imposed upon either properties or profits was astoundingly small. The distribution of profits was not locally controlled in any way, so that income sent from Puerto Rican sources to outside individuals or corporations remained untaxed by the local government. Even when such income, under certain stipulations, was locally taxable, there was a high degree of successful evasion on the part of continental investors and owners. Rafael Cordero supplied evidence to the Americans Bailey and Justine Diffie (in the composition of their book on the island, *Porto Rico: A Broken Pledge*) proving persistent under-assessment of sugar properties in the island in relation to their real value.[25] The Clark Report, in substantiating the charge, noted in addition that evasion was facilitated by the fact that, first, the local legislation did not provide ways and means of compelling non-residents to make tax returns and, second, the insular tax authorities had never taken advantage of the federal laws permitting them to examine the federal income tax returns of mainland corporations doing business in the island. The insular government was at last driven to the expedient of imposing a special levy on the sugar exporter in 1923, but a survey undertaken by the local *Asociación de Agricultores* discovered that the sugar *centrales,* with very few exceptions, simply passed the tax on to the farmers by means of a bare-faced insertion into the *colono* contracts.[26] A telling indictment of the gross inequality of the tax burden came, finally, in the recommendation of the Clark Report—hardly noted for the revolutionary tone of its findings—that there should be set up a special tax on wealth passing out of the island and that, from the mainland side, Congress should act favorably upon the recommendation that the federal authorities pay to the island territories, including Puerto Rico, the maximum amount of the deduction allowed continental citizens for income tax paid to such territories.[27] But the Report did not indicate what methods might be employed to persuade the Congress so to act.

Third, and finally, there was too heavy an emphasis altogether upon the political aspects of the new "freedom" that America had brought to the island territory. A reading of the large American literature on the island, both official and unofficial, with few exceptions gives the distinct impression to its reader of Americans alternately purring with pride in the thought that they have "given" political liberty to the Puerto Ricans and shaken with anger at the possibility that the Puerto Rican may be "ungrateful" for the gift. Yet it is doubtful if the majority of Puerto Ricans, the agricultural proletarians, discovered any real difference in their political life, save, perhaps, for the grant in 1917 of American citizenship. It is even more doubtful if political liberty could mean much to a people who had never savored it during the Spanish period and who could not possibly view it through the spectacles of an American constitutional liberalism. Liberty for them was centered around social and economic experience; and from this viewpoint American rule had meant little indeed. When a New England Brahmin orator like Whitelaw Reid spoke of "the almighty Yankee Nation" undertaking "the extension of ordered liberty in the dark places of the earth,"[28] the glittering rhetoric, for the Puerto Rican patriot, would have to be set against the fact that some three decades after its utterance the social condition of his island, in the adjective used by the Clark Report, remained "deplorable." Under America as under Spain, Puerto Ricans were governed by an alliance of business corporations, high officials, and local professional politicians; and the burden was perhaps made even more intolerable because of the self-righteous attitude that the American government and people brought with it.

The absence of positive citizenship marked both regimes. Some of the keenest American observers, for example, had argued for the planned growth of a system of peasant proprietorship, allied with a system of rural cooperatives, similar to that of Denmark. But, again, little was done along these lines. Only too frequently the problems of the new territories were dismissed as the deserved reward, or the necessary misfortune, of peoples who could not be expected to exhibit the economic virtues of Americans; Whitelaw Reid's contemptuous reference to "Chinese, half-breeds, pagans, and all" was typical. It was rarely inquired, if these charges were true, why the conquistador ancestors of Puerto Ricans had earlier exhibited entirely different traits or why, even more pertinent, similar blameworthy habits seemed, in the contemporary present, to be prevalent among the Carolina and Tennessee mountain descendants of the original "pure-blooded" English stock of the Middle Atlantic states. Even when American official effort to help showed itself in its most energetic and attractive form in Puerto Rico, as in the program of public education, its administrators did not appear to consider the grave implications of placing the attainment of education in front of the problem of insuring whether its possessor, later on, would enter an employment environment wherein the education could be effectively put to use.

Even the most undemocratically minded of Americans residing and working in the island could not escape the fact that in a colonial society the more lucrative and comfortable appointments gravitated to the outsider rather than to the native candidate. One American journalist who saw himself as a "calm and neutral observer" could not refrain from wondering "why the sweat-stained laborers in the cornfields should be seen wearily tramping homewards to a one-room thatched hovel to share a few boiled roots with a slattern woman and a swarm of thin-shanked children while the Americans who direct them from the armchair comfort of fan-cooled offices stroll towards capacious bungalows, pausing on the way for a game of tennis in the company compound, and sit down to a faultless dinner amid all that appeals to the aesthetic senses."[29] This contrast was a familiar daily scene in the lives of the laboring poor, whereas the political benefits of American rule were something that took place far off in San Juan; and there is a famous short ballad by Luis Lloréns Torres that tells of the simple countryman whose earthy skepticism about these benefits remained immovable in the face of the blandishments of the city *pitiyanquis* who pestered him on his visit to the great metropolis. The fact that the capital city had gained by 1914 a reputation, under American standards of hygiene, of being one of the cleanest of modern cities[30] could have had little meaning for a population that was still overwhelmingly rural. The grant of American citizenship was no doubt received with real enthusiasm, as the remarkable record of island voluntary recruitment into the national armed services after 1917 sufficiently testified. But citizenship in itself did little to raise the living standards of the average Puerto Rican, and it could hardly compete in importance with the rapid proletarianization that the rule of the sugar and tobacco corporations set under way. A planter Senator who was himself sympathetic to the rural masses as they confronted this unhappy prospect recognized it as the prime reason for the growing popularity of the Socialist Party in the country after 1920. The *jíbaro* has affiliated himself to that party, he told the *Ateneo Puertorriqueño* in 1922, "not because he has been convinced by a doctrine that he cannot understand, but because he is attracted by its promise of an immediate improvement in his material life; in much the same way as the early converts to the Christian message placed their vision and hope in the promised spiritual prize of the life beyond."[31] The warning was all the more suggestive because its author was convinced that a socialist solution for Puerto Rico was wholly wrong and that, on the contrary, the solution lay in state encouragement of a class of small landowners and growers after the French rural model. But such warnings went unheeded as being nothing much more than an exaggerated fear and remained, therefore, merely occasional expressions of social consciousness on the part of exceptional individuals. All in all, the Puerto Rican people would have been justified in feeling, by the time the New Deal program arrived in Washington in 1933, that the transfer of sovereignty had meant nothing much more for them than that they had been brought up out of the Spanish land of bondage in order to perish in the American wilderness.

The Politics of Survival: 1898-1932

EVERY conquered people must learn the terms of accommodation with its masters. If it is sufficiently unreconciled it may, of course, attempt open revolt, like the Italians against the Austrian yoke or, before them, the Netherlands provinces against the Spanish. If, however, it is disposed to accept its subordinate status in the hope of improving upon it by gradual peaceful concessions from the dominant country, then its political energy will be devoted to the search for ways and means of extracting these concessions. Such a relationship may terminate in the ultimate incorporation of the territory into the political and constitutional system of the governing power, in which case— as with Scotland after the Union of 1707—the colonial connection is replaced with the organization of a common government and a single political community. Or the relationship may continue as a permanently unequal one, so long as the leading groups in the colonial society are willing to accept the "mother country" as a trustee for their interests; this was the case with the British crown colonies throughout the nineteenth century. Yet even where the juridical relationship is mutually satisfactory there will usually remain problems of cultural accommodation not, on the historical evidence, easily resoluble. Eighteenth-century Scotland, for all of the finality of the English connection, was not free of such problems, as a reading of Scott's *Waverley* proves. A people may welcome the economic improvement that comes from a political connection yet deeply resent the acculturating process that is certain to accompany it. In such a situation, the peculiar province of the local political parties is, in part, to become the vehicle of the resentment. The struggle for extended internal self-government is then enmeshed with the struggle for cultural identity. Indeed, the one may become the prisoner of the other.

Something of this sort occurred in the history of Puerto Rican political parties after 1898. Each different stage in the development of local attitudes to the Americanizing process was reflected in the diagram of local political formations. The first brief period, between 1898 and 1900, witnessed a honeymoon idyll, with both of the newly constituted parties, the Republican and the Federal parties, vying with each other in their ardent declarations of Americanism. Muñoz Rivera's remark, on his return from his American trip of 1899, that he had come back from a nation whose power was the astonishment of the world, was indicative, and all the more so since the Barranquitas statesman, "the man of the mountain," had never really completely lost the distrust of the outsider endemic in the mountain region from which he had come to take up his first journalistic work in Ponce. A growing disappointment with the new form of government created for the island by Congress in 1900, however, laid the ground for the second period of open political resistance and of an increasing insistence upon the dangers of a full-blown Americanization of the *Patria Chica*. The creation of the Unionist Party in 1904, combining the old Federal Party with dissident Republicans, marked the turning point, for its endorsement in its program of that year of political independence as one feasible status, among others, for the island was the first declaration by a political group that a separatist status could be viewed as a possible solution to the problem. The political strategy of this period centered around the struggle for the liberalization of the instruments of government; first after 1900 and then renewed, after 1917, with the Congressional passage of the second Organic Act. A new element was introduced into the strategy with the emergence onto the political scene of the Puerto Rican Nationalist Party—actually founded in its original and less radical form in 1922—dedicated to a neo-fascist *risorgimento* of violence against the American "usurper" and regarding all peaceful methods of change as a traitorous appeasement of American imperialism. The wheel came full cycle in 1940 when Luis Muñoz Marín, son of Muñoz Rivera, carried his new Popular Democratic Party into power and then began to undertake the gradual revision of his father's creed of *autonomismo* which was to culminate in the formulation, after 1950, of the present-day commonwealth idea.

Certain things must be noted about all this. The change from Spain to America imposed upon local political leadership the need for a drastic reorientation both in its political methods and in its ideological bearings. Long-standing programs became obsolete overnight. New perspectives loomed ahead as a traditionalist Catholic monarchist rule was replaced by that of a neo-Puritan industrial democratic society. Puerto Ricans now had to learn, from the point of zero, how to live with Americans, to understand them, to please them. The political pilgrimage to Madrid was succeeded by that to Washington. It now became urgent to learn the art of winning friends and influencing people in the northern political capital, equally necessary to seek out the liberal elements of America that would be willing to champion the

Puerto Rican cause. The American equivalents, as it were, of the eminent Spanish republicans who had supported the cause of the overseas provinces before 1898—Pi, Salmerón, Ezquerdo, and others—had to be sought out and converted to that cause. For that purpose, naturally, a command of the English language was absolutely essential, so that a high premium was immediately placed upon the readiness and ability to master it. The Socialist leader Santiago Iglesias, who later became Resident Commissioner in Washington in 1932, had had an amusing interlude with the American troops in 1898 because of his utter absence of English; he was later to record how American military officers had invited him to address the crowd in front of the town hall of Carolina at the moment of formal occupation without suspecting the kind of speech that a young Spanish anarchist would be likely to make on such an occasion. A leading political figure, again, like Antonio Barceló gradually lost his hold on the Liberal Party during the 1930's in part because his limited command of English made it difficult for him to maintain vital contacts in Washington. A political leader, conversely, who knew the language well was at a decided advantage, and a considerable factor in the formidable success of Muñoz Marín and the *Populares* after 1940 was his long New York residence and the easy bilingualism, not to mention the plethora of friends in the city's liberal circles, that it gave to him. A corollary of this was that it became of some importance to the local party headquarters to have go-betweens who could interpret Americans and Puerto Ricans to each other. Naturally enough, this role came to be played by politically minded permanent American residents on the island, and the annals of insular political conflicts record their names—Henry Dooley, Walter McK. Jones, Muna Lee, James Bourne, Ruby Black, Earl Parker Hanson, Thomas Hayes. Finally, just as Creole leadership had been driven to prove its loyalty to the Spanish cause as vociferously as possible, so under the United States it exercised its genius for rhetorical utterance in its declarations of loyalty to the American cause. The result was frequently depressing—to read the story of how a young and brilliant Spanish anarchist-radical like Santiago Iglesias changed slowly into an American labor politician of the Gompers type is to be made forcibly aware of the debilitating effects, for example, of the older forms of American anti-intellectual craft unionism. Sometimes, more happily, the results were merely comic, as when in 1917 the island electorate astonished all America by anticipating the Volstead Act with a popular electoral endorsement of liquor prohibition. Whether comic or depressing or even, as frequently was the case, of real benefit to Puerto Rico, it was at least certain that these professions of loyalty were set in motion by the presence of new masters who arranged the definite terms of the new relationship.

Puerto Ricans of all parties had confidently expected these terms to be the democratic best of the American tradition. No single factor, then, subsequently so shaped the character of island politics as the fact that the governmental institutions introduced by the Congress for the island bitterly disappointed those great expectations. There was some reason to assume, in 1898, that the central constituent element of American constitutional development—the establishment of territories destined soon to graduate, after a period of apprenticeship, as states of the Union—would govern the unfolding constitutional status of the new overseas territories. This was assuredly the assumption of the Puerto Rican political leadership; the Federal Party *Manifesto* of 1899 anticipated that the island would temporarily become a territory with all of the accompanying rights, less the power to elect Senators and Representatives to the Congress, and that it would only be a matter of time before that transitional stage ended in full statehood.[1] It was not an unreasonable assumption, for the traditional constitutional pattern of the Union had recognized only the two basic status types of the provisional territory and the matured state. The precedents were powerful: both Louisiana and Florida had been promised ultimate statehood in the treaties that arranged their transfer to the United States; a similar stipulation had even been included by Secretary of State Marcy in the 1854 treaty annexing the non-continental Sandwich Islands; and the schemes prior to 1861 for the purchase or annexation of Cuba had almost all looked to the same result.[2] Nor was it unreasonable for the Puerto Ricans to assume that Congress (1) would also consult with them on the new form of government to be installed, and (2) would grant them, to begin with, at least nothing less and probably something more than the degree of self-government that Spain had granted them as an autonomous state in 1897.

All these hopes, however, were belied. There was no consultation with the local political will, except for whatever secret conversations with Puerto Rican lobbyists there may have taken place in Washington back rooms. There was no attempt to solicit any formal expression of island thought, as was obtained at the very same time in the Australian case, when the British government undertook to accept the Australian federal constitution of 1900 from the hands of an Australian constitutional convention subject only to the right to make minor modifications. Nor were the final results of Congressional meditation a matter for local jubilation. Both of the Organic Acts, of 1900 and of 1917, were a far cry, almost painfully so, from a grant of full internal self-government. Apart from the undemocratic structure of government that they erected, they were deficient in at least three ways in which the Spanish Autonomy Charter of 1897 had promised real advance. The Charter had guaranteed special Puerto Rican participation in the negotiation of Spanish commercial treaties likely to affect the island's economy; the American Organic Acts reserved that power unilaterally to the Congress. The Charter could not be amended without the prior consent of the island legislature; the Organic Acts reserved the amendment power, by implication, to the federal body. The Charter, finally, had conferred upon the island the right to full electoral representation in the national parliament; the Organic Acts did no more than grant it the right to elect a Resident Commissioner in Washington, who attained, after 1904, the status of a territorial delegate to Congress but who remained without the power to vote. The general ability of Spain, as indicated by her later history, to maintain these concessions was of course open to doubt. But Puerto Ricans could hardly have been expected to take that view of the matter in 1900. And the fact remains that the glaring disparity between the two respective grants of power was quite properly quoted by Puerto Ricans as evidence of American failure to live up to the promise of its liberal tradition in its dealings with its new colonial possessions. Nor should sight be lost of the fact that although circumstances in no way justified it the island was left under a military form of government, with military governors, for two long and humiliating years before Congress finally moved to pass the 1900 act for civilian rule. How real the humiliation was can be gathered from the story related by Cayetano Coll y Toste who, in his capacity at that time as government secretary, suggested in conversation with Governor George Davis that a battalion of Puerto Rican soldiers be formed by the new regime, only to be told by that blunt soldier that, if formed, all its officers would without question have to be Americans.

The legislative-executive machinery of government installed by the Congressional legislation was no more pleasing to Puerto Rican self-esteem. Puerto Rican parties and politicians not only had to learn to live with the American power (which they were quite willing to do) but they had to learn adjustment, in addition, to institutions that cramped and confined their freedom of movement. The Foraker Act of 1900 created the office of the presidentially nominated Governor, assisted by an Executive Council at least five of whom had to be native inhabitants of the island, with the remaining six offices open to American appointees. The legislative branch was composed of a House of Delegates, elected by universal suffrage, and the judicial branch of an insular Supreme Court appointed by the President with the advice and consent of the federal Senate. The Jones Act of 1917 retained the gubernatorial office but amended the legislature to make of it a body of two elective chambers, the Senate and the House of Representatives, while the executive branch was also reformed to become an Executive Council of whose members—by a curious bifurcation of the nominating power—five were to be named by the Governor and the remaining three by the President. Two things are of special note in these arrangements. To begin with, the executive branch, in both cases, was constituted as a powerful executive institution largely insulated from popular legislative control or supervision. This end was achieved, in the Foraker Act, by making the executive at one and the same time a cabinet and the upper legislative body, enjoying thus both executive and legislative powers, but safe from any sort of gubernatorial or popular control by virtue of its being appointed, in all of its eleven offices, by the President alone. The same end was achieved, in the Jones Act, by guaranteeing that three of the most important cabinet officers—the Commissioner of Education, the Attorney General and the Auditor—would be appointed by the President and that furthermore they would exercise broad grants of administrative power over vital sections of local public policy. In both cases, the cabinet was in effect an imperial office protecting the American metropolitan interests against the locally elected legislature. The majority of its members, including the Governor, were responsible not to any local will but to an external authority, the President of the United States, while the power of the latter was only checked, theoretically, by the shared nominating power of the federal Senate. Congress, ironically, was willing to create in San Juan the sort of Hamiltonian executive it was almost constitutionally incapable of encouraging in Washington.

The second point to be noted is that this machinery of government, in both grants, slavishly copied the American myth that (even granted a strong executive) political sovereignty should be fragmented on the basis of the "separation of powers" principle. This was especially so with the 1917 statutory arrangements, which repeated for Puerto Rico the Washington scheme of separate executive and legislative branches calculated to fight each other rather than to cooperate with each other. Muñoz Rivera clearly perceived in his remarks on the arrangement how the doctrine of mutual checks really meant the certainty of negative government, and that it would have been far better, had the American political mind been favorable, to set up a cabinet similar to the one granted to Canada in the British North America Act of 1867 or, indeed, to the one granted to Puerto Rico herself by Spain in the reforms of 1897.[3] His fears were amply borne out by the history of the political struggles in San Juan in the years after 1900. Until

1917 these struggles were waged around the efforts of the House of Delegates to diminish the undemocratic concentration of authority in an Executive Council composed in the main of American appointees (the first two Puerto Ricans to be appointed to its membership as departmental heads had to wait until 1914 for the recognition). After 1917 they centered around the fight of the two popularly elected chambers to enlarge their powers within a constitutional instrument which had been deliberately designed, as its author Senator Jones acknowledged in the Senate hearings on the bill, to check the elective element[4]—as if that element were not indeed sufficiently checked by the dual veto of Governor and President over its proceedings. Puerto Ricans accepted much of all this with characteristic patient long-suffering and even good humor (for years after 1917 there was a popular song in the island entitled "Bill Jones"). But neither the patience nor the humor could entirely hide the tide of bitterness that swept over them as they contemplated the degradation of the democratic dogma in their island society.

The answer that America returned on the issue of the constitutional status of the new territory turned out to be a grievous blow to Puerto Rican hopes. This of course constitutes one of the great debates in the history of American constitutional law, and cannot be fully repeated here. But perhaps few opinions of the United States Supreme Court have been more curious than the massive deviation which it charted, in the famous Insular cases, from the hitherto leading concepts of national constitutional development, as the difficult problems emerging out of overseas territorial acquisition came to its tribunal for settlement. The central question that faced the Court in these cases was of course nothing less than the embarrassing one of seeking out the appropriate legal doctrine which would help to reconcile democracy with empire. It had a hard time, a Puerto Rican scholar has acidly observed, "trying to reconcile the considerations of expediency involved in the imperialistic venture with the fundamental postulates of American constitutional democracy. As usual, the conclusions were reached on political and economic grounds but clothed with the precarious respectability of legal phraseology that betrays its rationalizing function."[5] For what the Insular cases did, in sum, was to break arbitrarily, and often on spurious grounds, the territory-state dichotomy that had hitherto been assumed to govern the entrance of new units into the federal organization, and nowhere better stated than in Taney's dictum in the *Dred Scott* case that annexed territory "is acquired to become a State, and not to be held as a colony and governed by Congress with absolute authority." By its invention of the doctrine of "incorporation," creating a new distinction between "incorporated" and "unincorporated" territories, the Court was enabled to declare an anomalous status for the newly acquired territories and, consequently, to proclaim that the constitutional precepts restraining the acts of President and Congress were no longer to apply with reference to these regions. The Constitution, the court declared in *Downes v. Bidwell*, did not immediately embrace in its entirety the people of an annexed area, nor bestow upon them the privileges of American citizenship.[6] The real power over these people, then, *Dorr v. United States* decided, was not the declarative command of the Constitution but rather the fiat of Congress as it flowed from the territorial clause.

The Congress, under this argument, had been delegated to serve as the "constitution" for Puerto Rico and the new Pacific possessions, and the sole restrictions upon its behavior in that role were "such constitutional restrictions upon the powers of that body as are applicable to the situation."[7] The ambit of Congressional power clearly rested upon the definition offered at any given moment of "applicable" powers and provisions, and in *Downes v. Bidwell* Justice Brown attempted to allay the "grave apprehensions of danger" felt by "many eminent men" by enunciating a distinction between the "fundamental" guarantees of the Constitution which must prevail everywhere and the non-fundamental guarantees which Congress might presumably abjure and need not extend to "unincorporated" territories unless it wished to do so.[8] The distinction was at best an ambiguous one, and none of the leading cases managed to arrive at an authoritative pronouncement conferring any real precision upon it. What was "applicable" and what was not remained to be decided, in the result, by the vagaries of judicial opinion from time to time. Thus it became evident throughout the next two decades that the "fundamental" rights for Puerto Rico did not include the right to indictment by grand jury, the right to trial by jury, or the usual limitations upon the powers of federal taxation. Most Puerto Ricans cognizant of all this argument instinctively resented their relegation, by means of esoteric judicial doctrine, to an anomalous and second-class status and would have agreed with Justice Harlan's opinion in the Downes case that the idea of "incorporation" had about it some occult meaning difficult of apprehension.[9] The nice wit of Mr. Dooley put it more irreverently in the observation, summing up the Insular cases, that, abroad, the states of the Union are states and the territories are territories, but God knows what they are at home.

What did all this amount to? The sovereign and proprietary rights over Puerto Rico ceded by Spain to the United States in the Treaty of Paris were in effect transferred to the American Congress, leaving that body free to govern the island as it saw fit, with the sole and vague restraining admonition that there were certain limits beyond which it ought not to proceed. But these limits themselves were in fact left to be defined by Congress itself, which thus became the real arbiter as to the "applicability" of the language of the Constitution to the tropical wards. A Congressional political science grew up, accordingly, which could deny Puerto Ricans (as in the Foraker Act) the right to select and supervise their legislative and executive officers or the right (as in the Jones Act) to be protected by the Bill of Rights in all of its amplitude. The grant of American citizenship to Alaska was deemed sufficient by the courts to warrant recognition of that territory as an "incorporated" area, while it was considered insufficient in the case of Puerto Rico, failing an express statutory declaration to that effect by Congress. The island became, to all intents and purposes, a dependent ward of the Congress, subject to Congressional whim and lacking the means of effectively challenging or influencing that whim. It became the prisoner of "Congressional government," with all the notorious limitations of that concept in the American scheme of things.

Finally, the reasons advanced for thus relegating the island, in company with the Philippines, to a second-class status within the federal family were derived from subjective cultural considerations not immediately self-evident in the federal Constitution. It was argued, as in Justice Taft's majority opinion in *Balzac v. Porto Rico* (1922), that Puerto Ricans, like Filipinos, were people "living in compact and ancient communities, with definitely formed customs and political conceptions . . . distant ocean communities of a different origin and language from those of our continental people,"[10] almost as if the ethnic composition of that "continental people" was a pure Anglo-Saxonism instead of being the polyglot melting pot it had already become. Or, again, the supposed "incapacity" of Puerto Ricans for self-government was invoked as a reason, usually accompanied with observations upon the corrupt nature of politics under Spanish rule. The proper answer to this latter charge, of course, was that the capacity of any people for "self-government" rests in the last resort upon the practical opportunities that are given to it to undertake the experiment. In any case, the corruption of Spanish politics was perhaps not fundamentally very different from the impurities of American politics at the close of the Gilded Age. The "great game of politics" in the American city, indeed, could teach even Latin politicians some new tricks of the trade. It is at least certain that the Puerto Rican *caciques* learned as early as 1900 the American technique of gerrymandering;[11] while a Puerto Rican publicist properly noted that the vote selling of island politics could not be anything new to American city dwellers used to vast and widespread electoral corruption in their own politics.[12] The absence of a democratic tradition in the island was fact enough. But the lesson to be drawn from it, surely, was that the habit of self-government should be accelerated, not delayed, by American official policy. Puerto Ricans, as Henry Carroll urged in his Report, were surely better prepared in 1900 for self-government than were the people of Mexico or the colonies in Central and South America that had earlier emancipated themselves from foreign domination. They would learn the art of governing through the only possible way of having its responsibilities laid upon them.[13]

This sound advice nevertheless passed unheeded. The fear of cultural contamination by "non-Western" peoples, the argument of geographical propinquity, the insistence that Congress possesses ample constitutional power to acquire and govern new territory absolutely at will, all were pressed into the service of denying the doctrine that the territories ought to be accepted ultimately as new states. The general sentiment was expressed, with characteristic literary bombast, by Whitelaw Reid in his commencement address to Miami University in 1899. "It was," he stated, "a Continental Union of independent sovereign States our fathers planned. Whoever proposes to debase it with admixtures of States made up from the islands of the sea, in any archipelago, East or West, is a bad friend to the Republic. We may guide, protect, elevate them, and even teach them some day to stand alone; but if we ever invite them into our Senate and House, to help to rule us, we are the most imbecile of all the offspring of time."[14] The sentiment received an equally patronizing expression in the message of angry vehemence with which President Taft, during the Puerto Rican constitutional crisis of 1909 let loose by the refusal of the local House of Delegates to pass appropriation bills in the hope of exacting new Puerto Rican legislation from Congress, castigated the local political leadership for even daring to query a happy guardianship on the part of the United States that should more suitably evoke from them expressions of congratulations than a posture of "ingratitude."[15] The Puerto Rican patriot, as he looked at the political institutions and the constitutional status with which the Congress had saddled his country, might have been forgiven for suspecting that, with the transfer from Spain to the United States thus effected, the new presbyter had turned out to be but old priest writ large.

The Puerto Rican political genius had to fit itself into this framework of things as best as it could. It had to deploy itself within a general environment of confusion, uncertainty, irresolution. It was obliged to work in the dark, for its anomalous status constituted, in the bitter phrase of José Coll Cuchi, a flag without a constitution, citizenship without suffrage, and a state without representatives. Spain had been an autocracy behaving autocratically; the United States was a democracy behaving autocratically. The distinction was a vital one for a people who believed with such uncritical enthusiasm in the glittering ideals of American liberty and justice; for even among many Puerto Rican Nationalists (as with the political thought of Martí in Cuba) there was a large streak of romantic republicanism that tended to accept the American Creed at its face value. Nor could the American people themselves resolve the dilemma thus posed by abjuring those democratic values, for their moral passion has been too real to permit such a cynical strategy. No American President could thus forward to his appointee in the Governor's palace in San Juan instructions comparable to Napoleon's well-known observation to his nephew, the Grand Duke of Berg, on the occasion of the latter's taking over one of the imperial dependencies, that his first duty was to himself (Napoleon), and his second to France, and that all his other duties, including those to the country placed under his charge, were subordinate to these.[16]

Yet the end results of national policy in the Caribbean territory did not seem to be very much different on this account. If there was not outright cynicism there were at least indifference, ignorance, and arrogance frequently masquerading as policy. Not much more, perhaps, could have been expected from what was essentially an amateur exercise in colonial administration. The real rulers of the island were the House Committee on Insular Affairs and the Senate Committee on Territories and Insular Affairs. Only a tiny minority of their memberships could be relied upon at any time to take an active interest in the island's affairs, and only too often the interest, when it appeared, stemmed from a desire to discredit the incumbent Washington administration. Senator Fall's remark at the time of the Congressional hearings on the legislation of 1917 for the island, that "very few members of the Senate understand what they are attempting to legislate about at all,"[17] indicated the general apathy when insular affairs came up for consideration. Puerto Ricans, altogether, had to endure the worst weaknesses of the system of Congressional committee government. Nor were the executive arrangements that were made for them any more palatable, for after the switch to civil government in 1900 the national management of their affairs had been left in the hands, incongruously, of the Bureau of Insular Affairs of the War Department and remained there until it was transferred to the Interior Department in 1934. This, in itself, almost looked like a calculated insult.

In any event, its consequences were hardly more pleasing than the record in the neighboring American Virgin Islands of government by the Navy Department which government agency, equally incongruously, had been made responsible for the rule of that island group from 1917 to 1931.

All this helps to explain the almost pathological preoccupation of the island political parties with the issue of its constitutional status. The politics of this period were, in fact, simply a never-ending variation upon the theme of status. The position of the islanders—American citizens (after 1917) without a state to live in, lacking any identity in international law, without even incorporation of their territory—was monstrously anomalous. The prevalent stances on the question before 1898 under Spain—*autonomistas, incondicionales, separatistas*—were prevalent after 1898 under America, only under different titles—Unionists, Republicans, Independents. The rules of the game had changed somewhat, but the game itself remained the same. One result of this was to create a vested interest in exploiting the status issue, in milking from it as much political credit as possible, on the part of the *criollo* political leadership. The advancement of personal political fortunes could always be profitably secured by taking a fierce stand on status, one way or the other. This is why so large a part of all of the party programs and pronouncements of the period —collated by Dr. Bolívar Pagán in his two volumes on the history of the local political parties—were consumed with statements on the issue; with, perhaps, the occasional exception such as the 1915 platform of the Socialist Party. This is why, too, so much of the political history of the period was an elaborately executed ballet wherein the active parts were played by an elite group of professional politicians around the narrow and sterile but dramatic status theme, switching membership from one group to another as the interests of the moment dictated, engineering party splits and mergers, issuing sonorous *pronunciamientos* in which the plangent rhetoric only faintly disguised the single enduring motive of political preferment.

This was the background, in essence, of the formation of the *Alianza* between the Unionist Party and the dominant Republican group in 1924 and of the *Coalición* between the dissident Republicans and the Socialists in the same year. Both of them were simply factional alliances entered into for the purpose of winning elections; and they resulted, in 1924, in what was perhaps the most scandalous election in the entire history of the island during the American regime. The same background was there, too, behind the irrepressible *personalismo* of politics. From the first organization of insular parties, the leader's manifesto rather than the party's platform became the rallying point of partisanship. The party zealot became known by the name of his leader—*Barbosistas, Muñocistas, Dieguistas.* The parties, especially the Unionists and Republicans, were generally agreed on similar programs, for up to 1913 they both supported the principle of federal statehood. The only thing that really separated them was the personal rivalry between the two leaders, Muñoz Rivera and Barbosa. So much was this the case that a not unpopular idea throughout this period played around the possibility, as Matienzo Cintrón suggested in an important speech as early as 1902, of liquidating these two major parties in order to permit the local political will to present a united front in the presence of its difficulties.[18] The idea finally flowered, in a way, in 1924, into the electoral alliance of the two groups, but, significantly, only after the two great leaders had disappeared from the scene. The preoccupation with the status problem also helped to encourage the unfortunate dominion of the legal mind in Puerto Rican politics. For the problem was of a constitutional complexity to appeal to the quasi-theological bent of the legal mind, with its temptation to subordinate the defense of principle to the presentation of a brief.

It is another way of saying all this that the unnatural concentration upon the status issue, however justified it may have been by the inescapable reality of American colonialism, was at the same time a useful device for maintaining the status quo in Puerto Rican society and politics. It helped to rationalize the rule of the classes over the masses. It presented an ideal excuse for sacrificing social and economic issues to political and constitutional issues. Like the question of the monarchy in Republican France after 1875 or the question of Church disestablishment in England before 1914, it was an easily enlivened issue calculated to divert attention from more urgent but less dramatic problems. The sole difference in the Puerto Rican case was that the politics of status turned out to be a closed monopoly of the elite groups since the rural and urban poor remained unexcited about an issue they could not easily or readily identify as a cause of their poverty. Their traditional passivity alone enabled their Creole leaders to sacrifice the real to the spurious causes. The early growth of the socialist movement, it is true, suggests that it might have given a more radical turn to politics (it is significant that at the height of its appeal the Socialist Party could poll nearly one quarter of the total vote in the 1920 elections). But the alignment of the Socialist leaders with the local Republicans in 1924 revealed that, like too many other political leaders, they were ready to allow social and economic matters to be obscured by the status frenzy. From that date on, the party declined into just another group on the pro-American side of the debate. The worker and peasant remained, as much under America as under Spain, the claque (to use Santiago Iglesias's early phrase with reference to the pre-1898 period) that applauded or hissed the rival political sections of the colonial bourgeois class. They would have to wait until 1938 before a new political leadership emerged, in Muñoz Marín's new party, to give priority once more to their needs.

In the meanwhile, neither the *Alianza*—in power from 1924 on-wards—nor the *Coalición*—in power after 1930—did much to cater to those needs. On the contrary, they did much to frustrate their satisfaction, for none of the factions comprising their respective memberships were in any real way sympathetic to the needs. Both the Republicans and the Unionists were prepared—the first in the years after 1900, the second in the period after 1919—to collaborate with American governors for the purpose of hobbling the trade union and labor movements; and the Unionist Resident Commissioner in Washington actively helped to export the "Red Scare" panic of post-war Republican America to the island. His official biographer has styled Barbosa "a man of the people." But there is little in the Republican leader's record to suggest that he worked primarily in the defense of working class interests; and his well-known stand on the race question in the island could be seen as little more than a battle conducted in the interests of the colored professional middle class group to which he belonged. Muñoz Rivera was perhaps more sympathetic. But he failed throughout his public life to use his enormous personal influence with his party to turn sympathy into a program; and just one year before his death he could confess to a party colleague that the whole party leadership, by reason of its "inexcusable silence," had in effect become the accomplices of the business class in its uncivilized treatment of the workers.[19] Neither Muñoz Rivera nor Barbosa ever seem to have thought in terms of an independent working class movement; which explains why, to take a single example, the Republican Party could attempt to take over the new *Federación Libre* in the early years after 1900 as part of their political machine. Even the more radical type of anti-American *independentista* politician, who might have conceivably been more sympathetic to that movement, failed to be so, and José de Diego could in fact go so far (when he was Government Under-Secretary in 1898 in the brief Muñoz Rivera cabinet) as to argue that, San Juan not being Barcelona, the Puerto Rican laborer needed more education before he could be allowed to be exposed to "subversive" ideas.[20] The politics of the period altogether reflected the battle that the colonial bourgeois class had to wage on two fronts, the first against the American power, the second against its own working class. In that battle its various factions were prepared, from time to time, to sink their differences in temporary alliances, pacts and unions. But the underlying principles of the game were rarely more elevated than the variations upon the theme of indiscriminate electoral promise-making satirized, for an earlier period, in Fernández Juncos's figure of *Don Bonifacio Político*; nor indeed, with some exceptions, did it produce a type of politician that was much better than the examples contained in the zoological classification of small-town and rural mayors that the same author put together, after the manner of Cuvier, in his *Los Alcaldes.*

And even within this general formula there were wheels within wheels. The politics of survival, simply because it was short on principle, could as easily involve collaboration with as opposition to the imperial enemy. Historically, every colonial power has been able to find collaborationists prepared to support its policies in return for the ribbon to stick in their coats. This was so with the Tories of the American Revolution, with the parliamentary opposition in Canada after 1867 which preferred their country to become an American satellite rather than continue as an independent state, with the "Loyalists" of Northern Ireland. It has been the case equally in the Caribbean. A West Indian nationalist noted as early as 1886, in the case of the British Caribbean, how that fact helped to divide the local society. "Besides the absurdity of the nominated element," he wrote of the British crown colony system, "there is the consideration that it tends to keep up an English or 'home' party in each island and consequently to maintain diversity instead of unity among the inhabitants of the colony. The colonist who looks to Downing Street as the *fons et origo* of honor and of lucrative public employment naturally becomes case-hardened against local public opinion, and is prepared, as is only too often seen, to sell not only his own principles but his neighbors' liberties for a consideration."[21] This was also the case in Puerto Rico, under both empires. In both the Spanish and American periods there emerged a group of *incondicionales* who wanted the complete assimilation, cultural and political, of the subordinate by the superordinate society. Politically, this entailed the incorporation of the local party groups into the organization and structure of the respective national parties, and consequently the sacrifice of their regional character to a nationalizing process. Thus, under Spain, the Liberal Party of the island yielded up its separate identity to the Spanish Liberal Party, while under America the Republican Party did likewise in its relations with the G.O.P. Yet it is unlikely that the fruits of this strategy were at all plentiful, since both Madrid and Washington tended to govern through the party groups that won the local elections rather than through the local affiliates of the national

administration parties. Culturally, the *incondicionales* tried to make
the island over as a carbon copy, first, of Spain and then of America.
The extreme illustration of this aim, under the American regime, was
the egregious folly of replacing Spanish with English as the medium of
instruction in the public school system, in the hope that one day
Puerto Ricans would forsake their native tongue for an alien language.
The policy had the signal result of creating a veritable Pandora's box
of linguistic and psychological problems that still continue—as the
reopened debate on the language question in 1962 showed—to
plague the island. No account was taken of the fact that in contrast
to the complex population of Hawaii, where the English language has
served as an integrating and leveling force, the Puerto Rican population was homogenous with a dominant language sufficiently adequate for world-wide contacts. The economic dependency upon the
United States was thus accompanied by a psychological dependency.

Politicians, especially the local Republicans, became "exaggerated
Americans," joined in the American political ritual of ancestor worship (Jorge Washington became a national figure) and eulogized the
American flag for which they developed something of an emotional
fixation. Even today few spectacles in Puerto Rico are more comic
than that of a Fourth of July patriotic address delivered by a statehood orator. They thereby gave impetus to the fashion of praising
things American and decrying things Puerto Rican. Thereby, too,
they encouraged in their people a deprecating attitude to their own
cultural worth and an absence of national self-respect carried to the
point where they were almost persuaded, like Peter on the morning
of Calvary, into a denial of their own self. The effect of all this was
to convert both the idea of political independence and that of cultural
self-identity into concepts regarded as "disloyal" and "un-American."
Nothing was perhaps more revelatory of this identification than the
slow metamorphosis in the political thought of the Unionist Party
during the three decades following the American occupation. The first
platform of the party in 1904 had accepted independence, equally
with statehood, as a legitimate terminus for the island's constitutional
growth, either of which could be attained by a gradual extension of
internal self-government. By 1912, however, the party's leader had
come to the conclusion that independence, far from being a practical
proposition, had in reality become a purely abstract ideal serving only
to appease the Puerto Rican sense of honor. By 1922 Muñoz Rivera's
successors in the leadership had become convinced that the ideal was
safely expendable, and the platform of that year finally abandoned it
for a milder program of autonomous self-government, thus leaving
the torch of an independent republic in the custody of the ghost of

José de Diego. The price of collaboration had thus become the abjuration of any radical policy that could be regarded as "anti-American." Puerto Ricans were thus learning the hard truth that the American Congress, like the Hebraic Jehovah, was a jealous god that brooked no rival.

The nature and record of the American Governors of the island during the period merits a separate note. Although there was nothing in the provisions of the Organic Acts to debar the appointment of a local candidate, all the Governors until 1947 (when the Elective Governor Act put an end to the system of presidential nomination) were Americans, with the single exception of Governor Piñero in 1946. Being the chief custodian of political power, the Governor wielded a more than disproportionate sway in the machinery of colonial government. After 1917, it is true, the Puerto Rican politicians eventually succeeded in curbing his powers and in requiring him to work through subordinates acceptable to them; the fierce struggle with Governor Mont Reilly between 1921 and 1923—precipitated by his harsh policy of refusing to accept Unionist nominations for office so long as that party continued to include the plank of independence in its program—finally settled that principle. But the very conflict that was involved in asserting the principle served at the same time to keep the figure of the Governor in the center of the political stage. His qualities, both as a person and as an administrator, therefore continued to be of paramount importance for the island and for the growth of its public policy.

Looking at the roster of the names, it can hardly be said that they were a dazzling success. The appointment, to begin with, did not carry the prestige of the Philippines gubernatorial post, so that it failed to attract men comparable to Philippine governors like Taft or Henry L. Stimson. Most of its occupants were imposed upon the island without special or careful consideration of their qualifications and without consultation with local opinion. Within a period of less than forty years some fifteen successive Governors occupied the post, and except for two who had served respectively as department head and executive secretary to a preceding Governor, every one of them came to the island as a stranger to its people and to their problems. Even when they were comparatively successful—Governor Towner, for example, or Governor Theodore Roosevelt, Jr.—it was less because of a wise nominating procedure than it was of a happy accident of personality. Only too frequently the office was used as a rich plum in the spoils system of American politics, while the custodianship of the War Office meant an additional pressure group in the form of elderly retired naval and military gentlemen anxious to spend the twilight of their days south of Miami; as late as 1939 the appointment was given to Admiral Leahy as he made his way from naval retirement to, finally, the American ambassadorship to the French wartime Vichy regime. Not even a President as liberal as Franklin Roosevelt was immune to the poison of "the machine" when it came to appointments to the territorial governorship; and Jim Farley has related how in 1940 Henry Woodring was ousted from the War Department because of his reluctance to approve the sale or transfer of Army planes to beleaguered Britain and was offered the Puerto Rican governorship as an obvious consolation for his wounded feelings.[22] The governorship, in brief, was a pawn of Washington politics. There was no Colonial Office to give shape or direction or prestige to such territorial posts. At best there was an understaffed and poorly financed Division of Territories in the Department of the Interior. Nor did Washington apparently learn better with the years, for the last continental Governor of the island, Rexford Tugwell, arrived in San Juan as the last stage in the public life of a dedicated New Deal official who had become, from the viewpoint of harmonious executive-legislative relationships along Pennsylvania Avenue, a serious liability to President Roosevelt as early as the end of the first term in 1936. For it is difficult to believe that the Tugwellian ego would have long tolerated the humiliating obscurity of a minor appointment on the outskirts of the tributary empire had it been at all possible for it to continue exercising an important role as a member of the praetorian guard at the Roman center.

The New Deal's loss, of course, was Puerto Rico's gain; and Governor Tugwell was of a moral and intellectual stature to take proper appraisal of his predecessors. "The comfort-seeking, middle-aged Governor," he observed of the type, "who had usually not been much of a success at home—speaking now of none in particular but only of the type—who had sought only a job for political duties well done in Iowa, Indiana, or Michigan, and who found himself involved in the complex intrigues and conspiracies of insular politics, always falling into traps, fearful of his Washington support, which the 'outs' in Puerto Rico early learned how to undermine, especially if they were monied 'outs,' was one of the unhappiest figures imaginable. He had usually come with good will, vaguely feeling himself a little superior, necessarily, to a conquered people, but had nevertheless tried hard to ingratiate himself with the influential 'better classes.' That these hated him for his superior feeling, and for the fact that he represented an alien overlordship, and while smiling blandly in his face, would gladly stab him in the back, he soon found out to his dismay. And he had no weapon with which to meet it. He soon became a member of a small alien set of Federal officeholders, with a little isolated society of their own, existing in a foreign land with what grace they could. There is not much evidence that any of them were aware of a vast mass of farmers and workers who hated the same selfish upper classes so many of whose members were ready to cut Governors' throats. These were potential but unused allies. Even if it had occurred to some Governor—and perhaps it did—such an appeal was hardly possible across the barriers of language, culture and tradition; if it was ever tried tentatively it never came to anything. So Governors lived in the palace with a few fiercely resented continental assistants, and the real life and management of insular society went on outside their knowledge, to say nothing of their control."[23]

Viewed thus, it is not difficult to understand why most Governors became either nonentities who were laughed at or whipping boys who were used to cover up the failures of the governing political elites. One sought to immortalize his name by signing a bill legalizing cock-fighting with a tail feather. It is rumored that another, on leaving San Juan, decamped with a set of exquisite heirlooms on loan for exhibition at the palace. Governor Mont Reilly—a protegé of the questionable Ohio Republican organization—earned for himself not only an opprobrious nickname but also the fierce hostility of all local groups. Governor Hunt—in the caustic phrase of one local statesman—laughed like a sick and decadent Mephistopheles, while Governor Post could never be heard to laugh at all. Governor Robert Gore—hand picked by Jim Farley—managed, within a brief year of the office, to earn for his contribution to American-Puerto Rican understanding the felicitous title of "Gore's Hell." Some Governors devoted their genius and time to cultivating their favorite panaceas for the island's ills. Theodore Roosevelt, Jr., was enamored of the idea of the family farm, to be aided by a Homestead Commission, but inflated land values killed the scheme. Governor Blanton Winship, in his turn, imagined that mass poverty might perhaps be alleviated by the official sponsorship of the Ponce de León Carnival. The language barrier was rarely broken through; indeed, Governor Roosevelt discovered on assuming the office in 1929 that not to speak Spanish had become almost an unwritten rule of policy on the part of the American regime, an attitude presumably founded upon the idea that the master-servant relationship could best be maintained by forcing the Puerto Rican to speak in English or to use an interpreter.[24] And even when the "condition of the people" question did manage to engage the sympathetic attention of a Governor—it is impossible to read Governor Roosevelt's account of his stewardship without appreciating, for

all of its naiveté in parts, its tone of active and warm concern for the
forgotten masses of the island—the sentiment could rarely flower into
a positive policy because, first, its silent assumption was always one
of American benevolence and, second, it withered away in the inevitable abuse showered upon it by politicians who resented an alien
intrusion into what they viewed as their own private bailiwick.

The escape from this dilemma only too frequently lay, for the
American, in constructing a rationalizing image of American "decency" foiled by Latin "untrustworthiness." One American newspaper
publisher concluded, after a tour of the Caribbean region in 1914,
that "the United States handles colonies better than any other nation"
but that, in return, the local political leaderships "take delight in
insulting us"[25]—and his words would have been heartily endorsed by
most of the American occupants of the Spanish throne room in the
gubernatorial palace. What they failed to see, of course, was the
simple truth that good intentions pave the way to purgatory when they
seek to operate an intrinsically indefensible system; that, in effect,
the management of empire by a democracy is a contradiction in terms.
Puerto Ricans who were pro-American talked in grandiose terms of
Puerto Rico playing the role of middleman of the Americas, being—
in the phrase of Rafael Hernández Usera—the voice of Spanish culture in the United States and the defender of the free spirit of the
United States in Latin America. But only too often the emphasis of
the ideal seemed to change when Americans took it up, to become
a policy in which Puerto Rico, in the phrase of Governor Roosevelt,
would be "so to speak, our show window looking south."[26] The only
logical, but impossible, role that the Puerto Rican Governors could
have set for themselves would have been that of presiding over their
own liquidation. Being ordinary men, however, they exhibited little
readiness to see their position in that manner. The observer of their
collective record, individual spurts of imaginative energy apart, is
obliged to conclude that, had they been required, like outgoing
officials under Spain, to undergo the ordeal of the *Residencia*—the
rigorous examination of an outgoing governor's record by the Council
of the Indies—few of them would have passed through it unscathed.
He will be reminded, even more, of the remark that Selden once
attributed to a wise pope, that men seldom think what a little foolery
governs the whole world.

The New Deal Experiment

THE decade of the 1930's, with the Democratic victory in 1932, witnessed a protracted struggle to extend the promise of the New Deal to the Puerto Rican dependency. This entailed at the same time a determined effort to readjust the emphasis of insular communal effort away from the political and more toward the social and economic problems. For the most seminal problem of any society is the social one, as indeed the most eminent of all Puerto Rican leaders once emphasized.[1] But none of the local parties, including Muñoz Rivera's own Unionist group, had shown itself sufficiently statesman-like to forego the handsome dividends to be gained by playing politics. The favorite strategy was to maximize the dividends by adopting the anti-American pose with the local electorate and the pro-American pose with the national. The political group favoring federated state-hood, in particular, made a special point of cultivating a professional "Americanism" which only too often was a cloak for the satisfaction of the crude thesis that the more lucrative plums of public service appointments should be conferred by "cooperative" American Governors upon the "loyal" groups of the society. Both the *Alianza* and the *Coalición* survived successfully for years on this strategy. The end result was (to use Adam Smith's sentence) a "paltry raffle of colony faction," with the natural confusion induced by the American failure to announce any definite policy for the island's constitutional future being exploited by the political class to further its own ambition and to protect the vested interests of the propertied classes to which it was affiliated.

The economic reformist, like the younger Muñoz, or the impartial public servant resolutely determined to achieve administrative efficiency, like Dr. Padín in the Department of Education, were denied any real chance to undertake the economic and administrative reha-bilitation of the society; not infrequently their ambitions were derided as "un-American." The chief energy of government went into marginal and often wasteful projects which did nothing to tackle the source of the social disease as distinct from its symptoms; an *Alianza* Unemployment Commission that finally terminated its labors by the publication of a voluminous report which consisted mainly of copies of Australian labor reports and legislation was not unrepresentative. Even the most basic of governmental functions—tax collection, public health protection, education, police protection—were performed with scandalous inefficiency. In one way, all this was part of the Spanish legacy. "None of them," wrote an American observer of the class of public officials in 1899, "except the scattered few who have been educated in the United States, have ever been in intimate contact with the working of republican forms of government, while every man who has held a Spanish position is conversant and thoroughly imbued with the spirit of a spoils-system combination so extensive that it puts to shame the most halcyon days of metropolitan aldermen in America."[2] In another way it was a part of the general Republican doctrine of negative government that had prevailed in Washington for most of the period during which the island had been American territory. It is instructive to note, with reference to that latter point, that a large bulk of the recommendations of the Brookings Institution report of 1930 dealt with suggestions for the rationalization and the consolidation of the insular machinery of government and administration on the assumption, supposedly, that social crisis should be met primarily by a policy of financial retrenchment and administrative reorganization. Much of the Puerto Rican tragedy, on the eve of the New Deal, can be understood in terms of this dual inheritance of Spanish monarchism and American republicanism.

A challenge to both forces slowly emerged after 1932. On the continental side, it arose from the realization on the part of the New Deal administration that the old policy of cautious political liberalization and economic drift had to be supplanted with a policy of extending to the colonial territories the growing activities of the federal spending agencies. The Brookings Institution report had already recommended the extension to Puerto Rico of all federal aid currently extended to the states. But the report's listing of the various items of that aid—the Smith-Hughes Act for the promotion of vocational education, the Fess-Kenyon Act for the rehabilitation of disabled industrial workers, the Clarke-McNary Act covering cooperative farm forestry and the Smith-Lever Act relating to cooperative agricultural extension work—only served to indicate how inadequate such aid then was and how it tended to concentrate upon mild rehabilitation programs only.[3] The problem now was to reinforce this with the larger horizons of the New Deal public works agencies like the WPA, the AAA, the REA, and so on. The transfer of Puerto Rico in 1934 from the War Department to the Department of the Interior under Harold

Ickes created the necessary change of administrative atmosphere. The outcome of that change was the establishment of the Puerto Rico Emergency Relief Administration under the local directorship of James Bourne, replaced, in 1935, with the more ambitious Puerto Rico Reconstruction Administration directed by Ernest Gruening. The first, however, was not much more than an expanded public works program (for all of the social idealism of its local officials) treating the problem as a depression emergency instead of the chronic maladjustment of a land-hungry and sugar-dominated economy that it was in reality; it was estimated that at the height of its activities the agency was giving direct or indirect relief to 35 percent of the island population. The second was a much more imaginative attempt, on the part of continental and local New Deal planners alike, to organize a single over-all reconstruction plan based at once upon a frank attempt to break the sugar monoculture that held the island in a vise and upon a determination to replace federal "handouts" with social justice as the foundation of effective rehabilitation.

The attempt took the form of the so-called Chardón Plan—named after its chairman, the able Chancellor of the University—which envisaged, via the machinery of a semi-public corporation similar to the Virgin Islands Company, the enforcement of the 500-Acre Law, rural resettlement, diversification of agriculture, the encouragement of cooperatives, rural electrification, rehabilitation of the stagnant coffee and tobacco areas, the government purchase of at least one sugar mill to be operated as a yardstick for regulating future relationships between the *colonos* and the millowners, and, finally, the genesis of a Puerto Rican industrialization plan through the sponsorship of a local cement plant. For a variety of reasons nonetheless the basic economic revolution envisaged by the plan's architects failed to materialize, and most of its individual projects were carried through on an experimental level only. Yet no one can read the story of the PRRA, especially in the early years before 1940, without the keen realization that it was a dramatic and noble effort to bring the best qualities of the mainland New Deal to a stricken and neglected colony—its reforming zeal, its recognition of the bankruptcy of "free enterprise," its zest for innovation, its eagerness somehow to replace politics with planning, its willingness to experiment both in ideas and in administrative methods. It laid the foundations for the reform program, after 1940, of the *Popular* government. It undertook, through the devoted efforts of the capable Attorney General Benigno Fernández García, the legal battles that made possible later the final expropriation of the sugar latifundia. Its low-cost housing program became the forerunner of the remarkable post-war mass housing schemes of the Commonwealth government. Its Planning Division undertook the first empirical studies which later became the research basis for the industrialization program. Above all, the schemes gave new hope to Puerto Ricans who had begun to despair of American responsibility. For the first time the federal government allocated massive subsidies to the island, addressed the genius of its ablest officials to the island's problems, became conscious, most of all, of its tremendous moral obligation to its Caribbean citizens. To read the enthusiastic account of the work by one of the ablest of its federal participants,[4] or the revealing confessions of a cabinet member like Harold Ickes as a result of his Puerto Rican journey during the period,[5] or the account of Mrs. Roosevelt's relentless personal investigations into the darker corners of the island life,[6] is to be made aware, altogether, of the fact that the passivity and orthodoxy of traditional Washington attitudes were beginning to be replaced by a new sense of urgency.

The new Washington mood was matched by a new island mood. To begin with, the return of Luis Muñoz Marín from his self-imposed American exile in 1931 brought to the liberal-nationalist cause all the great gifts of a slowly maturing leader who had learned, in a curious combination of talents, both the ethic of social radicalism in the politico-bohemian circles of New York and the ability to move knowingly around the bureaucratic labyrinth of Washington. He used the talents, in his dual capacity as Liberal Party Senator after 1932 and editor of the San Juan newspaper *La Democracia,* in the passionate services of his people towards the creation of a situation in which the national government could be persuaded, as he expressed it in a private letter to Mrs. Roosevelt, to fight the Puerto Rican problem "not with doles but with social justice, operating within an economy that shall be as far as possible planned and autonomous."[7] Muñoz was equally at home in either idiomatic Spanish or English. He understood American sentiments. He could talk their own language to American politicians, in much the same way as in the struggle going on at the same time for Indian national independence Congress leaders like Nehru and Krishna Menon could bridge the gulf that separated them, politically, from the British governing officials by the common bond of an English public school educational background. And his association with the New Deal planners, Ickes, Wallace, Tugwell, Hopkins, the President himself, became a part of his own intellectual education, enabling him to get away, finally, from the sterile preoccupation with political status and its consequent distortion of the real problems. In this education, moreover, Muñoz was accompanied by the new Creole group of rising intellectuals in the island who possessed the same bias: economists like Rafael Cordero, sociologists like José Rosario, university administrators like R. Menéndez Ramos, not to mention American residents like the geographer E. P. Hanson who, in attitude and thought, were in complete sympathy with the island liberal cause. Mr. Hanson, indeed, became so excited by the Puerto Rican challenge that he was finally to leave his federal service for a more lasting dedication to its solution.

There was, finally, the new growth of a real professional ethic in the island middle classes. There was the growing tendency for parents to send their sons, some of them their daughters even, to American educational institutions rather than the Spanish, thereby counter-balancing the cultural-literary reactionary tradition of the Hispanic academic world. Mrs. Dorothy Bourne trained the first group of local social workers. Dr. Padín, an Americanized Puerto Rican in the best sense of the word, helped in his own figure to establish a new prestige for the school teacher, carrying on the fine work of his predecessor Juan B. Huyke, the first Puerto Rican to be appointed Commissioner of Education. Dr. Carlos Chardón, even before 1930, had made an international name for himself as scientist-consultant in the general field of agricultural economics. Miguel Guerra-Mondragón, the local representative of the American Civil Liberties Union and one of the key research men in the sugar reform program, did much to rehabilitate the generally low public estimate of the insular legal profession. All of these individuals, in both their personal and public capacities, helped slowly to build up new standards of public service, always woefully low in a colonial society and made more so, in the Puerto Rican case, by the fact that there was not present, as there was in the neighboring British Caribbean islands, a professional corps of colonial civil servants who, for all of their real defects, were possessed of a deep sense of public duty and a massive incorruptibility. They helped, too, to break down somewhat the preeminence of politics as the leading industry of the society. They helped, as a consequence, to counteract the socially debilitating habit of leaving political expression exclusively in the hands of the professional politicians. They set the stage in brief, for the New Deal once its *élan* made itself felt in the island.

Yet for all of its promise the New Deal episode in Puerto Rico was a disappointing one. On the face of it, it ought not to have been so. It had the active support of the President behind it. Muñoz Marín had direct approaches to the White House not enjoyed by many powerful continental political leaders. There was little of the bitter Congressional opposition which was later to be directed against the *Popular* social reform program; even as late as 1943 a Bourbon Republican as

adamant as Robert Taft could be so impressed by the peculiar difficulties of Puerto Rican change as to lend his support to the program
of government-supported industrialization.[8] There were, of course,
hostile Congressional excursions to the island even in the heyday of
New Deal executive-legislative cooperation, and Mr. Hanson has described the comic visit of Senator King of Utah in 1936, as chairman
of the Senate Committee on Territories, which was chiefly characterized by the Senator's hapless cross-examination of astonished Puerto
Rican urchins for the purpose of measuring their competence in the
English language and therefore the degree of their "Americanization."[9] But this was the exception, not the rule. Even so, by 1939,
when the federal appropriations for PRRA began to feel the ax of
economy, all the toil and effort had little enough to show for themselves. Of the 57 million dollars that had been plowed into the island
during the five years of PRRA operations, over 50 percent had been
spent on labor or personnel services; relief cases aided by the agency
had increased from a figure of 126,000 to a total of 222,000; while
with the single exception, perhaps, of the hydro-electric program
under the direction of the Puerto Rican engineer Antonio Luchetti,
none of its projects had ever really managed to become an enduring
or important part of the Puerto Rican scene.[10] As Muñoz Marín said
of its predecessor, the PRERA, it did little more than hold a mirror
to the existing social system and reflect its outline faithfully.

Most of the research undertaken throughout the period, as a matter
of fact, was done through federal units like the Federal Experimental
Station at Mayagüez for the more efficient production and organization of the sugar industry, and thereby helped to perpetuate the evil
consequences of an alien-held monoculture. There was, of course,
much imaginative promise in many of the PRRA projects—the experiment in publicly administered sugar production at the Lafayette sugar
central, for example—but they failed mainly as a result of the drastic
reductions of federal funds with American entry into war in 1941.
The deliberate reorganization of rural community life, again, aimed
at ultimately regrouping the isolated rural population into a type of
organized village community that had been recommended, among
others, by the Clark Report, finally resulted in the birth of at least
three new communities of that character: La Plata, Castañer, and
Zalduondo. But this was a beginning only, the communities were pilot
projects only and in any case after 1942 they ceased to be even this
as they were turned over by the federal Selective Service agency to the
Civilian Public Service sponsored by the historic peace churches, to
become minor social welfare enterprises staffed by American conscientious objectors. The war focused fresh attention on the island, but only

because of its strategic importance for the defense of the Panama Canal and American shipping lanes, and because of the presence of extensive American fortifications. The New Deal, in effect, died in Puerto Rico in 1940 as surely as it died in the continental United States. By 1945 the best that a couple of sympathetic American observers could offer to the stricken land was the pious hope that it should await a "renewed and greater effort" towards a solution of its problems on the part of "all Americans" imbued with "Christian ideals."[11]

What accounts for this disappointing failure? In some measure, it was because the New Deal at home was not a coherent plan to reshape American society root and branch so much as it was a hasty and empirical response to sudden crisis; and it could be no more abroad in a dependent territory than what it was at home. In some measure it was because the Rooseveltian policy, fundamentally weakest in any sense of theoretical content or direction, sought to do no more than patch up an anarchic capitalism, so that the private ownership of the means of production was left substantially untouched. The economic and cultural dominance of industry was therefore repeated in Puerto Rico in the form of the dominance of the sugar complex. In neither case was the situation at all seriously challenged by a reform program which was, on the one side, a nostalgic resurgence of economic Jeffersonianism in its campaign against "big business" and its predilection for the "small man" and, on the other, a crusading liberalism feeling that "something ought to be done" but lacking any clear signposts to direct and channel the reforming energy. Indeed it was a curious irony of fate that the one New Deal "brain truster" who was identified in the public mind with designs of converting the program into a corporate collectivism along planning lines was the Rexford Tugwell for whom the Puerto Rican governorship in 1941 was one more stage in his gradual alienation from the decision-making centers of the Roosevelt regime as that regime moved slowly but inexorably to the political Right. The power of Franklin Roosevelt thus was the fruit of crisis; it was not the expression of a responsible democracy seeking with forethought to adjust its productive to its consumption capacity. It is true enough that "the Roosevelt revolution" witnessed a large expansion in production. But two qualifying facts must be noted. The first is that, until 1941, there was large-scale unemployment; it was the tremendous spurt given to national production by the war preparedness and war production programs, more than any domestic defense mechanisms invented by the New Deal, that finally brought full employment to the American worker and employer. Secondly, the direction of capital investment and growth in the New Deal was mainly towards government undertakings in the form of relief and public works projects rather than towards the investment of funds in genuine business activity. If the New Deal replaced an old order with a new order, the distinction was a minor and not a major one. The "new order" was not new with reference to the basic property structure of the economic system but only with reference to the degree of public supervision of economic activity. It helped, perhaps, to civilize the public behavior of the American businessman. But it did not in any serious manner restrict his private power.

What was true of the center of the New Deal was even more true of its circumference. One of its first measures in the island was to apply the organized scarcity program of the National Recovery Act and the Agricultural Adjustment Act by means, in part, of the Jones-Costigan Act of 1934 which placed insular sugar production on a quota basis. The legislation had a dual effect. It compensated the sugarland proprietors for artificial restrictions on production while it failed to make provisions to compensate the sugar cane workers and small producers who were thereby displaced from productive employment; and it placed a drastic limitation upon Puerto Rican sugar refining capacity which persists to the present day. The restriction upon crude sugar output was further encouraged by the free trade bias of the New Deal administration, yet it could only have had disadvantageous consequences for the raw-materials producers whose products depended upon the maintenance of a protectionist tariff. This was especially so for Puerto Rico, since from the very beginning the local economy had been forced into becoming a tariff-protected subsidy economy debarred, by Congressional legislation, from organizing a multilateral trading relationship with any market outside the American market. It was for this reason that a Puerto Rican leader as New Deal in his outlook as Muñoz Marín could be apprehensive of Democratic victory in 1932 since he feared the consequences for the island of the low-tariff, free trade ideology of the Democratic Party. The abrogation, in effect, of the Hawley-Smoot tariff in 1934 more than justified such fears, since in its roots it reflected the desire of the new administration to give priority to Cuban sugar requirements in return for increased American exports to that island. The offshore areas like Puerto Rico were thus sacrificed, first, to the interests of the rival Cuban producers, mostly subsidiaries of United States companies, (for the sake of the foreign-relations considerations of the State Department) and, second, to the interests of the cane and beet-sugar producers of the continental United States; the latter wielding the double advantage over Puerto Rico of having their own voting representatives in the Congress and a greater facility in organizing powerful lobbies in the national capital.

But the subordination of the Puerto Rican sugar interests to those of Cuba and Louisiana did not mean by any means the danger of their liquidation. For the policies pursued within the island followed in the main those pursued on the mainland by the Department of Agriculture. In the States this meant the replacement, in increasing measure, of the small farmer by the large commercial farm, whether in cotton or wheat, meat production or dairy farming; for the sole survivor of a program of artificial restrictionism under federal regulatory auspices was the big organization that could afford large capital expenditures and could wait for returns on investments. In Puerto Rico this policy meant the survival of the large sugar corporations, like those of the Serralles family empire, and the disappearance of the small cane farmer. The corporations, true enough, complained bitterly about the tariff reduction. But even that was not a heavy blow, for an analysis of their profit returns during the period makes it abundantly clear that they did not suffer in any serious way.[12] It was equally clear, however, that neither the *colono* nor the sugar worker was obtaining, by means of higher wages or better living conditions, any sizable share of corporate earnings that were in large part obtained at the expense of the continental sugar consumer through the operation of the preference and subsidy systems.

These conclusions are more than justified if a glance is taken at the history of local efforts at the time to obtain that share. The story has been told in detail by Dr. Thomas Mathews in his volume on *Puerto Rican Politics and the New Deal.* Much of the record, of necessity, concerns itself with the initiation and decline of the so-called Chardón Plan worked out by the federally appointed Puerto Rican Policy Commission, under Dr. Chardón's chairmanship, in the summer of 1934 with the assistance of James A. Dickey, the permanent AAA representative for the island, and Department of Agriculture experts. The Plan as it emerged envisaged nothing short of a complete rehabilitation program that would attack the central disease of the society rather than play around with its symptoms, as had done the federal relief projects. The heart of it lay in its proposal to undertake the public operation of a pace-setting segment of the sugar industry aimed at sharing the profits equitably with worker and farmer and at setting up a system of subsistance homesteads for food production and small cash crops. It did not go as far as Tugwell's earlier proposal for socializing the entire industry and running it, by means of a government corporation, along somewhat the same lines as a Soviet collective farm.[13] It was radical enough, nonetheless; and it went to the heart of the matter in its author's statement that "I firmly believe that nothing substantial can be accomplished here unless we face the ever-absorbing sugar interests."[14] The appointment of the well-known liberal Ernest Gruening as Director of Territories in the Interior Department and as Administrator of the Chardón Plan in the island seemed to insure that the program would be actively prosecuted under the guidance of a determined New Dealer. Yet despite all these auguries of success, the vast enthusiasms generated in all sections of the local community, even including initially the Republican-Socialist right-wing political groups, had by 1938 been quashed. Two keen American observers, writing from a radical liberal viewpoint, had described the colonial situation in the island in 1931 as a "broken pledge." It was still possible for two other American observers, writing this time from the viewpoint of a Christian progressivism, to describe the island in 1945 as an "unsolved problem."[15] For all of its bold language, the New Deal promised by the federal planners had somehow gone astray.

To some extent, the reasons were to be found in the nature of the federal structure of American national government. At least three departments of the executive branch—War, Interior and Agriculture—had responsibilities and interests in the island. The sprawling Federal Emergency Relief Administration under Harry Hopkins also had a concern insofar as the funds for the island relief projects had to come from its budget. The unavoidable outcome of this bureaucratic pluralism was divided authority and divided responsibility. Departmental jealousies and rivalries made necessary the unsatisfactory device of the multi-departmental committee, with all of the inevitable delay in decision making: the Interdepartmental Committee for the Economic Rehabilitation of Puerto Rico set up by the President in June 1934, with members from Interior, Agriculture, the FERA, the Farm Credit Administration and the Treasury, was a good case in point. There was at no time any real coordination. Departments took unilateral decisions without consultation with others; the unfortunate decision of the Department of Agriculture, for example, to send a technical specialist to the island in 1934 who (unbeknown to the Department) had earlier alienated Puerto Ricans by his racial prejudice and who was even *persona non grata* with the benign and tolerant Dr. Chardón, did serious damage for a while to the local program. The program, once again, was slowed down by the stubborn fight of the head of the old PRERA in the island to resist the incorporation of that agency into the new PRRA and to retain its independent identity. The attempt failed; but it managed to eat up energy and spirit that should have gone into the New Deal as a composite whole. Valuable time was wasted as plans already publicly accepted by the Administration got temporarily lost in the Washington jungle; for a time the Puerto Rican author of the rehabilitation program was even driven to the undignified and unpleasing task of lobbying personally in the capital for its rapid implementation. Even then, the implementation too often depended upon the dramatic move that bypassed the lines of departmental command, such as Muñoz Marín's stirring telegram to the White House which succeeded in producing a Christmas message for the island population from the President himself. Dr. Gruening, as head of the PRRA, had to compete with the forty-eight states and the other outlying dependencies for funds and patronage, and his first encounter with Harry Hopkins on that matter in 1935-1936 left him with the distinct impression that he and Puerto Rico had been sacrificed to the Administration's need to spend heavily in the mainland states during an election year.[16] This rift between Gruening and Hopkins was quickly followed by a rift between Gruening and Ickes, to the point where the latter finally persuaded the President to terminate the independent status of the PRRA by placing it, in 1936, under the jurisdiction of the Interior Department. There was not even wanting the cloak-and-dagger touch that made certain episodes in Washington's dealings with the island read like a chapter out of a Dashiell Hammett story. The Secretary of the Interior used his private investigating funds to send a special investigator to San Juan in the guise of an inquiring tourist to report on Governor Winship in 1935;[17] while two years earlier Governor Gore had committed an unpardonable faux pas by bringing back to the island as a member of his entourage a disreputable American newspaperman who had composed a series of hostile articles on Puerto Rico in the *Baltimore Sun* back in 1925 and who was subsequently obliged to flee the island with money obtained by acting as a lobbyist in the insular legislature for the local slot machine business interests.[18]

The eighteenth-century character of American federalism as a system of government thus entailed a basic absence of centralization and continuity for the New Deal in Puerto Rico. Even more important, however, were contributing reasons within the island itself. In Washington there were bungling and incompetence, in San Juan there were overt and covert sabotage and opposition. For the first time since the American occupation, the island's propertied forces faced—as did their continental counterpart—a progressive Administration determined to clip their historic power and prerogative. As a class of wealthy individuals, their record of civic patronage and responsibility had been miserable indeed. They had left none of the bequests or endowments to cultural or educational institutions that would have indicated the existence of a cultured patrician elite in the society. After four decades under the new regime there was a library in San

Juan built by Carnegie funds, but none anywhere built by Puerto
Rican munificence. The University derived its support from the student body, the insular Treasury and sundry federal funds. A rich
member of the Spanish colony had earlier perpetuated his name by a
grant of land for the Pedro Arzuaga y Peraza tuberculosis sanitorium,
but the example had not been followed. The tendency of the Creole
rich to spend their wealth on European travel, before 1898, was followed after that date by a tendency to spend it in the American holiday
resorts. At the same time, a very real habit of conspicuous expenditure
characterized their spending habits in the island; a private correspond-
ent to the Brookings Institution investigators remarked upon the fact
that the island, far from being poor in terms of its total income, could
boast of a fairly large money-spending class "which makes one wonder," he concluded, "if the absentee landlord who, it is claimed,
should spend his money on the Island, would really help Porto Rico
any by staying there and wasting his surplus in racing, boxing, cock
fighting, as so many of the residents do."[19] The Puerto Rican masses,
it is obvious enough, did not even enjoy, as some sort of compensation
for their poverty, the spectacle of a Venetian oligarchy using its
wealth in the service of either an elegant and sophisticated profligacy
or of a lavish adornment of the public society.

It was natural enough that this class of Creole wealthy should see
in the New Deal a serious challenge to their power, to their insular
assumption that they, as a class, had been ordained by nature to rule
the uncomplaining and submissive *jíbaro* and *agregado*. Politically
they were the Puerto Rican Tories, the counterpart of the "rock-
ribbed" Republicans in the north. They were, however, counterparts
with a difference, for the peculiarities of island politics worked in such
a way as to guarantee them the effective control of the insular political
scene for the entire period up to 1940. The major parties, true
enough, were affiliated with one or another of the American major
parties, to the point of enjoying delegation rights in the national
nominating conventions, even recognition in the distribution of federal
patronage. But this did not guarantee that the trends of national politics would determine those of local politics, for while party management in the insular-national relationship was largely in the hands of
resident Americans in the island, the "old hands," Puerto Rican control in insular organization was all but complete. This explains the
seeming paradox that while in 1932 the progressive forces swept the
continent as a whole they remained a divided minority group in San
Juan for the next eight years. This meant two things: First, that the
local "new deal" had to be initiated and largely continued by American liberal elements, with, of course, their Puerto Rican sympathizers,

and, second, that they had to embrace this task in the face of growing opposition from champions of the old order who remained in strategic command of the local legislative houses in the form of the Republican-Socialist Coalition.

The record of that opposition was at least an outstanding example of uninspired reaction. It successfully delayed action on the sugar plan, and the insular government had to wait until 1940 before the Superior Court judgment, in *People of Puerto Rico v. Rubert Hermanos,* finally granted it the right to enforce the agrarian law. It used its legislative majority to cripple the work of the agencies as much as possible, even to the point of attempting to sell to Washington an alternative "plan" guaranteed to stultify any progressive advance by setting up a rehabilitation corporation so organized as to insure the permanent control of the local legislature over the federal recovery program. It deployed its investigating power to initiate an inquiry—regarded by Ickes as "highly improper"—into the workings of the federal New Deal agency on the island. It lobbied sedulously by means of delegations in Washington. Even the office of the Resident Commissioner in Washington, being in the control of the Coalition, was pressed into the service of the anti-progressive cause; and it is the final sad comment upon the meaninglessness of Santiago Iglesias's "socialism" that, as the person occupying that post during the period, he lent himself to the strategy, even going so far as to obtain the insertion into the *Congressional Record* of a highly unreliable and hostile report on the Chardón Plan. Finally, no single move could perhaps have so emphatically underlined the gross opportunism of the opposition to what was, after all, a mild social reform program as the clumsy effort of the sugar producers' association of the island to counteract federal action by offering to Rexford Tugwell, then Under-Secretary of Agriculture, an appointment as its permanent representative in the field of public relations.[20]

Yet, for all this, the tragedy of the island lay within itself. For the events of its own political history during these years played directly into the hands of reaction, domestic and federal, and contributed in their repercussions to the ultimate disintegration of the reconstruction program. The first tragic event was the murder by Nationalist gunmen in February 1936 of the young and popular chief of police, Colonel Francis Riggs, so untypical, in its stark brutality, of a society remarkable for the comparative absence of serious violence in its public life. The second event was the "massacre" of Palm Sunday, 1937, in which the semi-militarized police were given an unfortunate opportunity to take revenge for the Riggs murder by firing upon an unarmed demonstration by the Nationalist Party in the southern town of Ponce. The

two events together had the effect of sharpening the already deep
tensions of colonial life and of destroying for good the working alliance
between the New Deal in Washington and the liberal groups, led by
Muñoz Marín, on the island. Behind both ugly episodes there lay the
resurgence of the Creole Fascist-Nationalist movement led by the
fanatical genius of Pedro Albizu Campos, whose virulent hatred of the
Americans has been reported to have gone back to an unfortunate
experience at Harvard University during the period of the First World
War. The frustration and hate, the political megalomania and the
perverted idealism of its individual members have been described in
the novel *Los Derrotados* of César Andreu Iglesias. Many of them
were members of the *falangista* groups set up in the island by Franco
agents, interested not so much in a genuine struggle for democratic
independence as in fomenting a neo-fascist attack upon democracy
itself. Their program, in reality founded upon hatred of the American,
carefully avoided any rational discussion of problems; it was enough
to insist, as the party did after 1941, that "when the Japanese have
defeated America, then Puerto Rico will have her independence."[21]
As with their European counterparts, there was the same mask of
hate, the same hostile and psychotic nationalism; what was distinctive
was that the Puerto Rican crypto-fascism took on the guise, in addition, of an exaggerated pride in things Spanish, the display of Spanish
coats of arms, the pathetic aping in personal behavior of the mannerisms of the Spanish grandee. All of this in its turn was all the more
grotesque because for many of the members, who were colored, these
peculiarities were an expression of their shame of color. Electorally
they were insignificant: when they carried their cause to the polls in
1932 they received less than 5,000 votes out of a total population of
nearly two million people. But because they symbolized the magic
appeal of independence their emotional attraction was boundless. In
a period when no leader in insular politics, not even Muñoz, could
afford publicly to slight the ideal of independence, they could pose
with some small measure of plausibility as loyal patriots fighting the
imperial power. The consequence was that they managed to distort
every issue, to inhibit rational discussion on the insular problems,
to compel every rival party to echo their rabid anti-Americanism or
run the risk of being pilloried as traitors to the insular "honor."
Fundamentally, they were sterile in theory. As one of the acquaintances of their leader aptly remarked, the Nationalist *cacique* was
gifted in his ability to foretell the past and look back at the future.
Their fervid nationalism nevertheless, couched so much in terms of
an outmoded Byronic romanticism, helped tremendously to subordinate once more the social question to the political. They contributed

much to the wall of misunderstanding which gradually erected itself between Puerto Rican liberalism and American liberalism. Above all, events played their game for them.

To begin with, the Riggs murder had the immediate effect of hardening New Deal attitudes to the island. The temptation was easy for the Washington powers, removed a thousand miles from the scene, to blame all Puerto Ricans for the murder and to see it as an act of cowardly ingratitude for all that America had done for the territory. The President began to get tired of the whole affair. Even a New Dealer as pungently liberal as Harold Ickes began to weaken in his faith in the island. The immediate expression of the decline of confidence was the so-called Tydings Bill of 1936 providing for an insular plebiscite on the question of independence as a means, in effect, of ridding the nation of an embarrassing encumbrance. In part the measure was sponsored by the conservative Maryland Senator almost as an act of revenge for the murder of Colonel Riggs, who had been a close friend. In part—although this was not known until the revelations of the Ickes *Diaries* published in 1954—it was originally suggested by the cabinet itself and drafted in the Interior Department.[22] In any case it was an unfortunate measure, since it was founded upon nothing more substantial than a feeling of angry petulance in the national government; Secretary Ickes could even persuade himself that if the island electorate should vote against independence "then such agitation as has been going on in Puerto Rico would be put an end to for probably twenty years."[23] Nor was it in any way a fair or honorable proposition, since its economic provisions—providing for a gradual subjection of Puerto Rican products to American tariff requirements at the high rate of a 25 percent annual increase—meant that political independence would be accompanied by almost certain economic ruin. An economy that had been deliberately made dependent upon the American market would now be turned adrift into a murderously competitive world trade market, while the American moral responsibilities accumulated as a consequence of that policy would be jettisoned under the pretense of granting "freedom" to the colonial ward. "The bill," observed Muñoz Marín bitterly in a letter to Ickes, "gives Puerto Ricans a very clear impression of being designed to obtain the mandate [for independence] from the Puerto Rican people under threat of literal starvation or a continuance of the present colonial status."[24] The whole tone of the measure, as well as the subterfuge involved in its Congressional presentation, suggested that the Administration had moved decisively to the right in its dealing with the island. It was moving from economic reconstruction to political "loyalty" as the lodestone of its Caribbean policy.

This was evident, more than anywhere else, in the slow transformation of Ernest Gruening during this period from a crusading liberal into an American super-patriot. The evidence of the change painfully mounted: the open break with every island liberal of note—Muñoz, Chardón, Padín; the "purge" of liberals in the PRRA administration in the island; the questionable procedures involved in the indictment of the Nationalist leaders after the Riggs murder on the illiberal ground of "political sedition"; the quiet reconciliation with the local conservative forces, including Governor Winship. Secretary Ickes was finally moved to a characteristic private explosion of angry disillusionment. "Gruening," he wrote in his diary in November 1936, "from being a liberal, has apparently decided that the mailed fist is the proper policy in dealing with these subject people. He has gone completely in reverse. He is on the outs with all of his former liberal friends in Puerto Rico. . . . I think that it is a poor time, in view of the substantial progress that we have made in bringing about better feelings toward the United States on the part of Spanish-American countries, to resort to extreme measures in Puerto Rico."[25]

Despite such misgivings, however, policy continued to be less, not more liberal. It led, in the end, to the complete alienation of the island liberal groups. The Ponce Palm Sunday affair and its aftermath of violent emotionalism drove the last nail into the coffin of any healthy mutual cooperation. Although on a lesser scale, the affair has subsequently played a role in the Puerto Rican political psychology not unlike that of Amritsar in the Indian Congress psychology after 1919. In both cases an act of violence left behind it a cancerous sore infecting the harmonious adjustments of practically every problem between both sides of the colonial nationalist struggle. The report of the Puerto Rican episode published by the American Civil Liberties Union, based upon the on-the-spot investigations of Arthur Garfield Hays, although candidly recognizing the incipient fascism of the Nationalists, placed the blame squarely on the shoulders of the insular government and justified the conclusion of the ACLU board of directors that the representatives of the federal government in the island had been guilty of "gross violation of civil rights and incredible police brutality."[26] Washington, however, including the President himself, preferred to see Ponce as a further proof of the presence of "un-American" elements and responded with a reassertion of "Americanization" as the proper remedy for the disease. The years between 1937 and 1940 consequently witnessed the gradual sacrifice of the original New Deal reform program to that sterile prescription of cure. Few things could have so dramatically highlighted the retreat as the President's letter of appointment to the new Commissioner of Education, Dr. José Gallardo, in 1937. "What is necessary," Mr. Roosevelt wrote to his nominee, "is that the American citizens of Puerto Rico should profit from their unique geographical situation and the unique historical circumstance which has brought to them the blessings of American citizenship by becoming bilingual. But bilingualism will be achieved only if the teaching of English throughout the insular educational system is entered into at once with vigor, purposefulness and devotion, and with the understanding that English is the official language of our country."[27] The integrity of the President notwithstanding, the proper comment upon his observations is that they were addressed to an appointee whose main recommendation for the appointment appears to have been his political activities in support of the local Democratic Party organization as an obscure young professor of Spanish in a South Carolina college; and that as new Commissioner of Education he was prepared to subordinate the educational program of the island to what was, essentially, a political purpose.

So, once appointed, the new Commissioner rapidly moved forward to purge from the educational system all persons known either for their *independentista* views or for their critical attitude to the educational program. The policy was accompanied, at the more general level of insular developments, by a new and open identification with all the elements in the society, even the anti-Puerto Rican sections of the American community, that had never really accepted in their hearts the full application of the democratic idea to the island. Dr. Chardón finally was driven to resignation from public life, and he assuaged his bitterness by undertaking a lengthy tour of the Spanish Main and the mountain interior regions of Venezuela and Colombia, and thereby gave to Puerto Rican science and literature the charming record, in diary form, of a remarkable peregrination.[28] In his absence his voice was replaced by others less benign: the American scientist employed at the Federal Experimental Station who could observe of his Puerto Rican colleagues that "many of them are highly intelligent and some are good administrators but a careful view of their scientific contributions indicates that they are unimaginative in natural sciences";[29] or the American director of the same station who could describe the local university as "anti-American" merely because some Nationalist Party leaflets had been discovered on the desk of one of its faculty members;[30] or the Jack Dempsey who could observe, on a swift visit to the island, that the three million dollars spent by the PRRA on university buildings could have been directed more profitably to the construction of more hotels and race tracks, so that the island could become a southern extension of the Florida tourist circuit;[31] or the Americans in the island who castigated Mrs. Roosevelt because she insisted on exposing the worst aspects of San Juan slumdom to her accompanying entourage of newspapermen and photographers during her island visit. All of these were variations on the general theme of American colonialist attitudes. Even Harold Ickes himself was not immune to the general infection; and his exchange of correspondence with Commissioner Gallardo in 1943 suggests that he himself could believe that the entire educational program of the colony could be set by the issuance of political directives from Washington offices.[32] These were all expressions, in different ways, of the naive distinction —running throughout a book published on the island around this time, Trumbull White's *Puerto Rico and Its People*—between the "restless radicals" who spoil things with their criticism and the "men of understanding and thoughtfulness" who could be relied upon to be loyal Americans. It had become painfully clear by 1940 that the *élan* of the New Deal had been lost in Puerto Rico as much as on the mainland and that if it were ever to be revived on the island it would have to be through an indigenous radical leadership determined to solve the local problems by local means and on local terms.

It is easy to see, in retrospect, what went wrong. The New Deal had grown up as a movement of response to American problems. It was transferred to Puerto Rico without much recognition of the truth that methods which succeed in a national democracy may not necessarily succeed in a dependent colony. What was "liberalism" for Americans became, at best, "enlightened imperialism" for Puerto Ricans. This was better than unenlightened imperialism; but it was imperialism, nonetheless. The entire effort was predicated upon the assumption, so "un-American" itself, that good government could be made into a respectable alternative for self-government. The imperialism of neglect had merely been exchanged for the imperialism of liberal paternalism. "Thirty years of neglect and even economic exploitation," Dr. Mathews concludes in his able study of the experiment, "were to be undone by government planning and regulation. However, this new policy had its drawbacks. Neglect was exchanged for excessive management. The idea that the Puerto Rican had to be watched, directed, and managed was apparent. He had to be shown what was to his benefit. When a discontented few showed signs of rebellion the island as a whole was then threatened by the Tydings measure."[33]

The ideological framework for a viable American imperialism, in fact, was lacking. An American writer, Alpheus Snow, had written a curious book in 1902 in which he had attempted to prove, in some six hundred pages of neo-Hegelian argumentation, that the dispositive and regulatory powers vested in the President and the Congress by the original constitutional grant of 1787 had foreseen and authorized the emergence of a federal empire wherein the relationships between the Union and its insular dependencies should remain permanently one of trusteeship, so organized institutionally as to guarantee that the dependent parts would enjoy the "distinct community life" made necessary by their "isolated position."[34] The thesis never stopped to inquire whether the growth of the American popular democracy since the adoption of the Constitution warranted such grandiose conclusions. Certainly there was no Puerto Rican leader of any note in 1940 who would have been prepared to accept such an anti-democratic argument; nor had any sizable section of American opinion shown any readiness to embrace such a high Roman concept of American imperial responsibilities. The absence of an ideological commitment to empire naturally entailed, in its wake, the absence of any sustained effort to build up any sort of special and permanent machinery for the government of the new empire. Snow's enthusiasm had led him to suggest that imperial obligations should be met by a radical alteration of the form of the federal government so as to permit the establishment of a Secretary of State for Imperial Affairs, aided by an advisory Imperial Council, with the general aim of substituting the unsatisfactory jurisdiction of Congress, which he rightly castigated as unfit for the purpose, with an administrative structure guided by experts.[35] But the New Deal, Jeffersonian in its liberalism as it was, never got beyond the timorous suggestion of a Central Council, incorporating an advisory committee for each overseas territory, under the chairmanship of the bureau chief in the Interior Department.[36] Even this mild degree of reorganization failed to materialize, and the collapse of the Puerto Rican New Deal may in some measure be traced to the failure.

Puerto Ricans, as a result, never knew the real focus of responsibility for their governance. There was a fatal absence of any proper machinery of consultation between the federal headquarters and the local offices. The office of the Governor continued throughout to exhibit—apart from the quite separate fact of the notorious lack of sympathy for the New Deal program on the part of either Governor Gore or Governor Winship—a dualism inimical to positive leadership, for its occupant was at once the agent of the federal executive power and the co-trustee of the local realm. The ironical paradox, in sum, lay in the fact that a proper discharge of the imperial responsibility required the existence of some governing body, something after the manner of the old Spanish Council of the Indies, to exercise a continuous and vigilant control over the governments of the dependencies; while the seminal principles of equality and liberty governing the

American experience made it forever unlikely that such a structure
of imperial supervision would ever stand a chance of getting itself
adopted at the national center. Inevitably the Puerto Rican people
were obliged to pay the price of that paradox.

1940 and After: The Populares

CLASSICALLY, the anatomy of colonial nationalism passes through various and successive stages. It begins with a stage of psychological dependence upon the governing power; affiliates itself to the progressive and friendly elements of that power; assumes that the solution to the colonial problem involves merely the transplanting of the best in the metropolitan culture to the dependent society. The strategy of the *turno en el poder*, used by Muñoz Rivera during the last decade of the Spanish regime, was founded upon this frame of reference; and in the British Caribbean a generation later it was reflected in the well-known slogan of Captain Cipriani in Trinidad that "what is good enough for the British Labour Party is good enough for me." A further stage is reached when these great expectations are disappointed, either because the progressive forces in the metropolitan society fail to come to power or because, once in power, they are tempted to forget their colonial allies. When this point is reached the colonial nationalist movement must accept the alternative of dying a slow death or of seeking out new sources of support in the mass base of its own society. It no longer sees itself as a suppliant begging aid from the sovereign power but as a nationalist task force, secure in mass support, demanding that charity be replaced with justice. If the demand is refused, the situation can rapidly deteriorate into the ugly arbitrament of armed conflict, as in the cases of post-war Indonesia and Algeria. If it is met with real sympathy, it can set the stage for a policy of statesmanlike accommodation between both sides, as in the case, most famously, with the withdrawal of the British Raj from India in 1947.

By 1938 Puerto Rico was beginning to reach that latter stage. In one way disillusionment, as already noted, had set in as early as the first decade of the century. But, even so, local leadership still continued to believe in American good will and to rely upon American liberal policies. It was not until the obvious failure of the New Deal that it began fully to emancipate itself from that reliance. For by 1938 the New Deal in the island had declined into a bureaucratic activity dealing with the accidents rather than the essences of a colonial society. The national Administration had turned its back upon the only group in the community which understood and was willing to cooperate in the task of creative social renovation. The Independence Bill of 1936 had effectively split the Liberal Party open, dividing it into the radical wing that wanted political separation at any cost and the moderate wing that wanted an honorable independence which would guarantee the full discharge of America's economic responsibilities to the island. The bill confronted a young leader like Muñoz with a cruel dilemma, for to support it would be to embrace economic chaos, to oppose it would be to turn the radicals against him as a puppet of the colonial regime. In any case the issue led ultimately to his open break with Barceló in 1937. In the meanwhile the bill turned the elections of 1936 into a spurious and distorted referendum on independence. The confusion thereby created is perhaps best demonstrated by the quixotic effort of Muñoz to persuade his party into a boycott of the election; for if, to the Latin mind, the tactic could be romantically likened to the act of Cortes in burning his boats on the beach at Vera Cruz, to the more practical mind of the Senator's American friends it seemed like a questionable device certain to result in the disapproval of his powerful Washington connections.[1] What is beyond doubt is that these connections, by introducing the Tydings measure, became directly responsible for the continuation in power for another four years of the reactionary Coalition, and contributed thereby to the rapid decline of Muñoz into the condition of the disappointed leader of a routed faction. Increasingly after 1937, moreover, the federal Administration was caught up in the gathering storm of the Second World War and in Puerto Rico, as much as on the mainland, the social-reform New Dealers were slowly being replaced by the new bureaucracy of experts in national defense and international affairs. The local government was left in the hands of the old-style alliance of professional *políticos* and a pliant Governor. Nothing progressive was likely to come from machine bosses who were specialists in working the extralegal system of petty intrigue and patronage into which, for want of positive popular leadership, the colonial machinery of government had deteriorated; or from a Governor—in the person of the retired Army General Blanton Winship—who, in the words of a Puerto Rican critic, regarded the island as an extensive Southern plantation with the sugar men as his foremen and the people as good or bad folk as they did their work and accepted their livings without or with complaint.[2]

Henceforth, it was clear enough, the Puerto Rican "revolution" would have to be carried on by Puerto Ricans. The year 1940 is quite properly regarded as the real turning point in the island transformation since it witnessed the successful seizure of the citadel of legislative power, with a slender plurality, by the new party—the *Partido Popular Democrático*—founded by Muñoz in July 1938 after an unsuccessful attempt to bring together the estranged factions of the old Liberal Party into a new united front. The story of the genesis and organization of the new party in those two brief years is nothing less than astonishing. It had to face and surmount the vulgar contempt of the established parties, perhaps nowhere better expressed than in the open letter in which Antonio Barceló, as an aging politician of the old school, condescendingly advised the young Muñoz to remember that the formation of a new party was not child's play and demanded qualities which the writer clearly felt did not belong to the eager novice.[3] It had to break away from the Puerto Rican habit of political leadership through family cliques or, not much better, the misplaced sentimentalism which could persuade the Liberal Party in 1944, for example, to nominate the daughter of the then deceased Barceló as its new president-leader, with not very happy results for that declining movement. There were, in addition, deeply entrenched habits of electoral corruption to overcome, in particular the sale of votes for a small sum of money or a new pair of shoes, so much accepted, indeed, by public opinion as a natural element of politics that in 1940 two of the island's leading newspapers had no difficulty in sponsoring a competition offering prizes for the best accounts of violations of electoral regulations in the previous election of 1936.[4] The new party could not hope for the handsome donations from the sugar industry that usually helped to finance most insular political groups; and for years *La Democracia*, the party organ, was run by means of gifts from more well-to-do party sympathizers and of devoted effort on the part of a persistently underpaid staff. The party's intellectual echelon of school and university teachers also found that its members had to pay a harsh price, sometimes including dismissal from their posts, for their political affiliation.

Above all, a new party that sought to launch not simply another change in governmental personnel but an entire fundamental social change was faced with the exacting task of changing the whole colonial climate of thought. It had to meet head on the debris of psychological fatigue and cynical disillusionment left behind by the avalanches of Spanish and American dominion. The Washington psycho-complex of the older generation had somehow to be replaced with a vigorous self-confidence within the individual Puerto Rican. Puerto Ricans, hitherto, had looked outside for help; they now had to look within, discover their own inner resources. That, in itself, was no mean task, for a reading of books like José de Diego's *Nuevas Campañas* or José Coll Cuchi's *El Nacionalismo en Puerto Rico* makes it painfully evident that even the most ardent of separatist Puerto Rican politicians found it more congenial to conduct a running battle with Washington than to undertake the hard task of mass political education throughout the island. The task was hard, of course, because of the massive apathy of the island people, an apathy too often mistaken by outside observers for a merely charming docility. Even a report as devoid of revolutionary sentiment as the Brookings Institution study had been impressed by that phenomenon. "There is a degree of submissiveness to misfortune and a lack of class feeling," its authors observed, "that to an outside observer is difficult to understand. Perhaps it is the widespread illness, perhaps it is the background of slavery and feudalism, perhaps it is the extreme poverty, perhaps the terrific impact of the periodic storms that carry all away with them and make human effort and ingenuity seem like naught, that explains the passive helplessness of the rural community."[5] The recommendations of the Report, of course, rested upon the silent premise that the sickness it analyzed required remedial action by the outside power in Washington. The time had now come, however, for action by the Puerto Rican social force itself.

The story of the political-educational campaign waged by Muñoz between 1938 and 1940 has been told frequently. What is necessary to stress here is the absolutely unique character of that campaign. It was unique because the party platform—taking a tremendous gamble in colonial politics—studiously avoided the status issue in order to concentrate upon a fully fledged program of economic reform. Other party platforms had advocated such before—the 1936 platform of the Socialist Party, for example—but there had been little evidence of any real determination to struggle for their fulfillment; and the Socialist Party, in any case, was at once the prisoner of its Republican senior partner in the Coalition and the victim of bitter internal quarrels that terminated with the eviction from its membership of the important leader Prudencio Rivera Martínez in 1939. Hitherto, again, the sociology of insular politics had revolved around political parties *de nombre*, characterized by an absence of effective island-wide organization, with their directorates centered in San Juan and blossoming momentarily into life at election times. Not the least of the massive changes introduced by the *Populares* was to get away from the debilitating atmosphere of the capital. San Juan had been throughout the citadel of conservative officialdom, so that it had been rare indeed for any anti-government party to win an election within its boundaries; and the practice had arisen, beginning under Spain, for such parties to hold their important meetings, including their foundation meetings, in the towns outside San Juan: Ponce, Mayagüez, Caguas, Arecibo. The *Populares* carried this one step further with their mass electoral campaign among the people, and especially the majority element of the poverty-stricken agricultural laborers. With rigged-out sound cars in the fashion of Huey Long, Muñoz campaigned throughout the length and breadth and in each tiny hamlet and *barrio* of the island. It was a campaign of informal conversation, with very little of the empty rhetoric that so often persuaded other politicians to mistake oratory for thought. It used a simply worded catechism to drive home its message. Its intimate democratic manner has been happily captured in the memoir later written by the ambulatory typist of the caravan, all the more engaging because of its convincing simplicity.[6] What one catches in its reading is, in total, the portrait of a new leader. We see him sleeping in heavy fatigue in the back seat of the ancient automobile that serves both as hotel and office as it travels the twisting mountain roads between one meeting and another; castigating a local party leader for disobeying his strict orders not to encumber a tight schedule with a prepared banquet; singing, with driver and typist, his favorite song, Rafael Hernández's "La Gaviota," as they travel from a mountain town into the capital; breaking down, little by little, the armor of polite yet deep suspiciousness which was the normal attitude of the Puerto Rican countryman to the entire gallery of politicians who had so often betrayed him; above all, establishing a rapport of warm camaraderie with his mass audience, all the more effective because it came from a strange ecstasy, within him, of compassionate identification with the men and women whose votes he sought. As one reads the record of the unorthodox campaign one begins to realize that Muñoz possessed, like all truly great leaders, the capacity to evoke in his followers a massive loyalty and an affectionate adulation that no reverses can diminish or hostile force pollute. The *Popular* lieutenant who, in a harangue in the theater of the small municipality of Maricao in the western highlands, invoked the image of "God in his heaven, Roosevelt in the United States, and Muñoz Marín in Puerto Rico," was only paying a pardonably extravagant tribute to the magic appeal his leader had been able to establish among all sections of the society.

The narrow victory of 1940 was followed by the tremendous landslides of 1944 and 1948 and a prolonged tenure of power that now matches (in 1963) the American Democratic reign after 1932. Much of the *Popular* program and policy have of course changed during this period. It is worth emphasizing at this point, however, those of its achievements which seem to have become an integral and permanent part of the national culture. Its emergence as the first genuinely nationalist party in the island has stood the test of time, if not perfectly, at least remarkably well. For if the movement started as the defender of the *jíbaro*—as its emblem of the *pava*, the peasant hat, indicates— it soon grew to embrace a whole cross-section of the society—cane cutter, dockworker, university teacher, professional man, Negro, and Hispanic white. "A worthwhile leader," one thoughtful Puerto Rican told an American inquirer in 1938, "will not come in on a wave of hatred and violence. He will not secure his following through attacks on specialized groups. He won't be representing any group such as the Negroes or the Catholics or the sugar interests. Instead, he'll regard the entire interest of the Island, and he should go farther than that and think in terms of a world society."[7] Muñoz could with good reason claim to be the fulfillment, in his person, of that prophecy.

It is true enough that with the consolidation of the new party's victory the old rift between the more moderate and the more radical *Populares* (many of the latter dear and close comrades of Muñoz in the days of political exile) on the status issue began once more to evince itself as early as 1943; and some of the latter group were later, like Géigel Polanco, to break with their leader. Even so, the remarkable feat of being able to appeal successfully to economic common sense was sufficient, in its electoral results, to enable the party to push through its reform program after 1940 and thereby to lay the foundations for the later industrialization program. Aside from this, it remains still an open question as to whether even the *Popular* magic will be able permanently to resolve the conflict which in many Puerto Rican hearts burns still between a natural desire for independence and a fear of the hardships that would assuredly lie in its wake. The reinvigorated debate on status set off by the admission in 1959 of Alaska and Hawaii to the Union, and excited further by the 1962 decision to hold a plebiscite on the question, suggests that the magic is comparatively helpless to appease the preoccupation with status. Alongside that failure there must be placed, on the debit side of the *Popular* achievement, the failure to complete the psychological release from United States tutelage. For the retreat from independence has meant a fatal return to the old game of appeasing Washington; so, today, the San Juan leadership remains silent on the United States naval-military grip on the island, in much the same way as even an earlier separatist leader like José de Diego was willing to allow a United States protectorate over an independent Puerto Rican Republic, even to the extent of guaranteeing an American right of armed intervention in the event of internal disorder.

More permanent, perhaps, has been the moral cleansing of the insular political life, commencing with Muñoz's appeal to the *jíbaro* to let personal gain yield to moral principle in the exercise of the vote; although even there note would have to be taken of the subsequent growth of a widespread "spoils system" within the Commonwealth governmental structure, as revealed by the series of articles in the *San Juan Star* during 1962. The *Popular* leader's trenchant observation, during the 1938-1940 campaigning period, that the citizen who sold his vote was like a *jíbaro* who would throw away his *machete* in the midst of a fight struck a responsive chord, so much so that the habit has subsequently become so rare as to warrant front-page news attention when it occasionally erupts. "We were like the crabs who get caught in the traps," a local workman told Dr. Sidney Mintz some years later. "I can remember the mayoral candidates here in Cañemalar giving people a new pair of pants or two dollars for the promise of a vote. The crab walks into the traps to get the sweet cane, but in the end he is caught and boiled. So we would sell our votes for new pants and suffer for several more years."[8] The moral purgative that Muñoz applied to the higher social levels was to introduce, as had his father before him, a new note of serious and dispassionate discussion into the political debate. Like his father, his versatile mind recoiled with impatience from the sterility of the *políticos*, their literary, archaic, and socially reactionary preoccupation with obsolete concepts. They lived, as it were, in some sort of hypnotic trance which prevented them from seeing things as they were. Lamentation for a dead past or, slightly better, academic argumentation over a dying present, deterred them from creative analysis of the future. They showed little interest in economics. They confounded literature with politics. If they had a sense of liberty, it was oligarchic and not democratic in character. The more extremist of them committed the mistake of what Marx called "playing with revolution." In retrospect, it is the supreme achievement of Muñoz Rivera and Muñoz Marín to have pointed out at least one way out of the impasse thereby created.

The chief task of every political leader who has captured power is to translate ideology into legislation. A reform program requires him to reshape, sometimes build up from nothing, the administrative machinery and the public services. He must recruit a whole corps of technicians and specialists to clothe the outlines of his legislative program with the concrete detail of statutory and administrative forms. He may have to meet the hostility, perhaps even the sabotage, of old-fashioned civil servants to whom a device like a planning board or a statistical office seems the prelude to socialist revolution. If he has been a professional insurrectionist, like Lenin before 1917, he must

learn to substitute the art of governing the state for that of overthrowing it. If, like the British Labor Party after 1945, the successful party
inherits the services of a profoundly conservative civil service establishment, it must invent new measures of administrative government
to bypass the dangers of reluctant cooperation. Whatever the particular historical environment, the leader of a party seeking large-scale
social reconstruction must possess, both in himself and in the men
and women he gathers around him, what Walter Bagehot in his
essay on Sir Robert Peel styled a "morbid sense of administrative
responsibility."

The *Popular* majority in Puerto Rico after 1941 faced most of these
hazards. Even more: it inherited all of the handicaps of colonialism.
For colonial government, by its nature, is negative government. It
places a high premium on the maintenance of "law and order" and on
the avoidance of "disturbances." The real center of power remains in
the home offices, whose personnel have an inclination always to believe that their wisdom is superior to that of the distant officials in
the field, and who tend, in addition, to measure the quality of a governor or an administrator by his ability to keep his particular bailiwick
out of the news. The local governmental machine is consequently
limited to a narrow, simple apparatus designed to maintain the stagnation of equilibrium. The Puerto Rican case in 1941 was no exception to the rule. The Organic Act of 1917 which laid out the
machinery of government had from the very start inhibited active and
efficient control of the insular business. It imposed what amounted
to a triple veto upon the local legislative will—of the Governor, the
Congress and the President. It set up a corporate cabinet—the Executive Council—which was fatally divided in its membership between
those who were appointed by the President and those who were
appointed by the Governor. Theoretically conceived as an advisory
council to the Governor, it had long since become a *político*-domi-
nated institution utilized to reduce his power and to establish control
over him on the part of the insular Senate by means of the device of
senatorial confirmation of cabinet posts. This end had been achieved,
as Governor Roosevelt described in his memoirs, by the unusual use
to which the "advice and consent" clause of the Organic Act had been
put by the insular Senate. That clause, in the American Constitution,
has been used as a rarely employed veto and not as a power to initiate
cabinet nominations. The colonial complex, however, worked to give
it a different usage. "In Puerto Rico," wrote Governor Roosevelt, "the
political leaders saw at once that a powerful weapon had been placed
in their hands. They argued that as the governor was not elected by
Puerto Ricans but appointed by the President, their position was not

comparable to the states in the Union and that, therefore, the majority party had the right to refuse to confirm any nominee of the governor for no other reason than that he was not a member of their political groups. The result normally was that either the governor surrendered to the majority party the right to name his cabinet officials, maintaining merely a veto power on improper selections, or a long and complicated struggle ensued."[9]

This situation was made worse by the fact that even the spending powers of the government, more particularly the liberty of the Governor to shape an independent fiscal policy, were drastically curtailed by the anomalous status of the Auditor, removed as he was from local control by his appointment by the unilateral decision of the President (joined with the federal Senate); in other words, the vital fiscal power resided in part in the hands of an official who could be persuaded either to become a rival to the Governor or a willing instrument of legislative obstructionism. The unity of outlook that alone can make a cabinet work smoothly was thus seriously imperiled. The constitutional bar upon the redistribution of agencies within the executive departments further inhibited governmental efficiency, since it denied to the chief executive the power to reorganize departments in the light of new conditions. There was no rational recognition anywhere of the proper lines of authority that should divide the manufacture of general policy from the detail of administration in working governmental structure; the fact, for example, that the Commissioner of Education was at the same time the President of the Board of Trustees of the national University was one of the central reasons why, over the years, that institution was compelled to sacrifice academic integrity to systematic exploitation by the professional politicians. All in all, by 1941, insular government had bogged down into a private war, or at best an armed truce, between an obsolete executive and a hybrid executive-legislative opposition. The situation had been rationalized, on the American side, by the traditional assumption of American liberalism that a weak executive was a necessary ingredient of "liberty" and, on the Puerto Rican side, by the feeling that a posture of hostility toward an alien executive was a proper proof of patriotism. The upshot altogether was that Puerto Rico in 1941, more even than Washington in 1932, confronted twentieth-century problems with an eighteenth-century machinery of government. A modernized executive, genuine civil service reform, a rehabilitated legislature, the recognition of administration as a new branch of government—all of these had to be tackled if the *Popular* program was not to get lost in the sterile negativism of colonial politics.

It was a fortunate accident that the *Popular* victory should have coincided with the appointment of Rexford Tugwell (in 1941) to the gubernatorial office, following the brief internship of Guy Swope, the last of the Farley type appointments. Without doubt the ablest of all American governors in the insular history, Tugwell brought to the office an array of gifts no predecessor could have matched: academic eminence, an intimate knowledge of the working of modern government, a quiet integrity, tenacity of purpose, social idealism, and, not least of all, an extensive experience in a variety of top administrative posts in American public affairs, culminating in the chairmanship of the City Planning Commission of New York. He came to the island, moreover, already deeply versed in its particular problems; his liberal spirit predisposed him, from the beginning, to lend himself and the power of his office, insofar as its imperial character permitted it, to enthusiastic fulfillment of the *Popular* economic reformism; and he possessed a large historic sense that allowed him to see the affairs of the tiny possession within the broad perspective of the emergent public society of the twentieth century of which he had been so ardent an exponent. The result was a working alliance between the Governor and the *Popular* leader that managed to overcome pretty successfully the built-in defects of the machine they had to work, and to push through a remarkable program of change between 1941 and 1946. "Outside of the strong backing which he gave Muñoz," an observer otherwise critical of the New Dealer has written, "Tugwell's really great personal contribution to Puerto Rico's reshaping was that of the political scientist who could take a revolutionary philosophy and program and translate them into definite government structures and actions. He knew how to create and run a government machine to accomplish great things. Muñoz and his followers did not—until Tugwell taught them. . . . He could not teach them anything about decency and honesty in government: those things were already present in the quality of the men who had assumed control with Muñoz. But the complex and yet efficient working structure of Puerto Rico's present government, as one of the most socially effective found anywhere on earth, is Rexford Tugwell's great achievement on the island. And even his bitterest enemies, in Congress and out, cannot deny the desirability of such a government—or deny him credit for creating its complex machinery."[10]

The best account of that change is still to be found in Governor Tugwell's own story in his volume *The Stricken Land*. No other book written on the period begins to match it in its detail or its interpretative power; Professor Lugo-Silva's volume is at best a mere chronological narrative of the most famous of the American administrations in the island.[11] The story makes it evident beyond doubt that whatever affirmative and progressive possibilities the gubernatorial office possessed were pushed to the limit under the touch of Tugwell's urge to get things done, to change the tone of the colonial climate. In the area of administrative legislation, there were placed on the statute book a budget bureau, a central statistical service and a planning law (in the form of the Planning Board Act of 1942), the last item setting out for the first time in insular history the concept of the island as one single area for planning purposes, thus superseding the archaic mechanics of some seventy-seven municipal governments in an island barely one hundred miles in length. Only two important measures failed to win legislative approval—a revision of the civil service law in order to establish a merit system and a statute modernizing the insular police; the first grounded on the rocks of political patronage, the second was lost as a consequence of the Puerto Rican fear about having a more efficient police system under the control of a continental governor. In the area of substantive legislation there was, first and foremost, the forceful Land Law (actually passed in 1941 under Governor Swope but largely based, in its far-reaching recommendations, on the findings of the committee, under Tugwell's chairmanship, which Secretary Ickes had appointed in 1940 to inquire into the administrative responsibilities under the 500-Acre provision of the Organic Act), which gave to the new Land Authority the legal power of eminent domain against the sugar corporations and the power to buy lands condemned through legal proceedings. It should be added, since Governor Tugwell's particular contribution is here being emphasized, that the Land Law also included a new and interesting idea in the field of land tenure by providing for the establishment of "proportional-profit" farms which would retain the benefits of large-scale and scientific production at the same time as they advanced the interests of the sugar workers; this sprang directly from Tugwell's inventive work, earlier, in the creation of semi-public plantation operations in the Mississippi Delta country and some of the Southwestern states under the Resettlement Administration of the early New Deal.

To all this there must be added the establishment of a Minimum Wage Board, the creation of a Transportation Authority and a Communications Authority, the reorganization of the administrative structure of the University of Puerto Rico, the birth of the Water Resources Authority (which by 1946 had done on a lesser scale, in the form of the new hydro-electric projects at the Dos Bocas and Garzas dams, what the federal government had done at Boulder and Grand Coulee); and, finally, the organization of a new island-wide Housing Authority, merging into one body the various insular and federal authorities that had been dealing with the problem since the passage of the National

Housing Act of 1937. The matter of housing, indeed, was a vital nerve center of any Puerto Rican transformation, for all previous efforts to alleviate the growth of the vile slumdom of the coastal towns had not been sufficient to accommodate even the annual population increase of the island, and as late as 1943 the Office of Information of Puerto Rico could report that some 75 percent of all insular families lived in substandard dwellings.[12] The Development Company and the Development Bank, enacted into existence at the same time, provided the institutional bodies requisite to an industrialization program. The Company was conceived as a direct medium for starting new industrial activities, the Bank as a means of filling the gap in Puerto Rico made by the failure of private bankers (for whom sugar seemed to be the sole attractive investment field) to build up investment institutions for the long-term crediting of a diversified economy, and by the failure, concomitantly, of local property to spend its wealth in any way as domestic venture capital. Finally, there was the establishment of a program—of which the creation of a School of Public Administration in the University was a part—for training the administrative talent necessary to staff this expanded machinery of government. "The truth was, at this time," observed Governor Tugwell of the beginning of his tenure of office, "that the *Populares* were very weak in technical ability. The party had a mass of loyal men and women at the bottom, a middle layer of local agitators and workers, small politicians—the useful cement of affiliation—but it had almost none of those in the middle class who carry on the paper work and do the technical jobs of modern civilization. These had to be recruited; and Muñoz, in his eagerness to reward party loyalty, was falling into the old Puerto Rican fault of putting a technical label on an incompetent individual and expecting him to do a satisfactory job. That had been one curse of the island. And it had brought the government service, the University, and even business, to a level incredibly below the demands of the situation. It now stood in the way of recruiting."[13] Altogether, the program was a magnificent accomplishment. It furnished two things that Puerto Rico had never before experienced: it laid down the outlines of a master plan for tackling the insular problem as a single whole, replacing the varied mosaic of agencies which since the New Deal period had underpinned the insular economic life. And it offered an ethic of public service to Puerto Ricans, especially of the younger generation of professional men and women, who had begun to transcend in their outlook the small coin of political patronage and strategy which for so long had kept the island a small-time "machine" combining American forms with the Latin political spirit.

It was not, of course, a battle without enemies. To begin with, there was the impersonal enemy of historical time and place. A great war, as the British experience after 1940 showed, is rarely an appropriate time for radical domestic reform. Social experimentation is, of brute necessity, sacrificed to national survival. Especially so for Puerto Rico, since the island formed part of the Caribbean ocean frontier so that, increasingly after 1940, the interest of Washington in the region became overwhelmingly strategic in character. The routines of war and blockade, of organizing vital supplies, civilian defense measures, military recruiting and training, replaced those of socio-economic reorganization. "My duty as the representative of my country in Puerto Rico," the Governor noted, "was to shape civil affairs, if I could, so that military bases, which might soon (before they were ready) have to stand the shock of attack, were not isolated in a generally hostile environment."[14] Attack was no empty possibility, for throughout the critical year of 1941-1942 the island was virtually isolated from the mainland by the Nazi submarine command of the Caribbean passages. Large sections of Tugwell's autobiography concern themselves with the appalling difficulties arising out of that ugly situation. There was the special problem of catering for the food demands of a population used to an artificial reliance upon huge imports of cheap foods from the American market. There was the problem, added to that, of keeping open the shipping lanes and of insuring that their cargoes concentrated on the necessary priorities of a people left in helpless isolation; and this, in turn, meant an open struggle with a local monopoly of import merchants whose instinctive greed drove them toward the surreptitious import of luxury articles for the well-to-do local consumer. There was the problem, to be worked out in collaboration with the local Army and Navy leaders, of securing effective defense measures for an island which, strategically speaking, lay wide open for the kind of occupation by carrier task force that was to characterize the Japanese advance in the Pacific area; and, with the Army and Navy building up their supply and operational bases on an outlying island far from continental support, the grim episode of Pearl Harbor can never have been far from the Puerto Rican consciousness.

All of this, naturally, involved the local government in the endless frustrations—a minor war in itself—of dealing with the terrifying jungle of new war organizations and agencies that proliferated in Washington after 1941 to supplement the machinery of a federal government geared for peace rather than for war. The frustrations, inevitable in themselves, were accentuated by two additional factors unique to the Puerto Rican situation. In the first place, Governor Tugwell was in large part shut off from fruitful communication with Washington as the major citadels of the national capital were taken

over by "dollar-a-year" men completely out of sympathy with his outlook. Second, there was the archaic character of American colonial
government, pitilessly exposed in such a crisis; for there was no one
single Colonial Office through which a governor in the field could
relay his pleas for aid and expect ready and unwavering support.
Governor Tugwell was thus driven to the expedient, for what it was
worth, of corresponding directly with the President on the basis of
the theory that, like a British colonial governor in his relation with
the Crown, he was the personal representative of the President rather
than an official of the Interior Department. But the theory had little
foundation in reality, if only because the monarchical character of
the Presidential office, and the killing burden it thereby entails for its
incumbent, made it quite impossible for President Roosevelt to act,
in addition, as a colonial Secretary of State. What in fact occurred in
wartime Puerto Rico was a splendid illustration of the fatal absence
of coordination in a government system founded upon the tenet of
divided powers. The Governor, unlike his counterpart in Barbados
or Jamaica, was not the sole and unquestioned executor of the imperial power. The power was, rather, irrationally shared out between
a variety of insular representatives of federal departments and agencies, both civilian and military, who viewed themselves not as subordinates of the Governor but as co-equals clothed in their own
independent federal authority. They were not always prepared to
take orders from him. In cases of conflict they were ready to appeal,
as they did, to their federal superiors against him. They were in the
position of undertaking independent policies with which at times the
Governor disagreed—the refusal of the Navy lords, for example, to
recruit Puerto Ricans—but for which he was held responsible by local
public opinion. The complete absence of any settled and decisive
relationship between Puerto Rico and the United States added fuel
to all this, for federal officials on the island were thus encouraged to
treat Puerto Ricans any way they pleased; Pedro Juan Soto's novel
Usmail is a disturbing account of the sufferings of the people of the
small island of Vieques as it was virtually turned into an American
service training camp. The absence of any of the directive unity that
marks out a genuine colonial system was perhaps a compliment to the
American anti-colonial tradition. But, in crisis, it was cold comfort
indeed. And it could never excuse a situation in which a governor
was subjected, as Governor Tugwell keenly felt himself to be, to
virtual trial at the behest of federal bureau and service representatives
within his own jurisdiction. He possessed, in brief, responsibility without the power necessary to match it.[15]

There were, in addition to this, personal as well as impersonal enemies. The familiar resistance of propertied classes to any real threat to their privilege was compounded by the sociological fact, in Puerto Rico, that the economy was less advanced and therefore its civic sense less mature; and there was no middle class of size and consequence to perform its traditional role in Western civilization of constituting, in Aristotle's phrase, the salvation of the state. The Puerto Rican upper class after 1940 repeated what its continental counterpart had used as strategy after 1932: the vicious campaign of personal slander against the President was repeated, on the smaller island canvas, in the form of scurrilous criticism of the Governor by all the forces of local reaction—the Franco supporters, the sugar interests, the newspapers, the old moneyed families who saw themselves as the guardians of the Hispanic, perhaps royalist, tradition, the city mercantile class embodied in the Chamber of Commerce. They were joined, of course, by their American Republican friends. In particular, the opportunity was seized by the Governor's old Congressional enemies—Senators Taft and Vandenberg, Congressmen Cole and Crawford—to pursue their long vendetta against him in his new appointment. The alliance of insular and federal forces was enough to persuade both the Senate and the House to send subcommittees of their respective Insular Affairs committees to the island during 1943 to investigate the charge that a vast socialist conspiracy was under way and that it was designed ultimately to include Puerto Rico in an infamous *Plan Caribe* of the Caribbean islands as a federated whole in which, among other things, Puerto Rican preferences in the American sugar market would be seriously jeopardized. No one can read the volumes of material thrown up by the investigations without becoming convinced of two things. The first was that the intellectual content of the anti-Tugwellian propaganda hardly rose above the level of an amateur rendition of the anti-bureaucratic simplicities of the Austrian school of "liberal" economists. On the Puerto Rican side, its paucity of mind is sufficiently exhibited in the pamphlet, composed in atrociously garbled English, written by Frank Torres, a member of the Executive Board of the Puerto Rico Bar Association, and so feebly argued as to have been rejected as a prospective article even by the editors of *Liberty* magazine.[16] On the continental side, the House Committee Report of 1943 allowed itself to degenerate into the thesis that the growth of limited planning powers proved the existence of intent to establish a totalitarian dictatorship in the island. The thesis was indeed so much an exercise in simple-minded illogic that its earlier presentation to the Senate subcommittee had provoked as conservative a member as Senator Taft into the irritated declaration that it was no longer regarded as unconstitutional that a modern government should under certain circumstances own and operate power systems.[17]

Or, again, it is only necessary to read the autobiography of one of the Governor's own official subordinates who secretly conspired to undermine his authority—Attorney-General George Malcolm's *American Colonial Careerist*—to appreciate the good fortune of the American reading public in not having been inundated more frequently (as have the British public for generations) by the sort of memoir-literature of retired colonial officials, replete with schoolboyish humor and pompous self-congratulation, of which it is a prime example. Yet for all of its intellectual infantilism, the opposition possessed real political strength. It was sufficient to persuade the House Agriculture Committee in 1942 to stipulate, with incredible irresponsibility, that moneys to be spent in the production and distribution of food in the island should not be used so long as Tugwell remained Governor.[18] It was sufficient to persuade Senator Vandenberg, in 1943, to introduce a bill seeking to terminate immediately the office of Governor of Puerto Rico, and thereby to seek a legislative removal of an appointed official in violation of constitutional principle.[19] It was sufficient, finally, to allow Representative McGehee, in 1944, to propose a House resolution which endeavored to obtain presidential removal of the Governor on the sole ground that he had been instrumental in bringing to the University of Puerto Rico the services of the aged and mild liberal Robert Morss Lovett on the occasion of the latter's outrageous eviction from the post of Government Secretary in the American Virgin Islands by a hostile Congress.[20]

The second fact that comes out of this record is one, perhaps, of unhappy paradox. A home government of a colonial empire is rarely prepared to relieve a local governor of his post save in extremely critical circumstances. There is no insurance, therefore, that a local reform movement like that of the *Populares* will come into power with the surety of a sympathetic governor. The governor could be a Gore or a Winship or a Tugwell. It was the good fortune of Puerto Rico, in one sense, that the federal New Deal delayed some eight years in appointing a convinced New Dealer to the Puerto Rican office and that, in turn, the local political situation delayed the advent to power of a reformist party for about the same period of time. A Muñoz in local Senatorial control in 1933 or, conversely, a Winship in the Fortaleza in 1941 could have had disastrous consequences. Yet what appeared to be a happy coincidence turned out in reality to hold seeds of danger. For the Tugwell appointment had the effect of placing an invaluable weapon into the hands of the Puerto Rican enemies of the *Popular* program. It enabled them to disguise their resistance to local democracy under the plea of combatting the "un-American" rule of a political survivor of the early days of the New Deal. It gave them a name and a reputation known—as that of Muñoz was not known—to their Congressional allies. It became all the easier to label the *Popular* program one of socialistic planning when, in reality, it was not so much socialist as a fresh example of a Latin American agrarian radicalism seeking to replace corporate latifundia with a system of individual agricultural smallholders. The net result was that the continued presence of Tugwell as Governor proved harmful and embarrassing to the island. This aspect of the situation has not always been fully appreciated, if only because the Governor's personal account tends throughout to see his Puerto Rican struggle as a Caribbean extension of his earlier duel with anti-New Deal congressional circles rather than as one episode only of the fight of Puerto Rican property and privilege to destroy the Creole challenge to their authority. It is perhaps possible that the campaign to obtain Congressional approbation of a bill to grant the Puerto Rican people the right to elect their own governor was denied final success until 1947 because of the fact that Tugwell was one of its leading sponsors. It is at least certain that although Muñoz was wrong in anticipating a national Republican victory in 1944 he was right to take note of the fact that sometime after 1938 the New Deal had lost its earlier reforming zeal and had discovered—as the advent of the businessman into the wartime agencies after 1941 showed—a new modus vivendi with American capitalism. In such a situation, and certainly after the Republican capture of the Congress in 1946, the advantages of the Tugwell appointment rapidly faded in comparison with its liabilities. It is to the credit of the Governor that he himself recognized that fact and resigned in 1946. It is worth adding that his subsequent relationship with Puerto Rico has been that of an eminent visiting scholar annually offering at the University *conferencias* that amount, in reality, to an affectionate testimony to the continuing memory of Franklin Roosevelt.

It is possible, indeed, to see the Tugwell volume on Puerto Rico as the epitaph of enlightened colonialism. The Gruening record, earlier, had demonstrated how easy it is for the usage of colonial authority to make of itself the graveyard of liberal reputations. The man who is liberal at home, suddenly thrown into an exalted position as member of a colonial governing autocracy, only too easily acquires an authoritarian instinct. What at home are seen as the greatest virtues soon became, in a different environment, the most heinous offenses. The phenomenon has been a well-known one in the British colonial empire. "That snobbishness," a West Indian critic has written, "which is so marked a characteristic of the Englishman at home, in the colonies develops into a morbid desire for the respect and homage of those over whom he rules. Uneasily conscious of the moral insecurity of his position, he is further handicapped by finding himself an aristrocrat without having been trained as one. His nose for what he considers derogatory to his dignity becomes keener than a bloodhound's, which leads him into the most frightful solecisms."[21] Similar psychological processes have been at work in the American colonial dependencies, relieved only slightly by a more explicit anti-colonial tradition and by the fact that a wider variety of industrial types have tended to migrate from the mainland.

The significance of the Tugwell interlude in Puerto Rico is that while it managed, in the figure of its leading actor, to be free of the cruder manifestations of snobbishness, it did not succeed in ridding itself of the more subtle assumptions of American pre-eminence. It is not unfair to say that the Governor's book is written from the implicit assumption that its author was the leader of the Puerto Rican reform and Muñoz Marín his chief legislative lieutenant. It records not so much the indigenous Puerto Rican struggle as the permutations (recorded in an almost Proustian prolonged mode of accumulated detail on accumulated detail) of the Governor's mind and spirit as he fights his myriad enemies. There is throughout a tone of calm condescension to the *Popular* leader, who is seen as the unstable and erratic poet-politician irritatingly refusing to yield to the American political scientist's more mature wisdom. The remark that Muñoz "provided my administrative toys; but I was always bucking his political judgment"[22] catches the spirit of the trained neo-Fabian planner who is basically skeptical of the very existence of politics and politicians. It would be difficult to imagine a political and social climate less susceptible to such a perspective than the Puerto Rican, with its veritable industry of politics. It is not too much to say that the Governor saw the whole scene in terms of another Rooseveltian drama in which he played the role of the President and Muñoz, as it were, that of Speaker Sam Rayburn, without ever fully appreciating that the genius of Muñoz made such an allocation of roles fantastically unrealistic. The failure to see this was due, to some extent, to an irrepressible egotism. For *The Stricken Land,* it must be confessed, is a difficult book to read with any patience. It has all the loose disorganized character of a manuscript that is at once a rambling private diary, a series of high-minded observations on economics, political theory, and public administration, the memoirs of a public servant and a running commentary on both American domestic politics and the events of the Second World War; and all of it composed, moreover, in the portentous and prophetic style of an American liberal who sees himself, perhaps, as the inheritor of the mantle of Henry Adams. The New Deal thus finally came to Puerto Rico not as a consciously planned colonial policy but as the expression, in large part, of the self-image of a refugee from its half-forgotten pristine period. No governor before Tugwell tried so valiantly to meet, as far as his temper allowed, the aspirations of Puerto Rican patriotism. No governor, consequently, helped to illuminate so vividly the grotesque archaism of the system he was requested to operate.

Tugwell was, in sum, a liberal seeking to work an illiberal system. But the liberalism, American best as it was, was unprepared to go as far as Puerto Rican discontents required. It could be prepared to accept a morally questionable plan, at the outset of the governorship, to occupy both the post of Governor and that of the University Chancellor and then be quite unable to see that the local storm set loose by the announcement of the plan was something more than the injured self-esteem of disappointed native candidates for the University office.[23] To defend the plan to Secretary Ickes as a means of freeing the University from politics was, even more, an amazing lapse of judgment, for the plan was calculated to do exactly the reverse.[24] Nor did the recommendations presented by the Governor to the President's Committee on the revision of the Organic Act (appointed in 1943) present any more concrete evidence of willingness to meet Puerto Ricans all the way on the matter of full internal self-government. The chief point of those recommendations concerned the establishment of a Commissioner General to be appointed by the President and with a status equal to that of the Governor (who would now be popularly elected), and the creation of an Advisory Council, half Puerto Rican and half continental in its composition, charged to report on general problems of economic rehabilitation and political progress. None of the American committee members, including Governor Tugwell, saw that with such a Commissioner and such a Council they were taking away with one hand what they were conceding with the other. It is even more surprising that the Governor should have found himself able to dismiss the very natural Puerto Rican objections to this continuation of colonialism in new guise as just another temperamental exhibition of Puerto Rican *dignidad*.[25] The limitations of New Deal liberalism—to take a final example—were aptly demonstrated in the closing pages of the Tugwell autobiography, where there is composed a quite uncritical acceptance of the claim of the British Colonial Office to have inaugurated, with the Colonial Development and Welfare organization for the colonies, and, later, with the 1945 and 1947

Colonial Office Despatches on West Indian Federation, a "new colonial policy . . . infinite in its powers of expansion, positive in its scope of achievement." Yet both British academic comment and progressive political West Indian comment were pointing out, at the very same time, the emptiness of that claim and, in particular, the failure of the Colonial Development and Welfare organization to attack Caribbean problems of basic economic structure as distinct from mild public works and social welfare schemes. The organization's leading premise, the assumption that the West Indian colonies were to remain what the Moyne Commissioners described as the tropical farms of the British nation, seems not to have been noted by the American admirer. Nor was there any recognition of the fact that the new West Indies Federation, as the events of the years following its inauguration—until its demise in 1962—have made clear, was regarded by Great Britain as a means, under the guise of granting federal nationhood to the colonies, of abdicating her continuing responsibilities to the region. There are times, indeed, when the reader of the Governor's volume (one of whose loudest complaints must be the affront contained in the fact that a volume of some seven hundred pages lacks a table of contents) begins to suspect that what troubled its author, in truth, was not that American colonialism existed but that it did not comport itself with the dignity and efficiency of the British or Dutch models in the neighboring islands.

For the "revolution of 1940" was written, not by Governor Tugwell, but by the *Populares* and their impressive leader. They had shaped its vital center, the agrarian reform law, long before the New Dealer's arrival; and the law even received his reluctant admiration. They had invented the concept of commonwealth status as the third way out of colonialism (as they at least saw it), distinct from independence or statehood, long before he championed the idea, and it is perhaps worth noting that, in later years, he has moved towards the solution of statehood. Most importantly, the *Populares* brought into the insular life a new moral atmosphere so that by 1948, after two terms in office, their greatest achievement was to have begun the liquidation of colonialism as a psychological institution. Determination to change Puerto Rico by themselves came to replace, albeit slowly and not even completely, eagerness to follow the lead of the federal power. For all of his radical language, Governor Tugwell thought in terms of a beneficent American leadership; they thought in terms of Puerto Rican leadership. Their instinct was sound. "If you mean to please any people," wrote Burke, "you must give them the boon which they ask; not what you think better for them, but of a kind totally different."

Henceforward Puerto Ricans and Americans would continue to work together, but the relationship, as far as the Puerto Ricans could make it, would be one more of equality and less of subordination. It would become more and more difficult for Americans to assume that one of their own kind was more eligible for a local appointment simply because he was American. Correspondingly, it would become easier for them to assume that a Puerto Rican candidate might even be fitted for federal appointments within the island, as the subsequent record of appointments to federal agencies in San Juan has borne out. It would be more difficult, altogether, for them to adopt, albeit unconsciously, the "missionary complex" as they came to the island, an attitude long endemic in the American visiting worker, as the reading, for example, of a book like Mrs. Blythe's *An American Bride in Porto Rico*—the title in itself speaks volumes—published early in the century by the wife of an American Protestant missionary makes painfully and abundantly evident.[26] Within Puerto Rico itself, the hitherto untapped capacity of local men to take on posts of responsible leadership now began to be used for the first time. That process would meet with bitter opposition; Representative Cole's contemptuous comment of 1943—"Why has Governor Tugwell selected twenty-five dollar a week drugstore clerks and one thousand five hundred a year geography teachers to fill six and eight thousand dollar positions as heads of these new authorities?"[27]—sufficiently revealed the social snobbery behind the opposition. Step by step, however, the class of office holders drafted from the continent would be supplanted by Creole candidates whose old bitterness at being denied their proper place in the sun would now begin to evaporate. Certainly, by the end of the 1940's it would no longer be possible for an eminent Puerto Rican to repeat the statement made in 1937 by the then President of the insular Senate to the effect that he wished he had been born elsewhere and that he was training his son to be an engineer so that he might, if he so desired, leave the island. Correspondingly, a new temper of proud independence would grow up to persuade able Puerto Ricans that self-respect and personal integrity should no longer be so freely sacrificed in the desire to obtain desirable appointments in the federal establishment. Rafael Picó's finely worded letter of November 1945 to the Secretary of the Interior, withdrawing his candidacy for the post of Commissioner of Education for the reason that he objected to the restrictive conditions placed upon it by the federal Senate, indicated well enough that the new generation of younger Puerto Ricans now controlling the local government had emancipated itself from the bad colonial habit of accepting without question everything that came from the ruling country.[28] It is for this reason, perhaps, more than any other, that the period after 1940 is to be regarded as the decisive watershed separating the Puerto Rican past from the Puerto Rican present. It was by no means the end of colonialism in the island. But it was at least the end of its negativist period.

PART II

THE PRESENT

Operation Bootstrap: The Advent of Industrialization

THE period after 1945 marks the turning point in the Puerto Rican transformation. The Tugwell governorship had set a pattern for legislative-executive cooperation in common tasks; and the Elective Governor Act of 1947 ended once and for all the distorting influence in local government of the nominated alien executive. The experience in the PRRA and later in the work of wartime organization had helped train a corps of administrative assistants who could become the timber of the Muñoz cabinets. The institutional machinery appropriate to organizing a radically fresh balance between output and people in an underdeveloped economy, to replacing stagnation with growth, had been set up by means of the far-reaching legislative program of 1942. The Social Science Research Center of the University made its own valuable contribution to the general problem—a contribution sometimes too easily forgotten—with the publication of specialist studies in the areas of labor economics, manpower analysis and occupational structure: Dr. Simon Rottenberg's *Labor's Role in Industrialization,* for example, or the study by Ray and Darling on *Manufacturing Occupations in Puerto Rico.* What remained to be done was to direct all of this into the creation of new income-producing processes by means of a planned industrialization program. This, simply put, was the purpose of "Operation Bootstrap," the "battle for production" that gathered its momentum slowly after 1945 and that had entered into a sufficiently rapid rate of growth by the middle 1950's to become the main stimulus in transforming a declining agrarian economy into an expanding industrial structure.

All this was naturally not self-evident at the end of the war in 1945. With a few exceptions due to wartime developments there had been little change in the insular economy, and reports on its sicknesses, like the Bartlett Technical Paper on *A Development Plan for Puerto Rico* of 1944 or even Harvey Perloff's volume of 1949 on *Puerto Rico's Economic Future,* were not much different in their analysis—although startlingly different in their policy recommendations—from earlier reports such as the 1934 *Report of the Porto Rican Policy Commission*. A land-use pattern centering around the sugar monoculture still prevailed, with all of its hazardous consequences—concentration on a lucrative cash crop, the use of the best lands thus for export purposes, the failure to produce subsistence crops for local consumption, the continual extension of cultivation to increasingly marginal soils. The situation had been rendered even more precarious by the fact that by 1940 the competition of mechanized beet and cane sugar both in the continental states and in the duty-free offshore areas (Hawaii and the Philippine Islands), combined with relatively high production costs as compared say with the Cuban industry, had caused the Puerto Rican industry to come to a relative standstill. It could thus no longer provide a positive stimulus to the other sectors of the economy. The tobacco industry likewise was in a state of decline as a consequence of long-term changes in world smoking habits as the cigar came to yield in popularity to the cigarette during the 1920's. The traditional high-class Puerto Rican coffee, again, once the delight of the European gourmet, never recovered from the loss of its world markets during the First World War, and the loss was not compensated for by a United States tariff protection wall (coffee not being an American industry). Nor had any of this created, in response, an effort to exploit, by the planned development of a local truck farming industry, the export possibilities latent in the Puerto Rican fruits such as avocados, pineapples, papayas, grapefruit (once a flourishing industry until it was practically destroyed by the competition of United States domestic producers), guavas and mangoes; the exaggerated dependency upon the United States export market had thus created a gross violation of the principle of regional specialization.

Two additional factors helped to aggravate the situation. The first was that, apart from the corporate sugar latifundia, the insular agriculture was characterized by an almost feudal pattern of technical equipment and skills, since the family-oriented farm structure inhibited the growth of a rationalistic-competitive spirit. "Puerto Rican agriculture," the Bartlett Report observed, "is a picture of extremes. On the one hand are large sugar corporations employing modern techniques of scientific management, and on the other is subsistence farming based on primitive methods. Between these two extremes there are small-scale commercial agricultural enterprises."[1] The second factor relates to the unbalanced character of an economy that had very little to show of pure industrial activity. The cultivation, processing and distribution of agricultural products remained the chief activity, with some 39 percent of the employed population directly engaged in farming and more than 25 percent of those being employed in so-called "manufacturing" occupations which dealt in fact with the processing of agricultural products. Most of the banking, finance, and large-scale commercial activities were likewise concerned with the servicing of the agricultural sector. Nearly half of the labor force, moreover, classified in the "industrial" sector were overwhelmingly the women employees of the evil sweatshops of the home needlework industry financed by absentee mainland capital and managed by local business entrepreneurs. Nor were the wholesale and retail trades any more genuinely industrial, being in fact little more (as the ubiquitous Puerto Rican highway grocery store showed) than monuments to a high level of disguised unemployment and an extreme inefficiency of distributive arrangements within the island. The hazardous dependency upon agricultural production was graphically illustrated, finally, in the statistics of the insular export trade, with sugar contributing (in 1946) some 48 percent of the total, tobacco some 13 percent, rum just over 7 percent, and needlework products nearly 16 percent.[2] Puerto Rico was clearly in the general category of primary-producing countries exporting for a world market and subject to international price fluctuations and political arrangements beyond their power to influence. Nor was this offset by any sizeable public sector of economic activity more within local control; by 1944 the governmental enterprises of the insular regime accounted for only 1.2 percent of total net income—proving, incidentally, that the characterization by its critics of the Puerto Rican economy under the New Deal as one of "state socialism" constituted an extravagant example of poetic license.[3] Furthermore the society was marked (in 1946) by an income distribution so grossly imbalanced that 11 percent of its families received over 42 percent of its total income while some 2 percent of families commanded 18 percent of the same total.[4] Though not a "sugar island" as perfectly as Barbados or Martinique, Puerto Rico was at the mercy of the same Caribbean sugar industry, and it was just about as true to say of its condition as Márquez Sterling had said earlier of Cuba that "Sugar cane does not make colonies happy, or a people cultured, or republics opulent; and the independence we won in the war against Spain we must consummate in a war against sugar cane, which perpetuated in the golden island, as an inexhaustible tradition, the despotism of the major-domo and the hatred of the slave."[5]

The transformation of all this into a burgeoning neo-industrial society, and the resultant transformation of the entire island climate of opinion from one of despair to one of hope, is by now a well-known story frequently retold.[6] By 1953 the governmental program of aids and incentives known familiarly as Operation Bootstrap had brought over 300 manufacturing plants to the island; more than 25,000 new jobs had been added to the island payroll; and the average annual net income per capita had risen from $122 in 1940 to some $426 thirteen years later. By 1957 industry had supplanted agriculture as the major income-earning ingredient of the economy; by 1958 the total of new factories established had reached 500, and over 660 two years later, providing altogether 45,900 new jobs; while by 1959 the establishment of two oil refineries, along with the Union Carbide Company decision to manufacture ethylene glycol in the island (to be followed, possibly, with the growth of a synthetic fibers and plastics industry), had laid the basis of an industrial petro-chemical complex which promised to relieve the economy of a dangerous reliance upon tantalizingly mobile light industries. The latest available statistics indicate that per capita income has risen to the level (in 1960) of $677 in comparison with $341 in 1950 and $122 in 1940: still below that of the lowest of the states of the Union, Mississippi, but nonetheless a remarkable improvement. The Commonwealth government planners have postulated for themselves the goal of a family income of $2,000 for the island population by 1975, an income sufficient, in their view, to provide incentives powerful enough to bring about the final cessation by that date of the out-migration of island citizens to the stateside employment market. By any standards, even that of a post-war world economy generally expansionist, it has been an impressive achievement. And particularly so when one recalls the prevalent note of harsh despondency about the island's future in most of the literature, official and otherwise, that dealt with the issues barely a generation ago.

For that literature had assumed, almost without exception, the static character of the insular production and consumption processes and so could advocate little more, in its varied prescriptions of cure, than variations upon the twin themes of birth control and migration. The Brookings Institution Report (1930) observed that "population has outrun the capacity of the present economic resources and organization to furnish full employment and satisfactory living conditions."[7] The report of the Puerto Rican Policy Commission (1934) referred to the pressure of population increase as "appalling" and "implacable." The Zimmermann Report (1940) flatly stated that "the people of Puerto Rico have reached an impasse—overpopulation."[8] The Report of the National Resources Planning Board (1942), finally, concluded that since the island was presumably deficient in mineral resources it would have to continue to rely upon an agricultural economy.[9] All these conclusions in one way or another stemmed from the grim pessimism, natural enough in a way, of observers confronted with the spectacle of a dense and growing population on an island with few natural resources. Even so, they tended to carry certain generalizing assumptions about Caribbean "human nature" and "tropical" economies quite belied by subsequent experience: that tropical countries are unsuited to manufacturing enterprise, that the state ought not to interfere with economic processes, that successful industrialization requires the presence of local raw materials for processing, that—more fundamentally—agricultural pursuits are somehow "natural" while manufacturing ones are "artificial"—the latter presumption nicely exemplified in a sentence in the Chardón Report that "these emigrants should go to settle farm lands, not to be exploited as wage laborers." Dr. Arthur Lewis has pointed out how this laissez-faire philosophy, borrowed incongruously from a prosperous Victorian British free-trade capitalism, has crippled the capacity of official circles in British West Indian society to look at their own economic problems with fresh imagination; and the report on *The Development of Primary and Secondary Industries in the Caribbean Area* presented in 1949 by the British section of the Caribbean Commission helps one to realize to what a degree the official mind in the colonial islands of the region has been until only very recently the prisoner of this ideological naiveté.[10] The Puerto Rican achievement since 1945 must be seen in the light of the fact that until only yesterday the architects of insular policy were caught in the same obsolete framework of ideas.

The Puerto Rican planners saw from the first that they had to make do with what they had. They saw, even more, that what they had should be converted into an asset rather than being deplored as a liability. The tariff assimilation of the island economy into that of the parent country had compelled Puerto Rico to buy its imported goods almost exclusively from American exporters; but at the same time it opened up avenues of a duty-free Puerto Rican export trade to a ready-made market. By the same token American investment capital could be attracted to the island with the assurance that it could sell its products in the familiar continental market rather than merely in a restricted local market; conversely Puerto Rico would benefit vastly, since all available experience in the formation of capital in underdeveloped economies goes to show that success largely turns upon the ability to break into an established foreign market and that this in itself is normally an expensive and hazardous undertaking. Finally, the population excess of the island could be seen, not as a frightful neo-Malthusian danger to demographic stability but as the potential reservoir of a low-cost factory labor force. It could be used as a means of attracting the large-scale labor-oriented industries which had already exhibited a readiness (in the movement of mainland industry from the major United States manufacturing belt into the southeastern states area after the late 1930's) to shift the location of their operations on the basis of labor-cost differentials. The manual dexterity and the demonstrated eagerness of the average Puerto Rican worker to acquire new industrial skills made the prospect seem all the more feasible. All that was needed to convert these possibilities into going realities was an initial breakthrough from a static to a dynamic economics. "In general," observed Perloff in his incisive study of the situation at just that point in its history, "the poverty, the crowding, the prevalence of diseases, the malnutrition, the lack of adequate educational, recreational and cultural facilities—in short, the conditions under which the vast majority of Puerto Ricans live—are not conducive to a high degree of individual development. As is true in so many other places, the poverty of the Puerto Ricans creates the very conditions which are in large measure the cause of their poverty. To break this circle and create the conditions for human improvement is the goal toward which strenuous efforts in Puerto Rico are currently being directed."[11]

Dr. Teodoro Moscoso has divided the development program into two phases.[12] The first phase, from 1942 to about 1950, was one of government-built and operated plants (cement, glass bottles, shoes, etc.) undertaken primarily as a means of proving to private capital the feasibility of profitable industrial enterprise in the island. Some of the plants—the glass bottle center, for example—were probably conceived erroneously after a false mental image of American capitalism as being an economy of typically huge mass production plants only. In any case, the effort decisively proved the point that if (as in Puerto Rico) the available local capital fights shy of industry and if in turn (as again in Puerto Rico) the government is unprepared to recruit that capital by coercive measures, the sole alternative lies in the invention of measures to persuade the established United States manufacturer to locate in the island. The elaboration of such measures constituted the second and more lasting phase of the program. This has involved the introduction of tax exemption to new industries established in 1947 and after, especially designed in its clauses to benefit the American manufacturer who moves from the continent to the island. It involves also the rental of industrial buildings; the recruitment of specially trained personnel; the negotiation of labor contracts; the maintenance of Commonwealth offices in the leading American cities; the issuance of an imaginative literature on the advantages of setting up shop in the island; and, not the least important, special aid and guidance to the prospective client concerning the general environment of statutory regulation within which he will be obliged to conduct his enterprise. The considerable difficulties of making a real success of all this should not be overlooked. It has meant assiduous planning of a sort even more arduous than that undertaken, say, by Great Britain in 1945; for whereas the British welfare-state planners inherited an already mature capitalism with which to work, the Puerto Rican planners had to start almost from scratch. Established industry is notoriously conservative in the matter of new geographical location; indeed it rarely moves except under the pressure of vast economic dislocation, as in the major industrial societies after 1929. What Dr. Arthur Lewis has said on this score with relation to the British Caribbean applied with equal force to Puerto Rico in the beginning: "They speak frequently," he observed in 1950 of West Indian nationalist politicians, "as if manufacturing in the West Indies offered a large profitable market which greedy foreign capitalists are anxious to rush in and exploit. They discuss industrialization in terms of the close restrictions which they would like to impose upon such capitalists, and they oppose monopoly rights, tax holidays and other incentives which some governments are now considering offering. The facts are exactly opposite to what they suppose. The West Indies does not offer a large market. There are very few manufacturers who wish to go there. Having regard to the highly developed industrial centers which exist in many parts of the world, offering every convenience, and to the many governments which are now trying to attract industry, it would be surprising if any large number of manufacturers were willing to go to the West Indies without being offered substantial concessions."[13]

The experience of the subsequent decade in Jamaica, in British Guiana, and in Trinidad has amply proved the truth of these remarks. It is to the credit of the Puerto Rican leadership that its members did not permit such ideological rigidity to blind them to the realities of the world they lived in. They saw that, as beggars, they could not be choosers. They recognized, as the colonial nationalist movements are more and more recognizing, that both American reform liberalism and British Labor socialism had had very little need to preoccupy themselves with the difficult problems of initial capital formation and technological development because they came into power, in their respective societies, in economies where the problems had in large part been solved earlier. At least in the first stage of their economic planning, the underdeveloped economies would have to concentrate upon the issue of capital accumulation, something which, as Marx pointed out, had been solved for the advanced economies by their exploitation of colonial resources. The easiest way to solve it—although it would seriously compromise later lines of public policy for the host countries—was to invite the overseas businessman. For this to be successful meant, in turn, again to use Dr. Lewis's words, that the potential industrialist would have to be offered an extra inducement and a friendly welcome rather than a maze of restrictions and an atmosphere of hostility and suspicion.

New social policies of course require new institutional forms. The Elective Governor Act in Puerto Rico released the island governorship from its earlier humiliating status of executive agent to the President. But it left untouched the colonial machinery of government with which the elected governor was still expected to work. The revision of legislation and administrative regulations which had been outmoded by economic progress—the commercial code and corporate law, for example, or financial and insurance law—now became an urgent necessity. As early as 1942 the creation of the Planning Board, with its various powers of control and direction in the areas of urban development, slum clearance, fiscal planning and public works, testified to a willing recognition of the truth that the careful evaluation of pace and scope in an industrialization program, as well as a workable system of priorities based upon social need, was essential to prevent its benefits from becoming the monopoly of private influence and privilege. The Development Company, also formed in 1942, was reorganized in 1950 to become the present Economic Development Administration, popularly known as Fomento, in response to its change of character from being originally a body concerned with the direct corporate management of industrial enterprises to a regular department of the government, operating more and more as a regulatory and guidance agency. The Bureau of the Budget was revamped to provide the fiscal centralization appropriate to island-wide planning, and its Organization and Methods Division began the slow process of familiarizing a comparatively young and inexperienced civil service with modern management techniques and, more generally, with the concept of the service as a body of professional men and women concerned primarily with the public interest. Alongside these there was established a welter of new public corporations, such as the Land Authority, to take on the growing responsibilities of positive government; although it ought to be noted here that the device of the public corporation was in large measure adopted not so much because of a recognition of the flexibility offered by it (although that was there) as distinct from the orthodox government department, as because the controlling Organic Act had expressly debarred the creation of new executive departments. All these developments in administrative structure laid the foundations for the more far-reaching changes that were to take place after 1949 with the adoption of a general reorganization bill by the insular legislature and the subsequent production of a series of reports made by the Rowe Commission for Reorganization in 1950.

How far has all this succeeded? To begin with statistical measurement, the application of a costs-and-benefits analysis to the general Fomento program confirms the impression that it is efficiently carrying out its purpose of generating additional net income for the economy, to the extent indeed of producing some 25 dollars of net income for every single dollar of invested program cost. The total cost of the program during the first five years of the life of the Economic Development Administration (1950-1951 to 1955-1956) amounted to approximately $30 million, while during the same period the Commonwealth Treasury collected approximately $106 million in public revenues as a result of the program. The record is uniformly impressive in direct benefits (by way of increased income figures) that accrue to the resident population, in the net additions to local government revenue created by the new factory enterprises, and in the indirect benefits which take the form of increases in the volume of activity in areas such as retail and wholesale trade, construction work, transportation developments, and other public services. In the economy as a whole, total production (in terms of 1954 prices) rose by 123 percent from 1940 to 1955, while the annual rate of growth from 1947 to 1955 was 6 percent, a rate in excess of those of most other countries for which data are available, and all the more remarkable in that the expansion was maintained during a period which covered the end of the Second World War and the Korean hostilities.[14]

The estimated costs of the Fomento program do not of course include the expenditures of governmental projects on highways, schools, electric power, and so on, nor were these projects originally undertaken for the express purpose of furthering the industrialization program. Nevertheless these expenditures have played an important role in attracting investment capital since they have provided the high capital outlay on basic services which an underdeveloped economy must inevitably spend during the early stages of industrial growth. Given the social welfare bias of the Commonwealth government, these expenditures would have been made anyway. But they have had the happy coincidental result of aiding the industrialization program, since Fomento plants, for example, may be able to choose their locations more freely because of the existence of a first-class highway system or, again, be able to hire a comparatively well-educated labor force because of the priority enjoyed by education in the local welfare expenditures. Likewise the tourism program (administratively a part of the total EDA program) has generated a sort of psychic income for the economy, in the sense that its capital expenditures (for example, on the construction of the Caribe-Hilton Hotel in San Juan) have helped to produce a favorable atmosphere of physical comfort and pleasing surroundings for the visiting industrialist who is contemplating a business venture in the island. Some Fomento planners have tended to speak in terms suggesting that the welfare program could not have made its appearance without the prior success of the development program. Not only is this historically incorrect, but it also sets up a quite meaningless dichotomy between the two. For in an economically underdeveloped area, especially, increased productive employment is invariably conditioned by a large essential services program, and conversely the continuing enlargement of such a program comes to rely to a great extent upon the new wealth created by the increase in jobs and occupations. To think otherwise is to embrace, as it were, a heliocentric view of the problem in which all things revolve around the sun of the Fomento headquarters.

The exceptional character of all this development has in itself produced, in the form of official and quasi-official literature on the island, a peculiar commodity unique in itself. For it would be difficult, even in the field of modern governmental propaganda, to match the rhetorically self-congratulatory note of the Puerto Rican literature. The official side of it is perhaps understandable, for it is the function of every modern public relations office to persuade the public that they are living for the best in the best of all possible worlds. What is more difficult to condone is the sort of volume written by private authors that becomes a hymn of praise set in terms of a sycophantic adulation more usually reserved for the orthodox Communist appreciations of the Soviet Union. One example of the genre is Earl Parker Hanson's *Transformation*, characteristically entitled, in its second edition, *Puerto Rico: Land of Wonders*. The sincere enthusiasm of the volume, both for Puerto Rico and Governor Muñoz, is real and affecting enough. Its effective exposure, in addition, of the myth of environmentalism as applied to the tropics is a welcome rebuttal of the schools of medical and demographic thought which still seek to attribute the degree of retardation in tropical societies to climate or resources rather than to the nature of the prevailing social and economic structure at a given historical moment. To go, however, to the opposite extreme of a romantic subjectivism is no less an unscientific mode of analysis; and it is the chief weakness of the book that in a florid and overdramatized way it portrays the Puerto Rican "revolution" as a Herculean task carried through almost singlehandedly by Muñoz, in collaboration with the creative genius of the Puerto Rican "people."

The implication that without Muñoz there would have been no change is a doubtful one, and it is possible that, with him or without him, the attenuation of colonialism would have occurred anyway. It is a pleasant change, of course, to read a book on Puerto Rico that does not purvey the thesis that its people are an embodiment of all the "Latin" defects. But it hardly seems any more persuasive to argue, as Mr. Hanson's enthusiasm frequently leads him to do, that they are a paragon of all the democratic virtues. It is unfortunate that the book should have been the major source of information on Puerto Rico for that large section of middle-brow America that likes to gain its knowledge of public affairs from the mentally undemanding magazines of the Luce journalism empire.

There are, particularly, three general considerations to be emphasized in evaluating Operation Bootstrap and the eulogistic literature— of which Mr. Hanson's book is only the most popular—that it has spawned. In the first place, the uniqueness of the development may be easily exaggerated. The Commonwealth government, after all, has done nothing much more than what most modern governments do in all ambitious underdeveloped countries by way of assistance to new industry. In one way, indeed, the policy is as old as the emergence of commercial capitalism in the Western European countries, for it echoes much of the way whereby the Tudor monarchs nurtured new industries in sixteenth-century England or whereby Colbert, in the next century, laid the economic foundations of the age of Louis XIV. Even compared to contemporary policies in the industrialization of backward areas the Puerto Rican program is in many ways conservative. It has not utilized the familiar device of direct subsidy. It has not itself supplied capital in any really lavish fashion; the Development Bank, like the local branch of the Reconstruction Finance Corporation, has pursued a conservative lending policy, with the typical banker's aversion to any policy of "dangerous" or "unsound" risk taking. The extent of direct government fiscal aid to the private investor has been certainly far more limited than the aid granted by the United Kingdom governments in their development program for the British depressed areas after 1945.

It is another way of putting this—and this is the second point—that the main outlines of the local industrial picture have throughout been those, at best, of a state-aided capitalism after the American fashion. If there has been a "revolution," it has been in the mild sense only of the gradual diversion of major capital enterprise from the agricultural to the industrial sector. There may not have been, as already intimated, any alternative to reliance upon the expatriate private investor. But the consequence, in part, of that reliance has been the growth of a public policy that keeps public expenditures within the social welfare limits acceptable in the United States economy. The intervention of the state in the economic process certainly cannot be regarded as a radical development, unless it be seen within the ideological framework of the dogma of economic individualism which dominated European and American capitalism for only a brief period, historically speaking, between 1850 and 1900. Seen from the viewpoint of the deliberate recruitment of the state power by classical capitalism for the three centuries of its growth after 1500, the Puerto Rican economic-political complex takes its place as merely another exercise in neo-mercantilist public policy. And although there is much pompous talk in Puerto Rico about the function of "planning" in policy-making, there are in fact curious gaps in the actual planning that has so far taken place. There is, for example, as yet very little planned location of the new industry, and this has given rise to a real inequality of the benefits unleashed by industry between different geographic regions. Thus the small towns of the interior hold more than one third of the total population, yet only about one sixth of the new industrial jobs have been made available to them.[15] The island newspapers are perennially full of stories concerning their economic plight, and the situation is not in any way remedied by the primitive method of political pressure that is brought to bear upon the insular government by the frequent visits of small town mayors to the office of the Governor in San Juan.

There is, then, a seeming paradox between the spectacle of the American cultural anthropologist seeing the island as practically the last primitive rural community in flux under the American flag and that of the Puerto Rican leadership proudly insisting upon the modernity of the society. The paradox, however, is seeming only, once it is remembered that the effects of industrialization have been unevenly distributed. The distribution has been uneven, indeed, in a dual sense. First in a geographical sense, for it is still possible for the visiting scholar to describe isolated rural communities, as does Dr. David Landy in his volume on *Tropical Childhood*, living out their lives in response to the traditional compulsions of the sugar-cane economy and only indirectly touched by the insular economic changes. Second, in a monetary sense, for there is much ready evidence to show that significant new income inequalities are rapidly growing up with the new wealth. Most of the available statistics, suggestively enough, concentrate upon absolute increases and say little about the relative distribution of "fair shares" between different income groups. For to report that between 1941 and 1953 there was a doubling of the average annual income of workers, or that while in 1941, 81 percent of working-class families had an annual income of less than $500 the percentage had declined in 1953 to 7.4 percent tells the student nothing about comparative benefits between different classes. In the absence of data it is fair to assume that the "income revolution" in Puerto Rico, as in the United States, means not a genuine redistribution of shares between the various income groups but (as the researches of Kuznets and Jenks have shown) a continuing inequality even when increased tax rates for the upper income groups are taken into account.

Nothing perhaps testifies more to the ideological conservatism of the Puerto Rican program than the general state of the insular agriculture. It might have been thought that any felt need to appease the prejudices of the expatriate private investor would have been comparatively weak in the agricultural sector. Yet it is in this sector that the retreat from an earlier radicalism has occurred most strikingly. It had become evident by 1954 that the state policy of redistributing sugar lands as *parcelos* to the landless proletarian had not worked out. The life style of the rural squatter remained much the same as before; the promise of the "proportional profit" farms as the harbinger of a genuine rural cooperative organization had failed to materialize, itself the outcome, in part, of the failure of the earlier experiment of the land cooperatives of the nationalized Lafayette *central*; direct government aid, in the form of agricultural subsidies, as in the case of the coffee industry of the western highlands, had helped the farmer and the landowner rather than the agricultural laborer; while the entire southwestern country region remained still a stricken land, lacking the modernized road and communications system that its producers badly needed.[16] It is true that achievements, as they are, have been remarkable enough. The program of bringing drinking water to the island villages, to take an example only, deserves the comment of the Ecuadorian delegate to the United Nations General Assembly in the course of that body's debate on Puerto Rico, that it was an achievement which many Latin American countries would be happy to be able to boast about. The general health of the rural population has also certainly improved vastly, especially if it is compared to the gruesome list of diseases afflicting the population, including tetanus, dysentery, asthma, gonorrhea and yellow fever, contained in the handbooks of rural medicine published during the last years of the Spanish regime. At the same time, even so, the island sugar industry remains in the doldrums, so much so that it has become almost an annual event for it to fail to produce the federally fixed quota. The depletion of the agricultural labor force has gone on without interruption, and agricultural leaders have begun to demand fiscal concessions comparable to those granted in the industrial field to pioneer enterprises. Public hearings within recent years have witnessed the growing popularity of the idea that the legal prohibition upon the employment of minors should be at least partially abrogated; employers in both the sugar and the coffee industries have endorsed the idea, socially retrogressive though its implementation would surely be. A comparable idea, equally reactionary, that the present tax on sugar employers that contributes to the insurance fund of the industry should be abolished, has also been mooted by the President of the island Farmers' Association.[17]

Agriculture, indeed, in all of its branches still awaits a separate agrarian code and possibly an autonomous Agrarian Institute which would guarantee it some sort of equal consideration with industry. It awaits the sort of bold reform program that would fit it as a separate entity into the insular economy as a regional whole. Yet all the evidence suggests that the readiness of the *Popular* leadership to consider unorthodox measures for the relief of agriculture has gradually given way to the precept that agriculture, like industry, must be judged by the orthodox yardstick of entrepreneurial profitability. The Governor's important speech of April 23, 1959, to the island legislature clearly revealed the bias that any future land reform will have to be estimated in terms of its ability to pay its own way and not primarily in terms of its social benefits.[18] The leading idea of the comprehensive report of 1953 written by Nathan Koenig and his associates of the United States Department of Agriculture and related Puerto Rican agencies is the reversion to the family-size farm in agricultural undertakings; yet all experience, both within the Caribbean and outside, forcibly suggests that peasant agriculture based on the family holding constitutes the Achilles heel of all economic development programs. Practically every West Indian island bears the ravages of uneconomically small holdings worked on inadequate technical knowledge and part-time employment; while almost every minimum-wage committee hearing on agricultural industries in Puerto Rico testifies to the temptation of the private *colono* to offset heavy capital investment with low wages. Nor is the idea, propounded in the later report of Donald O'Connor, that agriculture should be rehabilitated, especially in sugar, by the use of the same devices that have been employed in the industrialization program, any happier from the public interest viewpoint. For it would mean the expenditure of vast amounts of public money (the O'Connor report anticipates a figure of $100 million) more likely to benefit the rural employing class—as, indeed, has been the case with the subsidies already paid out to the sugar industry and with the large-scale irrigation projects carried out over the last few years—than to benefit either the agricultural proletariat or the general public.

In this field of public policy, at least, there seems little readiness in San Juan to go beyond the ideas traditionally prevalent in Washington. The idea of land reform along the usual Latin American lines has exhausted itself, for the Puerto Rican experience has merely served to reinforce the lesson of the earlier experience of the Mexican reform movement, which is that, a redivision of lands once made, population increase upsets the new balance within the next generation; and that since agrarian conflict is thus only assuaged and not solved, the main result of the reform is to consolidate, in Puerto Rico as in Mexico, the new ruling political elite that has been the leading agent of the reform. Nor should sight be lost of the fact that, this being so, Puerto Rican agriculture has signally failed in offsetting the exaggerated dependency upon the American continental food market through the development of a flourishing local food production program. Part result, part cause of that failure is the high prestige value of the imported canned foods as compared with the low status of the frequently far superior fresh native fruits; a gross distortion of values fostered, in turn, by the food pages of the local newspapers that mostly concentrate on the continental dishes and menus as compared to the Creole ones, frequently, again, far more pleasing. Nor has the growth, since 1931, of domestic science courses in the schools, both urban and rural, done much to counteract this snobbishness. As a result, Puerto Ricans are driven to overspend on their food expenses; much, for example, of the thirty million dollars that they spend annually in importing frozen meats, butter, and eggs could be saved by the planned growth of a local farming industry. In the absence of such an industry, they continue, like many colonial peoples, to produce what they do not consume and consume what they do not produce.[19]

The third and final glossary to be made on the island experiment concerns its status as a representative model to be copied by other poorly endowed areas as they seek to obtain their share of the wealth of nations. There is a recurring theme in the approbatory literature to this effect, and it is frequently tied in to the strategy of world politics with the claim that Puerto Rico is "the answer" to Communism within Latin America. The recent history of the territory is thus presented in terms of the "rags to riches" imagery so dear to the American imagination; a book like Ralph Hancock's *Puerto Rico: A Success Story* is a typical example. How far is this line of argument legitimate? The more one studies the Puerto Rican situation the more it seems to be an argument at once factually evasive and morally questionable. It is the latter because it reduces the island to the status of a pawn in American foreign policy making. It makes of it what Governor Theodore Roosevelt, Jr., once styled "the American show-window to the south." To the extent that the United States, for example, by way of federal expenditures, is willing to finance such a purpose it becomes difficult to believe that a prize exhibit can properly be regarded as a representative sample. And the argument is in doubt, factually, because it does not frankly admit to the special and quite unrepresentative factors that have accompanied, indeed in themselves made feasible, the Puerto Rican transformation. There is the fact, immeasurably most important and from which most others flow, that the island economy, in the words of the local Planning Board, is "in effect, an economic region" of the United States and "not a separate economy."[20] The economy thus has no foreign exchange or monetary problems, in the sense in which such problems afflict most independent nations making their way in the dollar-dominated field of international trade. It has the tariff-free American market wide open—within the limits of intra-market competition with the individual states—to its products. The American investor has the assurance that his capital, in going to Puerto Rico, does not go beyond the familiar hazards of investment within the Union itself. The economy even enjoys special arrangements—such as the mandatory return of federal excise taxes to the Commonwealth Treasury, and the extension of certain federal grant-in-aid programs to the territory without the concomitant responsibility to pay federal taxes—unknown to the individual states. This last item, in particular, cannot be underestimated as a potent factor in Fomento's success, since it means that, unlike any other individual segment of the United States economic complex, Puerto Rico is in exclusive command of its own public revenue system, so that it can offer complete tax exemption as an inducement to the American investor. The relative paucity of local savings available for investment in industrialization has in its turn exacerbated the reliance of the economy upon external, i.e. American, sources of financing; in the single field of housing, for example, it has been estimated that both private and public ventures have depended almost exclusively in their operations upon the American sources of capital formation, as the statistics of external loan assistance amply demonstrate.[21]

But above all, of course, there is the fact of the vast quantities of economic aid—in the form of grants, loans, credits, guarantees, and services, as well as the fiscal privileges here cited—which the peculiar political and economic relationship of the island with the United States makes it possible for the insular government to receive from Washington. No careful estimate has ever been made of the grand total of moneys that the island thus receives from the dozens of departments, agencies, and bureaus of the federal government that do business with San Juan; but the total aggregate of all of the federal services and programs thus made available—welfare benefits, highway appropriations, sugar subsidies, low-cost housing project loans, federal employee salaries—must amount annually, at a conservative estimate, to something between $150 and $175 million. In addition, the federal government pays the full costs of the island's defense, its postal system, its weather bureau, and its commercial and diplomatic relations with foreign countries, with the consequence that, freed of such expenses, the Commonwealth government is enabled to spend all the more generously on its own elaborate education, welfare, health, and housing programs. One interesting aspect of all this is the emergence, over the last few years, of a feeling on the part of the federal staff in San Juan that the official Puerto Rican insistence on the indispensability of the association with the United States has gone hand in hand with an official policy of withholding from the insular electorate these facts of United States financial participation in the insular progress. The angry protest of the regional administrator of the federal Housing and Home Finance Agency to the chairman of the Commonwealth's Urban Renewal and Housing Corporation, referring to the failure to give credit to the federal aid in the public advertising of that Corporation—aid that amounts to nearly $300 million in federally insured mortgages and nearly two thirds of the cost of all urban renewal projects in the island—speaks volumes for the deep resentment that this effort to make political capital out of American economic aid has engendered.[22]

Not the least consequence of all this is that there is a peculiar quality about Puerto Rican industrialization that further belies its usability as an exportable model. That is the fact that, being so thoroughly dependent upon the continental economy, the industrializing process is not of the classic North American–Western European variety centering around the mass production of goods with a heavy industrial base. It is, rather, a basically distributive entity, characterized typically by the proliferation of companies undertaking the sale and consumption of goods produced in the United States economy. Its "new men" are clerks, managers, salesmen, and advertising publicists rather than production technicians; and their work largely concentrates upon sponsoring, and catering to, the new consumption habits of the Puerto Rican buyer. The island, in brief, is a busy distributive outlet for the stateside manufacturer, so that whereas years ago it was deluged with cheap "seconds" from the continental factories today it has become an important importer of their leading commodities. There is, then, a dangerous divorce between the production and the consumption ends of the total situation the implications of which are easily overlooked because of the free-trade relationship between the ruling and the dependent economies. The implications, however, could be serious for an independent Puerto Rico.

Puerto Rico's naturally favorable factors for industrialization are shared, of course, by her Caribbean neighbors. But all of her artificial advantages that flow from her American connection belong to her alone. The Puerto Rican planners thus have confronted practically none of the difficulties that face planners in these other economies. They have not been compelled, like Soviet Russia in one generation and China in another, to industrialize at the grim price of imposing crushing sacrifices upon their people by means, for instance, of denying them satisfactory supplies of consumer goods in order to build up a heavy capital-goods industry. That perhaps explains why the theme of austerity plays such a small part, if any, in the official utterances of the Commonwealth government. The prosperity that the Puerto Rican planners have managed to invoke has thus been an overspill, as it were, of the American system in its post-war expansionist period. They are naturally to be congratulated upon seizing so enterprisingly the opportunity thereby presented to them. But it is at best naiveté, and at the worst mendacity, to suggest that their achievement can constitute a model for emulation by others. For the United States to spend on Latin American countries the money matching on a per capita basis the aid given to Puerto Rico would involve a massive expenditure that neither the American people nor the American government has shown itself willing to accept. Latin America can assuredly industrialize. But the task will have to be based upon programs designed to utilize the advantages inherent in each particular region, and not founded upon a superficial analogy.

The study of the Puerto Rican economic metamorphosis—it is clear enough from this line of argument—must therefore address itself to the peculiar problems that arise from its peculiar genesis. Those problems divide themselves into two categories. There are (1) those that flow from the external relationships with the outside world, that is to say, with the American superordinate society, and (2) those that flow from the society's own internal relationships, especially the character of the new social forces, including the new class relations, that have been set in motion by the impact of industrialization. The first part of the inquiry must seek to determine the possible dangers of too heavy dependency upon American capital sources for the continuing industrialization program of the economy which, after all, has only barely commenced. Discussion on that point has been regarded, up till only yesterday, as treasonable to the sacred canon of Puerto Rican progress, and indeed has only become respectable with the decision of the chief lieutenant of the Governor, former Speaker of the House Ramos Antonini, to identify himself openly in 1961 with the local group of small retailers in their economic struggle against the American-sponsored large shopping centers. The appointment at the same time of a professional economist, Dr. Carlos Lastra, to the post of Secretary of Commerce in the Commonwealth cabinet is further proof, since he is known to be sympathetic to the viewpoint of the small-business outlook, that open debate on this vexed matter can no longer be seen as the evil doing of what Mr. Hanson likes to style the "stuffy academicians" and the "doctrinaire idealists." The second part of the inquiry must seek to estimate whether the new internal realignments of social class, and especially the changing relationships between a new employer class and a new industrial working class, promise, as some of the more enthusiastic friends of Puerto Rico have suggested, the formation of a new and healthy national community or whether they will introduce the social tensions and the economic conflicts that have invariably accompanied the growth of capitalism (even on a popular basis) elsewhere. It is obvious enough that the two things are enmeshed together in a common web of circumstance; and it does not require much close observation in the island to realize to what a degree the ordinary daily thought of the society is conditioned by the cords that bind it to the continental land mass. It is equally obvious that the answers that are given to the solution of these problems will help to determine the success or failure of democracy within the island society in the next generation. For the democratic idea is of very recent growth in the society, and much of what there is of it has only too often assumed that the growth of the democratic ideology is necessarily coincidental with the acceptance of the American Way. That identification is there, to cite only one example, in a pro-American book like Rafael López Landron's *Cartas Abiertas a el Pueblo de Puerto Rico* of 1928, and it characterizes much of the contemporary Puerto Rican literature.

Nor only that. The advance of democracy in Puerto Rico, as in any comparatively underdeveloped economy undergoing an industrializing transformation, is bound up with the advance of industrial productivity and industrial institutional forms much more than is the case in those older societies where the socio-cultural effects of that transformation have long ago been assimilated into the web and woof of the national existence. The strains and stresses of the change are bound to place a heavy burden upon democratic processes as yet only in their infancy. The transition from the bucolic to the machine age requires intermediate stages, and it is difficult to imagine bucolic placidity quickening into frenzied modernity without imagining status ideas, often of great crudity, as the intermediate stage. That is especially the case when, as in Puerto Rico, the rising groups of the middle class are much more interested in those status ideas than they are in the "democracy" to which they pay such fervent lip service. Their paranoic fear of relapsing into rural poverty makes of them fierce social conservatives, while their newly-found social ambitions drive them into anti-democratic political positions: the attack of the organized industrialists' groups upon labor representation in the local legislature is symptomatic. The vulgar materialism of their life-style— as Ricardo Alegría has remarked, the bar has replaced the book as the status symbol in the new Puerto Rican middle class household— shows plainly enough that for them democracy, as they understand it, has little to do with the higher cultural life. This as much as anything else explains the secular religion of "machine worship" in those groups, the recurring theme in the local propaganda literature of Puerto Rico *en marcha*. It explains the temptation to find short cuts to luxury, often at the price of sacrificing other social values not presently in high repute. This in a way is the reason why the social and cultural consequences of a rapid industrialization have not received the attention by the Commonwealth policy makers that they deserve. Industrialization has been seen, only too often, as an end in itself. It is curious to note that the attitude goes back beyond 1940 to the attitudes of the burgeoning class of manufacturers in the island under Spain. There is a lyrical passage of Cobdenite enthusiasm about the factory system in the report of the Industrial Commission of Ponce that was originally intended for the colonial ministry in Madrid and was turned over to Henry Carroll for inclusion in his separate report of 1899 on the industrial and commercial condition of the island. "In all the countries of the world," the Ponce reformists wrote, "manufacture is the source of progress, well-being, and morality. Of progress, because it contributes in the highest degree to general education, as well as to general wealth. It educates the people in the performance of work, cultivates their mechanical aptitudes, and elevates them in the social scale. In manufactories the proletariat is converted into a workman. Of well-being, because it affords employment and the means for supplying the material needs and enjoyments of life to the poor by lowering the revenue taxes, which bear heavily upon the contributors, and it reduces the price of the necessaries of life. Of morality, because of the numerous opportunities it affords for work. It does away with vagrancy and the evils of vice. It educates mankind in the practice of good habits, and especially elevates and dignifies woman, to whom it opens a wider field than that of ordinary labor as a domestic, and enables her to turn away from the inducements offered by houses of ill fame."[23]

There is still much of this glowing optimism in the official literature of the Commonwealth promotional agencies. It remains to be seen whether the optimism is justified. It remains, even more, to be seen whether the attempt to sugar the pill of industrial changes by the rhetoric of the Governor's pet scheme of "Operation Serenity," seeking as it does to raise general culture levels so that all Puerto Ricans may enjoy the vast treasures of both the Spanish and the American heritage, will turn out to be successful. For, as things now stand, there is an obvious failure to coordinate the bootstrap and the serenity themes, and a consequent discrepancy in their relative abilities to shape actual lines of policy. It remains yet to be seen, this is to say, whether contemporary Puerto Rico can manage a reasonable marriage between those two opposites within the broad framework of the profit-making principle more successfully than did early Victorian England or the United States after the Civil War.

The Problem of Economic Dependency

PUERTO RICANS as a whole have evinced little doubt of the advantages of American imperialism over Spanish imperialism. For they have benefited enormously in material terms with the transition from the one to the other. Basically this has been because Spanish imperialism, by 1898, was a contracting imperialism already breaking up (as Cuba showed) under the force of centrifugal and disintegrating tendencies, whereas American imperialism was an expanding one—at the beginning indeed of its outward push. The first was moreover a semi-feudal mercantile imperialism, content to stifle the economic development of its colonies by tying their trade and commerce (as were Puerto Rico's to the very end) to the dominant interests of the home merchant class. American imperialism was that of a free-trade economic power ready and able to afford the economic development of the territories it occupied in such a fashion as to develop their people also. It is true that it was never a capital-exporting imperialism to the degree that Britain proved to be in India. But it has never had any objections to capital exporting when the opportunity has arisen. At the same time, American imperialism has always been diluted by the omnipresent democratic thought patterns of the national existence. Even during the Manifest Destiny period Americans have never been able to divest themselves of the libertarian views which are the premises of Franklin's satirical essay on empire, *Rules by which a Great Empire May be Reduced to a Small One*; in practice they have been guilty (as in Puerto Rico) of some of the policies caricatured in that essay; but Spanish imperialism had been guilty, before 1898, of practically all of them. So that, although an expanding imperialism and therefore tempted to a positive abuse of its power, the American economic expansion was not accompanied, as was the expanding imperialism of Nazi Germany after 1933, by the brutal habits of a conquering master race.

The problems of American investment in Puerto Rico (and of Puerto Rican reliance upon that investment for a continuing industrialization program) are of a different order from those confronted

189

by the other dependent islands of the Caribbean. The problem of the British islands, for example, is to persuade British governments to abandon once and for all the outmoded Victorian principle that the grant of political independence, within or outside of the Commonwealth, must entail the cessation of continuing financial aid from London; and the lesson of the contrast with the financial liberalism of the United States in Puerto Rico has not been lost upon the West Indian political leadership of both Left and Right political persuasions.[1] The Puerto Rican problem, then, is not that of a dearth of American capital, private or public, within the island so much as the implications that flow from the practical monopoly of such expenditures in the external aspect of the economy. The monopoly is so absolute as to deserve repeated emphasis. The bulk of external trade is with the United States market and is only made possible because of free access thereto. The principal credit facilities and federal transfer payments are made through the machinery of federal law. The receipts of unilateral transfers from the United States are highly important. Puerto Rican agricultural workers migrating seasonally to the mainland remit annually to their families a sum of some $6 million. Veterans' income is considerably larger, for the Veterans Administration, serving some 114,000 veterans in the Puerto Rico and Virgin Islands area, disburses a total of $60 million a year to them by way of medical services, pension benefits, building and home loans, educational benefits, and readjustment training. The Social Security Administration, in its turn, pays out annually something like $50 million to some 135,000 taxpayers in the island, covering retirement payments, survivors benefits, and disability payments. These transfers—including the federal government's payments to both the Commonwealth government and local business—add to the total purchasing power of the economy a sum equal, on the average, to 10 percent of the gross Commonwealth product for the postwar period.[2] Nor must it be overlooked that during the last decade approximately 50 percent of the difference between island imports and exports has been financed by the transferred income accumulating from these various sources.

The case of general out-migration to the employment centers of the mainland again underlines the same lesson. For reasons easy enough to understand, the Puerto Rican migrant chooses the continental United States above other non-Spanish places for either temporary or permanent residence; the Puerto Rican colony recruited in the 1890's by the Hawaiian sugar producers and the more recent minor migration to the neighboring American Virgin Islands, with a particularly heavy concentration in St. Croix, alone qualify the generalization. In the decade after 1942 the total migration to the mainland amounted to some 249,918 persons; since 1945 the annual average rate has been near the figure of 40,000; while most recently there has been a marked decline as the Commonwealth advertising effort in the United States begins to have the unexpected consequence of bringing back native sons attracted by the glowing reports. In the light of the fact that a chronic unemployment rate persists—Edward Corsi has remarked that insular unemployment is worse, still, than that of the mainland economy in the depths of the great depression of the 1930's[3]—the importance of unrestricted migration to a major industrial economy as a safety valve cannot be underestimated. Nor does it make any crucial difference, from an economic as distinct from a human viewpoint, that the Puerto Rican migrant becomes the exploited base of the sprawling industrial complex that stretches from southern New England to northern Virginia and that he rarely manages to obtain a white-collar or administrative job—as the reports of the New York State Commission against Discrimination frequently attest; the important thing, from the economic viewpoint, is that the job opportunities are there. Nor does it really matter whether the migration factor is seen as a deliberate policy of the insular government, as some critics aver, or as merely a happy accident of the American labor market, as the Puerto Rican economic planners prefer to see it. The fact is that the freedom of movement of persons between the island and the mainland is there, flowing from common American citizenship, and is inevitably taken into account by the Puerto Rican planning and manpower agencies. Any Congressional move to limit the flow—by placing it on a quota basis, for example—would play havoc with the island economy.

Some of these factors—the seasonal earnings of migrant agricultural workers from the island, for example—are perhaps in themselves incidental to the industrialization program. Migration, certainly, is more important, regarded in its more permanent aspects. Yet the real key to Fomento success lies elsewhere: first, in the ability to offer full tax exemption, both corporate and personal, to the American industrialist, and, second, in the existence of a low-cost labor force which permits savings in production costs by means of the wage differential. This second item belongs, more properly, to the discussion of the role of labor in the Puerto Rican industrial picture. The first item, however, focuses attention on the fragile and hazardous foundations upon which the industrialization of the island has been based. Without that weapon, to begin with, even the measure of success so far attained would not have been possible. "There is no reason to believe," a former Fomento economic adviser has written, "that, in the absence of something as dramatic as complete tax exemption, Puerto Rico could have participated in the benefits of this boom (the postwar boom of the American market) to any significant extent. Even the federated states of the south and west which have done so have not accomplished this without effort, and before the Fomento program got under way the extent to which Puerto Rico was unknown on the mainland was the most favorable aspect of its public relations situation there."[4] The continuing success of the program must apparently rest in large measure upon the persistence of the tax advantages, either by way of their periodical renewal or their conversion into a permanent element of public policy. Yet it is precisely there that the serious problems begin. For apart from the domestic consequences of exemption within the continental economy—it frustrates the fair distribution of the national tax burden and creates grave and harmful inequities in the tax structure—the cessation of the privilege would almost certainly mean the departure of some firms. And even if the privilege remains, it can hardly hope to remain a permanently attractive magnet. There is already a growing American suspicion that the device, along with others, seriously threatens to erode the continental tax base, which may lead to restrictions upon its continued use.[5] The Kennedy administration's tax bill of 1962, indeed, seeking to control the large-scale tax evasion of corporations with overseas operations showed how seriously Washington takes this problem; and nothing could have better illustrated the utter dependence of the Puerto Rican industrial program upon continuing goodwill in Washington than the desperate efforts of a Commonwealth lobbying team, led by the Governor himself, to persuade the Treasury tax officials and the appropriate congressional committeemen to exempt Puerto Rico from the provisions of the bill.

As a method of economic planning, again, the tax exemption device encourages a coercive tendency in other countries to follow suit, and as this occurs the comparative advantage of one country will tend to decline. Thus Mexico is already streamlining the device; Jamaica and Trinidad are consciously copying the Puerto Rican pioneer industry legislation, with tax exemption as the major feature; while the recent announcement by the Curaçao government of a similar program, but immeasurably strengthened by the probable inclusion of that Dutch Antillean economy in the new European Common Market, would mean that firms locating there could serve the European market from behind the free tariff wall.[6] The competition arising from such developments can perhaps only be offset by governmental effort to diversify both the incentives for investment and the areas of investment. It is all the more significant, then, that there is a tendency on the part of American businesses in Puerto Rico to be extremely reluctant to revert to a taxable status or even to construe tax exemption as a short-run program and, on the side of the Commonwealth government, a tendency to exhibit what one observer has described as "a tax-exemption state of mind."[7]

But there are more far-reaching considerations even than these. The tax exemption device merely happens to be the most favored weapon in the armory of interstate competitiveness within a system of economic federalism. The Puerto Rican experiment can be properly assessed only if it is seen within the federal framework that cabins and confines it. It must be seen within the federal scheme, subject to the disadvantages as well as the advantages of that scheme. For the entire experience of the American economy has conclusively demonstrated how a federal political form, splitting up sovereignty into little pieces, seriously inhibits the growth of a national economic policy that will safeguard the legitimate interests of each component unit of the union on a basis of equality. It places a high premium, as a form of association, on artificial or non-economic factors; it penalizes the more backward areas; it sacrifices the national concern to sectional interests or to powerful economic groups. Instead of a national policy of planning national resources along rational lines there is substituted a harsh competition between the individual states or the different geographic regions for the favors of private industry. The result, as is well known, has produced a national economy at once anomalous and ill balanced in character. The process that converted the South into an economic colony of Northern business for almost a century after the Civil War is only the best-known example. But the more recent transformation of the New England states into a new "depressed area" as their industries have gravitated in recent years to the "new South," or the stultification of a unified natural resources policy within the Department of Agriculture because of the opposition of the powerful farm associations, or the failure to initiate a national policy for the preservation and development of the great Western lands because of the success of "private federations" in their use of individual state legislatures as defense mechanisms in the struggle against federal regulation—all of these are more recent examples that exemplify how much the federal structure permits chaos to pre-empt cosmos in the economic life of the nation.[8]

The system works, altogether, to place the interstate private business organization in an advantageous bargaining position in its relations with the state police power. Recent years—to take a single example—have seen the president of the General Motors Corporation publicly threatening to locate new automobile plants in more "sympathetic" states like Ohio should the Michigan legislature accept the proposals of the governor of that state for increased rates of corporate taxation; and the episode has been matched, in Puerto Rico, by the callous threat of the president of Bull Lines to refuse to continue carrying refined sugar from Puerto Rico to the mainland ports should the Federal Maritime Board fail to approve his company's application for yet another increase in freight rates.[9] This is a hazard at once peculiar to and persistent for the Puerto Rican industrialization program. There is nothing to prevent the leadership of any American-controlled enterprise within the island from speaking to the government of Puerto Rico in a similar tone should it be decided at any moment in San Juan to adopt a more radical tax policy in the territory. It misses the point to argue that there is no institutional reason why Puerto Rico should possess an internally integrated industrial pattern so long as she remains within the federal structure, any more than should individual states like Nevada or Rhode Island,[10] for those states in themselves suffer from the economic disadvantages of federalism. Even more: if the Puerto Rican achievement is assessed, not in local but in comparative federal terms, it has to be admitted that after more than a decade of struggle its average income per capita—$622 in 1961—was still just over one half of that of the two continental states, Arkansas and Mississippi, with the lowest averages on the mainland, while both of those latter states continued to possess substantially more manufacturing employment and more employment by government than Puerto Rico.[11]

The scaffold of advertising and promotion put together by the skilled staff of the Fomento organization is impressive enough. But it has been more than matched by the more enterprising of the individual states. There is little evidence to show, moreover, that those states, as rivals with Puerto Rico for investment capital, are prepared to accept the repeated assurances of the Commonwealth government that a job created in Puerto Rico is not a job vacated on the mainland. When indeed the Congress granted Puerto Rican exemption, in 1940, from the federal minimum wage law it is possible that the Puerto Rican economy was at that time so backward that Congress did not stop to consider that its industries would become aggressively competitive with those of the mainland market. They have now, in fact, become so; and the decision in 1960 of the leading Fomento official to transfer his headquarters from San Juan to New York, designed, in part, to lobby the mainland "blue chip" companies more effectively, underlines the fact. "We only want, and need," Governor Muñoz has written in an argument addressed to the American labor movement, "our proportionate share—and it is relatively infinitesimal—of the new capital that is generated each year in the United States so that we can provide the jobs, the decently paid jobs, our people need."[12] But all that has been proved so far is the fact that (1) the "proportionate share" can only begin to be provided in a period of national economic expansion (a serious recession on the mainland would play havoc with the Puerto Rican industrial outlook), and (2) there is no known or available mechanism, except the brute power of competition, to determine at any given moment what constitutes a "proportionate share" of available venture capital for Puerto Rico or any other segment of the national economy.

It is in the nature of federalism, in brief, that a local or provincial political power, in the absence of an overall national policy of economic planning allocating fair shares to all on a rational basis, is helpless to control the movements of a private economic power which, by its technological character, cuts across state and provincial boundaries. And Puerto Rico is peculiarly helpless, even more than the individual federated state, since its geographical position lends a new dimension to its vulnerability. The transportation costs of finished products to the continental market, for example, are often fatal to a local plant and sometimes wipe out its competitive advantage on the score of labor costs—a fact noted by the *Wall Street Journal* in 1957 and not denied by the Puerto Rican Fomento organization in its spirited reply.[13] The American manufacturer, again, is not bound to his Puerto Rican venture by any special ties. Even when he is genuinely anxious to assist the industrialization program his sentiment may be overwhelmed, as was the case with the closure of the Sylvania Electric Corporation in 1958, by the termination of an important contract elsewhere and the decision (in that particular case) to sacrifice the Puerto Rican plant to the two major plants in Brazil and Pennsylvania.[14] Or he may discover that there are administrative difficulties involved in maintaining communications between an island plant and a distant continental headquarters; this was the main reason, apparently, for the unpopular closure in 1960 of the large Paper Mate plant in the south coast town of Salinas, communication between that point and Santa Monica, California, being simply too difficult and uncertain.[15] Nor will the willingness of management to help transfer a handful of the Puerto Rican employees to the continental plant, as did in fact occur in that last instance, do much to offset the drastic decline of local trade and commerce that its departure means for the community. There is, again, to look at another aspect of the problem, no vital waterway in Puerto Rico to be controlled at any price, such as Suez or Panama. It is true that there are stable political conditions in the island congenial to the peace of mind of the outside business investor, of which official incentive advertising makes much. But the importance even of this factor may perhaps be exaggerated, for the absence of such conditions has not seriously discouraged American investment of massive proportions in the Latin American countries, especially in potentially rich economies such as those of Venezuela, Brazil, and Argentina. Most Latin American revolutions, as a matter of fact, have frequently been nothing much more, from this viewpoint, than palace revolutions that have left substantially untouched the working agreements between the political regimes and the foreign business interests. Further afield, indeed, the famous Düsseldorf Agreement of 1939 between the central trade associations of the British and German industrial interests is a classic instance of the economic friendliness that may prevail between national societies that, in their political relations, are even on the verge of open conflict. American business in the Latin American and Caribbean fields has frequently exhibited an equal readiness to cooperate with regimes which, from the Puerto Rican viewpoint, are politically reprehensible. It takes the threat of outright expropriation, as in revolutionary Cuba, to bring about a change of attitude; and even then the record of American business attitudes to Mexico in the late 1930's and the 1940's suggests that even the act of official expropriation of foreign properties, so long as a satisfactory rate of compensation is agreed upon, need not permanently destroy amicable commercial relationships.

There is yet another point to be made. Throughout the entire American period of rule, and especially since the New Deal era, the island economy has been to all intents and purposes a subsidy economy. And since the federal contributions have been largely haphazard and ill directed, they have not helped the island toward a genuine planning revolution designed to take care of its long-term economic needs. The benefits accruing from them, significantly, have occurred in an almost completely accidental manner, as in the case of the large fiscal returns on the rum tax during the war period and the financing of the vocational training program through the GI Bill of Rights after the war. "The people of Puerto Rico," Professor Perloff has observed, "have become adjusted to an income level deriving in very large part from a flow of funds into the island which is not directly related to the sale of goods through normal channels or returns on investments abroad. This is not a very sturdy foundation, and the reduction of federal emergency outlays in the island can have unfortunate consequences, *unless* the export industries are built up rapidly and the productive plant and equipment is expanded so as to broaden the base of the economy."[16] Those conditions have still not been completely fulfilled, and thus the Fomento planners continue to see migration as a crucial factor in their considerations and clearly anticipate, also, that in the event of any really large-scale desertion of the island by American firms they will be able to fall back upon an extended federal public works program.[17] But both of these alternatives are peculiarly unsatisfactory. A policy of dependence on migration is limited on at least three counts: its continuance is always uncertain, it can generate (as it already has done) hostile social and political repercussions in the United States, and it is likely, considering the nature of the migrants, to affect adversely the productive capacity of the island. A public works program, likewise, is notoriously deficient anywhere, since it aims at relief (like the old PRRA before 1940) rather than at removing the causes giving rise to the need for relief. In spite of these drawbacks, the Puerto Rican bureaucracy chooses to accept these alternatives. Or perhaps, more accurately, its "choice" springs inescapably from the single governing fact that whether with a sugar economy in one generation or an industrializing one in another the local power has had to fit itself into the requirements of the American national concern.

In more general terms of course we are witnessing here a classic example of how the economic laws that govern the relationships between superordinate and subordinate societies operate in such a way as to tighten the vise of economic dependency. There grows up an entrenched institutional arrangement of commercial and trading connections which forces the lesser economy into a narrow and one-sided reliance upon the greater. In the Puerto Rican case not only is the island frustrated in any efforts to diversify its global trading relationships, but it is also to this extent made far more vulnerable to the repercussions of economic recession on the mainland. The establishment of any firms and technicians other than American is practically paralyzed by the strict enforcement of the federal immigration legislation, a fact recently emphasized by the remarks of the Economic Adviser to the Italian Embassy in Washington.[18] The relationship creates an unfavorable balance of trade against the local economy; and it is not enough to argue here with the Puerto Rican Planning Board that such an unfavorable balance is not of necessity an index of economic weakness and to cite as supporting evidence the case of the United States itself between 1790 and 1873,[19] for the comparison ignores the crucial fact that the American economy during that period possessed massive raw material resources, as yet unexploited, whereas the contemporary Puerto Rican economy possesses no such reserves of strength. Industrial development, as a consequence of all this, tends (as a Fomento director has confessed) to rely almost exclusively upon imported raw materials, to sell mainly on the continental market, to use local materials rarely, and generally to be integrated into the American industrial structure rather than into the Puerto Rican economy.[20] If to all this there is added the fact that in all of the strategic sections of the economy in its connection with the continental mainland—shipping, air traffic, immigration control, postal communications—the power to make or break rests either with the federal Congress or with one of the federal regulatory commissions, the degree of Puerto Rican subordination to the continental scheme of things becomes translucently clear. The general result is what Gunnar Myrdal, speaking of the problem generally, has termed an "enforced bilateralism," insuring the continuing hold upon the lesser economy even after political liberation from the colonial status has been completed. Despite the very considerable economic advantages that accrue to the dependent country as a result of the connection, at the end of the process it is certain to mean a considerable economic disadvantage, since it tends to worsen that country's terms of trade by artificially restricting the scope of the markets where it buys and sells. The one great asset which final liberation from the economic dependency will mean will be the liberty of the society to regulate its economic life according to the interests of its own people, since it will then be capable of its own intelligent interference with the play of forces in the international economy.[21]

The Puerto Rican *Populares,* truly, have worked with magnificent energy and devotion towards lifting their people up by their own bootstraps. But they have been not so much planners, in any traditional collectivist sense, as imaginative industrial promoters seizing vigorously what they can obtain from a game whose rules they have had no share in shaping. Their economy, resultantly, has become more and more tied to American capitalist enterprise. As much as in the pre-1940 period, it is subject to widespread absentee ownership in its means of production. Indeed, the old type of sugar absenteeism has merely been succeeded by a new type of industrial absenteeism. The absentee landlord of the old days has been replaced by the absentee shareholder of the new. And the rationalizations of the absenteeism have not altered much, for the arguments that were once paraded to defend the sugar interests of the United States are now advanced to justify the American industry interests. The end result may not have been consciously desired by the architects of the "new" Puerto Rico. It is nonetheless real for all that.

It would be difficult to estimate with any exactitude how widespread and far-reaching are the manifold consequences of this situation. The more direct and obvious consequences are frequently of real benefit. The American employer, especially if his enterprise is of some corporate size, like Woolworth's or Eagle Drug, brings with him civilized employer attitudes that are a welcome contrast to the socially unconscionable small local entrepreneur, although he has not yet begun to match, in social welfare schemes for his employees, the impressive record of a firm like Cadbury in Jamaica or Olivetti in Italy. When an oil refinery or a rice-milling concern comes to the island it brings with it, because of its size, standards of business administration and personnel management that help to modernize local entrepreneurial attitudes. But there are other effects, more indirect and more subtle, which are less desirable and which altogether conspire to create an environmental atmosphere which influences local public policy. There slowly grows up a feeling that the local government, thoroughly dependent upon the outside investor, must do nothing to alienate him or to sacrifice his "confidence." It must sustain a "favorable" climate, lest it kill the goose that lays the golden eggs. This means that legislation with any radical twist must be carefully eschewed. Just as in political relations with the United States the local leadership must orient its strategy to the political currents dominating the Washington scene, so in economic relations it must avoid any policy that might begin to look to apprehensive investors like "socialism." It must be admitted that the Puerto Rican leadership is at least frank about this. "A special case of contradiction between development policy and welfare policy arises," the EDA Administrator has cautioned, "if economic development is to be financed largely by private sources. The modern tendency to finance welfare schemes through progressive taxation then comes into conflict with the necessity for high profits to provide both an incentive for capital investment and a fund out of which such investment may be expanded in the future. . . . There is some difficulty hindering government participation in industrial ownership so as to engage directly in this capital accumulation, certainly short of an all-out socialist program. Such a socialist program, for its part, would probably seriously hinder eliciting the participation of outside capital in most cases."[22] It is easy, reading between the lines of that statement, to recognize how, speaking bluntly, the full freedom of the Commonwealth government to shape its own public policy is conditioned by its economic subordination to the national capitalist economy. A government in San Juan which at any future date was more to the left than the present *Popular* administration would rapidly find itself in trouble, and the spectacle of the American administration taking reprisals by way of reduced sugar allocations against Castro's Cuba in 1960 and, later, a full blown trade embargo has emphasized that lesson to the Puerto

Rican observer. What is at present only an abstract truth could then become a pungent challenge.

All this is evident in a variety of ways. It is there in the fact that the major decisions about investment policy in the island, and also continuing policy once a plant has been established there, remain with the top management in the continental offices of the concern. It is there in the "go slow" policy on a radical location-of-industry plan in the island, for a "go ahead" policy has so far been inhibited by the fact that the upper managerial echelons of American plants are overwhelmingly staffed by Americans who are reluctant to settle outside of metropolitan San Juan in sites where the amenities of life would be far beneath their expectations. A proper balance, eminently desirable on social grounds, between town and countryside is thus in part frustrated by the desire of the American managerial group and their families to enjoy the semi-touristic "good life" they read about in the resplendent Commonwealth government advertisements in the *New Yorker* magazine. It can even contribute to the closure of an enterprise; the failure of the large Textron textile plant in Ponce in 1957 was due in large measure to difficulties in obtaining proper managerial talent in a city area where American-style comforts have so far done little to break down its drowsy social conservatism.[23] Because, to take a further example, most of the housing program, both public and private, is financed by American loan capital, there is a premium placed upon the private ownership concept, reflected in the government's new policy of selling rental units in public projects to tenants and of eliminating taxation on personal house properties beneath the $15,000 level. But it is reflected more drastically in the fact that little has so far been done to curb the depredations of the cheap builder and the real-estate speculator in the land boom which is flourishing especially in the expanding urban perimeters. The pressure both of population increase and of social advance has produced in Puerto Rico a telling demonstration of the pre-emption by private owners and developers of increased land values created entirely by social processes. More than in a country like the United States (which originally invoked the eloquent confusion of Henry George's preachings on the issue) the intense land hunger prevalent in a geographically circumscribed land area such as Puerto Rico calls aloud for the planned use of land as a public utility. Nothing short of a nationalization policy could deal with the problem satisfactorily.

The *Popular* government, however, has shown little inclination to apply the public utility concept, or even to adopt the comparatively mild controls advocated by a liberal American planner like Harvey Perloff in his book of 1949.[24] Both the recent hearings of the Public

Service Commission and the Collett-Clapp Report of 1959 on transportation and communications services reveal a profound disappointment, both on the part of the consumer and of government itself, with the failure of the privately owned Puerto Rico Telephone Company (a subsidiary of the International Telephone and Telegraph Company) to undertake the long-range planning and the scale of reinvested operational capital to meet both the present demands on the service and the anticipated large increases in that demand as industrialization proceeds apace. Yet government has been no more adventuresome in this matter than in that of industrial location. There is nothing to indicate that it is ready to contemplate the expropriation of the company as the means of providing for an essential public service, a plan mooted long ago by Governor Tugwell. The public hearings conducted in 1961 by the Senate special committee unearthed some remarkable examples of administrative inefficiency and gross neglect of subscribers' complaints on the part of the company—deficiencies which indeed, had they been those of a government department, would have been vociferously acclaimed as conclusive proof of the folly of public ownership. The outlying small town communities, as the loud complaints of the island mayors show, have hardly begun to enjoy the services of a modern telephone system. In such a situation, characteristic of absentee-controlled utility companies in colonial economies, attitudes to public ownership deemed orthodox in the United States appear peculiarly archaic; thus forces as generally conservative as lawyers and attorneys have supported government expropriation of the Puerto Rican service, a support, interestingly enough, that echoes the observation of one of the Puerto Rican governors under the Coolidge Republican administration in 1925 that, with respect to electrical transmission and distribution, "private or corporate development primarily for profit would be an abandonment of every obligation of duty which the Government owes to the people whom it serves."[25]

The vexed question, finally, of the complicated transportation problems of greater San Juan within a fiercely expanding urbanism offers a final proof of public policy weakness. The last decade has seen a major "face lifting" in the road system of the city and its environs, and the end result perhaps justifies the lyrical approval of observers from other Caribbean islands—Jamaica, for example, where the road systems remain hopelessly antiquated.[26] But it has become abundantly clear that what is grandiloquently styled "urban planning" by the Planning Board and the Department of Public Works is nothing much more than a construction program premised almost uncritically upon the limitless automobilization of the economy and certain to produce within a generation, or perhaps less, the grievous traffic problems already afflicting metropolitan areas like New York and Los Angeles. The Puerto Rican planners, however, show no more eagerness than most of their continental counterparts to face up candidly to the truth that only an efficient public transit system operating on a service basis and not, like the Transportation Authority now, on an earning basis, can ever hope to meet the appalling dimensions of the problem; for this would involve a direct confrontation of the cult of the private automobile, with all the challenge to the entrenched interests of the United States automobile industry that it would assuredly mean. Yet Puerto Rican conditions are quite suitable for the mass use of the bicycle—widely used in other Caribbean cities like Georgetown and Port of Spain—if only the prejudice in favor of the private automobile, fed by all the massive advertising of the American industry, could be combatted. It may perhaps be unfair to put all of the blame for this, as does Dr. Sam Wallace in the lively rebuke of his public lecture of 1961, on the Planning Board, for there are vital factors contributing to urban sprawl—the tax structure controlling the use of undeveloped land, for example—which are outside the scope of the Board. In the meantime, however, San Juan, built, like Manhattan and San Francisco, on a narrow strip of land and likewise facing specific limitations of space, becomes more and more a tropical microcosm of the concretized-motorized nightmare which Los Angeles has already become. It is ironic, so pressing is the problem, that even normally conservative voices in the community see no alternative but to accept openly a systematic policy of subsidized public transit.[27]

It is possible that much of this general situation gains strength from the limited concepts of "planning" that guide the Puerto Rican situation. Those concepts have in large part been borrowed from the Chicago school of planning in which both Professor Perloff, its leading theorist, and Governor Tugwell have had a hand. "Planning" is used by that school as a generic term "to refer broadly," as Perloff puts it, "to the ways in which men and women, acting through organized entities, endeavor to guide developments so as to solve the pressing problems around them and approximate the vision of the future which they hold."[28] The emphasis is thus placed on planning as an administrative instrumentality; it is certainly something far less radical than the traditional usage of the term in socialist literature. The definition takes the general purposes of a society for granted as they are set by the controlling social and political forces and seeks merely to offer the methods that are most appropriate to their fulfillment; it centers, again in Professor Perloff's words, on the making of decisions and scheduled effectuation of policies. The planner, within this concept of his task, does not seek to challenge the business civilization, but merely at best to blunt its rough edges. He even begins to believe that to do anything more than this would be "undemocratic"; thus one of the leading spirits behind the growth of the Planning Board in Puerto Rico can assert that a "master plan" is wrong if it attempts to "dictate" to private interests, for the word "master" does not seem to fit into a democracy. The business of the planner is to cooperate with the private developer, and likewise the developer with the planner, which means "profit on both sides."[29] The entire Fabian tradition of planning is thus almost casually swept aside. As a result the Puerto Rican planning processes center around the establishment of zoning and subdivision regulations, the issuance of building permits, the review of capital improvement projects, the construction of thoroughfares, and so on; anything beyond this is rejected as "idealistic" or "undemocratic." The planner is thus denied any real power to address himself to what, in the sprawling growth of greater San Juan, is the massive driving power of the profit motive as it stimulates the building contractor, the real estate speculator, the finance company. He may challenge business interests in minor ways—the conversion of major town thoroughfares, for example, into one-way traffic arteries (which irritates the local merchant class). But because he works in a society protected by the American flag he is unable to challenge those interests in any big way; so, as one Planning Board official has put it, he cannot experiment with the Russian method of controlling urban population growth by debarring the entry of new families into the peripheral areas of existing city complexes.[30] The reason may explain the failure to grapple with the urbanization problem. But it would be difficult to accept it as reason in itself to explain the failure of the planners to provide adequate public facilities such as schools, playgrounds, parking areas, and community centers in the new housing developments—a puzzling lapse in the light of the fact that Puerto Rican life has traditionally centered around the community habits of the open *plaza*; or to plan for a series of extensive public parks; or to compel builders to construct adequate drainage for the mass housing they build—a health official has estimated that at least twenty major housing developments in the San Juan area are seriously deficient in the provision of septic tanks; or to undertake proper regulation of beach areas in the public interest, after the fashion of the Beach Control Authority set up to meet a comparable problem by the Jamaican government; or, finally, to make room in the linear spread of San Juan–Santurce for the provision of a civic center worthy of a great city.

The Puerto Rican planners may indeed not consciously adapt their policies to what they conceive to be American preferences. They may not even feel any sense of constraint to the degree that they themselves have made these preferences a part of their own convictions. Even less is it true to say that American preferences are crudely foisted upon them from outside. It would be more exact to say that, as with all subordinate jurisdictions, the planners tread warily in all those fields where the controlling jurisdiction has the power to make its displeasure felt. There are, after all, many unattractive elements within the local society that contribute to policy failures. Politicians, as elsewhere, resist the advance of the planners, and it is a well-known fact that the eradication of urban slum areas like the San Juan eyesores—which have been quixotically named by their residents with titles hardly pleasing to the American public mind: *Checoslovaquia, Corea, Sierra Maestra*—has been slowed down by the willingness of politicians to see a source of electoral strength in obtaining essential services like light, water, and improved streets for the slum poor. The fact remains, however, that the supervening federal power is so pervasive that it becomes elementary political wisdom on the part of local leadership to consider its interests and outlooks. In certain fields this power is embedded in the political-constitutional relationships between the island and the national capital. The extended authority of the federal regulatory commissions is a case in point. In airline transportation, in shipping, in labor relations of an interstate character, in sugar production and, more recently, in petroleum manufacture, the island is subject to federal institutional control, either by Congressional legislation as in the case of the controlling coastal shipping legislation or by agency regulative power. Every one of these controls has given rise, in the relations of its operators with the government of Puerto Rico, to a record, generally speaking, of bureaucratic reluctance to meet Puerto Rican needs with any degree of alacrity. The present air carrier service to and from the island is the end result of a protracted struggle, from 1943 onwards, by the local government to secure adequate and reasonably priced air transport, so much so that the present-day cheap tourist flights were originally forced upon the major lines (Pan-American and Eastern) by the government's resort to non-scheduled carriers after 1945; and even today the government has so far failed in its attempt to obtain from the Civil Aeronautics Board comparable cheap passages from the island to European destinations. Agricultural policies, in their turn, are influenced by the dependence upon federal grants-in-aid, and the Resident Commissioner of the local government in Washington has noted the serious dangers present in the fact that, as he puts it, the scientific use of Puerto Rican land depends entirely upon decisions reached in a Washington government office.[31] The system of the sugar quota is well known. But the operating principle that inspires it—that Puerto Rican interests must yield to continental interests—governs other commodities as well. The recent issue of the restrictions placed by the federal government upon imports of crude oil from abroad in order to protect the national domestic producers showed how Puerto Rico, although not included in the program, could nevertheless be prevailed upon to promise the federal administrators that it would not permit itself to become a refuge for foreign exporters seeking to evade the federal government's purpose.[32]

Some of the instances of federal control of course are not really of serious consequence; when, for example, the Fomento advertising writers are obliged to eliminate from a rum promotion campaign the portrait of an American feminine tourist sipping an island alcoholic mixture, following the protests of the American producers' association, it is no more than a minor irritant and merely provokes wry Puerto Rican comment on the vagaries of the American puritan conscience. Other instances, however, evidence a far more pervasive control of the insular economy. This is especially and notoriously the case in the matter of maritime shipping. The statutory requirement that Puerto Rican exporters must ship their products to the American market by American shipping means, in effect, that they are at the mercy of four large steamship companies organized in the powerful shipping cartels of the United States Atlantic and Gulf–Puerto Rican Conference and the Pacific Coast–Puerto Rican Conference, exempted by the United States Shipping Act of 1916 from the application of the federal anti-trust laws. The prolonged crisis in which the Commonwealth government has been embroiled one way or another since 1946 with respect to this situation makes a depressing story. The shipping companies have successfully requested frequent rate increases throughout the period without consultation with the local government; the increases have been extravagantly high, amounting, for the brief period of 1956-1959 alone, to an addition of some 27 percent on many imported popular consumer goods; the increases have also entailed, as the Commonwealth Manufacturers Association has pointed out, serious difficulties for many local industries dependent on low transportation costs to make a profit for themselves; and, in spite of all this, the Federal Maritime Board has authorized the increases notwithstanding, as studies by the Ports Authority of the Commonwealth government appear to show, that in almost every case recurring demands for rate increases have gone far beyond concurrent increases in operating costs. All this emphatically demonstrates the presence of at least one fragile element in an industrialization program that relies for its continuing success upon an overseas communication system controlled, to a degree of some 85 percent, by American shipping companies entirely impervious to local control or regulation.[33]

The larger implications of this situation are worth noting. "The coastwise laws," write Daniel Marx and Samuel Eastman in their authoritative study of 1953, *Ships and Sugar*, "in substance require the people of Puerto Rico to support an American instrumentality, American flag shipping, in a manner which is tantamount to taxation without representation. This is not to say that this is necessarily unfair, for the American merchant marine also contributes to the defense of Puerto Rico, but merely to state what the incidence or impact of the coastwise laws seem to be."[34] It is hardly surprising that the Commonwealth government has been giving serious thought for some time to the creation of its own mercantile marine. Certainly the optimistic expectation of the Fomento chieftains in 1955 that a "dramatic reduction" in the cost of door-to-door surface transportation to the mainland may be possible "within the next few years"[35] has not been fulfilled in any way in the period following its utterance; in fact, it has been seriously reversed. Nor does it appear likely that the creation of an independent merchant carrying service by San Juan would receive the necessary federal approval—any more than it had been possible for the federal government of the now defunct West Indies Federation to break away from the restrictive clauses of the United Kingdom–United States Air Services Agreement of 1946 as a condition of forming its own independent national air carrier so vital as such an independent service was to the Federation's tourist trade. In the meanwhile, the Puerto Rican difficulties with its maritime connections continue to symbolize the ridiculous paradox that the Caribbean, as a region of intense maritime activity, has never been able to create its own navies and merchant fleets.

It would be easy to make out of all this an imposing indictment of American imperialism. The *Movimiento Pro-Independencia de Puerto Rico*, one of the insular separatist organizations, has estimated that the island economy is in thrall to the United States in as many as thirty-eight different ways and that even the ways which are on the surface apparently beneficial to the islanders—federal agency expenditures, for example—are in reality only a partial compensation designed to benefit the dominant power.[36] Much of the argument is sound. What is more, the apprehensions are shared by an increasing number of Puerto Ricans and it is simply not good enough to say, with a government economic adviser, that the concern is limited to a "declining, almost minuscule, group of doctrinaire *Nacionalistas*, who have no other stock in trade."[37] The important recent speech of the late Ramos Antonini, Speaker of the House, graphically invoking the construction of a 38th Parallel against the expansion of the American supermarkets in the island towns, should be sufficient to emphasize the lack of both accuracy and generosity in that kind of assertion by Puerto Rican officialdom. But to go beyond reasonable criticism of Puerto Rican dependency upon the American market and to deny that the connection has brought very real economic advantages is to indulge in an exercise of nationalist chauvinism. The United States Tariff Commission Report of 1943 concluded after an exhaustive study of the whole question that the gains derived by Puerto Rico from the relationship have on balance outweighed the disadvantages. The point to be made against the American connection is in fact a little more complex. Its benefits have been and continue to be very real. What is wrong is the simple fact that the benefits have been accidents rather than essences of the crucial dependence of the local economy at every step upon the policies pursued by the metropolitan power—a fact usually overlooked by these apologists who continue to employ the findings of the Tariff Commission Report as arguments against the ideology of Puerto Rican independence. Those policies reflect continental trends and continental interests, and Puerto Rican gains are not so much deliberately calculated as accidentally derived from them. This is particularly true in the matter of the tariff. Puerto Rico had no representational or consultative role to play in the original formulation (in 1900) of her incorporation into the tariff system, and ever since that date she has had to obtain what crumbs she could from an arrangement that has throughout been utilized as a weapon of American national economic policy, sometimes political policy. Thus there has always been the fear that Cuban sugar would be granted preferential rates (as was indeed the case between 1934 and 1939, when it enjoyed a tariff rate some 52 percent lower than other foreign rates), or that a lowered rate on Cuban rums would encourage the dumping of unaged and non-matured brands into the continental market from Havana (as was the case between 1942 and 1945). Changing national policies that might make or break a local industry must always be anticipated: the local rum industry was thus only made possible by the vast consumer market suddenly opened up by the repeal of Prohibition at the beginning of the New Deal period. An enlarged free-trade policy on the part of Washington could work real damage to the new insular industries—just as the grant-aided economies of the British Eastern Caribbean area, as well as the newly independent countries of Trinidad and Jamaica, see their protected status within the United Kingdom consumer market threatened as Britain seems to be moving nearer (1963) to membership in the European Common Market. It is the declared policy of the Puerto

Rican government, in the light of all this, to insist that ideally the tariff should reduce rates on the raw materials and primary products which its manufacturers import and refrain from reductions on competitive foreign manufactured goods. The Puerto Rican high propensity to import—continues the official line of argument—itself largely occasioned by economic assimilation into the continental commercial and industrial structure, can only be offset by a continuing increase in export goods, from which the Commonwealth Treasury may be enabled to accumulate external reserves as a source of financing the resultant balance-of-payments deficit. But this requires that the island's special difficulties shall be properly taken into account when federal tariff policies are shaped and that, further, a greater degree of flexibility should be accepted in order to meet those difficulties.[38] The future of Operation Bootstrap depends upon whether the federal policy makers meet those expectations with sympathy. That remains still a matter for the future. But it is worth noting that the argument closely follows the argument of the group of Ponce manufacturers who presented an extensive report to the colonial ministry in Madrid in 1898 and which was later incorporated by Henry Carroll in his separate report of 1899 on *The Industrial and Commercial Condition of Porto Rico.*

One disturbing fact, in this respect, deserves separate comment. The Commonwealth government must deal, in its nexus with Washington, through the medium of the federal regulatory commissions which hold sway over so many of the federalized insular activities. Yet it has become abundantly evident that, in their administrative policies, what was originally intended to work as a federal regulation of corporate business has become a federal protection of corporate business. Professor Cushman concluded, in his definitive study of 1941, that, in the particular instance of radio, the Federal Communications Commission has throughout assumed that "what is best for the radio industry as a business enterprise must also be best for the country" and that the commissions have in general been staffed by men who have had a "substantial stake in the status quo; they do not wish to be disrupted, and it is natural for them to feel that wise planning should avoid radical changes."[39] A generation later, things have not much improved from the viewpoint of the consumer. Professor Marver Bernstein's more recent examination has reinforced the earlier critical conclusions, and makes clear that the insulation of the commissions from political and partisan influence has merely served to make their directors more responsive to the pressures of the regulated groups. Studies like those of Professor Clair Wilcox and of Walter Adams and Horace Gray likewise reveal how much of the administrative application of the anti-trust legislation has been under-taken on the basis of the premise that the established rights of cor-porate property must not be seriously abridged, with the consequence that the giant corporate enterprises of American life have gained many of the privileges accorded to the regulated utilities without at the same time having to accept the restraints imposed upon the latter.[40]

To Puerto Rico this is a matter of essential bread and butter. For the regulatory commissions—if all this is true—are unlikely to re-spond at all sympathetically to the arguments of so liberal a plaintiff as the Commonwealth government. In the latest report on the com-missions, that of James Landis to then President-elect Kennedy in 1960, the harshest passages refer to two of the federal agencies—the Civil Aeronautics Board and the Federal Maritime Board—with which Puerto Rico has had relationships at once close and disappoint-ing. Those referring to the CAB speak of "the intrusion of influences off the record that appear to be determinative of pending cases" and of a "failure to do forward planning of the type necessary to promote our air commerce to its desired level of efficiency"—which may help to explain why the Board so far has seemed more willing to listen to the United States Navy than to the Commonwealth government in the latter's campaign to open up the Navy-occupied island of Vieques to commercial aviation. A remark on the FMB—that "a fog of secrecy also surrounds many actions of the Board and no articulate standards seem to have developed with respect to *ex parte* presentations"—may also help to explain the general neglect on its part, already noted, of vital Puerto Rican interests.[41] The ineptitudes of Congressional gov-ernment in the island (as the history of successive visiting Congres-sional committees has unhappily catalogued) are thus being followed by the ineptitudes of commission government.

For the commissions are geographically remote from Puerto Rico. They do not hold hearings in San Juan as at least the committees of Congress sometimes do. Their members know practically nothing of Puerto Rican problems; the committees of Congress have at least pro-duced a small core of members who have made it their special busi-ness, like the late Representative Fred Crawford, to inform themselves exhaustively on the problems of the dependent territories. There exists no machinery of government to insure that Puerto Rican nominees will be named to their memberships, Congressional pressures and Presidential patronage being indeed the main forces behind appoint-ments. The truth is of course that as Puerto Rico has grown eco-nomically, its problems have become less susceptible to solution through the traditional channels provided by the federal-state system. The device of the office of the Resident Commissioner in Washington may have been good enough fifteen years ago, for its functions were not much more than those of a Puerto Rican lobby looking out for federal handouts. But as Puerto Rican industrialization has come more and more into conflict with important continental economic interests the device has become pitiably inadequate. Puerto Rican nominees have managed to get to the top in the federal agency offices situated in San Juan—there is hardly one such agency that is not administered by a Puerto Rican official—because there have been channels through which their interests have been advanced: the Commonwealth government itself, the local committee of the national Democratic Party, the local Statehood Party affiliated to the national Republican Party. But no such channels exist in Washington; in particular, Puerto Rico lacks the major device of the state Congressional delegation with which the individual states defend their interests at the federal center. A minor reform of course will occasionally improve the system from the Puerto Rican viewpoint; thus the reorganization plan which in 1961 reshaped the Federal Maritime Board so that its promotional and regulatory functions, hitherto illogically mixed up together, will now be separated can only do good for Puerto Rico. The basic defect, however, remains, and if the economic dependency of the island upon the national economy is ever to be terminated it will assuredly not come about through the instrumentality of the commission method of government.

It is hardly a matter for astonishment, in the light of all this, that concern about the more hazardous aspects of Operation Bootstrap has recently blossomed into a hotly debated issue of basic public policy. The concern has received its most eloquent expression in the speech, already noted, of the late Speaker of the House to the San Juan Lions Club. The leading theme of that speech was, simply put, that the emergence of a "balanced economy" in the island was threatened by the dangerous readiness of Puerto Rican merchants and entrepreneurs to sell out their businesses to the extravagant offers of the big American concerns, with the dual consequence that, first, the means of production become more and more concentrated in the hands of a few groups and, secondly, these groups being non-resident Americans and American corporations, a system of absentee ownership grows up in which the vital decisions about production and policy are made by groups immune to local control or influence. Increasingly Puerto Ricans, both of the business and working classes, are alienated from the controlling economic power behind the industrialization program; they become, in the phrase of one Puerto Rican business leader, spectators rather than actors in the great economic drama that is taking place in the society.[42]

Of the essential justice of the charge there can be little doubt. Recent government reports have indicated that 78 percent of all investment in the economy is made by outside American interests and that only one out of every four factories is in Puerto Rican hands. Nor is that offset by any sizable degree of Puertoricanization of the managerial operation of the plants. The percentage of Puerto Ricans in the top echelons of the managerial elite was somewhat less than 20 percent in 1958, a percentage far lower—to make a comparison with the policies of a number of British concerns with extensive manufacturing and trading interests in Africa and Asia—than that of foreign businesses elsewhere in the developing economies of the world.[43] The consequences are far-reaching. The American manager is frequently unprepared to meet the labor-management problems that flow from the different cultural background of his employees; the case of the manager of the Standard Products Corporation, whose unsympathetic attitude to the Puerto Rican women under his charge provoked the complaints of the Retail Clerks Union, is not unrepresentative.[44] Much more important, production and employment decisions are made in stateside head offices which cannot be expected to have much sentimental regard for Puerto Rico or for the social consequences likely to be created by those decisions. It is thus beside the point for the local newspapers to write laudatory articles stressing the fact, for example, that with the exception of the top three executive officers a sugar plant like the famous *Central* Aguirre works with an all-Puerto Rican supervisory staff,[45] for at the critical juncture where top-level decisions are made the responsibility lies still with the continental directorate. The external directing forces will naturally respond to the incentives that the Commonwealth government offers them. But the response will always assume the paramountcy of their own interests and convenience. Dr. Joseph Airov's study of the location problems of the synthetic fiber industry, to take one example of many, thus suggests that a decision to locate in Puerto Rico as against the mainland would depend entirely upon the consideration that the island could offset high fuel and power costs with its low labor costs; but it is evident that the island would have no power to influence the decision, at any step, should the labor costs advantage decline, as in the long run it must.[46]

But there is more to it even than this. A protest like that of Ramos Antonini is, at best, a sentimental appeal to the patriotic instinct of the Puerto Rican businessman and it fails to comprehend the basic character of the problem because it lacks a theoretical understanding of the laws that guide the flow of international private capital in the modern world. In particular, there are two general considerations that help to throw some light on the Puerto Rican case. The first is that the capital invested tends to go into the production of goods for export rather than for home consumption in the countries where they are manufactured. The economy of the underdeveloped country is thus directed to the export of selected products only. And this is aggravated in Puerto Rico by the fact that the economy of the United States, being largely self-sufficient, produces not only equipment but also raw materials and food products, so that the dependent colonial economy, unlike those of the British colonies, is even denied the advantage of becoming a specialized raw material or food producer for the continental consumer market. The increases of consumer expenditures by the Puerto Rican buyer means, then, an endlessly spiraling demand for durable items not manufactured in the island, with the consequent loss of income that a struggling economy can ill afford. One reflection of this condition is the reckless use of credit in Puerto Rican consumer habits, undeterred by any sort of governmentally imposed austerity program; the recent remarks, indeed, of the Secretary of Commerce on this problem suggest that government anticipates that the "education of the consumer" will be taken in hand by the very business forces that benefit from the absence of such "education." The second consideration is that although absentee capital operating in Puerto Rico notoriously makes for itself an enormous rate of profit—there was some anxious public comment in 1961 on the announcement by the president of the Commonwealth Oil Refining Company that its operations had netted a total profit of over $6 million within a period of six months—there is nothing, apart from the international civic sense of the owners, to guarantee the reinvestment of the profits for additional production within the host economy. The right to repatriate capital and return profits is not accompanied by any obligation to reinvest, such as might perhaps be guaranteed by an international code of behavior binding on the foreign investor. "Because the impetus of rapid growth is being given through the use of imported capital," noted a Puerto Rico Planning Board advisory paper in 1958 on this whole problem, "there exists the danger that withdrawal of income received from this investment may slow down the overall rate of growth of the economy. At the present time this flow back of income is relatively minor but is likely to develop into magnitudes of major proportion. Thus, it is conceivable that this flow may reach the level of $350 million per year as compared with about $70 million today. It will tend to grow faster than the overall economy since it is concentrated in the newer and more dynamic sectors of the economy. To offset this, a program designed to interest local capital in sharing in the growth of the economy is important and to create the opportunity for reinvestment of capital of foreign corporations is necessary."[47]

Local capital ownership, of course, is a favorite nostrum in this type of discussion, and it constitutes the single leading proposition in the Ramos Antonini speech. As a solution to the problem, however, it is open to serious doubts. It would of course be more susceptible to local political control. But this would depend, in turn, upon the willingness of the local political will to exercise the control. In Puerto Rico, at least, there has been little evidence to suggest any radical exercise of such control; the legislature, to take a single example, has signally failed to take any remedial steps when serious unemployment is caused in the depressed town of Humacao by the decision of a local sugar enterprise, the *Central* Ejemplo, to remove its milling operations to other sites in the island.[48] There has been much talk lately about legislative control of monopolies in the economy through the active implementation of the existing anti-monopoly laws patterned after the federal Sherman Act; but the sad history of the federal trust-busting legislation does not warrant any great hopes about better success in Puerto Rico. The attitudes summed up in the Ramos Antonini speech, in fact, constitute simply a sentimental plea for "little" business as against "big" business, the commercial retailers, in the particular case at issue, against the large supermarkets, and for Puerto Rican business as against American business. But neither distinction is valid in any economic terms. "Little" business cannot realize the savings inherent in large-scale production, nor offer the cheap products en masse made possible by that style of production for which, moreover, the Puerto Rican consumer has shown a marked preference. Nor is there any evidence to suggest that the Puerto Rican businessman is likely to treat either the Puerto Rican consumer or employee more generously than his American counterpart; indeed, because he understands his own working classes better it is possible that he would be able, from the psychological viewpoint, to treat them worse. "I believe," Ramos Antonini declares, "in the necessity of the supermarkets but I do not believe in their glorification." The sentiment sounds fine, though it is difficult from any economic viewpoint to draw a hard and fast line between necessity and glorification. But it remains at the moment the dominant sentiment in the burgeoning Puerto Rican debate on the issue. Until it is exhausted, as a sentiment, the debate will be prevented from moving forward to the position where it is seen that the real distinction to be made is not between "little" and "big" business or between Puerto Rican and American business but between the principle of the private ownership of business on the one hand and that of its public ownership on the other, whether through the medium of a local public economy in Puerto Rico or of an international public economy of which it could be a constituent part.

The Role of Labor

In Puerto Rico, as in all underdeveloped economies, the role of labor in socio-industrial change is crucial in a peculiar way. The process of industrialization at once forces radical transmutations upon the existing organization of the labor force and adds new elements to the force itself. It calls for new skills. It introduces new conditions of technology and communications. It precipitates vast and often unanticipated social and cultural changes. Thus in Puerto Rico, although it is erroneous to say, as do some of the more romanticist critics of Operation Bootstrap, that the factory employment program has caused rural depopulation and the drift of manpower to the coastal city slum areas, it is true that it has accelerated processes already well under way before 1940. Industrialization, in turn, poses a serious question of psychological adaptation to industrial employment conditions, although, from this viewpoint, Puerto Rico has been fortunate, since factory employment and the factory system that creates it have not meant (as with industrializing change in more classically primitive economies) a sharp break with a preindustrial past. The wage system and the depersonalized character of large-scale employment have been features of the insular economy for decades, and the growth of the new factory sector has represented an extension of the boundaries of the labor market rather than the creation of a new type of market with its own internal dynamic. In any case, sociological investigation has fully annotated the remarkable ease with which the Puerto Rican worker has adapted himself to factory life; Dr. Peter Gregory has discovered that both for financial and psychological reasons the vast majority of island proletarians view their translation to industry as a permanent one, with perhaps the single exception of older workers with previous agricultural experience who appear to anticipate a return to a landowning status as either a concession to nostalgia or as a sort of partial retirement.[1]

Problems likely to produce more real difficulties for the insular transformation exist rather in the realm of the long-term role of labor than in that of its immediate adjustment. There is the question of minimum wage legislation, for example, for the strongest magnet that has attracted expatriate capital, after that of tax exemption, has been lower wage costs offered by an economy of significantly lower living standards and lower monetary expectations. There is the question of labor productivity; the demographic picture of the island, to illustrate, indicates a heavy burden upon the economy of non-adult, non-productive persons insofar as it shows that only some 28 percent of the total population—as compared with some 39 percent of the mainland population—can be included in the civilian labor force.[2] There are, finally, the problems, first, of the organizational structure of the island trade union movement, threatened as it currently is by the intrusion of new technical method and new managerial practice, and, second, of the entire relationship, as yet almost totally unexplored by any serious thought, that is likely to develop in the future between the labor movement, the twin forces of government and politics, and the American corporations that in large part own the new factories.

No single one of all of these issues emphasizes so vividly the peculiar difficulties of labor in a developing economy as that of the wage level in industry. The "basic dilemma," as the authoritative Nathan Report of 1955 phrased it, is that of organizing a reconciliation between, on the one hand, "the need for low-wage incentives to induce new investors to come to Puerto Rico, and on the other hand limiting unfair competition with mainland industries by existing and even prospective employers who would exploit Puerto Rican workers through submarginal wage levels. Minimum wages that are too high can destroy existing industries and discourage new investors. Minimum wages that are too low will harm Puerto Rican workers and give Puerto Rican industries an advantage over their mainland competitors. Therein lies a major ingredient of Puerto Rico's minimum wage policy problem."[3] The low labor costs, natural enough in an economy where massive unemployment still exerts an enormous depressive pressure on wage levels, have naturally appealed to the labor-oriented industries of the mainland. Even where the tax exemption incentive has been the more powerful reason for a Puerto Rican location choice it ceases to have any meaning unless profits are initially made, and since savings in costs are not to be derived from either lower transportation or lower raw-materials expenses they must come from the labor source. The pressure on a low wage level is enhanced by two additional factors. The first is that many of the industries so far attracted have been the "fly-by-night" New York and New Jersey business adventurers searching for a quick profit from low-paid and ill-organized Puerto Rican workers; the remarks of the head of small textile plants in the interior towns of Aguadilla and Camuy on the impossibility of continuing profitable production as local wages rise are suggestive on this score.[4] As these smaller investors are replaced by larger firms this sort of consideration will naturally tend to decline in importance. But the second factor will not so readily disappear since it applies to both types of investor. For both of them appear to insist on more favorable prospects for profits before taxes when they ponder on an industrial project in the island than when they consider a comparable project on the mainland; just as, in the matter of floating loans in the mainland financial markets, Puerto Rican public institutions find themselves compelled to pay higher interest rates to American investors who demand higher returns from Puerto Rico. In the long run, insular labor has to meet the costs of overcoming this psychological deterrent to investment by a willingness to accept a considerable wage differential, so that the weekly pay of the Puerto Rican worker, industry for industry, is barely one third of the pay of his counterpart on the mainland. Much of the local discussion on the role of labor in Operation Bootstrap thus gathers around the problems relating to the minimum wage factor.

It is sometimes alleged, in that discussion, that the Commonwealth government has a vested interest in permanently keeping down wage levels as a continuing investment incentive. The charge has been forcefully presented recently by James Hoffa of the Teamsters Union.[5] The record of the government in the whole field of labor relations and social welfare legislation belies the accusation. Its system of wage setting by administrative decree, now covering some 75 percent of the employed labor force and operating through the agency of the Commonwealth Minimum Wage Board, has been the major instrument in raising the take-home pay of local workers since its inception in 1941. Most of the wage reviews have concerned industries not covered by the comparable federal procedure, but there have been times (as with the review of sugar industrial wage rates in 1943) when they have set minimum wages higher than those established by federal fiat. It is true that most of the increases have coincided with revisions of the mainland minimum levels, indicating that federal precedents tend to influence and guide local administrative trends. At the same time, the Commonwealth government has exhibited a genuinely pro-labor attitude in a variety of related fields. It has set up, by legislative enactment, a fund from which compensatory payments may be made to workers displaced by mechanization in the sugar industry, largely financed by special taxation imposed upon the sugar companies; and the example has been more recently followed by legislation to cover dockworkers likewise affected by technological changes in the shipment of sugar cargoes from the island coastal cities.[6] Protective legislation has also been adopted in the varying fields of industrial safety, group insurance for small farmers, and vocational rehabilitation of disabled workers; while the latest item in the category of legislative measures against discriminatory practices in the employment field concerns itself with older workers who find themselves penalized by their age. The legislative findings on this latter point took cognizance of the fact that discrimination against workers over forty-five has reached alarming proportions in American industry and that its extension to Puerto Rico, already noticeable, can only entail grave social consequences.[7] Even more: the immaturity of the union movement in the island has meant that most of pro-labor legislation has come from government rather than from pressure of union leadership. In a number of fields—technical education for workers, workers' adult education, the conquest of illiteracy, the provision of accounting service and advice by the Department of Labor to unions that request it—the initial stimulus has come from official sources rather than from the unions. For example, the *exposición de motivos* of the legislation presented by the *Popular* party legislative group in the legislature in 1957 for the purpose of facilitating union participation in the governmental process;[8] or the cordial relationships that have always prevailed between the Governor and American liberal union leaders like Walter Reuther or David Dubinsky; or a characteristic public expression on these matters such as the Governor's speech of 1956 to the International Ladies Garment Workers Union[9]—all these show that the formal guarantees of union rights contained in the 1952 Constitution of the island are something more than an empty recognition of what is *au fait* in a modern liberal society. It is not unfair to say that the *Popular* government, although not ideologically left wing in any real sense, has clearly done far more for the working class of the society than did the former Socialist Party during the latter's shared tenure of power in the decade before 1940. After all, what could be expected from a "socialist" party whose leader, then Resident Commissioner in Washington, could denounce Governor Tugwell as a "sworn foe of free enterprise"? The decline of that party, leading to its final disappearance from the political scene as a serious contender for electoral support in 1948, shows how the Puerto Rican worker has been satisfied to accept the leadership of a political party—the Popular Democratic Party—which, like the Democratic Party in the United States, has always been pro-labor but never laborite.

The crucial question, then, does not concern any supposedly anti-labor bias on the official side. It revolves around the question, rather, of whether the official policies of economic growth, postulating an enlarging influence of American capital and a deepening reliance

THE ROLE OF LABOR

upon its continuing good will, will not make the Commonwealth government in the long run the prisoner, even though reluctantly, of that influence and good will. The official stand on the vital minimum wage issue already suggests that the government feels that it must follow the attitude of mainland capital rather than that of mainland labor. Not, indeed, that there is no merit in the arguments that are invoked to justify this stand. They have been sympathetically stated at length in the Nathan Report on *Evaluation of Minimum Wage Policy in Puerto Rico.* An unconditional application of the federal wage standards, granted the enormous difference between American and Puerto Rican productivity rates, would have the effect of wiping out a number of local enterprises and substantially curtailing employment. It was for this reason that the concept of a fixed minimum, embodied in the federal act of 1938, was in 1940 abandoned by Congress for Puerto Rico and replaced with a flexible system, based on an industry-committee procedure which would promulgate separate rates for each island industry engaged in interstate commerce. The federal legislation was accompanied at the same time by similar local legislation, thus providing the island with a dual system of wage revision, with all the additional protection that it means for the island worker. The slow rate of mechanization in the local industrial pattern in part justifies the absence of parity, for it will probably take a decade or more for that rate to begin to match the mainland rate and thereby justify the application in the island of the general federal minimums. To precipitate that application at the present time would have the effect of halting further industrialization. The Nathan Committee estimated, in 1955, that such a procedure would nearly double wage costs on the average in the local manufacturing industries and that the then ruling federal minimum of one dollar an hour "would be disastrous" for the Puerto Rican economy. Nor is it evident that the minimum wage operates in the island as it does on the mainland as merely a floor rather than a ceiling for wage rates; indeed, the available evidence—as in the significant proximity that prevails between average and legal minimum hourly earnings—strongly suggests that without the contribution of the wage committees, both federal and insular, within the period since 1940 wage levels would have remained drastically lower than their present position. If industrialization is to continue there can be no alternative policy to that of continuing the present flexible system for the foreseeable future.[10]

That may well be so. There are other factors to take into account, however, which perhaps preclude the permanency of the flexible system. Puerto Rico is not a "primitive" economy. It is, rather, a sophisticated economy more and more approximating to the mainland system in many respects. The arguments, accordingly, that justify the statutory repression of wage rates in an economic system like that, for example, of American Samoa, where the arbitrary imposition of anything like American wage rates upon a casual and almost wholly untrained labor force could only have unfortunate socio-cultural consequences,[11] can hardly apply to Puerto Rico. The price structure of the economy is almost wholly Americanized, so much so that federal employees domiciled in the territory enjoy a bonus as a means of offsetting a living-cost rate that is in fact even higher than that of the mainland. In effect, this means that the Puerto Rican worker, especially the urban worker, is expected to pay mainland commodity prices with sub-mainland wages. It is unlikely that he will be willing to accept this imbalance unendingly. And indeed it is actively expected that as the trade union movement grows in strength it will rapidly move towards a demand for the discontinuation of exemption from the federal statutory requirements in the realm of wage rates. The demand has already been openly stated as policy by both the local and mainland union movements. The public statement, indeed, of the AFL-CIO that the differential wage rate has made of the island a "refuge" for unconscionable employers and that, in the long run, the wage exemption system must cease,[12] can only promise an increasingly intensified drive by mainland labor to fight the device. What a weak local unionism cannot do a powerful mainland unionism can seriously hope to achieve; and the fact that one of the most aggressive recent campaigns for unionization within the island has been undertaken by the morally tainted Teamsters Union will have little effect in halting the process; a casual truck driver living on a hazardous contract system is hardly likely to be impressed by the reproduction in the leading island newspaper of the findings of the United States Senate Committee on labor malpractices. For if the national union movement is prepared to challenge differential wage returns even in "backward" territories like the Ryukyu Islands or special areas like the United States Canal Zone on the strength of the general principle that exemptions from the federal legislation are usually motivated by the desire of American firms to establish plants where they will be able to exploit a surplus labor force at substandard wage rates,[13] employers operating in Puerto Rico can hardly expect to be met with a less stringent attitude.

This union challenge, in turn, will be accompanied by a growing hostility on the part of mainland corporations which begin to feel the pinch of competition from trade rivals based on the island, competition certain to increase as an accelerated pace of mechanization and modernization in Puerto Rico inevitably results in a growing degree of direct competition with mainland products. So serious is this probability that the Nathan Report terms it "not a pleasant prospect to contemplate," which will have to be frankly faced sooner or later. "It is not an exaggeration to say," that Report concludes, "that Puerto Rico must either live with a continued or even rising mass unemployment or must capture a rising share of the mainland market among a limited but growing variety of products or the rate of migration to the mainland must increase substantially over past levels."[14] There are, as already noted, grave social objections to a reliance upon migration, while the tremendous consumer expectations already unleashed among the Puerto Rican consumer body cannot now be restrained except at the price of serious social and political disturbance. The inference is clear that the way ahead lies with enlarged industrialization. As this occurs, the mainland forces working against Puerto Rican economic and fiscal privilege will give a new importance to the role of labor in the local industrial revolution.

That process is indeed already well under way. It is there in the volume of criticism directed at the minimum wage procedures during the Congressional hearings of 1955, which resulted in the introduction of the device of the annual review, designed to accelerate the advance of the local wages to the federal level. It is there in the growing dissatisfaction in the island with the revisionary procedure as a whole, both insular and federal. The time periods between revisions have frequently been excessively lengthy (so important an industry as retail trade had no wage revision for a whole decade between 1945 and 1955). There has been a marked lag in some industries where minimums could have been increased more expeditiously without retarding industrialization; in this respect, the cycle of revisions undertaken by the Commonwealth Wage Board has tended to lag behind that undertaken by the federal jurisdiction.[15] A Commonwealth legislative committee, again, has drawn attention to the fact that the composition of the federal committees is so drawn up as to guarantee a permanent minority representation for local personnel, whether labor or capital[16] (although it might be added as a comment upon that observation that there is no guarantee that a locally dominated board would do better by the Puerto Rican worker than an outside-dominated one). What is certain in any case is that those industries which at present have a high labor cost in proportion to other costs in their enterprise will rapidly be driven (as competition from other low-cost areas, like Asia, increases) either to close down or accept radical technical changes designed to neutralize inevitable wage increases. The traditional needlework industry of the island provides, let it be noted, a classic illustration of this economic truth: the critical decline in its employment figures, from a total of 61,000 employees in 1950 to just under 4,000 in 1957, shows how an industry that has traditionally made its way for half a century with sweatshop conditions of a primitive "domestic industry" type becomes compelled to rationalize or die as its workers acquire adequate defense mechanisms against continuing exploitation.[17] In the long run, altogether, wage disparity will have to yield to tax exemption as the prime weapon in the armory of the Puerto Rican leadership in its effort to keep ahead in the competitive struggle of American economic federalism.

All this brings to the forefront the entire question of the Puerto Rican union movement, its policies, its structure, its self-image in the national future. It raises the question, too, of the attitude of the political and administrative rulers of the territory to the present and future functions of the movement. This second consideration is of paramount importance in itself, for the long reign of the *Populares* and the monolithic character of their politico-governmental machine means that the posture adopted by them on any question takes on a weight and authority denied to all alternative postures. It would be impossible, beyond doubt, for any government to destroy the organized labor movement, weak as it is, as was decisively proved by the failure of the effort of the local reactionary bureaucracy—retained, mistakenly, by the Americans after 1898—to break the new *Federación Libre* of those days. It would be equally impossible for a government leader to attempt to intimidate the union movement by a threat to deport a prominent union official, as Muñoz Rivera threatened Santiago Iglesias in 1900.[18] The contemporary problem concerns itself, rather, with the nature of prevailing views about the status and function of organized labor in an underdeveloped economy on the threshold of becoming a modern industrial democracy.

David Ross's article of 1957 (written in his capacity as consultant to the Economic Development Administration) may properly be regarded as a representative expression of the official view on the problem.[19] The article argues, basically, along three lines: (1) that trade unions belong fully only to advanced industrial societies; (2) that they generally stand in the way of economic progress since they are invariably opposed to technological innovation; and (3) that in any case so long as government adequately safeguards the workers' interests through minimum wage and other legislation little need for trade union activity arises. A mere glance at the monumental history of the Webbs on trade union history in England will show how illusory is the first proposition; for unions, historically, have been a feature of all societies based on a wage relationship between employer and employee. In the Caribbean itself, powerful unions have been in existence in the British islands since the great riots of 1937-1938, despite the fact that those islands still await the advent of full industrialization. Unions like the Barbados Workers Union, in fact, have been a power nucleus from which progressive political parties have emerged in a purely agricultural economy. In Puerto Rico itself the union movement goes back sixty years to the early efforts of the young Spanish anarchist Santiago Iglesias to unionize into a single whole the embryonic workers' clubs which were granted permission to exist, under military supervision, by the Spanish authorities. With the legal recognition of unions finally secured in 1902, the path was cleared for what became for the next two decades a running war between the unions on the one side and the government, the police and the American sugar corporations on the other. Between 1918 and 1932 more than 130 separate unions came into existence with a total membership of more than 40,000, covering practically every sector of the economy. They were basically immature organizations, vexed by all of the problems—described by Dr. Rawle Farley in his pamphlet on *Trade Unions and Politics in the Caribbean*—that plague embryonic unions in a quasi-industrial economic order. But they were there; and they served a real purpose. It is true that the present-day unions—to take up David Ross's second point—the stevedores and the sugar workers for example, have steadily opposed the introduction of more efficient work methods, so that the docks of San Juan and Ponce and Mayagüez remain woefully inadequate for serving the vital sea lanes between the island and the mainland ports. But worker attitudes are always a function of the employment environment. So long as full employment is a utopian dream the worker will justifiably suspect that technological innovations will mean job losses. Nor has much effort been made to seek out his enthusiastic cooperation; labor-saving devices, when they have been introduced— as in the case of the "turnabout" trailer boats in the docks in 1958— have been introduced without previous consultation with the unions involved and without any effort to educate the worker in the full meaning of their installment. The Commonwealth government has sought to cushion the impact of such devices by its compensation legislation; but the unions have indicated that they consider compensation for a mere limited time period insufficient to meet the earning losses involved in worker displacement.[20] What is needed at this point is a conscious search for ways and means of giving the worker, as distinct from the technical expert and the administrative official, some real consultative function in the industrialization program. It is heartening to note that the legislative majority of the local

House of Representatives has willingly recognized the need, and has insisted that there must grow up a more direct and daily relationship between the government bureaucracy and the electorate. But little has been done to implement the principle through institutional forms, and the temper of the administrative group, as distinct from that of the legislative group, tends still to be that of a technocratic determinism which is merely impatient with the irritating conservatism of the unions and their leadership. Nor should it be overlooked that the worker and his cause become the targets of frequent public homilies and admonitions while the comparable conservatism of the older middle-class professions is noted, if noted at all, in tones of muted discretion. There is evidence, finally, to suggest that there is a growing temptation to accept the new American myth that the new technology of automation will involve self-generating social benefits without recourse to human volition or social control, and that it will be likely to discover as ready an audience in Puerto Rico as in the mainland centers.[21] Such an attitude, if widespread enough, could be fatal to working class hopes.

Nor is it a persuasive argument to say, in the third place, that trade unions lose much of their value in a labor-oriented governmental program. That sort of argument rests upon a narrow utilitarian conception of the trade union as a mere defense mechanism of the worker in industrial relations. It fails to appreciate the more positive function of the trade union in modern society as at once the social fulcrum of the worker's industrial life and the potential source of a burgeoning professional ethic in the world of labor. Ross's viewpoint here is that of the economic consultant who sees the union only as an unwelcome intruder in his own sphere of economic engineering. But that engineering by no means holds the complete answer to the present discontents of the Puerto Rican worker. It has as yet failed to exorcise the scourge of mass unemployment. It holds out the glittering promise of handsome returns by 1975 for the average Puerto Rican family; but the skeptic is obliged to point here to a tendency towards excessive optimism in the statistical prognostications of the government planners as they seek to prophesy the future family income level or the future savings habits of domiciled corporations. The statutory defense of wage levels, again, ceases to have any meaning as soon as a particular industry reaches the minimum wage level—already the case with a number of industries (even by 1955 the then current federal minimum figures already applied to the banking, insurance, finance, radio broadcasting, and dry docks industries).[22] As soon as this happens, any further advances must come from collective bargaining processes, a job which will increasingly devolve upon the unions. And even where the federal wage committees, as already noted, tend to be more activist than the Commonwealth committees, that can only be at best an uncertain reed to lean on; and the Finley study of the record of the National Labor Relations Board in the years after 1952 amply documents the growing conservatism of that agency as its members have come to see their function as the protection of management rather than as the defense of the employee and thereby to betray, if unconsciously, the original intention of the New Deal legislation.[23]

Once, then, the union movement is seen as a social force inescapably concerned with the total good of the society of which it is an integral part it becomes pertinent to emphasize the larger dimensions of the Puerto Rican transformation. For not even the most ardent champion of the Commonwealth government—save perhaps E. P. Hanson—could propose the thesis that its programs have fully solved the social ills, old and new, that plague the society and that increasingly become the natural concern of a socially conscious union leadership. There is the breakdown of agriculture and of the way of life that accompanies it. The ravages of that breakdown in the private sector have already been noted; it is enough to add that in certain areas it has gone so far as to threaten the re-emergence of the old type of the "company shop" whereby the small-town merchant, working in league with some of the sugar *centrales,* reduces the sugar-cane worker to the status of a debt-ridden "captive client."[24] In the public sector there is the failure of the Land Authority to obtain for the agricultural laborer the "new deal" it originally set out to accomplish; the recent rash of complaints on the part of its employees in its "proportional profit" farms in Vega Baja and Barceloneta on a whole series of problems ranging from the Authority's use of its reserve funds to its policies governing the use of common pasture grounds indicate that the manager-employee relationships in such a public enterprise are not much healthier than those prevailing in private concerns;[25] and there has been, beyond that, widespread and illegal diversion of lands originally assigned to the agricultural unemployed to the benefit of professional people and even members of the legislature.[26] Dr. Elena Padilla's more general study of the land program concludes that the profit-sharing plantations have not decisively bettered the cane worker's living standards and that the employees have failed to acquire a sense of participation either in the ownership or the management of the enterprises.[27] Indeed, if care is not taken, the idea of the "proportional profit" farm, like that of the land cooperatives before it under the old Puerto Rico Reconstruction Administration, will be allowed to die from legislative apathy and will become, as a United States Department of Agriculture expert has said of that earlier concept, a great social experiment abandoned without a recording of scientific data and therefore incapable of becoming a basis for sound judgment for future planning. This field in itself constitutes an enormous challenge for organized labor.

And of course there are others. There is a legion of problems relating to the public health and social welfare fields of vital concern to the Puerto Rican worker. Only a minority of the total population— just under 23 percent—are covered by health insurance schemes, whether of a group non-profit character like Blue Cross or of a restricted subscription membership like the Association of Teachers plan. The record of the Commonwealth, especially in the provision of public health centers, has been remarkably enlightened. Even so, an authoritative report has recently pointed out that the Puerto Rican sick get only one third, in terms of expenses that are paid for them, of what the continental United States hospital patient obtains; that an ill-paid and insufficiently trained nursing staff is inequitably distributed throughout the island, so that metropolitan San Juan enjoys a nurse for each 400 inhabitants while a small town like Orocovis has only a nurse for each 11,500 inhabitants; and that in general the majority of Puerto Ricans do not have available to them medical-hospital services that are safe, well cared for, well equipped and sufficiently staffed.[28] The care of the mentally sick remains in an almost primitive stage, a fact made all the worse by the existence of a public opinion that has traditionally seen no shame or humiliation in the public display of mental and physical deformity. There is as yet no public clinic system, after the fashion of the psychiatric ward of New York's Bellevue Hospital, to which attempted suicides can be directed for help, despite the fact that the suicide rate in the island has always been high, with an alarmingly high percentage, by world standards, among younger people. One happy exception, perhaps, to this generalization has been the remarkable transformation during the last few years of the old insular insane asylum in Rio Piedras from an almost medieval institution (known to the public for years as the *manicomio,* the madhouse) into an up-to-date psychiatric hospital. The condition of the insular prisons is probably not much better than what it is in most of the American states; at least a former leading official of the system has testified that there was (in 1959) no program of prisoner rehabilitation and no really successful program of vocational occupational training for prisoners.[29] The science of child care, again, is only just beginning; and two visiting American experts have drawn attention to the gross deficiencies of the insular public health authorities with relation to prevailing policies concerning the care of delinquent children in industrial homes and the more general problem of juvenile delinquency.[30] The care of the aged, finally, leaves much to be desired. The proportion of aged people who benefit from the rare program such as the rehabilitation program of the Vocational Rehabilitation Division of the Department of Education is pitifully small; chronic ailments long unattended too often make of the average older Puerto Rican a sickly and complaining person; while, on the more general level, he is puzzled and bewildered by rapid social changes which gradually rob him of the status of the venerable patriarch afforded him by the older cultural milieu, not to mention the cultural loss involved in the entertainment-revolution whereby radio and television have tended to replace the older habit of vigorous conversation in the town *farmacia,* the neighborhood store, and the *plaza.*[31]

These problems are only examples of what affects the Puerto Rican worker at every step that he makes. His own institutions, accordingly, must at once move to deal more actively with them and to claim a right to do so. The union must be seen not simply as an instrument of defense against the employer but, more positively, by members and outsiders alike, as a social movement to which no social problem is alien. The movement must accept as a natural fact a position where its leaders speak on all national problems as of right; it is symptomatic that at present no labor leader thus speaks for labor as someone like Jorge Bird or Salvador Caro speaks for business and as Chancellor Benítez speaks for education. It is no belittlement of the Puerto Rican economic planners to say that, as a type, they have been far too much cast in the mold of benevolent paternalists willingly to accept the positive role of the trade union. Their emphasis, natural enough perhaps, has been upon the physical and economic facets of industrial change, and too little attention has been paid to the social, cultural, and psychological consequences of the fierce penetration of a quasi-folk society by the institutions of the most perfected industrial capitalism of the modern world. There has been almost a temptation at times to dismiss such attention as the quaint preserve of the university intelligentsia. The little man, as a consequence, has had small chance to participate in the changes so deeply affecting him. He has been a passive recipient, not an active collaborator. There has been little planned effort, as Professor Charles Rosario has pointed out, to educate him into an understanding of the socio-cultural results of industrial change, or to replace obsolete values with new ones that might help him, functionally, in integrating himself into the new order of things.[32] And even where the trade union has been accepted by the policy makers it has been accepted less as a partner than as a ward. Even that acceptance should not be taken too much for granted; it is well known, for example, that the attitude of at least one former cabinet member, the head of the Water Resources Authority, was one of outright hostility to the union, the Electrical Industry Workers, operating within his department, despite the fact that the collective bargaining agreement between the union and the authority goes back to 1942. The government as a whole, in fact, holds to the idea that collective bargaining potentially endangers the public safety and therefore has no place in government offices. It is only necessary, in rebuttal of that view, to point out the illogicality of a position that denies the right of collective bargaining, as well as the right to strike, to employees in government departments and grants it, by way of Articles 17 and 18 of the insular Constitution, to employees in government agencies operating, in effect, as quasi-private concerns (which latter include, in Puerto Rico, areas of the national life as vital as transport, electrical energy, and water supplies).

The wider social significance of the union movement has thus tended to be overlooked. It is characteristic, to take one instance only, that the article on "Labor's Role in Industrialization" contributed by Professor Rottenberg to the 1953 issue of the *Annals* of the American Academy of Political and Social Science—an issue devoted to a eulogistic account of the Puerto Rican democracy—should contain only a single passing reference to trade unions and utterly neglect the wider horizons of potential union contribution to the national life of that democracy.[33] The bias has been typical of most of the economic experts and consultants who have perennially invaded the island; few of them have possessed the larger look that comprehends the full sociology of the economic process. It is probably wrong, of course, to charge the leadership of the Planning Board, as one critic has done, with the assumption that "all problems are economic ones" and that the social problems accompanying economic change may be dismissed as "apparently trivial."[34] It is nonetheless interesting to note that, in defending themselves by drawing attention to the literature that they have put out in recent years on those social problems, the Planning Board leaders list a series of documents that include nothing on the trade union movement in the industrialization process.[35] Even the Governor's cherished scheme of "Operation Serenity," designed to insulate the Puerto Rican workman against the corroding materialism of a fully Americanized society, could become distorted, in hands less humanistic than his, into simply a means of marshaling a docile and malleable labor army for the use of the business class. And even accepted at the value placed upon it by the Governor's own sympathetic nature it seems hypocritical to request the Puerto Rican proletarian to dedicate himself to the "serene life" before he can even afford a good single daily meal, and especially when he has before him the rather elaborate ostentation with which his government officialdom conducts its own social functions.

All this means a challenge to the territorial officialdom. But it means an even more serious challenge to the insular labor movement in its present condition. For, as a movement, it is weak, disunited, immature. Its leadership is almost wholly untrained, for it has been throughout the province of labor lawyers often unscrupulous in their search for handsome fees. Both at the local and territorial levels the union organizations have become so much the instrument of labor politicians in their struggle for political spoils that apathy rather than enthusiasm tends to be the overriding tone of the rank and file membership. Effective organization has been made difficult, in the agricultural sector, by the peculiar character of sugar cane work, for being generally unskilled and marked by discontinuity in employment—there is the annual agony of the *tiempo muerto*, the off season when workers are laid off—it seriously inhibits the value of weapons, like the strike, that are more effective in an industrial setting. The remark of a Puerto Rican sugar cane worker—"A strike is like war: each man must be for himself"[36]—indicates the attitude union organizers have had to face in attempting to construct a united front against the employer interest. Peculiar difficulties also beset unions in the new industrial plants, for it is not easy to unionize a factory whose owners can threaten to leave the island if labor costs increase, and much of the more recent work of the Ladies Garment Workers organizers in the textile and clothing plants have been frustrated by the mere presence of the threat. It is not surprising that as late as 1947 the island's agricultural workers, aside from the cane areas, had hardly been touched by unionism, for too much of the work in coffee and tobacco was still performed by *agregados* or ambulant *peón* labor; nor any less surprising that by 1958 only some 27 of the 455 new industrial plants had been organized and only some 35 percent of the total labor force belonged to a trade union.

The relationship between the island's union movement and that of the United States has been something of a mixed blessing. There has been real aid from the parent body, ever since the American Federation of Labor responded in 1900 to the appeal of Santiago Iglesias for help by setting up a special fund for union work in the newly acquired territory.[37] But the aid has been inevitably accompanied by the intrusion into the island of the organizational rivalries that have historically divided the American labor movement, with the added consequence that the local movement has been fragmentalized into warring factions, the *Federación Libre de Trabajadores* and the *Confederación General de Trabajadores*, affiliated, respectively, to the American Federation of Labor and the Congress of Industrial Organizations. Their subsequent merger into the single *Federación del Trabajo de Puerto Rico*, following the historic merger of the two mainland organizations, has been a fictitious rather than a real unity, reflecting mainland rather than island developments. Even this unity has been violently strained by the decision of James Hoffa and his colleagues of the Teamsters Union in 1959 to convert Puerto Rico into a stage from which to deploy a war of revenge upon the AFL-CIO for their earlier expulsion from that body. More lately the divisive tendency has been accelerated by the rising debate on the proper function of the mainland unions in the island. There has grown up a feeling that those unions exhibit features—failure to translate contracts and union constitutions into Spanish, excessive preoccupation with the issue of Communism, the practice of "carrying the dues north"— which are inimical to Puerto Rican interests, and the feeling has resulted in the creation of movements like the *Central Unica* and the *Sindicato Obrero Insular* designed to combat the "invasion" of the mainland unions. The ambition, in some ways, is laudable. But a false nationalism may too easily beguile the Puerto Rican worker into the assumption, for which there is very little foundation in fact, that labor "czars" of his own kind will treat him more generously than the American variant. He might well recall, indeed, that his greatest leader was the Santiago Iglesias who, as a young Spanish traveler, stopped off at San Juan in 1896 for what was originally intended as a short visit and remained to become, as his autobiography testifies, the tremendous organizer of the cane workers against the American sugar corporations.

It is clear enough that Puerto Rican unionism faces grave demands upon its gifts of energy and leadership. It must set out to unionize fully the labor force. It must make its own contribution to the achievement of a full-employment economy: the unemployment rate oscillates, to take the figures for 1960, between 8.3 percent and 15.6 percent. It must convert the rights of labor specifically guaranteed in the Bill of Rights of the local Constitution into realities for the entire working-class population. The principle of the union shop, as guaranteed in the model contract of 1960 between the Water Resources Authority and the electrical and irrigation industry workers, must be made to cover all undertakings. Employment practices that penalize the Puerto Rican worker, such as the tendency of San Juan hotels and night clubs to give preference to continental artists, must be challenged by the local union force. The maritime unions have a duty to join in the effort, hitherto deplorably unsuccessful, to put an end to the practice of "runaway" ships that pay substandard wages by registration in low-standard countries including, in the Caribbean area, Honduras and Panama. In the home field, again, the union movement must put an end, if possible, to the divisions that cripple its capacity to contribute to the larger national life; the fusion in 1960 of the four dockworkers' unions into a single district council, with the general organizer of the International Longshoremens Association acting as its coordinator, is a step in the right direction. It must, more generally, build up its own statistical and educational services, as the more progressive mainland unions have done. Up to now the appearance of union representatives at wage committee hearings in San Juan has not been impressive, being characterized by vague and imprecise evidence painfully reflecting the absence of economic data and statistical knowledge. The movement, in fact, needs a whole new corps of trained leaders. The work of the Labor Relations Institute at the national university deserves a reference in this connection, for under its succession of able directors it has worked wonders in the field of union education, not least of all in organizing field trips of selected students to neighboring Caribbean countries. It is heartening to note the recent gift of the Ladies Garment Workers to the Institute, designed to create scholarships in the field of union leadership. Trained leadership of course will have to go hand in hand with applied research on the labor movement as a whole, a field relatively neglected by both the American and the Puerto Rican social scientist. The monograph published in 1947, and based on a survey undertaken in 1941-1942, on incomes and expenditures of wage earners in the island, under the financial sponsorship of the Work Projects Administration, was in fact the first island-wide survey of its kind ever undertaken in the American regime; and Puerto Ricans still await comparable research in more up-to-date form on working-class income benefits from the industrialization program, as well as on things like union structure, social background of union leadership, and so on. An expanding program along these lines should do much in the long run to supplant the present type of labor boss who wields an almost unipersonal authority in his union and whose power is made all the more unchallengeable by the fact that there is hardly a single union in the island in which the electoral process is safeguarded by the method of the secret vote.

The movement must adapt its thought processes to the demands, technological and social, of an industrializing economy. This means a new and rational attitude to mechanization, work-output problems, labor productivity, even labor-management relations, the latter of which incidentally stand in danger of becoming the monopoly of mushrooming management counseling firms and the mumbo-jumbo of their managerialist "philosophy." It must recruit the new social groups of white-collar and blue-collar workers into its ranks, the employees, for example, of the new American-style drugstores, supermarkets and fashion shops (like the Franklin chain) that are growing up in San Juan and the suburban areas. This requires, in turn, a healthy alliance between manual and clerical workers; the passage, in the 1958 convention of one of the local dockworkers' unions, of a resolution taking note of the alleged effort of the Commonwealth government to "break" unions in the governmental structure, especially in the controversial Department of Education, was a welcome sign of a burgeoning sense of interoccupational unity.[38] There must come, at some point, a real effort to create an independent labor press, at present nonexistent. That deficiency must be seen in the light of the fact that, as a trade union leader who is also head of the Evangelical Council of Puerto Rico has testified, neither of the island's two leading Spanish-language newspapers can be relied upon to give a fair hearing to the voice of labor.[39] On the contrary, they specialize in sensationalist reportage of the more violent scenes of strike actions; and union officials have recently protested against the persistent press campaign which seeks to persuade the reading public that the wage increases, minor enough, permitted by the minimum wage law and its successive amendments will mean economic disaster, a generalization at once vicious and unjustified when it is remembered that the closures and sales to foreign interests of the sugar *centrales* over the last forty years have been caused not by excessive wage labor costs but by the readiness of their owners to sell out at handsome profit rates.[40] All in all, Puerto Rican labor must turn more and more to itself and its own genius to defend working class interests. Its leadership requires a professional competence so far generally lacking; that is why, to come back to the minimum wage method, labor representation in the federal committees organized by the federal Wage and Hour Administration is defective because the great majority of Puerto Rican labor leaders do not possess the requisite command of the English language, while in the local committees organized by the Commonwealth Minimum Wage Board the defense of union interests frequently falls, by default, into the hands of the "public interest" members since the unions, unlike the employers, are unable to afford the services of accountants, business agents, lawyers and economists.[41]

Organized labor, this is to say, must begin to seek out a genuinely independent status for itself. The weaknesses of the contemporary movement spring in large measure from its willingness to lean heavily upon government aid and patronage for far too long, so that its

capacity for virile and self-sufficient growth has been seriously compromised. From the very beginning it surrendered too easily to the
temptation, endemic in all Latin American societies, of becoming
the ward of a bogus social and political radicalism in the *peronista*
fashion. The original intention of following the Gompers strategy of
using the labor vote as a means of exerting pressure upon the established political groupings, of "rewarding friends and punishing enemies," was very early (in 1902) yielded up to an electoral alliance
with the new *Unionista* party; and when that failed it was replaced
with the establishment in 1915 of a separate Socialist Workers' Party
which, in its turn, had become so successful by 1936 that it was,
electorally speaking, the largest single political entity in the island.
With the decline of that party, the habit of political affiliation was
transferred after that date to the new *Popular* party, so much so that
the new *Confederación General de Trabajadores* formed in 1940 was
nothing much more than the union annex of the *Popular* organization. That new union, in its turn, however, was sacrificed, like its
predecessors, to the demands of politics, as the expulsion in 1946 of
its pro-independence wing sufficiently showed. This remains the general pattern still. It might perhaps change, however, with the more
recent arrival in the island of the big aggressive mainland unions such
as the Teamsters, the Seafarers International, and the Ladies Garment
Workers whose representatives, being paid and appointed by the
mainland offices, neither depend upon local politics nor seek to make
a livelihood out of it.

It is true enough that this general practice of reliance upon the
professional politician and the party organization has in large measure
been enormously beneficial to the Puerto Rican worker. Apart from
the minimum wage legislation there has been a wider range of protective legislation covering topics from child labor to industrial safety.
The principle of collective bargaining has been vastly stimulated and
aided by the free conciliation and arbitration service provided by the
Commonwealth Department of Labor; in 1958-1959 alone some
57 percent of the 100,000 union members in the economy were
affected by contracts in which that service had intervened.[42] At the
same time, even so, the more far-reaching effects of this dependence
have been somewhat less constructive. Labor unity has been sacrificed
to political maneuver, as the unhappy history of the *Confederación
General de Trabajadores* from 1940 until its dissolution in 1954
showed. Union leaders have been tempted to devote more energy
to congenial politicking than to union work. The record of the late
Ernesto Ramos Antonini as a public figure bears out that truth, for
the resignation of that important *Popular* leader from active union

work in 1951 was a tacit admission that there were serious difficulties lying in the way of anyone seeking to combine the two roles of career politician and labor organizer. This, however, is the exception and not the rule; and organized labor in the island has a long way to go before it can play the American role of a powerful pressure group or the English role of a strong partner within a political party of its choice. The result is that events that seem, on their face, to favor labor frequently turn out to be its undoing. Even victories at the polls sometimes turn out to be sterile. That has certainly been the case in the past. By a cruel paradox, indeed, the electoral success of the Socialist Party spelled the doom of a strong unionism. The remark of Santiago Iglesias to his followers—that it would be better to act in response to realities rather than see all destroyed for the sake of principles that cannot be put into practice[43]—meant, in effect, an acceptance of the political pragmatism which throughout all Puerto Rican politics has been used to justify the sweet smell of political power, the *turno en el poder*. The struggle for public office, in the words of one observer, became transformed into a contagious disease.[44] Too much of a genuine working-class program was lost through making too many concessions to that struggle. This is why today the greatest ambition of a union leader is to become a small town mayor or, even better, the mayor of a large city, like Carlos Juan Cintrón, the one-time mayor of Ponce. The final goal, of course, is a seat in the legislature, like Hipólito Marcano in the insular Senate. This is why, too, as union and political leadership become at once fused and confused, the objectives of the union side tend to lose out to those of the political side when a conflict between them arises; a case in point is that of mechanization, where the stand of the *Popular* party chieftains is difficult to reconcile with that of the unions. This is why, again, innovations of any kind are likely to come from the government and not from the unions; why, for example, all presently available evidence on union corrupt practices, as on the docks, comes from reports of legislative committee inquiries and not from a union movement ready and eager to cleanse its own Augean stables.[45]

This leads to a second point. Some deep thought has to be given to an entirely fresh examination of the relationships that should obtain between unionism and politics. It would be fatal of course to copy the American practice of a radical divorce between the two. Labor ought not to isolate itself from political life on the basis of a false analogy with American conditions. It must seek, on the contrary, to create its own independent political expression in which there will emerge a more equitable balance between the industrial and the political wings. This in any case is almost sure to take place sooner or later as the quiet reorientation of the *Populares* towards the interests and outlook of the island's business and professional groups makes it unlikely that their leadership will ever advance forward to a radical collectivism. The American problem has been that of unions too little concerned with politics; the Puerto Rican problem has been that of unions too much concerned with the less pleasing aspects of politics. From now on, every effort to divide the insular labor movement by splits engineered on grounds of political strategy in the interests of the professional politicians must be resisted; there is much to be learned from the failure of the Commonwealth government over the last few years to oust the Teamsters from the territory by lending quiet official aid to the rival AFL-CIO Seafarers International Union. It must be recognized that even public ownership, as in the case of the *Popular* agrarian reform, fails unless it is accompanied by the planned participation of the workers in the managerial direction of the enterprises, something that has not been attempted in the insular industrial life despite the fact that the cooperative movement in the island goes back to 1873. The individual worker must be enabled to gain the fullest measure of public recognition as the backbone of the society, a recognition still frustrated by a social value structure which has not ceased to identify manual labor with social degradation. For if, before 1898, the average Puerto Rican proletarian would have deemed it an enormous pretension on his part to claim public office for himself or for his fellows,[46] this sense of apologetic inferiority has only been mitigated, in the sixty years that have followed, to allow that privilege to the elite of his leaders who climb to social recognition, via political power, on his back. When, too, any of his kind before 1898—like Ramón Morell Campos—had the honor of being presented in the socially exclusive *Ateneo* it was only on the condition that he joined in the applause of the work of the men regarded by *Ateneo* values as the national poets and patriots.[47] So today a worker usually gains political prestige only at the price of allowing himself to be absorbed into one of the political groups enjoying a practical monopoly within a rigid electoral framework.

If all this is to change there must be finally a revolution of doctrine within the ranks of labor. For it has never really sought as a movement to acquire a solid theoretical foundation or to anticipate the society that is being formed around it in terms of understanding and not merely manipulation. Even with Santiago Iglesias, there was nothing much beyond an eloquent confusion of disparate and ill-digested ideas gathered indiscriminately from Marxism, Spanish syndicalism, and American labor of the Gompers style. This fact probably accounted for the bizarre circumstance whereby the early Socialist

Workers Party of the island could affiliate to the American party of Daniel de Leon without knowing hardly anything of that body's Marxist position and believing vaguely that "socialism" was something akin to the moral teachings of the historical Jesus.[48] The subsequent growth of the working-class movement in its later alliance with the *Popular* party added nothing more precise in the way of ideology, for even in the early days of that party, before it had irrevocably committed itself, sometime after 1946, to an economic program tied to the American business economy, it had been not so much socialist in its orientation as New Dealish, with changes adapted to the local Puerto Rican environment. All in all, this ideological eclecticism, however much it made political relationships with Washington easier, had the effect of isolating Puerto Ricans from the Latin American progressive movements. It is suggestive that the only hint of Communist ideological influence throughout the period of American rule comes from occasional pamphlets written by obscure island essayists now quite forgotten—the various pamphlets, for example, of José A. Lanauze Rolón, including such titles as *El Fracaso del Nuevo Trato*, *El Mal de los Muchos Hijos*, and *Porqué somos Communistas*. It is equally suggestive that the launching of the new monthly magazine *Combate* in 1958 followed by the establishment of the Institute for Political Education, symbolizing new trends of thought and action in Latin American and Pan-Caribbean radical liberalism, should have been centered in San José, Costa Rica, and not in San Juan. Puerto Rican labor, if it is to become an intellectually and morally creative force, must seek consciously to remedy this situation. It is not enough that it should undertake various social services for its members, although this is a laudable enterprise, as the establishment by the local Transport Workers Union of the first workers' hospital in the island shows. It must seek, in addition, to establish the first principles of a new society lest it become, like most unions in American life, nothing more than just another pressure group in a society where pressure has largely replaced principle as the mainspring of the national experience. If it fails in that task, it will have little choice but to remain the weak recipient of an insular managerial revolution espoused and controlled by the emergent alliance of "big business" and "big government."

Class and Community

INDUSTRIAL revolutions, historically, create new social classes. They mobilize new social energies. They set up new lines of class demarcation. They may brutalize a society because they fail to replace the culture styles they destroy with healthy new ones, as was the case notoriously with early Victorian England. They may add new impetus to forces that have already commenced the process of community disorganization, such as the rural depopulation and cycles of migration that have created in Puerto Rico, as in most other "underdeveloped" agrarian economies throughout the modern world, the vast disease of urban rootlessness. They stimulate the rise of urbanism and thereby contribute to the decline of the countryside typical of the impact of industrial capitalism on all of the Western societies. They may be accompanied, as in Russia after 1917 or India after 1947, by a social ethic that attempts to make man the master rather than the servant of the new social relations in which he is involved; or they may simply let the new acquisitive instincts released by applied science and higher income levels have their head. In any case, there is a new ferment generated in the body politic which plays havoc with established personal and social relationships.

Puerto Rico has been in many ways a microcosm of many of these changes—so much so indeed that its people have become the research object of a whole corps of American social and cultural anthropologists. Probably no modern people have been placed under the sociological microscope so relentlessly and so arbitrarily as those of this small Caribbean island society, or provided so much opportunity for the composition of solemn doctoral dissertations by American university graduates. A vast corpus of specialist literature exists, as a consequence, upon practically every facet of insular society and culture: familial organization, the patterns of courtship, systems of land tenure, the ecology of production, culture change, population trends, market organization, social psychology, child rearing, and so on. No student of Puerto Rican life can afford to ignore the literature, for in many ways it has replaced speculation with scientific research as the basis of the controversial debate on change and culture that presently agitates the society. At the same time, the student will do well to enter at least two caveats as he examines the literature. The first is that there are not wanting signs that the average Puerto Rican citizen, as he becomes more and more exposed to the pretentious questionnaire and interview techniques of the sociologist, begins shrewdly to suspect that it all amounts to an academic version of imperialist condescension and that its inarticulate assumption is that his "peculiar" or "abnormal" characteristics must be exhaustively catalogued before they yield to a higher, that is, American form of "civilization." The second caveat concerns the intrinsic character of the research. Much of it belongs to the category of fruitless and sterile surveys that are so endemic among modern government agencies and academic institutions. Much of it is the sort of solemn "research" that laboriously proves the obvious, or rephrases it in an incomprehensible mumbo-jumbo of pseudo-scientific terminology, or carefully gathers together, mainly through the art of exhaustive footnoting, the findings of other workers in the vineyard.

So the pungent realities of Puerto Rican life become frozen into arid concepts such as the "change-prone person," or the "folk-urban continuum," or "status perspective and achievement," or "interpersonal competence." Or, even worse, the realities are deployed in the construction of vast theoretical structures of sociological theology, usually concerned with the methodology of social investigation, which are deceptively imposing. It is only necessary to compare the cold scientism of the volume composed by the team of Columbia University cultural anthropologists in 1956, *The People of Puerto Rico*, with the warm humanism of a volume like Edith Clarke's *My Mother Who Fathered Me,* which attempts to undertake a similar inquiry into the subcultures of Jamaican rural society, to appreciate what this means. In the latter book the method of scientific inquiry does not stand in the way of showing the Jamaican people as they live now; in the former volume, the method—culminating in a pretentious effort to construct "Hypotheses of a Developmental or Diachronic Typology" —becomes almost the central purpose, with consequences essentially dehumanizing. We obtain a system, we do not see a portrait, of the Puerto Rican people. We see social categories rather than persons. Individuals lose their unique identity as they become "interviewees." The truth portrayed in this style of literature, however real in itself, is, as it were, statistical rather than poetic. The impalpable congeries of the hopes and fears of the different groups of the society have somehow escaped sympathetic attention; and it comes as a surprise to note a reference to a source as unscientific as a novel by Evelyn Waugh in an otherwise characteristic academic discussion of problems of Puerto Rican population control.[1]

There has been nothing in the insular history, it goes without saying, to prevent the island from becoming a class society, of the Spanish conservative-bureaucratic type in the first instance and of the American liberal-rationalistic type in the second. Neither process, Hispanization or Americanization, has of course resulted in an exact photostatic copy of the metropolitan way of life in the colonial society. But in both cases there existed political and social attitudes in certain of the insular groupings which assumed the desirability of such an end result. In both cases those elite groups actively espoused that purpose. The central drive in social and political life under Spain came from the Spanish loyalist group fleeing from the South American Nationalist revolutions; although their number in San Juan was small (Colonel Flinter put the maximum figure in 1833 at seven thousand) they were so much above the average of the population that they established their position of leadership with ease. They were reinforced by the Spanish emigrants from Spain itself, and even after the transfer of sovereignty to the United States the monthly arrival of young Spanish emigrants—the *gallegos,* as they were indiscriminately termed by Puerto Ricans—seeking clerical work in the mercantile houses of their compatriots was an event on the San Juan docks. Under American rule, in turn, the control of the educational and political relations of the island by Americans for the first four decades of the century guaranteed that American ideas about the sanctity of business enterprise and its concomitant class structure based upon income inequality would prevail without question. The trustees of that process today are the 51,000 "continentals": Puerto Rican residents who have been born in the continental United States, and who now live in the island.

The class structure of contemporary Puerto Rico derives from that background. At the top there is the class, Spanish and to some degree aristocratic in origin but rapidly becoming Americanized in its social habits and expectations, of the prominent San Juan wealthy families. Their economic foundation is that of ownership and management in commerce, finance, government service, and the more modern professions. There is as yet no directory of their names, but they would expect to be included in the Social Register which it has been reported is about to be launched in San Juan by a young Spanish social adventurer in search, apparently, of a lucrative career. As executives and officials, the menfolk of the class are enmeshed in a hierarchical business structure of which the positions of final command are invariably located in the United States, so that a high premium is placed upon a fluent usage of English, a generous hospitality towards the visiting chieftains of the American company headquarters and, in general, a sympathetic understanding and perhaps personal emulation of the values and habits of the American business class. Many of them, indeed, are "new men" who earlier accommodated themselves willingly to that general process as American cash-crop and marketing capitalism began to take hold of the economy, especially in the sugar kingdom; and their way was made easier by the reluctance of the "old" families, especially in the coffee and tobacco regions, to change their mode of life, families who resisted the new orientations indeed with the comforting rationalization that sugar was "American" and coffee "Spanish." The price of this sort of resistance can be high, as was the case with the older Spanish-type importing houses of commercial San Juan, for it has meant their gradual replacement with the new chain outlets and supermarkets that have not been hampered by outmoded concepts of business paternalism. For the entrepreneur who has been ready to adjust, however, the rewards have been plentiful. It means, in housing, a luxurious residence in the elegant Condado-Miramar section of San Juan and possibly a weekend vacation house at the beach or in the mountains. It means status and esteem in the elaborate complex of the best circles and prominence in the social events that are extensively reported in the social pages of *El Mundo*. The children of this class will be educated in the high-class private schools that stress English as a preparation for the later collegiate education in, overwhelmingly, American colleges; in 1956, out of a total of 115 men of the parental generation in this class group, 56 had attended American schools as compared to only 12 from Spanish schools and 32 from local Puerto Rican schools.[2] Not the least crippling of the social consequences that this entails is the inability of the local state university, so far, to obtain from this group the moral support and the financial endowments it has every right to expect from its members.

The womenfolk of the class constitute a noticeable group in themselves. As young ladies, the *pacto de amor* that unites them to the eligible young men of their class or, frequently, to the junior officers of the American Naval Base or to the Ivy League escorts they have met in their residence at the North American finishing schools, will receive its proper publicity in the island press. For many of them, their social debut will take place at the ball with which the select *Casa de España,* founded in 1934, celebrates the anniversary of its foundation. The social launching will also include initiation into one of the snob sororities—and that many of those bodies are in no way connected with the educational institutions of the society indicates sufficiently that they do not even pretend to visit any embarrassing mental exertions upon their devotees. There is the usual trip to Europe, usually with parents; for, as the planned group tours annually sponsored by the University indicate, Puerto Rican youth has not yet learned, as its American and English counterparts have learned, the habit of undertaking that great adventure alone. As wives and junior matrons, the women of this group will participate in the sort of conspicuous social unemployment that well-to-do women everywhere indulge in. Clubs like the *Hijas Católicas* or the *Club Cívico de Damas* or the *Unión de Mujeres Americanas* exist to provide essentially secular activities, such as the organization of benevolent charity schemes or the entertainment of a visiting Latin American artist like Pedro Vargas or a talk by the local Spanish Consul, for their members. Much of all this, it will be appreciated, is a feminine-oriented way of life that reflects, as distinct from its American counterpart, a marked preference for Hispanic recreation values, an easygoing sense of duty to the family household, an uninhibited enjoyment of children. Because, too, the type of the confirmed bachelor is not as yet widely tolerated in the society the matron enjoys, correspondingly, a more solid status; it would be easy to envisage a Puerto Rican George Apley but somewhat more difficult to envisage a Puerto Rican Cash McCall. In socially objective terms, of course, the members of this class, both men and women, are a dependent bourgeois class deriving their economic raison d'être from their connection with the metropolitan business civilization. They tend, therefore, to be one of the groups in the society that are most receptive to the influx of American ideas.

Beneath them there exist the rising middle class groups. In part these are the older professions, both in city and small town, of law and medicine, and the traditionalist groups of rural landlords and retail merchants. In part, however, they are the new professions in process of formation, the new occupational types thrown up under the influence of new national and social institutions: the government schoolteacher, the modern officeholder, the technical civil servant, the professional salesman. They reflect the growing professionalization and the more intensive division of labor of an industrializing society; so, even in the older professions, the Victorian tradition of the Creole doctor who was also a writer or poet of some real local fame—José Gualberto Padilla, for example, or Dr. Cayetano Coll y Toste—is being supplanted by the type of the medical specialist; while the more recent writer or playwright in the field of the arts, Andreu Iglesias, say, or René Marqués, is also more of a practicing professional than his predecessors. There are subgroups that are entirely new, such as that of the Puerto Rican native-born general managers (some 69 of them in 1958) employed in American-owned Fomento plants.[3] Expanding institutions like the three universities of the island provide a modus vivendi for the native intelligentsia, for under Spain there was no such center for the outstanding teacher like Rafael Cordero or the philosopher-educator like de Hostos. Most of these middle class groups, however, are business-oriented. They eagerly embrace change, for they are anxiously trying to "make the grade" socially. More than any others, they are the responsive nomads who yield up readily to wherever the objective of maximizing production and consumption calls them. Their homes have moved from the traditional *plaza* house to the suburban villas of the new *urbanizaciones* such as Dos Pinos, Altamesa, El Commandante, and Beverly Hills. Their home interiors, apart from those of the university group, will have little of culture in them and at the lower levels will tend to be filled with the bric-a-brac of cheap popular Catholic art. The general decline in the older habit of including servants' quarters in middle-class homes reflects at once the new competition of factory employment for working-class girls and the replacement, in any case, of domestic servants with the American-style household gadgets. Because the average house lot also tends to be pitifully small there is little room or need for the services of the "house boy," so much a part of the Jamaican middle-class scene. The denizen of these new urbanizations may perhaps feel a vague nostalgia for the small town or the rural hamlet from which he has generally come. But it is open to serious doubt as to whether, offered a choice, he would exchange the new life for the old.

All of these homes, at all levels however, will offer testimony, by way of the radio, the television set, the refrigerator, and the household appliance of all kinds, to the enormous increase in consumer expenditures during the last two decades of which they are at once cause and effect. The increase can best be appreciated from the statistics of expenditures on the items of food, automobiles, medical expenses, toilet articles, sports goods, and so on: between 1940 and 1955, to cite two representative examples, total consumer spending on house furnishings and equipment rose from $5.9 million to $17.2 million, and that on recreation goods and services from $8.8 million to $64.5 million.[4] The new house, the new car, the latest television set, the outdoor equipment for "gracious living" have all been seized upon, as in American suburban life, as the glittering symbols of status. Consumer habits, altogether, released by the decline of the traditional restraints imposed by rigid class status upon occupational choice and behavior patterns, offer in themselves a fascinating study for the social psychologist. Just as, fifty years ago, the mark of having socially risen in island society was the ownership of shoes, today it is likely to be the ownership of durable goods or a formal wedding ceremony or a place for one's son or daughter at the University. There is an ostentatious show of the new possessions; for many years it was the habit to exhibit the refrigerator in the dining room as a piece of furniture for all to see, until the television set took over the place of honor. A new prestige of shopping grows up; for, previously done by proxy through servants, it has now become the socially acceptable thing to do for the middle-class housewife, with the consequence that the glittering supermarket replaces the ill-kept and badly housed public market as the fashionable retail outlet. Food habits, then, are also changing, although the native popular dish of rice and beans still retains its honored status as Puerto Rican standards of feminine beauty, bordering on obesity to American eyes, give way only slowly to the American image of the slim feminine figure. Property owner-ship, all this is to say, becomes more and more a mark of social esteem; as can be appreciated from the rise in expenditures on owner-occupied dwellings for the period of 1940-1955 from some $17 million to some $71 million, and on tenant-occupied dwellings from some $12 million to some $28 million. There are, naturally, serious gaps in this development; many individuals of the $2,000-$4,000 income group, for example, suffer from the fact that they are not eligible for public housing and yet cannot afford the private housing schemes that have not reached down below the $4,000 income level.[5] So pervasive, however, is the general appeal to self-betterment and social elevation—one of the latest middle-class private developments asks its clients, in its snobbish advertising, to join in the suburban luxury of the new Golden Age of Puerto Rico—that the gaps do not generate resentment so much as a more frantic effort to bridge them on the part of these rising groups.

There are, finally, the various gradations of the insular working class. The average Puerto Rican, after all, still remains a proletarian, rural or urban. He has small chance of owning the means of pro-duction with which he works (when he has work to do), whether it be in the older or the more modern industries. If he belongs to the rural poor his conditions of life have undoubtedly improved since they were described, more than a decade ago, in the studies of Professor Hernández-Ramírez (1947) and Felix Mejías (1946).[6] Since that time, too, he has had some chance to enter the new groups of the factory-employed workers, for even as late as 1949 those groups were so little in evidence that the authors of *The People of Puerto Rico* volume did not consider it necessary to include a chapter on them in their study, or at least a separate discussion. Despite the presence of a great deal of occupational inheritance there is today, as Melvin Tumin and Arnold Feldman point out in their study of social mobility, a remarkable amount of job movement taking place among the categories of service workers, semi-skilled and skilled workers, and clerical workers, much of it based upon the new career ambitions unleashed by the public educational system. There has been taking place, in fact, a very real structural transformation of the economy and its work structure, evident in the single fact that within the last generation the percentage of the insular labor force engaged in domestic and personal services has declined from 20.5 percent to 9.8 percent, while those engaged in manufacturing and mechanical industries have increased from 8.4 percent to 23.7 percent. It is true that many of these new worker categories are still unprotected by law against the exploitation of higher income groups as they strive to struggle upwards; the attempts recently to unionize maids and servant girls in the San Juan area spring, in part, from the fact that save for compulsory federal Social Security payments and local accident insurance there is no requirement on the part of the employer to limit working hours, provide adequate salaries or make any concessions on matters like vacations and sick leaves.

These new workers on the labor market manage, nevertheless, to achieve a vast degree of occupational mobility, although the higher the social rank, of course, the sharper is the incidence of mobility. An energetic individual may start a small country store and so elevate himself to the shopkeeping class of a small town; this indeed is a real possibility in the tobacco and mixed-crop economy of the central highlands region where the process of mass proletarianization has not gone so far as to eliminate, as elsewhere, the "small man" type—the independent truck farmer operating with government aid, for example —or to wipe out entirely the functional value of education as an instrument of social mobility. Or, again, a woman from the underprivileged groups may better herself by becoming a teacher in the vastly expanded school system built up by the government since 1940. Or the child of poor parents may become a struggling white collar worker by dint of a great family sacrifice that enables him to gain the necessary letters of credit in the form of a training certificate from one of the technical schools that have come into existence, especially in the town areas, since veterans' educational benefits began in 1945, or from one of the private commercial schools that cater to the middle class aspirations of those who dream of escape from their class prison and the enjoyment of better things. The lucky young man, again, may obtain an appointment in the insular police force, a prized goal in a society where the police enjoy so high a prestige that both good looks and political influence, according to popular legend, are indispensable conditions of entry. Or the lucky young woman may gain a position in the new and glamorous occupation of airline hostess, although it must be admitted that the major American airline companies serving the island have so far shown little liberalism in their hiring of Puerto Rican candidates, certainly nothing to compare with the forward looking policy that made it possible for the neighboring British West Indian Airways to be the first airline in the world to employ a Negro stewardess.

There are again marginal occupational groups that manage precariously to straddle the new class alignments. There are the *choferes,* the drivers of the public cars that serve as cheap, popular interurban transportation throughout the island (their preference for the station wagon has meant an interesting decline in the social status of that vehicle). There are the truck drivers who service the rapidly expanding construction industry (usually paid by the load and therefore some of the most fiercely reckless of road users). If the members of both of those groups can meet the heavy monthly payments on their American vehicles they earn, psychologically, a compensation as mobile wage earners who have escaped the drudgery of the cane fields and the discipline of the factory. Beneath them, in social estimation, are the lottery-ticket vendors, the street peddlers, the itinerant barbers, all of them attaining a sort of individual independence at the price of constituting a loose group of social "floaters" sustained by very little of a sense of group consciousness. But all of these situations, especially these latter ones, are accidents rather than essences of the social system. They maintain at best a few groups on a pittance; they do not constitute a definable social class. They do little to assuage the fear of being thrust back into the ranks of the unemployed or of the socially disinherited that is a brooding omnipresence in the daily lives of most of their individual members. One of the ugly testimonies to that fear are the shack slums that are set up, almost overnight, by the hordes of squatters and their families on any piece of available ground that becomes vacant in the town districts. It is perhaps suggestive, on this score, that the government agencies responsible for urban renovation have recently announced their abandonment of their policy of complete slum clearance for one of mere "rehabilitation" of existing slum areas.

All this must be set, finally, within the framework of the general social trends within which this changing class structure lives and moves. The island society, as the authors of *The People of Puerto Rico* conclude at the end of their exhaustive study, is changing from an agrarian two-class orientation to a modern industrial country. The capital basis is shifting from the ownership of land to industrial, bureaucratic, and commercial activity as preferred styles of economic activity. Sociologically this means the displacement of the traditional ruling groups like the non-corporate sugar *hacendados* and the older type of rural middle class by new groups—the city-based businessmen, the capitalist ranchers, the official bureaucrats—whose members have had little compunction in adjusting their style of life to rationalizing trends. Culturally, it means the gradual diffusion of American-style cultural practices to the point where they begin to create new uniform patterns of behavior and attitude characterized, collectively, as a process of "Americanization." It would be easy of course to exaggerate the scope of these changes. Cultural tenacity, after all, is a real thing; at least the authors of the Columbia University study were so strongly assured of its power that they felt it to be legitimate, as late as 1949, to analyze the whole society in terms of its older regional subcultures rather than in terms of a monolithic whole. The coffee region around the western mountain township of Lares, for instance, still retains many of the older hacienda features and the political power of its "old" landed gentry has not yielded as readily as elsewhere to newcomers. The agricultural laborer still works there within the old web of hierarchical relations. On the other hand, regions like the sugar areas of the north and south coasts where the capitalist revolution of technology has been felt most deeply have seen the rise, in more perfect form, of impersonal managerial hierarchies and a wage-earning landless proletariat dependent on absentee capital and tied to the credit complex of the local company stores. And even within the cultures of the littoral sections there are significant differences still, shaped largely by historical background; thus, because land concentration processes have not developed so rapidly in certain south coast areas as in certain north coast areas the former possess a distinct group of *colonos*, or small cane farmers, not present in the more homogeneous class system of the latter. Similar differences are to be observed in matters such as ritual kinship, religious affiliation, the niceties of social ranking, and the habits of political voting. Or, again, the historical accident that made of the north coastal stretch of beaches around the village of Loíza Aldea a landing ground for the illegal entry of slaves under Spain has left behind in that area today an economic oasis of fishing villages inhabited by a heavily Negroid population and, in the shape of the colorful *fiesta de Santiago Apóstol*, an isolated phenomenon of Puerto Rican religious life in which the cult of popular saints seems to be connected with the ancestral memory of the old African war gods.

Yet all this, however important it is for the cultural anthropologist, cannot disguise the general truth that in one degree or another the entire insular society is being forcibly repatterned by the institutional changes wrought by modernization. The replacement of domestic, self-contained agriculture with cash-crop production for the outside market characterizes all subsections of the economy. "All socio-cultural segments of the island," the Columbia study acknowledges, "are becoming more alike in their cash-mindedness—their dependence upon wages, the purchase of manufactured goods, the decline of home industries—their stress on individual effort, their utilization of national health, educational, and other services. . . . The town middle classes of business and professional people which are expanding under the influence of the new national institutions are everywhere very similar. The growth of a cash economy and the availability of new goods and services have provided a further condition for the diffusion of cultural practices. The diffused traits are those of industrial civilization, especially in their American forms."[7] There is little evidence to show that the diffusion is seriously resisted by any important group. Indeed, if Professor Vidich's portraiture of the social values conquering in a typical urban-rural community like the Trujillo Alto area is at all representative, it indicates that all groups, from one social pole to the other, have passionately embraced the new production ways and the new consumption styles accompanying them, even when acceptance involves serious indebtedness in the effort to maintain the fierce pace.[8] A romantic might see in all this the unhappy advent of "materialism." But this would be a profoundly mistaken position. In the first place, the argument often presupposes the existence of some happier Puerto Rico that is now being lost, in much the same way as romantic critics of the English industrial revolution presupposed a "Merrie England" that had been destroyed by the "dark satanic mills," historically a dangerous misconception of pre-industrial England. In the second place, it prejudges the pursuit of economic welfare as being somehow morally dubious, whereas, in reality, as the Puerto Rican essayist Enrique Laguerre has aptly noted, aspiration for material goods is a legitimate aspiration in all human beings.[9] It would be more proper altogether to say that the Puerto Rican transformation has been a quantitative rather than a qualitative one. For despite all the brave talk from San Juan about the birth of a "new civilization" in the island, what is in fact emerging is a new parallelogram of socio-economic forces defined less by customary folkways than by the "folklore of capitalism." This is the one seminal fact from which all discussion about the Puerto Rican future must of necessity proceed.

How does all this affect the problem of an effective and healthy community life—what the Union Party platform of 1922 referred to as "the sole and fundamental problem; all others are inherent therein because they converge towards the organization of the individual for his relations with other beings in the formation of communities that make up a people and a nation"? There is a great deal of semi-official literature which is ready to suggest, in almost lyrical terms, that the *Popular* welfare program, including the "self-help" campaigns among the country people undertaken by the Division of Community Education, is on the way to solving the problem; all that is needed is more of it.[10] More generally, the welfare philosophy of the Commonwealth government presupposes, as it were, an umbrella of national unity (what Adolphe Roberts, speaking for the neighboring British West Indian area, has termed a "nationalist liberalism") that will bring all groups of the society together into a harmonious *puertorriqueñismo*. And, indeed, much of Puerto Rican social history since 1940 supports the claim. In education, social welfare, the growth of the co-operative moment, the conquest of sickness through the remarkable system of public health centers, there has been tremendous headway. More importantly, the entire atmosphere of lethargy and hopelessness of the pre-1940 period, not very different from the general paralysis of spirit described by liberal patriots like de Hostos and Baldorioty as characterizing the Spanish period,[11] has been replaced by the sense of optimism that comes from the presence of great energy in a national government. To read volumes like Dean Fleagle's *Social Problems in Porto Rico* (1917) or Arthur James's *Thirty Years in Porto Rico* (1927), written by socially conscious Americans, and then to compare the social evils they describe with the welfare policies inaugurated since 1940 to tackle them, is to be made aware of the genuine social liberalism of the Commonwealth leadership.

But the crucial question concerns itself not with the energy but with its ultimate direction. Puerto Rico is rapidly graduating to the status of a modern business society. But there is plenty of evidence to suggest that this is very far short of being the organic community free from deep tensions and conflicts predicated in the Union Party 1922 statement. The old local loyalties are giving way to a new mosaic of social classes that are building up new allegiances, and although the charming habit of the *fiesta de ausentes* attempts to sustain the older sentiments it is not much more than an annual celebration of the "home town" sentiment for those who have left their birthplace behind them. These new allegiances, in turn, are class and professional rather than community-oriented in their nature. The new class of businessmen reminds the observer, in its individual types, of the prototype of the prosperous entrepreneur to be found all over Latin America. They are frequently more American than the Americans they seek anxiously to ape; they belong to Rotary International or the Elks or the Lions clubs; they have a subscription to *Time* and *Life* magazines; and, like nothing so much as some latter-day Latin American Babbitts, they naively subscribe to the "rags to riches" mythology when it has been largely replaced, in its original American habitat, with the more sophisticated dogma of "the organization man." The San Juan business clubs, interestingly enough, not so long ago applauded a visiting American "huckster" who lectured them on the virtues of the Andrew Carnegie form of capitalism; his name, appropriately enough, was Napoleon Hill.[12] The spending habits of this class of man, again, are as yet hardly touched by *noblesse oblige*. A Puerto Rican wealthy man in the last century might have built up a family library; his modern successor is more likely to buy up a baseball team or, as with Cobián, a string of movie theaters. A professional man like Angel Ramos collected, a generation ago, a fantastic library collection on the history of the Napoleonic era; it would be difficult to meet such a bibliophile in the contemporary professional classes. The single well-known exception is Luis Ferré, the Ponce industrialist who is at the same time an art patron in his own right and the chief benefactor of the Catholic University at that city; and he comes at once from an "older" family and from a city commonly regarded as being more socially "conservative" than the capital.

Nor do the new middle classes exhibit any larger sense of social obligation. Many of their members are recruited, via university education, from the small town petit bourgeois groups. But, as they rise, they develop a defensive attitude towards the mass population. They lose the camaraderie which at least helps compensate the poor for their noisy squalor. They are anxious, indeed, to leave the thought of poverty behind them. It is worth noting, as a Caribbean comparison, that the isolation of the Jamaican middle class from the masses, so well defined in Kingston life, was recently dramatized by the publication by the University College of the West Indies of a report on the appalling conditions of life among the Jamaican Rastafarian community; and it is a safe gamble that a comparable report on the conditions of life in the San Juan slum districts would be received with a similar sense of shock by the Puerto Rican middle class. For if the Puerto Rican social climber graduates into one of the professions he is likely to see his new status less as an opportunity to serve the public good than as an avenue to personal advancement. For far too long a period most of the professions have protected themselves from too much outside interference by organizing themselves, with legislative approval, into *colegios* that exhibit an almost medieval sense of corporate jealousy. The final ambition, in a profession like medicine, is to establish a lucrative private clinic, so much so that the practitioner who abjures the ambition in order to devote a lifetime of service to the poor, like Dr. Guillermo Barbosa in old San Juan or, before him, Dr. Esteban Vidal y Ríos in Ponce, is pointed out as a unique and unusual person. The possibility of a high professional ethic in that field must also be seen in the light of the fact that there is a noticeable migration of Puerto Rican physicians to the United States and that, because graduates of approved medical schools are there accepted more readily, there is a danger that the better men will leave and that those from the lower quality schools of Cuba, Spain, and Latin America will remain in the island.[13] The local Medical Association dare not, of course, oppose the extensive public health services that play so large a part in the local health picture. But short of that it has vigorously opposed the efforts of the Secretary of Health to ease the chronic shortage of doctors for staffing those services by means of waiving the citizenship requirement so that non-United States doctors may be recruited by the department. The usual charges of "socialized medicine" have been made, on which the proper commentary is, first, that the shortage has in large part been created by the losses involved in the fact that many government-employed doctors move without compunction to higher-paying private practices after completing their public service obligations and, second, that, as a matter of fact, the trend in public policy has been to encourage recourse to private medical care wherever possible, so much so that the percentage of the population dependent on the public services has declined from 90 percent in 1935 to 67 percent in 1958.[14]

Other professional associations are no more liberal in their attitudes. Too many of them are concerned almost solely with the protection of their corporate interests. This helps to explain why the College of Dental Surgeons has done so little since its inauguration in 1941 to meet the serious deficiencies in the provision of dental attention for the Puerto Rican people, so much so that as late as 1954 the population-dentist ratio in the community was below even that of the worst provided of the American states, South Carolina.[15] There is the same professional exclusivism that is unwilling to extend a generous welcome to the needy foreign practitioner seeking work and refuge in the island; and in defense of its interests it is ready to invoke the most perverse of logic, exemplified in the argument of the local Dental Association that there is in reality no scarcity of dental service in the island because scarcity is to be defined not in terms of the statistics of population-dentist ratios but in the existing "demand" for service— which in effect means of course the "demand" only of those who can afford to pay for it.[16] It is suggestive, again, that the local bar has been so far singularly unsuccessful in producing great legal luminaries and that a passion for the protection of the civil liberties of unpopular minority groups has been almost completely identified with the single person of Dr. Santos Amadeo. It is at least true that years of covert complaint about the academic standards and the administrative practices of the University Law School finally culminated, in 1959, in the appointment of a special committee of inquiry.

The spirit of selfish corporatism is compounded, moreover, by two general factors. One is the general dislike of, perhaps contempt for, manual labor inherited from the pre-industrial Hispanic tradition that pervades the community. Everyone wants to be a *caballero*; few readily accept that there can be a dignity of labor. Hence the characteristic schedule of occupational preferences, which leads, as the second factor, to the dangerous imbalance of occupational recruitment within the society. The law schools, many of dubious quality, are crowded with candidates for whom a law degree means a lucrative appointment in government service. The newer scientific professions still await an equal public esteem. Few Puerto Ricans know of the great work of a botanist like José Otero in the field of Caribbean mycology or of a public servant like Milton Cobin in the sphere of tropical botany; the newspapers carry off and on impassioned defenses of the agronomist from whose now neglected ranks, it is argued, much of the membership of the commercial and administrative classes has sprung; few Puerto Ricans are attracted to the profession of geology, and of the seventeen geologists working in the island in 1960 only two were native Puerto Ricans; and, as a final example, a young arts graduate whose amateur interest in meteorology becomes so keen that he accompanies the Navy air squadron assigned to hurricane detection within the Caribbean area is regarded as so unusual that his story becomes front-page news in the island newspapers.[17] Not only work but also its institutionalization within the field of labor becomes suspect; this is perhaps why the former head of the insular police force was reported to resent fiercely the imputation that officers under his command were willing to contemplate the organization of a union in order to protect their interests. Nor is it fully appreciated that this trait, perhaps tolerable in a more traditionalist economy, becomes an anachronism in a society that has accepted the world of industrial work as the answer to its problems.

In such a society there can be little real interclass solidarity. There is interclass mobility. And even this takes place within clearly demarcated limits. The occupational structure, as defined by Tumin and

Feldman, exhibits a high degree of circulation in the varied groups between service workers at the bottom and business owners at the top, but the process is circumscribed by the presence, at the very top and bottom, respectively, of the professional and semi-professional groups and the groups of unskilled laborers and agricultural day laborers, both of which are relatively closed occupations. The groups at the social bottom may indeed possess a great deal of positive social hope in their attitudes; but the fact remains that the chances of their social rise are slender indeed. More generally speaking, there is not here the equality of opportunity to justify the characterization of the society as one that guarantees the *carrière ouverte aux talents* at all levels. The outstanding professional man may, once in a while, come from the ranks of the small-town poor, as did Angel Ramos, the newspaper magnate, in the years after the First World War; but that is an exception. A more representative example of what happens would be the figure of the well-known actor José Ferrer, the economic basis of whose success springs from the fact that he was born the son of a Puerto Rican lawyer and a sugar plantation heiress. There is, again, a powerful sense of *puertorriqueñidad* that affects all classes. It is the fact, nevertheless, that the feeling has very little power to shape actual patterns of life and behavior. There is a great deal of class segregation in those patterns. The new housing programs, for example, separate the income groups from each other in a new way. To pass through a higher middle class urbanization like San Gerardo and then through the proletarian ghetto of the vast 28,000-person Llorens Torres housing project is to be made keenly aware of the fact that, even in such a tightly circumscribed island society, there can be a serious division between "two nations" living apart from each other.

Even the habits of recreation and entertainment take on a similar segregationist tone. The more elegant movie theaters tend to run the Hollywood product and the cheaper ones the products of the Madrid and Mexico City studios, a distinction reflecting in turn an inequality of opportunity in the chance to learn the English language. Historically, there seems to have taken place a real decline in the habits of common enjoyment over the last half-century. For, today, the patron saint *fiestas* of the island towns seem to have little of the raucous and turbulent carnival spirit prevalent in the earlier days of the 18th and 19th centuries, the boat races and horse races, for example, of the old San Juan Bautista festival in San Juan itself, or the fancy costumes, the Moorish clowns, the very social licence itself of the fiesta of Santiago Apóstol as they were described, a half century ago, by José Antonio Daubón in his *Cosas de Puerto Rico* (1904). Even the annual Casals Festival, initially acclaimed as a national act of cultural renaissance, has tended to become a middle- and upper-class affair as its prices remain impossible for the vast untapped mass audience; and, in a way, it is symptomatic that a sport like horse racing should enjoy an independent administrative authority for its regulation while the Casals Festival, from the beginning, has been a subsidiary of the Puerto Rico Industrial Development Company and its chief administrator, the executive vice-president, is at the same time a financial vice-president of that Company, with unfortunate consequences for the status of the Festival as a non profit-making cultural undertaking.

The *obrero* and the *campesino* concededly benefit vastly from the work of the welfare officer, the home economist, the family adviser, the rural librarian. Yet the tone of much of the work done by these types is neo-Victorian in its genteel condescension, in its assumption that its beneficiaries are to be firmly guided into paths deemed praiseworthy by the social experts. "What Puerto Rico has to fear most," a friendly critic has remarked in this respect, "are not her problems, but that her problems might some day be solved—that the lower classes will obediently become sterilized to lower the birth rate, that industries and middle class will proliferate, and that the friendly and passionless world promised in the pamphlets of the Division of Community Education will come to be."[18] That manipulation of the masses indeed has been carried over from the "old" Puerto Rico to the "new," for it has been at the heart of the societal role played by the agricultural laborer, the *jíbaro*, throughout both the Spanish and the American periods. The authors of *The People of Puerto Rico* have summed it up nicely. "In many ways," they write, "the image of the *jíbaro* has rationalized his exploitation by other socio-cultural groups. Since he was natively shrewd, the town merchant was morally free to try to deceive him. Since he was said to be lazy when working for others, means to make him work had to be found, and these means could be justified. Since he was so well acquainted with nature's remedies and was supposed to be inherently healthy, he presumably did not require medical services. Since he was natively intelligent and resourceful, educational facilities were said to be wasted on him. And since he is a child of nature, rural roads, modern housing, schools, radios, high wages, and too much governmental service were said to ruin him. Civilization tempts him to leave the land. It disrupts his healthy value system with new wants, making him dissatisfied with his lot. As a consequence he leaves the healthful environment of the countryside and becomes a social liability as an urban slum dweller."[19]

All this of course has its own historical roots. It goes back, in one way, to the rural isolationism of the *jíbaro*'s life from the colonial

beginnings, so that there was never much of a collective village life—
after the pattern of the remarkable "free village" system that flourished
in the Jamaican mountain districts after the abolition of slavery in
that island in 1834—to provide the physical foundation for a vigorous
community consciousness. But neither the present-day shack slum
areas of the coastal cities nor even the new urban dwelling areas with
their bleak concrete uniformity are successfully filling that gap in the
present. Both of them present a grim picture of cultural disorganization; the *urbanizaciones,* especially, have been allowed to sprout as
sprawling areas on the margins of existing urban concentrations instead of being seen, in the British fashion, as "new towns" to be
planned in their own right as independent communities. In the meanwhile a floating population of rootless persons has become rather
well defined. There are the small-town and city prostitutes, the vast
majority of whom come, according to the study done a generation
ago by Professor José Rosario, from either the ranks of the unemployed or from the class of domestic servants who prefer a life of
dismal prostitution to that of an ill-paid and badly treated menial in
an autocratic household.[20] There are the drug traffickers described,
as a type, in one of Emilio Diaz Valcárcel's short stories, *Las pálidas
noches.* There are the criminal juveniles returned from the Harlem
social jungle. There are the vendors of the local sweets who perambulate street and highway with their unhygienic carts. There are even,
perhaps, the restless student types whose abrupt translation from
island interior to mammoth university campus is not made any easier
by the spiritual and intellectual poverty of the town cafés and boarding houses in which they spend much of their time: a slice of Puerto
Rican life immortalized in the *Cuentos de la Universidad* of Emilio
Belaval. Many of these groups, of course, are the victims of the general trend of rural depopulation, for it has been estimated that by
1975 the number of rural families in the island will have declined by
some 45,000 and the number of urban families increased by some
100,000; and that the present imbalance between urban population
and adequate housing accommodation may not be resolved satisfactorily until 1970.[21] The general result is to breed new problems of
social disorientation as yet not fully grasped by government policy
makers or adequately appreciated by the more fortunate social groups.

There are two additional and aggravating factors to be noted in
respect to all this. The first involves the historical fact that throughout
local history there has been a chronic *desempleo cívico,* a fatal deficiency in a sense of communal obligation on the part of the socially
comfortable. Spanish rule actually encouraged social selfishness. "The
sort of government used here," wrote Edward Emerson in 1834,

"exempts the private man from the trouble of taking any pains about the management of public affairs; he has only to let the state alone, and mind his own business. I mean that no man here will be drawn away from studies or the contemplations he may love, by any patriotic notion of being compelled to raise his voice or write his volume about this measure or the other; no nullification party, no U.S. Bank party, no caucuses interrupt him. Even the apathy and the no less remarkable ignorance of the people aid in rendering the solitude of an educated man more complete."[22] The solitude is less complete today, of course, yet its legacy remains. To publish a slim volume of romantic verse, or deliver a *ponencia* on Puerto Rican "culture" defined in a narrow literary sense, or read a lyrical piece on the *presencia jíbara* at the *Ateneo de Puerto Rico* remains for many still the thing to do. The habit must have deep roots in the insular psychology, for it has survived the ridicule that has been directed at it by Puerto Ricans themselves—in the little piece, for example, of Manuel Fernández Juncos, *Yo quiero ser Poeta*. The growth of the social sciences, especially in the universities—an ideal most famously advanced throughout nineteenth-century Latin America by the Puerto Rican intellectual Eugenio María de Hostos—has helped to counterbalance this temper of literary gentility. Even so, the Fabian habit of dispassionate research into all aspects of the insular life is still so rare that the formation in 1958 of an Institute of Social Investigation by a group of private citizens was publicly admired as an event of unique significance. It is symptomatic, again, that when at long last a full-scale inquiry was launched during the same year to examine the state of civil liberties in the insular society it should have been government-sponsored and undertaken by an official committee of the legislature. Altogether the civic instinct has been so fragile a plant that, apart from the usual political opposition, the Commonwealth government has rarely been obliged to submit itself to the healthy surveillance of an independent *civisme*. Social conscience withers in such an environment. It will certainly be some time yet before the middle and upper classes of the society begin to show that active concern for the common people which Salvador Brau urged upon their forebears some three quarters of a century ago in his eloquent pronouncement on *Las Clases Jornaleras de Puerto Rico*. It may be longer yet before they are impregnated with the noble ideal of a neo-Kantian private and social conscience which it was the self-appointed mission of de Hostos, in his *Moral Social*, for example, to teach his fellow countrymen.

The second factor to note is that as the social system becomes more heterogeneous a sharper sense of identity begins to emerge in people. But it is not the awareness of a *summum bonum*, the *idem sentire de republica* envisaged by Brau and de Hostos. On the contrary, it is a feeling of occupational and group identity and, significantly, recent years have seen growing proof that the feeling will increasingly express itself through the medium of organized pressure groups of the American type. Bodies such as the Puerto Rican Coffee Producers Cooperative, the Association of Sugar Producers, the Puerto Rican Medical Association (in its recent dispute, for example, with the local Blue Cross Association) already adopt such a posture—so much so indeed that the local legislature has recently moved to look into the economic aspects of the practice of lobbying at the local capital. A body, again, like the Association of Teachers is heavily politicized and tends to view the Secretary of Education as its own private emissary within the cabinet. The establishment, quite openly, of a political party backed by the Catholic Church in the election year of 1960 might also be seen, indeed, as an unusual expression of the Church's attempt to save the principle of religious instruction in the state schools. The wave of strikes throughout 1959-1960—teachers, taxi drivers, stevedores and sugar workers, among others—suggests that new tensions are growing up between employers and labor. The appearance of a public correspondence of angry protest over the high cost of living points to a sharper sense of mutual distrust between producers and consumers, although it is doubtful if the suggested schemes of a Better Business Bureau or a "consumers' revolt" will succeed any more in the island than they have in the States.[23] The bitter complaints, again, of the class of small shopkeepers against the invading chains of large supermarkets indicates that, as big business moves in, little business—as in the States—will be driven into a desperate struggle for survival. The old cleavage, to take a final example, between the landed gentry and the city commercial interests promises to be replaced, as new class lines harden, with a new alliance between the big landowners and the urban business groups. It is difficult, in the light of all this, to take seriously the enthusiastic claim of a visiting American publicist, Stuart Chase, that Puerto Rico has invented a "new dimension" of partnership between business, labor, and government.[24] The blunt truth, on the contrary, is that as the struggle for economic survival thus proceeds the society will discover that in the place of the myth of social unity hitherto prevalent in insular attitudes there has been unleashed a Pandora's box of competing class and group aspirations it may take more than the emotional invocation of *puertorriqueñidad* to assuage.

A word is in order on the character of the communal psychology behind all of this. Industrial society, as Durkheim has pointed out in a well-known analysis, is unique in that it releases in its members voracious and essentially limitless appetites for material goods and satisfactions. It sweeps away the inhibitions that persuade men willingly to accept denial of those appetites. The consequence is certain to be a massive frustration, at once personal and social, if the productive capacity of the economy cannot at once meet the rising consumption demands and if, too, the ruling ideology of the society does little or nothing to school or curtail the acquisitive temper in people. Since these two aggravating conditions are present in Puerto Rico the island is a classic illustration of the materialist appetite run riot. Its very proximity to the North American world and its unprotected exposure to the psychologically clever advertising of the "hidden persuaders" and the "image merchants" of that world has made it a ready victim of the disease. A tremendous barrage of programs and propaganda also within the society itself, both from governmental and private sources, advertises the desirability of change and progress. The ambition of almost every Puerto Rican, therefore, becomes an anxious hope that he may join in the game, an apt slogan of which is the motto of a local radio advertising program, *Vivir como rico y pagar como pobre*. The ascendant classes have uncritically embraced the consumption modes that accompany the game; the exquisite horrors of too many of their new home interiors, purchased from the various "House Beautiful" stores, are the result of what happens when the power to buy is not matched by the possession of aesthetic discernment. Widespread recourse to credit and indebtedness becomes, in Dr. Arthur Vidich's phrase, the index of widespread status panic; and a 1951 study of consumption habits in the income groups above the $2,000 a year level asserts that at this stratum Puerto Rican families carry a considerably larger volume of current debt than people of similar incomes in the United States.[25] The individual worker likewise is becoming a slave to the routine of work as the advertising machinery that engulfs him persuades him that the good things in life are the gleaming material goods that money can buy for him. What has been styled in American life the "myth of the happy worker" thus becomes added to the already large number of myths that afflict and confuse the popular imagination.

Looked at from this angle, it seems at times as if the society is nothing much more than a culture of anxiety. Puerto Ricans speak jestingly of *la lucha*, the struggle, in much the same half-serious, half-comic way that Americans joke about "the rat race." To note the tensions of the new middle-class variant of the struggle for existence, in themselves of alarming proportions, is to understand some of the economic factors lying behind individual sickness, both organic and psychiatric. For the husband, at this level, faces an exhausting day of income-gathering to meet a load of monthly payments on household goods, while the wife undertakes a round of frivolous social activities that constitutes the Achilles heel of her existence.[26] A similar struggle takes place at the lower social levels, and indeed is further complicated by the cultural fact, as Dr. Peter Gregory has noted in his studies on local worker attitudes, that the Puerto Rican worker suffers from a sensitivity to the judgments of others so intense that cordial relationships with the owner or the manager in the workshop become utterly indispensable to his peace of mind.[27] To look at the bizarre combination of squalid huts and television antennae in the fetid slums of *El Fanguito* and *La Perla* is to be made forcibly aware, at the same time, of the distorted social values to which the struggle is dedicated. It provides little room for class fraternity. At times it seems that about the only thing that holds the various social classes together is the hope of making a killing in the state lottery or in the illegal *bolita* games. The taste for gambling, indeed, appears to be one facet of general consumption habits that has remained constant throughout the last two decades of socio-economic change, so much so that today, as sixty years ago, the habit remains, in the language of Walter Weyl's description at that earlier date, so widespread that it may almost be said to have taken the place which in other countries is taken by the habit of saving.[28] Or, to go further back, it is clearly a living inheritance from the Spanish period when, as Charles Emerson noted in his letters from San Juan, the addiction to gambling was so widespread among all classes that governors were compelled to overlook the open violation of the colonial legislation that attempted to outlaw it.[29]

What is dismaying about all this is not so much the burden of frustration that presses so heavily upon all classes as the attitude which takes it for granted. The authors of the Columbia study impassively conclude their volume on a note of frightening anthropological determinism. "The individual," they write, "is inevitably caught in conflicts in the course of this reorientation. The security of his older extended family and fixed position in the social hierarchy is weakened before new goals can be realized. The new goals in themselves almost inevitably carry frustration, for the doctrine of unlimited upward mobility can never be wholly achieved by any one individual, or even largely achieved by any group of individuals. Frustration, insecurity, and even serious neurotic and psychosomatic symptoms may be so widespread as to constitute national characteristics. But they are characteristics of a set of human relationships that are rapidly changing—and changing toward patterns that contain inner contradictions and instability."[30] The class structure of business civilization is here taken for granted as a law of Puerto Rican social development. The frustrations that come from the present inequality of productive capacity and consumer demand are seen as being almost permanent in character; yet many of them are due to the quite separate fact that there is no public policy that seeks to assure "fair shares" of the total insular wealth but only, in its place, an emphasis upon efficient capital formation and overall economic development, with distribution left pretty much to chance. In the viewpoint represented by the Columbia study social forces are seen, in some pseudo-Marxist fashion, as manipulating people without people being able, in turn, to manipulate the social forces. There is no appreciation, consequently, of the possibility that the Puerto Rican people might be able to carry through their industrial revolution without of necessity accepting the values of American capitalism; and the failure springs from the assumption, central to most of the work done by American scholars on the island, that Puerto Rico will remain tied to the American system. Yet the psychological liberation of Puerto Ricans may depend in the last analysis upon willingness and ability to break away from that connection, for until the break is made the destructive tensions will continue between the productive capacity of a poor economy and the consumer demands of the rich American economy. All in all, the Puerto Rican patriot might well be justified in concluding that until now the American social scientists have analyzed his society and that now it is his business to change it.

And even when, as does at times happen, the American academic observer does feel apprehensions about the directions of Puerto Rican change, his prescriptions of cure hardly sound convincing. Thus the authors of the Princeton University study on social mobility are clearly worried over the growing "Americanization" of life values in the "new" Puerto Rico. So, they offer as consolation the conviction that there still remains a "margin of freedom" created by the fact that the Puerto Rican traditional concept of the equal moral worth of all men, added to traditional family relationships, may yet counteract the process. They suggest that the "deliberate attempt to maintain the older ideal theme of *dignidad,* while, simultaneously, the new orientation to production is causing market-minded themes of personal evaluation, represents an attempt to create a culture with several major orientations to which equal dominance must be accorded."[31] Doubt is cast upon the presumption of "equal dominance," however, by the fact, as is testified by the Princeton study itself, that the newer system of values is slowly but surely gaining dominance over the older system.[32] Cultural themes in themselves have little power to reshape society. They must have behind them the energy of a group or a class

of some strength of its own. But the social class that has traditionally
been identified in the Puerto Rican imagination with the theme of
dignidad, the class of rural folk, has throughout been a class, as the
above-quoted Columbia study makes evident, that has been done
things to by others rather than doing things itself. It is not a strategically located class, as have been other classes elsewhere that have been
able to soften somewhat the impact of the capitalist spirit: the country
gentlemen of Victorian England, for example, or the solid peasantry
of Republican France. If successful resistance to modernization along
American lines is to be launched it will have to come from groups that
are more centrally involved in the process of modernization themselves. Even more, they must bring with them leading principles that
are something more solid, more closely related to economic realities,
more meaningfully contemporary, in brief, than the charming images
of rural socialism.

It is evident—as a final comment—that Puerto Rico can hardly
be classified with any accuracy as a "plural society" in the sense in
which that concept has been applied by Dr. M. G. Smith (following
the famous original use of the concept by Furnivall in his work on
the colonial Far East) to modern Caribbean society.[33] For there is
little in Puerto Rican life to make of it, in Smith's language, "a
culturally divided society" in which "each cultural section has its own
relatively exclusive way of life, with its own distinctive systems of
action, ideas and values, and social relations." It is, on the contrary,
a homogeneous society; it has little in the way of racially distinct
groups; nor has there developed, historically, a pure slavery form to
give rise to breakaway communities, like the Bush Negroes of Surinam
or the Maroons of Jamaica, which have been, and to some extent still
are, states within the state. It is true that the image of the *jíbaro* as
the symbol of a common tradition has played merely an expiatory
function in the society as the modernizing groups dream of a rural
innocence they have forever lost. At the same time, however, there
is without doubt a common conviction of a *puertorriqueñidad* that
cements the society together. The pluralistic theory tends toward
an over idealization of subordinate subcultures as compared with the
whole society and its general will; but—apart from the moral dangers
involved in that perspective—Puerto Rican society has been characterized throughout by a marked absence of a vigorous local community sense that might have provided a foundation for the localist
prejudice. The formal communities, especially the county-like *municipio,* are weak and amorphous groupings, with the real center of
localist loyalty being the *barrio* neighborhoods. If there is indeed

pluralism in Puerto Rican life, it is the more modern variety based upon occupation, and reflecting the interests of socio-cultural groups quite independent either of land or race. The lines of division, that is to say, are horizontal rather than vertical. It is therefore probable, as Professor Charles Wagley has suggested for the Caribbean as a whole, that the more fruitful mode of investigation into the problem of social unity in Puerto Rico will revolve around the study of non-localized associations such as trade unions, political parties, religious organizations, sports and social associations, and so on.[34]

Whether a modern form of pluralism can of itself produce a viable social contract in the society depends, of course, upon other factors, mainly a willingness of the new rising groups to subordinate their newly found private interests to the public good. It is worth noting in this respect that what passes for cultural pluralism in Caribbean life is in many ways class stratification of a Westernized form, as the studies of Lloyd Braithwaite (1952) and Raymond Smith (1956) have shown in the cases of Trinidad and British Guiana. There is evidence to suggest that even in a society like Trinidad, where the East Indians have traditionally been regarded as almost beyond the pale of social respectability, new class alignments are beginning to replace the more simple racist alignment. This can be seen in the rise of a professional East Indian middle class capable of showing a more sophisticated political outlook as its members come to have more in common with the Creole middle class and less with the East Indian poor of the rural counties. It can also be seen in the phenomenon, annotated in much recent fictional literature, of the Creolization of the East Indian as urban manners become national in their scope. A similar process is evident in British Guiana, where the readiness of rich East Indians to vote for the white d'Aguiar party in the 1961 elections in that territory suggests that race rapidly gives way, under pressure, to the appeal of economic interest. The threat to Caribbean social unity, this is to say, does not come from the presumptive instability of the culturally diverse community but rather from the new pull of class allegiance as modernization and nationalist self-government together combine to replace the colonial ruling classes with new local ruling classes.

Puerto Rico, like the whole Caribbean, faces this sort of problem. But there is little reason, at the outset, to accept the pessimism of the "plural society" thesis. For that thesis exaggerates the differences between cultural and ethnic groups in a society and underestimates the factors that serve to transcend those differences. The inherent tendency of the "plural society," as Furnivall and his followers have seen it, is to run to social atomization as soon as the hand of the metropolitan rule disappears. The prognostication is open to serious doubt on at least two counts. In the first place, its emphasis upon cultural separatism did not allow it to appreciate fully how much a subordinate society can take from the metropolitan society. Thus in Puerto Rico the atomization process, if it took place at all, would certainly be offset by the fact that all groups in the society, even the political separatist groups apart from the Nationalist Party, accept the American ideals of democratic government and popular sovereignty, just as, in the case of the former British West Indies, it will be offset by the universal acceptance by all groups of the values of British parliamentary democracy. The new tensions of the developing class structures will be there of course; but at least they will move within the framework of accepted politico-constitutional rules. Secondly, since every society in a sense is a pluralistic society—as, indeed, the difficulties of the Furnivall school in deciding the criteria of pluralism show—there is no necessary hostility between national patriotism and cultural diversity. They may complement each other, not destroy each other. This is evident enough, to take a final Caribbean example, from the case of Jamaica, where the stubborn survival of narrow clannish loyalties in some elements of the Chinese and Syrian groups, nursing fantastic stereotypes against all other groups, has not precluded the growth of an all-embracing Jamaican nationalism of a peculiarly marked intensity. So long as these factors prevail it is reasonable to expect that, as Puerto Rico moves forward with the rest of the Caribbean away from metropolitan rule and influence, the end result will be social cosmos rather than social chaos.

Family, Religion, and Color

THE argument at this point faces the issue, profoundly controversial, of the cultural revolution that is taking place in Puerto Rico as the society comes more and more under the sway of American mores. The discussion divides naturally into two parts: (1) an estimation of the scope and nature of the changes actually taking place and empirically verifiable, and (2) an examination of the implications of change in the area of ideas and values. Much of the sociological analysis of the society, as already suggested, has tended to avoid the second part of the discussion by retreating into an ivory tower of "diagnosis" and "prediction" without appreciating the truth that, if only by a deliberate silence on the controversial matters, it lends the strength of its findings to the dominant, i.e. American forces leading to culture change. To say, in defense, that "while the social scientist cannot establish the superiority of one value over another, he can assist in implementing given values,"[1] is to beg the vital question as to whether the "given" values are those of the local population or of a supervening community. That line of argument fails even more when there is a question, as there is in Puerto Rico, of one set of values being in conflict with another. Be that as it may, the evasiveness is there in the literature, so that it would be almost (although not quite) true to say that the facts of change get discussed by the American sociologists while the ethical implications of change, centered around the discussion of "Americanization," are canvassed by the insular intelligentsia.

It is not difficult to state the facts, in some detail, of insular sociocultural change. Ever since Charles Rogler's pioneer study of the small town of Comerío in 1940 there has been a steady stream of meticulous research appearing in print. There are gaps, of course— the realm of race relations, for example, where the conspiracy of silence on the part of most Puerto Ricans has been respected by the American analyst. It would be difficult, again, granted the power of Catholic prudishness among all classes, to conduct anything like a Kinsey investigation of sexual behavior in its more intimate aspects; and the oral contraceptive experiment conducted among Puerto Rican

working-class housewives by the local Family Planning Association
in recent years is not to be confused with such an investigation. These
qualifications, however, do not seriously frustrate the possibility of
making fairly dogmatic generalizations about culture change in the
society, despite the occupational tendency of academic investigators
to insist upon more and more "verification" through more and more
"research." Most certainly the qualifications do not absolve the investigator from the duty of relating the "facts" that he unearths to the issues
that trouble the thoughtful Puerto Rican. For we are dealing here not
with merely a straightforward case of cultural transformation. It is
something far more controversial: a case of cultural imperialism. The
economic dependency and the political ambiguity of the island, in its
relations with the American power, have gone hand in hand with a
deep sense of cultural loss and distortion. A culture of Hispanic,
Indian, and African elements has been exposed, without let or hin-
drance, to the American Protestant Anglo-Saxon culture. The economic and political advantages have been, and are still, very real. But
they have been obtained at a heavy cultural price, for they have
had the end result of creating a cultural gap between Puerto Rico and
the other societies of the Greater Antilles archipelago without genuinely incorporating the island into American cultural life. Puerto
Ricans have thus been unable to identify fully either with North
Americans or with fellow Latin Americans. To analyze the territorial
society without fairly confronting this issue is to compose Hamlet
without the Prince of Denmark. Yet much of the work, otherwise
praiseworthy, of the Social Sciences Research Center of the national
university has managed to do that; while it is astonishing that E. P.
Hanson's book can discuss the island's transformation at length without even mentioning Antonio Pedreira's book on *Insularismo*, the outstanding expression, so far, of Puerto Rican intellectual uneasiness
in this whole matter. What is now needed is that the facts of transformation shall be related to the great moral issues of cultural identity
and national self-determination. Perhaps the entire problem must be
seen less "scientifically" and more humanistically, for Beatrice Webb's
remark that the sociologically possible is not always the ethically
desirable has a peculiar relevance to the Puerto Rican discontents.

Of all insular institutions none has felt change so severely as the
family. Traditionally the Puerto Rican family, at all levels, has been
a variant of the older forms of European familial organization, relatively unaffected (as compared with the family in other Caribbean
societies) by native Indian or African Negro customs. Its source in
European Catholicism has given it a male authoritarian ideal in which

the husband has played the role of unquestioned *paterfamilias* and the wife, especially at the proletarian levels, has had almost a chattel status. A whole corpus of folkloristic rationalization has grown up—in the areas of child rearing, courtship practices, marital relations, the social function of the family—to buttress the consequent inequality between husband and wife. The woman is viewed as being inherently inferior to the man; she is even seen as suffering from a mental debility and a moral weakness which require an elaborate system of masculine checks upon her freedom of movement. The twin complexes of virginity and *machismo*, the Puerto Rican form of male chauvinism, operate, with a relentless persistency, to construct and maintain a rigid wall of psychological separation between the sexes at practically every stage of life. The first, firmly rooted in the Catholic Virgin Mary adoration, surrounds the Puerto Rican girl from infancy onwards with a repressive atmosphere of cloistered virtue. Courtship, when finally permitted, is parentally regulated; premarital sexual experience is effectively denied by a social taboo so deeply entrenched in the communal psychology of sex that its transgression on the part of a bride is visited with a humiliating return to her parents or occasionally with more violent chastisement; and the emotional frustrations generated by this jealous protectiveness lead to a high rate of early marriage, seen by young girls as the sole means of escape from parental tyranny. *Machismo*, on the other hand, not merely encourages but almost demands premarital sexual experience, only too often with prostitutes, on the part of the adolescent male as a sort of *rite de passage* into the state of manhood; and after marriage it no less demands a sort of Falstaffian braggadocio in which a premium is placed upon the ability of the man to become a *conquistador de mujeres*.

It is easy to see how all of this stands in the way of a healthy and rational relationship of the sexes, both within and outside of the marital state. Husband and wife, especially in lower-class Puerto Rico, approach their union from completely opposite points of view. The wife envisages the fulfillment of romantic expectations that are in turn fed by the peculiar tensions of courtship; the husband seeks, on the contrary, a mother-substitute in his marital choice, for there is a great deal of psychiatric evidence to suggest that the outward show of masculine virility hides a real tendency to infantile dependence upon feminine power. The husband comes to marriage already sexually experienced, if perhaps crudely, the wife comes to it not only with an appalling ignorance about sex but, even worse, with a traumatic fear of its mechanics. The opinions collected by Dr. J. Mayone Stycos and his associates from a group of lower-class married women, and Kathleen Wolf's revealing description of the sort of half-hysterical, half-prurient pre-wedding party that is thrown by her married friends to a bride-to-be in the middle class of the smaller towns,[2] suggests that there exists on the part of the woman a fear of sex relations so profound as to affect seriously the possibility of marital equilibrium. At the worst, this can mean a complete failure of any sort of democratic partnership, and Dr. Stycos has argued forcefully that one major reason for the non-appearance of rational fertility control in the proletarian family is to be found in the complex of mutual suspicion which in its turn prevents any sort of open discussion between husband and wife on the matter of sexual activity. At the best, it can lead, under certain circumstances, to a position where the woman plays a role of spurious authority. "Attitudes," Dr. Wolf writes of rural middle-class women at this point, "will vary from somewhat contemptuous amusement at men's antics to an irritated discussion of how to handle men when they are drunk or enraged. The tone of motherly solicitude in which these conversations are couched betrays the fact that in domestic crises men, in spite of their masculine assertiveness, fall into the role of rebellious but dependent children, while their wives take the role of irritated yet indulgent mothers."[3]

There are certain particular points to emphasize about all this. In the first place, there is a wide, almost schizophrenic, gulf between ideal and reality in marital relations. For the woman marriage, whether formal or consensual, is entered into in almost a Romeo-and-Juliet frame of mind, while the man only too easily sees himself as an irresistible Don Juan entering another adventure. But the reality of marriage, particularly in the lower-income groups, has little of the mythical Latin flavor about it. On the contrary, its whole tone strongly smacks of Calvinist puritanism. The Virgin-child complex converts the figure of the wife into an ideal to be adored rather than a partner to be lived with; and the consequent strain frequently becomes unbearable, as, indeed, the high rate of suicide at this social level appears to bear out. Nor is the violence only directed at self; the young father—returned, significantly, from a New York residential experience—who murdered his baby child in an interior small town merely because she was, from his viewpoint, of the wrong sex, revealed to a shocked society the terrible destructiveness that is latent in *machismo*.[4] The female respondent who told an interviewer that "They fall in love as I did and think heaven is coming, without knowing that what really comes is hell"[5] summed up, in her turn, the acid cynical bitterness that must overwhelm many women who flee from the tyranny of parents only to discover that they have embraced the worse tyranny of a husband. The highly stylized passion of the courtship, designed as it is to facilitate the almost universal struggle with the hostile parents of the *novia*, is rapidly replaced with casual indifference, so much so that it is a frequent complaint with many Puerto Rican wives that their husbands no longer care for them. The complaint, moreover, is likely to be heard at all social levels. For there are few common activities to bind together the partners even of many a middle-class household. The uneasy balance of interests reflects itself in the sexual segregation that takes place so conspicuously at parties in middle-class homes, with the men discussing politics in one group and the women discussing children in another. It is true that dream and reality do not always converge in the family sociology of most societies. But the discrepancy in the Puerto Rican case is enhanced by the fact, first, that there is little of the American habit of "competitive dating" to give young people a better chance to establish relationships of a genuine compatibility and, second, that the pattern of puritan modesty forbids the free exchange of opinion which is basic to any rich and satisfactory marriage.

The second factor to note is that, flowing as a corollary to all this, too many marriages skate almost habitually on the thin ice of jealousy. With the proletarian family it is more often male jealousy, for paradoxically the preoccupation with the idealized purity of women goes hand in hand with a wide suspicion of their easy surrender to temptation. With the professional classes it is rapidly becoming, in the American style, a feminine jealousy too, as the wife begins to resist the traditional "double standard" under the influence of more liberal American ideas. At both levels the wife is expected to conform to a set of behavioral values associated with approved definitions of a "good" wife. To attend a movie unescorted, to dance with a man other than one's husband, to entertain an abstract idea, even to permit a male friend of the family into the house in the absence of the husband—these still, for many wives, are acts tantamount to marital infidelity. Wives are under the keen scrutiny of men who, as a class, are almost pathologically sensitive to imagined "insults" to their spouses; more than one unsuspecting American has made a casual and harmless joke about a wife only to find himself confronted with an explosion of uxorious rage. Divorce, of course, is now socially respectable; the Governor himself is a divorced man. Even so, the divorcée still suffers such a real social penalty and becomes, much more than in American life, so much an open target for sexual depredation that not infrequently she moves to the States in search of a more tolerant climate of opinion. There is some significance, too, in the fact that whereas the marriage of an American girl to a Puerto Rican male is infrequent that of local girls to American males is quite popular and widespread. For while American sex norms have their own peculiar stresses and contradictions, there can be little doubt that many Puerto Rican women find in an American husband an easygoing tolerance and a readiness to accept them as an equal that they miss only too often in their male compatriots. Far too often the Puerto Rican male appears to them as an immature person who does not so much love women as the self he asserts by conquering them.

The sociological imagination frequently fails to appreciate the large moral question of sex equality that lies behind all this. To see the detail of Puerto Rican courtship, for example, as nothing much more than a cultural mechanism whereby the girl learns early to subject her personality to that of her prospective husband is not good enough.[6] For the vital questions begin exactly at that point. As the extended kinship family begins to be displaced by the American type of individualistic family the woman begins to experience a new birth of freedom. She already enjoys a more egalitarian status in the working-class households of the rural lowlands and the urban districts, where the more congested living quarters, the better educational facilities for children and the chances of outside employment for women all conspire to qualify the traditional pattern. There even begins to emerge, in some of these households, the economically and emotionally independent woman characteristic of the robust peasant types of the French and British West Indies. This, in its turn, is accelerated by the rapid emancipation of the servant class as factory employment competes with the old-fashioned household drudgery of domestic service. Every socially conscious Puerto Rican must welcome this particular change, since, as a former Secretary of Education has reminded the island's social welfare workers, the servant is a relic of slavery which ought to disappear, not to mention the fact that as the middle-class woman finds it more and more difficult to obtain a servant she is driven to do chores herself, like looking after the children, which can only serve to strengthen, not weaken, the family structure.[7] The change is naturally more pronounced in its upper-class manifestations. The university co-ed who comes from a small town soon learns to appreciate the more liberal atmosphere of Rio Piedras, even with the handicap of supervised living in the town *pensionados* and the convent-like college *dormitorios*. The habit of the chaperone is in rapid decline in the city life; it is no longer poor form for a girl to smoke in public; and the elaborate play of delicate flirting in the Sunday evening *paseo* of the Ponce *plaza* has almost declined into a quaint tourist attraction. The universities offer a new professional opportunity: in 1957 there were some 236 women members in a total faculty of somewhat more than a thousand in the national university. The total employment picture, indeed, promises a new economic independence to women of all groups; as early as 1955 there were 184,000 female wage and salary workers in the economy, compared to a total of 467,000 male workers; and of these, 22,000 were in government service, 36,000 in the service industries, and 15,000 in the clothing and apparel industries.[8]

Even the men's world of politics has been successfully invaded. Feminine politicians like María Libertad Gómez and Felisa Rincón de Gautier have made names for themselves in the *Popular* movement, while the dramatic actress Mona Marti has added her own flamboyant attractiveness to the *Independentista* ticket. In the field of more general public affairs, the Governor's wife is a veritable Eleanor Roosevelt in her role as insular first lady: Mrs. Jaime Benítez is quietly effective in her role as the University Chancellor's wife; Nilita Viéntos Gastón is an able literary critic; while Jane Nicole de Mariani devotes herself to the thankless task of combatting the menace of noise in the society. The churches have been slower in their recognition of women, but they are moving in the right direction: the local Methodist Church recently ordained its first woman minister. The professions, at other points, continue to resist the process. It is a real anomaly, for example, that as late as 1958 there were only six women superintendents out of a total of seventy-five in the Department of Education, notwithstanding the immense preponderance of women— some 80 percent of the total—in the ranks of the teaching profession.[9] There should be more women in the higher governmental spheres: the legislature, the mayoralties, the ranking federal posts. Many of the women in these new fields of feminine enterprise, it is true, are single or widowed, but that is a familiar stage, soon passed through, in the history of all movements of feminine emancipation. The more representative figure becomes, increasingly, the young married woman who is at the same time an energetic professional; one thinks, offhand, of someone like Sandra Rivera, the young theater director who learned her trade at the Pasadena Playhouse, or Piri Fernández de Lewis, the President of the *Ateneo*. All of these, as a type, know how to combine professional zest with feminine serenity; for although psychiatry booms in San Juan as elsewhere the Puerto Rican professional woman has a long way to go before she exhibits the notorious frustrations and tensions of her American counterpart. What remains to be done now in the island is to move forward towards the more mature stages of the process. They could perhaps be no more aptly announced than by replacing John Stuart Mill's *Essay on Liberty* (read to death by the social sciences students of the University of Puerto Rico) with his *Essay on the Subjection of Women* in the University curriculum.

The emancipatory process is likely to be resisted, with few exceptions, by the Puerto Rican masculine world. It has been argued, at the theoretical level, that the substitution of Catholic by Protestant norms can only mean the exchange of an easygoing Catholic attitude for an inflexible puritan rigor engendering dangerous psychological conflict and repression.[10] This may be so, particularly in the area of work attitudes. It is suggestive that a Puerto Rican intellectual of the last century who was much influenced by liberal Protestantism could at one and the same time describe, in his memoirs, his own pleasure at joining in tropical night parties, singing the *aguinaldos campestros* as he and his companions rode through the Puerto Rican hills, and criticize the habit of the *fiestas patronales* because they encouraged the laborers to be lazy.[11] But the argument omits the vital consideration that Catholic tolerance of human nature has reached, traditionally, to the sexual behavior of men only and that Protestantism, though like most organized religions it has been inhospitable to any genuine equality of the sexes, has been far more favorable to a limited freedom for the woman both in social life and in the life of the churches. At the practical level, the emancipatory process is met by stubborn resistance, frequently rationalized by the erroneous belief that American women are "loose" and that American influence must therefore be fought. Nor does an American education always help. There are many Puerto Rican professional men who have come back from a stay of three or four years at Harvard or Chicago with all the old phobias about masculine superiority untouched. It is probable that the growing minority of husbands who relinquish these phobias do so as much through natural feeling as through intellectual assent to the idea of equality.

It is sometimes argued, in the literary debate on the idea, that the Puerto Rican woman herself does not want change; although the evidence is suspect once it is remembered that most Puerto Rican literature, with the exception of the occasional poet like Julia de Burgos or the historian like Isabel Gutiérrez del Arroyo, has been a man's literature. But this thesis too is untenable, and no more convincing proof could be offered than the fact that, as the investigations of Paul K. Hatt (1952) and J. Mayone Stycos (1955) show conclusively, an overwhelming majority of working class women would like to reduce the size of their families drastically. The attitude, in the words of one of them—that children for the rich are even a recreation, for the poor man they are always a burden—seems to be sufficiently widespread to be able to counteract the powerful sentimental predilections of a traditionally child-centered culture.[12] It is for this reason that it is irresponsibly misleading to denounce planned birth control (as does a critic like Felix Cohen) as a "value judgment" made by people who do not like Puerto Ricans,[13] for the need for such a population control method is urged not merely by such hypothetically wicked anti-Puerto Rican investigators but is even more ardently accepted by the women of Puerto Rico who know the social and physical costs of excessive child bearing. The demographic statistics indicate, too, that as the reduction in births is canceled out by a reduction in deaths, thus doing little to lower the rate of natural increase in population, the current pace of growth, given the already high population density, could wipe out the benefits of the industrialization program within a generation. The stage is clearly set for widespread birth limitation through social planning. It could have nothing but beneficial results both for the freedom of the individual Puerto Rican woman and for the happiness of the family as a whole. The Puerto Rican male who resists all this is patently fighting, like King Canute with the waves, a losing battle.

The question of religion in the island society is obviously related to the question of the family. The inherent brutality of Spain was no more apparent than in the utter failure of its state church to meet the social question before 1898. The deficiency even today of a widespread and enlightened public opinion in the society goes back to the church's failure either to challenge the caste system of overseas Spain (of which indeed it was an integral part) or to undertake the moral or mental elevation of the masses. The observation of the chaplain of the American army of occupation at the time of the transfer, that the island was a Catholic country without religion whatever and that the sacrament of confirmation had not been administered for many years in a great part of it, indicated the lethargy almost certain to overcome a hierarchy that for some four hundred years had had no competition whatsoever; for it was not until the very last years of the regime that Protestant churches were permitted in Ponce and the island of Vieques, and even this was allowed only because Queen Victoria had petitioned the Spanish Crown at the request of a few English immigrants in those places. The isolation was fatal, for it left the religious welfare of the Puerto Rican people to the mercies of an expatriate clergy whose sympathies were wholly Spanish. The failure to establish a local university was only one price that the colony had to pay for the ecclesiastical monopoly in the field of education; and it was perhaps ironic that the demand of the local liberal forces for such an institution was made in the very year, 1810, in which what is today the splendidly situated University of the Andes in Mérida, Venezuela, was granted collegiate status. Perhaps even worse was the failure of the colonial church to take a stand on the slavery issue under Spain; Alejandro Tapia y Rivera has recorded in his autobiography the damning fact that whereas there had been occasional lawyers, like Hernández Arvizu, who had been prepared to defend the slave, the Spanish clergy, like the clergy in the southern states of the American Union, defended the institution as one ordained by divine law.[14]

The American passion for popular education naturally meant an immense improvement after 1898. Even American military governors looked around for means of converting Spanish barracks into American schools. The Protestant missionary complex, of course, was impossibly condescending, as Mrs. Blythe's book abundantly shows. But it was a real advance, nonetheless, upon Spanish clericalist indifference. It showed an enthusiastic concern for the common man. Even more, it undertook—especially after the formation of the Evangelical Council in 1919—to train a native Puerto Rican ministry, a policy that Spanish Catholicism had never countenanced lest it encourage an anti-Spanish religious nationalism. The policy has been intensified as the older Protestant churches—the Episcopalians, Baptists, and Methodists—have been followed in the insular proselytization by the more energetic "hot gospel" sectaries like the Pentecostalists, the Disciples of Christ, and Jehovahs Witnesses. To listen in to a "store front" church meeting or a private house meeting characterized by much raucous hymn-singing is to understand how evangelical fundamentalism, in Puerto Rico as elsewhere, can appeal to a rural proletariat because it affords, unlike either the Catholic or the orthodox Protestant churches, a democratic congregationalist experience for the socially disinherited.

There have been, in fact, two distinct stages in the religious history of the island since 1898. The first stage encompassed the introduction and growth of the orthodox American Protestant churches, working through their mission boards and heavily subsidizing their Puerto Rican enterprises because of the absolute inability of the local proletarian congregations to become financially self-supporting. This meant, in effect, a system of religious colonialism. The second stage grew out of a nativist reaction against an American Protestantism that was middle-class in its outlook and financial organization and therefore tended to be a religious expression of the territorial dependence, political and economic, upon the United States. The major Protestant churches continue, even today, to be dependent upon the continental mother churches; the Episcopalian bishopric is occupied still by an American incumbent; many pastoral letters, especially in the city areas, are sent out in English; and the Evangelical Council can still think it appropriate to stage a mass revivalist meeting in a San Juan sports stadium in which Billy Graham, through an interpreter, addresses a large Spanish-speaking audience. The more popular pentecostal groups have thus flourished in response to the emotional needs of a people too uninhibited in their attitudes to be satisfied with American Protestant middle-class norms. They have not acquired, of course, the colorful eccentricity of such cult religions as the Jamaican Rastafari or the Trinidadian Shango groups, nor do they have political overtones comparable say to the Rastafari creed which sees contemporary Caribbean society as the oppression of the black man by an alliance of white and brown Babylonians to be ended only by Ethiopian repatriation.[15] They have no sense of alienation from Puerto Rico itself. Rather their prime function is to provide for the cash-dependent Puerto Rican poor, both rural and urban, a sense of emotional security in a changing world. They thus reflect, like the more quaint cargo cults of Melanesia, the cultural disturbance of more backward peoples as they are driven to comprehend the modern Western technology that is gradually overwhelming them.

All this has meant the breakdown of traditional Catholicism. In part, this is due to the general secularizing trend that has undermined formal institutional religion the world over. In part, however, it is due to local reasons. Historically the Catholic church, especially in regions like the island's south coast, has suffered from its identification with the upper class. After 1898 its Hispanic stamp made adjustment to a new society difficult; indeed the continuing persecution of the Protestant churches in Franco Spain suggests that had Catholicism in Puerto Rico had the opportunity it would have remained equally uncompromising towards the "heretic." Its priests continued to remain anti-social. They either actively opposed or remained indifferent to innovating movements like Prohibition and the Social Purity campaigns. They sought to resist the Protestant proselytizing of their more affluent parishioners with the argument that "only the poor people are Protestant."[16] They fought against the intellectual enlightenment of the masses; even the American priests among them could meet the tragedy of earthquakes by leading candle-light processions to appease the wrath of the Devil and by insisting (in one case) that the people of the town had brought the tragedy upon themselves by persisting in the removal of a former priest for grossly immoral conduct.[17] Even under Spain the church had done little to instruct its adherents in the intellectual foundations of the faith, so much so that many of them had turned to the "superstition" of the popular saint cults, with an occasional touch of African cultural influence, as in the Loíza Aldea *fiesta* on the north coast. Since 1898, inevitably, the combined pressure of the formal separation of church and state and the new American Catholic hierarchy, the latter less mystical and more pragmatic than its Spanish predecessor, has helped to stay the decline. The present-day American priests are generally recognized as being more liberal than the Spanish clerics, more ready to fraternize with their flock, more willing even to recognize women as equals and not (as the popular Catholic magazines still insist) as creatures mentally and biologically inferior to men. There is now a Catholic university; and more native clergy: in 1958 the Order of Redemptorists installed its first three native-born priests. Even so Puerto Rico at best is a Catholic society in a cultural sense only. Catholic festivals, such as those of the patron saints of the individual towns, have become almost entirely recreational. Many of the religious societies, frequently of American origin, like the Holy Name Society and the Knights of Columbus, reflect the secularization of activities. Even the integrity of Catholic dogma begins to weaken under American influence, and it is a suggestive sign that Bishop Fulton Sheen's syndicated newspaper column, so neo-Protestant in its "peace of mind" emphasis, appears regularly in one of the territorial newspapers.

All in all, the message of the traditional churches, both Catholic and Protestant, falls far short of satisfying the clamant needs of Puerto Rican life. The chief weakness of Protestantism is that it has been an American middle-class morality exported without alteration to a land where the middle class, as it is known in the United States, has hardly existed until yesterday and even now is in an embryonic form only. The dilemma was candidly stated by the American hierarchy itself in its analysis of 1942, summing up some forty years of evangelical effort. "The ministry which the Evangelical Church has introduced to the island," it noted, "is a middle-class profession, alien to Puerto Rican society and to the economic structure and life of the community."[18] It tried to fit an ecclesiastical structure used to the free will offering as its financial basis to a society where gross poverty and the economic practices of the Catholic church made it a hopeless anachronism. Its outlook was shaped to urban congregations, while the Puerto Rican membership was overwhelmingly in the rural field. Its ministers had been trained to cater to city churches made up of middle-class people. "How far can homiletics, church history, dogmatics and systematic theology," the report asked itself, "prepare a man to serve a rural community in which only one-half of the people are literate; over one-third are out of work for sometimes more than six months of the year; four-fifths are in debt; three-quarters are weakened by hookworm, malaria, and other parasitic infections; and a majority are squatters who have practically no knowledge of how to use the soil to grow food crops and most of whom are undernourished, listless and hopeless. This is typical Puerto Rico."[19] It makes much more sense to develop a corps of local pastors around a rural-centered social service organization; and the way has already been shown by the remarkable work of institutions like the Presbyterian church farm at Quebrada Limón and the Friends social settlement center at Castañer.

The Catholic church, similarly, although more genuinely national in its scope of operations, is hardly national in any really representative sense. Its faith has hardly been more than skin-deep with the vast majority of communicants. The astounding array of virtues traditionally assigned to the *jíbaro* in the local romantic literature—generosity, wisdom, patience, hospitality—have always been less religious than folk-patterned. There is a noticeable absence of religious taboos against the use of contraceptive devices on the part of the general population, and Catholic teaching is so little regarded in that area of personal behavior that to take it seriously may be taken popularly, in the sharp words of one observer, to be a sign of mental weakness.[20] And even belief is at least half-magical in its roots. Thousands of faithful who flocked to a supposed miraculous appearance of a Virgin Saint in an island village seemed to have been motivated less by a spirit of Catholic veneration than by a pathetic search for cure from crippling illness and infirmity.[21] Finally, the wide prevalence of various forms of spiritualism in the society (tending, at the higher class levels, to merge into theosophical societies) shows how frequently many Puerto Ricans turn for catharsis to a set of beliefs unequivocally condemned as spiritually dangerous by the church. The relationship between the spiritualist session and mental therapy is a real one, especially for those Puerto Ricans who suffer, through their personal neuroses, from the failure of their society to build up a cohesive community consciousness. For many of them, too, setting up as a medium provides an avenue of social mobility not readily available through other means. Not least of all, spiritualist membership, in the *Fraternidad Surcos* for example, affiliated to the International Spiritualist Federation of London, provides a focus of social identity for many people who become socially lost in a rapidly changing economy. Just how widespread the appeal of spiritualism may be can indeed be judged from the fact that even the free thought of one of the leading writers and politicians at the turn of the century, Rosendo Matienzo Cintrón, could finally wander off into a confused spiritualism feeding on the questionable ideas of Lombroso and Alex Kardec, so much so that at least a fifth of his edited writings and speeches were devoted to the topic.[22]

It is surprising, considering all this, that the relationship between religion and politics has not been closer than it is. It might have been

expected that, under Spain, a nationalist Catholic movement would
have grown up, like Gallicanism in seventeenth-century France, and
that under the United States it would have grown even stronger, in
the same way as Irish nationalism in the nineteenth century was
strengthened by the conflict between a Catholic subordinate society
and a Protestant dominant power. Spanish religious policy stifled the
possibility before 1898, although an autonomist-minded bourgeois
class did exist as its possible social base: one of the first acts of the
Lares insurrectionists of 1868, after they had seized control of that
mountain town, was to compel the local priest to hold a solemn mass
for them in the cathedral. As for the American period, the Vatican
policy of appointing Spanish or American candidates to the island
bishoprics has not yet fully yielded to the local Catholic sentiment in
favor of Puerto Rican candidates. Two of the three island bishoprics
—the metropolitan see and the Ponce prelature—are occupied by
Americans; and a Puerto Rican bishop, Monseñor Alfredo Mendez,
was only finally appointed to the Arecibo position in the ecclesiastical
reorganization of 1960, for the first time since the days of Juan
Arizmendi in the years before his death in 1820, the sole nativist to
hold such an appointment for some four hundred years of the church's
residence in the colony. The early period after 1898 did produce,
true enough, a resurgence of Catholic strength as many persons came
to see Catholicism as a symbol of traditional Puerto Rican values
threatened by Protestant America. But the feeling did not persist in
any real manner, largely because the insular Catholicism itself became
somewhat "Americanized" as the structure and personnel of the
American congregation began to replace those of the Spanish.

That is where the matter stands today. So much, indeed, is that the
case that it is now extremely doubtful whether the key to Puerto
Rican culture (whatever it might have been in the period immediately
after 1898) is the conflict between a local Catholic way of life and
a dominant American Protestant culture. The truth of the matter is
that within the last sixty years there has taken place a dual process,
the "Americanization" of Catholicism and, to some extent, as already
noted, the Puertoricanization of Protestantism. That can be seen in
the way in which the earlier drama of struggle between the Catholic
priest and the American missionary has given way to the struggle,
nowadays much more common, between the Catholic priest and the
Puerto Rican religious journeyman of ultra-revivalist leanings. It can
be seen in the fact that not only are there few nativist Catholic clergy
but also a disastrously slow effort to train them; so, a local Catholic
source is obliged to admit, after seeking to prove that the policy of
the Puerto Rican ecclesiastical province has been to seek out a native

clergy ever since the early sixteenth century, that if all expatriate clergy, nuns and bishops, were to leave the island it would mean an exodus of over 500 persons, leaving behind a tiny number of about 70 Puerto Ricans.[23]

Above all, however, this general truth can be seen in the details of the revival, in 1962, of the controversy about the status of the English language in the island schools, especially in the Catholic parochial schools. For in that argument, centering around whether English should be taught only as the leading foreign language or should become the general language of instruction, the Church revealed itself as the new defendant of the compulsory Anglicization of the schools, taking over, indeed, where the United States federal government had left the matter in 1949. Not only did there seem to be present a deliberate policy, on the part of the hierarchy, to discourage teaching in the autochthonous language, but also an attempt, on the part of certain groups of nuns, to persuade the parents of pupils even to speak English at home; and the protesting correspondence of lay groups cited the revealing case of a group of Puerto Rican children in one school who petitioned their Spanish-speaking priest to confess them in English. The protest, it is worth noting, based itself upon (1) the natural right of parents to determine the cultural bent of their childrens' education and (2) the general sympathy of Papal directives and church tradition to local cultures. It was a protest, moreover, of a non-political character, transcending political alignments. The entire episode, made even more ugly by the crass intrusion of Congressman Adam Clayton Powell in his capacity as chairman of the House Education and Labor Committee, showed how alienated the official Catholic establishment is from at once the local vernacular and the local culture patterns of which it is an expression. When, indeed, as the statistics unearthed by the controversy revealed, only four out of a total of forty Protestant schools teach in English while, of the Catholic schools, at least fifty-four out of a total of ninety-two use the outside language as the vehicle of instruction, the emptiness of the traditional claim that Catholicism is the Puerto Rican religion *par excellence* is more than proved. The Roman church on the island, clearly enough, is less and less the church of the people. That fact, perhaps, may explain the recent phenomenon of the conversion to the faith of a number of university intellectuals; for as the Church becomes less popular its appeal might be increased for the spiritual snob. But in any case there seems little possibility at the moment of a Romeward Oxford Movement coming out of the university city of Rio Piedras.[24]

For all of these reasons, and more, the local political parties have never seen the religious question as the question of the day. The status question has always pre-empted any other. Apart from that, it must be remembered that the United States came to the island in 1898 with relatively clean hands as far as the religious issue was concerned. There were not, as in the case of Ireland, three centuries of brutal military occupation and economic landlordism to leave behind a legacy of irrepressible hate which manages, even now, to sustain the fatal political partition between Ulster and the Republic. Thus the Puerto Rican religious divisions today have little to do with economic or political ones. The leader of the pro-American Statehood Republican Party is also a leading Catholic layman. The President of the *Independentista* party is a Protestant, although there has always been a militant Catholic group within that party seeing independence as the mode of salvation for a Catholic Puerto Rico. There was a circle of *libre pensadores* in the *Popular* party at the beginning, but not enough to make of the party an openly anti-Catholic group such as the Argentinian Liberals. This perhaps explains why the birth control program of the government has never become a full-blown official campaign to popularize control methods, despite the fact that, from what is known of public opinion on the matter, such a campaign might enjoy considerable success. It is at least certain that an official clerical attack upon a *Popular* candidate accused of virulent animosity toward the church does not prevent his successful election to the legislature.[25] Similarly, a *Popular* leader may openly confess to an early youthful agnosticism for which he now claims, in wiser old age, to be carrying his cross of penance, like some new Simon of Cyrene; but this does not prevent him from insisting, at the same time, that the legitimate principle governing church-state relationships should continue to be the American doctrine of the complete separation of the two authorities.[26]

If there is indeed any religious question per se it concerns this issue of church-state separation. And even there the local Catholic position —stated most recently with reference to the relevant legislation of 1940—does little more than echo that of the continental Catholic congregation in its demand for freedom to undertake religious instruction in the state schools. The entire issue was thrashed out in the debate in the Constitutional Convention of 1951-1952. A reading of that debate makes it evident beyond doubt that (1) the majority of the convention delegates, of all parties, were determined to protect the religious neutrality of the state power, so much so that the clause of the 1952 Constitution containing that desideratum is even more distinct in its language than the famous clause of the American Constitution; and that (2) it is therefore impossible to read into their attitude that they meant to permit a policy, especially in education, of "cooperation" between church and state which would at least allow the "free time" formula practiced in some of the American states. Nor is this all. The claim of the Puerto Rican bench of bishops that the federal precedent does not fully apply because Puerto Rico is a "Catholic" country is hard to accept in the light of the facts. There are at least 500 Protestant churches, with an active and militant membership of some 250,000 parishioners, in the island. The religious heterogeneity is indeed so self-evident and the merely habitual character of so much Catholic "belief" beyond doubt that it would be true to say that the Roman church in the island can no more claim to be the "national" church than the Church of England can claim to be so in the United Kingdom. In any case, there would seem to be very little danger, in reality, of the state authority being used in the island against the Catholic church. On the contrary. The federal Congress amended an already favorable section of the 1952 Constitution by requiring that educational policies may not be so formulated as to jeopardize the position of the private church schools.[27] The official birth control program, of which the orthodox Catholic leadership makes so much strident fuss, limits itself, with excess of caution, to the passive offering of contraceptive advice to patients who request it, so much so that some students have suggested that the usefulness of the program has thereby been seriously impaired. There is a widespread practice, especially at the municipal level, of the political authorities placing public facilities at the disposal of the Catholic church, especially on the occasions of the saints' day festivals.[28] And at every level, including the ceremonial functions of the central government, there is a distinct tendency—derived from the days when the church could command unhesitating respect from the secular authority—to favor the Catholic hierarchy in the matter of invitations to participate in celebrations.[29] That hierarchy certainly is not in anything like the precarious position of the French princes of the Haitian church who, for over a century, have had to face, on and off, the fierce hostility of that island republic's Creole political leadership. Whatever hazards confront organized religion in contemporary Puerto Rico, of a surety they do not include the hazard of a Bismarckian *Kulturkampf*.

Nothing of all this is in any way invalidated by the unusual and startling intrusion of the church into partisan politics in 1960 with the creation, openly backed by the bishops, of a Christian Action Party. For to justify that action, unleashing as it did a frenzied uproar remarkable even by Puerto Rican standards, with the declaration, in the words of the Chancellor of the San Juan diocese, that the Governor and his party were "openly attacking" religion is to ignore in quite crass fashion the general record of the *Populares* in all matters affecting religion. It ignores equally the generally respectful attitude of the average Puerto Rican citizen to the religious experience; there is very little agnosticism in *Popular* rank and file members who could respond to the bishops with the declaration "My heart is with God. My vote with the Popular Democratic Party." Clerical endorsement of a political party, including the open employment of priests in the task of helping to register it so that the rosary should appear on the ballot paper, may indeed prove in the long run to be the gravest error committed by the church in its entire territorial history. For none of the reasons that have justified the rise of large and important Christian Democratic parties in post-war Western Europe—the presence, for example, of powerful Marxist parties openly embracing anticlerical principles and the possibility, therefore, of open persecution of religion by governments formed by those parties—exist in Puerto Rico. It is consequently unlikely that the new party will ever manage to recruit the mass following of such parties—the MRP, for example, in the French Fourth Republic. If the events of 1960 are any foretaste of things to come, the new Catholic political strategy is far more likely to generate a popular anticlericalism of the Latin American variety hitherto unknown in insular politics. There are signs already that, in the unlettered, it will evoke the suspicion that the cause of religion is not necessarily the cause of the church and, in the educated laity, a severe strain on conscience as its members seek to reconcile their filial loyalty to the church with their knowledge that a politics founded on religious lines of division can only mean unhappy strife for the community. Not even the declared agnostic can derive much pleasure from all this, for J. N. Figgis's remark (with reference to the European experience) that political liberty is the residuary legatee of ecclesiastical animosities has little meaning in a society where that liberty is already a full reality in the scheme of things. Reasonably minded Puerto Ricans might have said farewell to their 1960 election year with the observation of one Catholic layman that the only way to avoid the evils of anticlericalism is to bury clericalism.[30]

The characteristic trilogy of the Caribbean social drama has been family, religion and color. The frontier conditions of Caribbean life made the family a fragile institution at best. The sugar and slave economy, uprooting whole generations from their African background, gave rise to the esoteric cult religions—voodoo, obeah, the saint cults—of the Afro-Caribbean variety. Racial intermixture, finally (the inevitable consequence wherever the sex drive finds itself in a slavery environment), produced the massive complexes of color psychology in the regional life, with serious results both for the quality of personal self-esteem and of social life.

There is a widespread belief in Puerto Rico that whatever the family and religious situations may be there is no local problem of race prejudice. The belief usually adopts one of two methods of evidence. The first is to argue (as José Celso Barbosa and Tomás Blanco have done) that if there is discrimination it exists only in "social" or "class" areas, a phenomenon plausible enough, perhaps, in the light of the cultural heritage of Spanish pride of class. The second is, overtly or by implication, to accept the North American criteria of discrimination, based as they are upon an open black-white dichotomy, and then apply them to Puerto Rican conditions: the method is implicit, for example, in the 1959 Civil Liberties Committee report on racial discrimination. The general consequence of both modes of argument is to facilitate an optimistic tone whenever the problem is discussed. The optimism is frequently accepted un-critically by outside observers or even resident Americans as proof that all is well; thus, Professor Henry Wells can sweepingly assert that there is "an almost total absence of deep-rooted value conflicts: the island has always been notably free of racial tension, religious controversy, and class antagonism."[31] The reluctance of the individual Puerto Rican to discuss racialism, in particular with Americans, is in part justified, perhaps, by his suspicion that most Americans are prejudiced in one degree or another. It does not fully explain, however, the quite powerful taboo on such discussion within the local community itself. Nor does it in any way justify the conclusion that, if prejudice exists, it must be due to the growing influence of American attitudes.

What, in truth, is the position? To begin with, insular history has been such as to ameliorate the harsher features of race relations. The rapid growth of the free mulatto class and the degree of racial inter-marriage have already been noted, facilitating, in part, the emergence of the new social order of post-slavery Caribbean life, the Creole society of the classic form, even before the advent of legal emancipation. It is true that slave rebellions were not unknown and that Spanish liberalism, as compared with British or Dutch policies, must not be exaggerated. It is true nonetheless that none of those rebellions reached the grim magnitude of the St. Johns revolt of 1833 or that of St. Croix in 1848. And it is an astonishing fact, as the Spanish Cortes was told in the 1873 debates on emancipation, that Puerto Rican slaveowners themselves petitioned for emancipation, against the inclination of the mother country.[32] All of these factors contributed to a marked improvement in the social role of the freed Negro in the second half of the nineteenth century, as compared with worsening conditions throughout the first half. The names of Barbosa, Morell Campos, Carrión Maduro and Pedro Timothee testify to his social mobility. He was still debarred from the police, the magistracy, and business. But the independent professions welcomed him, and at the proletarian level there were real opportunities. Henry Carroll reported in 1900 that of the eleven working class representatives who testified before him at that time nine were Negroes, all of whom, with one exception, could read and write and were decently clothed.[33] The observation takes on some further significance in the light of the fact that white labor tended to survive in the Puerto Rican coffee and tobacco economies and worked side by side without friction with Negro labor, encouraging thereby a widespread habit of intermarriage, especially after 1900, between the white highland laborers and the colored coastal people. The *hidalgo*-like contempt for manual labor was there, of course; but at least colored and white workers shared the opprobrium together. Equally, the fact helped to shatter the myth— an article of faith in all of the apologetic literature on slavery—of the innate inability of the white person to undertake physical labor in the tropics.

These factors help to explain the contemporary situation. They accelerated an amalgamative process between the races, so that there has grown up an entire vocabulary (as throughout Latin America) of terms indicating with nice exactitude the degree of color discoverable in any given person. There is very little, in the Puerto Rican Negro, of the belligerent militancy of his counterpart in the United States. The term "Negro" itself is more one of endearment in personal relations, even between whites, than it is one of derogation; significantly, too, there are no equivalents in Spanish of the opprobrious epithets "nigger" and "coolie" that are in such common use throughout the former British West Indies. There is full political equality for Negroes, to the extent that where there are colored Puerto Ricans in the Legislature, like Leopoldo Figueroa or the late Ernesto Ramos Antonini, they are there not as trustees of a supposed "Negro" vote but as high-ranking members of the leading political parties. Creole society in the island has many features in common with the social structure of a southern American state like Louisiana, but it is markedly different in that there is no elaborate complex of political oppression against the Negro citizen to make possible the emergence of a white paternalistic "nigger lover" like the late Governor Earl Long. Both the local Socialist Party and, after it, the *Popular* Party have been instrumental in widening employment opportunities for dark-skinned Puerto Ricans in, for example, the teaching profession and the police force, including the higher echelons of the latter group. In the field of religion, again, there admittedly is a temptation on the part of light-colored groups to equate witchcraft and magic with Negro groups; but at the same time the Negro middle class is an accepted part of congregations, both Catholic and Protestant. African elements, if any, have been assimilated, not isolated. At least one of the most revered patron saints of the island, the Virgin of Monserrate, is unmistakably dark-colored and the fact has entered some of the popular devotional verse:

> *Virgen de Monserrate,*
> *Virgen de Hormigueros,*
> *dime quien te ha dado*
> *tu color moreno.*

And all this, finally, is reinforced by the fact that there is an increasing degree of racial anonymity going on as anatomic characteristics popularly designated as Negroid become less and less conspicuous in the individual heavily colored person, with the exceptions of certain population pockets in the island.

But how far does all this amount to a genuine racial democracy? Very little, perhaps, in any complete way. For racial tensions do not have to assume the forms of physical violence or of overt segregationism or even of open political expression before they can be said to exist. In Puerto Rico, as elsewhere in the Caribbean, they express themselves more subtly through the vehicle of racial intermediacy, the discreet yet very real sense of color snobbishness based upon the awareness of "shades." So, whereas in the United States one drop of "colored" blood designates one as a Negro, in Latin America and the Caribbean one drop of "white" blood can launch an individual on the road to social acceptance as white. The consequence of this difference is of course to protect the Caribbean colored person from the evils of "white supremacy." At the same time, it also serves to impose upon him a heavy burden of emotional insecurity. For the American Negro, save for the tiny minority who "pass," remains a defined Negro; he is what he is; he knows where he stands; his Puerto Rican brother is daily confronted with the torture of an ambivalent racial identity. "If the mulatto looks more like a white person than a Negro," Dr. Rogler has noted, "he is socially defined as a white person, providing his accomplishments so rate him." His self-appraisal therefore revolves around his success in obtaining that badge of social recognition. In a more mysterious procedure, perhaps, he shares with the American Negro the half-conscious envy of "whiteness," the conviction of its utter desirability. If he is curiously silent about it all, it is because he fears the problem and therefore attempts to hide it within himself. But that he is quite right to be aware of race mixture, and of its social penalties, is evident enough in the number of popular sayings that are illustrative of an attitude of, at best, genial contempt towards the colored person: Professor Rosario has collated them and put them together in his study of 1940.[34] The ramifications of the attitude run deep and wide throughout the society. As early as 1901 an American social service worker could report that in the charity schools of the island it was looked upon as a degradation for any but Negroes to do housework.[35] An American visitor could write in a home journal in 1922 that it was curious that Puerto Rican Negroes seemed to be Republican in their political sympathies; and the local rival party press was quite willing to reprint the observation as a means of taunting its opponents.[36] During the 1930's and 1940's, again, an important psychological reason for the widespread recruitment into the extremist Nationalist Party was the insecurity feeling of the mulatto who could never determine whether he hated the white American or the obvious Puerto Rican Negro more. The type furnished material for many of the party's leaders. Styling themselves white and vehemently denying Negro ancestry, they were clearly enough victims of a virulent sense of racial shame, disguising itself under a spurious and comic invocation of things Spanish. They perhaps saw themselves as the custodians of the old Spanish colonial tradition, without appreciating that a Spanish grandee, had he ever witnessed their aping of his manner, would have dismissed them as arrogantly as the Napoleonic nobility of the First Empire discounted the abilities of the Haitian black leadership after 1800. The sentiment led them into a grotesque perversity of values, as when, for example, they could attack Senator Chavez of New Mexico as a "cultural hybrid" who had betrayed his own Mexican "race" in order to seek success in North American politics.[37] More recently, the trilogy of plays produced by the playwright Francisco Arriví has dramatically portrayed the trauma of race shame that afflicts the mulatto group; in *Sirena* the figure of the mulatto girl who undergoes facial plastic surgery in order to win the love of the white man she adores speaks eloquently for the emotional price the group has to pay for living in a multi-racial society not yet come to satisfactory terms with its color question.

The characteristic form of racial discrimination thus is "shade" discrimination. It is not less real because it is more difficult to decipher than the American forms of discrimination. Nor does it make it any less illiberal to call it, as does Tomás Blanco in his essay of 1942, "social" and not "racial." Nor indeed does the use, however charming, of characteristic euphemisms to refer to racial admixture—*pardo, moreno, trigueño*—disguise the fact that social acceptance goes hand in hand with the degree of whiteness in skin texture. "A person who has marked Negro physical characteristics," Dr. Raymond Scheele writes of the upper class, "and is therefore described as a Negro, may have high income, great political power, and advanced education, yet on racial grounds may be excluded from the inner circles of intimate family life, Greek letter sorority or fraternity membership, and the more select social clubs. He may attend political affairs, be a guest at the governor's palace, and be invited to political cocktail parties, because people wish to cultivate his friendship, but he would probably not be asked to a girl's engagement party or other more private functions."[38] Wealthy white men may marry light-skinned mulatto women without loss of status, but their wives will rarely achieve equal social recognition. The wives in other unions may bring wealth to the husband, if he is comparatively poor, in exchange for which they will receive the socially desirable attribute of whiteness. Correspondingly, marriages of white men to dark mulatto or Negro women can carry with them a strong moral stigma not so easily overcome; and, significantly enough, a great many of such unions tend to be undertaken by resident Americans of liberal leanings. There is, then, no absolute bar on marital admixture, so that the society has not given birth to the class of "poor whites" so prevalent in the Leeward and Windward Islands groups, where the ravages of consanguine degeneracy can be seen today in the modern descendants of the seventeenth-century French and English emigrants. The real bar in Puerto Rico comes from the existence of an elaborate and subtle system of informal social pressures and prohibitions based upon an ambivalent attitude to color. There are alumni groups of professional men of dark color who "feel more at home" with each other than they would with their white associates. There is, of course, no open denigration of color. On the contrary, there is almost an official code of feminine beauty that applauds the favorite style of the woman who is neither too dark nor too white; as the song goes:

> *Lo mas que me gusta el café*
> *Que de la trigueña me cuela.*

But neither, on the other hand, is there a complete and harmonious acceptance of color. That is perhaps why the colored Puerto Rican will sometimes seek refuge in the claim that he is "Indian" or "Spanish" or "Latin." That is perhaps why too a poet like the late Luis Palés Matos, who identified himself in his work with the Afro-Antillean Negro cultural tradition and thus broke away from the traditional aping of European poetic forms, has been attacked by his fellow countrymen as an artist who sought to deny that Puerto Rico, unlike the other Caribbean islands, was "white by blood and by culture."[39] It is not then surprising that the colored Puerto Rican has rarely responded, in any number, to the invitation of men like Betances and Barbosa to adopt an attitude of open racial pride. He prefers, still, to remain—in the phrase of Pedro Timothee—a pampered servant in an alien house than to become master in his own. The pride of race yields, still, to the atmosphere of color worship.

All this, in turn, threatens to become worse, not better, as the society becomes more industrialized. For industrialization everywhere, and especially in its early stages, works to unloosen the nuts and bolts that hold a traditionalist society together. Spanish feudal traditions (which include slavery and anti-Moorish feelings) tended, as Professor Rogler has pointed out, to perpetuate a closed caste system in the colony and by its discouragement of the competitive process and spirit to play down sharp racial and class struggle. That has changed; and is certain to change even more as industrialization speeds up the appeal to individual self-interest and self-assertion. Even before 1940 there was evidence to suggest a great deal of frustration on the part of colored university students who found their professional advancement limited by prejudice.[40] They could move up the social scale through personal achievement. But the movement was always relative; their final position rarely corresponded to that of the white person of comparable achievement; and only too often white persons of inferior social standing obtained privileges denied to colored persons of superior standing. The readiness to accept all this is certain to become diluted as the percentage of candidates for professional preferment (via mass education) grows. The Puerto Rican who told Christopher Rand that "on the mainland, there has always been a lot of social mobility and a lot of color discrimination, here there has been little social mobility and little color discrimination" quite properly was emphasizing a connection between the two phenomena that is sure to increase in its effects as sharpened economic competitiveness and heightened social ambitions throw people more and more together. The volume of discriminatory practices discovered by the investigators of the Civil Liberties inquiry of 1959—in the college fraternities and sororities, in certain private schools, in the luxury tourist hotels, in the higher-priced housing developments—shows that prejudice has reached serious proportions and by no means justifies the rather tepid conclusions of the inquiry itself in its General Report.[41] The legislative enquiry during the summer of 1963 added further evidence concerning discriminatory employment practices on the part of local banks.

It is of some interest to note, in this respect, the puzzled conclusions of the authors of the Princeton University study on social mobility. Their refined statistical analyses yield, for them, little evidence that skin color matters in Puerto Rican life, but the "testimony of common sense," they confess, suggests otherwise: being Negro or white clearly does matter when dealing with status-conscious members of the middle and upper classes.[42] As American forms of discrimination press upon these more ambivalent forms the Puerto Rican who regards himself as white will increasingly find himself in the cruelly ironic position of being himself subjected to the prejudicial techniques he has hitherto utilized against the dark-colored persons of his own society. He will then have to decide whether he will accept that position as a necessary price of retaining political and economic ties with the United States or whether he will join forces with those persons in a common front against prejudice. If, of course, those ties are retained then it follows that the decisive factor in the shaping of future race relations in the island will be the development of race relations in the United States.

This raises, finally, the question of immediate public policy. The Civil Liberties report has advised against the extended use of the public police power. Speaking of discrimination in the "private" field of *casinos* and some civic associations, it argues that government pressure would be "unnecessary" and would only arouse feelings of "hostility."[43] Similar language is employed by the Princeton University study to arrive at a similar cautious conclusion: the attention paid to skin color, they assert, is "heightened to critical awareness at the fringes and the interstices of personal relations, where public policy is not an issue, and where public controls are not available."[44] The argument deserves two comments. In the first place, it runs counter to the principle, emphasized most recently by the American courts in the cases relating to the administrative applications of the desegregation rulings of 1954, that the vitality of constitutional rights cannot be allowed to yield simply because of disagreement with them, nor their practical exercise be nullified by threats of public disturbance. To argue otherwise is to hold up the application of the law to ransom by any group that allows its feelings of "hostility" to get the better of it.[45] Secondly, as far as Puerto Rico is concerned, the Commonwealth government has itself already legitimized the use of the public power in this field with the passage of the Civil Rights Act of 1943, reinforced later with the constitutional guarantees of the 1952 Bill of Rights. The tendency of all modern legislation is clearly to enlarge the scope of "public" as against "private" jurisdictions in the whole area of the liberty of the subject; indeed the very definition of what constitutes "private" relationships is rapidly changing as it becomes clear that the distinction between "private" and "public" behavior is psychologically and sociologically unsound, since all "private" acts are imbued with "public" consequences. To take just another Puerto Rican example, Chancellor Benítez entertains the visiting Negro writer James Baldwin at a well-publicized luncheon, but the powers of the University Chancellorship are not used to crush the discriminatory practices of a number of the University fraternities. There is little reason to believe that discrimination will of itself disappear without the more coercive machinery of the state being invoked through the medium of statutory measures adequately enforced. It is worth noting increasing parliamentary and public sentiment for such measures in Great Britain following the outbreak of the Notting Hill race riots of 1959. It is difficult to believe that the Puerto Rican experience will point to any other conclusion.

It is evident enough from what has been said that in these basic matters of family, religion, and color the Puerto Rican society is essentially *sui generis*. There is a formal Catholicism. But the real religion of many Puerto Ricans is spiritualism, while the widespread habit of consensual marriage still successfully resists the orthodox marriage ceremony on the ground, as many of the Puerto Rican common people feel, that once married there is no possibility of divorce. The democratic family unit after the American style is increasingly modish with the new middle-class groups, and an advisory manual written for young Puerto Ricans—Celia Bunker's *Con que vas a Casarte?*—is a straightforward Spanish-language variant of the usual popular American handbook on love and marriage. At the same time, the change is frequently only skin-deep. The older assumptions always reassert themselves in crisis, based as they are upon the Spanish concept of sex relations inherited from the Arab influence on Spanish civilization. The popular vocabulary on those relations still sees them as, in essence, a battle between the male conqueror and the female conquered; there is the monotonous regularity of the various stages of the relations—the aggressive passion of the *noviazgo*, the calamitous abuse of the honeymoon, the premature indifference of married life; and instead of the democratic discussion that is supposed to heal marital rifts there is, more usually, the popular strategy whereby each injured partner runs home to parents and relatives in the extended family system, from whom each recruits sufficient sympathy to arm them for further warfare at home. More generally speaking, there are numerous areas in which, frequently with little logic, there are hidden reserves of cultural traditionalism. In food matters, for instance, the standard Puerto Rican mixture of rice and beans maintains its priority in the family menu, so much so that, as a recent report has noted, its low protein value accounts for the fact that the percentage of children suffering from diseases of intestinal parasites is substantially the same today as it was forty years ago.[46] The official secular religion of the society emphasizes the desirability of economic change and social modernization. But for many Puerto Ricans on the bottom rungs of the social ladder those processes involve so much tension and even outright catastrophe that they abjure them by turning to their own private schizophrenic worlds, as the prevalence of *ataques*, the kind of seizure so much a part of the local psychiatrical picture, proves. Change, and resistance to change, must also be seen in the light of the general fact that Puerto Rican society is one of *chisme* (gossip) and *bembeteo* (humorous comment), so that the fear of being exposed to "what people will say" inhibits many a person from openly accepting a new solution to an old problem. And to all of this, in itself sufficiently complicated, there must be added the ultimate complication of the fact that all Puerto Ricans, subjected as they are to a cross-pollenization of cultures, must learn to live in two worlds at the same time. Even now, after so much attention from the arch-priests of social psychiatry, it is difficult to estimate exactly the price of that dual existence in terms of broken faith and divided loyalty.

The Debate on "Americanization"

As WITH all great empires, twentieth-century America must sooner or later face the bar of world opinion. As she becomes a world power her civilization begins to permeate all the cultures that come under its influence. Men begin to discuss the "Americanization" of their world as earlier they discussed the influence of the British Empire or the "Romanization" of the ancient world. The unique feature about the discussion in Puerto Rico is that it has gone on for half a century or more before the present-day's wider discussion began and that the evidence it contributes to that discussion it contributes as a society which has been wide open to the Americanizing process without any defenses worth speaking of. Here, in one way, the world may see as in a microcosm the shape of American things to come. Here in some sense are possible answers to one of the seminal questions of the age: as American influence, combined with that of the forces of modern machine technology, spreads wider and wider, must it of necessity destroy the cultural diversity of a pluralistic universe and replace it with a drab uniformity? Some of the Puerto Rican literature answers the question in much the same mood of apocalyptic hatred with which the unknown mystic author of the *Book of Revelation* castigated the Roman power of the first century. Some of it responds with an adoptive Americanism so ultra-patriotic as to satisfy the stringent demands even of the Daughters of the American Revolution. In its representation of the entire gamut of feelings from acceptance to rejection, indeed, the Puerto Rican discussion provides the architects of American foreign policy with an almost perfect case study of what they must expect to meet as they help try to convert the twentieth century into the American century.

The cultural impact, of course, was recognizable from the moment of transfer. Some of it was immediate and obvious—the revolution in sports, for example; even before 1898 baseball had been a popular game and after that date it rapidly became the national sport: the first United States professional team to visit the island, Dave Driscoll's All Americans, came as early as 1914. Some of the change was less apparent, and slower in revealing its consequences. The decline of the small town, for example, only became conspicuously obvious after the Second World War, when the new mass housing programs accelerated the decline of the old *plaza* life that had moved an early American visitor to a fond remembrance of Browning's lines on the pleasures of Italian town living.[1] It took some twenty years or more for the old town boarding houses, redolent of native food and elegant furniture, to be replaced with the raucous, neon-lit American-style bars and café-restaurants, but the change has been completed long ago now; while the early Victorian charm of the old Mallorquina Restaurant in San Juan is all that remains of what was once a lively rendezvous, in the Paris or Madrid manner, of the cream of the insular intellectual, artistic, theatrical, and political circles. In the realms of property and sex relations—the twin bastions of any social order—change in the first was almost immediately effected with the intrusion of American capital into the sugar business, while in the second the victory of change has perhaps been less emphatic. Change in general had gone so far by 1923 that when it was decided in that year to publish *The Book of Puerto Rico*, a voluminous collection of essays on all aspects of insular life and experience, it was felt appropriate to publish it as a dual text, in both Spanish and English.

Much of the change, naturally enough, took place during the first generation of the century and passed by uncatalogued in any serious way. The island and its problems apparently had little attraction for the American writers. The first full account in English of island government and politics was probably Knowlton Mixer's book of 1926, and even then it was a pedestrian account. No visiting American historian managed to do for the island what Henry Adams, out of his Polynesian visit, did for Tahiti in his scholarly memoir on the last queen of the great Tera dynasty in the twilight of its rule as it was superseded by the French and British imperial systems in the Pacific. On the Puerto Rican side, moreover, most of the older people who clung with a pathetic tenacity to the old order and its ideals have left the scene, which makes it easier for those who today resist the Americanizing process to fashion a romantic myth of island life under Spain. Typically, the book that more than any other has symbolized the nationalist protest against the process of assimilation, Pedreira's essay on *Insularismo*, was published in 1934, at the very moment when the traditional order it eulogized was on the threshold of final decline. It is perhaps also typical that no book has yet been written as an *apologia pro vita americana* as the American civilization touches and reshapes the Puerto Rican character. For just as the etiology of change has been taken for granted by so many, so too its consequences have been too uncritically accepted as proof of the necessary "modernization" of the insular life, as evidence of what one American educator who was also an early dean of the University of Puerto Rico blandly termed the "growing pains" of the island.[2] There are signs, however, that the unconscious arrogance of this attitude can no longer hold automatic command of the field. It could be assumed, once, that the burden of proof in the debate lay with those who resented the Americanization of the society. It is now apparent, however, that it may now rest with those who envisage for the Puerto Rican citizen the role of a *petit-yanqui* in the Caribbean basin.

From the outset, the debate deployed itself between the Hispano-philes and the Yankeephiles, between the champions of the *personalidad nacional* and the *absolutistas de la cultura occidental*. Much of it, naturally enough, was little more than a romantic nostalgia for Spain. A book like Vicente Balbás Capó's *Porto Rico a Los Diez Años de Americanización* (published in 1910) was a frank white-washing of Spanish rule and a naive defense of Spanish cultural supe-riority, even to the point of deploring the replacement of the brutal Spanish method of garrotting with the only slightly less brutal Ameri-can method of hanging in the realm of criminal punishment.[3] At its other extreme, the literature exhibited a condescending optimism about the ability of the average Puerto Rican to "make the grade" as a good American. "While it may be a long time," wrote an early American observer, "to mold this man into a self-respecting, useful franchised citizen of the United States, it can be done, for the reason that he is docile, obliging, appreciative of favors and, best of all, possesses an inbred courtesy and politeness and an equability of tem-perament which permit him to readily absorb new ideas."[4] In between those two extremes there was sandwiched the argument, frequently resting on biological or genetic analogies, which believed that the supposed hereditary traits of the Puerto Rican people—chivalry, sympathy, a mystic sense of life—could be grafted on to the practical traits and the love of fair play of the American people. This last thesis probably goes back to the beginning of the American occupation and has certainly now become the favorite slogan both of the Common-wealth government and of the American forces that want to retain the insular-continental connection.

Of these attitudes, the one that happily welcomed Americanization was by far the most characteristic for the first two or three decades after 1898. The initial response of the islanders was to accept the American regime cordially, since it brought with it, so it was believed, a practical sense of democracy that had been known only to a few informed persons in the island before, and even then merely as abstract truths unrelated to their daily experience.[5] Americans at least were an active people. It was only natural that the active spirits of the local society—those, for instance, who under Spain had formed the membership of bodies like the *Sociedad Económica de Amigos del País*—should have welcomed the galvanizing push and social dynamism of the American spirit as those influences tended to sweep away what Pedreira termed the habits of "tropical laissez faire." The American ideals of personal and social betterment meant a real difference after the massive indifference of the Spanish official attitudes. The grant of American citizenship in 1917—although opposed by the Unionist Party on the ground that it compromised the struggle for independence—reinforced the general feeling of gratitude to the new ruling nation. Americans at least seemed, at their best, to care about the Puerto Rican condition. The care, of course, was frequently couched in terms of a vague and sentimental liberalism, and well-meaning efforts at friendship—Roy Schuckman's pamphlet of 1954, *Puerto Rican Neighbor*, is typical of the attitude[6]—often suffered from overtones of a cloying neo-Christian fraternalism. But the improvements worked by this attitude were undeniable, so much so that there was hardly any significant group in the society that genuinely wanted to put the clock back, with the exception of the Spanish patrician families in the island who clung to the old *hidalgo* conviction that social recognition could not be purchased merely by money.

By 1930, however, the earlier enthusiasm was beginning to wane. Educated Puerto Ricans like Antonio Pedreira and José Padín began to ask themselves whether the price paid for Americanization, however advantageous economically, was not questionably high. Their Hispanic background, with its philosophical bent, encouraged them to query a civilization where the gifts of organization, industry, and technique flourished but where, in de Tocqueville's sentence, the love of the beautiful was sacrificed to the cultivation of the useful. They sought out a definable Puerto Rican "character" and "tradition" that might be preserved against complete erosion. The best-known statement of their position was, and remains still, Pedreira's volume of 1934. The volume merits some extended attention because it has done for a whole generation of Puerto Rican intellectuals what the *Education of Henry Adams* did for the American liberal after its publication in 1905; and Pedreira's skepticism, like that of Adams, had its roots less in a democratic distrust of business values than in the distaste of the gentleman for the commercial spirit. Starting off with an almost racialist thesis of insular history, Pedreira laments the decline, as he sees it, of the *fermentación patriótica* under the American suzerainty. He does not deny the material achievements of the regime. But he insists that they have helped to engineer the moral degradation of his society. He urges, in an almost Burkean phrase, that the proper dimension of culture is one not of length or breadth but one of depth.[7] Judged by that criterion, alien rule has sapped the sources of Puerto Rican collective action. There are more schools and offices, but also more crimes, more suicides, more personal dishonesty. American influence has centralized social life and destroyed, except in towns like Ponce, the older tradition of local recreation. The American tempo has brought about the decline of the arts of dance and conversation. The springs of public service dry up; and now the country has no figures of outstanding public men to carry on the great record of the Puerto Rican patriots. Above all, the "sordid utilitarianism" of the American spirit has worked a pitiable intellectual vulgarization. For democracy means the sovereignty of the mediocre man and the decline of the intelligentsia. It rewards the inept and punishes the wise. It even vulgarizes politics: for to be a politician yesterday was to undertake a patriotic duty, today it is a mere profession. Yet all this, Pedreira concludes, is merely a moment of transition in the insular life. The task, in this moment, is to undertake a "reaffirmation" of the unique values separating Puerto Rico from the United States, even from the rest of Latin America; for in the rich musical score of the Spanish tradition Puerto Rico sustains her own special note.[8]

The complaint holds much of real merit, and sums up the essence of the cultural-nationalist position to the present day. It may well be that its annotation of the despair and sadness of life in a colonial society is far less valid in the changed Puerto Rico of the 1960's. It is no doubt true, too, that much of the argument is false insofar as it tends to see change as the odious result of American rule instead of flowing from the very nature of the twentieth century of which the island is a part. But the real criticism to make is of a somewhat different nature. The seminal error of the argument resides in its conservative presuppositions. In reality, it is a tract against "democracy" and only perhaps anti-American because America happens to be the major protagonist of "democracy" in the Western Hemisphere. It commits the mistake, common to all Platonically conservative thought, of making *a priori* assumptions about the nature of democracy and the democratic man and then seeking to coerce the facts into the straitjacket of the assumptions. It mistakes the degradation of the democratic dogma for the dogma itself. For what has shaped Puerto Rico since 1898 is not the pure democratic spirit but—quite a different thing—the capitalist-democratic spirit of America. The "sordid utilitarianism" Pedreira arraigns is not the necessary fruit of democracy but of the American acquisitive society. His is the protest, to be exact, of a cultured mind against the social rule of the majority, whether the majority be American or Puerto Rican. He opines, in a suggestive sentence, that if Ortega y Gasset had been a Puerto Rican he would have written the *Revolt of the Masses* twenty-five years earlier.[9] The remark reveals how too many Puerto Rican minds have been seduced by that too-famous book to embrace a social theory that converts any mass political movement into the road to the mass-totalitarian society. Nor is it clear how the adulation of the Puerto Rican "people" is to be reconciled with that attitude. The argument, altogether, can become too easily the reactionary affectation of an intelligentsia anxious to preserve an older Puerto Rico in which the masses "know their place" and accept it with all the deference of the *jíbaro*, whose native grace is compared, in his favor, to the studied mannerisms of the "educated" person. The customary values Pedreira wanted to preserve are those—dancing, horse riding, acting, witty conversation— of a leisure-class stamp and not obviously identifying marks of a Puerto Rican "national character." The nationalist thesis, here as elsewhere, may become simply a rationalization of the interests of an intellectual class seeking to evoke a local past that cannot be recovered and in which, as one critic has noted, it was only necessary to know the titles of books and the names of authors in order to be labeled a distinguished person and where the poor, although hungry, always respected their social "betters."[10] That the criticism can be angrily rebutted as a libel on the whole Creole intelligentsia perhaps suggests that it scores a real point.[11]

Despite the fact, therefore, that Pedreira's volume is one of the very few by Puerto Rican intellectuals that has managed to say something quite original about the national ethos (his eulogy of the eighteenth-century denunciation of Spanish colonial rule written by the Spanish bishop Fray Iñigo Abbad shows that he is no mere frustrated Hispanophile in a New World society), its influence has succeeded in popularizing too many myths about the nature of modern society. His distinction between "culture" and "civilization"[12] enables him to draw an artificial distinction between "spiritual" and "material" values, with their respective custodians in the shape of "intellectuals" and "technicians." Even worse, the conclusions drawn from that dubious distinction are that (1) the United States is a "materialist" culture while Puerto Rico is a "spiritual" culture and (2) the impact of the materialist culture upon the spiritual culture, via industrialization, may perhaps be so arranged that the latter does not lose its "spiritual" elements; the argument has been recently reiterated in Dr. Eugenio Fernández-Méndez's essay, *Filiación y Sentido de una Isla*.[13]

Of the first conclusion it is enough to say that it is one of the favorite distortions of the complexity of American life (often based upon a Caliban-Prospero dichotomy that is more impressive in its literary cleverness than in its sociological truth) purveyed by many of the European intelligentsia, and that the geographical proximity of Puerto Rico to the American scene makes it all the less excusable in the case of the island intellectuals. Nor should sight be lost of the fact that by defining culture in a narrow philosophico-literary manner the critic of the American scene is enabled to deny the contribution that the American inventive spirit has made to world culture, in its widest sense, in the form of jazz and, at their best, of the movies. The second conclusion in its turn fatally misunderstands the real nature of the transmission of culture that occurs between interacting societies. To believe that it is possible to change the technological foundations of a society and leave untouched its cultural superstructure is to engage in naive utopianism. Yet much of the local debate is preoccupied with "protecting" the local culture against the Americanizing touch. It engages in a studied admiration of the *jíbaro* (there is, indeed, a whole defensive literature on that theme that goes back to Manuel Alonso's essay of 1849, *El Gíbaro*) at the very moment when industrialization, rural depopulation, and emigration are working together to make the type increasingly obsolete. Much of all this, of course, is a romantic idealization of the Spanish tradition. Yet not the least ironic aspect of the process is that it idealizes as the most loyal representative of that tradition the very class of workers who were the most despised and neglected of all island groups in the harsh reality of Spanish Puerto Rico.

The cultural-nationalist theme, resultantly, is frequently one of an angry and narrow-minded xenophobia. Its champions insist that the government-sponsored Casals Festival of 1957 possessed no real meaning for Puerto Ricans because native musicians like the Figueroa Quartet were not invited to participate in it.[14] A University journal publication, *La Torre*, is fiercely denounced because a statistical analysis of its pages reveals that only a small portion are devoted to local themes by local authors, as if aesthetic truth can be arithmetically assessed.[15] A curious set of critical values can suggest that a local patriotic composition like Rafael Hernández's *Lamento Borincano* ought to be classed with the Beethoven Fifth Symphony.[16] It can be broadly hinted that evil forces must be at work if the Puerto Rican candidate for the Miss Universe contest in Long Beach, California, is not awarded the supreme honor.[17] Even the theme of "local boy makes good" is pressed into the service of nationalistic sentiment; so that, on the one hand, the homage done by the national university to Don Juan Ramón Jiménez, an adopted son only of Puerto Rico, takes on the bizarre dimensions of necrophilism in the room dedicated to his memory in the University library; while, on the other hand, Don Pablo Casals is presented to the world by the Commonwealth government not only as the supreme cellist that he is but also as a great Puerto Rican in a style reminiscent of a Hollywood studio's frenetic advertising of a major star. A linguistic purism tries to exorcise Americanisms from the local Spanish:

> *Me habré americanizado*
> *Que casi, casi, he olvidado*
> how I must write the *español?*

without fully appreciating, first, that the most virile and creative of languages, contemporary American among them, have been born of continuous selective recruitment from a variety of sources and, second, that the local Spanish itself, the popular *Boricua*, is in itself the linguistic outcome of the complete disappearance of élite Castilian with the departure after 1898 of the Castilian-speaking ruling élite and of the filling in of the gap with a "corrupt" popular speech recruited, in its varied sources, from lower-class Spanish dialect, the speech habits, possibly, of African slaves and, more recently, the widespread absorption of American-English terms. There grows up, again, a neo-Jeffersonian assumption that the "real" Puerto Rico is agrarian, not industrial, that agriculture is natural while industry is artificial, and that only in a traditional economic activity like the coffee culture is there to be found "the true Creole-dom of the Puerto Rican people";[18] it is happily forgotten, or perhaps not even known, that many of the coffee growers who originally commenced the industry in the last century, especially in the Utuado-Lares-Aibonito triangle, were not natives but Corsican immigrants. Or, again, to come back to the literary aspect, the fact that a book like Maria Teresa Babín's *Panorama de la Cultura Puertorriqueña* fails, when listing the roll call of local artists and writers, literally to include everybody, added to the fact that the author writes as a resident Puerto Rican in New York, can be cited by small-minded critics as evidence of "insult" to the native culture.[19] And, in its more extreme manifestations, all this becomes only too easily an irrational anti-Americanism that might even persuade itself to believe at one point, on the basis of an unfortunate letter written by the United States Secretary of War in 1898, that the main purpose of the United States in coming to the island has been to use it as a dumping ground for American Negroes and thereby as a means of solving the American race problem.[20] All in all, much of the literature in this entire field has about it an aroma of self-pity, of injured vanity, almost indeed of a masochistic pleasure in the contemplation of the tragic sorrow of a defeated people. It will have to become something more before it is a positive and democratic nationalist ideology coming to grips rationally with Americanization.

For such an ideology will have to accept the fact that in the history of Western civilization, at least, generous enthusiasm for the external influence has been the *sine qua non* of continuing creativity in a society. All of the national variants of that civilization have been the outcome of intermixture—the French, the Italian, the English and, not least of all, the contemporary American. Their history has been proof of the dangers of the closed society—as against the open society —as it received its classic expression in the Tenth Book of Plato's *Laws*. What is known, indeed, as Western civilization would not be what it is without the rich influences of the Jewish and Islamic worlds which extended, at the height of their power, from Baghdad, through Palermo, to Cordoba; and a Spanish-speaking nationalism should remember that the decline of Spain in modern times goes back to the misconceived effort to destroy the Arabic element of its medieval heritage. On the other side of the Puerto Rican coin, the American civilization itself owes much of its varied richness to its manifold European sources. National societies that have sought to insulate themselves from extra-national influence have done so at the price of grotesque self-stultification. This is the key to modern Portugal (whose backwardness is reflected in the backwardness of its African colonies), to Franco Spain, to nineteenth-century China and, in some measure, to contemporary Russia. They are tempted to embrace a sort of nationalistic chauvinism. They rewrite history to fit the new claims; the most famous example, of course, being the attempt by the Russian Communist Party after 1940 to annex the whole national history, so that Ivan the Terrible, Kutuzov, Peter the Great and their like become the new presiding deities of the national Pantheon. There is a not dissimilar effort in the sort of historical literary criticism composed by Puerto Rican literary historians, in which the importance of any single figure is almost exclusively estimated in terms of his attitude to the problem of national emancipation. There is no reason to believe that the moral difficulties which Americans created for themselves by embracing the dogma of "Manifest Destiny" would not be repeated, on a smaller scale, for a Puerto Rico that pursued the same path. The disease, of course, occurs in a variety of forms. It is there in the belief that Puerto Rican and American traits (never really scientifically defined) can fuse to fashion a new culture. It is there in the almost paranoiac anger at any criticism coming from the outsider, even where, as in that section of Alfred Kazin's other-

wise perverse article on his visit to the island that analyzes the national trait of "docility," the criticism may be entirely justifiable. It
is there in the impassioned defense of the small nation as the source
of culture, while the big nation is seen only as a source of power;
and a monograph like Mariano Picón-Salas's *Apología de la Pequeña
Nación,* for all of its cosmopolitan temper, fails because in comparing
Puerto Rico with classical Athens or the Italian city states of the
fifteenth century it assumes that geographical size, rather than any
other factor, has been the leading element in the establishment of
those civilizations.[21] The nature of the Puerto Rican future must be
sought from a more persuasive historical and sociological mode of
analysis.

Does this then mean that Puerto Rico must resign herself to a
continuing Americanization? Far from it; for so to assume would be
to accept a depressing cultural determinism. To say that civilization
grows out of culture contact is one thing. To say that a subordinate
society must therefore passively accept every external influence is
quite another. For what has happened in the Puerto Rican case is
that the noble concept of cosmopolitan influence has been, in reality,
reduced to the influence of an *occidentalismo exclusivista* and that
the latter, in its turn, has been corrupted into the even narrower
influence of the American business civilization. It is true to say that
much of the island's transformation is the general modernization of
the times. But it is no less true that the modernizing process has
passed through an Americanizing filter before it has reached the
island society. The cultural impact, like the economic, has been
unilateral rather than multilateral. There is much solemn discussion
about the island's place in the *cultura occidental.* But in point of
fact the outside influences to which the island has been exposed have
so far been those emanating almost exclusively from the United
States. Puerto Rico has never really been given a fair chance to prove
what she might become under the influence of a variety of cultural
forces.

This is eminently self-evident from the emptiness of the prevalent
assumption in the debate that the island's Spanish traits can be
married to American traits to give birth to a new cultural form. The
assumption, properly speaking, is a twofold one. The first is that the
future will witness a cultural partnership, as it were, based upon a
mutual recognition of the equality of the participating members. The
second is that the island society can be regarded as a latter-day custodian of Hispanic values within the Caribbean region. Both, frankly,
are exercises in pious hope rather than statements of reality. As far

as the first is concerned, it is true that a sort of cultural pluralism does exist in American life. But where this is so the cultural segment survives often on sufferance only and it must confront, all the time, the pressure of everything American to absorb it into a democratic cultural totalitarianism. Many of the elements that have refused or have been unable to accept absorption have been relegated, like the American Indian, to a bitter and bleak struggle for existence on the margins of the national life; while those that have finally accepted have been compelled, like the Mormon Church, to do so at the price of yielding up the very beliefs and attitudes—the Mormon concept, for example, of the self-sufficing economic kingdom—that have been their distinguishing characteristics. The American record in Puerto Rico since 1900—whatever the future may hold—does not warrant any more optimistic conclusions about the Puerto Rican place in the national picture. The Puerto Rican child, from the beginning, has been taught American rather than Puerto Rican history. His attributes have been built up in a colonial atmosphere, where the mass media have portrayed to the populace a culture that is not their own and to which they have been taught to attribute everything that is worthwhile in their experience. The very linguistic symbols of merit and authority become those of the dominant power; thus the Puerto Rican student still manages, only too frequently, to address his teacher as "Mister," rather than *maestro* or *profesor,* as if the teacher were an American. Nor is this applicable to the past only for, as René Marqués has pointed out, the ancestral sense of helplessness in the individual Puerto Rican is still psychologically worked upon through modern methods of education that are only somewhat more subtle than those used previously.[22] Since the burden of taking on the inconvenient aspects of communications between the ruled and the rulers has always been the compulsory lot, in colonial situations, of the ruled, Puerto Ricans have been compelled to learn English rather than Americans Spanish. The depreciation of the local culture has encouraged a corresponding self-depreciation in individuals. For some it has taken the form of a blind submission to the American style, expressing an urgent drive, frequently only half understood by its victims, for identification and incorporation with the elite of the governing power; and the guilt feelings thereby engendered have frequently been covered up by the device of identifying Puerto Rico with "Western civilization" rather than with the United States, so that terms like this and others—"the crisis of the West," "Western culture," "the free world," and so on—play a therapeutic role in the psychology of that type of Puerto Rican. For others again the response to a situation so basically intolerable to sensitive spirits and so power-

fully buttressed by all the institutions of the society, private and
public, political and economic, has been a retreat into feelings of
bitterness, inferiority, chauvinism; and the life of a spirit like Pedro
Albizu Campos is a tragic monument to those elements in Puerto
Rican politics.

Even when the individual American in the picture has been
genuinely liberal, the liberalism has only too often blandly assumed
the natural superiority of American values (just as, in the case of
the British Caribbean, even the sympathy of British Fabian Socialists
with local aspirations has been grounded on the assumption that West
Indian nationalism ought to perpetuate English modes and manners).
The matter of race is an apt illustration. Americans liberal on everything else have drawn the line (with some individual exceptions) at
accepting the Latin principle of race mixing. It has been a widespread,
and quite unscientific, belief among them that the mixing engenders a
decline in mental and physical capacities, and Dean Fleagle felt compelled to issue a stern warning about its "degenerating effect" on
family life in his book of 1917.[23] Nor is this a thing of the past only,
for Alfred Kazin's crass reference to "Step'n Fetchit sloth" in Puerto
Ricans suggests that there may sometimes lurk a latent anti-Negro
prejudice underneath the gleaming armor even of the New York
Jewish liberal. The Peace Corps is supposed to have been one of the
more imaginative ideas of Kennedy liberalism, but the liberalism did
not prevent the organizers of the Peace Corps training camp in Puerto
Rico from countenancing the insulting suggestion that individual
Puerto Rican *independentistas* should be asked to play the role of
anti-American critics, like nothing so much as sparring partners, to
the young members of the Corps. More generally, much of the liberal
American literature on the islanders tends to exhibit an air of generous
paternalism, but paternalism nonetheless. It is full of the sort of remark—that young Puerto Ricans who have come to American universities "have shown themselves to be fully equal to Orientals and
other students from other lands," or that the underlying traits of the
average Puerto Rican, "even though they may not be such as to build
empires or produce Shakespeares, are qualities of which his peers in
the world community stand in great need"[24]—which infuriates thinking Puerto Ricans even more than a posture of rank hostility. At best
the attitude tolerates Puerto Ricans; it sees them, in the indignant
phrase of one of the victims, as just "damn nice stupid people." The
fact that the island's white highland laborer has certain historical
analogies with the cabin dwellers of the Southern Appalachian region
of the United States has encouraged an attitude towards him not unlike the popular American attitude to the "hillbilly." None of this,

all in all, looks like an American readiness to welcome the Puerto Rican as an equal partner in a joint cultural enterprise.

There is not much more truth in the second assumption that Puerto Rico can be viewed as an overseas crucible of Hispanic culture. The Spanish legacy, as already noted, did not transplant to the island any of the outstanding features of Spanish life—a ceremonial urban culture, a complex bureaucracy (except in the military government), a sophisticated agricultural economy. Nor did it introduce any of its imposing civil and ecclesiastical hierarchies, as it did in its Mexican and Peruvian viceroyalties: the missions of the religious orders, the great peninsular universities, the tradition of splendid architecture, both civil and religious. There was nothing like the strong institutional fabric of the continental colonial societies to form a foundation for later emancipation from peninsular suzerainty. The psychological consequences of all this have been momentous, not least of all the continuing dependency of the Puerto Rican spirit upon external deliverance and the comparable failure to look inwards for national salvation. So, if there are unique Puerto Rican characteristics, it is profoundly misleading to expect them to be Caribbean echoes of the original Hispanic. Indeed the expectation is grossly unfair, for it presupposes a sort of tribal ancestor worship of merely snobbish utility. The American critic who compares the twentieth-century Puerto Rican with the sixteenth-century *conquistadores*, to the disadvantage of the former, rarely pauses to reflect upon the conclusions that might be derived from comparing his own type with the independent American farmer we read of in the pages of Crèvecoeur. The modern Puerto Rican must be judged by what he is, not by what his ancestors were: the warning applies to both the Puerto Rican and American cultivators of the myth of Puerto Rico as a bridgehead between two world cultures. Consequently the attempt to explain the island culture and institutions as a crossing between two growths of pre-established national entities, the one Spanish, the other American, unavoidably results in shallow analysis. The metaphor has too easily seduced even critical observers, so that the cultural reality—that Puerto Rico exists as a local Creole culture in its own right, not merely as a tropical mirror of metropolitan European or American societies—is too readily lost sight of. For what has really taken place in the last sixty years is not the growth of an ideal common life shared on equal terms by both Puerto Ricans and Americans—the ideal was typically expressed in a book like Juan Bautista Soto's volume of 1928, *Puerto Rico ante el Derecho de Gentes*—but the relentless imposition of American standards upon a dependent society helpless to resist the process. The islanders have been expected to accept, and have accepted, many of the characteristic American attitudes. But there is little evidence that Americans have been willing to learn anything from a society most of them have never heard of except in derogatory terms.

All this is not mere speculation. A reading of an article like Daniel Boorstin's of 1955 in the *Yale Review* suggests that even the American intelligentsia—not to mention the American people as a whole—are far from appreciating the position of the Puerto Rican cultural nationalist.[25] It is Boorstin's chief contention that the Puerto Rican intelligentsia is mistakenly seeking to organize a renaissance of an *alta cultura puertorriqueña* which in fact does not now exist nor existed previously. There is a "communal myopia" abroad because Puerto Ricans refuse to recognize this fact and instead seek mistakenly to create a flattering image of themselves in a past which has none of the justifying elements of the French or English or Italian past. What they should do, on the contrary, is to recognize their limitations and learn to live with them. In particular, the business of their intellectuals is not to undertake a strenuous quest for culture but to help develop the "social resources" of the society. For in Puerto Rico, "as elsewhere," Boorstin writes in a curious sentence, "the literary classes possess a terrible power to impose on the community an aimless malaise." If in Puerto Rico they agree that "for a people to discover the utility of one of its natural limitations is worth a dozen patriotic hymns" they will help to guide the society along proper lines. They will contribute, especially, to helping their countrymen get rid of a "needless frustration" that comes from seeking to be what they never can be.

For a historian who elsewhere, as in his study of American colonial beginnings, has sought to minimize the influence of ideas upon events, the assumption that the Puerto Rican "frustration" is to be traced to, and is largely facilitated by, the *idées fixes* of its literary class is odd indeed. For if it is true, as Emerson insisted, that all men are the prisoners of ideas, it is no less true that ideas or intellectual élites do not, of themselves, create frustrations insomuch as they help to verbalize frustrations that arise from the collective experience of a people. They do not so much impose presuppositions upon a society as reflect its preoccupations. Their concern in Puerto Rico with the issue of political status is not, as Boorstin imagines, an unfortunate error so much as it is the inevitable outcome, in intellectual life, of a colonial situation; and his presumption that the concern, perhaps once justified, is no longer necessary because the achievements of Commonwealth status since 1952 have "solved" the status issue is, after all, a presumption which is denied by considerable portions of the local electorate and political leadership. It is worth noting too that the concept of history behind this line of criticism is basically Whiggite. Puerto Rico, we are told, has no "history" worth speaking about. But it is clear that by "history" Boorstin means a Churchillian sort of high political drama. "Puerto Rico's political history," he writes, "lacks even a single revolution or civil war of intense drama or of decisive significance. Its cultural history has produced few monuments (with the notable exception of the fortress *El Morro*). Its institutional history has produced few striking phenomena."[26] There is no mention here of economic or social history; the cultural life of the common man is airily passed over without a reference; and the argument almost reduces itself to the narrow literary thesis that the most vital element in history is the intellectual debate on "the large issues of political theory." The advice comes ill from an American whose own society's debate on the "large issues of political theory" produced, in its time, nothing more fundamental than the collected essays on administrative statecraft that are the *Federalist* papers. The argument becomes all the more questionable when the Puerto Rican citizen is told by its author that the island has no history and, almost in the same breath, is congratulated on the fact since it means that, "unencumbered by the baggage of a magnificent past, Puerto Ricans can discover grandeur in improving the present." This fanciful distinction between past and present—as if both were not integral parts of the basic continuity of any society— is not the least puzzling of elements in an argument that is full of quixotic fancies.

The real offense of the argument, however, is its tone. It dismisses with an amused disdain the official and non-official cultural programs that are carried on by institutions like the *Ateneo* and the Institute of Puerto Rican Culture. But a great deal of those programs does not go beyond the sort of enterprise that the Ministry of Works and the National Trust, for example, undertake in Great Britain: the protection of historical monuments, the preservation of rare manuscripts, the care of great houses, the encouragement of archeological and historical research, art exhibitions, public lectures, and so on. To watch the *teatro rodante* of the University putting on a classical Spanish play or the *Ballets de San Juan* a program of classical dance to entranced audiences of the ordinary Puerto Rican people in small town *plazas* throughout the island is to be made aware of the powerful sense of beauty that resides, too often repressed by the harsh struggle of life, in the Puerto Rican common man, profoundly humanist as he is; to be made aware too of the fact that the programs constitute a new relationship between government and the arts after the fashion of the old WPA program of the American New Deal. Boorstin's attitude here seems somewhat ironic when it is remembered that the literary and cultural aspirations of his own American society for a century after independence were treated by the English and European literati with exactly the same cavalier contempt that he expresses for the contemporary Puerto Rican effort. What is more, that contempt quite naturally evoked, in response—as the experiences of Harriet Martineau and Dickens in America showed—an excessive American sensitiveness to the foreign critic not at all unlike the contemporary Puerto Rican attitude to the outside commentator. In a sense, after all, Puerto Ricans are only appropriating for themselves the lessons of that *Address on the American Scholar* in which Emerson exhorted his countrymen to throw off their stance of awed deference in the face of an effete European culture and to create their own tradition on native grounds. Boorstin's attitude makes sense only if it is presumed that what Americans did in one century Puerto Ricans may not attempt in another.

Much of the Puerto Rican search for a cultural identity, it is true, is comic enough. But such searches are not successful overnight. It took a century or more before the Emersonian plea, in the American case, was answered with the growth of the naturalistic novel and play in the twentieth century. It is the cardinal error of traditional and established national cultures to identify their particular brand of art and literature with a universal Hellenism and to caricature the efforts of new emergent societies to create their own unique style. Yet nothing is more pluralistic than culture. There is nothing peculiarly Puerto Rican in asserting, as a Puerto Rican critic of Boorstin's essay has aptly declared, that every country possesses its own history just as every individual, however humble, possesses his own biography; and the purpose of the Puerto Rican intelligentsia is not to exalt their national past but merely to evaluate it.[27] The search would only become dangerous, and warrant Boorstin's strictures, if it meant in Puerto Rico something akin to the absolute return to the past of the advocates, for example, of the Islamic state in the politics of contemporary Malaya and Indonesia. But, in reality, it is far from being that, if only because there exists no priestly-educator caste to give it sense and direction. No Puerto Rican writer or artist denies that he belongs to the army of humanity. He simply insists that he sees no necessary denial of his loyalty to the general staff in recognizing that, first and foremost, he belongs to a small platoon within the larger membership.

For variety is the spice of culture as well as of life. It is no treason to the world community that Italy is distinguished by a tradition of opera, or France by one of theater, or America by one of film. It is the chief fault of the "Westernizers" in the Puerto Rican debate that they appear to possess the image of an abstract transnational world culture which leaves little room for individual national idiosyncracies. Or, even worse, they welcome the full flood of Americanization as if the individual Puerto Rican had no other role to play than that of Caribbean salesman for "the American way." This is especially the sentiment of the Statehood-Republican elements. They are anxious to forget the Puerto Rican past in order the better to embrace the American future. They cannot see that ideally the Puerto Rican, in Governor Muñoz Marín's sentence, ought not to succumb to an enervating nostalgia for the past nor yet to an arrogant forgetfulness of what he owes to the past.

What are the chances that the local society will pay serious heed to that advice? Quite frankly the social and psychological legacy, the accumulated debris of colonialism, seriously inhibits the chances. In Puerto Rico as elsewhere colonialism has meant (1) the exportation to the colony of the less attractive features of the metropolitan society, and (2) a temptation on the part of too many sections of the colonial people willingly to receive those features, as their own traditions have been weakened by colonial rule. Thus both continental and Puerto Rican American sentiment have contributed to the process. It is evident in a number of ways. In architecture, for example, there has flourished no distinctively tropical Puerto Rican style, utilizing the Hispano-Moresque motif, to match the astonishing art of the new Brazilian architecture—with the exception, perhaps, of the earlier University buildings in Rio Piedras or the new Union Church in San Juan. The Capitol building which houses the Legislature is simply another imitation, exemplified in most of the American state capitals, of the federal pile in Washington, while too many of the business and office buildings erected since 1900 have been inappropriate copies of the New England Colonial or Kansas Renaissance styles. The concretized bleakness and army-barracks uniformity of the new mass housing developments are a peculiar horror which have to be seen to be believed, for the building contractor and the real estate agent have been permitted to organize—unrestrained by any really comprehensive town and country planning—a barbaric destruction of natural beauty in the name of "progress." The remark of the vice-president of the IBEC Housing Corporation—that he dare not entrust the survival of a tree to a worker in charge of a bulldozer[28]—sums up much of what has happened in recent years to the splendid beauty of the island. No less an authority than the Dean of the

Harvard School of Planning and Architecture has spoken with horror
of the brutal mutilation of the old tree-lined highways that the Puerto
Rico Telephone Company has been permitted to perpetrate throughout the island and, more generally, has warned against a slavish imitation of the Western industrialized societies by the new colonial nations
that even goes to the extent of copying their mistakes.[29] The American
confusion of bigness with greatness, in fact, has been accepted all
along the board, so that the big television set, the luxurious ranch
house, the "insolent chariots" of the Detroit automobile manufacturers
proliferate in San Juan as much as in any continental city. A certain
amount of cultural loss, naturally enough, there must always be as
the price of the "open society." But much that could have been
saved in Puerto Rico has been needlessly sacrificed. Leonard Bernstein has noted that a genuine Puerto Rican musical tradition could
have been developed to offset the saturation of American jazz and
Cuban mambo.[30] The famous *plenero* Canario has related how the
Puerto Rican *plena* was revived from obscurity by his own almost
singlehanded effort, and his description indicates how much the *plena,*
like the Trinidadian calypso, has in its time been a running commentary by the Puerto Rican artist upon the public events of his
society.[31] It is nothing less than comic, again, that the local *tradición
navideña* of the Three Kings, the *Magos de Oriente,* should have been
superseded on the part of Puerto Rican families by a stupid fanaticism
for the Santa Claus figure, entirely inappropriate as that figure is to
the *ambiente tropical* of Caribbean life.[32]

Some of the more lamentable elements of the insular life, of
course, cannot be attributed to the American spirit. The Puerto
Rican tolerance of strident noise, for example, is always difficult
even for Americans to comprehend, and much of life in the island is
spoiled by the frightful assault upon the eardrums that is thereby
perpetrated. The finding of the National Safety Council that the
accident rate on the island highways is double that on the continental
roads testifies to the appalling recklessness of the local traffic. All
early writers on the new possession from the very beginning remarked
upon cruelty to animals as a widespread feature of the local scene.
The Puerto Rican aesthete likes to think of the *homo americanus*
as the enemy of culture, yet there is a real strain of philistinism in
much of the Puerto Rican character itself. The story of how the
citizens of one local town set out, soon after the American occupation,
to "beautify" their *plaza* by destroying four beautiful *flamboyán* trees
and filling in the holes with cement may be apocryphal, but it is met
with so frequently in the literature on the island that it would appear
to be not entirely libelous in its implications. The delicacies of tropical

sight and sound—some of them, like the singing *coquí,* quite unique to Puerto Rico—have been affectionately described by Tomás Blanco in his book on *Los Cinco Sentidos;* yet much of what he writes about is being unceremoniously destroyed by the changes of the new Puerto Rico. Nor could any responsible sociologist be persuaded that Americans or American influence are primarily responsible for many of the special features of local society and politics—the almost Oriental passion for "face saving," the minor nepotism that persuades many to be *Popular* party supporters in order to hold down a government job, the habit of *personalismo,* the courteous evasiveness in personal relationships which the superficial observer frequently mistakes for dishonesty.

Yet the fact remains, having said all this, that the Puerto Rican tone, in popular culture habits at least, is set more and more by the American mass media. What is grandiloquently announced as a "renaissance" by the Commonwealth government's advertising witch doctors is not much else than a tropical reproduction of the American styles in business, entertainments, and family living. "Culture grafting" has really meant the enthronement of social advancement measured in the acquisition of property and the psychology that goes with it. The dross, of course, has a dress of clever rationalizations to make it presentable, usually purveyed to the local credulous audience by mediocre visiting American speakers and lecturers, just as in the American case itself the second-rate English novelists have inflicted their mediocre talents upon the continental audiences ready to applaud them. Nor is this just the petulant complaint of an outsider. The 1960 platform of the governing party permitted itself, perhaps rather late in the day, to a searching and critical reappraisal of a "revolution" which, in its own words, bids fair to multiply consumers' goods rather than create a "good civilization." Its main thesis, that the new prosperity is not producing "more tranquillity, more serenity, more education, a better civilization, but simply a multiplication of consumer goods, many of them unnecessary," makes the essential point. Everybody knows, too, that the criticism reflects the private doubts of the Governor himself, who almost certainly must begin to feel, as he leads his people into the temples of gluttony, like nothing so much as a puritan in Babylon. It is all the more unfortunate, therefore, that the *Popular* platform does not at all indicate the methods that might be invoked to cure or to ameliorate the social malaise that it thus analyzes.

There are two additional factors that help to make matters worse. The first is the character of the island's resident American community. The second is the impact of organized tourism as a big business operation upon the social climate of the island. Of the first, the "underlying aloofness" of the American *colón* was noticed from the very beginning by American travelers.[33] It is only necessary to read today his favorite English-speaking papers in the island to learn that, as a type, he still retains a basic "continental" attitude to the island, for everything in the island life—its politics, its traffic and police problems, its social and educational services—is discussed in these papers on the basis of persistent comparison with American standards. With few exceptions the American in Puerto Rico regards himself as marooned on a strange island far from home. He has rarely come to it in the spirit of the European immigrant coming to the United States as a land of freedom and opportunity. In the main, he is a plant manager or a salesman or a technical specialist, and he will have little of the catholic liberal training that would enable him to see his Puerto Rican neighbors as something more than "quaint" Latins who are on the road, eminently desirable, of becoming Americanized. He will generally restrict his social life to the American community, much of the temper of which is set by the naval and military personnel of the local United States service installations; and it is enough to read, for example, the odd views of a high-ranking officer like Admiral Gallery on the censorship of "pornographic" literature to realize that the attitude of the community to local controversial questions will not be remarkable either for liberal feeling or intellectual power. The average member of such a community will send his children to English-speaking schools like the Commonwealth School, will learn little Spanish, and will read the stateside newspapers (the *Miami Herald,* probably, rather than the *New York Times*). His wife will tend to suffer the well-known ennui of the colonial wife; a flurry of correspondence provoked by the violent anti-Puerto Rican outburst of a self-styled "bored Operation Bootstrap wife" in 1958 suggested relief for her in the usual unimaginative round of work in the YWCA, Red Cross drives, Garden Club projects, hospital aid schemes, and church activities.[34] There is, on the whole, little effective identification with Puerto Rican life, little real understanding of Puerto Rican problems. The gesture of courteous recognition to the Puerto Rican tradition—the full-page homages, for example, that the First National City Bank pays every so often to the figures of the Puerto Rican literary and cultural past in the local newspapers—remains the exception rather than the rule.

The type of the American bohemian, of course, is not unknown and gives rise to an occasional outburst of Hemingwayesque enthusiasm in which it may be suggested that Puerto Rico officially sponsor the art of bullfighting or launch an Armada against the Dominican Republic in its Trujillo period. But the more usual attitude will be that of the newly arrived office manager who sadly complained that the island had the *merengue*, bolero, and samba but lacked "good western style square dancing."[35] Nor is the more liberal American absent from the scene; indeed, he has a real place in the history of the *Popular* party. Nor, more latterly, is he averse to making radical utterances in areas of discussion where others, more angelic, may fear to tread; thus a visiting liberal like Professor Boris Stanfield has run foul of the local business community as he has gratuitously appointed himself some sort of tropical Jeremiah rousing lethargic Puerto Ricans, with a combination of astonishing belligerency and comic indiscretion, to an awareness of the grave responsibilities that await them, as he sees it, in the world of Russian-American power politics. But this type is a drop in the larger bucket. For all of his liberalism, the American in Puerto Rico is still inclined to see the Puerto Rican neighbor as a candidate for graduation in the school of American civics. The inclination encourages him to exaggerate the readiness of Puerto Ricans to embrace all things American; a local critic has thus pointed out the naiveté of putting on in San Juan a heavy theatrical diet of eight English-speaking Broadway plays in as many weeks without appreciating the fact that even educated Puerto Ricans who know the language well might not follow the idiomatic complexity of a Broadway play in sufficient numbers to warrant such a grandiose scheme.[36] No American in Puerto Rico of course, it is fairly true to say, will have about him the sort of devitalizing personal corruption described in Stevenson's stories of the white man in Polynesian society. One can only "go native," after all, in a society whose irrefragable primitivism provides the opportunity to go beyond the boundaries of no return. But neither, on the other hand, is the domiciled American likely to emerge, in any sizable number, as the champion of the Puerto Rican patriotic principle. There has been no equivalent of a Lawrence in his ranks. Nor has he produced, in literature, a Camus capable of painting the Spanish-Antillean atmosphere of the colonial element in the larger national life. His reaction, indeed, to Alfred Kazin's critical article would suggest that he is liable to respond with some violence to any visiting fellow American who utters public criticism of Puerto Rico, not because the criticism is false but because it has the effect of fouling the local American nest. His ultra-American passion also explains why his local press could deluge the late Ramos Antonini with fiercely denunciatory language because that political leader had dared to bring into the open the question of absentee wealth in the local economic development and thereby destroy the myth, carefully cultivated by that press, that all Puerto Ricans, save for the separatists, gladly welcome all things American.

Nor is the cause of liberal America in the territory aided—to note
the second aggravating factor—by the rapid development of San Juan
as another Miami Beach in Caribbean tourism. It has been official
policy not to envisage the tourist trade as a possible competitor to
industrialization as the major dollar-earning element of the economy.
But no country can for long escape the moral consequences of a
flourishing tourist program. These consequences are already flowering
in San Juan. The public display of the ostentatious wealth of the
narrow streak of congested hotel civilization on the San Juan seafront
serves only to dramatize by contrast the slumdom of *El Fanguito* and
La Perla. The socially undesirable types that flourish on the unwhole-
some fringes of the tourist hotels—the gambler, the "con man," the
pseudo-bohemian, the tropical beachcomber—have become well
established. It is true that the sort of human wreckage, the "white
trash," to be found in bars in less pleasing spots of the Caribbean is
not conspicuous in San Juan. The lowest form of human existence in
the Puerto Rican capital, indeed, will tend to be Puerto Rican, the
human wretch who survives by drinking a fierce mixture of raw, cheap
rum and Coca-Cola, for whom Puerto Ricans have a special name,
el atómico. At the same time legalized gambling rapidly demoralizes
the tone of any society in which it is permitted, as the cultural pauperization of Havana proves after it became, with the passage of Prohibition in the United States, the headquarters of the American crime and
gambling syndicates. The carefully regulated gambling casinos of the
San Juan hotels, it is true, subjected as they are to the keen scrutiny
of a governmental inspectorate, have not yet made the city into another pre-revolutionary Havana. But it is at least arguable that a
secretive gambling system, carried on in highly luxurious saloons, has
the effect of further segregating the tourist from the local population
and might carry as undesirable consequences as the raucous public
gambling of the Las Vegas variety.

The tourist dollar admittedly aids certain groups. But it also serves
in its general effects to exacerbate income differences within the economy. It generates a new imbalance between the production and the
entertainment industries. It creates new and glaring contrasts between
local poverty and tourist conspicuous consumption; the elegant para-
pets of the San Juan tourist palaces almost overlook the fetid slums
of the San Juan city districts. Income inequality is reinforced; the
remark, on that score, of a Jamaican trade union leader in the 1958
debate in that island on the issue of possible legalized gambling in its
North Shore tourist hotels—that a hotel waiter in Montego Bay may
earn a weekly wage as low as seventy shillings in a hotel where an
evening meal may cost the tourist guest eighty-four shillings—could

be duplicated in San Juan. Tensions increase when hotel managements favor American over Creole entertainers on the singular assumption that the tourist prefers it that way, and there are signs in
Puerto Rico that local artists even as well known throughout Latin
America as Bobby Capó may find it difficult to obtain an assignment
on the big night-club stages of their own capital city. Continental
tourist shops begin to oust working-class families from the Spanish
houses of the old city and replace them with tourist sales items that
sell at enormously inflated prices. Whole stretches of public beaches
become alienated to the private hotels at the cost of much local resentment; Brazilian success in preventing this process in Rio de Janeiro
seems not to have been noticed. It is true that there is very little of the
open color bar that makes out of the Bahamas a white international
tourist ghetto. But there is a covert "shade" bar; and there is certainly
a class discrimination which makes most Puerto Ricans feel that tourism is a high-cost enterprise from which they are excluded. The feeling
perhaps accounts for a growing demand that the tourist planners
ought to encourage the construction of smaller and cheaper motel
services throughout the island and the preservation of the older style
of town *pensionado* that is being driven under by the huge tourist
palaces. The demand could profitably take note at the same time of the
proof offered by Jamaica that a successful tourist industry can be built
up without the device of legalized gambling to lure the American
spender. Tourism, altogether, introduces the worst values of American life, not least of all the scabrous tittle-tattle about "personalities"
that goes on in the syndicated columns of the professional gossip
columnists of the Walter Winchell variety and is echoed in Puerto
Rican circles by pathetic imitations like Tony Beacon's *San Juan
Diary*.

It is only natural that the American image of Puerto Rico takes on
something of all this. The advertising campaign of the Commonwealth
government in lush magazines like *The New Yorker* reinforces the
portrait of the island as a tropical tourist paradise, "an island in the
sun" in the worst Hollywoodian manner. The society takes on the air,
in the words of an American tourist visitor, of a place "for a select few
who stay within the walls of beauty and cleanliness maintained by
natives who live out of sight in depressing hovels, while somewhere
United States manufacturers turn out tax free merchandise for United
States consumption at an excellent profit and employing only nice,
bright men and women imported from the States."[37] Or again the
island is lavishly advertised as a new bilingual and bicultural society
in which the children of the new Puerto Rico speak both English and
Spanish, talk about Cervantes and Walt Whitman, and read the *New*

York Times as well as the local newspapers. An American "old hand"
who in his lifetime taught for a generation in the island's small town
schools and who was, until his death, the Librarian of the national
University aptly commented upon how much of an Alice in Wonder-
land distortion the claim really is, if only because the number of university women students who read the *New York Times* could have
been easily accommodated in his own small office.[38] Behind all this
there hides a continuing desire, perhaps only half-consciously felt by
its practitioners, to appear handsomely in American eyes, to be accepted by Americans as legitimate contenders for the prizes to be
gained in the game of Americanism. Its leading premise was stated as
far back as 1916 by an outstanding Puerto Rican educator—long
identified, ironically enough, as one of the most nationalistically
minded of Commissioners of Education—in his remark that "this
island will remain an intellectual and spiritual as well as an economic
dependency of the United States. . . . The stimulus and inspiration for
continuous growth must come from without. They will come from the
United States."[39] The prophecy, so far, has turned out to be true.

That recognition of the unity of economic and cultural dependency
is perhaps the heart of the matter. Economic subserviency breeds cultural subserviency. The reliance upon American investment, both
public and private, stimulates anxious efforts to please by the imitation of American folkways. It is a basically humiliating condition,
especially for a pride so virile as the Puerto Rican; so much so indeed
that the motivation of the factor of economic dependency, stressed so
much by Puerto Ricans, may in fact be, as Renzo Sereno has suggested, simply a device to present a rational piece of fiction in place
of openly recognizing an intolerable reality. The end result is a psychology of ambivalence that oscillates between an uplifted national
pride and a haunting sense of inferiority. It makes for a latent anti-
Americanism; and one day, perhaps, an American sociologist will
compound a theory to determine how many drinks a representative
Puerto Rican must consume at a cocktail party before his released
inhibitions permit an open expression of the sentiment. For the American resident on the other hand, the situation frequently generates an
imprecise guilt which in its own turn is hidden by a continuing self-
assurance about the benefits that Puerto Rico gains from the American connection or, more indirectly, by a mode of conversation that
endlessly debates why Puerto Ricans drive recklessly or use physical
gesticulation as a mode of argument or indulge in the habit of
unpunctuality so irritating to the American Protestant work ethic.

It follows from all this that only a root and branch emancipation
from dependency, both economic and political, can hope to end the

ambivalence and lay the groundwork for a spiritual independence. Given that, the Puerto Rican spirit will be free, first, to nurture its own special contribution to world civilization and, second, to accept or reject American influences on a basis of free and uncoerced choice. The local pride in the local tradition will then be enabled to express itself without the distortion that comes from American rule; for the present temptation to trumpet abroad even the most obscure of Puerto Rican writers and artists as unappreciated Dostoevskis or Bernhardts is in large measure a fruit of the psychology of all colonial peoples. Local enthusiasm for the local success should then be freed of its present tone of defiant glee; for if Puerto Ricans seem to exaggerate the success of native sons abroad—whether it be Rafael Cintrón's European chess victory or Sixto Escobar's boxing prowess or even Miss Rita Moreno's encounters with the Los Angeles police—the exaggeration is pardonable after a fifty-year period during which local views and values have had little opportunity to be heard and respected. Nor should the fact be overlooked that in their hero worship the islanders tend to acclaim an operatic star like Graciela Rivera or an actor like José Ferrer, a musician like Sanromá or a baseball hero like Orlando Cepeda, rather than their business leaders. The Governor is as much admired in his role as a poet (he is *el Vate*, the Bard) as he is in that of a politician-statesman. These are healthy and civilized preferences. But they cannot of themselves fully contribute to world civilization until they have behind them the backing of indigenous social and political forces, until, that is to say, the island frees itself from the incubus of a political and economic relationship with the United States that virtually ties it hand and foot to the most powerful business civilization of the century.

For the truth of the matter is that as the Americanization of the society proceeds apace its isolation from other cultural influences becomes more and more pronounced. Apart from the odd trip, the insular artists and intellectuals are starved of any fruitful contact with the Latin American world. The fact that the general output of the Institute of Puerto Rican Culture is weak in the field of painting, so powerfully resurgent elsewhere in the Caribbean in Mexico and Haiti, and strong in those fields that are not Pan-Caribbean in character—mural decoration, wood sculpture, lithography, and poster art—suggests a regrettable separation from what is going on elsewhere. Everything, increasingly, is seen through the American perspective. The strident tones in which so many Puerto Ricans congratulate themselves upon enjoying political "stability"—which really means the protection afforded by the virtual protectorate of the

United States military power—shows how deeply they have removed themselves from a sympathetic identification with the Latin American peoples. The humiliation, frequently self-imposed, of that situation is no better exhibited than in the spectacle of the Puerto Rican statehood fan pleading with the American people to take on an assimilative policy which would mean the erosion of all the social and cultural characteristics which distinguish his people from those of the United States. In such a context, people come to despise their own virtues. So, there are private hospitals in San Juan where all signs are in English despite the fact that the staff are overwhelmingly Spanish-speaking. The man in the street will convert himself into a pathetic comedy as he tries to parade the little store of mangled English phrases he has somewhere picked up. The comic strips in the newspapers are all of them American, with Spanish titles, even although some of them, "Blondie," for example, or "Bringing up Father," portray the type of abject American husband so far removed from the Puerto Rican male's image of himself. Criticism will be heard of Bobby Capó because the song with which that local artist and songwriter welcomed Mrs. Kennedy on her state visit to Mexico seemed "disrespectful," whereas in truth what that amusing episode proved was the profound dissimilarity between Puerto Rican and American ways of appraising feminine charm. It is hardly surprising that disgust with all of this, and what it symbolizes, drives many thoughtful Puerto Ricans to retreat into inner private worlds. For some, it is political intrigue; for others, gossip, and rumor-mongering; for still others, concentration upon arid scholarship in local fields, like the debate as to exactly where Columbus landed on the west coast of the island and on which topic whole books manage to get written. The dominant social tone becomes that of an egotistical individualism, only assuaged by the increasingly uncertain assurance about a common *puertorriqueñidad* which becomes more and more of a nostalgic dream as it loses touch with the harsh realities of change.

For no society, unless it be trapped like the Puerto Rican, has of necessity to confuse modernization with Americanization. The confusion has arisen in Puerto Rico because of the artificially unilateral connection with the American power. There is evidence to suggest, indeed, that over the last sixty years the connection has resulted in a very real pauperization of Puerto Rican intellectual life. The new middle classes are assuredly less world-conscious than their predecessors before 1898. It is only necessary to read through the catalogue of the library of the *Ateneo Puertorriqueño* in 1897, the last year of the Spanish regime, to realize how closely in touch with European culture were the San Juan Creole professional groups at that time;

for the list includes the works of the liberal historians like Lamartine, Renan, and Edgar Quinet and of the Romantics like Victor Hugo, Zola, and Perez Galdos.[40] The American connection has undoubtedly narrowed the intellectual horizons as it has cut off Puerto Rican minds from the wider European and Latin American influences. The task of the future is to re-establish those broken ties. Political independence once achieved, the task should not be difficult. Puerto Rico would be received in her own right in world civilization. The learning of foreign languages would become a first claim upon a rejuvenated educational system; so that not only would the teaching of English be freed from its present political overtones but the Puerto Rican child, in addition, would learn to master those other languages, French, Dutch, and Portuguese, that surround him in the Caribbean and Latin American worlds. The island, thus receiving new creative influences, would in truth become the "crossroads of the Americas"; and what is now an empty phrase could become a living truth.

The Machinery of Government: Executive, Administrative, and Judicial

IN NO field of the Puerto Rican experience has the American impact been so deeply felt as in that of political and administrative institutions. The separation of civilian and military powers, so much an American principle of governance, was completed in the territory after 1900. The Organic Acts of 1900 and 1917 initiated important phases of administrative reorganization in the local machinery of government. More important, perhaps, the "revolution of 1940" inaugurated a conscious drive to streamline the administrative structure in accordance with the new demands of enlarged internal self-government; and the Elective Governor Act of 1947 was logically followed by extensive reforms in organization and functions so that the public service and the legislative-executive system would mirror the gradual transference of power from the federal center to the Caribbean circumference. These reforms, following the earlier spurt given to administrative modernization by Governor Tugwell, were summed up in the *Report* of the Commission for Reorganization set up by the local Legislature in 1949, and put into effect by legislative statute the following year. The new Constitution of 1952, following the general terms of reference of the federal Congressional Public Law 600 of 1950, clothed the reforms with the cohesive framework of an instrument of government created and adopted (in part) by a local Constitutional Convention (contrasting significantly with the old colonial method of inaugurating the West Indies Federation of the British islands some years later by the promulgation of their new federal constitution through Imperial Orders in Council from the top in London). All in all, administrative reorganization in Puerto Rico in the years since 1940 has shaped a structure of public government almost ideally suited to the demands of positive planning in the modern democratic state. Its architects have been able to push through the reorganization with an ease that must be the envy of any administrative theoretician who has had anything to do with the modernization of government in any of the American states. For state and city governments in most of the states exhibit features of an almost medieval backwardness, as any examination of the New England township or the Midwestern county, as they have been faced with the demands of modern technology and communications, will readily prove. Puerto Rico by contrast has become almost a model of modern public administration.

Why is this? Some of the reasons speak for themselves. The Spanish heritage of strong centralized rule has left its mark, despite the fact that no American governor could have behaved as dictatorially as the Governor Sanz who under Spain was responsible for one of the most hated gubernatorial terms in the island's Spanish history. There has been no period of economic individualism in the insular history to give rise to a "folklore of capitalism" equating public planning with an evil betrayal of economic laws. There is today party government in a British rather than American sense, so that once administrative reorganization becomes majority party policy its legislative ratification goes through without significant opposition. The strong party discipline of the *Popular* Party, added to the fact that that party has had unchallengeable control of both legislative and executive branches since 1949 (and for all practical purposes since 1941), means that differences between the two houses of the Legislature get resolved easily and that the power of extra-parliamentary groups to influence legislative determination is reduced to a minimum. It is true that in the early days under Governor Tugwell reorganization was passionately assailed by both visiting Congressmen and local opposition leaders as a daring plan to build up a mighty bureaucracy that would seek to bypass the restrictive provisions of the Organic Act, and the Tugwell autobiography is to a large extent a prolonged account of the battle that ensued. But the conditions which really stimulated that situation—the latent parliamentary civil war endemic in a colonial regime where there is a popular Legislature and an expatriate executive, and the Congressional vendetta against the figure of Rexford Tugwell—have now disappeared. The Governor can no longer be pilloried as a meddling outsider. And, in the person of Governor Muñoz Marín, his chair is occupied by a past master in the art of imposing forceful leadership upon his cohorts without driving any part of them into resistance. Strong central government thus does not have to encounter the suspicion (as in Cuba or Haiti) that it is a possible vehicle of personal dictatorship. Nor is it hamstrung—as in the case of the now defunct West Indies Federation—by the sort of conflict between center and periphery that is almost a natural law in federal structures. For all of these reasons, inventive experimentation has characterized the governmental field in the territory more, perhaps, than in any other single segment of the insular life.

"Energy in the executive," wrote Hamilton, "is a leading character in the definition of good government." For the reasons already cited, the office of the Governor in Puerto Rico has been able, in the last brief generation, to expand its authority along Hamiltonian rather than Jeffersonian lines to a degree unequaled in any American state government or even, perhaps, in the presidency itself. The powers and functions of the Governor—in his fourfold capacity as chief executive, chief legislator, party leader, and official head of state—are so wide in scope that the office is one of the most powerful under the American flag. Only the President and perhaps the Governor of New York can be said to exercise comparable authority within their respective jurisdictions.[1] The particular reasons for this have already been assessed. More generally there is the fact that both under Spain and America the local citizen has been trained to rely far more heavily upon his government than has been the case on the mainland. This was recognized as an important element by the Commission for the Reorganization of the Executive Branch in 1949. Now that he is no longer the favored appointee of either Madrid or Washington, that Committee's report observed, the people of the island "now expect the Governor in addition to all his statutory and legal duties, to his ceremonial and symbolic functions, to his political and party leadership, to do certain things for them that they cannot do for themselves. . . . They expect the Governor to guide the economy of Puerto Rico so that the standard of living be raised, that the pains of poverty be diminished, and that both agriculture and industry prosper and that political freedom may be realized in terms of social and economic betterment. . . ."[2] The expectation has grown logically from the demands that an underdeveloped tropical economy makes upon its government. Even a Republican Congressional report on the matter is driven to the conclusion that such an economy, characterized by grim overpopulation, persistent seasonal unemployment, considerable illiteracy, and a grotesque urban slumdom cannot afford the luxury of the negative state.[3]

In line with all this the executive article of the local Constitution places the plenitude of executive power into the hands of the Governor by eliminating the old Executive Council that had shared the power with him under the terms of the Organic Act. By the repeal of the important Article 34 of that act, Public Law 600 removed the veto of the United States President over insular legislation and so gave to the Governor's office an independent dignity it had not previously enjoyed. The Governor is granted the power—not available to the American chief executive—to veto items of appropriation bills. He possesses (since 1949) a wide discretionary power, such as that granted to the President in 1939 and 1945, to propose reorganization plans and thereby has a free hand within limits to arrange the division of work throughout the executive branch as he sees fit, and thus altogether to make himself master in his own house. He enjoys all the conventional powers assigned to chief executives in the American state scheme: the power to execute the laws, to appoint his cabinet members with senatorial advice and consent, to call special legislative sessions, to veto legislative proposals, to exercise the power of pardon (although this is limited, happily, by the constitutional prohibition of the death penalty in local criminal matters), and to proclaim martial law, although this, too, is limited by the provision that, once such proclamation has been made by the Governor acting in his role as commander-in-chief of the local militia, the Legislature "shall meet forthwith on their own initiative to ratify or revoke the proclamation"[4]—a qualifying clause not unimportant when it is remembered that episodes like the attempted Nationalist Party uprising of 1950 make it not altogether an academic power. The office of the Governor, again, is not limited by any restriction upon occupancy, for despite a spirited debate on the issue the Constituent Assembly of 1951-1952 refused to accept any constitutional limitation. To do so, the majority of delegates felt, would be to interfere with the popular general will in its support of a uniquely popular leader, although they might have added, from a less theoretical position, that it would impose upon Puerto Rico the waste of ability that makes of American ex-Presidents wandering ghosts on the national political stage. The Latin fear of *continuismo* in government was in any case overridden by ultra-democratic considerations.[5] The unusual clause governing the succession to the office also lends it new strength, since it provides that a vacancy shall be filled by the person of the Secretary of State of the cabinet.[6] Not only does the provision save the executive branch from the rivalry between Governor and Lieutenant-Governor that so frequently bedevils American state politics, but it also ensures that in the event of a vacancy the office shall be filled by an official who, as a departmental head and a cabinet member in his own right, will be able to insure some effective continuity of policies with which he has been intimately acquainted. The office altogether has sufficient power and prestige to make it an excellent tool for any Governor who wishes to make of it an instrument of positive national leadership. This being so, it hardly makes any difference that, in a less imaginative moment, the Constituent Assembly should have written into the Constitution the cumbersome and, in a democratic system based upon universal suffrage and the party system, the utterly obsolete device of impeachment.[7]

In the pursuit of his duties the Governor has the assistance of

(1) the cabinet, or Council of Secretaries, and (2) the staff agencies which comprise the Office of the Governor. The former body, surprisingly enough, has no specific powers granted to it and is, indeed, merely the Governor's "advisory council" in its collective capacity. The subordination of the cabinet to the chief executive, in fact, has gone as far in San Juan as on the presidential level in Washington. In part, this is due to the questionable reputation that the cabinet, as a corporate body, has had in the older colonial administrative structures, in part to the sheer force of the Muñoz Marín personality in its human aspects. The upshot in any case has been what most observers agree to be an unhealthy centralization of authority into the hands of an almost monarchical chief executive. Even an observer as habitually cautious as Professor Henry Wells has ventured to suggest that "one hears it said that the men around Muñoz are sometimes too deferential to his views and too hesitant about arguing with him and telling him home truths; and this may well be so."[8] Certainly most of the important *pronunciamientos* of official policy tend to see daylight as personal statements of the Governor rather than as cabinet or party decisions. Certainly, too, no cabinet member participates openly in the debate on the leading question of political status (apart from occasional statements of a non-controversial character) and only the Resident Commissioner in Washington, perhaps, matches the Governor in his contributions, as a student of constitutional law, to that issue. The 1962 decision to hold a plebiscite on that issue, profoundly important as it was, seems to have had its genesis in the Governor's European tour immediately preceding its announcement, and there was little evidence to suggest that it had been the subject of cabinet consultation, let alone cabinet decision. The cabinet, again, in its principle of recruitment tends to be a body of technical and professional specialists rather than a group of "all-round" men. There has been a tendency to appoint (as is currently the case) an economist to head the Department of Commerce, a doctor the Department of Health, an engineer the Department of Public Works. This perhaps explains why one cabinet member can enunciate the limiting doctrine that the business of the Economic Development Administration is merely to "set up factories that will create jobs for the thousands who do not yet have them." This is perhaps why too the same type of departmental technocrat is so peculiarly sensitive to outside criticism; unfortunately the sensitivity is encouraged by his insulation, because of the separation of powers, from the rough and tumble of legislative politics. Nor is he encouraged to widen his sympathies by an executive structure that centralizes so much power into the hands of its leading figure. He gets little chance to become a generalist able to put the specialism of his

departmental task within the larger framework of the national policies. A former Secretary of Justice has complained about the discouragement of individual initiative that ensues from the merely consultative character of the executive council.[9] The embarrassing episode of 1955, in which a prominent cabinet member was obliged to announce that he had not read his ghost writer's speech on the matter of American-Puerto Rican cultural relationships delivered to a visiting American audience and that, on second thought, he could not agree with its thesis takes on an almost poignant appearance in the light of the open secret that he had been driven to that humiliating expedient because of the Governor's disapproval of the speech.[10] In a system of matured constitutional ethics, such pressure on the part of the cabinet chief would normally call for the cabinet member's resignation. The monolithic character of the *Popular* movement indeed both as government and party is aptly illustrated by the fact that throughout the Governor's three terms there has not been a single cabinet resignation accompanied by a public airing of differences of opinion on a controversial matter. To sum up: under the colonial regime the "cabinet" tended to be the rival of governors; in the regime of internal self-government it has become the creature of governors.

In Puerto Rico as much as in the United States the doctrine of cabinet collective responsibility is conspicuous by its absence. The paradox, however, is that the factors which in part justify this fact on the American side are not at all so prevalent on the Puerto Rican. There is very little of the institutional jealousy between legislature and executive that so often works for deadlock in Washington politics. The former Speaker of the lower house had pointed to the remarkable fact that 95 percent of the legislation submitted to that chamber by the Planning Board gets approved readily by both majority and minority votes.[11] Suasion over the Legislature, as a matter of fact, is parliamentary rather than congressional in its completeness. Party strength in the lower house is almost exactly reflected in the composition of the Senate, so that there is very little of the inter-house bickering that inhibits Congressional unity in the federal capital. A parliamentary executive, it follows, would fit all this like a glove on a hand. A collegial type of cabinet would do much to rectify the defects of the present arrangement. The pious observation of the Rowe Commission Report that presidential one-man government reflects "the best experience of chief executives in many places and in many times" was founded on a regard for American experience only, and in any case failed to recognize that the system does not provide the collective responsibility and the rapidity of action that the cabinet system provides. If the art of government is regarded from the managerial and not the legal aspect it is clear indeed that it would be more efficiently conducted if the leadership of the chief executive were re-inforced by the genuine team work of departmental cabinet colleagues who possessed a real responsibility.[12] As things now stand, the Puerto Rican cabinet has somewhat more of a fixed constitutional status than the one ruled by the American President—but only somewhat; and in practice it is the replica of the federal body that was frankly envisaged by the Rowe Commission.

The difficulty remains, nevertheless, of inventing the means of converting the local cabinet into the quasi-parliamentary body recom-mended by the critics of that Commission. The authors of the advisory report made to the Constituent Assembly by the University School of Public Administration recommended the formation of a cabinet possessed of the "representative quality, prominence and authority that would necessarily be a consequence of an increased share of responsibility and interest in the growth of the government as a whole."[13] But this is a vague recommendation. Nor is the report any less vague when it insists in the same paragraph that such a cabinet could be obtained by appropriating "the advantages of the parlia-mentary system without accepting its basic principle" of the members of the cabinet being at the same time members of the legislative body enjoying the latter's confidence.[14] For it is surely their status as popu-larly elected politicians, with their own independent strength both in their party and in the legislative body, that enables such individuals to assert their "prominence" and "authority" in the parliamentary system. That is the lesson undoubtedly of the British experience. It is the lesson, in the reverse, of the American experience, for even cabinet members of the Roosevelt administrations as strong-willed as Henry Wallace and Harold Ickes were unable to secure for themselves the "prominence" and "authority" automatically enjoyed by the leading cabinet colleagues of the British Prime Minister. It is not to be expected that a popularly elected chief executive will regard him-self, in the company of men who owe their position solely to his nomination, as merely *primus inter pares*. He is more likely to see them, as Governors in the former British West Indies have viewed the nominated members of their legislative councils, as "King's Friends" whose function is one of unanimous and uncritical support of the executive. It is perhaps significant that the only Puerto Rican executive member who ranges over a wide area in his public utter-ances is the Resident Commissioner for Washington, who is popu-larly elected and whose popular election indeed predates historically that of the Governor. The desideratum of the School of Public Ad-ministration Report, in brief, could only be attained perhaps by substituting popular election for executive nomination as the recruiting principle of the cabinet. Many of the conditions of political life in Puerto Rico, as indicated, already anticipate such a solution. But it is doubtful, unfortunately, if their existence is sufficiently powerful to override all of the reasons, psychological, historical, and cultural, that favor the continuation of a single executive along American lines.

As things stand, consequently, the administrative reform measures pushed forward since 1947 have rationalized and strengthened the Office of the Governor without doing much to rehabilitate the cabinet along modern lines. The creation of the Bureau of the Budget in 1942 as an executive fiscal weapon; the incorporation of the Planning Board into the Office of the Governor in 1950 as a staff component; the establishment of the Organization and Methods Division in the Bureau of the Budget; the enlargement of the Governor's staff services, including the use of the device of the "administrative assistant"; the shifting of minor and petty routine duties from the Governor's shoulders—until 1949 he was required, among other things, to authorize and personally sign some 350 travel orders a year for government officials and employees and to authorize, some 300 times a year, executive branch officials to make international telephone calls[15]—all of these measures have contributed to transforming what was until only yesterday a cramped colonial institution into an efficient instrument of progressive executive leadership. They constitute the modernization of an executive system that becomes urgent once self-government replaces external control. The Puerto Rican experience has thus been used as a guide as, somewhat later, the crown colony executive in the British islands like Jamaica and Trinidad has been supplanted by a full-blown cabinet system topped by the office of Premier. The reasons for the change, in Puerto Rico as elsewhere, have been twofold. In the first place, economic transformation requires administrative transformation. In government as in nature the form follows the function, not the function the form. It is hardly conceivable that Puerto Rican industrialization could have gone forward so rapidly if a government structure designed to maintain a balance of power between American governors and local *políticos* had remained in existence; or if, to take another example, essential services like electric power, water supply, and vocational education had been the responsibility of the myriad municipal governments. Secondly, the colonial structure of the Organic Act of 1917 had become, by 1947, a negative and not a positive set of institutions. It had developed all the vices of "Congressional government" with none of its virtues, driving the whole system back to the sort of government by committee made notorious, in early American constitutional history, by the pitiful record of the Continental Congress. Jealousy of the colonial Governors had encouraged the vicious habit, in the Legislature, of circumventing their authority by devices such as the creation of "segregated" funds sealed off from gubernatorial control. The price that the island paid for all this was grim indeed; in Governor Tugwell's phrase, Puerto Ricans committed governmental suicide by smothering an alien executive. The real achievement of the last decade and a half has been to create a machinery of government which promises an end to that sterile process. It has done little to bring either the cabinet or the Legislature up to date. But at least it has created a modern executive.

It follows from all this that the Puerto Rican governorship is one of the busiest offices under the American flag. Governor Tugwell's collected papers reveal a sufficiently heavy burden when it was a colonial executive. Its democratization has naturally served to make the burden even heavier today. As head of government, the Governor must supervise all departments and agencies as best he can, and it is doubtful if he really has time fully so to do, despite the habit, recently borrowed from the Kennedy administration, of requiring weekly progress reports from all departmental and agency heads. He receives all sorts of delegations, including those supplicating his office for economic aid for their depressed towns. He is the recipient of memoranda and letters from varied sources: the Police Association pleading the economic difficulties of its members, the Mayor of Guanica outlining the beach destruction that has taken place as a consequence of oil dumped from a passing Italian freighter along the southern coastline, friends of Albizu Campos, the imprisoned Nationalist Party leader, seeking his release, or local groups protesting the presence of United States military installations in the island. The Mayor of San Juan relieves him of many social functions, for that remarkable lady politician dispenses social entertainments with all the zest of the late Mayor Jimmy Walker of New York. But he cannot escape all, and his calendar is always liberally full of speaking engagements, whether it be to the San Juan Lions Club or important visiting conventions or the inaugural session of the Caribbean Organization. Then there are all the calls on his services as party leader, for he is the *líder máximo,* the dominant personality in the internal dynamics of the party structure he has so largely himself created. Not least of all, there are all the demands of foreign affairs. For although, in constitutional theory, the Governor has no jurisdiction in external relations, in practice he plays a not unimportant unofficial role. He receives visiting dignitaries at *La Fortaleza,* from state governors and touring Congressmen to lecturing academicians and Papal Nuncios. He is regularly consulted on Latin American affairs by Washington administrations, especially if they are Democratic; while his own speeches on those affairs are widely noted. He may exchange important correspondence with the President, as in the exchange of letters with President Kennedy in July 1962 on the proposed plebiscite. He will receive invitations of a kind not usually sent to state governors: to the 1962 independence celebrations, for example, of Trinidad and Tobago. The usual prestige that comes to him, then, as a governor is thus reinforced by whatever measure of "international personality" his own Commonwealth State Department is able to secure for the territory. It is not surprising, then, that there are many duties that require a trip abroad: a stay at Cambridge in order to deliver the Harvard Godkin lectures, a visit to New York to speak with Mayor Wagner on the problems of Puerto Rican migrants, an official state visit to Jamaica, the flights to Washington made particularly necessary by the dependence of the Commonwealth upon Congressional good will, the acceptance of an honorary degree from Brandeis University. It is small wonder that the Governor hides away as frequently as he can in his well-protected country home in Trujillo Alto.

In Puerto Rico as elsewhere the modern state is the administrative state. Sir Henry Taylor's dictum that "he who administers the law is in very truth the master of it" applies as forcefully in San Juan as in Washington or London. The quality and behavior of his bureaucracy is of primary importance, accordingly, in the life of the ordinary Puerto Rican citizen. The growth of the public services in the society has been, in effect, the growth of the central government, and many functions elsewhere performed by local authorities have been perforce taken over by the government: police, fire control, education, health and welfare services, and so on. The temptation of the professional public administration analyst (whose reports on the island are legion) has been to view the island as one large municipality. To the degree that government has accepted this predilection it has encouraged the growth of the principle of efficient authority as against that of the principle of democratic participation.

The public service, in its modern form, is of course in its infancy in the society. The transition from a "spoils system" to a merit service did not really occur until the passage of the Personnel Act in 1947. That act created the grades, competitive, non-competitive, and exempted, of the present-day service, as well as the Office of Personnel, headed by a Director who thus became the chief administrative officer of the service, replacing the old system of government by commission. Dr. John Honey's definitive thesis, *Public Personnel Administration in Puerto Rico,* has described in detail the far-reaching consequences of the act. Within three brief years it stimulated the growth of full-scale, trained personnel offices within the several larger departments and agencies; stimulated, through the vigorous use of the powers of the new Examining Board, the elimination of the excessive use of the provisional appointment, one of the major evils of the old system; carried through the schemes for a rational pay plan and classification system, both of which had had their genesis in the earlier work of Guillermo Nigaglioni, former Commission Chairman, and of the Public Administration Service of Chicago, so that the insular employee was finally assured some reasonable system of classifying his abilities and some reasonable monetary goals to work for; started the embryo of a rational placement system that would fit the right man into the right job; and laid the foundations, in collaboration with the University School of Public Administration, of a training scheme, both of an in-service and formal educational character, which could encourage in the civil servant the idea—completely lacking in 1945—of an honorable career in government service based upon technical skill and a professional ethic. The new regime began, too, to look into the vagaries of the government scholarship system, hitherto existing without any centralized control, with the result that the system had frequently been operated out of context of the most pressing needs of the local service and with little effort made to give to the taxpayer any information on his sizable expenditures in that field.[16]

A decade and a half seems a period sufficiently long to justify a stock taking of the changes at once conceived and carried through by the administrative oligarchy since 1947. Some changes have been dramatically successful. The habit of using a government appointment as a sideline to something else has gone—a remarkable achievement in itself when it is remembered that in 1944 almost one half of the classified service was composed of temporary employees lacking even the minimum qualifications and managing to get themselves retained beyond the legal time limit by means of political influence.[17] The prestige of the insular service has grown with reform, so that the older tendency of insular employees to prefer federal employment in the federal agencies situated in San Juan has gradually given way to a pride in their own service. Most important of all perhaps is the fact that the idea in itself of an extended merit and professionalized service has by now found support in both official and popular attitudes. The early reluctance of Muñoz, as legislative leader, to accept the idea—as opposed to Governor Tugwell's reformist zeal—gave way to enthusiastic approval as his own political position improved, and by the time of Governor Tugwell's resignation he was insisting upon the necessary distinction between the functions of the political party and those of the government under the new conditions. His welcoming speech at the foundation ceremonies of the new School of Public Administration at the University in 1945 was devoted in the main, indeed, to a concise definition of the different functions of political party and administration in the new Puerto Rican democracy. Dr. Honey has concluded that, following this lead, most politicians had accepted the new system within some five brief years after its inception, although the habit still remained of candidates arriving at government offices with letters of endorsement from political friends.[18] The new system, that is to say, had finally entered the Puerto Rican psychology as a piece of permanent institutional furniture for the insular life, as distinct from the earlier reforms of 1907 and 1931 which had been, in the absence of popular support, expressions of the concern of individual American governors for a civil service along American lines.

Much, even so, remains to be done. It would be surprising, after all, if the new system within so brief a time span had begun to match, say, the British civil service in organizational maturity or general sophistication. There are still serious deficiencies in the quality of personnel beneath the level of major agency and departmental heads and their key subordinates which are frankly recognized by Puerto Ricans themselves. The training program in collaboration with the University School of Public Administration has done much in this field; and it is not an accident that one of the most authoritative commentators on the problems of the insular service is Dr. Pedro Muñoz-Amato who, of all the Directors of the School, gave it its original quality and direction, especially insisting upon a general liberal arts program which would give, ideally, to the public servant a humanistic Social Sciences education. But the School is itself only a decade and a half old. It has tended to concentrate, since 1947, upon becoming a school of graduate study, thus being forced to lessen its concentration upon the in-service training program of departments; there may be too much of an emphasis in its curriculum upon the more technical aspects of public administration; there is some evidence of quite serious student dissatisfaction with the dull and repetitious teaching, often involving the laborious reading of long extracts from textbooks, on the part, especially, of the part-time members of the faculty. Finally, the rapid turnover of its teaching personnel, especially through the lure of more attractive appointments in government service (one of the former staff members of the school was, until only recently, a young associate justice of the Insular Supreme Court, while one of its former Directors is now an assistant Secretary of State in the Commonwealth government) and in private business (another of the former Directors is a leading figure in the local home construction industry), has inhibited it from becoming the pervasive influence throughout the ranks of the service and upon public opinion that it should have become. This, too, is all the more disturbing since the twin sources for the recruitment of trained governmental personnel remain still the official scholarship program and the School of Public Administration. There are also two chapters of the American Society for Public Administration in the island, but their influence on government, naturally enough, is not as yet comparable to that of the Fabian Society on the British civil service over the last eighty years. The basic principle itself of the merit system—the full coverage of all civil servants by its provisions, with perhaps the exclusion of top policy-making officials appointed by the Governor—has been compromised from the very beginning by the division of the service into its three classes. As of today the principle awaits its wider application and in particular the fuller utilization of one of its basic features, the public announcement of vacancies, in order to eliminate favoritism in appointments. Reform might even go so far, as the Director of Personnel himself has suggested, as to question the prevailing judicial doctrine, based upon a famous opinion of Justice Holmes, that government employment is not to be seen as a constitutional right, for the doctrine can be used by an unscrupulous government to deny the right to work as an equally vital doctrine in modern life.[19] The whole merit system, furthermore, is presently artificially restricted and justice demands its further extension to cover the more than one-half of the insular public employees—some 29,000 out of a total of some 57,300—who are in the non-competitive and exempted grades; while there are entire categories of employees—in the Department of Education, the University, the Police Department, and the Water Resources Authority—who are denied the protection of appeal to the Personnel Board or to any comparable body of a judicial character. They must fall back on what protection they can obtain from trade union efforts. But there is a great deal of discrepancy and absence of uniformity in both the legal statutes governing employee union rights and in the attitudes of various departmental leaderships to these rights. The whole system badly needs the creation of service-wide uniform rules and principles. But neither the Personnel Board nor the Public Service Commission is specifically entrusted with such a task in their respective statutory declarations of functions. How far such a uniformity of rule and principle has been frustrated by departmental autonomy is made evident, again, by the fact that there are agencies like the Land Authority and Fomento that are characterized either by a complete absence of regulatory principles or by a dangerous informality in employment procedures.

The various reports of the 1959 Civil Liberties inquiry indeed would seem to indicate even more serious defects in the administrative branch. The constitutional guarantees of the Bill of Rights, it is estimated, do not in reality apply to more than one third of the total government employees, who, in addition to all municipal government employees saving the San Juan municipality, are at the mercy of illegal discrimination and personal favoritism coming from their agency and departmental heads. "Although the attitudes of departmental and agency heads," observes the report on *Problems of Civil Rights in Personnel Administration,* "are generally satisfactory as far as the protection of the basic rights of public employees is concerned, there are still sporadic failings of discrimination on personal grounds, for reasons of racial and sex prejudice, and on account of political beliefs. Some departments systematically exclude women, with no clear justification by way of lack of qualifications. There is a noticeable scarcity of Negro persons in certain posts and subdivisions. The practice of not admitting *independentistas* prevails still in many areas."[20] A "loyalty oath" of peculiarly wide reference demands not only allegiance to the Constitution but also to the laws of the *Estado Libre Asociado.* It is true that there has been no mass investigation of employees comparable to that unleashed in the federal civil service by President Truman's Executive Order of 1947. At the same time, the government openly prohibits the recruitment of candidates of known Communist or Nationalist leanings without any effort to state publicly the grounds, if any, for so doing. It is not unknown for departmental chiefs summarily to dismiss individuals merely for their known attachment to the rhetorical abstractions of the Nationalist ideal or to impose the severe penalty of dismissal for the comparatively mild offense of distributing during office hours literature which has included, among other items, an appeal to President Truman against the continued use of the atom bomb.[21] Even the use of intemperate words in the midst of the excitement of the attempted Nationalist revolt of 1950 has been regarded as sufficient ground for severance from the public service, although commendably the Personnel Board later annulled the departmental action.[22] This sort of arbitrary behavior is encouraged by the presence in certain departments, notoriously in the Department of Education, of wide discretionary powers enjoyed by the departmental heads in matters of promotion and transfers of personnel. In a society as highly politicized as Puerto Rico such powers can always be used in the service of party orthodoxy. Nor is the danger merely theoretical. The 1950 cases in the Department of Education, in which two teachers of outstanding and lengthy service were dismissed by the Secretary without explanation and hearing, demonstrate how easy it is for a departmental officialdom to destroy the professional career of public servants when there are no procedural guarantees (as in the case with all personnel in the non-competitive grades) to protect them against political discrimination. It is at least an alarming state of affairs when over forty percent of the teaching profession believes that appointments and promotions in their field are made less with reference to individual merit than to political influence.[23]

The administrative branch, as a matter of fact, has managed to solve a number of problems. But it has been signally unsuccessful, so far, in securing the principle of the political neutrality of the public servant. There is no clearly defined higher service, like the British Administrative Class, whose advice helps to shape policy but who must yield, in the final resort, to ministerial decision. There is in fact a nebulous region in which there is no precise line of demarcation between the professional career official and the political head. This not only contributes to confusion about the *locus* of responsibility but also denies to the service as a whole the leadership and example that come from the existence of a top echelon of eminent permanent officials. Such leadership and example will be difficult to furnish and sustain as long as the government bureaucracy as a whole shares the conviction that professional advancement and security of employment depend upon loyalty to the governing political party. And there is persuasive evidence that such is indeed the case. The practice of requesting "voluntary" contributions to the *Popular* treasury from office holders—a practice that goes back to the beginnings of popular government in the island—still prevails despite sharp criticism from the Personnel Board; and the illegality of the practice, at least on the part of the municipal authorities, is cynically got over (as the ingenuous letter of the treasurer of the Popular Democratic Committee in the town of San Lorenzo illustrates) by turning over the responsibility of collecting the tribute to a Popular Democratic party functionary.[24] The use of public resources for *Popular* party uses (as late as 1948, at least, the practice was sanctioned by the Governor in correspondence later introduced as evidence in the hearings of the Civil Liberties inquiry of 1959) continues to be a major abuse of government facilities for partisan ends, and might in itself constitute indeed a new type of pressure on the electoral process to replace that of the open purchase of votes challenged by the *Popular* Party a generation ago.[25] It is not unfair to say, altogether, on this point, that the sharp

distinction made years ago by the Governor himself, in his capacity
at that time as Senate President, between the functions of a political
party and those of an administrative machine, based upon a clear
recognition of the boundary lines that ought to be established between politics and administration, remains still, today, a theoretical
distinction in many ways, with the entrenched government party committing many of the offenses contained in that lecture inaugurating the
local School of Public Administration.

It has been argued by some critics—by Dr. Muñoz-Amato, for
example—that the best solution to this general problem lies in (1) the
increased self-discipline that will come from the better education
of the public servant and (2) the relaxation of the tight restrictions
that presently, by virtue of the local application of the federal Hatch
Act provisions, surround the overt political activities of government
personnel.[26] The first solution is at best very long term. It has
taken something like a century since the publication of the seminal
Trevelyan-Northcote Report for the British civil service to acquire its
present standards of sophistication, integrity, and incorruptibility. It
would be utopian to expect Puerto Rico, with no administrative history
to speak of and with very little cultural tradition of a leisured gentleman class to fall back upon, to match those standards in any short
time period. It does not require cynicism, again, to be skeptical of
the practical efficacy of the well-meaning Ethical Codes that the Commonwealth government has drawn up for its various branches within
recent years, for few things appeal so readily to the Latin political
mind as the prolific production of beautiful sentiments on "democracy" and "democratic" behavior. Those Codes, certainly, have not
prevented the conversion of the San Juan city administration into
a political machine, with a vast network of *Popular* Party *barrio*
chieftains being subsidized from public funds under their guise as city
employees. The second solution, which would entail the promulgation
of norms of permissible political behavior on the part of public servants at present absent from either the Personnel Law or the regulations of the Personnel Board, would involve, first, the lifting of the
present restrictions upon civil servants accepting political candidacies
for political office (unless they resign or accept unpaid leave of absence) and, second, possibly copying the distinction that is made in
the British case between the various grades of the service insofar as
permitted political activities are concerned. But there is a crucial
difference between the British situation, where the political non-
partisanship and the public anonymity are already fixed elements in
the public service, and the Puerto Rican situation, where both of
those elements are at present only theoretically recognized. As a gen-

eral principle, general public trust in an official who runs for political office could easily be undermined by political statements made during a campaign; even more, such statements could easily compromise the authority of his executive position within the government, should he return to his post. The more apt comparison, if comparisons are required, perhaps ought to be made with the case of mid-Victorian England before the advent of the great Gladstonian reforms. The prime need, surely, in Puerto Rico is to emphasize as far as possible the clear separation of politics and administration, even if that means a certain inflexibility of policy and procedure. The British case is one in which the idea of a non-political service has probably been carried too far. The Puerto Rican case is one in which the idea has not yet been carried far enough. To allow certain categories of the service the privilege of a paid leave of absence for the purpose of seeking an elective office would only serve to encourage the insidious habit of politicizing professional occupations that is already one of the major afflictions of the Puerto Rican society. The recommendation of such a step is probably the outcome of a rather uncritical Anglophilism that has infected American (and therefore Puerto Rican) political science circles. Altogether it will be some time yet before the Puerto Rican career official begins to enjoy either the assured social status or the professional dignity of his British counterpart.

None of this is to belittle the very real accomplishments of the insular government service. Puerto Rican standards of public morality are impressive enough when contrasted with the widespread cynicism of Americans about the conduct and attitudes of their high federal officialdom. Apart from the scandals of the Department of Agriculture and Commerce unearthed by legislative inquiry in 1958 there have only been heard charges of minor peccability—the fraudulent sale of automobile licenses, for example, by certain employees of the Motor Vehicles Division of the Department of Public Works. What is lacking, rather, is a recognizable professional ethic. The civil service, like many of the private professions, tends to be too inbred. There are not enough of the independent civic organizations, like the American Civil Liberties Union in the States, to act as friendly but sharp critic. The device of the public corporation has been widely used. But it has not been used as a means of creating an avenue of public participation in affairs, for many of the corporations do not even possess a board of directors, part-time or whole-time. Nor has the device been used as a means of encouraging the habit of voluntary public service, so much a nursery of active citizenship in Great Britain. The 1952 Constitution and statutory law together indeed authorize the Governor to nominate a formidable total of around six hundred posts, including some four hundred officials of the executive branch, and the appointing power of the chief executive thus runs from appointment to minor posts such as justices of the peace and district court marshals to positions such as the Racing Commissioner in charge of island horse racing, the seven members of the Commission for the Betterment of Depressed Communities, the three members of the Commission for the Hearing of Municipal Complaints, to take examples only. Yet the disturbing aspect of this growth of the appointing power—apart from the consideration that it could produce a new "spoils system" outside the merit system—is that it appears, in its exercise, to be based upon no consistent or recognizable principle of selection. Examination of the rules governing appointments in the enormous variety of boards, agencies, and advisory bodies now existing in the administrative structure—fully listed in the *Manual of Organization of the Government of the Commonwealth of Puerto Rico* originally put together as a public service by the University School of Public Administration and subsequently taken over as an official responsibility by the Bureau of the Budget—shows that they fluctuate between direct gubernatorial nomination, sometimes requiring senatorial confirmation and sometimes not, selection by departmental heads, nomination by town mayors (as with the Commission for the Port of Mayagüez), selection by professional associations, group representatives selected by the Governor, and (as in the case of the Government Employees Association) a sort of multi-departmental selective process in which individual members are appointed by state officials as varied as the Chancellor of the University, the Controller, the Chief of Police, the Speaker of the House, the President of the Senate, and the local Supreme Court Chief Justice. All of these bodies, moreover, are permanent committees, so that there is little of the habit of using expert opinion and advice in *ad hoc* committees that do not contribute to excessive bureaucratization, and which has been such an outstanding feature of Dr. Williams's reform government in Trinidad since 1956. It is probable, too, that the social circles from which selections are made are severely restricted, leaving little opportunity for the ordinary man and woman to serve and probably encouraging, too, the habit of plurality which is so marked a feature of the "new patronage" in the British public service.

Something must be said, finally, of the internal atmosphere of governmental life. Much of the service literature, the *Boletín de Gerencia Administrativa*, for example, is heavily saturated with the influence of American public administration teaching, with its emphasis upon "human relations." Yet there are certain Puerto Rican traits of character that resist the American orthodoxies. There is a strong pride of person that leads to an almost pathological obsession with status. It often stands in the way of acknowledgment of incompetency of any kind, for a heavy premium is placed upon not offending the susceptibilities of colleagues. In administrative work it generates a reluctance in top officials to delegate responsibility to subordinates, even an insistence on dealing personally with the trivia of office business. The authoritarianism of personality in the office head that is thereby let loose is in its own turn encouraged by the deferential attitudes of his subordinates; it is enough to read the printed copies of prayers and good resolutions that cover the desks of so many secretaries in government offices, many of them couched in painfully abject terms, to realize that, if ever the revolt of the masses takes place in Puerto Rico, it will assuredly not be led from the ranks of the governmental clerical grades. Excessive regard for the feelings of colleagues may thus at the same time go hand in hand with excessive disregard for the interests of subordinates, particularly glaring in the widespread slackness in certifying the classification of employees once their probationary period is terminated, a practice that seriously compromises the legal status of the employee in the service as a whole. There is something of this temper, too, in the general sphere of service relations with the public. Too many departments which deal directly with the public do so through the medium of employees lacking training in the art of dealing with it; thus, to take one instance, the chaos that accompanies the annual renewal of automobile licenses in the Motor Vehicles Division illustrates a deplorable absence of any sense of successful public relations. Insufficient effort goes into the regular education and information of the public; thus, to take another instance, the general consternation occasioned in 1961 by the decision of the Planning Board to impose a six-months moratorium upon further construction in the San Juan area was met, late in the day, by an explanatory exposition by the Board's Director through film and television media. There ought, in fact, to be regular radio and television talks to the public by departmental chieftains as a permanent feature of government-public intercourse. More generally, the fierce drive to get things done on the economic-industrial front has fed the temptation to take short cuts, to justify lapses in the observance of statutory regulation and administrative rule (there have been complaints about the Planning Board's land classification program and about the general atmosphere of public hearings conducted by the Board examiners) with the plea that nothing ought to stand in the way of modernization. Institutions like the church, the press, the university have been seen by the propagandists of modernization as inferior, as they contribute to that end, to the institutions of government. All progress, indeed, has been seen, only too often in the official literature, as the direct consequence of the industrialization program; a vulgarized form of the theory of economic determinism even asserts that culture itself flows from the industrial base; and critics are summarily dismissed as disgruntled idealists who comprehend little of the nature of economic growth. These attitudes are certain to continue until, both psychologically and institutionally, the gulf that divides the governmental machinery and the general public is effectively bridged. Until, that is to say, what the preamble to the local Constitution styles "the free participation of the citizen in collective decisions" becomes more of a reality and less of a pretty phrase.

In no area is reform so urgent, perhaps, as in the administration of justice. The least satisfactory aspect of the "revolution of 1940" has been that relating to the machinery of justice and the manner in which the machinery has been deployed in the treatment of the minority groups of the society, especially the Communists, the Nationalists, and the *Independentistas.* Lord Acton's dictum that "The most certain test by which we judge whether a society is really free is the amount of security enjoyed by minorities," constitutes the crucial test of the glittering generalities of formal guarantees, including those of a Puerto Rican Bill of Rights whose relevant section, with regard to this vital problem, is copied almost literally from the First Amendment of the federal Constitution. The test has been made all the more severe in the Puerto Rican case because of the challenge to the local sovereign power of the series of attempted Nationalist revolts in the period between 1936 and 1950; and of the repressive legislation, especially Law 53 of 1947, generated by the atmosphere of fear and political hate arising out of those attempts.

So far as the ordinary citizen is concerned, the insular judicial system has much to commend it. Both in its substantive and procedural aspects it is based fundamentally upon Anglo-American precepts of jurisprudence, notwithstanding the presence of certain Spanish elements. Not only does it reproduce the classic institutions embodying those precepts—the jury system, clear and distinct procedural rules, habeas corpus, a police system under civilian control—but in some respects even improves upon them. The right to bail on the part of accused persons is an absolute one. Since 1939 the right of accused to legal aid has been sedulously insisted upon by the courts. The Commonwealth Bill of Rights, in its turn, goes much further in many ways than many other modern juristic statements in safeguarding the liberty of the subject, for it is humane in the best Puerto Rican tradition. It prohibits incarceration for any period exceeding six months prior to trial; guarantees that a failure to testify may not be used in court as evidence or presumption of guilt; provides that suspension of civil rights, including that of the right to vote, shall cease upon termination of any term of imprisonment; outlaws the practice of wire tapping; and, most humane of all, prohibits the death penalty.[27] And it is only necessary to read the catalogue of social and economic rights guaranteed by the Constitution, including the right to work, to housing and medical care, and to "social protection" in the event of unemployment, sickness, old age, or disability,[28] to realize how far its authors—in their theoretical presuppositions at least, for practice lags far behind—have progressed beyond the assumptions of liberty secreted in traditional liberalism and still accepted as articles of faith by much of American public and political opinion.

Yet all these, gathered together, are admittedly at best an oasis in the heart of a desert. The fact, in itself, that the insular Penal Code (adapted almost in toto in 1902 from that of the state of California) has not been revised in any important way since its adoption suggests that there is much room for improvement at the present time. Its one fundamental defect is its inarticulate acceptance of the Anglo-American common law tradition of the nineteenth-century schools of criminology, with a resulting general failure to set crime within its proper context of social and psychiatric conditions. The prison system —to take a single example—reflects that bias, for the Secretary of Justice himself has publicly acknowledged the failure to put into motion any system of modern prisoner rehabilitation.[29] The institutions of probation and parole are utterly deficient on account of a shortage of an adequately trained staff of professional workers. The system of the justice of the peace has in large measure broken down since the largely amateur character of the appointees frequently results in grave errors on their part, especially in the important field of the initial determination of probable cause in the early stages of judicial prosecution. The essential justice of the jury system, again, is frequently brought into question by the fact that jury panelists only too often have relationships with the police that compromise their impartiality. Nor should it be overlooked that much of this, especially the failure to recognize fully the socio-psychiatrical environment of crime, is made all the more unfortunate by the general cultural fact that there is an extremely close relationship in Puerto Rico between crime, mental illness, and poverty. That is why there is more than the usual percentage of criminal eccentricity—the high rate of incest, for example—which makes Puerto Rico at times sound not unlike the more isolated sections of traditionalist New England life. Law, in general, still lags far behind culture in the island life.

Nor does the insular judicial system as a whole (reorganized by the 1952 Constitution and subsequent statutory legislation) furnish proof of a larger eagerness to accept the norms of the contemporary sciences of criminology and legal administration. The Constitution makers set up, against the urgent plea of their advisory commission, a judiciary recruited on the principle of executive nomination. Yet that principle maximizes the possibility of political considerations intruding upon the appointment and promotion of judges. While this has, so far, not been the case so much with the local higher courts, it has definitely been so at the lower levels, if only because political influence has had time to entrench itself ever since the Organic Act of 1917 introduced the principle of nomination by the executive. While, therefore, that principle may be superior to that of popular election (so widely used in the individual states of the Union) it possesses its own fatal weaknesses. Certainly, for a generation or more, the Puerto Rican judicial bench at the municipal and district levels has been selected, in effect, at the discretion of local legislators and party committees. Judicial reorganization will have to accept sooner or later a mixed principle of selection, in which the Chief Executive will be aided by an appellate judicial commission whose major responsibility it shall be to draw up lists of recommended candidates for executive consideration. This is the chief element of the so-called Missouri Plan, increasingly winning approval from American professional judicial circles. The present situation in Puerto Rico, in which nominations to the lower courts are in effect made on the recommendation of the Secretary of Justice, a member of the political cabinet, is in every way deplorable. The difficulties experienced in 1960 by persons seeking to obtain the necessary judicial approval of inscriptions for the newly launched Catholic Action Party of that year sufficiently testify to the abuses that are latent in the system.

The severest criticism of all, however, must be reserved for the prosecuting and law-enforcement agencies. The exhaustive report by Santos Amadeo and Victor Vargas Negrón on *The Criminal Phase of the Administration of Justice* pens its harsher passages of criticism when it discusses the powers and duties of those agencies. The system of public prosecution centers around the corps of district attorneys and prosecuting lawyers named by the Governor with the advice and consent of the Senate and subject to the administrative control of the Justice Department. Their powers amount to fearsome proportions, for they include those of helping to issue warrants for arrest and fixing bail as well as taking depositions of prisoners and generally supervising the interest of the public authority in court. They can even accuse a magistrate who has refused to issue an order for arrest, as well as possessing the power to accuse a public functionary when he has committed an offense in the course of his duties. Not only are these powers far in excess of any carried by public prosecuting bodies in most modern democratic societies, but in Puerto Rico they are utilized in the worst spirit of American courtroom prosecution. The American rather than the English concept of the state prosecutor has been followed, so that the Puerto Rican Justice Department lawyer or district attorney behaves, like his American counterpart, like nothing so much as an official inquisitor in a star chamber proceeding. He is not likely to remember the injunction of the United States Supreme Court, in *Burger v. United States*, that his concern in a criminal prosecution should be not that he win a case but that justice should be done. He habitually resorts to confessions elicited by means of various degrees of coercion, nor is the accused protected from that evil by the right to a preliminary investigation, after arrest, before a magistrate. There is much to be said for a reform which would explicitly reject as admissible evidence any confession made to police officials, as is, for example, the case in India. The Puerto Rican Supreme Court has at least taken official note of local police methods of physical coercion in the obtaining of evidence.[30] It is evident enough that the liberty of the subject is seriously threatened, all the time, by an excess of zeal in both prosecuting officials and police and that the dictum of the federal Supreme Court, in the McNabb case, that "zeal in tracking down crime is not in itself an assurance of soberness of judgment" must be secured by means of effective curbs upon police powers. The series of confessions extracted from hundreds of prisoners in the mass arrests effected at the time of the 1950 and 1954 Nationalist uprisings showed how political animosity can precipitate such abuses. But it is palpably obvious that the abuses grow out of, more generally, a prevailing atmosphere in the law enforcement agencies in which their members conceive their task as an act of war against crime (especially matters like gambling and illicit rum manufacturing), and wherein the ends justify the means. The more explosive outbursts of that habit are perhaps infrequent. But when they do occur they expose underlying traits that bode ill for the future of civil liberty in the society. When trained observers can conclude that the compendium of abuses committed by the law enforcement agencies acting together in the affairs of 1950 and 1954 can only be properly compared to the conduct of the police in the Union of South Africa in arresting for treason citizens who did not subscribe to race segregation in that society,[31] it is clear that there exist the makings of a latent public authoritarianism.

The policeman and the attorney, of course, are agents only. They take their cue, naturally, from their administrative chieftains. The fault then, if any, rests not with them but with the general behavior pattern of the administrative branch in the recent past, since, say, the abortive student strike at the national university in 1948. The record has been painstakingly analyzed in Dr. David Helfeld's report on *Discrimination for Political Beliefs and Associations* of 1958. It is, in its worst moments, an unhappy record. The mass arrests of hundreds of persons without proper procedure; the use of moods of national panic to punish political enemies, usually at the local level of affairs by small-time political "bosses"; the holding of suspects incommunicado for lengthy periods; the excessive use of military show through the deployment of the National Guard; the illegal practice of finger printing of suspects; the detention of members of the *Independentista* Party without proof of sympathy on their part with Nationalist Party violence; armed searches and seizures without proper authorization: it all indicates a marked contempt for the judicial process that is characteristic, in many ways, of emergent national societies where there has occurred a serious imbalance between the development of the executive branch and the growth of the judicial system. Yet the really disturbing aspect of the Puerto Rican matter is that all this could have happened only because (1) the particular policy of the Commonwealth government in especially critical moments, mainly motivated by a momentary panic in high circles, took the form of safety measures that were wholly disproportionate to the real danger to law and order that was involved, and (2) the general legislative policy of the government constituted, over the years, a consistent pattern of limiting civil liberties for hated minority groups through invocation of the questionable doctrines of "bad tendency," "guilt by association," and "advocacy"—as against incitement—of "seditious" activities.

The first point was fully brought out in the interrogations of leading government officials by the Civil Liberties inquiry of 1958. There appears to have been no plan worked out by government in anticipation of the major 1950 event. Its reaction consequently was one of improvised and needlessly repressive measures concocted in what appears to have been a mood of panic. Mass incarceration was resorted to on the unreliable basis of a list of "subversives" allegedly drawn up as far back as the days of Governor Winship. A large display of military force via the mobilization of the National Guard was effected, despite evidence that the "revolt" had little popular support, if indeed any, and consisted merely of a series of violent and separate disorders fully within the capacity of the insular police forces to handle. Large numbers of citizens who had nothing to do with the events were deprived of their civil rights. Most significant of all, there was no evidence, some eight years later, that the administrative officials responsible had learned anything from the experience. Both the police hierarchy and that of the Justice Department sought, ignobly, to avoid blame by charging each other with being the prime source of orders throughout the critical period. "No critical analysis," observes Dr. Helfeld, "had been made by either agency following the uprising to determine if civil rights had been violated, and if so, to what extent, and with what justification. . . . Every measure taken was justified by what was considered the overriding demands of public safety. On the one hand, there was an absence of thought about alternatives which could protect public safety at a lesser cost to civil rights, or alternatives compatible both with safety and civil liberty. On the other, there was a readiness to take refuge in formalities, and an unwillingness to face the substance of things."[32]

The second point—that of general legislative-executive intent—is exemplified best in the history of the anti-free speech act, Law 53, of 1947. The law, typically, was uncritically copied from the provisions of the federal Smith Act of 1940. It was introduced into the Legislature with no prior notice, so that it was accompanied by only a summary and unprepared debate in the lower house. An analysis of the eighty-four cases brought to the courts under its provisions until its gubernatorial repeal in 1957 constitutes an illuminating case study of the way in which even a liberal minded government may persuade itself into imposing grave limitations on free speech under the guise of defending the public safety. There were cases in which men were imprisoned simply on the ground of uttering vague and exaggerated oratory in defense of the Nationalist cause. Men like Enamorado Cuesta were imprisoned and later released without trial for nothing more than quoting a famous revolutionary utterance, of the nineteenth-century Puerto Rican radical Betances, on his newssheet's masthead. Nationalist party members, as in the case, most famously, of Ruth Reynolds, were charged with seditious conspiracy on grounds no more convincing than attendance at party meetings and participation in a mass ceremonial oath of the organization. Convinced Communists, as in the Marrero case, were charged with preparing for the violent overthrow of the government whereas, both in fact and theory, they could not possibly have condoned such an un-Marxist procedure as the basically amateurish acts of "playing with revolution" which the 1950 revolt and the 1954 shooting in the federal Congress exemplified. Imprisonment was imposed, again, as in *People v. Montalvo et al.*, for behavior no more alarming or illegal than attendance at religious ceremonial functions to commemorate the heroes of the Nationalist martyrology since 1868. There can be little doubt, all in all, that the government prosecuting forces were animated by a spirit of fierce

political hostility to minorities and individuals, and that the Nationalist terror was exploited in the service of the hostility. "Under a facade
of legality," the Civil Liberties report has concluded, "we find the
legal system infiltrated by a spirit of vindictiveness and exaggerated
sense of danger, which deleteriously affects the police, the *fiscales*,
trial courts, juries, and even to a certain degree the Supreme Court.
As administered at the trial court level, we find Law No. 53 used as a
dragnet to punish members of hated minority groups, with the crime
defined in a highly expansive manner to reduce or eliminate the problem of proof."[33]

Two footnotes must be added to this discouraging conclusion. The
first is that the record failed to yield, on the part of any member of
the insular Supreme Court, condemnation of or protest against—in
the manner of a Brandeis or a Black—the relentless erosion of the
free speech guarantees of the Constitution that all of this encompassed.
The second is that, although the particular law, No. 53, has been
subsequently repealed, this does not at all mean that the official attitudes that originally made it possible have in the meanwhile been
replaced by more liberal ones. On the contrary: all the evidence suggests that they are still there. The Legislature has indicated no readiness to compensate individuals unjustly victimized in the aftermath
of the Nationalist fracas. The only reform to take place in a police
agency devoted to the investigation of the political opinions of private
citizens is that its title has been altered from that of Division of
Internal Security to that of Division of Intelligence. The conclusion
of the Amadeo-Negrón report that "the police of Puerto Rico lack the
leadership necessary to convert them from an inexperienced force into
a competent agent of public order"[34] remains still an invitation to
serious reform within the service. The control of traffic offenses is
scandalously desultory. There is a real police persecution of members
of separatist groups; even the University in Rio Piedras, as the shock-
ing gun slaying of one of its younger officials by a disgruntled university police employee in 1962 showed, is not above using the morally
questionable device of the plainclothes investigator for the purpose of
patrolling the political activities of students. There is, even more, a
distinct tendency for leading members of the executive branch of government to protect individual police officers who have been convicted
by the courts of the offense of perjury in the over-zealous pursuit of
their duties. Nor have the public utterances of the former Superintend-
ent of Police, couched in tones of a pronounced bellicosity, tended to
stimulate the habit of frank self-criticism. The whole system clamors
for independent investigation, something, for example, along the lines
of the recent Willink Royal Commission report on the constitutional

position of the police in the United Kingdom. It remains to be seen whether the series of educational courses for selected police force members recently launched under a joint agreement of the Police Academy and the University School of Public Administration will turn out to be a real beginning of a real reform program.

There is a widespread feeling, as the recent report of the advisory Citizens' Committee suggests, that all this calls for far-reaching reforms in the insular system of government. There is a real danger, generally, that to the degree that administrative rulings are influenced by political sentiments there will grow up a class of civil servants characterized by the moral sentiments of state inquisitors. The present administrative machinery appears, so far, to have been an ineffective check to that process. The Police Commission, for instance, has not shown much independence of mind. Resignation from its membership on the ground of disagreement with policies—like that of Enrique Córdova Díaz—has been rare indeed. The Personnel Board has been more vigorous. But it failed, in the Schafer and Suárez cases, to protect civil servants who were separated from the service on grounds so flagrantly unfair that, on appeal, the insular Supreme Court had no difficulty in ordering reinstatement in both cases. The Supreme Court, in its own turn, has not always acted with the necessary vigilance surely to be expected of it, and responsible critics within the legal profession itself have publicly drawn attention to the Court's failure, out of timidity or a mistaken concept of "freedom of the press," to protect the privacy of the investigating and prosecuting procedures against the journalistic temptation to hold "trials by newspaper."[35] The student of the Puerto Rican legal process will remember, in that respect, the unfortunate scandals of the Hoyos and Fournier cases. The record, finally, of the Public Service Commission has been one of a dismal neglect of duties, especially those concerned with the supervision and regulation of public services. The present state of telephone services in the economy is directly traceable to the Commission's laxity in permitting rate increases over a number of years without requiring adequate guarantees from the telephone company for large-scale capital expenditures in anticipation of steadily rising demands for the service. It took, indeed, a sustained campaign by the island newspapers and a vigorous inquiry by a local Senate committee to expose the full record. The enlargement of the legislative investigating power and the exercise of a more forceful public opinion may indeed be the answer to this whole problem.

As far as these wider problems of the civil service are concerned the green light must be given to a number of reform measures. The whole subject of executive nominations to appointments must be regularized so that it is based upon public standards of propriety and good practice; in particular the "grapevine" methods of recruitment, so inevitable in small societies, should as far as possible be orderly and systematic, and as widely known as possible, so that nominations may come from all quarters. The sense of devotion to public duty is something of course not always susceptible to plans and programs, for it grows out of the general atmosphere of a society. It can bear official encouragement, however, and it is heartening to note the development of the program of annual prizes granted to civil servants within the government on the basis of rewards for suggestions for administrative improvements, presided over by a central committee. Going beyond that sort of thing, there must be full freedom for employee union organization. The Director of the Personnel Board is on record as being in favor of the British device of the Whitley Council. But the British experience of the device since its inception after the First World War has not been hugely successful, and certainly proves that it is no substitute for independent employee representation. The external problems of the service, particularly its relations with the public, call for attention. In a society where government plays so large a part as employer there is too frequently a tendency to regard a government job as a safe investment rather than as an outlet for professional zeal. A revolution in local government, outside San Juan proper, is long overdue. The changes that would be necessary in that field have been listed by the Puerto Rican chapter of the American Society of Public Administration.[36] A new penal code needs to be adopted to suit modern conditions. The method of the grand jury, stripped of many of its powers since 1925, could profitably be revived in the area of criminal procedure. The recommendation of the Civil Rights Committee, finally, that a permanent Civil Rights Commission be set up as a standing watchdog of civil liberties, has much to commend it.[37] It is only doubtful whether the very limited powers that the Committee envisages for such a body—those of a study-making and generally educative character—would not leave it too weak to exercise any real influence. The experience of the American states that have set up fair employment practices commissions since 1945 would appear to suggest that the experiment can do little real good unless the commissions are something more than merely advisory bodies or simply receptacles for the grievances of private citizens. There is indeed a remarkable discrepancy between the gravity of the problems unearthed by the special investigations of the Civil Rights Committee subgroups and the mildness of its final recommendations.

What is required, as the Committee elsewhere remarks, is a thoroughgoing overhaul of the executive and administrative branches of the government. The reforms of 1949-1950 were limited to structural reorganization. A new study would cover all aspects of public administration, and it would do so in the light of the new conditions that have come into being since the adoption of the 1952 Constitution. One particular problem of increasing gravity should certainly be dealt with, namely the question of service salaries throughout the whole range of government offices. For the effect of the economic boom of the last decade has been to widen the salary gap between public and private employment to such an extent that one of the main crises within government is that involved in recruiting and maintaining government personnel of the highest caliber at scales of financial reward that are far below those that can be obtained in the non-public fields. The able lawyer in the Justice Department, the skilled engineer in Public Works, the first-class economist in the Planning Board all find tempting offers from outside and increasingly accept them. The Secretary of Health is paid a salary—$14,000—that is only one half of that received by his counterpart in New York State and a fraction only of what his abilities could obtain for him in private practice, while there is a chronic shortage of executive ability in practically all departments—there are at least twenty key postions in the University, for instance, that are either unfilled or inadequately filled. This problem in itself cries aloud for a thorough survey. What is needed, without doubt, is the acceptance of some sort of doctrine of "fair comparability" between the public and private sectors such as has gradually evolved in the British system as the result of the recommendations made by a series of commissions and committees since the report of the Priestley Commission of 1955. For while it is true that the principle of remuneration in a public service should never be primarily that of the classic economic principle of supply and demand, the public servant at the same time cannot be expected to live as ascetically as a Christian saint or a Platonic philosopher-king. The doctrine of public duty, if it does nothing to ameliorate this problem, is in fact being employed to justify serious income inequalities; and there is much to justify the suspicion that this is what is happening in the Puerto Rican case. Not the least of the evil consequences of this fact is the growing practice of government officials to leave the service in order to accept more lucrative appointments in the private sector. It would be of some public interest to know the inner story of this practice, for it occurs most frequently with officials of those government bodies—Fomento, the Economic Development Administration, and so on—who deal closely with United States business firms settling on the island. It has within it the germs of a potential conflict of loyalties.

The final impression of Puerto Rican public administration is thus one of mixed colors. The habit of departmentalism has meant that progress has been erratic, fluctuating greatly between different agencies and departments. The one single most important consequence of the modernizing process, as Dr. Honey early insisted, has been to increase enormously the quality of employee morale within the service. "Formerly," Dr. Honey observed of the government employees, "they were inordinately worried by the threat of political turnover, by demands for contributions to the party in power, by wage and leave uncertainties, and by a sense of the insignificance and mediocrity of public employment."[38] Yet many of those factors still persist, as the later evidence shows, and Puerto Ricans still await the full statement by the Commonwealth government of the policies governing public employment requested by Dr. Honey in his list of final recommendations. There remains still a serious imbalance of power between the bureaucracy and the rank and file; it is suggestive, to cite a single example, that the members of even one of the most privileged groups of the service, the police, are required to wear a heavy wool uniform ridiculously inappropriate to a tropical climate. There is still too little of close intimacy between government services and the public; there is no reason, to cite an example again from the police system, why larger public support for the force should not be obtained by the formation of a civilian auxiliary police organization to be affiliated with the regular body. At the same time, there are many bright aspects. The rights and duties of government officers are publicly discussed in a responsible fashion. The Governor symbolizes, in his own figure, the type of the ideal public servant. Above all, the entire structure of government is increasingly subjected to careful scrutiny as it becomes an object, in its myriad aspects, of academic inquiry. A glance at the titles of the various theses composed by students of the School of Public Administration and the School of Social Work at the University shows how wide the scrutiny is, for they include, among others, dissertations on local police administration, the need for a new department of Social Security, probation work in San Juan, the psychological impact of compulsory retirement upon government employees, the delegation of legislative powers to municipal corporations, the court conciliation service, the Association of Teachers as a pressure group, and so on. And, not least of all, there is the unique significance of the fact that, in sponsoring the Civil Liberties inquiry of 1958-1959, the Commonwealth government has been among the very first of governments in the modern world to have sponsored voluntarily an independent investigation into its own domestic record, in this case under the auspices of the General Assembly of the United Nations. It is a precedent that could profitably be emulated by other societies.

The Machinery of Government: The Legislature

THE Legislature in Puerto Rico, as already indicated, has played a role in insular government at once subordinate and distorted. Subordinate, because it has never been able to assert itself with any lasting success against an alien executive power. Distorted, because it has been driven —like the old House of Assembly in Barbadian constitutional struggles—to believe that the legislative function is preeminently one of pillorying government measures. That was at once the case with the old House of Delegates under the Foraker Act of 1900 and with the lower house of the Legislature under the Jones Act of 1917. The legislative prestige further suffered from the existence, during the direct colonialist period, of a triple veto upon its deliberations: that of the President, that of the local Governor, and that of the federal Congress. Important administrative offices were sealed off from its control. It suffered, too, from the general American belief that the legislative task could be treated, by those who practiced it, as an accessory to a legal practice or a business career and not as a full-time occupation; and the clause of the Organic Act stipulating that the Puerto Rican legislative regular sessions should begin on the second Monday in February and close not later than April 15 naturally led to the bad habit of over-numerous special sessions and a general neglect of the legislative duties it was supposed could be dealt with in such a laughably short period. It is only since 1952 that the Puerto Rican citizen has been enabled to read a full report of legislative business thanks to the new constitutional requirement that the Legislature shall publish a daily record of its proceedings, despite the fact that the struggle to obtain such a service goes back to the still-born resolution of the old House of Delegates on the matter in 1903.

As a consequence of all this, it is no news that the Legislature in the island has enjoyed little public esteem throughout its history. It had some eminence when the present Governor was majority party leader in the Senate before 1948, but it soon became a junior partner of the executive branch once his gifts were transferred to the elective governorship. That process, combined with the general worldwide decline in the prestige of legislative assemblies, helps to explain why the Legislature in San Juan is today almost ludicrously sensitive to outside criticism and why its proceedings, except when the perennial status issue comes up for discussion or when it debates the explosive issue of alleged governmental maldistribution of funds (as in the case of relief funds for the victims of the Humacao hurricane disaster of 1960) or when it takes an unprecedented step (such as its vote of censure against President Eisenhower's alleged interference in local politics in the same year), are so scantily reported in the local press. The coverage of legislative speeches by *El Mundo* certainly is not at all comparable to that provided for other Caribbean readers by papers like the *Trinidad Guardian* and the Jamaica *Daily Gleaner*.

The 1952 Constitution establishes a Puerto Rican Senate and a House of Representatives, both elected every four years by "equal, direct and secret universal suffrage." Informed opinion, it is worth recording, was strongly in favor of a unicameral system at the time of the Constituent Assembly deliberations, and reported along those lines in its advice to that body.[1] For there is no federal system in the island to justify a second chamber. Nor do there exist in the society any traditional interest groups that could present a claim, justifiable historically, to coexist institutionally with a popular legislative assembly, as is the case with those European countries that possess a royalist and aristocratic background. Two additional reasons, however, have usually been advanced in Puerto Rico, as elsewhere, to justify a second chamber. The first is that the presence of such a body serves as a brake upon the intemperate and hasty legislation likely to come out of a popular assembly. The second is that the twin deliberations of two bodies, in place of only one, guarantee a more satisfactory statutory result. The first argument assumes a rash and importunate lower house impatient of any careful discussion of proposals coming before it. A glance at the legislative history of Puerto Rico would hardly appear to prove the point. Speaking of the American period only, it took the Legislature, in conjunction with the executive, some thirty-two years before it accepted the principle of votes for women. It waited some four decades or more before it acted to enforce the provision of the 1900 Organic Act against large landholdings. Although it had no constitutional responsibility for educational policy for a large part of the period, it failed nonetheless to adopt a firm stand on the vital question of the teaching of English in the school system. Anyone who bears these facts in mind would be tempted, indeed, to solicit a technique for accelerating the passage of legislation, rather than for delaying it. Nor is the second reason any more persuasive. Debate of two bodies tends not so much to improve the quality of legislation as to lessen it, since a second chamber which is not prepared to be an utter nonentity has a vested interest in elaborate amendment of legislation coming from the first. The technical revision of legislation, on the other hand, can always be done by a specialist arm within the popular house itself. If the powers of the second chamber are less than those of the first, the result of dual consideration is delay; if they equal them, the result is deadlock.

The second chamber in the Puerto Rican experience, in any case, has never promised to match the American Senate in the quality of its leadership. Throughout both regimes it has been, quite deliberately, a chosen body for protecting the interests of the imperial power. This was so both with the Council of Administration under the Spanish Autonomy Charter of 1897 and with the Executive Council of the Foraker Act of 1900. The insular Senate created by the second Organic Act after 1917 was not so patently the same thing. But the making of it a directly elected body, differing from the lower house only in matters of age and residence qualifications, almost entirely obliterated any reasons that might have hitherto justified a second house. The popular governorship (1947) and then the partial grant of self-government (1952) quite destroyed the need for a senate safeguarding metropolitan interests. Henceforth the question of bicameralism or unicameralism would have to be debated on the grounds solely of its application to the special Puerto Rican conditions. Symptomatically, however, the question was not really seriously thrashed out in the Constituent Assembly of 1951-1952. It was decided, almost axiomatically, to maintain a popular senate. The reasons presumably were (1) the fact that, at the time, personal rivalry between the presiding officers of the two existing houses made it difficult to eliminate one of the posts and (2) more generally, the tendency of most Puerto Rican political thought to imitate uncritically the American institutions of government, even to the point of appropriating their obvious defects. The result here as elsewhere, has been to place a barrier in the way of really creative thought.

The Legislature is thus composed of a Senate of 32 and a House of Representatives of 64 members. These numbers, however, may be increased by virtue of the unique constitutional provision which ensures, by a method of limited proportional representation, that when the majority party returns more than two thirds of the legislative membership a special increase in the number of seats shall be arranged in order to provide additional representation for minority parties.[2] The total of the additional seats, however, shall not go beyond the point of ensuring that the minority party or parties shall be able to seat 9 members in the Senate and 17 in the House. This

quite remarkable arrangement has the advantage of helping to counterbalance the monolithic control of the Legislature by one party that has
been characteristic of the local electoral scene at least since 1940; in
1948, for example, 55 of the total of 58 members elected were members of the Popular Democratic Party. It has been estimated, on the
basis of the 1948 electoral returns, that this measure is likely to
reduce the representation of the dominant party by over 20 percent
and to increase that of the minority parties that meet its condition
of reward correspondingly. Whatever be its statistical outcome, the
moral lesson is the more important, illustrating as it does a sense of
magnanimity on the part of a majority party that is certainly rare in
Latin American politics. Combined with the new social and economic
rights provided in the local Bill of Rights and with the 1957 legislation setting up an electoral fund to help subsidize political parties
from public funds, it reveals a capacity on the part of the local majority leadership to rethink old problems in new terms which, irrespective of the merit of those particular reforms, might have been
carried further in the constitution-making process. As things now are,
however, the Legislature reflects the orthodox American state government pattern in its main outlines. Its total membership will be, at a
minimum, less than a hundred. It is difficult to see how such a small
body benefits from bifurcation into two houses. Nor is it easy to
appreciate readily the advantages that come from duplicating at every
step the procedures of legislative business. The advantage in any case
of a senatorial discussion of legislation that will be radically different
from discussion in the lower house is stultified by the fact that party
strength in the one tends to reflect almost exactly party strength in
the other. A strong party discipline further ensures that the twin
majorities of the governing party, at least, will act as a single group.
Puerto Rico, in effect, has a two-chamber Legislature which to all
intents and purposes deports itself as a unicameral parliament.

As in American state government, then, the insular Legislature
hardly excites the enthusiasm of the observer. It is overshadowed by
the executive. The dramatic achievements that make "front-page
news" are those of the planning and development agencies. The most
pressing problem that faces its leadership, then, is that of enlarging its
prestige both with the other branches of government and with the
electorate at large. It must be able to attract to its membership, as it
presently does not do, the cream of the island's talent. The able
university graduate or teacher goes more readily into law or government service in the executive and administrative branches. With a few
exceptions, Federico Cordero, for example, he rarely embraces the

legislative career; and this particular example is not a strong one in the light of Cordero's confession, at the time of his abrupt resignation, that he felt he possessed neither the aptitude nor the sense of vocation that would justify the continuation of his legislative career.[3] The average age of the Senate is 55.9, that of the House of Representatives 48 years: not too high, but high enough apparently to give the youth branches of the *Popular* Party a feeling that the younger elements are not sufficiently represented. There is an open avenue of promotion from the ranks of local mayors and assemblymen (a total of 26 in the membership of 1958), hardly a happy phenomenon when the low estimate in which small-town government politics is held in insular opinion is remembered. An analysis of the occupational background of the membership of the 1950's reveals not only the typical American phenomenon of the excessive representation of the legal profession (some 32 lawyers out of a total bicameral membership of 96) but also a high proportion of agricultural proprietors (16) and of trade union leaders (7), the latter being usually labor "bosses" controlling a handful of unions. There is a pronounced weakness in the representation of the academic world (the nine teachers were from the lower educational levels) and of the technical world: the professional class members came from the older professions like medicine (2), journalism (5), and pharmacy (3). Lawyers, farmers, and businessmen clearly enough dominate the insular legislative scene, reflecting, in part, the tight hold of the merchant and farmer class in the municipal structure of government outside the capital city.[4] The official language of debate being Spanish, there are, naturally enough, no Puerto Rican residents from the American community who are members of either house. Yet there have been such members in the past: Elmer Ellsworth after 1941, Walter McK. Jones after 1922, and Frederick L. Cornwall very early between 1900 and 1904: the latter, incidentally, was obliged to address the legislature (in those days the House of Delegates) through the medium of an interpreter. A fourth candidate recently emerged in the open effort of Earl Parker Hanson to obtain the Popular Party nomination for a Senate seat in the 1960 elections; but the attempt was abandoned by its author after a characteristic single-handed newspaper campaign of strident self-advertisement. The glaring absence of continental Americans in the legislative function is not the least of the weak links in the chain.

The decline of legislative standing is best seen in the field of legislative-executive relations. It may be too much to say, with a local critic, that the legislative membership is one of mediocre men and that it is a rubber stamp of the executive; just as conversely it may be too much to reply, with the legislative leadership, that such an accusation constitutes an insult to the Governor, the Legislature, and the people of Puerto Rico themselves and that it calls for a full apology.[5] But it is true that all the dice are loaded in favor of powerful executive control. Although the recommendation of the Rowe Commission for the establishment of a Council of Economic Advisers has not been followed up (the federal precedent, in any case, has not been a happy one) its other recommendations for strengthening the executive arm have by now been implemented to make up an impressive armory of weapons to use against possible legislative revolt. The Bureau of the Budget prepares an annual model budget that is usually accepted by the Legislature with only minor modifications. The Finance Division of the Planning Board prepares, in turn, a six-year financial program which, by anticipating long-range goals, seriously curbs the possibility of subsequent independent action on the part of the Legislature. The Governor's secretariat processes administrative bills to be presented to the Capitol building, fits them, even more, into an elaborate priority system, and thus undertakes itself the function of pre-legislative arrangement of business which the Puerto Rican constitutional writer de Hostos had once imagined the Legislature doing for itself by means of the device of the *Precámara* suggested in his treatise on *Derecho Constitutional*. The "Governor's lobby" of executive staff members keeps in close touch with legislative leaders during the passage of bills proposed by the Governor. Because there is none of the party sectionalism which in the United States makes competing and often mutually hostile wings out of the Congressional and non-Congressional elements of the major parties, the legislative groups in Puerto Rico cooperate willingly with the party leaderships. The *Popular* legislative leaders thus maintain a close liaison with the government. It is symptomatic of the liaison that, surprisingly, the General Secretary of the *Popular* Party should at the same time be a senatorial member of the legislative group. Legislative procedure is geared, even more than in an English-style party assembly, to the expeditious passage of government business. An opposition representative has wistfully noted that there is nothing in the local Legislature to compare with the device of the "filibuster" in the American Senate, and that although apparently absurd it is in reality an important device for the successful deployment of legislative minority interests.[6] One consequence of this inability of the minority groups to pose any serious threat to the official bureaucratic machine is that legislative debate tends to run off tangentially into abstract and interminable discussions on general issues. The *turno de la posteridad* is one price among others that the legislative arena pays for imposing both upon its minority groups and its individual members a feeling of helpless frustration. It might be added that this fact alone would be ample reason for rejecting the proposal, popular with the majority of legislators, for the radio and television transmission of debates. It would require an almost superhuman modesty for the average member, who is an orator at heart, to resist the temptation such a process would present.

For any legislative control over the executive and administrative offices worth talking about hardly in fact exists. The Constitution repeats the usual prohibition against the mixing of the legislative and executive functions and thereby incidentally puts paid to any idea, such as that advanced by the advisory group to the Constituent Assembly, that would establish a mixed cabinet having the leaders of the legislative houses in its membership for the purpose of maximizing cooperation between the two branches.[7] So, in San Juan as in Washington, the ability of legislative and cabinet memberships to understand each other is limited to the occasional committee hearing where the administrative official appears as a witness rather than as a fellow parliamentarian, with all the room for friction latent in that fact. With the huge difference, of course, that the local Legislature is not, as in Congress, a rival power with potent strength to assert its co-sovereign status with the executive. Its law-making function works well. But its function as either a channel of grievance or as a steady critic of governmental policy and behavior is generally unsatisfactory.

That this is so is evident in a number of ways. It is there in the fact that, with regard to their memberships, the Central Committee of the *Popular* Party and the majority legislative caucus of the two chambers are in fact virtually the same body. It is there in the fact that the Governor's appointive power is generally unchallenged by the Senate; in the period between 1952 and 1958 it is the astonishing truth that only one out of 761 appointments submitted to that body was rejected outright, and even then it was hardly a significant case, dealing as it did with a proposed member of the Board of Accountants. It is there, again, in the tremendous decline in the use of the gubernatorial veto power since the imported American governors were replaced with locally elected governors. It can be seen, finally, in the character and history of the legislative investigating power. The power on the whole is insufficiently used as a means of keeping government on its toes: between 1948 and 1957 the House undertook only some forty-six investigations, of which in any case only four related to the executive branch, while between 1949 and 1956 the Senate in its own turn completed no more than sixty-seven investigations, of which again only seven concerned the executive.[8] There has been little here to compare with the mammoth investigations that the Legislature, when it was a colonialist body, conducted into the scandals of wartime rationing of scarce commodities during the early 1940's. It is a scandalous omission of legislative duty, to come more up to date, that the grave violations of citizen rights perpetrated by the government in 1950, and again in 1954, failed to provoke a legislative inquiry and that the country had to wait until 1959 before it obtained a full and impartial analysis of the matter from the Civil Liberties inquiry of that year.

The 1958 legislative inquiry into the scandals of the *División de Industrias Pecuarias* of the Department of Agriculture and Commerce laid bare, it is true, a number of administrative irregularities among the high officialdom of that department, including the evasion of Personnel Board rules in the appointment of employees and the use of fraudulent practices for the purpose of obtaining "kickbacks" of money for the *Popular* Party. But it has to be added, first, that the inquiry was only undertaken after successive reports of the Controller had directed attention to the matter and, second, that there was no legislative protest when one of the senior officials implicated by the evidence was subsequently elevated from his post as Director of the Bureau of the Budget to that of the Secretary of the Treasury. What was equally revealing was the tone of elaborate apology with which the legislative commission set out to undertake the daring task of investigating an administrative agency; it is almost as if its members were anxious not to be accused of seeking to embarrass the government in any way.[9] The revelation of administrative malpractices of a much less heinous character in the case of a British government department at about the same time (in the Crichel Down affair) led to a thorough debate in the House of Commons and the dramatic resignation of the cabinet minister concerned. Neither consequence occurred in the Puerto Rican case. To observe in defense that the investigating power can become, as in recent American political history, a source of "sterile conflict," intergovernmentally, is a laudable sentiment enough on the part of a Puerto Rican investigating committee.[10] But the observation confuses the abuse of a valuable device in a constitutional form of government with its legitimate use; and such a spirit of timidity has hardly been responsible for the outstanding achievements of the proper use of the federal investigating power in recent years in areas as varied as crime, radio and television, and the independent regulatory commissions. The local Puerto Rican government, altogether, stands in dire need of a temper of vigorous independence on the part of the Legislature.

Nowhere perhaps is this need more clamant than in the field of the public corporations. When the corporate device first began to appear in the island, after 1942, the prevailing assumption (reinforced by Tugwellian Fabianism) was in favor of its independence, as far as possible, from normal executive and legislative control; and, in particular, freedom from the highly centralized procedures—budgetary, procurement, personnel—of the then present government system was viewed as being indispensable if the flexibility of the corporate device was to be fully utilized. Subsequent experience, however, has demonstrated the danger of independence seriously compromising both at once legislative responsibility for, and executive direction of, public policy. Yet it is astonishing, in the Puerto Rican case, that reforms have concentrated almost wholly upon reasserting executive sovereignty and have done little indeed to meet the problems of agency relationships with the Legislature (the chapter on "The Role and Relationships of Public Corporations" in the Rowe Report of 1949 concerns itself exclusively with relationships with the executive branch). The statutes setting up the agencies frequently require that administrative regulations shall secure legislative approval before going into effect. But the provision, too frequently, is a dead letter since the Legislature possesses no means of effective supervision— a committee on delegated legislation, for example. Thus the Planning Board, on its own admission, functions in effect as an autonomous body, with practically no executive or legislative supervision to speak of.[11] The British practice of an occasional full-dress debate or of a parliamentary investigation of the public boards, resulting in things like the Hebert Report of 1957, could profitably be copied. In addition, there should be a series of legislative committees paralleling the corporations, the business of each one being to keep a sharp eye on one particular corporation. This in turn would naturally require a modern system of committee technical and specialist aid which at present does not exist, for the Office of Legislative Services created in 1954 offers the services of only a small staff, composed of three lawyers, one of whom is Director, three economists, and various office personnel. What is needed is something along the lines of the federal Legislative Reference Service as it was reorganized by the Legislative Reorganization Act of 1946, including—at present non-existent in Puerto Rico—an up-to-date legislative library. The Speaker of the insular lower house has recently urged the full recruitment of economists and other experts to the legislative advisory services on a much larger scale than presently is the case, so that when the Model Budget and the Six-Year Economic Plan are presented to the Legislature the members of that body will be able to discuss them critically and intelligently. The context of his remarks clearly indicated an apprehension on his part that the present facilities for genuine legislative participation in the policy-making process were grievously inadequate, so much so that too many legislators turn with relief to the more satisfying task of looking after the "parish pump" interests of their constituents.[12] Some means, to sum it up, must be found for penetrating the curtain of mistrust and misunderstanding which at the moment divides the administrative commissars from the elected politicians.

There is one special facet of all this that merits some closer attention. It concerns the power of legislators to obtain information from the administrative agencies so that the elected representatives shall be enabled more properly to fulfill the functions that are legitimately theirs, first, of educating public opinion, and second, of knowledgeably criticizing public policy. The whole matter was thrashed out in the important debate of 1953 on the occasion of the revision of legislative rules governing the transmission of questions from either house to government departments and agencies. The debate indeed was so important that it is worth noting in some detail.[13] It arose out of the legislative majority's decision to amend the important Rule 18 of the parliamentary *Reglamentos* so that in place of an automatic House or Senate approval of a member's request or petition for information (by way of an approved resolution) without opposition or debate, the new practice would curtail the right by providing room for objection against such requests or petition. The debate, carried on simultaneously in both houses, was suggestive for the light it threw upon the government party's preconceptions about the function of the majority and the minority in a democratic popular assembly. The presuppositions appear to have been two: first, the business of a legislative majority, it was agreed, is to push through a stream of legislation based upon the mandate received from the popular will, the business of a legislative minority to scrutinize that legislation as a participating critic. It is not the latter's business, in this view, to seek to continue the electoral debate on alternative policies; thus in the Puerto Rican case the debate on political independence is assumed to be closed because the electorate has rejected the protagonists of that idea at the polls. The legislative task now simply is to debate the majority program; the minority's function is limited to supporting or attacking that program.[14] Second, it was assumed that an unrestricted power of petition to executive departments and agencies would lead to a "paralysis" of government as a whole. Executive officials would be inundated with mountains of detailed requests for information, the proper answering of which would be at once costly and time-consuming. A single senator or representative, had he the mind, could thus both embarrass the executive branch and compromise the good name of the Legislature.[15]

Both presuppositions are curious doctrine, to say the least. The first rests upon a supposed separation of detail and principle that is quite artificial, for it is difficult to see how an opposition can adequately criticize a government measure without invoking its own suggestions for an alternative policy. It would be impossible, to take one instance, for a question of educational policy like the teaching of English in the insular schools to be debated without referring to the status question, for the one clearly rests upon the other. The thesis, in effect, employs the theory of the popular mandate—the basic theory, if it has any, of the Popular Party—to seal off critical discussion of the majority program; and among other things it has been in fact invoked at times by the majority spokesmen as a reason for denying public hearings on proposed legislation.[16] It may be conceded that, being in control of government, majority business must come first. But the argument defended here would go further and limit the opposition, in truth, to boundaries of debate set by the proposed agenda of the majority group. The second presupposition is even more indefensible, for it resides upon nothing less than a fanciful exaggeration of purely imaginary dangers. The majority "floor leader" of the House argued that unrestricted petitioning could mean, if applied to the American system, that a single Congressman could demand the full details of atomic energy from the Atomic Energy Commission, thereby imperiling national defense; or that, in the Puerto Rican case, a Representative could reduce the right to farce by requesting the names of all persons born in the island since 1900. Is it reasonable, he asked, that a single legislator could thus compromise the dignity and prestige of the legislative assembly by such an arbitrary demand? The answer is simple: all parliamentary privileges run the calculated risk of being abused; and a practical use cannot be abrogated on the merely problematical possibility of future misuse.

In any case, there is no evidence in the parliamentary experience of either France or Great Britain of governmental "paralysis" resulting from the liberal question-time periods that both have provided, traditionally, for the legislative cross-examination of ministers. Similarly, in the Puerto Rican case, if it is feared that the excessive use of the privilege of questioning would overstrain departmental capacity to answer, then the difficulty can be met by increasing departmental staff rather than by curtailing parliamentary privilege. The senatorial leader of the *Independentista* Party quite rightly pointed, in the debate here being described, to the fact that the doctrine here invoked would paralyze not the government machine but the democratic right of minority speakers to seek out information on, for example, the reasons that guide the Fomento executives in their choice of New York advertising agents, or the guiding principles behind problems such

as the location of new industries, or the nature of overseas markets
for local products, or the holdings of the insular Social Security Fund
in excess of the legal maximum: all of them questions that have
actually been raised in recent legislative history.[17] If again the British
House of Commons permits some 20,000 questions annually to be
presented to ministers, can it be seriously argued that a much smaller
number of petitions in the Puerto Rican Legislature (some 169 in
1940 and some 21 in 1951) would endanger the efficiency or
stability of the government?[18] To ask the question is to answer it. It
is difficult not to accept the conclusion that the real reason behind the
revision of legislative rules was a desire on the part of the legislative
majority to cut into the parliamentary rights of the minority groups.

More than that. The debate, held at much the same time, on the
power of either house to require the discharge of bills from committees to the floor betrayed a similar readiness to believe that the
minorities would abuse any parliamentary weapon—in this case the
right to argue, in five minutes, the pros and cons of a discharge motion
—for partisan ends. Again, it is an essay in insubstantial improbability
that is invoked to justify an illiberal end. The opposition Representative who scathingly asked whether the Legislature really imagined
that the problem, for example, of independence for Puerto Rico could
be adequately discussed in successive periods of five minute debates
properly estimated the worthlessness of the proposition. The facts, as
distinct from the theory, of insular legislative history, indeed, point
to a tradition of willingness on the part of most minority groups over
the last fifty years to use their privileges with circumspection.
Throughout that entire period, moreover, there was no effort on the
part of the majorities to restrict those privileges. This was the case
with the early massive majority of the Unionist Party, as also with
that of the *Alianza* later, and, later still, with that of the *Popular*
Party itself in the period between 1944 and 1952 when it reigned in
the Legislature almost unchallenged. Nor was there any effort at
restriction even during those periods when the fever of faction and the
spirit of political animosity have been more intense than is the case
at the present time: the 1928-1932 period, for example, before the
foundation of the Liberal Party, or the 1941-1944 period, when the
Popular Party's slender majority depended upon its ability to retain the
fragile adherence of the three members of the *Partido Unificación*.[19]
It is hard to believe that the spirit of the political debate has so
changed that the classic rights of the present-day legislative minorities
need to be trimmed.

Indeed present conditions, if anything, cry out not for their limitation so much as for their enlargement. The vast increase of delegated

legislation tends more and more to insulate the administrative official-dom from legislative surveillance. This, in the Puerto Rican case, may not be so much of a handicap for the legislative majority members, since they can obtain most of the information they desire through extra-official methods and the intimate relations they enjoy with the executive leaders, natural enough in a geographically tiny society. But for the minority members it is a barrier which stands in the way of obtaining the detail of knowledge without which criticism of departmental policy is almost useless. Nor is it enough to suggest, with the majority floor leader of the House, that the knowledge can be obtained by requesting the appearance of a departmental head before the appropriate legislative committee.[20] For such appearances are too intermittent to permit the continuity of information that is desirable; they cannot fully substitute for the detail of a written answer; and in any case the excessive pressure of committee work on legislators (sixteen committees in each house) further lessens the value of the committee room as an area for extended cooperation between the two branches. There is throughout the majority attitude as it emerges in these debates a strong presumption of the moral unreliability of the opposition groups, a feeling that since those groups are present, overwhelmingly, in the legislature because of the constitutional guarantees covering minority representation they must now behave, rather like new boys at school, with a circumspection appropriate to their status.

Much of all this, in its ideological roots, is the result of the doctrine of the majoritarian mandate as the basis of legislative representation which, as already noted, is about the only piece of theory the *Popular* Party can be said to have adopted. Once it is accepted that the government is only doing "what the people want" it becomes easy to accept the further argument that the majority legislative program is not so much a partisan one as it is that of a benevolent government concerned only with the national "good" of the "people," and that criticism of it almost takes on the quality of treason. A further corollary of the argument insists that there is a peculiar obligation of strict party discipline on the part of legislative party members, so much so that the history of intra-party conflicts within the insular parties reveals an almost unanimous assumption on the part of rebels and dissidents that any serious quarrel with their party leaderships generally requires their resignation, not merely from the party, but from the Legislature itself. Professor Robert Anderson has annotated the various leading cases of the last two decades—involving the early Báez Garcia case of 1942, up to the more recent cases of the Susonis and Francisco Díaz Marchand. The discouragement of the formal minorities is thus matched by the usage of the mandate theory to crush any sort of continuing minority dissent within the parties themselves; the party rebel, carrying on his own guerrilla war against his own leaders, challenging party orthodoxy and generally enlivening legislative debate, and who, as a figure, is so much in evidence both in the United States Senate and the British House of Commons, is thus conspicuous by his absence in the Puerto Rican legislative councils. It is at least heartening that, in the more recent case of Representative Carlos Westerband, expulsion from party membership by the Republican Party Territorial Committee following his open invitation to his party leader to resign, has not been followed by his resignation from the Legislature despite the feeling of his party leaders that he had a moral obligation so to do.[21]

The local Constitution reiterates the orthodox American principle of the separation of powers. There is, equally, the same prohibition against the mixing of legislative election and administrative appointment. The document includes the categorical statement that the "legislative, judicial and executive branches as established by this Constitution shall be equally subordinate to the people of Puerto Rico."[22] The former Speaker of the island lower house has noted how the doctrine was originally borrowed by the American Founding Fathers from Montesquieu's theory; although he neglected to note that that theory, in its turn, had been based upon the French thinker's famous misunderstanding of the realities of the English eighteenth-century constitution. What indeed is surprising is that the Puerto Rican constitutionalists should be defending the doctrine at a time when both in the United States and in Puerto Rico the growth of modern government has completely bypassed it. The fact can only be explained perhaps by their inherent tendency to copy the American constitutional language, to regard America as the exclusive source of authority. For although the academic advisers to the Constituent Assembly ranged in their various reports over a vast variety of alternative experiences in modern democratic government, the delegates to that body generally tended to stick close to American precedent, with a few single exceptions. It is possible that their fear of Congressional disapproval, not entirely unfounded, kept them within the limits of constitutional conservatism.

One of the most important of local commentaries upon their handiwork is contained in the speech made to the House of Representatives in February 1955 by its late Speaker.[23] Originally provoked by the almost casual remarks of a Supreme Court justice concerning the dangers of legislative intrusion into the judicial sphere, it expanded into a lengthy eulogy of the separation of powers doctrine and an impassioned plea for its continuing observance by all three branches. Much of its substance, on analysis, is unobjectionable. It properly explodes the fiction that the doctrine means an absolute divorce of powers rather than a deliberate intermixture. Indeed, when in the Puerto Rican case the Legislature (via the Senate) confirms judicial appointments, creates and abolishes courts, except the Supreme Court, and may even, by special legislation, amend or repeal rules of evidence in certain cases, it is obvious enough that the legislative branch has an ample power to intervene, if it so wishes, in the affairs of the court system.[24] There is recognition, too, of the quasi-judicial powers of the "fourth branch" of government required by the administrative complexity of the modern state. So that it is all the more astonishing when Ramos Antonini goes on to admonish his fellow citizens to hold firm to the eighteenth-century formula of "harmoniously balancing," in his phrase, the three traditional branches of the "total power" of the state lest that power be used arbitrarily and tyrannically. How the balance is to be reconciled with the hard fact that in the Puerto Rican system the executive is far and away the most powerful branch is not explained; nor is any effort made to determine whether it is in fact possible to retain a system of "counterpoise" between legislature and executive when their respective memberships are held together in the vise of an iron party discipline. It is doubtful, as a matter of fact, whether the dogma of "checks and balances" could for long coexist with such a political condition; since, as a dogma, it presupposes a fundamental jealousy between the two branches that can rarely be transcended by a common and unifying political leadership.

All this becomes even more puzzling when the Speaker goes on to claim that of the three branches the legislature is the "most powerful." The sole theoretical proof that is advanced to justify the claim is—in itself merely negative proof—a recital of Madison's rejection of the overweening claims of the judicial branch in the early American experience. As far as the Puerto Rican realities are concerned the paramountcy, once again, of the executive must be called to mind. This is not to deny that the Speaker is correct when he deduces from the general grant of power to the Legislature the conclusion of an ample legislative investigating power, even to the point where that power may be used to request a stay of judicial proceedings. The power is real enough in Puerto Rico; the authoritative case is the precedent established in 1943 by the special legislative committee set up at that time to investigate the matter of the liquidation of the *Teritorial y Agrícola de Puerto Rico* and *Comercial de Puerto Rico* banks. What is at issue is not the existence of the investigative power but whether its use by the Legislature helps in fact to substantiate the claim that the legislative authority is the "most powerful" branch of the insular machinery of government. It has already been suggested that this, in truth, is not so. We are confronted here with the paradox of a grandiloquent defense of the investigating power and a practical usage of the power that is utterly disappointing. The very vehemence indeed with which the defense is conducted suggests that its basis is that of an injured legislative pique rather than a positive determination to assert legislative sovereignty in deed as well as in theory.

The real need perhaps is not so much for legislative sovereignty as it is for a more activist assertion of legislative independence within the existing framework of executive preeminence. For executive preeminence does not have, in any way, to mean legislative subservience. For all purposes of legislation the British House of Commons is the instrument of the cabinet. But the episodes of May 1940 and of October 1956 abundantly prove that in critical moments it can unseat an unpopular Prime Minister, while in between those dramatic heights it performs its regular function as sharp critic of government and channel of citizen grievance with admirable dispatch. The critics who speak of the "passing of Parliament" underestimate its genius, when aroused, to put the executive in its place. In part that is a matter of a collective parliamentary pride that rises above party loyalties. In part it is a readiness in crisis to revolt against the party line, as did the group of Conservative members who voted against Mr. Chamberlain in the vital war debate of 1940. Revolt of that nature of course is the rule, not the exception, in the case of the United States Congress, and at least one Puerto Rican legislator has reminded his colleagues of the virtues embodied in the fact that a Republican Congress may be the violent critic of a Republican administration or that a Democratic administration, like that of the second Roosevelt, may have to rely for its Congressional support upon an alliance of the liberal wings of both parties.[25] Such an American role, in the nature of things, the Puerto Rican Legislature cannot hope to emulate. But a British role would not be beyond its reach.

Such a role, however, is at present stultified not only by constitutional limitations but also by the general climate of opinion within which the Legislature works. The curious concept of the legislative role of minorities that prevails within the ruling legislative circles has already been noted. Even more disconcerting than this, however, is the equally curious concept of parliamentary protocol that appears to prevail in the same circles. The concept permeates a book like Néstor Rigual's *El Poder Legislativo de Puerto Rico,* which reads more like a eulogy of the legislative branch than a critical estimate of its place in the Puerto Rican machinery of government. By starting off with the assumption that the highest desideratum in the life of a legislative body ought to be the existence of cordial relations between all party members, the author is enabled to conclude that dissident parliamentary groups which attack their leadership suffer from harmful complexes, erroneous suspicions and preoccupation, in general, with petty matters for which the only recipe is (in the best Latin rhetoric) comradeship, tolerance, and understanding.[26] By thus seeing the problem as psychological rather than political in character, the argument manages to ignore completely the whole question of the need for independent-minded "back-benchers" in a legislative assembly and of the evils that flow from their subjection to routine party discipline. It is not surprising, then, that it leads in turn to an uncritical apologia for the habit of the caucus in Puerto Rican legislative government. Yet all the Puerto Rican evidence available suggests that the rule of the caucus helps to silence both minority and dissident groups, so much so that, as Rigual himself notes, the legislative history is full of the history of such groups, often giving themselves mockingly ironical names—the *Ku-Klux Klan,* the *Solid South,* the *Sierra Maestra*—that in themselves suggest the presence of deeply felt frustrations. The results of this system of government by party machines are manifold. Energetic members like the young (and lately resigned) Federico Cordero, who has been responsible in large part for the establishment of the committee investigating citizen complaints about negligent construction in home-building enterprises—an investigation marked by the refreshing innovation of holding committee hearings in the housing developments themselves rather than in the Capitol building—have found themselves being viewed as "uncooperative" members. Relations with the press are not too good, and one reporter has been moved to observe that trying to obtain data on the expenses incurred by the holding of special legislative sessions is like trying to get the address book of the Central Intelligence Agency. Legislative action can be swift when the leadership so wishes, as in the case of the extraordinary removal of the two elected Christian Action Party members in 1961 on the ground of fraud in the registration and voting processes. That action, indeed, was not only extraordinary but also punitive. For, as the American Civil Liberties Union pointed out in an advisory letter, the charge of attempted coercion of voters is extremely difficult to prove since the line that divides coercion from persuasion is hard to draw; and in the light of a complete absence of relevant legal precedents within the federal jurisdiction, the Puerto Rican legislative action might easily be construed as an attempt to deny to a religious organization its constitutional right to form a political party and present candidates for office.[27] Yet other issues, surely of comparable urgency, are neglected or allowed to become the object of extra-parliamentary agitation. So, to itemize only a few, issues such as the continued holding by the United States armed services of military installations in the old San Juan enclave that are now militarily obsolete, the refusal of the United States Navy to relinquish unused land on the island of Vieques in order to facilitate the economic rehabilitation of that depressed island area (demanded by a body as socially respectable as the Puerto Rican Chamber of Commerce), the high profit rates of United States corporations participating in the industrialization program, the extent of the disease of family nepotism within the government service (which some critics believe to be widely advanced), the inflationary effects of uncontrolled credit and installment-buying facilities on the local economy: all receive little or no notice within the legislative arena.

It would be palpably utopian, in the light of all this, and much more, to believe that the Puerto Rican legislative branch is a House of Commons or an American Senate. It would be more exact to say that the Capitol building has about it the unpleasant aroma of typical county courthouse politics. For, to say the least, the Puerto Rican legislative politician is in truth an "old hand" at the political game. "The fact is," wrote an American observer as far back as 1906, "that the American politicians sent to Porto Rico were usually outclassed in point of experience in politics, and general knowledge of public affairs, by their Porto Rican comrades. Very naturally, the equal, or the superior, soon wearied of the equal, or the inferior, as a teacher; and especially when he realized that his teacher ought to be in school himself." "It must be remembered," the same observer continued, "that these Porto Rican politicians had for years been 'playing the game' of politics, not alone in their local controversies, but for generations, each in turn, had combatted as shrewd politicians as were engaged in the political or diplomatic controversies of Europe."[28] The remarks apply equally well to the present-day Puerto Rican practitioners in the local legislative politics. There is the same cleverness in utilizing any situation to further the political interest; perhaps the best illustration of that genius is the way in which the visit of Charles Lindbergh to the island in 1928 was converted into a means of pushing the Puerto Rican cause in the federal Congress, culminating in the astonishing letter sent to the Washington Resident Commissioner by the local legislative leadership, in which authorities as various as the National Research Council, Dr. Lyman Abbott,

Elihu Root, President Coolidge, and H. G. Wells were pressed into the service of the cause.[29] There is the same comic sensitivity to press criticism, nicely enough exhibited in the display of righteous anger to which the insular Senate treated itself in 1951 as a consequence of some critical observations printed by the island's leading newspaper and which should in any case have been made the business of a Committee of Privileges.[30] There is the same cavalier disregard for priorities in legislation making, so that, more recently, the Legislature has found time and money enough to authorize the manufacture of a bust of Jesus T. Piñero, the first elected native governor, but has found neither time nor money to implement the long-standing plea of Senator Santos Amadeo for the creation of a joint House-Senate civil rights permanent committee along the lines of the federal Congressional committee.

Above all, of course, there is the smell of legislative malpractices. They have recently been under close public scrutiny as a result of the remarkable pieces of detective journalism undertaken by *The San Juan Star*. Both the *Popular* and the Republican Statehood parties have been guilty of the illegal use of legislative budgetary funds for the purpose of large-scale political patronage, with such funds being used for the payment, among others, of party administrative officers, young members of the *Popular* Party Youth being groomed for future leadership, party public relations men, and a large number of political ward heelers disguised as office workers, janitors, and messengers on the legislative payrolls. The fact that at least four government party legislators have their wives on the House payroll hints at a possibly wider practice of nepotism, and certainly casts an ironic light upon the spectacle of Puerto Rican politicians angrily criticizing the vulgar intervention of Representative Adam Clayton Powell, the "proconsul from Harlem," in the insular politics, especially when that Harlem Democrat's record for irregularities in the expenditure of public funds is called to mind. The weakness of the local Republican party as a legislative opposition is somewhat explained by the fact that the party's legislative group, by its collusion with the government legislative leadership in the allocation of funds for political purposes, has thereby made itself financially dependent, in part, upon the *Popular* Party and thus sold its right to adopt a critical attitude. Nor did either party group much enhance itself in the public eye by its panic-stricken response to the publicity attending these revelations, culminating in the amazing spectacle of the Legislature deciding, after an all-night frenzied meeting, to cut its budget by over half a million dollars as an act of self-atonement; accompanied, in turn, by a joint statement of the House Speaker and the Senate President which, for sheer

Pecksniffian hypocrisy, must equal anything in the history of the morals of American politics. The picture, altogether, that emerges from the evidence is that of a pedestrian legislative assembly composed in the main part of part-time solons enjoying their public posts as handsome political plums, taking little interest in legislative affairs, as the dismal record of their committee attendance shows, and leaving the real business of the Legislature to be conducted by the charmed inner circle of the government party leaders. It will assuredly take something more than the fancy of the Speaker of the House of Representatives for occasionally delivering learned homilies on the historical growth of the legislative process of the Western world since the medieval period to rescue the Puerto Rican Legislature from the low esteem in which it is presently held throughout the society.[31]

Some wholesale reform of the Legislature is clearly one of the pressing orders of the day. It would require a number of things. It would mean, in the realm of party, some widespread relaxation of discipline within the legislative groups, some serious criticism, therefore, of the sort of special pleading that defends the present caucus system as in books like that of Néstor Rigual. It would require some decline in the present legislative tendency to use its powers to consolidate private occupational interests—the chemists, for example—by means of statutorily created *colegios*, and an increased readiness to see itself as the representative of the national will, and so moving more harmoniously with the changing currents of public opinion. This could mean a more positive legislative contribution without seriously upsetting the present balance of legislative-executive relationships. For, as things now stand, the investigating power—the essential tool for creating that contribution—is used to inquire into games of chance or insular hospital facilities or traffic problems without any show of really dramatic success in dealing with any of these problems; nor should it fail to be noted that the legislation controlling at least the first of those problems penalizes the Puerto Rican poor while it leaves untouched the well-to-do. Even a problem as minor as that of the strident abuse of the loudspeaker in commercial advertising appears to be beyond the ability of legislators to control, notwithstanding statutory powers that go back to 1937; and one consequence of their failure is that San Juan, as the head of the police force has remarked, runs the risk of becoming one of the noisiest cities in the world.[32]

There are, naturally, some bright spots in the record. The so-called "Ramos Antonini Plan" of 1954 was an imaginative attempt to replace the traditional pork barrel methods of appropriating money for expenditures on local projects with a comprehensive plan that would require individual legislators to draw up careful estimates in collaboration with the Planning Board in San Juan and with the local planning boards on the district level, and thereby avoid the fractionalization and frequent waste that have hitherto accompanied the use of assigned funds. The public hearings, again, of the Joint Legislative Committee in 1957 on the crisis in the sugar industry were a fine illustration of the civic value of open legislative inquiry. But the pressure of legislative duties prevents committees from pursuing the method very frequently. Only too often the legislative instinct lies dormant. Even when a case arises such as the resignation, belatedly, of the President of the Senate in 1956 as a consequence of charges made against him concerning a possible conflict of interests between his legislative duties and his activities as a legal adviser to some of the big private firms of the economy in suits brought against them by the Commonwealth government, the Legislature has failed to take appropriate action through, for example, a Committee of Privileges. In that particular case indeed the matter was originally brought to public attention by the assiduous criticisms of the Speaker made by a fellow legislator through the medium of privately paid pieces in the local press. It was left to the Governor, moreover, in his capacity as party leader to set up a committee for drawing up a suggested Code of Legislative Ethics (although, interestingly enough, the report of that committee has never been published). So long as this passivity characterizes the legislative branch it will have little chance of becoming the "most powerful" branch of the governmental trinity. It might not even become, as it ought to become, a more energetic partner of the executive.

One device of quasi-legislative control over the administrative and executive branches deserves special notice. That is the Office of the Controller, created through the appropriate clause of the legislative article of the Constitution. Its incumbent is appointed by the Governor with the advice and consent of the total number of members of both houses (a useful condition that ensures the occupant of the office shall be a public-spirited citizen free, as far as is humanly possible, from partisan bias). He is charged with the auditing of the revenues, accounts, and expenditures of the Commonwealth and its agencies and instrumentalities, including the municipal authorities; and his reports and recommendations are referred to one of the permanent joint committees of the Legislature. He holds the office for a tenure of ten years and can only be removed (like the Governor himself) on grounds of treason, bribery, and misdemeanors involving moral turpitude.

It would be difficult to overestimate the practical importance of this office. It has authority and independence. It is removed from party control. It performs at once the functions of a General Accounts Committee and a Select Committee of inquiry, as those offices are known to the British House of Commons. Its assured annual budget of approximately $500,000 and its varied staff of some 125 persons, including some 80 examiners, gives it an *expertise* not enjoyed by any legislative committee. The reports of its incumbent since its inception have covered an enormous variety of matters: the fiscal practices of municipal government authorities, the use of public funds, the internal administrative practices of practically every government department at one time or another. Particular reports have dealt with charges of personal favoritism in the appointment of clerical workers in the Department of Agriculture and Commerce, the illegal occupation of land lots held by the Land Authority, the misuse by a public hospital director of municipal property and personnel for his private clinical practice, irregularities in pensions payments by the Retirement Board of the Association of Teachers, the alleged use of forged hotel receipts by the Mayor of Ponce on the occasion of official trips to the United States. But it is as much the unique reporting power of the office as it is the substance of its reports which makes the influence of the office in insular public administration so far-reaching. For not only is its holder enabled by the legal and constitutional grant of his authority to publish the examiners' findings and recommend corrective action in his audit reports; even more, he is authorized by law to publicize the findings by way of news releases to the press and radio. Wrongdoing thus receives the full glare of modern publicity, and there can be little doubt that during the last few years the method has done much to inculcate a higher sense of rectitude and circumspection on the part of the Puerto Rican public servant. This is evident enough in the reactions of violent indignation that the Controller's office has at times provoked from government circles, especially in municipal government where corrective measures have been needed more urgently perhaps than elsewhere. A public figure charged with misdemeanors feels obliged at times to carry his defense, in turn, to the press himself; that was the case with the President of the Teachers Association in 1955 and with the Mayor of Ponce in 1959. The resultant exchange of views may not satisfy the aggrieved official. But it publicizes the facts and lets daylight into the inner recess of government offices the operations of which are only too frequently hidden from public view by the occupational temptation of the official mind to persuade the public that all is for the best in the best of all administrative worlds.

Undeniably there are dangers in the Controller's power (a power denied, incidentally, to the Controller General of the United States) to publicize the findings of his examiners, and especially to make public the names of officials or employees in connection with unethical or illegal behavior. It is beyond doubt a harsh medicine. Improperly used, it could become a means of seriously compromising the reputation of persons named by a Controller who conceived of himself as a sort of revolutionary committee of public safety. His immunity to executive or legislative control (the Governor has consistently refused to interfere with the Office, against strong appeals to do so) renders him accountable, in reality, to almost nothing save his own sense of justice. It is true that officials are granted an opportunity to see findings and defend themselves, on request, in a meeting with the Controller before a report is forwarded (in cases that seem to merit it) to the Department of Justice for possible legal action. But this precaution was not adopted in the Cintrón case of 1959; and even when it is resorted to it has little power to stay the publication of the findings. While it is true, again, that the Controller cannot be blamed for exaggerated or inaccurate press accounts, such accounts do grow out of his official releases.[33] Most serious of all, there is the question as to whether it is a desirable practice, from the viewpoint of the principle of civil service anonymity, that the names of public servants (as distinct from those of elected persons or political heads) should be dragged into public controversy. It would seem more healthy if such names could be withheld from press releases and that disciplinary action be left to the department or agency or corporation head who receives the report. If action is held up at that point, there is room for action on the part of the Governor (who also receives all reports) and of the Legislature. There is certainly a need for fuller legislative debate on reports. It is not enough, in any case, to dismiss the problem here posed by referring to the well-known reputation for integrity of the first incumbent of the office.[34]

With some such measures to safeguard against abuse, however, there is much to be said for the retention of the office. Its very unpopularity is an index of the real service it performs. In a society where the culture trait of deference to authority encourages an uncritical acceptance of hierarchical organization and an easy adjustment to centralized power on the part of officials at every level, it is a tremendous advantage to have such an office empowered with a quasi-judicial independence and a constitutional authority to compel, under pain of contempt, the attendance of witnesses and the production of papers and records. Its value is especially obvious in the light of the continuing unsatisfactory state of affairs throughout the field of local government in the territory. The last few years have witnessed a series of charges brought against local mayors throughout the island con-

cerning electoral corruption, arbitrary behavior in employment practices, violations of fiscal regulations, general neglect of duties, and so
on. To some extent the charges have been the fruit of bitter intra-party
factional struggles, to some extent the result of a failure to resolve
conflicts between the central and local authorities in matters such as
the joint control of the municipal health centers. In addition, there is
the general reluctance of the local politicians to accept the authority
of the island Legislature. The open quarrel in 1959 between the Association of Mayors and the Senate Housing Commission revealed the
depth of that feeling. The creation by the Legislature in 1955, in turn,
of a special *Comisión de Querellas* possessing wide powers of interference in muncipal matters, including the power to divest a mayor
of his office under certain conditions, only served to inflame the feeling more, since the Association of Mayors sees in the Commission an
illiberal amputation of the legitimate powers of the local municipal
assemblies. In all of this, the real issues become clouded through the
fog of shrill accusations of politics and personalities. The need for
an impartial investigator is self-evident, and especially so when the
Legislature and its committees become embroiled as participants in
the disputes. The Office of the Controller, much more than its predecessor, the office of the Auditor of Puerto Rico, fully serves that purpose. So long as adequate safeguards exist against the misdirection of
its powers it should continue to guarantee that Puerto Rican government will be less a government of men and more a government of
laws.

Something must be said, finally, of the record of the Legislature
with reference to the legal framework that it has set up for the existence of political parties within the society. For the quality of legislative work clearly depends upon the quality, and indeed the essential
variety, of its membership. Looked at in this way, there can be little
doubt that many of the defects of the Puerto Rican legislative record
spring directly from the unusual stringency of the electoral laws governing the registration of new political parties and their ability to gain
a place on the electoral ballot. The so-called "ten percent rule"—
whereby an aspiring new party must obtain a number of signatures
equal to ten percent of the total number of votes cast for the office of
the Governor in the previous election and representing three quarters
of all electoral precincts within the island—effectively disenfranchises
the really small and unpopular party groups as well as denying to them
the financial aid of the electoral subsidy law, for it means, in effect,
that each of such groups must be able to obtain about 80,000 signatures before getting on to the ballot, no mean task. The general effect
of the rule, as noted elsewhere, means that the registration process

becomes a political game, with the pressure on the party managers and the ward captains becoming so heavy that it easily encourages exaggerated claims, abuse of procedures and even outright fraud. It is true that the requirements were relaxed both in 1947 and 1952 to facilitate the registration of minority groups. But there is evidence to suggest that, in the 1952 case, this was done in order to please a dissident group of no dangerous proportions within the ruling *Popular* party itself;[35] while more recently the decision to reimpose the more exacting requirements appears to have been motivated by a fear, in both the *Popular* and the Republican Statehood parties, that the more radical groups of the nationalist ideal in the island may be successful in obtaining a place on the ballot. Apart from the effects of this patently discriminatory attitude on the state of parties, its repercussions on the legislative scene have long been apparent. The parliamentary battalions are too fiercely disciplined; the figure of the "independent" is almost unknown; views that do not command a large following in the electorate are denied a voice in the legislature and, even worse, are encouraged, because of the ballot difficulties, to direct themselves into underground non-electoral channels; and there is so little real turnover in the legislative membership, so few new faces making their appearance, that the fact is used to justify the complete absence of any system of educating new legislators in their new duties.[36] So long as this system of electoral exclusion prevails the legislative branch will be denied the new blood, the fresh streams of energy that it needs if it is to become a serious rival to its executive and administrative fellows.

Parties and Politics

IT IS somewhat surprising that there exists so little literature on Puerto Rican politics and political parties. For the island is a politics-centered society; San Juan café society thrives on political gossip; and almost every citizen is a natural politican in much the same Latin sense of Max Weber's remark, somewhere, that every member of the Mexican army is a colonel. Yet there is no book as yet comparable say to Professor MacKenzie's study of the distribution of power within the major British political parties. There are of course the volumes of the *Historia de los Partidos Politicos Puertorriqueños* composed by the late Dr. Bolívar Pagán, one-time President of the now-defunct Socialist Party. But those volumes are less an original analysis of the parties and of their theology, internal structures, power struggles, and general *razon de ser* than they are a collection of party platforms, convention records, speeches, and parliamentary debates, valuable enough in themselves but held together merely by brief connecting narrative paragraphs. Similarly the volume of Reece Bothwell and Lidio Cruz Monclova, *Los Documentos, que Dicen?*, is documentary only and does not go beyond 1898. The contributions of politicians themselves to the literature have been in the main their writings as editors of partisan newspapers—Muñoz Rivera from the early *La Democracia*, Barbosa from *El Tiempo*. There is a certain category of book by practicing politicians—Vicente Géigel Polanco's *El Despertar de un Pueblo*, for example—that is extended political essay writing rather than empirical description of practical politics; while there are other books, of which the *Temas y Letras* of Samuel Quiñones, the President of the Commonwealth Senate, is a good example, that read more like the work of reflective literary gentlemen than of participants in the political hurly-burly. There have been no political autobiographies in any real sense, nothing comparable to the Nehru or Nkrumah self-portraits; and if indeed Governor Muñoz Marín should ever decide to publish a political memoir it should constitute a rare mine of first-hand information on the Puerto Rican "great game of politics."

It is symptomatic, granted the hero worship of that game, that most of the available books are the biographical exercises on the famous figures: the legion of books and pamphlets on Muñoz Rivera, the charming act of filial homage which is the work of Doña Pilar Barbosa de Rosario on her father, Teófilo Maldonado's *Hombres de Primera Plana*. Very little, if any, of the work put out by the Social Sciences Research Center of the University is addressed to explicitly political themes, being mainly preoccupied with economic, industrial, and anthropological questions. The Political Science Association of Puerto Rico has recently printed a select bibliography of some fifty-two doctoral dissertations and master's theses concerning the insular government and politics written at United States colleges and universities, but the vast majority of them are unavailable to the general reader. Professor Robert Anderson's unpublished thesis on *Party Politics in Puerto Rico* is perhaps the first attempt to analyze the structure of the local party groups from the viewpoint of a professional political sociology. But apart from that work, as well as a handful of journal articles by Professor Henry Wells and Dr. Thomas Mathews' volume on *Puerto Rican Politics and the New Deal*, there is little enough to help the student towards an understanding of the insular political situation, so different as that situation is from that of the individual American state.

That understanding must begin with an appreciation of the cultural context of the situation. For the culture of the insular politics, as well as that of insular family life, has been surprisingly adept at resisting absorption by the Americanizing process. The fact is not readily apparent to the casual observer because, ever since 1900, the local politicians have taken over both the terminology and the structure of the American parties. There is the same committee system, the same electoral system (with some modifications), the same public rhetoric. It is even possible for opponents to apply the language of baseball to political attitudes in a public exchange of views.[1] Yet the very vehemence with which attachment to the principles of American democracy is announced suggests that the psychological revolution away from Spanish to American concepts has by no means yet been fully completed. There is much evidence to warrant the belief that the Puerto Rican politician still thinks of parties, in the Latin sense, as vehicles of the "national revolution" or as custodians of the "national spirit." The sentiment is related to the special circumstances that surround the growth of nationalist political movements, not only in Latin America but throughout Asia and Africa as well. The nationalist party seeks not so much to develop a program on the foundation of an established social order as to reshape the social order itself. Thus the revolutionary movement, once successful, becomes the government in a special sense, frequently without real opposition. That has been the case with the PRI in Mexico, with the Congress Party in India, with the Peoples National Movement, more recently, in Trinidad. The "revolution of 1940" in Puerto Rico inevitably cast the Popular Democratic Party in much the same mold. Except for the fact that it did not rise to power as an insurrectionist movement, most of its other features stamp it as this sort of party. Its opponent, the *Partido Independentista Puertorriqueño,* undoubtedly sees itself in a similar light. The status of Governor Muñoz thus approximates more to that of Nehru in India or, earlier, Ruiz Cortines in Mexico than it does to that of a British Prime Minister or American President. His party likewise arrogates to itself the public image of the *familia revolucionaria,* with the corollary that criticism of its policies comes to be viewed at times not simply as dissent but also as a lapse of patriotic will. But the American connection, cultural as well as legal, inhibits the full growth of this attitude. The local political system, consequently, and its tribal totems and taboos are an ambivalent mixture of both the Latin "revolutionary" and the American "democratic" systems.

One single factor of paramount importance that illustrates all this is the factor of *personalismo.* Its roots go back to the absolutist political methods of Spain and, on the economic plane, to the personal authority of the *patrón* in the rural life of the society. In politics it expresses itself in the exaggerated role played by the leader, the *hombre-pueblo,* both within the party and outside it. It would be misleading to see it as simply a Puerto Rican variant of the "great man" theory of political leadership. That is the defect of Rexford Tugwell's more recent book devoted, in part, to a study of Muñoz as a leader, *The Art of Politics.* The phenomenon in Puerto Rico has tougher roots in the communal psychology than the concept of leadership has in Britain or the United States. Nor is it to be equated with the paternalism of the welfare state, advanced as that is in Puerto Rico. It is a paternalism in the more feudal sense of the political follower being the "man" of his "liege lord," although it has been buttressed of course by the judicious distribution of public services and appointments, especially at the district level, to the party faithful. It can reach proportions of real idolatry; the voter who declared at a 1956 public meeting, "The day that you die, Don Luis, I will hang myself," was only giving a bizarre expression to the sentiment. To some extent again it is a reflection of the authoritarian relationship between parents and children in the traditional family structure, for political affiliation has frequently been influenced by the traditional attitudes prevailing in the family home. The observation of one professional Puerto Rican politician upon another—"He was born *Unionista,* just

as he was born Roman Catholic and *ponceño*. He could not help
it"[2]—explains still a not unimportant factor in the shaping of voting
habits, despite the findings of researchers—Peter Bachrach's brief
analysis, for example, of the voting preferences of university students—that the potency of the factor is weakening within certain
groups of the younger generation.

To the extent that *personalismo* is reinforced by family influences
of course it becomes tied in with the habits of nepotism in colonial
politics. As far as the office of the Resident Commissioner in Washington is concerned, one of its former occupants who was hardly a
brilliant success in it, Bolívar Pagán, has confessed that he was in
effect handpicked by his predecessor, Santiago Iglesias, who happened
also to be his father-in-law. But a great deal of research needs to be
done on this question, admittedly delicate, before its contribution to
the growth of *personalismo* can be properly estimated. Whatever its
varied roots, however, the general phenomenon of *personalismo* remains a potent factor still in the Puerto Rican political fever and helps
to produce what one political leader as far back as 1897 described as
a politics of *andante caballería* in which the melodramatic hero offers
himself for the admiration of the masses. "The adversary," wrote
Degetau y González, "is not a man who thinks in a different or in an
opposite way to oneself, because thought plays a quite accidental role.
Ideas are hardly taken into consideration, and it is because of that
that the primary consideration in the estimation of political behavior
becomes whether Don Fulano is a hero, a great know-all and an
extraordinary personality, and whether Don Mengano is a liar, a fool
or a despicable person; or whether Perencejo acts only out of mere
envy and whether the patriotism of Don Sutanejo is of such a refined
quality that you can hardly see it. Or, again, attention is centered
upon whether this one has come to despise the generous friend who
presided over his very baptismal rites or that one has failed to satisfy
the good gentleman and enlightened patriot who has rendered such
and such worthy acts."[3]

The same critic anticipated in another passage the supersession of
all this with a rational politics. "We are now at a moment in history,"
he added, "in which sophisticated nations have moved on from cloak-
and-dagger politics, the sort of politics in which the melodramatic
hero offers himself for the admiration of the masses in a spirit of
knight-errantry. Thanks to the disappearance of great inequalities
going back to the caste system and to the constant diffusion of ideas,
the nation that needs heroes is crippled for modern life, which demands the diffusion among the social mass of a sufficient amount of
good sense, so that everybody, without any offense, may be judges of

what concerns all. That is why politicians are under an obligation, not to pose like knights in armor, but to present themselves like reasonable men, elaborating the rational foundations of their conduct before the bar of outside criticism."[4] It is the portrait of a rational democracy, entirely utopian in the Puerto Rico of 1897. But it might have been thought that the development of American democratic ideas, allied, especially after 1938, with the social and economic program of the *Populares,* would have brought it a little nearer reality. To some extent of course it has. There is a more informed electorate. Mere rhetoric—one thinks of the historic discourse of José de Diego defending the teaching of Spanish in the schools, in the San Juan Municipal Theater in 1915—is likely to be received more skeptically today. The 1960's are seeing the rise of an educated middle class whose professional and administrative sense is increasingly impatient with an amateur politics. There are even signs, as the 1962 plebiscite hearings showed, that many of the Governor's political friends are increasingly willing to speak out critically about his favorite scheme of Commonwealth status.

For all that, however, the politics of ideas anticipated by Degetau y González has yet to flower. For the *Populares,* from the beginning, did not really possess a coherent social philosophy any more than did the Rooseveltian New Deal that so much influenced them by reason of Muñoz's Washington connections. Indeed the strong empirical emphasis of the *Popular* program, its constant inveighing against "doctrinaire" attitudes, conspired to make it dangerously unphilosophical. The bias did not lead to the perfervid politics of the *pacto,* as it had done earlier with Muñoz Rivera, if only because after 1944 the *Popular* electoral landslides made it unnecessary. But it has led to a theoretical vacuum, so that there has been no debate of great ideas, no division between left and right groups, to counterbalance the Weberian omnipresence of the leader. The history of the changing ideological shifts in the party, when they have occurred, has really been significantly the history of the changing attitudes of Muñoz himself. Significantly too the only really sharp debate within the party has been the revival of the old status issue as the *Popular* claim to have "solved" the status problem has seemed less and less convincing to many party members. It is worth noting too that the one single issue of philosophical weight to enliven the government party recently is the one—church-state relationships—forced upon it by the open entry of the Catholic hierarchy into politics in the 1960 election year. To declare, officially, a vote for the government party a sin of disobedience was beyond doubt a fatal error on the part of that hierarchy, viewed with alarm by American Catholic prelates as conservative as Cardinal Spellman; but it had the virtue at least of lending a new lease of partisan enthusiasm to a party greatly fatigued by a long occupancy of power, even more, of driving the Puerto Rican voter to an examination of fundamentals he has hitherto rarely known.

The emotional power of *personalismo* is exemplified in another way in the failure even of the secularizing and unifying impulses of the governmental bureaucracy to overshadow the Governor or to diminish his appeal. The old habit of party policy being set by *pronunciamientos* issued at the will of the leader rather than by the parliamentary group of the party or by its scheduled conventions prevails still, as the case of the so-called Cidra Declaration of 1959 on the status issue graphically demonstrates. The consequent disregard for rule and regulation can be seen in the astonishing admission of the Civil Liberties Committee that its investigators were unable to locate a copy of the rules governing the internal affairs of the ruling party and its reluctant conclusion that the party either did not possess such rules or that if they existed they must be of a quite unsystematic character.[5] There appears again to be no provisions in existence to cover the succession to the party leadership. The widespread speculation on the future of the party once the Governor quits the scene is only one of the morally debilitating consequences of that fact; while, apart from this, free and vigorous discussion within the party on all kinds of issues hangs fire until the position of the Governor on any one of them has been ascertained. The "cult of personality" thus inhibits the growth of any system of democratic and popular party organization centered around, say, the emergence of an annual conference after the manner of the British Labor Party, which would allow a majority of ordinary party members to determine policy. Some critics have attempted to meet the problem by suggesting restrictive legal devices—the Statehood Party's suggestion, for instance, that the office of the Governor shall be made constitutionally incompatible with that of president or leader of a political party. But such suggestions miss the point that it is Muñoz's power as party leader and not his authority as Governor that enables him to keep the Legislature in a position of subordination to a unipersonal executive. *Personalismo* will decline in importance once the Puerto Rican public mind, both through education and experience, becomes sufficiently sophisticated to decide that the phenomenon has outlived its usefulness.

In the meanwhile *personalismo* naturally leads to a tremendous and unhealthy centralization of power within the local political parties. There are ever-present struggles between rivals for the control of party organizations: the rebellion of Muñoz himself against the

Barceló leadership in the Liberal Party after 1936, the gathering re-volt of the García-Ferré faction against the debilitated leadership of Iriarte in the Republican Party after 1948, finally successful in 1952, the dissatisfaction with the leadership of Concepcion de Gracia which has accounted so much for the break-up of the *Independentista* Party in the last few years. The struggle once over, the new leader takes over the unipersonal control of the party. But there is always the possibility of new rebellions, and the recent Westerband attack upon the García-Méndez leadership in the Republican Party is in one way only a repetition of the methods that the present leaders themselves used against Iriarte in their own earlier climb to power. The leader can thus be hoisted by his own petard; but it is the emphasis upon per-sonal leadership, even although it never becomes an open *caudillismo* after the Latin fashion, that remains the final emphasis. The struggles normally take place within the caucus rooms of the central party committees, followed by popular acclamation in the party assemblies, for there is little enough of the system of democratic election of the leader after the fashion of the British Labor Party parliamentary group. It is indeed significant that the one party which of recent years has attempted to set up a depersonalized leadership structure, the *Independentista* Party, has gained little for its troubles save its present state of calamitous disorganization. It follows from all this that dissent with the leader easily becomes identified with dis-sent with the party; a fact illustrated by the failure of Gilberto Concepción de Gracia, then a dissident *Popular,* to avoid a party schism in 1945-1946 by insisting that his attacks at that time were against Muñoz as leader and not against the party. There was, again, the quaint attempt in 1952 to assuage the wounds of inter-factional strife within the local Republican Party by the proposal to set up a collective leadership, Swiss-style, with a rotating chairmanship; but again the personal ambitions present were too clamant for the pro-posal to succeed. One peculiar consequence of that particular struggle is the present dual leadership of the Vice-President and President of that party, both of whose portraits appear side by side in the pictorial literature of the party. It remains to be seen whether that very un-Puerto Rican arrangement will for long withstand the pressures of the Puerto Rican political character.

The power of the central executive committees of the parties is evident in a number of ways. They have a wide constitutional recog-nition. Both the Electoral Law and the Municipal Code confer upon them extensive powers of intervention in the registration and voting processes. The Primaries Law of 1956—which is entirely voluntary and has only been utilized by the *Popular* Party—also gives them generously wide powers; perhaps this helps to explain why that law has failed to alter in any way the distribution of power within the parties, as was indeed the pessimistic prophecy of the academic study on the subject made by a University of Puerto Rico group in 1955.[6] A primaries law, in any case, which is used only at the discretion of the party leaderships and, in the *Popular* case, works in such a manner that successful nomination in the primary means certain electoral victory (as in the one-party Democratic states of the American South) is hardly calculated to strengthen the position of rebel groups within the parties. A similar monolithism appears in the power of expulsion wielded by the party central committees. There appears, here again, to be few regulations, if any, governing that power. In the case of the *Populares* certainly it would be difficult to discover a general rule or indeed a general concept of what party membership actually means, in the record of the expulsions of Vicente Géigel Polanco and Representative Díaz Marchand; for in the first case the individual left the party after being relieved of a position of confidence by the Governor, while in the second case the individual felt obliged to resign his legislative seat after being expelled from the party, instead of sitting out the rest of his term as an independent. In the later Gutiérrez Franqui case a leading *Popular* Senator resigned his seat after being exonerated from charges of anti-*Popular* acts in his private legal capacity. Two things are noticeable: one, the failure to separate parliamentary matters from party matters and, two, the failure to provide an avenue of appeal from the central committee's disciplinary power. In part the failures testify to the arbitrary nature of the party discipline. In part they exemplify the absence (as in American parties) of a coherent philosophy by which disloyalty may be objectively judged. The *Popular* high command even appears to entertain the idea that a dissident party member ought not to be expelled so much as be expected to place himself voluntarily outside of the party. But this is a play on words that only serves to disguise the undemocratic assumption that there can be no room for vigorous variety of opinion within a party.[7] The assumption is related, in one way, to the anti-liberal attitude implicit, at the legislative level, in the doctrine of the mandate.

Everything in Puerto Rico thus conspires to blur the distinction between government and party so basic to the Anglo-American democratic system. Critics have referred to this as the fundamental political problem of the society. Apart from the Latin "revolutionary" tradition, already noted, there is additional confusion flowing from (1) the almost unrelieved reliance of the individual citizen upon the central government and (2) the fact that the primordial element of the social order itself—its constitutional status—has throughout been identified with political parties. When the Constitution of the *Estado Libre Asociado* is openly claimed to be the handiwork of the governing party there develops a situation not unlike, in some way, that of the French Third Republic after 1875, when the constitutional order itself becomes a football of party animosities, leaving the rest of the national debate to go almost by default. Granted the Puerto Rican cultural-political legacy, it would be utopian of course to expect anything else; that is why the critics go wrong who deplore all this on the assumption that the only feasible system is the Anglo-American model. It is unfortunate, even so, that the tendency of Puerto Rican legislation has been not to counteract this exaggeration of the political party role, but to reinforce it; and this can be legitimately criticized.

The political parties in the island have broad powers. They recommend personnel to the State Elections Board; name the officials of the local registration boards; are officially designated as agents for the issuance of voting cards to the electorate; and are "controlled" by a primaries law which makes the decision to hold a primary election the entirely voluntary responsibility of the party's governing council. It would be astonishing if these provisions, collectively, did not bring about the politicization of the registration and voting processes; and that is exactly the case. The registration period is treated by the party workers as a pre-electoral rehearsal, and the attitude inevitably encourages them to bring heavy political pressure upon the voter. No one can have witnessed the degradation of the priestly office perpetrated by the Catholic church in the registration of the new Catholic Action Party in 1960, or in the same year the melodramatic antics employed by the leaders of the new Democratic Party to get their group onto the ballot, including the strategic use of yachts, helicopters, and steelbands, without a strong conviction that there is much to be said for replacing present procedures with an automatic registration of the voter based upon periodical census records; as was indeed recommended by a group of legislators in the Legislative Assembly in November 1958.[8] The constitutional warranty of a free and secret vote is grossly violated by a variety of methods; and when some 71 percent of local political leaders believe that such methods exist and help to coerce the free will of the voter[9] it is clear that electoral reform has a long way yet to go in the society. Not even the closed polling station, the unique system in Puerto Rico of herding voters into a voting place on election day and confining them there until they have cast their vote, has managed, severe measure as it is, to exorcise the widespread popular skepticism about the purity of the vote.

Nor is the subsequent campaign exempt from the skepticism. The use of public property for party campaign purposes has already been noted. The extensive malpractices on that score convert the constitutional prohibition effectively into a dead letter. The distribution of public services to the *Popular* districts, in preference to others, especially in the immediate pre-election period; threats to withhold public welfare payments from the politically recalcitrant; the use of local town halls as political clubs; the payment of minor items such as gasoline bills with public funds; the flagrant abuse of departmental publications in the service of party propaganda, of which the case of the publication *Semana* put out for schools by the Department of Education is only the most scandalous one: there is more than enough evidence now to prove that all of these practices, at one point or another, are fairly common throughout the campaign period and particularly so in the *municipios*. The distribution of hurricane relief funds has been under suspicion too; at least it is one of the jokes of insular politics that Providence appears to provide Muñoz with a hurricane every election year. All this is not to say that the massive landslide victories of the *Populares* since 1944 have been only or even primarily due to such practices as these, for that party enjoys sufficiently widespread support without really resorting to them. Yet no one who reads, for instance, the local legislative debate on the new Municipal Code of 1958 can fail to perceive a *Popular* temptation to cross the dividing line between local politics and local administration in the name of their national "mission." The local party committees have made themselves the real source of nominations to the local administrations, to the point of superseding the local legislative assemblies with an elaborate spoils system. One consequence of this has been that, over the last ten or twelve years, there have been violent power struggles in more than fifty municipal governments between elected Mayors and nominated party officials. The experience of the Mayor of Aguadilla between 1944 and 1948, reported by himself (in 1958) in his capacity as national representative in the lower house, is perhaps not uncharacteristic of the state of open political civil war that frequently ensues.[10] The grave damage thereby inflicted upon the prestige of local government has been defended (in that same debate) with the argument that it has been traditional practice for municipal employees to lose their jobs on the occasion of a new mayoralty, and that this ought not now to be changed because "tradition makes law, and not law tradition." It is only fair to add that the Majority Leader of the House sturdily rejected that line of argument.[11]

What is needed, all in all, is for statutory development to move towards a sharper separation between party and state. The average unlettered Puerto Rican citizen finds it hard to distinguish in his mind between the *Popular* government and the *Popular* party. Too much of recent legislation does little to help him. Indeed it serves to deepen his confusion, since in clothing the political party with quasi-official functions it gravely compromises the status of the political party as a voluntary association within a pluralist society. This is graphically so with the case of the Electoral Fund created by legislative fiat in 1957. Under the law the Secretary of the Treasury is empowered to pay out to each of the established parties an amount up to $75,000 each non-election year and up to $150,000 during an election year. Each party that elects to take advantage of the fund (and is eligible to use it) must set up a formal organization to handle party funds and render a monthly report to both the Secretary of the Treasury and the Commonwealth Controller. Only two parties elected initially to accept the aid of the fund, the *Populares* and the Statehood Party. The former party, as a matter of interest, spent the largest item of its first grant—some $26,000—on radio, film, and television propaganda, while the Statehood Party's largest item— some $27,000—was spent on paid political announcements in the local newspapers.[12] The premise of the law (similar to one once entertained by the first President Roosevelt)—to offset the financial inequality of competing political parties—is admirable enough, and has been acclaimed, in its Puerto Rican expression, by some American political scientists.[13] Yet the public subsidization of political groups is open to serious objections from the perspective of the argument that is here being proposed. It compromises the voluntary nature of a party. It discourages the habit of voluntary payments of individual dues that ought to be at the heart of party fund-raising. It tends to further centralize party organization, since the party officialdom will now have access to moneys which, by definition, will be denied to inside dissident groups. It tends to freeze the status quo insofar as it strengthens the existing parties as against new ones likely to emerge in the future; and this last point should be seen in the light of the excessively stringent conditions presently controlling the acceptance of new parties on the ballot. The history of established churches in the modern state is testimony enough to the reality of these dangers. At least the dangers were obvious enough to persuade the leadership of the *Independentista* Party against acceptance of the Fund moneys in their memorandum of 1957.[14] Nor does the decision of that leadership, two years later, to reverse its stand and accept the state aid alter the persuasiveness of its earlier argument.

There are, more generally speaking, limits to legislating successfully against the power of private wealth in a class society. The legal prohibition against "kickbacks" by public servants has failed drastically in Puerto Rico; and there is little reason to believe that the prohibition (contained in the Electoral Fund law) against excessive private donations to a political party will turn out to be any more successful against the influence of the rich patron than has been the case with the comparable federal legislation. In establishing a state fund the Puerto Rican Legislature has simply tackled a symptom of the larger problem of the influence of money in politics. And when it goes on to state, in the preamble to the law, that "it is profoundly in the public interest that political parties be free from the control of economic forces, private or governmental, which, upon becoming necessary for the financing of the normal legitimate activities of political parties, might gain a control or influence over them that would be inimical to the democratic ideal," the student of politics is tempted to offer two observations. The first is that any attempt to build a wall between economic and political power in any society, but especially in a business society, is easier said than done and assumes too readily that both can coexist as separate compartments divided in a watertight fashion from each other. The whole idea of such a separation is artificial and moreover, if steadily applied, would have the consequence, among others, of preventing the development within Puerto Rico of a new party system based upon a healthy and balanced alliance of party and organized labor. The second observation is that, even if separation were possible, the consequence of legislation after the Puerto Rican pattern might well be to substitute the influence of public patronage for that of private wealth. The remedy could be as unfortunate as the disease for it could destroy in time the very essence of a political party in a democratic society as a voluntary association depending mainly upon the devotion and the sacrifices, including financial, of the mass of its ordinary members. It could merely do nothing more than give a new economic support to the manipulators and the professional careerists in the political parties, and it is enough to watch the struggle between the leaderships of the rival youth groups in the *Popular* Party to appreciate how deeply imbedded is that tendency in Puerto Rican politics already.

Throughout the last generation there has been a revolution in Latin American political parties reflected in part in a revolution in party titles. As the question of national independence has given way, under the tremendous pressure of social forces, to the social question, the old party names, originally borrowed from the European party lexicon, have given way to names more appropriate to the new issues. Liberals and Conservatives, Democrats and Republicans, have slowly yielded to other more radical groups, the *Asociación Revolucionaria Americana* in Peru, the *Acción Democrática* in Venezuela, the *Frente Nacional* in Colombia, the *Colorados* and *Blancos* of Uruguay. The outstanding feature of Puerto Rican politics in one sense has been its inability to follow that continental pattern. It is true that the Unionist Party, by its name, sought after 1904 to personify a national front superseding partisan divisions, but the attempt failed. The Popular Democratic Party, again, sought after 1940 to transcend the divisions with its appeal to the "revolution of 1940." But its tremendous electoral successes have not enabled it, any more than its rivals, to escape the dark omnipresence of the status issue or to remain for long aloof from the need of attempting to slice that Gordian knot. The leading characteristic, then, of all three Puerto Rican parties today remains still the answers they seek to provide respectively to the problem of the Puerto Rican relationship with the American power. The local Republican Party, quite simply, wants federated statehood; the *Independentista* Party, full sovereign independence; and the *Populares,* a continuation of the present Commonwealth status. The leading issue, that is to say, mirrors the psychology of a colonial society. So powerful indeed is the tyranny of the issue that there is a prevalent belief that party ideologies that gather around it are somehow "natural" and that any others must be viewed suspiciously as being "artificial."[15] The accidents of colonial history thus become identified with the laws of political nature.

The rise of the *Populares* and their record of government have already been noted. Their main problem today is without doubt that of maintaining and expanding a healthy democratic climate of opinion within a monolithic party structure. The great achievement of Muñoz has been to hold together the varying factions of the party and to prevent any repetition of his own revolt, between 1936 and 1938, against the leadership of the aging Barceló in the former Liberal Party. For the secession of the *independentista* group, led by Gilberto Concepción de Gracia in 1945-1946, never promised to become that serious. Yet the party has paid a heavy price for that success. The structure of command at all levels remains posited upon the habit of *caciquismo.* The perennial conflicts between the local municipal committees and the district party legislators point to a failure to solve the problem of the party-government relationship at the lower levels. Nor is the moral tone of the party leadership at the *barrio* level very high; and the frequency with which the investigating and disciplinary powers of the central committee have been invoked in the last few years is a disturbing sign. Healthy and free debate between the various sections has been quietly discouraged or even repressed on the odd assumption, apparently, that "democratic" opinion means unanimous opinion. The best example of that attitude, of course, has been the now famous break between the Governor and Don Jaime Benítez, the Rector of the University and one of the Governor's former intimates. In many ways it has been a quixotic comedy of errors. For the Governor "withdraws" his "confidence" from the Rector in a characteristic *pronunciamiento* from his mountain retreat; but he fails to itemize charges beyond a vague reference to a *faena política* against his leadership within the University precincts; nor does he seek to use his appointive power in the University's governing council, the Superior Educational Council, to obtain (as he could) an anti-Benítez majority that could then proceed to unseat the offender. The Rector, on the other hand, maintains an Olympian silence; and, as far as is known, no attempt is made to use the machinery of the party to heal the rift or even to discuss its sources. The division is neither public nor private; it operates within the twilight zone of gossip and speculation, broken intermittently by an outburst of angry newspaper articles written by the thinly disguised friends or open partisans of each of the compelling personalities of the drama. Nothing could more fittingly illustrate at once the ideological indecisiveness of the party and once more the dangerous intermixture of party and government matters, for it has never been made clear whether the Governor's distrust of the Rector refers to the latter's position as a public official or to his status as a party member. The effect of all this upon the continuity of the educational process at the University has been one of almost incalculable damage.

The party in effect has become the prisoner of the government. In the phrase of one critic, the *Populares* have substituted the administrative process for the political process. The early enthusiasms have given way to the routine of office. There has been a noticeable shift from economic and social innovation to conservative constitution-making. The original appeal of Muñoz to the *jíbaro* to sacrifice the immediate hope of money in exchange for his vote for the long-term view has now been forgotten; and, sadly enough, the electoral appeal of the Popular Democratic Party is today a variant on the "you never had it so good" theme. The party machinery, after the American fashion, remains dormant except in election years. It was an odd coincidence at least that the flutter of "educational activity" set off by the party leadership in late 1959 took place at much the same time as the Statehood Party opposition was beginning openly to anticipate victory in the 1960 elections. The activity was impressive enough, for it included (as organized by the party *Comisión de Orientación Pública*) a scheme of day-long schools in which lectures and discussions would be held throughout the island by some eighty leaders, and intended to reach a total of some 20,000 leaders of rural and municipal party committees. For the first time in local political history, it was claimed, a political party two decades old undertook an exhaustive stocktaking of its past, present, and future by means of such a program.[16] That may be so. But as a program it hardly begins to match the remarkable program of adult civic education undertaken by Dr. Eric Williams and the Trinidad Peoples National Movement after 1956 in their now internationally famous "University of Woodforde Square." And if the *Popular* Party press (almost non-existent save for a fortnightly *Boletín Popular*) is compared with the PNM weekly newspaper, *The Nation*, at one time ably edited by the West Indian writer and historian C.L.R. James, it must be admitted that the Puerto Rican liberal-reformist movement has so far done practically nothing in the general and continuous civic education of its party membership. Nor are the administrative reforms within the top leadership structure that were announced in 1960 likely soon to mean much. For although they introduced vital changes—the enlargement of the Central Committee, for example, to include, in addition to the party legislative members, representatives from the constituency groups and mayoral candidates —it remains to be seen whether the replacement of the unipersonal presidency of the party with a presidential commission of seven persons, themselves to be elected by a presidential panel of nineteen persons and rotating in membership every three months,[17] will not prove to be such a complicated and cumbersome method of party government that leadership will revert, once again, into the hands of the Governor as party leader.

Time alone will tell. But, these reforms notwithstanding (including the further innovation of holding two general party conventions every four-year period), the old emphasis upon the mystique of personal leadership is certain to remain for some time. It is, of course, not a uniquely Puerto Rican phenomenon; the gradual metamorphosis of Mr. Manley in Jamaica from the Fabian intellectual of 1940 into the "Man of Destiny" of 1960 in the leadership of that island's Peoples' National Party indicates that this is perhaps a general phenomenon of Caribbean politics. But the whole cultural *ambiente* of Puerto Rican life conspires throughout to aid and abet the phenomenon. It is worth noting that a recent authoritative study on the morphology of the insular politics, Professor Anderson's *Party Politics in Puerto Rico*, warns that, however Mexican the Puerto Rican system may appear to be, the dominant party has yet to find the secret of successfully emulating the Mexican achievement of organizing the effective institutionalized continuation of itself as a movement transcending the personality of its leader and of therefore solving the urgent problem of the peaceful passage of party authority from one generation to another. So long as it fails there, Puerto Rico seems doomed to the continuation of a party politics ideologically empty and tactically relativistic.[18]

Professor Anderson does not spell out in detail what that is likely to mean. But the present state of the *Popular* Party, its loss of ideological direction, its growing patronage establishment, its ruthless politicization of government and administration, provides more than enough evidence for a dusty answer. No one single phenomenon could better illustrate it all than the nature of the political machine nurtured in San Juan by the well-known *Popular* Mayor, Doña Felisa Rincón de Gautier. "Doña Fela" has made herself into a leading *Popular* commissar by methods traditionally well-known in American city machine politics: the use of public funds for the distribution of gifts—shoes, medicines, petty cash—to the low-income masses of the San Juan slums; the inclusion of party "neighborhood deputies" on the city payroll; the enlarged budgetary expenditures during election years, and so on. She herself possesses the regal air to accompany all this, for her attitude to "her" people is not unlike the graceful condescension of a Castilian queen to her royal entourage. She throws parties for the San Juan poor in the most impeccable of benevolently feudal manners; possesses at once a taste and a flair for publicity; and collects citations such as "Latin American Woman of the Year" as avidly as other women collect hats or love affairs. The frequent absenteeism from her mayoral post that this involves is perhaps enough in itself to justify the growing dissatisfaction with the present method of mayoral election through the medium of a Board of Commissioners nominated by the Governor with the consent of the Senate. It is symptomatic of the lethargy that has overcome the *Popular* machine that an attempted defense of the city administration in response to the 1962 critical articles of *The San Juan Star* could not manage anything more intellectually persuasive than Earl Parker Hanson's pitiable plea that "virtually every municipal government of any consequence in the United States is also, and must be by the nature of things in our democratic system, a political machine."[19] A student of American municipal politics might be forgiven for thinking that a defense a little more plausible, even much more convincing, might have been made along the lines that, as the famous George Washington Plunkett once said of the New York Tammany Tiger machine, the machine politician at least goes down into the gutter to help the socially disinherited; for there is little evidence that the moralizing reformers of *The San Juan*

Star possess much of a concern for the denizens of the San Juan slum gutters. It only remains to be added that "Doña Fela's" colorful politics are occasionally interspersed with fascinating lectures that she gives to the local feminine clubs on the language of the ladies' fan.

All this, of course, is a particular example of a general malaise. Yet what is regrettable is less the general picture than the perverse arguments that seek to rationalize it. Thus it is a pity that Rexford Tugwell's recent *The Art of Politics*, which is in part a study of Muñoz, should give aid and comfort to the whole thing with its temptation to argue that the emergence of a leader of the Muñoz type resides upon half-mystical factors not readily susceptible to rational identification and discussion. There is, indeed, and especially on the part of American liberal political scientists, more than a tendency to pen a literature of exaggerated lyricism around the figure of Muñoz as a leader. For the truth is that, since his first great campaign of 1938, Muñoz has not so much led his people as followed their major prejudices. He has, in fact, elaborated a peculiar theory of leadership in which the abandonment of the independence ideal can be justified on the ground that a leader must only give the people what they want. The theory of plebiscitary democracy is thus used to rationalize the political status quo; nor is it apparently considered that, in a mass society of politically controlled mass media, the "people" may just as easily want what they get as get what they want. Those mass media in Puerto Rico have in fact been recruited in the service of a relentless propaganda campaign to vilify the idea of independence, to persuade the people that independence will bring economic chaos and political instability; and the resultant mass fear of independence has then been cited as proof that the people do not want it. The new debate so urgently needed on independence must first of all clear away this phobia. But there is little chance that the task will be undertaken by a government party which presently suffers, as did the British Conservative Party in 1945 and the American Democratic Party in 1952, from the lethargy that comes from an extended tenure of power.

The *Popular* Party suffers from being too long in power. The Republican Statehood Party suffers from being out of power too long. For it is the heir of the Coalition that governed until 1940 and has never really forgiven Muñoz the ouster of that year. Since then it has been obliged to rehabilitate itself and to widen its appeal, for, traditionally, its appeal—as with its first leader Barbosa—has represented only the opinion concentrated in the metropolitan zones of the coastal areas and rarely penetrated the high sierra of the interior. The rehabilitation has been purchased at a heavy price, involving bitter internal feuds and personal rivalries. For just as in 1924 the party had been split by the rivalry between Martínez Nadal and Tous Soto on the occasion of the latter's decision to take the party into a Unionist alliance, so in 1941 the death of Martínez Nadal was followed by a bitter struggle to inherit his mantle between the "old guard" and the newcomers. Not until 1952 indeed was the issue finally resolved when —as already noted—the present dual leadership of García Méndez and Ferré wrenched control from the hands of the old Iriarte group under rather bizarre circumstances. It is perhaps only the hope of an electoral victory, with the entry of Alaska and Hawaii into statehood, that prevents the wounds left from those struggles from opening up again.

Politically, the Republican program from the beginning has been a replica of American constitutionalism, even to the point of reproducing the obvious defects of the model; thus the Humacao 1914 platform of the party advocated the separation of powers between executive and legislature, a popularly elected Senate and the executive appointment of all agency heads with senatorial consent.[20] The party's favorite nostrums accordingly join together in seeking to curb the powers of government to an almost eighteenth-century level: the separation of local and central elections, a constitutional limitation upon gubernatorial re-eligibility after two terms of service, general reduction in taxation. Paradoxically the party also wants the compulsory vote, on the Australian model, something calculated to strengthen official power over individual liberty, and in spite of the fact that the percentage of voter abstention in the island—between 18 and 22 percent—is not alarmingly high. The sense of paradox disappears, however, if it is remembered that most of these nostrums spring not so much from a reasoned political philosophy (which the Statehood Party does not have any more, in the fullest sense, than the *Popular* and *Independentista* Parties) as from a desire to curb the powers of a hated Governor. For the local Republicans hate Muñoz no less frenziedly than their continental counterparts hated the figure of Franklin Roosevelt a generation back; and in fact they repeat against Muñoz in Puerto Rico the sort of ugly personal gossip that was launched against the President at that time by the Republican "primitives." It is not too difficult to meet *estadistas* who believe, or claim to believe, that the Governor is a dipsomaniac, or is becoming mentally unbalanced, or suffers from even worse diseases. Their intellectual paucity is further underlined by their persistent slogan that the Governor is a dictator. The truth is indeed that it is Muñoz and not his Republican opponents who has publicly denounced the real dictatorships of the Caribbean area. The Republican silence in that matter, as one critic has suggested, may be related to the fact that the party's vice-president has owned extensive business holdings in some of those dictatorships, notably the Venezuelan regime of Pérez Jiménez before its downfall in 1958.[21]

For—not to put too fine a point on it—the local Republican Party is the party of local wealth. For while analysis of the social origins of the *Popular* leadership reveals, it is true, a high percentage of men and women from the upper middle-class stratum, a large number of them at the same time are professionals and intellectuals of modest means; the Republican leadership, on the other hand, is one of extremely wealthy individuals. The leader, García Méndez, is president of a large sugar-making concern and prominent member of the Puerto Rico Sugar Producers Association. Its vice-president, Luis Ferré, is president of a large complex of industries in the Caribbean region and owner of the large cement industry in the southern part of the island. The leading island newspaper, *El Mundo*, has been generally Republican in its sympathies; but there is nothing in the social background of the Republican high command to compare with the rise of that paper's late owner, Angel Ramos, from an apprentice printer, coming from the humble township of Manatí, to the leading press lord of the society. Naturally enough, the hard core of the party's efforts centers around the demand for what is termed somewhat ambiguously "more representation" for the "economic power" in government. It is even possible that the demand for statehood itself plays second fiddle to that ambition. At least Theodore Brameld discovered, in his studies of selective public opinion, that there was a large consensus of thought which suspected that the statehood demand was to some extent used as a vote-getting strategy in order to restore power to the local top socio-economic class.[22] The party certainly agitates vehemently for the abdication of welfare programs to private enterprise, which would mean a return to the reactionary Republicanism of the old Coalition regime and, to take one example only, the replacement of the new Port Authority in maritime communications with the old private White Star Line.[23] The party's gubernatorial candidate, again, has spoken of a capital-labor relationship wherein the worker might be consulted in matters of factory discipline and organization but wherein, too, the decisive production decisions would still apparently remain the exclusive prerogative of management.[24] It is only fair to add that on this score the Ferré industrial philosophy is certainly ahead of the prehistoric attitudes to labor still affected by the more traditionalist island businessman, frequently of direct Spanish ancestry, and too is by no means behind the managerial attitudes to labor in the Fomento factories. Yet altogether the party "philosophy" is more that of the Taft variety than it is of the Dewey-Eisenhower-

Rockefeller variety. There is little evidence to suggest that the "new" Republicanism of the American political right since 1952 has penetrated its thinking. Nor is it likely that the opinion of one local writer that Ferré combines the austerity of a Lincoln with the dynamism of a Henry Ford is anything more than a pardonable exercise in partisan exaggeration.[25]

In the meantime the party hopes to benefit from the growing conservatism of the new booming middle-class groups that are presently enjoying the economic and educational standards provided by the changes of the last two decades. As the members of those groups crowd into their bright new concrete villas in the flourishing suburbia of *Villa Nevares* and *Puerto Nuevo* and *El Commandante* they develop all the psychoses of the insecure property owner, and, like English Puritan bourgeois families turning Anglican Tory in the Augustan age, they express their changing attitudes in the search for more "respectable" political affiliations. It is thus possible to see the heavier vote for the Statehood Party in the 1956 elections—its candidates doubled their total vote from 85,591 in 1952 to 171,910 four years later—as a protest vote of citizens on those new social levels. This is perhaps why the Statehood opposition openly asserts Muñoz's secret adherence to his old ideal of political independence, for nothing terrifies the instinct of local property more than the apprehension of constitutional severance from the United States. To portray the Governor as a Puerto Rican *fidelista* in disguise (however fanciful that may be to anyone who knows him closely) becomes a clever tactic, for it plays on the nerve centers of a real fear. That is perhaps also why the Statehood leaders refused to endorse, in contrast with the *Popular* and *Independentista* leaders, the horror of all Puerto Rican liberals at the attempt of Puerto Rican clericalism to deploy its preventive jurisdiction over the body of Catholic communicants in the open interests of a partisan political viewpoint; although it is heartening to record that the returns of the 1960 election did not justify the high hopes of that cynical strategy. Be that as it may, the new urbanized groups constitute a challenge to *Popular* leadership with their new social gentility. An analysis, for example, of the 1956 election returns shows that the government party strength still remains at its highest level in the rural areas and at its most precarious in the town areas. This is the prevailing pattern although there are curious exceptions: it is hard to understand why, for example, the mountain *municipio* of Adjuntas and the south coast *municipio* of San Lorenzo are anti-*Popular*. Correspondingly the Republican electoral strength is concentrated in the larger cities and their suburban outskirts, although it has to be noted that, despite the 1956 increases, the party strength has not yet equaled that of its predecessor, the old Coalition party, in the 1948 elections.[26] But the pattern is clear enough. It remains to be seen, within the '60s, whether the growing rural depopulation and the corresponding increase in the size of the urban populations will have the effect of finally reversing, in favor of the Republicans, the present distribution of voter preferences.

It is perhaps because of this situation of electoral flux that Republican strategy today appears to concentrate upon tactics rather than philosophy. The party activists address open letters to the public by means of paid newspaper advertisements. They lobby visiting American Congressmen by means of vigorous reception groups at the International Airport. They turn out, with others, to welcome the Kennedys on the presidential state visit to San Juan. They organize huge demonstrations, mostly composed of party members in comfortable automobiles. They buttonhole the visiting dignitaries of the American State Governors annual meeting; decorate their automobiles with "Estado 51" stickers; and try to match the annual trek of Puerto Ricans to the birthplace of Muñoz Rivera in the exquisite little mountain town of Barranquitas with an annual gathering at the grave of Barbosa in old San Juan. Above all, they have recently become adept at setting up a variety of "front organizations" that agitate as supposedly non-party supporters of statehood. So far there are the Council of Federal Employees (who have an obvious interest in statehood), the *Asociación Pro-Estado 51*, the *Acción Pro-Estado Federado*, and the *Congreso Pro-Acción Plebiscitaria*, the latter concentrating its activities upon propaganda for a Congress-sponsored plebiscite on the status issue. There will probably be more of these before the issue is resolved. Altogether it would not be unduly unfair to say that so far the party leadership has signally failed to throw up any leader of at once statesmanlike quality and personal magnetism. The party has seemed too much to be composed of men prepared to pay any price for the chance of electoral victory. Nor has it managed to draw to itself more than a modicum of outstanding intellectual support; there is no intellectual adherent of the movement who even begins to look like its Burke or its Hamilton. It is at least one of the lasting achievements of Governor Muñoz that from the beginning he has been able to attract to himself some of the outstanding intelligences of the society: Jaime Benítez, to begin with, and new able young men like Eugenio Fernández-Méndez, Carlos Lastra, Ramón García Santiago, Angel Quintero Alfaro, Pedro Muñoz-Amato, and José Trías-Monge. The Statehood Republican protagonists have yet a long road to travel in that respect.

Yet the real weakness of the party lies in the ambiguity that sur-

rounds its basic character. For it is at once a local movement of conservative forces seeking, as is evident from the public image of Ferré
himself, to confer upon the businessman a respectable political role;
and a pressure group battling for statehood within the Union and
being led, in that role, by the more professional type of politician after
the manner of García-Méndez. For many of its adherents it is simply
a vehicle for the attainment of statehood, an attitude aptly summed up
in the remark of one of its legislative members, Senator Santos
Amadeo, that if Muñoz were to accept statehood he himself would
become a *Popular* tomorrow. Yet so long as that end-result remains a
hope only the party, of necessity, functions as a political lobbyist for
local wealth and affluence; and the more, indeed, the dream of statehood remains unfulfilled the more certain is it that that aspect of the
party will more and more prevail. For, as things stand, the dream
seems as far off as ever. As long ago as 1928 a New England liberal
friendly to Puerto Rican aspirations pointed out that the gross disparity between the Congressional ill-treatment of Puerto Rico and the
pampered status of Hawaii had been due in large measure to the fact
that the Pacific territory from the very beginning had enjoyed the
leadership of a group of wealthy and powerful residents of continental
American stock to whom Congress would always listen, while Puerto
Rico enjoyed no such advantage.[27] The disadvantage still prevails, for
the families and corporations investing in Puerto Rico remain, overwhelmingly, absentee forces necessarily little interested in the politics
of the territory. Nor can statehood be accelerated, as it was in the
Hawaiian case, by playing upon the notorious Congressional phobia
about Communism; it would be difficult to cast Puerto Rican labor
leaders like Frank Chavez or Hipolito Marcano in the role of a Harry
Bridges, while not even the most frenzied efforts of Representative
Rubén Rivera Ramos have been able to discover a Communist plot in
the island. As a consequence of all this, the party is in a state of perennial turmoil. It is yet another illustration of the central disease of
insular politics that, every so often, newspaper speculation resuscitates
the possibility that rejuvenation can come about by the candidacy of
Don Jaime Benítez as a new party leader. It remains to be seen
whether such a possibility can emerge out of the many *alter egos* that
live together in the lively personality of the University Chancellor.

Certainly ever since the abortive Tydings Bill of 1936 independence for Puerto Rico, meaning a complete separation from the United
States, has seemed a feasible goal to one continuing section of local
political thought and opinion. The local custodian of the ideal, since
1948, has been the *Partido Independentista Puertorriqueño*. Elec-

torally, it has recently been on the decline, having been replaced in 1956 by the Republican Statehood Party as the leading opposition group. Its vote in that year indeed dropped catastrophically from some 126,000 to nearly a half of that figure, 86,101, and in only six towns did it manage to poll as much as 25 percent of the total votes cast; and that it fared no better in 1960 was in large measure due to the fact that all liberal opinion appears in that year to have gone in sympathetic support to the Governor in his stand against clericalist politics. What are the reasons for this? Before that question is answered it ought to be noted that the ideal of an independent republic has been an honorable one in the island for a century or more. It animated the liberal spirits under Spain—Ruiz Belvis, Acosta, Betances, de Hostos. It was the main reason why many Puerto Ricans supported the American intervention in 1898. It was accepted for years after that event by the early Unionist Party as a legitimate alternative to statehood and self-governing autonomy within the American system. It is true that Governor Muñoz, in his now celebrated Cidra Declaration of 1959, ruled out independence as a candidate for plebiscitary acceptance or rejection, and thereby dealt the party a brutal and illiberal blow calculated to place in jeopardy its very survival as a party legitimately seeking the support of the Puerto Rican voter. But, in doing that, the Governor showed himself to be possessed of a lesser magnanimity than his forebears of the old Unionist Party who, in their famous foundation meeting of 1904, allowed the paladin of the *independentista* faith, José de Diego, to make a belated but successful plea for the retention of independence as a feasible solution to the status question. As such, it cannot be dismissed by any arbitrary action aimed at denying to the party currently espousing the ideal its democratic opportunity to have its case tested, on a ground of equal chance, before the court of local opinion.

The fear of the economic consequences of independence is undoubtedly a major factor in the party's recent decline. People fear the effect of political separatism upon American capital investment and the whole future of the new prosperity under the industrialization program. The fear is certainly cleverly exploited as a means of dampening enthusiasm for independence. Yet it is probable that it is ill founded. For talk of Jamaican secession from the new West Indies Federation during the last two years has not slowed down American and Canadian investments in that neighboring Antillean island; and now that the talk has ended in actual secession it has yet to be shown that the withdrawal into a separate Jamaican independence will damage the economic growth of the island. Nor is there anything in the *Independentista* Party platform to suggest that, on gaining power, it

would seek to emulate the confiscatory program of the neighboring
Cuban Revolution. At the same time, even while this is so, it is true
to say that the party leadership has done little itself to mollify the fear.
It ought to address itself, at the least, to a study of the economic
consequences of independence; it ought to draw up plans covering the
successive stages within which the necessary economic adjustments
could be made with least damage to the economy; above all, it ought
to demand, as a leading item in its economic program, the arrangement of a long-term economic treaty with the United States whereby
the American power would be required to undertake a sort of Marshall Plan aid to the economy during the transitional period from
dependence to independence as a token of its moral obligations to the
Caribbean ward. But little enough along these lines has been attempted. Nor indeed are people reassured when the party attempts
to belittle the very real achievements of Operation Bootstrap. For to
argue that the island's inclusion within the continental free-trade system has benefited only two or three lines of local business is to ignore
the fact that the inclusion benefits the Commonwealth regime as a
whole to something like $150 million or $175 million each year and,
beyond that, the fact that the rate of general social return to government cost in the industrialization program has paid off with handsome
dividends for living standards as a whole (from 1950 to 1956, for
example, a total cost of some $30 million brought in a total benefit of
some $106 million).[28]

The party's appeal is further handicapped because in its social and
economic program it accepts the mixed-economy and welfare-state
policies of the government party and only recommends additions of
degree rather than changes of kind: a more careful concern for agriculture, a more "nativist" industrializing program, a more effective
control of absentee capital and the extension of public holdings for
the benefit of the small farmer. It is worth noting that the program of
the *Movimiento Pro Independencia* is not much more radical, for in its
own declaration of principles it advocates nothing more startling than
an economic system wherein workers shall be guaranteed some share
of profits and the employer a reasonable profit margin.[29] Very little
thus divides the independent-minded opposition groups from their
government opponent on these matters. Nor is it likely that a "turn to
the left" will come from a party, in the case of the *Independentistas*,
the leadership of which is largely composed of doctors, lawyers, artists,
and teachers; in the 1956 Legislature the nine party legislators included six lawyers, a fact that encourages preoccupation with politico-
constitutional questions rather than with economics. Nor again is a
radical theme likely to come from a party that announces itself as the

principal defender of a middle class which, according to the party argument, has been brutally proletarianized by the government programs,[30] for all the evidence supports the quite different conclusion that it is the government party that itself has become more and more comfortably middle class in its outlook. The more extremist Nationalist groups are no more genuinely working-class in their convictions and ideas; certainly the attempt of César Andreu Iglesias in his novel *Los Derrotados* to establish a relationship between the nationalist movement and the working-class movement fails to convince the reader. And as a last word on this matter, the generally middle-class character of the various groups seeking independence, their combination of social conservatism and political radicalism, is nonetheless real despite the fact that a rival *Socialist Association of Puerto Rico* was formed in 1956, for the announcement of principles published by that group was not so much socialist in any real sense of the word as just another rhetorical appeal to liberty, democracy and fraternity.[31]

The leading weakness of the *independentista* forces, until recently, has been their disability to construct a united front, as well as the fact that, lacking a striking leader, they fail to meet one of the basic requirements of a personalist politics. The *Independentista* Party itself was born out of a defecting element, the Pro-Independence Congress of the 1940's, within the *Popular* Party and in its own turn it has spawned its own dissident offshoots. There is at least one such offshoot, the *Movimiento Pro Independencia*, of a growing popular appeal, and other minor factions like the *Acción Vigilancia Patriótica* and the *Partido La Voz del Pueblo*; while there is a never-ceasing proliferation of small groups—the *Movimiento 30 de Octubre*, for example—that straddle the gap between the Independents and the Nationalists. The defeat of 1956 and, worse still, the crushing blow of the 1960 election in which the *Independentista* Party failed even to obtain the 10 percent of the vote required to maintain official recognition, have naturally encouraged bitter criticisms of the present leadership. It is said that they have allowed themselves to become a comfortable opposition group in the Legislature, neglecting the more urgent duties of a nationalist-libertarian party as the "bureaucratic appetite" has seized hold of them.[32] The fight on the national front has been placed second to the fight on the parliamentary front, with unhappy consequences; and there is a distinct note of anti-parliamentary syndicalism in the demand of the *MPI* group for a non-party workers' organization that would recommend electoral action or electoral abstention to its members as particular issues arose.[33] The decline of the leading independent party, indeed, is traced by some of the more *auténtico* spirits to its acceptance of a functional role in the parliamentary institutions set up by the 1951-1952 Constituent Assembly notwithstanding the party's original boycotting of that body at the time.[34]

That whole question, indeed, of what should constitute the proper strategy of a movement which is pledged to abolish a politico-legal machinery of government it regards as being wholly colonialist in character is the leading problem of the radical groups. The ideology of *retraimento*, of complete withdrawal from the parliamentary game, is one that in turn has attracted and repelled the *Independentista* Party, for apart from that earlier paradox of strategy there is the later paradox involved in first rejecting the financial aid offered by the state Electoral Fund on the ground of the old sentiment of Puerto Rican politics, *verguenza contra dinero*, and then later accepting it as pressures set in, after 1959, flowing out of pre-election anxieties. Nor is this fatal ambiguity of attitude restricted to the independent groups, for it also plagues the Statehood Party, as is evident enough in that party's decision to boycott the 1962 plebiscite, despite the fact that the party's parliamentary group had lent at least its presence to the legislative enactment of the machinery of the plebiscite. The ambiguity is similarly strikingly illuminated by the cruel dilemma faced by all of the independent groupings as they have been called upon to take an attitude, friendly or hostile, to the uncompromising terrorism of the extremist Nationalist elements. To criticize is to invite the charge of cowardice and treason; to applaud is to be charged with being friendly to a strategy of political assassination. The *Popular* Party can afford, in the twilight of its respectability, to taunt the *Independentista* Party with the support of murder on the occasion of that latter group's indirect praise for the Nationalist revolt of 1950; but the historian will remember that in his earlier independence days Muñoz himself was guilty of a similar ambiguity in his refusal to sign a statement openly condemning the Nationalist murderers of the local Chief of Police in 1936. In this sense Puerto Rican politics, all in all, are a politics of ambiguity. In part, this is ideological: if a party decides not to go for outright independence, it is caught in the web of the status debate, and that explains why so many insular parties have been able, without any apparent awareness of illogicality, to support two or even three alternative answers to the status issue at the same time. In part, it is tactical: on the one hand, to participate in the local machinery of government is to be suspected of colonialist collaborationism; on the other, to withdraw from participation (as Muñoz himself, at an earlier date, had once contemplated) is to court the grave danger of permanent isolation from the center of the insular affairs. The psychological ambivalence of a colonial people is thus reflected in an unavoidable political ambivalence.

The surprising thing is that, notwithstanding all this, the independent principle manages to survive as a virile idea. It is true that, as yet, it lacks a charismatic leader, so necessary in the small Caribbean societies. For Albizu languishes in prison as an aged and sick man; and Muñoz is the "lost leader" who has sought more and more to play the role of a public official of the imperial metropolis and less and less that of a patriot leader of his people, seeking less to forge a new nation than to find solutions to problems that are overwhelmingly American rather than Puerto Rican. There is evidence to suggest, however, that as the independent principle loses ground on the electoral front it is gaining ground on the educational. The cultural-literary meetings at the *Ateneo,* enthusiastically patriotic in tone, testify to the strong support of the Creole intelligentsia. Writers like César Andreu Iglesias and Manrique Cabrera produce weekly and daily journalistic columns of effective satire. *El Imparcial* vigorously attacks the Government, finds encouragement in its Director's visit to Trinidad on the eve of that territory's independence, compares the support of the principle of national independence in President Kennedy's letter of congratulation to Prime Minister Bustamante of Jamaica with the abandonment of the principle contained in the President's correspondence with Governor Muñoz at much the same time. At the same time, what Professor Anderson has called "the politics of patriotism" are sedulously pursued by the more activist pro-independent groups. The *Movimiento Pro Independencia,* in particular, has set about to establish an island-wide organizational and educational structure based upon the three-man cell unit and an ideology of a non-partisan popular struggle for independence, thus following the attitude of the earlier *Congreso Pro Independencia* of 1943. It holds regular mass meetings, celebrates the birthday of Albizu, pickets the local Puerto Rican residence of Representative Adam Clayton Powell, allocates special duties to each regional group of the national mission, sends its student affiliates to international youth conferences, offers legal aid and advice to members in trouble with the insular or federal investigating agencies and publishes a weekly organ, *Claridad,* and a lively *Carta Semanal.* Its leaders have clearly seen that what the independence struggle now needs is a long and intensive non-partisan educational campaign, turning its back at once on the sterile politics and the semantic turgidity of the colonial politicians and seeking a genuine support from people in all walks of life. They have at least brought a new militancy into a movement that has become far too languid. Nor should sight be lost of the significant fact that, in the *Mesa de Lares* of 1962, all of the various *independentista* forces have at long last been able to come together in a united front against the common foe. It remains to be seen whether that newly found unity can survive the crisis of the plebiscite that originally called it into being.

It would therefore be a profound error of judgment to believe that, whatever happens to its party expressions, the *independentista* ideal in the island will gradually disappear. The party expressions will no doubt continue to oscillate between a kaleidoscopic variety of groups. But its basic sentiment, that of a proud people yearning for a national identity, clear and distinct, seeking to become a coherent entity rather than a rootless multitude, is far too deeply entrenched, even perhaps in many members of the ruling party, to be lightly dismissed. There is a ready tendency to push its adherents summarily aside as impossible dreamers, or even something worse. The contemptuous remark of one local American journalist—that one of the movement's groups, the Puerto Rican National Liberation Front, is "a heterogeneous tide— bunches of old-line Nationalists, Castro inspired students, *independentistas* who have lost hope in the ballot box, maybe some Communists"[35]—is not unrepresentative. The ideal of independence of course has its lunatic fringe in the gunmen of the Nationalist Party. But they constitute a psychiatrical rather than a political problem, as a reading, once again, of *Los Derrotados* makes clear. Their emotional instability can be seen in that novel's character Marcos Vega, a man whose nationalism flows less from a reasoned faith than from the hatreds that the exploitation and injustices suffered by his father have left with him; how such types live on the edge of emotional breakdown is evident enough. The real harm they do is to furnish proof to the American citizen who knows little about the island that independence means terrorist nationalism. It is possible that even the average Puerto Rican citizen will be tempted into that facile conclusion, for there are powerful forces on the side of the status quo that are more than ready to tell him that independence for the island means inevitable social chaos, just as in the nineteenth century the defendants of the slavery issue in the Caribbean were ready to argue that abolitionism would mean a black Haitian civil war in every island that attempted it. Such misconceptions may hamper the ideal of independence; they can hardly obliterate it. Indeed there are signs that as the balance of membership within the United Nations shifts towards the newly emancipated nations of Africa and Asia that body will become less and less ready to accept the official United States view that independence is irrelevant to the Puerto Rican problem.

The American critic, again, who comforts himself with the thought that the independence groups have only small followings is likely to find himself being reminded, even by an official United States Congress document, that his own revolution of 1776 was carried through by an energetic minority and that in any case the moral worth of an idea ought not to be vulgarly assessed simply in terms of the numerical support that it can muster at any given time.[36] Nor should it be overlooked that the one great service that the *independentista* groups offer to their *patria chica* is their close association with like-minded political movements throughout Latin America, a service vital enough when it is remembered that the Commonwealth government has been signally unsuccessful in persuading even Latin American liberal opinion that Commonwealth association is an adequate substitute for national independence. For the *Popular* Party, as well as the *Estadista* Party, is United States-oriented, and that fact alone makes both of them suspect throughout the continent. The name of Albizu Campos remains still the symbol throughout the southern hemisphere of Puerto Rican freedom; and it is a fact, after all, that Albizu was the ardent champion of a larger Caribbean freedom—as his tour throughout Haiti, Santo Domingo, and Cuba in 1927 showed—long before those who presently vilify him in the Puerto Rican press had even become aware of a Caribbean problem. Much of the present-day activity of the *independentista* groups, naturally enough, concentrates upon the same appeal to international opinion. There is an appeal to the Foreign Ministers Conference at Santiago de Chile to look into the Puerto Rican case; a message of fraternal greetings to the Cuban revolutionary government; a declaration of support for Venezuelan and Honduran delegates in their effort to put the Puerto Rican matter on the agenda of the Third Conference of the Inter American Cultural Council; and efforts to persuade the General Assembly to include Puerto Rico in its debates on colonialism. There is too the occasional support that comes from a visiting friend from a Latin American political movement, although this is seriously inhibited by the difficulties imposed by the United States immigration authorities in San Juan. Altogether the activities give the lie direct to the criticism which decries the *independentistas* for grasping at a principle of sovereignty that has allegedly become largely obsolete in an internationalist world, for in their ability to see their struggle as possessed of international meaning, especially in the Spanish-speaking world, they show that it is possible to set a nationalist ideal within an internationalist framework.

But Puerto Rico still awaits a mature two-party system that puts first things first. The one, great, overriding reason for this has been, and remains, the colonial subserviency to the American power. A colonial politics is driven, ineluctably, to stress the national question to the detriment and neglect of the social question. The main preoccupation becomes constitutional reform; differences on domestic issues that cry aloud for attention are played down or perhaps never even fully aired; and party alignments are forced into an artificial straitjacket. All this, and more, has taken place in Puerto Rico. Despite Muñoz's bold assertion to his party convention in 1940 (in refusing to accept the party's candidacy for the post of Resident Commissioner in the federal capital) that the days of Washington direction were over and the days of local direction beginning, the preoccupation with Washington direction still remains as powerful as ever; and not even the *muñozcista* charisma has been able to subordinate the status issue permanently to the early *Popular* emphasis upon social and economic change. The opposition parties, in their turn, tend to neglect those social and economic issues in favor of the more attractive items, psychologically speaking, of their own special recipes for the status problem. It is true that their presence in the Legislature, as Professor Raúl Serrano has pointed out in his study of executive-legislative relationships, has greatly improved legislative work in general and legislative scrutiny of executive behavior in particular, and that they have helped thereby to compensate for the timidity that characterizes too many of the majority party legislators in their capacity as carriers of complaints to executive officials.[37] Nor can the value of that contribution be underestimated when, to take examples only, it serves to publicize the local Communications Authority's arbitrary denial of the right to use the insular telegraph service to a citizen wishing to protest, in mild enough terms, against the colonial subjection of Puerto Rico to the United States, or draws attention to the alarming use of private agents by the Internal Security forces to check on the political activities of students on the national University campus.[38] Even so, this is still something far removed from an opposition party grooming itself as the alternative government and identified with a concise philosophy on all domestic issues that differentiates it from the incumbent administration.

Nor can it be argued that this umbilical cord that keeps the practice of insular politics so closely tied to American developments is of unconditional benefit to the island. One American writer has attempted the thesis that those local parties that have favored independence since 1900 have been at once pro-Spanish and "conservative" in ideology, while the pro-American parties have been "liberal."[39] But this is a very untenable thesis, especially for the period since 1940. Certainly today the most pro-American party, the Statehood group, is hardly the most "liberal" ideologically; while even before 1940, when the thesis might have been somewhat more legitimate, the "liberalism" of the Unionist Party in 1922 (the year in which it finally abandoned the ideal of independence) was so fragile that its members could assure a visiting American that if the Socialists won the next election the United States would have to institute a military government to keep them down.[40] It is this continuous appeal to America, as if to a father figure, that inhibits the growth of indigenous philosophies on indigenous problems, uncomplicated by considerations of their possible repercussions in the federal capital. This dilemma will not be resolved, it follows, until the vexed question of political status is resolved. The one question cannot be discussed in isolation from the other, for Puerto Rican politics have been, in a very real sense, and remain still, a politics of status.

That fact in itself justifies a separate treatment of the status problem. But it is worth emphasizing here, in a little more detail, its repercussions upon the general spirit of the insular political game. The game is tied up with national politics in Washington in a way quite distinct from state-federal politics within the Union itself or from the relationships, say, between London and the newly independent nations like Jamaica and Trinidad. For the Puerto Rican politician who wants to succeed—unless, of course, he is an outright separatist—must tread a delicate path between the extremes of being either at once too pro-American or too anti-American. His enemies must not be able to brand him as a tool of Yankee interests; at the same time he must avoid the label of ultra-nationalist, unsympathetic to American needs in the area. He must learn to swallow the daily humiliations that accompany Congressional rule; and only when the humiliation becomes a deliberate provocation—when, for example, Representative Adam Clayton Powell threatens to use Federal educational funds spent in the island as a stick with which to beat the Commonwealth Secretary of Education—will he finally turn in righteous anger. Obtaining favors from Washington becomes an art in itself. So, Governor Muñoz publicly thanks Sherman Adams for that presidential assistant's aid in facilitating the passage of the Congressional law placing the power to nominate the Commander of the local National Guard in the hands of the insular chief executive, while the Governor's enemies resist the change on the ground that it will serve to increase the political pressures already existing in the appointments and promotions business of the Guard.[41] Or again, to take another example, a local *Estadista* delegate to the 1956 Republican nominating convention in San Francisco feels compelled to defend his good name by publicizing his role in the meetings of the platform committee, particularly in regard to his defense of the statehood for Puerto Rico plank, lest the local Territorial Committee believe the libel that he was instead languishing in a comfortable hotel room.[42] Similar considerations undoubtedly moved the Resident Commissioner for Puerto Rico in the federal capital to defend himself against charges that he had been comfortably installed by his government in the luxury of Washington's "Embassy Row."[43]

It is part of the same game that the independent-minded groups in the society become the targets of a fierce Puerto Rican Americanism. Their arguments are rarely treated to a fair or courteous analysis; and their motives, always supposedly "subversive," are mercilessly pilloried in the press. Every outrage of the civil peace is almost invariably laid at their door. So, the Mayor of Vieques, who leads the struggle against the United States Navy in that islet, is caricatured as a mock-heroic Sancha Panza; the life of Albizu Campos is rewritten by hostile journalists in such a way as to play up his racial animosity and to play down his reasoned criticism of American colonialism; while the authors of the widely noted *Documento del exterminio,* drawing attention to the building up of the territory as an American atomic arsenal, are treated to a furious indignation so violent that it is fair to believe that it has its roots in a morbid fear about possible reactions in Washington. Finally, the Puerto Rican anti-independents themselves launch a sustained onslaught upon the very idea of independence in itself, as witness the Governor's Godkin lectures; although it is fair to add that the extreme position of, quite logically, attacking also the idea of the American pro-independence movement of the 1770's has been left to one of their resident American sympathizers.[44] In such a way does the colonial become his own willing executioner. The Puerto Rican governing class thus presents the spectacle of being about the only colonial national group in the modern world that runs, in Rousseau's phrase, to meet its own chains.

All this, finally, must be put within the general context of the politics of federal largesse. For there are roots of economic self-interest underneath that betrayal. The tremendous volumes of money that accrue to the territory through the enormous variety of federal programs and services have placed their most potent tool into the hands of the San Juan politicians, and the story of how they have used it is in itself one of the most fascinating aspects of insular politics. It has been a federal patronage feeding in its turn the local patronage. Politicians have not resisted the temptation to vie with each other in the game of boasting who is most influential in Washington as lobbyist seeking the federal spoils. Muñoz himself rose to power by becoming perhaps the most astute of the lobbyists during the 1940's. And the game today is as virulent as ever. The Resident Commissioner in Washington dispenses, like any Senator, the privilege of choosing candidates for nomination to the national army, navy, and air force academies. He must defend his record, of course, against critics who aver they could do the job better, as the fierce exchange of correspondence with the local *Estadista* leader recently showed. The local Democratic Party Committee in San Juan has perhaps as its major function the task of securing the lucrative ranking federal agency appointments for deserving Democrats. The political opposition criticizes the Governor for failing to request Washington to declare the island a disaster zone in order to obtain the fullest amount of federal aid for local agriculture; in turn the Governor naturally advertises his success in searching out every possible federal hole and corner from which some new appropriation may be prized for the island—a grant for local airport expansion under the new federal Airport Act, for example, or for urban renewal under the federal urban renewal legislation. A political hopeful like José Benítez seeks to make his mark by establishing a local Democratic party to supplant the *Popular* organization as the rightful channel for federal patronage, and his taunt that the *Popular* Party is only "a local party that starts at Fajardo and ends at Mayagüez" is designed to prove that a local party without formal affiliation with one of the major continental parties cannot obtain all that the island needs from the federal treasure chests. It is a fitting comment upon the ethics of the whole game that Benítez, being defeated in that move, assuaged his disappointment by accepting a higher piece of federal patronage from the new Kennedy administration in the form of appointment to the post of Deputy High Commissioner of the United States Trust Territory in the Pacific (it would be interesting to learn how a Puerto Rican adjusts himself to being a South Pacific small-island potentate in an essentially colonial situation).

Looked at from this angle, Puerto Rican politics has been throughout a politics of mendicancy, with the Puerto Rican Lazarus, as it were, knocking persistently at the gate of the American Dives. Few episodes dramatize the moral dangers secreted in the relationship better than the story of the foundation, in 1911, of the College of Agriculture and Mechanical Arts in Mayagüez as part of the insular University. For that institution received its original impetus from the almost accidental discovery by the resident continental agriculturist D. W. May in 1907 that the provisions of the Morrill Act of 1862 could be made applicable to Puerto Rico, and a subsequent correspondence with the political leader José de Diego which resulted in a successful appeal by the local legislature for federal approval of the idea. A reading of the documents shows with painful clarity how the nationalist faith of the famous *separatista* yielded to the promise of federal aid and to the glory of bringing its benefits to his own home town.[45] The economic appetite thus dilutes political ideology. It would be easy for the critic of Puerto Rican politics to draw up a harsh moral indictment of the men who accept the dilution. What restrains him, in the final analysis, is a sympathetic awareness of the fact that the contrast between a Puerto Rican poverty and an American wealth so utterly flagrant must have meant—and still means— a moral temptation almost too pressing for ordinary human nature to resist.

The Problem of Political Status

No ONE single issue stirs Puerto Rican emotions more violently than that of status. It is, in truth, the issue of issues. Until 1940 it absolutely overshadowed all others, so much so that its tyranny over all political parties divided the insular political will and left the masses to be exploited by the unified interests of the big economic groups of the economy. The early years of the *Popular* "new deal" gave it a respite, but it returned, with the conclusion of that experiment sometime after the termination of the war, with all of its pathology and virulence. On no one single issue is the visiting Congressman or public official queried so relentlessly as on this one. Each time a Congressional committee journeys to the island to hear and collate the local view—the O'Brien committee of 1959, for example—it touches off a new explosion of passion and interest that sets up in turn a chain reaction of enormous extent. The theme is used by some as a stick with which to beat the Americans. It is used by others as a rationalization for inaction or passivity on the local level. Opponents cite constitutional authorities and precedents for their particular interpretations with much the same enthusiasm as the religious controversialists of the sixteenth and seventeenth centuries cited scriptural texts in the passionate conviction that the citation axiomatically proved the validity of their general argument. Indeed the analogy is not inapt, for there has grown up in the island a veritable secular bibliolatry on the issue. If to that there is added the further observation that in a geographically constricted society the atmosphere of the debate, as apart from its substance, takes on some of the overheated quality of political disputation in the Italian medieval city states, some fuller understanding of the situation may be obtained.

Some critics, Daniel Boorstin, for example, have claimed to see in the preoccupation with status a symptom of local intellectual sickness. No judgment could be more naive. It is astonishing indeed that a professional historian should so cavalierly neglect the historical roots of the preoccupation. For historically every society subordinated to an imperial power has been driven to examine the moral legitimacy of the subordination. This was the case with Italy under Austria, with Ireland under England, with Poland under Czarist Russia, with the American colonies themselves under Britain. Even from the Marxist viewpoint—so unsympathetic, doctrinally, to nationalism—the national question has always been seen as prior to the social question. "The nation," wrote Lenin, "is a necessary product, an inevitable form, in the bourgeois epoch of social development. The working class cannot grow strong, cannot mature, cannot consolidate its forces, except by establishing itself as the nation, except by becoming national." To adjure a people not to concern itself with the national issue (as does the line of argument pursued by Boorstin) is to ignore the nature of the entire growth of nationalism over the last two centuries. A local Puerto Rican critic has noted further that an attitude such as Boorstin's reflects in itself not any absolute truth that Puerto Ricans must learn so much as the peculiar status of the intellectual class in American society, existing on the uncomfortable margins of the society, regarded with suspicion by the general public and rarely itself participating in politics, and indeed frequently contemptuous of the political art.[1] The politico-nationalist passion of the Puerto Rican intelligentsia is certain to appear nonsensical to members of such a class. But history at least is here on the Puerto Rican side, for the search for national self-determination has shown itself to be historically a far more appealing thing than the internationalist creed of classical socialism. Thus socialism in nineteenth-century Norway only developed seriously after the separation from Sweden; until then the satisfaction of nationalist sentiment seemed more pressing than obedience to socialist principle. Thus the Italian liberals listened more to Garibaldi than to Marx until the Austrian yoke was lifted in 1859. Thus finally the internationalism of thinkers like Renan and Jaurès was, and still is, comparatively powerless to control the French working-class movement so long as patriotic Gallicization has been fed by continuing German occupations of the homeland. The record shows altogether that no nation can settle down to a serious examination of its internal problems or give its best devotion to internationalist ideologies so long as an unsatisfactory connection with a foreign power prevails. Let the critics who berate Puerto Ricans for being concerned with their national self-identity remember the lesson—to take two examples only—of Rosa Luxemburg's defeat by Pilsudski in her effort to prevent the Polish socialist movement from going nationalist and of the deployment of the Russian Communist Party, once Trotsky had been defeated by Stalin, as a weapon for the protection of the Russian national interest.

The Puerto Rican problem must be set within this general context.

Puerto Ricans were not born with a status complex; it was thrust upon them. If even the most casual utterance on the problem by even the most obscure or least influential of Congressmen or federal officials is seized upon to become "front-page news" in San Juan, that is understandable in the light of the fact that the island is still controlled by Congressional and federal administrative powers. If, again, the discussion revolving around the alternative schemes—independence, statehood, and the present commonwealth status—seems to reduce itself at times to a Scrooge-like estimation of the economic and fiscal advantages that the island would allegedly enjoy under any one of them, the temptation to think in such terms may be regrettable but it is eminently understandable once the degree of local economic dependency upon the federal government's general economic policies is borne in mind. No responsible Puerto Rican leader could ask his people to make the enormous economic sacrifices which the complete cessation of the present fiscal and economic privileges within the federal union would entail. When indeed the proponents of a better Congressional treatment for the District of Columbia point with some envy to those privileges, including federal tax exemption, it is evident that the island economy enjoys advantages not to be lightly abandoned.[2] Much of the almost paranoiac anxiety with which the status issue is debated only begins to make sense indeed if it is seen in the light of, one, the fear that Congress might at any time decide upon abandonment and, two, the feeling that conversely the economic-fiscal advantages will be used, as they have been used in the past, as a justification for the denial of political reforms. What in fact has happened is that America throughout has confronted the island population with a Hobson's choice between a political status that gives them food with shame or one that offers them poverty with dignity. Those Puerto Ricans, like the champions of the *estado libre asociado* since 1952, who argue that this dilemma has now in fact been resolved can only do so on the assumption that the commonwealth status form has been able to transcend the status complex. But the proponents both of statehood and independence deny that this is so; and the very vehemence with which the *Popular* spokesmen defend their thesis reveals how much their "invention" remains tied to the status complex instead of being removed from it in some Hegelian fashion understood only by the more philosophically mystical of their academic friends. The forms change; the basic passion remains. "The deep-seated Puerto Rican desire to attain a position of dignity and equality," a more objective observer has concluded, "has been demonstrated over and over in the past history of the island. The prolonged, often discouraging struggle for concessions from Congress, the classic debates over status, the insistence upon a compact with bilateral assurances—all are evidence of this ingrained need."[3] The need still awaits the prescription of cure that will finally assuage it.

The alternative of commonwealth status deserves analysis first if only because, unlike its rivals, it is a present reality and not a distant hope. A massive avalanche of literature exists as its apologetic: the Constituent Assembly debates of 1951-1952, the federal Congress hearings on Public Law 600 of 1950, the basic constitutional instrument of the Commonwealth, the official propaganda of the Commonwealth government, the extensive hearings of the federal Insular and Internal Affairs Committee of 1959, and so on. No state government has so bombarded the American government and people with justifications for its *raison d'être* as the Commonwealth government since 1950. Basically the argument asserts the decisive termination of colonial status with the passage of the federal and insular constitutional changes that took place between 1947 and 1952. The constitutional advances, in one way, have been real enough. Puerto Ricans retain American citizenship and, with certain exceptions, the amplitude of American civil rights. The right to compose their own instrument of local government has been conceded. American executive appointment to local offices has virtually ended. Puerto Rican citizens enjoy full freedom of movement within the Union and cannot be threatened (as have been African and West Indian migrants into the United Kingdom) with possibilities of restrictionist quotas upon their entry on the part of the imperial parliamentary power. (The nearest approach to such punitive legislation has been federal Judge Leibowitz's recommendation of a New York state law to discourage Puerto Rican migration by requiring one year's residence in the state before establishing eligibility for relief.) It is possible to see all this as simply the end result of a sixty-year-old process whereby Congress has progressively handed over successive shares of the Congressional governing power to the island. The *Popular* dogma, however, insists that it must be seen, and especially the 1950-1952 changes, not simply as a process of enlarged self-government that leaves the status issue untouched but rather as a fundamental "treaty" that changes the federal-insular relationship in such a way as to convert the island territory into a "free associated state" stripped of colonialist trappings. Its defenders have attempted to give it a theoretical respectability by acclaiming it as the latest step of a pliable federalism in the modern world that goes back to Proudhon and Locke and Althusius, and a historical respectability by tracing it back to the liberal-autonomist movement under Spain. The second argument is perhaps more persuasive than the first.

But neither of them in itself is conclusive evidence that the changes, when added up, guarantee a new relationship between the United States and Puerto Rico without any traces of subordination that are not mutually voluntary, or that, more extravagantly, they constitute a solution for the modern colonial problem on the global level.[4]

It is important to note the full nature of the official dogma. It has wanted—as outlined concisely by Antonio Fernós-Isern in his book of 1948, *Puerto Rico Libre y Federado*—the full democratization of the three branches of the insular machinery of government; a local constitution adopted by the Puerto Rican people, they alone to be empowered to amend it; the federal legislative power to be limited to action in matters exclusively and specifically reserved to the federal government, as in instances involving the states of the Union; Congress to cease the exercise of its plenary power; and all of this to be set forth in a new and bilateral organic pact, amendable only through mutual consent and not unilaterally. All this granted, and the United States–Puerto Rican relationship would take on the form of a local status of "democratic sovereignty," coexisting equally with the agencies of the federal government as those agencies exercised the functions specifically reserved to them by the agreement.[5] Subsequent elaborations of these "heads of proposals," as it were, have indicated that, for the *Populares*, the reserved federal power should be exercised only under extreme conditions, not as a normal function of routine relationships and certainly not as a means of interference in local government affairs. All this in its turn rests upon the fundamental premise of a theory of contract, Public Law 600 and its resultant Federal Relations Statute being viewed as a "compact" whereby the Congress knowingly made partial but irrevocably binding cessions of Congressional power to the island and knowingly agreed further that no element of the compact could be altered without the consent of both parties. "As we see it," Governor Muñoz has said, "Puerto Rico is a new kind of state, both in the sense of the United States Federal system and in the general sense of a people organized to govern themselves. It is a system of government and it is a new manner of relationship to the United States, as it could be in the case of any large union or confederation of political societies. . . . The idea of 'compact' determines a basic change in the relationship. It takes away from the very basis of the relationship the nature and onus of colonialism. It cannot be revoked or changed unilaterally. . . . So, the political status of Puerto Rico is one of free association with the American Union. It is a new way of abolishing a colonial status under the constitutional system of the United States."[6]

How far is all this believable? The inquiry must concern itself, when all is said and done, with two questions: (1) does the legislation of 1950-1952 in reality go as far as the *Popular* thesis claims? and (2) was it the intent of Congress, in passing that legislation, to change the constitutional status of Puerto Rico by means of ceding its constitutional power over the island in perpetuity? A careful examination of the evidence makes it difficult not to feel that the answer to both questions must be an emphatic negative. The formal title of the territory has changed, but it remains nonetheless a territory. Congress continues to hold its *pleins pouvoirs*. It is true that at the time of the adoption of Public Law 600 Congress refused to accept the so-called Johnston Amendment which would have required Congressional approval of all subsequent constitutional amendments in Puerto Rico. But it is equally true that Congress at the same time used its revisionary power to strike out sections of the local Bill of Rights offensive to its more conservative members, and that in addition it defined a perimeter of federal limits upon the local amending power with the clear implication that it had no intention of consenting to a permanent abdication of the federal authority. Indeed, as one Statehood legal authority pointed out in the 1951-1952 debate in the Constituent Assembly, the power of Congress to govern the territories is a plenary power not subject to the constitutional limitations that control the relationships of the federal government with the individual states. What is more: the power is inherent and inalienable and Congress, even if it wanted to, could not divest itself of it. To argue that it has so divested itself is to charge Congress with action it cannot constitutionally undertake. The very fact that by virtue of the Federal Relations Statute Congressional laws that are locally applicable will continue to apply and that, in turn, federal agencies in the island will continue to exercise administrative functions does not encourage the presumption of a complete bilateral relationship between the two capitals.[7] What was in reality achieved in 1952, according to a Socialist member of the Constituent Assembly, was a mild extension of internal self-government undertaken in the form of an amendment to the existing Organic Act. The constituent power of the Assembly, in that view, was by no means sovereign, for that body was nothing more than a subordinate parliament, met by an authorization of power momentarily conceded by Congress and to be used solely for the purpose of amending the Organic Act. The new Constitution that came out of that process, therefore, is revocable on two counts: first, through the power that Congress continues to exercise through the federal territorial clause and, second, through the power it exercises by virtue of Clause 4 of the Treaty of Paris of 1899.[8]

These, of course, are the opinions of the critics of commonwealth status, and are partisan. But there is evidence to show that the majority Congressional opinion tends to argue along similar lines. The vital Senate Committee report of 1952 makes it clear that for most if not for all Congressmen the federal power remains the higher law; while the statement of the Chief Counsel of the Office of Territories, reluctantly pressed out of him by persistent questioning from Senators Long and Malone, at the same time, is unequivocal in its admission that the plenary power of Congress, via the territorial clause, remains unimpaired as a final check upon the Puerto Rican legislative process.[9] Analysis of Congressional intent of course is a notoriously hazardous enterprise and in the Puerto Rican case it is made even more so by the absence so far of substantial judicial interpretation to lend clarity to the intent (although it must be added that, if such interpretation did exist, the previous history of judicial comment upon national legislation concerning the insular status is not of a nature to encourage the great expectations of Puerto Rican liberal thought). At the same time, the Congressional debates and documents are there. Professor David Helfeld's careful examination of their content leaves little doubt of the fact that there is at least serious discrepancy between what Congress imagined it was doing in 1950-1952 and what *Popular* spokesmen have subsequently claimed Congress was doing. At no time during those debates did any Congressional group conceive that it was seriously abrogating the Congressional review power; or that Congress was binding itself permanently not to intervene in local affairs under certain circumstances; or indeed that it was doing anything more radical than merely engineering an enlargement of the local self-governing power, as it had done previously in 1917 and 1947. Even the most liberal of Senators, Senator O'Mahoney, for example, did not want to go beyond the stance of "friendly paternalists" at once retaining a jealous regard for Congressional power and a deep conviction of the necessity, for Puerto Rico, of a continuing superior Congressional wisdom. The compact they agreed to did not appear to them to be bilaterally binding in any legal sense (whatever its moral compulsions might be). All this is certainly very different from the grandiose exegesis emanating from official San Juan. "The great bulk of the critical remarks made by the Congressmen," Helfeld observes, "would seem to indicate attitudes opposed to any irrevocable delegation [of Congressional power]. In contrast, sponsors of the constitution characteristically gave ambiguous, evasive, and incomplete answers to direct questions on the permanence of the allocation of power. Before an assumption of permanency may be presumed, the burden of proof would seem to rest with those who make the claim. Tested either by the existence of specific statement or overall mood that burden appears not to have been met."[10] "From the perspective of Puerto Rico," he continues, with equal discouragement for Puerto Rican optimism, "one attitudinal fact is clear: if the Senate feels strongly enough about a matter, particularly should a deep felt principle be involved, paternalism rather than confidence in self-government will dominate its decision. Those Senators who lean toward leaving the greatest degree of Puerto Rican affairs to self-determination appear to have a majority support of unstable and potentially wavering proportions."[11] No amount of clever word spinning—of which Governor Muñoz is an accredited master—can bridge that gulf between the *Popular* thesis and the realities of Congressional opinion.

Nothing indeed could illustrate all this better than the history of the "compact" since 1952. There has been a sustained campaign from San Juan to enlarge the local autonomy and decrease, correspondingly, the ambit of the Congressional authority. Aside from the fact that the very effort to liberalize a compact originally announced as an abolition of colonial status involves an obvious illogic, there remains the inerasable fact that the revisionist pressure from San Juan has been met throughout by a loud silence from Washington. The Commonwealth government has sought to have transferred to its authority all those functions remaining under the federal government which by their nature are not required so to be kept, culminating in the promotion of the composite Fernós-Murray Bill of 1959, the main provisions of which sought to replace the Federal Relations Statute with a new body of law to be known as "Articles of Permanent Association." The opposition of the local Statehood and Independent Parties to that effort has been understandable. What is significant is that the Congress showed, throughout the bill's history, little indication of yielding on any really serious point. The sole concessions it has made have touched the periphery rather than the center of the metropolitan power—the power ceded to the Governor, for example, to nominate, in place of the President, the Commander of the local National Guard. The local government has been granted Congressional consent to enter into interstate compacts with individual states in order to deal with problems like crime and juvenile delinquency. But on the more sovereign matters of local control over, say, immigration or currency or customs Congress has been immovable. And those items, after all, constitute as it were the testing ground of the *Popular* thesis, since they constitute at once matters over which the *Populares* have staked claims in their party platform utterances and matters of national concern which Congress, by nature and tradition, would hardly dream of lightly surrendering.

Nor is all this simply a matter of Congressional conservatism. It is, even more, a matter of federal administrative authority. He who administers a law, in Sir Henry Taylor's sentence, is in very truth the master of it. It is not without some significance, then, that much of the Puerto Rican effort to liberalize the 1952 "compact" has concerned itself with an attempt to increase the Commonwealth government's functions and responsibilities presently co-opted or shared by federal agencies. Apart from the clause seeking to lift the present statutory restriction upon the fiscal borrowing margin of the territory, most of the important clauses of the Fernós-Murray Bill were concerned with that attempt. But there has been so far little apparent readiness on the part of the federal agency officialdoms to relinquish willingly their respective sovereignties to local officials. Certainly the consensus of the written observations of federal departments on the Fernós-Murray proposals indicated an unmistakable hardening towards Puerto Rican demands. The Department of the Navy objected on the ground that the clauses relating to island land and water areas could create big problems for the military departments operating within the territory, if only because there is too vague a definition of what constitutes Crown Property areas threatened with transfer to the Commonwealth government.[12] The Department of State, it is true, supported the bill, with especially strong endorsement of the provisions seeking to eliminate the archaic practice presently governing the award of the credentials to the Puerto Rican Resident Commissioner in Washington—hardly an earth-shaking issue.[13] The Department of Health, Education and Welfare, on the other hand, drew attention to some of the grave constitutional implications of the bill. The disposal of excess federal property, its lawyers felt, was already sufficiently taken care of by the Federal Property and Administrative Services Act of 1949. They considered that the provisions concerning the transfer of navigable waters could result in the United States surrendering, with respect to Puerto Rico, powers which she would possess if the territory were a state of the Union. The contemplated transfer of federal duties and services to the Commonwealth government held, they thought, similar hazards. "While the condition of Presidential and Congressional approval," they wrote, "would appear to establish safeguards in this respect, Article VI raises the question whether a provision of this kind does not imply that there may be federal functions which, though properly exercisable as such by the United States in the several States of the Union, would be more properly performed in Puerto Rico by the Commonwealth as Commonwealth functions in view of the nature of the association of the Commonwealth with the Union. We assume that the implications of this article will be thoroughly explored in this connection."[14] The warning, though veiled, is clear enough; and the apprehensions behind it have been character-istic throughout of the federal administrative attitudes. When the Navy Department believes that certain of the Fernós-Murray provisions would stultify the application of gift and estate taxes and property lien laws to Puerto Rico;[15] or when the Attorney General's office considers that the provisions of the Submerged Lands Act and of the Outer Con-tinental Shelf Lands Act already cover other questions raised by San Juan;[16] or when finally the Justice Department fears that other of the Fernós-Murray items could mean that the United States might not be able to make a unilateral decision to exercise exclusive jurisdiction over a military reservation on reserved property,[17] it is clear that the federal agency mind altogether feels that the Puerto Rican draftsmen are asking too much too soon, that in making certain requests—the right of Puerto Rico, to take a further instance, to ask for certain reductions in the general United States tariff rates when applied to the island—they are requesting for the island special privileges denied to the individual states.

All the available evidence about Congressional intent thus points to the conclusion that, in passing the legislation of 1950 to 1952, Congress meant no more than to grant the island the right, within limits, to frame its own constitution, and that the federal agencies and departments have taken the intention as basic to their reading of the present condition of things. Congress had little if any intention of terminating its unilateral power with respect to insular affairs, and its view was subsequently fully expressed in the lengthy observations of Senator Jackson in 1959 during a gentlemanly exchange with Governor Muñoz. The Commonwealth thesis, the Senator argued, really meant that the hands of Congress would be tied by the concept of bilateral action, for if Congress could not legislate for the island without the express consent of the Commonwealth government it was carrying the demand for flexibility to the point where Puerto Rico would be able to resist federal authority in a way denied to the indi-vidual states; for Senator Jackson this was the "fundamental constitu-tional matter" which, if left unresolved, would compromise Congress in perpetuity.[18] The Commonwealth representatives might reply of course—as they have indeed done—that their demands at any future time would always be so reasonable that Congress in effect would not experience the sensation of being compromised; that the only federal property they might wish to take over—to take an example only— would be items like El Morro Castle, of historical rather than strategic importance. The answer surely is that the legal power of bilateral consent, once yielded, could not satisfactorily rest upon the accident of a reasonably minded government in San Juan. The American Congress, like some Hebraic Jehovah, is a jealous sovereign, so much so that the student of the matter begins to wonder whether the Common- wealth spokesmen have not been guilty of extreme naiveté in assuming that Congress would ever accept their radical thesis; certainly a read- ing of the exchange between Governor Muñoz and Senator Jackson reveals a separation of deep-set principle between the opposing viewpoints. And a reading of the testimony before the House Terri- tories subcommittee in May, 1963, on the later proposal to create a joint United States–Puerto Rican commission to study the problem strongly suggests that, four years later, Congressional skepticism re- mains as strong as ever.

For—to turn to the realities, once again, of federal public ad- ministration in the territory—the evidence throughout has pointed to a powerfully felt federal skepticism. The Resident Commissioner has pointed to the dangers lurking in the protected monopoly of the American shipping companies in the island's maritime traffic and in the fact that the scientific use of local land depends upon decisions reached in a Washington government office;[19] but no relief has yet come, in either case, from Congress. The Commonwealth govern- ment must still go to the Federal Communications Commission for the licensing of its radio and television stations; and the local Radio and Television Association, interestingly enough, has challenged the right of the Commonwealth Legislature to investigate this particular sphere on the ground that the Federal Communications Act of 1934 has preempted the field for the federal government, thereby—as found in *Dumont v. Carroll* and *Stahlman v. F.C.C.*—excluding local ac- tion.[20] There has been no brighter success in the attempt to secure the transfer of export liquor inspection from the federal Treasury to the appropriate Commonwealth agency. The mails remain with the federal Post Office, although many Puerto Ricans resent the fact that, among other consequences of this action, mailed literature sent to the island from the Iron Curtain countries is arbitrarily impounded by the postal authorities in San Juan. Nor have the federal courts been kinder to local feelings. They have failed to uphold, for example, the facile opinion of the Commonwealth Attorney General that the Supreme Court decision in *Nelson v. Pennsylvania,* establishing Con- gressional preemption in the field of anti-sedition legislation, does not affect local statutes; and the activities of the House Un-American Activities Committee in San Juan further show that Congress is as yet unprepared to accept the argument of the American Civil Liberties Union that the Congressional investigatory power cannot reach into the island save as a specific invitation from San Juan comes along.[21] In the conflict, again, between the federal and Commonwealth jurisdictions in the control of the industrial-relations field, the federal courts have as yet failed to concur in the Puerto Rico Labor Relations Board decision, *Hilton Hotels International Inc. v. Unión de Trabajadores de la Industria Gastronómica,* in which the full-blown thesis of the "compact" was invoked to argue that, since 1952, Puerto Rico has been invested with local regulatory powers not inferior to those enjoyed by the individual states, and that those powers, including control of labor relations, have ceased to be subject to federal regulation.[22] The federal courts, indeed, have in general exhibited no braver enthusiasm than the federal regulatory commissions for the transfer of services to the Commonwealth power; and in this respect it is finally worth noting the San Juan Federal Court decision that contracts relating to the rental and sale of houses in the territory under the guaranteed protection of the Federal Housing Administration cannot be controlled by competing regulations of the Commonwealth authorities, on the general ground that a national planning agency cannot operate efficiently unless it be relieved of restrictions emanating from local legislation.[23]

It is possible to say of course that the *estado libre asociado* is less in itself a permanent solution to the status problem than the promise of the future growth of such a solution; indeed what actually happens is that the *Popular* theologians tend to say that it is a permanent solution when speaking in San Juan and merely the promise of a solution when speaking in Washington. It is, in any case, a plausible enough thesis, and has been recently advanced by Professor Carl Friedrich in his 1958 lectures at the University of Puerto Rico.[24] From this viewpoint—the viewpoint of a potential creativity—the next line of advance is the unfolding liberalization of the present relationship through a series of institutional and administrative reforms. Some of them, by any liberal standard, certainly need no apology. There is the need to enlarge Puerto Rican participation in the federal legislative processes, for the present device of a voteless Resident Commissioner at the seat of the federal power is not only laughably inadequate but also a colonial anachronism (rather like the old-style colonial agent of the British Crown Colonies). There is the need to ensure that all applicable federal legislation shall only be applicable to Puerto Rico with Puerto Rican assent through appropriate machinery—the establishment perhaps of a concurrent joint committee system between the respective capitals or the organization of closer ties between the two executive branches. Or federal legislation, again, suggests Professor Friedrich, could be delegated in its local administration to Puerto Rican officials, as in the case of Switzerland. Such devices certainly would have the merit of supplanting the present unsatisfactory method of occasional and almost casual meetings between the Governor and the American President, such as the one that took place during President Eisenhower's brief stayover at the Puerto Rican Ramey Air Base during his 1960 Latin America tour. If changes could be promulgated along these lines, the argument goes, it would perhaps not be utopian to expect that the local popular institutions would begin to have more and more free play and that metropolitan interference would cease almost insensibly in local affairs. Professor Friedrich anticipates that such an outcome could probably materialize by 1975.

Is all this feasible? The argument, albeit attractive, is predicated upon assumptions that remain, so far, pretty fragile. On grounds of expediency alone the general temper of Congressional-administrative conservatism makes success of such a program highly doubtful. Even Congressmen as generally friendly to the Puerto Rican case as Mr. Roosevelt and Senator Douglas have begun to express doubts about the exemptions presently enjoyed by the island from federal obligations, exemptions that expose Puerto Ricans to charges of being "free loaders" at the expense of continental taxpayers. It is even more unlikely, then, that Congress could be brought to tolerate the more radical reforms suggested by Professor Friedrich that go beyond even the defeated recommendations of the Fernós-Murray Bill. We are told, for example, that the Commonwealth government should be given the right to refuse assent, if it so wishes, to any treaty the United States might enter into, and be further empowered not only to have separate representation in international bodies and agencies but also, again if it so desired, to carry on its own separate foreign policy, after, of course, reasonable consultation with Washington. This suggestion alone raises formidable questions. If power to dissent from treaties means power to dissociate the island from treaty obligations (as it must, if it is to mean anything) would it not seriously compromise the necessary unity of foreign policy, not to mention the ultimate responsibility of the President for those policies? And if it only means, as Professor Friedrich alternatively propounds, the right of the Resident Commissioner to vote in Senate debates, possibly by being accepted as a member of the Senate Foreign Relations Committee, would that be a concession of any real significance? Would an independent foreign policy permit the island—to take examples only—to criticize British imperial actions in UN debates, or recognize a left-wing government in Guatemala, or advocate the internationalization of the Panama Canal Zone? Would it permit Puerto Rico to deny its continuing assent to the conversion of the island, already rapidly taking place, into a center for United States guided missile experiments, or to the continued use of the territory as an American army and naval base? Would "reasonable consultation" with Washington mean a bar upon such actions? If so, the proposed freedom would surely be illusory. Merely to raise such questions is to emphasize the massive difficulties involved in such an argument. It is not too much to say that they go to the heart of the Monroe Doctrine as the basic foundation, as Americans see it, of continental security and defense; and the *contretemps* with Cuba has only encouraged American policy makers to emphasize the continuing sanctity of that doctrine rather than to contemplate its liberalization. Professor Friedrich's recommendations on this score are clearly as utopian as the ideas of statehood and independence that he so cavalierly dismisses as "impractical" for Puerto Rico.

The fact is that stripped of its philosophical foliage the argument of Professor Friedrich still leaves untouched the island's subordinate status. It still accepts the presumption that reform comes by way of American concessions. Why, for example, should Puerto Rico have to wait until 1975 for the full grant of internal self-government and self-determination? So to assume is to take for granted a Congressional timetable of change when elsewhere in the colonial world a more rapid pace is being set by the colonial peoples' movements: when, for instance, the neighboring West Indies societies of Trinidad and Jamaica, hardly dangerously revolutionary systems, have already received full Dominion status. Professor Friedrich, like the Commonwealth theoreticians, invokes the analogy of the British Commonwealth to buttress his argument (the young Henry Stimson had used the analogy as far back as 1912 when testifying before a Senate committee in support of a bill to invest Puerto Ricans with American citizenship). But surely the governing fact there is that the constitutional development of the dominions has gone so far since 1931 that even the moral obligations of the Statute of Westminster have long become obsolete and that Dominion status today means nothing less than the unrestricted possession of the total armory of national sovereignty; to the point where it becomes necessary, in Professor F. R. Scott's phrase, to speak of "the end of dominion status."[25] Dominion status thus allows full freedom in the matter of war; would Puerto Rico be permitted, so long as she remains "associated" with the United States, to remain neutral in an American war? The real trouble with arguments like those of Professor Friedrich indeed is that they are posited upon a theory of consent that is at utter variance with the facts. Hegelian-wise they play with the idea of a process of becoming which gets substituted for, is indeed almost identified with, the universe of facts. They assume a more or less binding obligation on both sides, moral rather than legal, to meet each other halfway. But the hard fact is that whereas Professor Friedrich speaks mysteriously of a "generic consent" to the terms of the "compact," most Congressional actions bespeak a readiness to read into the "compact" the more prosaic terms of ordinary commercial contract law doctrine. Congressional behavior altogether has obviously seen the term "compact" in the sense (to quote Governor Muñoz's description from a different context of argument) in which it is employed to describe the container of rouge and face powder in a lady's handbag. And there is little to suggest that Congress will rapidly move from that utilitarian interpretation. Looking indeed at the difficulties involved in seeking to apply the classic doctrine of contract to the Puerto Rican-American relationship the student is tempted to echo Sir Frederick Pollock's terse opinion of that doctrine as one of the most pernicious ideas in the history of political theory.

"If the matter could be worked out in such a way," Professor Friedrich hopefully opines, with reference to some of his proposals, "that the arrangement would not imperil the bonds of mutual affection and regard between Puerto Rico and the rest of the United States, it might be feasible." Yet surely the crux of the whole matter rests upon what definition at any particular moment Washington is prepared to place upon "bonds of mutual affection and regard." So far Congress has been reluctant even to accede to the mild demands of the Fernós-Murray Bill; almost every session of Congress confronts the Commonwealth government with a powerful challenge to its exemption from federal minimum-wage legislation by the American union movement; and Congressional investigating committees have been willing enough to abuse their power in order to brand the island (as they did in 1959) as a "nerve center" for dissemination of Communist propaganda throughout Latin America; nor has Congress shown willingness, in that last matter, to accept the thesis of San Juan attorneys that Public Law 600 has invalidated the constitutional legitimacy of the Congressional investigative power in the island.[26] None of this looks like a deep concern for "bonds of mutual affection and regard"; nor does it encourage optimism about the willingness of Congress to accept, for example, Professor Friedrich's proposal that the present Congressional power unilaterally to amend the local constitution shall be limited by granting the Puerto Rican public will an effective veto over amendments to which it objects. Until such a veto exists, however, the Commonwealth government, on Professor Friedrich's own admission, is unfairly subjected to unilateral Congressional interference in a vital matter; for he who can amend a constitution is the master of it. And that both Puerto Rican and American theorists feel this to be so is evident from the effort they take to invent desperate arguments to avoid that conclusion. It would certainly be desirable that Congress concede the Puerto Rican right to exclusive amendment, with the single proviso that such amendments be accommodable to the terms of the Federal Relations Statute and the federal Constitution. But until Congress takes that step there is no alternative except to conclude—as Henry Wells and Victor Gutiérrez-Franqui tacitly admit in their argument on this point— that the role of Puerto Rico throughout has been nothing more than that of a drafting agency for Congress.[27]

It may be said, more generally speaking, that the Congressional retention of the amending power, like the more general power of Congress to annul local legislation under the two earlier Organic Acts of 1900 and 1917, is no real affront since it will probably never be used by Congress. The answer, here, is twofold. In the first place, even if this be so, it ignores the psychological elements involved in freedom. Men live by symbols as much as by facts, and the humiliation of being subject to a superior will is none the less real because the will may lie dormant. Second, there is always the possibility, however slight (and, in any case, the ever-present apprehension of the possibility), that Congress may exercise the will. Those who like to compare the "new invention" of an American "creative federalism" in Puerto Rico with the British Commonwealth might be reminded, in this respect, that for some sixty years after the passage of the North America Act of Confederation Canadians fondly imagined that they enjoyed full freedom, until the grave events of 1926 showed that gubernatorial reserve powers generally considered ornamental only could be invoked to imperil the dignity of both cabinet and Parliament. MacKenzie King's important speech to the Canadian House of Commons on that occasion makes instructive reading today for Puerto Ricans concerned with Congressional powers over their territory.[28] It is not unexpected, therefore, in the light of all this that Puerto Rican critics have been skeptical of the Commonwealth analogy; and that they have seen in positions like those of Professor Friedrich an essential ambivalence in which their authors are boldly liberal in the abstract principles they cite and unhappily conservative in the facts that they propose to retain in their "final" solutions.[29] The portrait of an American expanding federalism emerging to solve the Puerto Rican status issue is impressive enough. But, on examination, one is tempted to remember Herbert Spencer's remark about a beautiful theory murdered by a gang of brutal facts.

Ever since 1899, when the newly formed Republican Party

promised in its platform that "The day shall come very soon when Porto Rico shall have a place among the several States of the Union as one of them," the ideal of federated statehood has never been without its institutional expression in the island politics. Party leaders have pointed to their prolonged American citizenship, to the Puerto Rican record of political stability, to their loyalty to the flag during all the wars of the period in which the United States has been involved (a Republican Party address to the Congress in 1919 pointed with pride to the fact that prosecution in the island during the First World War period for evasion of military duty or for infringement of the espionage laws was practically negligible, as a justification of their claims).[30] The passage of statehood bills for admission of Alaska and Hawaii has sent an electric current of new hope into the movement. For, prior to that, it had been usual to assume that non-contiguous territories possessing multiracial populations unassimilated to the American culture would never be accepted as new states by Congress. Senator Beveridge's dictum, that giving self-government to such populations would be comparable to giving a typewriter to an Eskimo and asking him to print one of the great daily newspapers of the world, had seemed to be irrevocable. But the barriers now are down; and there is undoubtedly a growing bandwagon sentiment among the island electorate for a rejuvenated effort to make of the territory, in the phrase of an earlier Republican Party statement, "a prosperous and happy American commonwealth."

The leading argument usually advanced against statehood is that of economic cost. It is part of the *Popular* catechism to assert unequivocally that the automatic removal of the present tax exemption and the immediate application of the federal minimum wage standard (which statehood would involve) would bring about the virtual collapse of the industrialization promotion program. Governor Muñoz, speaking on the basis of calculations made by his government economists, has estimated that statehood would compel Puerto Rico either to assume a fantastically heavy double income-tax burden or (in order to meet the new federal tax obligations) to cut down her own internal tax burden to a degree that would gravely impair the present structure of local social services. The 1959 report on the matter by the Bureau of the Budget estimated that statehood would cost the territory a total absolute increase of some $188 million in federal contributions, a truly formidable increase, percentage-wise, on the present obligations of the local taxpayer. Nor would this loss be offset by the comparatively minor increase—approximately some $32 million—in the Commonwealth budget that would accrue by means of increased federal grants-in-aid that would

come to the island as a state.[31] The Commonwealth government
estimates may be suspect; and it is certain that the Fomento agency
heads who told the visiting O'Brien Committee of 1959 that statehood would mean closing down their shop entirely were probably
guilty of irresponsible exaggeration. Nor is it yet a proven truth
that only exemption from federal taxation brings, and keeps, industrialists in the island. Nor, again, has it been proved beyond doubt
that as a state Puerto Rico could not hold up its end in competition
with other states for the patronage of business; there is much truth
in Luis Ferré's observation to the same O'Brien Committee that the
success of Florida over the last few years in attracting new industry
indicates that a state possessing no more natural resources than the
Caribbean island can succeed handsomely in that game.[32] Yet there
seems little doubt that even if statehood were not economic suicide
it would certainly entail, to begin with, heavy economic sacrifices of
no mean order. It is silly to ignore that truth. Thus it is not enough
to argue, as Luis Ferré again has done, that because Puerto Rico has
twice the number of children and aged people as the state of Okla-
homa it follows that, as a state, the territory would receive double
the amount of federal aid in public assistance which that western
state presently receives; for it leaves out the important qualification
that Puerto Rico, correspondingly, would also be obliged to double
its local contribution, through the matching device, before being
eligible for federal funds.[33] Nor, again, is it sufficient to argue that
the Puerto Rican capacity to carry increased tax burdens is proved
by the fact that Rhode Island, in size only one third the area of
Puerto Rico and with a lower total population, can afford to pay a
total of some $256 million in federal income tax; the analogy is in-
appropriate because the proper criterion of comparison is neither
population nor territorial size but the relative state of wealth of the
individual state.[34] The proper item to emphasize is the possible willingness or unwillingness of the Puerto Rican people to accept the very
real price they would have to pay for statehood.

Yet the real problem perhaps is not, after all, that of cost. Certainly
there is little in the history of territorial graduation to statehood to
suggest that Congress has ever regarded ability to pay its federal way
as absolutely indispensable to acceptance as a new state on the part
of a territory. And as far as local political attitudes are concerned the
difference between the *Popular* and Statehood positions, ever since
Governor Muñoz's Cidra Declaration of 1959, is now one of degree
only and not of kind. For by promising in that announcement that
when the individual income level of the island, as determined objectively by the United States Department of Commerce, becomes

equal to that of the poorest state in the Union the Commonwealth government will request Congress to terminate the existing fiscal arrangements and arrange for a plebiscite to be held to adjudicate between commonwealth status and statehood, the Governor in effect at once conceded (1) that the present incompatibility between statehood and maintenance of the rhythm of insular economic growth is temporary only and (2) that the *estado libre asociado,* far from being the new and final political solution it has been so dithyrambically applauded as, is in reality a halfway house based upon a transitional collection of economic facts.[35] It amounts to saying that the Republicans want statehood now, the *Populares* are willing to consider it later when they can agree that it no longer constitutes (as they now view it) a clear threat to insular living standards. This probably, of course, is tantamount to deferring the decision for another generation, for the territory is still a long way behind the poorest state. What is more, the projections made by the Planning Board with reference to the growth of personal savings and of the national gross product within the next fifteen years (concluding that by 1975 the economy will have reached an average living standard comparable to that of the United States in 1950) are essays in undiluted optimism, for they are founded upon assumptions about the savings pattern of the average family as it graduates to higher income brackets and about corporation habits in determining profit policies that are never elaborated in any detail in the technical reports. His Republican opponents consequently welcome the Governor's turnabout in favor of at least the ultimate possibility of statehood but suspect the motives that persuade him to hedge it with such a problematical qualification.

From then on, presumably, the debate on statehood would center around non-economic considerations—in the Governor's phrase, the "weightiest moral, spiritual and cultural reasons." On the Puerto Rican side they will almost certainly be mainly considerations of culture. The local Republicans will urge, as they now do, the full cultural assimilation to America; their opponents will style the idea, one way or another, cultural genocide. That there are large reasons for pause admits of little doubt. For it is open to serious question as to whether the Americanization of Puerto Rico can ever be any more successful than the French effort to obliterate all German traits from Alsace-Lorraine after its recapture from German occupancy. The particularity of the island has always been pronounced. Its neo-Hispanic traits were not overlaid, after 1900, with a popular colonizing movement from the mainland. The precedent of New Mexico does not really apply, since the Spanish and Indian groups of the old Southwest were (unlike Puerto Rico) isolated outposts of Hispanic

America encircled by a vast and comparatively empty land. The ties of Puerto Rico with the Latin countries, although not too strong, would not at the same time be that easily broken. It is possible indeed that the territory as a state of the Union would present the American people and government with a serious irredentist problem they have never before encountered. For just as the *incondicionales* under Spain endeavored to drown the local cultural personality in an ultra-Spanish connection, so today the Republican *incondicionales* seek to drown it in an ultra-American connection. In both cases there is present a basic absence of respect for the cultural ingredients of the national self, an earnest anxiety to prove the "loyalty" of the colonist to the governing power. This is why the Republicans throughout the American period have been foremost in emphasizing the material advantages of colonial ownership, taking the form, to take examples only, of requesting the colonial power to establish a naval base in San Juan,[36] or to locate an army brigade in the island,[37] or to recognize in general the strategic importance of the island at a time when the United States is experiencing difficulties with the maintenance of overseas bases in countries where political pressures are agitating for their removal.[38] They inhabit a universe of values in which the ability to speak English or the compulsory use of the flag salute in the schools become badges of a frenetic American patriotism, with themselves regarded as its only genuine local custodians. At the less political level it takes the form of subscribing to *Time* and *Life* magazines in their English language editions, of preferring the phonograph records of Nat "King" Cole murdering the Spanish language to the authentic Latin American product of Pedro Vargas or Lucho Gatica, of embracing tourism as a more important source of income than industrialization, so that the island may become the "Majorca of America," without being aware seemingly of the moral and social consequences of such a choice. And all of this finally to be placed at the service of American foreign policy in the Latin American hemisphere, in such a way that Puerto Rico as a state could become an interpreter of America's "sense of democratic values" to those Latin countries where a full appreciation of that truth is frustrated by the "false feeling, unfortunately widespread in Latin America, that the American considers himself a superior race."[39] Puerto Rico, in effect, would at once become a passive victim of the Americanizing process and a willing instrument in the hands of American foreign policy architects. This could mean, in the long run, the comparative dissolution of the Puerto Rican national individuality.

The final irony of all this is that, so far, the United States has shown little disposition to conciliate its Puerto Rican loyalists. The island Republicans are affiliated to the national Republican Party organization. But so far they have been unable to persuade that organization to accept a continuing and unequivocal support of statehood for the island; the party platform of 1952 included a promise of support, but that of 1956 omitted it. The primary value of a Puerto Rican delegation to one of the stateside nominating conventions, whether Republican or Democratic, seems indeed to be one purely of an entertainment value. It is doubtful if many Americans knew anything much about Puerto Rico until Judge Romany supplied a moment of laughter to the tension-bound Republican convention of 1952 by demanding a poll of the three island delegates; just as earlier, in the 1932 Democratic convention, the sole value of the Puerto Rican delegation appears to have been the opportunity it gave Jim Farley to place Mayor James Curley of Boston, then at odds with his own Massachusetts delegation, temporarily in its membership so as to ensure his eligibility to vote. The inclusion of Hawaii and Alaska does not necessarily mean that the "Bible Belt" would still not resist the gift of statehood to a heavily Catholic Puerto Rico, or that the South would not fight against the entry of a population containing a sizable Negro element. In any case, there is the argument of expediency: the record shows that Congress is prepared to endure the grueling trauma of a statehood battle just about once in a generation. If there is any chance then of a successful attempt on behalf of Puerto Rico it might not come much before the bicentennial anniversary of the adoption of the federal Constitution. And by that time, too, the statehood enthusiasts should be reminded, the process of administrative centralization (which makes the individual state today far less prestigeful than it was in 1898) will have gone even further, with the concomitant result of converting the individual state more and more to a position where, to use the description of Justice Roberts, it is less a coordinate sovereign and more an administrative district of the national government. As the prize comes nearer its suitors may discover that it glitters less resplendently.

Only a full-fledged independence perhaps can forever end the Puerto Rican magnificent obsession with status. Both the present status and that of statehood rest, in practical terms, upon continuing American good will. Each presently involves its respective protagonists in a humiliating search for favors from Washington. It is only necessary to read the acrimonious exchanges between the Resident Commissioner and the Vice-President of the Statehood Party in 1959 concerning their relative merits as lobbyists in the federal capital for the interests of Puerto Rico to appreciate how colonialism reduces its subjects to the status of anxious mendicants at the main portals of the ruling nation. The rosy anticipations of huge federal expenditures in their turn encourage a politics of patronage, so that it becomes of ever-present urgency for San Juan to anticipate, by intelligent guesswork, the trends of Washington politics; this is why, for example, Muñoz began to veer away from his Democratic connections after 1946 in the expectation of a Republican victory in 1948. The continuous need to anticipate what Washington will think, to court the federal power by not asking too much or too soon, to carry on a debate the essential terms of which are always set by Washington, has the accumulative effect of deepening the insular mood of a half-defensive, half-aggressive inferiority. Sometimes it takes the form of an exaggerated effort to please the representatives of the ruling power; sometimes it becomes a tendency to exaggerate, in public pronouncements, the hazards of the insular economy. The greatest blessing of independence would be to heal that one deep wound of the Puerto Rican human nature.

The entire discussion of independence has been throughout utterly distorted by an irresponsible exploitation of the fears it arouses with reference to its presumed economic consequences. For the sudden loss of the American subsidy, as well as the termination of the free-trade arrangements, would bring economic, and after it, perhaps, social and political chaos; of that there can be little doubt. But what is often lost sight of is the plain truth that the prevention of such a tragedy is an American and not a Puerto Rican responsibility. The insular economy's reliance upon free trade and federal subsidy is the outcome of American policy, and so is the general consequence of making the economy a subsidy economy based precariously upon the spending mood, at any one moment, of the federal Congress, and thereby preventing it from developing healthy and rational trading relationships with non-United States markets in the Caribbean and Latin American zones. Just as in the cases of Guam and the Philippines, the local unit after 1898 was forced, by that federal monopoly, to sell its agricultural products in a cheap market and to buy its industrial products in a dear one. Operation Bootstrap has not radically altered this economically irrational nexus with the federal continental system. For the Puerto Rican *independentista,* one general conclusion flows from all this. It is this: that the United States, by reason of these policies, now has a profound moral obligation to guarantee some measure of economic security to a politically independent Puerto Rico. It should take the form, ideally, of an economic treaty, accompanying the act of political autonomy, valid for a fairly long period and ensuring for that period both continued free trade with the United

States market and possibly a continued subsidy, by way of economic reparations, for a limited time period to be mutually agreed upon by both parties. Precedent for such an arrangement exists in the proposals put forward by the Trinidad government in 1960 for the continuation of United Kingdom economic aid to the former West Indian Federation when it would have reached Dominion status, to take the form of planned development grants.[40] American acceptance of the general principle behind such recommendations, moreover, is implicit in the economic development program of the 1960 Act of Bogotá.

No student of the Puerto Rican problem of course would lightly underestimate the massive difficulties involved in all this. It presupposes a quality of statesmanship that, whatever the general principles announced from Washington, has seldom characterized American practical behavior in the Caribbean region. Congress has so far shown little disposition, as far as Puerto Rico is concerned, to go beyond bills, like the Tydings measure of 1943, that offer political independence without economic aid. The executive branch in its turn has not gone beyond bald presidential announcements of a readiness to offer independence to the island at any time that insular opinion demands it. The single precedent of joint executive-legislative action in this field—the grant of independence to the Philippines in 1946—is not a reassuring one, to put it mildly, for the grant was accompanied by economic terms so onerous that they had the effect of making the new nation economically dependent upon the United States by means of unilaterally imposed statutory quotas on Philippine exports and of a fixed currency exchange rate highly unfavorable to the Filipino *peso*; not to mention the iniquity of a "parity provision" which prohibited Filipino discrimination against American commercial interests while failing to do anything about the removal of the mass of American discriminatory practices against Filipinos. Nor is the subsequent history of Washington-Manila negotiations on the question of American indemnities for war damages an encouraging one. Governor Muñoz has described in graphic terms the effect that a reading of the Congressional hearings on the Philippines Independence bill of 1946 had upon his political thinking. They convinced him, he has recorded, that the economic advantages enjoyed by Puerto Rico could not continue if Puerto Rico became an independent sovereign state; that political plank, he observed, would destroy the economic planks with the devastating fury of a tropical hurricane.[41]

All this, and even more, is true. That is why the present leaders of the island government urge that independence is an abstract concept and that it would be palpable irresponsibility to sacrifice the certitude of present benefits to the hazard of future problematical gains. The Burkean empiricism is persuasive enough. But before being overwhelmed by it at least two considerations ought to be pondered. The first is that there is a very real incertitude even about the permanency of the present economic benefits that flow from the Commonwealth relationship. If independence is "utopian," so is a Commonwealth status still incomplete, on the confession of its own architects, and still requiring an unending parade of requests for concessions and refinements from Washington. In both cases a struggle remains for the future and for the attainment of two differing concepts which at the moment remain, each of them, pieces of unfinished business. The choice confronting Puerto Ricans, then, is not (as the *Populares* would have it) one between reality and sentiment, but one between two competing sentiments. The second consideration is that what sacrifices a people is prepared to make depends at any time upon a number of variables. The sacrifice that Muñoz requested of the *jíbaro* in 1938—ceasing to sell his vote to the highest bidder—seemed heavy enough at the time, perhaps as heavy as those that independence might require a generation later. In 1938 Muñoz's request, too, was branded as "unrealistic" and "sentimental," in much the same way as the ideal of independence is branded today by its critics. It is the history of all minority ideas that, to begin with, their so-called "impracticability" is invoked as sufficient evidence of their utter madness, until new circumstances emerge to make them appear as sensible solutions to the problems that originally provoked their rise. This was the case, in the last Puerto Rican generation, with the *Popular* idea of social and economic justice. It could be the case, in the next generation, with the idea of national independence within the framework of an interdependent world.

The debate on status reached a new boiling point with the decision of the Commonwealth government in 1962 to conduct the long-awaited plebiscite on the matter, heralded by the exchange of correspondence with the President. Opinion about the motives stimulating the decision must of necessity be speculative, although it is worth noting that some local opinion saw in the decision an attempt on the part of the Washington administration, with Puerto Rican collusion, to forestall an adverse vote in the United Nations when the Committee of 17 concerned with colonial problems began to address itself to the Puerto Rican issue. Be that as it may, the now famous plan for the "culmination" of Commonwealth status, seeking to clarify the moral and juridical basis of the territorial association with the United States, provided once more a *mise en scène* for the favorite pastime of the Puerto Rican legal and academic classes, the deliverance of extraordinarily longwinded discourses of abstruse constitutional legalism. In one way, of course, the plebiscite was a step forward, since it signified the abandonment on the part of the governmental party of the peculiar thesis that its own series of electoral victories over the years had in themselves constituted a sort of favorable plebiscite for Commonwealth status—a claim properly dismissed at one time by the Chairman of the House Interior and Insular Affairs Subcommittee as "sheer nonsense." In every other respect, however, the plebiscite, in all of its complicated stages, was a regrettable error. For, as a device, the plebiscite is always unsatisfactory. It is alway difficult to separate the essential from the occasional elements of the question in hand; a rational debate gets clouded with emotions; the administrative regulation of the thing tends to get politicized, unless there be some sort of effective international supervision; the alignments of public opinion do not usually depart from the already existing alignments of partisan convictions; and very often the result of the voting, as was the case with the Jamaican referendum of 1961 on the question of continued membership in the West Indies Federation, fails to deliver an overwhelming majority one way or the other. To all that must be added, in the Puerto Rican case, the fact that the time-period involved was too short to permit of the exhaustive and lengthy educational movement so utterly necessary if the average island voter was even going to begin to understand a series of plebiscitary alternatives so legally abstruse that not even the lawyers could agree upon a common interpretation. No people, after all, ought to be requested to deliver a collective opinion on the momentous issue of their political destiny with such an absurdly short period of time at their command.

Yet there are more fundamental objections. It was patently absurd to plan a plebiscitary vote in which the voter would be asked to decide between the clearly defined formulas of statehood and independence and the vague, undefined formula of a "perfected" Commonwealth status which failed to itemize the constituent elements of "perfection": he would be voting completely in the dark. Nor did the later elaborations of "perfected" Commonwealth status, as they emerged out of the local public hearings, do much to clarify the position; in fact, they merely served to make confusion worse confounded. For what emerged out of that debate was a massive "grand design" of sweeping constitutional reforms to be presented in legislative form to the Congress and presumably having behind them the moral force of the overwhelming majority of the insular citizenship. Merely to list them is to appreciate their audacious quality: Puerto Rican participation in the national Presidential vote; a direct voice in federal actions affecting the island, perhaps including special representation in Congress; a

formal "reaffirmation" that Congress has abandoned its power to unilaterally abridge the Commonwealth "compact" relationship; and an
assurance that the "compact" is "permanent and irrevocable," presumably to be obtained by the passage of an amendment to the federal
Constitution. In their collected form, they clearly bring together the
minimum demands which the Puerto Rican governing class feel they
must have granted to them if the Governor's plea, in his letter to the
President, that the time has come to "eliminate any possible basis for
the accusation, which is made by enemies and misguided friends of
the United States and Puerto Rico, that the Commonwealth was not
the free choice of the people of Puerto Rico acting in their sovereign
capacity, but was merely a different kind of colonial arrangement to
which they consented," is at all to be met.

No student of American constitutional law is likely to underestimate the fact that all this presents one of the most drastic challenges
to the federal form of government since the historic southern attempt
at secession. Every single item of the scheme would assuredly arouse
a heated controversy, once presented to the Congress, for they all run
counter to the leading governmental concepts accepted by the American political mind. The Presidential vote item, like the claim for irre-
vocability, would require a constitutional amendment and the very
time period that that would involve would in itself be a serious disadvantage; apart from the fact that local participation in the Presidential
elections would immediately enmesh the insular political parties in the
web of the national political game. Insular participation in the exercise of federal authority concerning the local territorial matters, even
if it only meant, as Judge Pelayo Roman Benítez advised, something
comparable to the mechanism of Dominion consent to British laws in
the Commonwealth relationship, would revive once again in all its
fury the doctrine of local nullification and interposition with which
Calhoun sought to cripple the federal power over a century ago, and
President Jackson's classic rebuttal of the doctrine would apply as
much to Puerto Rican claims in one century as it did to South Carolina's claims in another. Once again, Puerto Rico finds itself claiming
entitlement to powers denied to the individual States of the Union;
and, in addition, there is evidence, this time, that the gross absurdity
involved in seeking to obtain from an increasingly conservative Congress a fundamentally new "compact" going far beyond the mild proposals summarily rejected by Congress in 1959 has its motivating
reason in the Governor's desire, natural enough, to leave behind him
a monument to his political genius. It was not surprising, then, that
once it became evident, by the spring of 1963, that Congress was cool
to the whole plebiscite idea the Commonwealth government sum-

marily threw it aside and turned its attention to the less radical scheme of obtaining Congressional consent for the setting up of a joint commission to enquire into the problem.

For, once again, the crux of the matter remains the powers of Congress and its willingness, at any time, to change them along basically radical lines. Puerto Rico proposes; but Congress disposes. The loose talk about "sovereignty" that characterized so many of the briefs presented at the local 1962 hearings on the plebiscite revealed an astonishing ability of Puerto Ricans to by-pass that uncomfortable truth, so disturbing as it is to their penchant for constitutionalist utopia-mongering. For that truth means at least two things that no plebiscite can hide. The first is that, the final disposition lying with Congress, everything really hangs upon the terms that Congress is prepared to attach to any of the three status formulas when the time comes for negotiation. Yet no one knows those terms; they remain unknown quantities. Ideally, the Puerto Rican voter, for example, ought to know whether Congress would be willing to accompany independence with a long-term treaty of economic aid, perhaps within the framework of the Alliance for Progress; equally, if he favors Commonwealth status, he has a right to know beforehand what items, if any, of the "culmination" program Congress would be willing to accept. Everything that is known, again, about Congressional views on statehood casts a pall of doubt over hopes of a Congressional willingness to accede to a pro-Statehood plebiscitary vote, even though that vote might have the moral force of an overwhelming plurality; that surely is the meaning of the blunt warning of Senator Clinton Anderson in his important letter to Secretary of State Dean Rusk that it is an erroneous impression to believe that statehood is primarily a matter for decision by the Puerto Rican people and that "such an impression, created by an officer of the Department of State in reply to a letter to the President of the United States might cause a great deal of misunderstanding and possible ill will if the plebiscite were to show that a majority of the people of Puerto Rico were in favor of immediate statehood at this time, yet the Congress were to refuse to grant it."[42] So long as this basic uncertainty prevails the Puerto Rican voter must feel at times that he is being made the plaything of a ridiculous comedy in bad taste. For to say the least, it is not fair, in the words of one angry citizen during the debate, to force a country to choose between one form of government (statehood) that is not yet attainable, and another (Commonwealth) that is not yet made perfect.

The second point flowing from the fact of Congressional supremacy is equally obvious. The Puerto Rican plaintiff, if he persists in asking for the moon, must devise ways and means of persuading Congress to give it to him. That explains the legalistic fancies of the plebiscite debate. Faced with the fact that there is nothing in American constitutional law that could make out of a local plebiscitary affirmation of one particular status an authoritative command upon Congress to grant it, proposals are advanced seeking in one way or another to bypass that obstacle. It is urged that any Congressional action to use its legal powers over the "compact" would make the Congress "internationally delinquent." It is suggested that an additional referendum be held to ratify the negotiations with the Congress, on the assumption, presumably, that the verdict of two plebiscites will be more morally pressing than that of one alone. Most fantastic of all in this jungle of juridical legerdemain, the idea is mooted that Congress should first recognize the sovereign independence of the territory, possibly by means of a Congressional resolution, thus leaving Puerto Ricans free to enter into any new relationship with the United States on an equal footing. It is not surprising, after all that, to be told, finally, by the Statehood adherents that San Juan should seek a constitutional amendment providing for territorial entry into the Union as a State, but with full safeguards for its economic structure and cultural framework. It is literally quite astonishing that after some sixty years of intimate relationship with American federalism there should still be such a profound misunderstanding of its general principles in the Puerto Rican mind.[43] So massive, indeed, is the discrepancy between the American reality and the Puerto Rican theory that the observer suspects that, in their hearts, the Puerto Rican governing class must know that in persisting in their policy they are in fact committing themselves and their people to a generation of further struggle with Congress. That is evident enough in the Governor's *cri de coeur* that his people must "ask and ask and ask again" if Congress denies their pleas. If that is what the future holds it is, in very truth, a bleak prospect indeed. It will condemn the Puerto Rican people to a permanent halt in the desert, in which they are offered a tantalizing Pisgah-view of their promised land but are forever denied an opportunity to enter it.

In the meantime the claim that the *estado libre asociado* is the "final solution" to colonialism becomes more and more flat, stale, and unprofitable. The very variety of the arguments that are pressed into service to justify the claim in itself raises some skepticism. At one point the Puerto Rican citizen is told that Commonwealth status is a final stage towards which he has been moving during some sixty years of a preparatory period in the school of democratic training, an argument that imposes a purposiveness upon Congressional policies it is very difficult for the student of Congress to accept.[44] At another point it is argued that because Puerto Rico has never been declared an incorporated territory—a prerequisite for statehood, if the case of Texas after 1836 be taken as the exception that proves the rule—it cannot qualify for statehood;[45] the argument is a good example of the fruitless inquiry into constitutional precedent that plagues the whole debate. Or again the Commonwealth lawyers attempt to build up an elaborate theory of mutual obligation contractually arrived at that is at total variance at once with the facts and with the more prosaic interpretation of the relationship to which Congress stubbornly holds. The local Attorney General's Memorandum of Law of 1959 thus speaks bravely of the gradual relinquishment of territorial powers leading, as he sees it, to a permanent divestiture of those powers; but the bubble is quite broken by the laconic comment of the federal lawyers that the general thrust of the relevant cases is to show that while Congress may throughout have thought that it should exercise its powers with great restraint, it has not intended to effectuate a permanent abdication of any part of its constituent powers.[46] The Commonwealth case is persuasively argued. But nothing can get the debate away from the single cardinal fact that Congress has insisted throughout, and still insists, upon understanding the vexed word "compact" in a narrow legal sense and not in a wide moral sense. Puerto Ricans have to be contented as a result with small concessions that are then blown up by the Commonwealth apologists into a significance out of all proportion to their intrinsic meaning or worth. And not the least favored of the devices employed in that exaggeration is to extract the most from each concession by making it the subject of a heavily politicized local referendum, as was the case with the debt-margin referendum of 1961. So, just as in the field of sociology the island has become a passive research laboratory, in the field of politics it looks like it is being rapidly reduced to the status of a permanent electoral college.

The Growth of Education

IN THE last analysis a society is no better or worse than its public opinion. That opinion in its turn at once creates and is created by the educational system of the society. These are truths pertinent to any liberal, democratic constitutional society. But they acquire novel meaning in the underdeveloped countries for a variety of reasons not so prevalent in the older societies. To begin with, the intellectual classes, in the broad cultural sense of the term, have played a far more important role in progressive political leadership in the younger societies. There has been comparatively little of a traditional reservoir of civility, of potential rival leadership from aristocrats or businessmen or trade-union officialdom; more, the professional groups have likewise been undermanned; with the result that the intelligentsia have enjoyed almost a monopoly in the movements of colonial agitation. They have been able, correspondingly, to shape the public opinion of their societies in a way denied to their counterparts in more structurally varied societies like England or the United States. In turn they have been the product (like the Anglo-Indian educated class under the British Raj) of an educational system originally built up by the colonial power, so that, as a well-defined student class, they were at once the beneficiaries of the cultural growth sponsored by the imperial regime and the natural source for the recruitment of a turbulent leadership in the national anti-imperial movement. Nor has the subsequent eviction of the imperial outsider ended all this, for the new nation established by colonial revolt swiftly turns to education as a prime target for its reforming zeal. The school, at every level, becomes inundated with demands for education, of any and every sort, on the part of the members of the lower social strata who have been released from the imprisonment of custom by the revolutionary appeal. To an extent as yet unknown, therefore, in the older societies (America perhaps excepted) the educational process becomes not merely a purely intellectual experience or, as in Britain, the privilege of élite groups, but a vehicle itself of social mobility, a badge of social status, a mechanism whereby new graduating classes learn not only to understand society but also to manipulate it.

The Puerto Rican experience has followed much of all this. Both in the Spanish and American periods the intellectual class led the nationalist struggle. The contribution of the medical profession has already been noted. But there was, too, the contribution of the class of unemployed lawyers who, together with the doctors and journalists and teachers, constituted in the island, as elsewhere, the first stage of a socially conservative constitutional liberalism demanding little more than a fair share in the national government under an imperial sovereign they were not on the whole inclined to challenge in principle. After them came the second generation of protest, that of a more virulent politico-cultural nationalism concerned far more than its predecessor with (1) the defense of the Creole culture against the "alien" imperial culture and (2) a more fundamental reorganization of the social and economic structure of the society. This second stage was mainly stimulated in Puerto Rico by the influence of the New Deal, assimilated by leaders like Muñoz in their exile periods in the radical-bohemian circles of Greenwich Village during the inter-war period. Its cultural side received emphasis from the group of teachers at the local university who were utterly Hispanic (with undertones of Falangist sentiment) in their sympathies, while its more socially minded side was encouraged by the New Dealer element among the faculty—young instructors, for example, like Jaime Benítez and the small echelon of public-spirited New England Americans. This helps to explain why one solid core of the *Popular* mass membership after 1938 came from the island teachers and why some of the more outstanding of the *Popular* senatorial leaders after 1940 were teacher-politicians like Ernesto Carrasquillo and Doña Juana Rodríguez Mundo who saw themselves as the champions of reform measures—the guaranteed annual salary, for example, designed to protect a hitherto defenseless group of citizens. Likewise, in the third stage of national advance—when the intellectuals as an indigenous élite become transformed into a new modernizing oligarchy as the imperial power yields up more internal self-government within the colony—the intelligentsia once again plays a more public role than its counterparts in the Western nation states. This is why, once again in the Puerto Rican case, the University can claim with proper pride that it has been throughout a nursery of local administrative and professional statesmanship; many of the outstanding leaders in government have come from its teaching ranks—Rafael Picó, Arturo Morales-Carrión, Sol Descartes, to name a few only; while it would be difficult to overestimate the contribution to the social energy of the society that has come, over the last dozen years, from the University's annual yield of two thousand graduates in practically every field of professional competence. Add to all this the almost solemn respect in which the *catedrático* is held in the local society—for there is little of the mood, half of tolerance, half of contempt, characteristic of the attitude of American public and American college students alike to the figure of the college teacher—and it becomes easy to see why in Puerto Rico as in most other emergent nations there has grown up a quite fresh appreciation of the Platonic maxim that the most important minister in the state is the minister of education.

The local progress in education since 1900 has been, by any standard, remarkable. The Spanish regime had introduced only the bare rudiments of a public education system, so that by 1898 some 77 percent of the population were still illiterate and some 92 percent of children in the 5-17 age groups (an astonishing percentage) were not attending school. Even then the system was poisoned by the government suspicion that the teaching force was always a potential source of heretical ideas; physical conditions were wretched and almost totally neglected by a local administration whose sole concern was that its statistical reports to Madrid should merely indicate some increase in the school population; teaching even at the secondary school level was based upon the almost medieval assumptions of Spanish pedagogy; and whatever existed of professional education was the result almost exclusively of private societies and of sporadic efforts of the Church. Just a short quarter of a century later there had taken place a really miraculous improvement, as a reading of the 1926 Report made by the Education Survey Commission of Columbia University (the first scientific analysis of the island's educational problem ever undertaken) makes abundantly evident. The improvement in part was eloquent testimony to the American passion for widespread democratic education, as opposed to the European elitist prejudice. From the very beginning the American Commissioners of Education pursued that passion, often to the dismay of the local educated class who wanted higher institutions of learning to be created before the extension of elementary education to the masses was undertaken. In part, again, it was equally a tribute to the enthusiastic response of most of the islanders to the new policies. The one bright spot, indeed, in the dismal story of legislative policies after 1900 was the consistent generosity of the Legislature in its educational appropriations; the percentage of total tax collections spent on elementary and secondary school education since 1899 has, with very few exceptions, remained around 25 percent.[1] This meant that once the initial period of American tutelage was over (psychologically already by 1920, although the office of the Commissioner did not pass to the appointing power of the local government until 1947) Puerto Rican educational leadership rapidly moved forward to horizons of endeavor even going beyond the vision of their continental instructors. For if American educational administrators like Paul Miller (Commissioner after 1915) and Thomas Benner (the first Chancellor of the University after its legislative reorganization in 1925) brought energy, resourcefulness and imagination to their tasks, their Creole successors, Padín, Chardón, Benítez, brought gifts no less great to the challenge that awaited them, in particular the need (1) to reconstruct the Department of Education along the lines of an educational philosophy adapted to the special wants and conditions of Puerto Rican life and (2) to transform the national University from a low-class teaching institution, not recognized by any of the associations which acted as accrediting agencies for American universities (its status in 1940), into a real center of higher education.

The growth of an indigenous educational philosophy was made difficult for a number of reasons. It had to emancipate itself from the leading principles of an American system which, however well meaning, were fatally inappropriate to the local scene. Those principles, however admirable in themselves as they sometimes were, were transplanted wholesale to the island after 1900 and amounted in reality to the inculcation of "Americanism," the extension of the school system, and the teaching of English. Disproportionate emphasis was placed upon devices such as patriotic exercises (originally introduced by General Eaton who, as a Civil War veteran, saw the territorial problem in terms of keeping the national unity intact, as some latter-day experiment in "reconstruction," by methods that would naturally suggest themselves to the military mind). The new curricula were fantastically unreal, so that the average child came to possess little information about health, hygiene, nutrition, the civic conditions of his people, and the natural and scientific world in which he lived; while music and the fine arts were almost totally neglected, despite the natural enthusiasm that the Puerto Rican common man had always had for them. The school organization itself was of doubtful value, for it attempted to impose the traditional American 8-4 plan upon an economy in which the majority of children at best attended school for a meagre four-year period. Neither curriculum nor organizational structure, again, made any distinction between the education of the rural child and that of the urban child, with the consequence (endemic all over the colonial Caribbean) that the former was sacrificed to the latter: as late as 1940 there was not a single secondary school in any of the forty-five rural municipalities that contained some two fifths of the total insular population. And all of this, bad as it was, was made even worse by the presence of two additional factors peculiar to Puerto Rico. The first factor was the almost Hobbesian sovereign power that was vested in the Commissioner of Education, so that instead of a coherent and continuous educational policy there was in its place a series of spasmodic and uncoordinated innovations introduced by successive Commissioners with little reference to guiding fundamental principles attuned to local needs. The local school system as a consequence became, in the words of its leading local historian, somewhat like the political status of the territory, a ship without a haven to anchor in, roaming the seas with no definite home port in view.[2]

The second factor, however, was far more tragic in the evil that it worked. It was, of course, the whole matter of the language problem. From the outset, the assumption—a fatally mistaken one—of the American educators was, in the words of Victor Clark's Report of 1899, that "There is a bare possibility that it will be nearly as easy to educate these people out of their *patois* into English as it will be to educate them into the elegant tongue of Castile. Only from the very small intellectual minority in Puerto Rico, trained in Europe and imbued with European ideals of education and government, have we to anticipate any active resistance to the introduction of the American school system and the English language."[3] This objective of compulsory bilingualism distorted the entire educational process for over thirty years. So essential was it deemed, indeed, that the attitude of a candidate for the post of Commissioner of Education to that question became almost the sole criterion of his assumed fitness for the appointment; and, naturally enough, each Commissioner's tenure of the post became identified, almost to the exclusion of all else, with his particular variation on the general theme of the teaching of English. For the most part the result was educational chaos. The use of English as a medium of instruction meant, as the 1925 Survey Commission pointed out, not only that children did not remain long enough in school to obtain a real mastery of English, but also that all other subjects suffered, both on account of the priority of English in the curriculum and on account of the transmission of those subjects in a broken and formalized English on the part of inadequately prepared teachers. One has only to read a short story like Díaz Alfaro's *Peyo Merce enseña Inglés* to appreciate the grotesque farce that teaching under such directives must have become in many country schoolrooms presided over by teachers who could only privately wonder at the awful folly of the instructions they received from the insular educational headquarters. The pedagogical problem became, frankly enough, a political issue. To criticize the policy was to expose oneself to charges of sedition and "un-American" attitudes. Even today there is hardly a

Congressional committee that visits the island that does not sooner or
later betray the presence of at least one member who angrily notes the
absence of a mastery of English in the island's common people as
evidence of dangerous secessionist ideas at work in the educational
structure. It has taken some two decades or more for most of the
American educators who have come to the territory to accept the fact
that English is, and always will remain, a foreign language in Puerto
Rico. "As an educator," Dr. Padín said finely of the problem, "I can
not accept English as a taboo or a Molochan deity. I deem it my duty
to challenge its claims and to adjust its place and function in the
curriculum, in the same manner as any other educational subject."[4]
This attitude has finally won out. But the wreckage left behind by the
unhappy experiment remains still to plague the Puerto Rican educational planner. To it must be traced the responsibility for both the
present inadequacy of much of the Puerto Rican populace in the use
of a full Spanish and their psychological resistance to the learning of
English. It is responsible further for the way in which government
policy on the teaching of English as a second language is still used as
a political football. Nor can there be little doubt finally that the difficulties presently encountered by Commonwealth educationists in their
attempts on the second language problem derive in part from the
failure of the American educational system as a whole to set up an
effective second language program for American school students. The
cultural evil that colonial regimes do clearly lives on after the extinc-
tion of their more overt political machineries. American political
federalism, in contradistinction to the Swiss or the Canadian, has
throughout demanded a cultural and linguistic uniformity that must,
in the present Puerto Rican case, be fatal to the *Estadista* dream of a
Spanish-speaking people pressing forward successfully as a claimant
for American statehood. It would be difficult to estimate the financial
waste, let alone the human waste, that this prejudice has exacted in
Puerto Rico over the last sixty years.

   It is urgent to stress all this for the reason that so long as the
island's political status remains unresolved the language, and therefore the educational, problems will also remain unresolved. For so
long as statehood is accepted as a feasible status at some future date
so long will its advocates insist that the cultural and linguistic refash-
ioning of the people, at least insofar as it means a complete mastery
of English, is a legitimate cost that must be paid for that status. So
long, conversely, that both *muñozcista* and *independentista* see the
political future in their own respective terms so long will they hold
that Puerto Rico needs no more than a working familiarity with, and
appreciation of, the American national language and culture. In the

meanwhile, the Commonwealth Department of Education must from time to time fight against the recurring efforts of Congressional politicians to revive the language "issue," as they see it; and it is still possible for President Roosevelt's unfortunate letter of 1936 to Commissioner of Education Gallardo to be cited in the local press in support of those efforts. The rectification of pedagogical error thus becomes the vindication of a cultural value, and will surely remain so as long as the political status question continues. Even the University of Puerto Rico still continues to use English in its two professional schools of Medicine and Dentistry, not merely as the language of classroom instruction but also, astonishingly, as the language used in all the schools' regulations, correspondence, public announcements, and even in informal relationships between staff and students outside the classroom and the laboratory.[5]

So long, once more, as Puerto Ricans retain their American citizenship a heavy emphasis will always be placed upon arguments of mere utility in support of the imposition of English—the argument, for example, that the island migrant to the continent will suffer less exploitation the better is his command of the language; the argument, as used by American educational advisers like Professor Hollingshead, for example, comes pretty close to urging that the insular educational system ought to be converted into a training school for the rational exportation of Puerto Rican laborers to the American employment market.[6] Alternatively, another argument frequently heard suggests that English should only be taught to those groups in the society that need it by reason of their professional or social position; thus class privilege manages to masquerade as pedagogical doctrine. Puerto Ricans cannot hope to escape this sort of thing until independence frees them from the artificial connection with the United States. Once that break is made, they and their educational guides will be able to address themselves to the rational and improved teaching of both Spanish and English, the first as their household tongue, the second as a leading additional language taught on its merits only. Until that is done, they will continue to suffer from a linguistic ambivalence flowing from their political ambivalence. "The money spent in attempting to turn this nation into a race of bilingualists ignorant and gullible in two languages," wrote Oliver St. John Gogarty of the attempt to introduce Erse into the Irish Free State, "would have given Dublin spacious streets and boulevards and restored it to the place it held as the Seventh City of Christendom before Napoleonic Paris was built." There is poetic extravagance in the sentiment. But it would be easy to forgive the Puerto Rican patriot who echoed it with reference to his presently not dissimilar predicament.

An educational policy for a free Puerto Rico would carry on much of the fine work undertaken in the last twenty years. It would continue the institution of the junior secondary school, known familiarly in the island as the second unit rural school, whose original establishment in 1928 and subsequent development marks one of the most significant events in the insular educational record. Significant in particular because it has placed primary emphasis upon the practical arts—agriculture and shopwork for boys, weaving and needlework for girls—and upon health work and social studies for the local adult population. This school has become the social center of the *barrios* in which it is placed and has consciously set out to become, in the words of the Commissioner's Report for 1945-1946, a laboratory wherein the child becomes a useful member of society and where he develops a social conscience of cooperating with his leaders in the elimination of prejudices that hinder the progress of the rural communities. Along with this there has gone the growth of vocational education, initially spurred on by the extension in 1931 of the benefits of federal legislation for vocational education to the island. The Division of Community Education of the Department of Education likewise has done wonders in the stimulation of adult education; one has only to look at its self-help program at the village level—commemorated in movies of some international fame—or at its rural library service run by volunteer librarians, or at its community leadership enterprises to be made aware of the massive enthusiasm at work in its dedicated staff. A Puerto Rican government that is democratic, finally, could not fail to pursue the truly Herculean achievement of the Commonwealth government in its devotion to the ideal of a popular, free education shared by all citizens capable of benefiting from it. The impressive consistency in the share of the Budget annually allocated to education—the 1960 Budget allocated 29 percent of its appropriations to education—would alone testify to the devotion. Certainly the Puerto Rican educational official has not been cramped in his style, as his British West Indian counterpart has been, by a traditionalist "Treasury mind" seeking financial retrenchment as the overriding criterion of administrative policy.

Even so, all this is a beginning only. Puerto Rican educational leaders face still a series of appalling problems. The relationship between income and attendance at the free public school is well known in the American federal system; and Puerto Rico is no exception. A recent study suggests, in its analysis of tests of schooling, that the number of Puerto Ricans in the under-25 age group who had had less than five years of schooling was 64.8 percent, compared with the national American average of 11 percent; while—another damning fact—some 39.7 percent of Puerto Ricans inducted into the military services in 1958 were unable to pass the mental test, with the consoling thought, if it be consolation, that five of the Southern states of the union showed even higher rejection rates.[7] The pressure of numbers on facilities remains heavy, and indeed gets heavier, so that some 17 percent of children in the 13-15 age group and some 55 percent of those in the 16-18 group receive no education at all. Of the 600,000 children, again, who are at school, nearly 30 percent are compelled, because of the dearth of facilities, to attend a half day only. The teaching load of the individual teacher is so crippling—there is one category of some 400 school groups where the average load per teacher is between 80 and 100 students—that the classroom must frequently become just an exercise in mass discipline. Part cause, and part result, of these conditions is the generally unsatisfactory atmosphere of the teaching profession; morale is certain to be low in a profession characterized by mass resignations—a Department of Education study reports that between 1953 and 1958 some 5250 teachers abandoned the calling.[8] There prevails still an unhealthy intermixing of politics and education. The Association of Teachers is openly divided between its official leadership and a *Movimiento de Renovación* that is mainly composed of Statehood adherents. The division has made of the recent annual conferences of the Association nothing much more than a series of strident shouting matches between the rival factions. There is a thinly disguised civil war, in turn, between the official leadership and the University administration, and it is not too difficult to see in the perennial disputes over educational theory and practice that divide both sides strong undercurrents relating to the war of nerves that has taken place for so long between the Governor's seat in La Fortaleza and the Rector's office in Rio Piedras. It is without doubt an unhealthy situation when the representative body of the bulk of the country's teachers can openly pillory the University administration as a political group seeking deliberately to sabotage the growth of graduate studies in the Department of Education at the University.[9]

To this political bias of the profession there must be added a social bias. No organized group in Puerto Rican life eulogizes more shrilly the ideal of democracy than the Association of Teachers. Yet no group is probably so conscious of its middle class aspirations and attitudes; most of its members indeed have entered the middle class through the University. They view themselves—as their negative attitude to the question of affiliation to labor unions indicates—as white collar workers above the common crowd. Their social sense rarely goes beyond professional self-interest; their Association's medical-hospital plan is one of the best in the island, but their public activities do not go beyond that point to embrace the democratizaiton of the larger society. There is evidence to support the feeling of one local observer that as teachers rise from the lower stratum families they tend to reveal intense hostility to lower-level habits; and a continental professional observer has suggested that it is probable that many of them evince invidious feelings of status in their feelings toward students.[10] This adulation of middle class norms, shared of course by other groups, bodes ill for the future of a genuinely democratic society. It inhibits the teacher, paradoxically, from undertaking collective effort to increase his salary rates, at present not much higher than that of the better-off factory worker, for such effort becomes identified with unionism. It helps promote the gulf of status that separates town and countryside. It is worth noting, there, that the report of the European advisory group of 1958 stressed the importance of rural teachers living in the communities where they teach, and that such a proposal has been proffered, on and off, for over a quarter of a century, certainly going back to Dean Fleagle's argument along the same lines in his book of 1917.[11] Above all, the middle-class prejudice places a high premium on the virtues of bureaucratization, so much so that in Puerto Rico it encourages an attitude of teacher passivity in the face of an educational system excessively centralized in its structure of authority. The centralization goes back to both the Spanish and American periods, when the habit of obeying commands from the top without question made the teacher's life something comparable to that of a private soldier in an army. Yet much of it still survives in a system and a period that loudly declare themselves to be democratic.

A great deal of all this goes back, in more general terms, to the fact that local educational theory and practice have been allowed to receive their mold from the leading orthodoxies of American education. From the very beginning the total reaction against the *damnosa haereditas* of the Spanish educational regimen precipitated a readiness to accept the American alternative. American educational pioneers like Eleanor Allen and Edith Flitcraft de Dastas, now long since forgotten, initiated the trend and it has never really been subsequently challenged. It would not be too much, therefore, to charge that one of the most grievous handicaps affecting insular educational growth since that time has been the willing subserviency to Teachers College of Columbia University in that institution's role as the Mecca of the latter-day progressive educational movement. Every article of the progressive credo has been practiced in the island; the island indeed has been a sort of experimental laboratory for that purpose. The consequences of that fact proclaim themselves in the contemporary system. There is the neglect of the gifted pupil in the name of democratic education; the sacrifice of substance to method, the conversion of technique into purpose, with the consequent erosion of exacting intellectual standards; the "life adjustment" that has converted a legitimate empiricism into a vulgar acceptance of the status quo; the subordination of individual development, always something of an anarchic thing, to "group persuasion" and "group dynamics"; the replacement of private studies with group projects, with all of their simulated realism and their accumulative destruction of the idea, traditional or not, that the chief aim of any wise education must be to educate the individual spirit within a body of learning, with a tradition and purpose behind it. There is the same religion of social activities in the school, and the same perverse logic which justifies them as equivalent to intellectual effort; nor is there absent the confusion about concepts of success and failure which leads educators into the dangerous argument that under a democratic system a child must not be permitted to "fail." All this of course is now well known to the American citizen who takes an intelligent interest in his children's school experience, if only because of the anguished public re-examination of progressive schooling that has been agitating the American public mind since the educational superiority of the Soviet system in the pure and applied sciences, if not perhaps even in the humanities, has become a demonstrable fact. The tragic irony of the Puerto Rican case is that the progressive canon is still embraced at every turn when its central premises are being thus openly challenged on the mainland. It is enough only to peruse the report on manpower shortages and education put out by the President of the Superior Educational Council to realize how much, even now, the Puerto Rican official mind is the prisoner of the narrow pedagogical doctrine that the business of higher education is to grant to its students the particular training which will fit them for immediate entry into the societal labor market; nor is that a theory only, for it embodies the tremendous social pressures that presently besiege the national University and that seek to persuade the University leadership into the idea that their primary function is to provide a manpower reservoir for the immediate functional needs of the economy. Puerto Rico might well become the last bastion of the progressive forces as they regroup themselves to defend an educational philosophy which, on the grounds of its own empiricism, has failed to meet the requirements of the national democracy.

That this is so is evident enough from a book like Dr. Theodore Brameld's study of life and education in Puerto Rico, *The Remaking of A Culture*, which has behind its findings the sponsorship of the College of Education of the University itself. The book, to begin with, is not so much Dr. Brameld's volume as it is a vast compendium of the recorded opinion on various local problems of two selected groups of "subcultural respondents" and "national leaders." It openly espouses, thereby, the exaggerated adulation of opinion as such, as if democracy were merely the patient excavation of opinions on the assumption that all opinions are born free and equal, irrespective of their relationship to larger truths qualitatively and not quantitatively estimated. The opinions are frequently interesting and throw much light on the intricacies of Puerto Rican social protocol. But it is difficult to accept the main thesis of the argument that education will be the sovereign remedy for the social ills it illuminates. When we are told that what Puerto Rico needs is an education that "not only attacks every problem germane to the nature of class relations, divisions, conflicts and objectives, but shares throughout in their solution" and, again, that "education is *not* the mere transmitter of the cultural heritage, however important this obligation may be; it is also and even more crucially remaker of the heritage,"[12] it is evident that at best the observations assume that an educational philosophy can stand above the class relations of a society instead of reflecting them and, at their worst, constitute a thinly disguised plea for the sovereignty of the professional educator in the manufacture of public policy. There is a sort of ecumenical liberalism at work here, anxious to consider every opinion, eager to believe that all social conflicts can be rationally resolved, passionate in its belief that education today, perhaps like religion yesterday, can unite the disparate groups of a class society. Yet when the liberalism analyzes the deep social snobbishness that accounts in Puerto Rico for the growing popularity of the private school among the new middle classes,[13] it is hard to believe that such powerful social prejudices will dissolve when confronted with a definition of freedom as the final goal of Puerto Rican culture that is so vaguely and widely phrased[14] that it could mean anything to anybody who cared to read his own convictions into its ambiguous framework. The book ends with a series of proposals as "next steps for Puerto Rican education," some thirty-eight in all. But, of all of them, it would be an arduous task to single out more than three that are primarily concerned with the intellectual substance of learning, the irrefragably minimum adventure of ideas; the rest are concerned with techniques, projects, pedagogical devices. For it is surely a debatable point as to whether a student will learn more about English literature by courses that utilize tapes, phonograph records, and films as the "principal instrument of learning" (Item 16) than by the earnest private reading of the great novels; or whether his understanding of international relations will be seriously increased by being confronted with Point Four visitors who would be used as "resource persons in the study of foreign cultures" (Item 9). The point to make is that, whatever the rights and the wrongs of the matter are, the Puerto Rican parent citizen is not really being granted the opportunity to find out. He has become the victim of American education in the same way as he has been made into the object of American government. It is heartening, of course, that there are signs of dissent. Thus a local journalist-academician can write favorably of Professor Arthur Bestor's critique of the high priests of American educational orthodoxy, and one of the leading educational theorists of the island can note that a considerable number of local educational leaders are beginning to suspect that in permitting itself to become a social-welfare agency the public school has brought upon itself confusion about its central mission.[15] But these are signs no larger than a man's hand. They are not yet the storm clouds of a full-scale revolt.

Puerto Rican higher education is served by the University of Puerto Rico and the two private institutions of the Inter-American University at San Germán and the Catholic University at Ponce. Both of the latter are smaller denominational schools, beginning, but only just beginning, to offer some healthy and much-needed competition to the national University. The future of higher education, for the time being therefore, is in effect the future of the state institution. Enough has already been said to reveal the prominent role that the University, like all collegiate institutions in developing societies engaged in profound metamorphosis, plays on the total insular scene. This explains why the political reforms of 1940 were followed by the educational reforms of 1942, with the reorganization in that year both of University structure and University purposes through the University Law of that same date. This explains too why the University has subsequently set out to reshape itself so that it could successfully play its role, in part, of a training ground for the personnel to meet the enormous demand for professional, technical, and administrative people unleashed by the industrialization program. An official report has estimated, so profoundly elastic is that demand, that by 1975 the economy will require a total of some 55,000 professional and some 67,000 managerial personnel. The Committee on Human Resources has likewise estimated that to fulfill this need the total University population will have to increase by some 20,000 above its present enrollment by 1975. Despite the notorious fallibility of prediction in these matters, there is little reason to disbelieve these estimates.[16]

Economic and social change, then, have been accompanied by

educational change. The change, under the imaginative guidance of Chancellor Benítez—appointed to the rectorial post only some three years after his graduation from the University of Chicago—has throughout laid emphasis upon three leading principles. First, it has set out to make itself felt throughout the entire society. For before the *reforma universitaria* the University was restricted, in its student body, to the sons and daughters of well-to-do families, a privileged group, dangerously undisciplined, frequently fascist in its political sympathies, and intolerant of any exacting mental demands. Enlarged now to over 21,000 students, part-time and whole-time, and buttressed by a generous scholarship program, the University today is a far more representative mirror of the society; within even a few years after 1942 one fifth of its students were children of manual laborers, one eighth of schoolteachers and one third of government employees. There is an ambitious extramural teaching program (that might soon flower into a system of community colleges), a fine cultural activities program, and an impressive policy, through the means of the mobile University theater, of taking the great plays of the Hispanic literary tradition to the audience of the small towns of the country. It is only necessary to look at the neighboring University College of the West Indies in Jamaica to realize the immense scope of the Puerto Rican enterprise, for whereas the latter serves all social classes its West Indian counterpart, dealing with a society of roughly comparable numbers, some three million people, has still to reach a student enrollment of one thousand and in temper remains too much a self-conscious institution studiously cherishing its Platonic isolation from the general community, a little corner, as its Anglophilist architects have seen it, in a foreign field that is forever Oxbridge. Secondly, in establishing its schools of pharmacy, engineering, dentistry, business administration, medicine, and natural sciences, the University of Puerto Rico has properly followed, Aristotelian-wise, the maxim that the education of the citizen should be accommodated to the special nature and constitution of his society. That could hardly be otherwise when it is remembered that admission to the University has become, for large segments of the population, one of the main opportunities, sometime the only opportunity, for social and economic enfranchisement.

Third, and finally, the University has sought to counteract the possible dangers secreted in that second point (it could lead to what a recent report on the University's School of Medicine has aptly termed the habit of "scientific atomization" in technically trained people) by exposing the freshman student to a liberal arts General Studies program concentrating upon the evolution of Western culture and the central problems of the contemporary social sciences. The practice of engaging prominent scholars elsewhere as visiting professors and lecturers, vastly stimulated by the present administration, has likewise worked to counterbalance the tendency to narcissism that is never far from the Puerto Rican professional mind. The outside influence has also been fostered by the work of the Social Sciences Research Center, where the continental sociologist and cultural anthropologist have found a hospitable atmosphere for studies ranging from the savings patterns of Puerto Rican families to the occupational aspirations of college students. The result has been that if, on the one side, the Puerto Rican historical collection in the University library is pre-eminent in its sphere as witness to a proper concern with the country's past, the liberal bent of the University leadership has stimulated, on the other, the growth of a body of empirical knowledge about the contemporary life patterns which, for all of the defects of the American sociological imagination, especially its habit of avoiding controversial discussion under the guise of a religion of fact collecting, is quite unique in the Caribbean. It is no longer true, in the words of the Chancellor's report of 1945, that "far more is known scientifically about the patterns of culture in certain sections of Samoa and New Guinea than about those of Puerto Rico; even Life in a Haitian Valley has been more carefully studied (by Herskovits) than has life in a Puerto Rican valley." All in all, the Chancellor can today rightly claim the institution he leads as an educational experiment on a cultural frontier. "To the tendency toward insularism," he has written, "we have opposed another, much more in accord with our age, with the spirit of our history, and with our aspirations for the present and the future; we have conceived of Puerto Rico as a community forming part of Western civilization, a frontier region where at one and the same time the best and the most diverse elements of our culture meet, and where in consequence it is necessary to take stock of the greatness, the temptations, the faults, and the possibilities of its way of life."[17]

How much, even so, is all this fact, how much the intoxicating rhetoric of the collegiate commencement address? In its academic standards the University, to start with, is still far from being the first-class institution of collegiate rank that it ought to be. Too much of its teaching, especially at the lower levels, must perforce preoccupy itself with correcting the unhappy limitations of entrants from secondary schools whose standards are much inferior to those of the secondary school products of the neighboring former British islands, for there has been nothing in Puerto Rico at all comparable to the Mico Charity in Jamaica and the Codrington Foundation in Barbados.

There is a serious gulf between basic and advanced courses, so much so that the General Studies faculty has very little opportunity to mature above the level of the freshman courses for which it is responsible. A director of the Basic Course in Spanish has referred to the pathetically limited command on the part of the freshman student of his own language and his general inability to use it as a vehicle of logical thought or verbal expression beyond the small change of daily conversation;[18] and the defects inhibit the growth of sophisticated discussion throughout the student's later college years. The American habit of assigned weekly readings from the usually dull college textbook so deluges the student that he rarely develops the art of independent reading, let alone that of building up his own private library of books. It is symptomatic that the University obtained its first real bookshop only in 1958, equally symptomatic that the libraries are used by most students as pre-examination study halls rather than as sources of learning. The new Student Center erected in 1960 boasts, among other facilities, an impressive bowling alley; yet the critical faculty member who scorns the set of values thereby portrayed might pause to reflect that things are not much more elevating in a Faculty Club whose Board of Directors can include the holding of an annual billiards and dominoes tournament among its important sponsored activities. The general practice, again, of the American-type "objective" examination produces all of the sad results attending its American usage: the temptation of the student to become little more than an intellectual detective; the handicap the method places upon the overly imaginative student whose tendency to see the complexity of an issue often defeats the "either-or" assumptions of the "true-false" question; and the failure, through the absence of sustained essay writing, to train the student in the discipline of putting his thoughts into his own words and style. The adjustment of grades to mass quality means that the exceptional student succeeds perhaps too easily, while the rest only too often remain individuals who are socially charming but intellectually unambitious. That lassitude is in turn encouraged by a University administration over-protective in its general attitude to the student body, nicely illustrated in the observation of the official report defending the introduction of the controversial scheme of regional colleges that such colleges would enable first and second year students to continue living at home and so continue to receive family help in the difficult years of adolescence.

But the most conspicuous example of bureaucratic coddling is without doubt the repressive paternalism with which the University administrators treat the matter of student political and intellectual activities. The student strike of 1948 provoked at that time an official restriction upon the general freedom of student activities that has remained in use to the present day. Political activities on the campus are banned; political speakers from the outside are denied access to college audiences and platforms; the general student council outlawed in 1949 has not been reinstated; and most of these prohibitions have their legal basis in amendments to the University Law made unilaterally by the Rector and the Superior Educational Council in 1950 without consultation with either faculty or student body. Nor is this grossly illiberal policy made any more palatable by a high-sounding administration ukase that permits student meetings and organizations only if they refrain from "partisan propaganda" and "indoctrination" and exemplify a "sincere attitude to a good politics" (whatever that may mean).[19] The injunction betrays an utter misconception of politics and political activities, for to assume the emergence of "political activities" that are not "partisan" is rather like requesting a system of marriage without sex. The criteria are too vague; they confuse "politics" with "controversy"; and they too easily permit the administrative officialdom to equate political activities that are "partisan" with political activities they do not like. Even worse: for in actual fact the regulations are interpreted in such a way as to permit meetings that are in reality partisan. Thus permission is refused to a student group to organize a faculty forum on the issue of the place of Puerto Rico in thermonuclear warfare, while the administration itself sponsors a series of campus lectures by Professor Carl Friedrich that constitute a thoroughgoing partisan defense of the Commonwealth government's official thesis on political status. In addition to all this, there has been a long battle to get the University hierarchy to respond to the appeal of the *Federación de Universitarios Pro Independencia* that they follow the lead of stateside universities such as Michigan State in declaring the ROTC system voluntary instead of compulsory, as is permitted, indeed, by the governing rules of the Morrill Act.

University policy of course cannot be separated from University structure. From the start, the University borrowed the chief features of the American state university system. Many of the difficulties that presently plague faculty-administration relations stem from this fact. There is, under the 1942 basic law, far too much reliance upon government, even to the point where matters normally regarded as being wholly University concerns, such as the administration of University finances and the supervision of University non-academic personnel, are largely controlled by respectively the Commonwealth Treasury and the government Personnel Board (a situation which, with reference to finance, was only terminated recently with a plan for University fiscal autonomy that permitted the academic center to be the sole overseer of its income and disbursements, subject only to an annual audit by the Commonwealth Controller). Change has been slower elsewhere, however. The University's structural organization, for example, fails to make a rational distinction between local campus government and central University administration, so that the Chancellor and the Dean of Administration exercise between them far too many responsibilities and far too many pedestrian duties that ought to be delegated to others: it is ridiculous, for instance, that the latter officer should be at once the leading administrative official next to the Chancellor and a campus authority concerned, among other things, with the orderly arrangement of campus vehicular traffic. There is a crying need for some sort of revitalized executive cabinet, concentrating solely upon University-wide policy, such as the Central Administrative Committee recommended in Mr. Burton Friedman's 1959 report on administrative reorganization.[20] In vital regions like the budgetary process, procurement and maintenance, investment of University funds, contract research, personnel administration, the University has failed so far to produce a corps of trained professional executives capable of meeting the demands of complex problems that have gone far beyond the power of adept amateurs to meet. Even comparatively simple things, like the establishment of a trained and uniformed campus police, too often come about as a hasty response to public indignation when cases of assault take place on the campus at night. Successive reports, both from the outside and within, have throughout the last few years again pointed to the gross defects in University library affairs, library facilities being, up to now, quite inadequate, both in quantity and quality of books, to serve the needs of a growing university contemplating extensive growth in its graduate programs. A report of the Faculty Representative has underlined the oddity of a library serving a Spanish-speaking university student body that possesses a drastic scarcity of books in Spanish in comparison to an overabundance of fiction in English, frequently of doubtful quality:[21] while some of the more severe passages in both the 1954 and 1959 reports of the Middle States Association on the University are those concerned with the state of the University library. The recent consolidation of the seven hitherto separate University libraries into a centrally administered system headed by a General Director of Libraries, and the appointment of an able library technician, John Ashton of Northern Illinois University, as Associate Director, promises at least a fresh approach to these problems. Not the least ironical aspect of all this, taken as a whole, is that the University has failed to provide for itself the professional executives it needs at the same time as it has provided, through its professional schools, the main bulk of trained career civil servants for the insular government. All in all it suffers from a structure of government that is virtually the same as it was twenty years ago, when there were fewer colleges and only a tiny fraction of the present vast student enrollment.

The really critical defect, however, lies in the fact that the sovereign authority of the University is shared, illogically and unsatisfactorily, between the Chancellor and the Superior Educational Council, the latter an extra-university lay board appointed, in the American fashion, by executive nomination from the Governor's palace and exercising delegated responsibility over large areas of the University life. The drawbacks of this division of authority have long been apparent. The Chancellor's authority, within the framework of his constitutional accountability to the Council, is far too monarchical. It is not sufficient to echo the more fanciful of the charges made against him by his critics to believe that the massive concentration of power put into his hands by the 1942 changes (which were originally conceived indeed as a wartime emergency), including the power, as general executive director of the University, to nominate and supervise teaching and administrative staffs, is fraught with danger. Too many officials are tempted to see their allegiance going to him rather than to the University; and one report has described the Dean of Administration as simply the *alter ego* of the Chancellor for the University centers outside the Rio Piedras complex. It is true that the two University Boards created by the same constitutional instrument possess consultative powers in internal administration matters. But the nature of their membership almost precludes a strong independency on their part since, with the single exception of a Faculty Representative chosen by secret ballot, they are composed of college deans who owe their own appointments to the Chancellor. It is not surprising that the Faculty Representative to the Rio Piedras Board should complain that too many matters, the construction of new buildings, the organization of divisions, the creation of new institutes or agencies, do not come to it for discussion, and that the most outstanding exception that he can cite is the inauguration of the new traffic plan for the University.[22] The frequency with which charges of non-consultation with the Boards and, sometimes, with departmental chairmen are made against the Chancellor's office, especially in the matters of faculty appointments, salaries, and leaves of absence, suggests that the machinery of University government at this point is gravely defective. There is much to be said accordingly for a root and branch revision of the 1942 basic law. The establishment in 1960 of two Academic Senates, combining in their membership elected faculty members and University Board members, with the former predominating in numbers, is a step in the right direction, since they give the faculties a voice and a platform they have hitherto been denied in University councils. The reform finally terminates a situation in which the faculties have had to work through the *claustros* on each campus, each of which were so large in their membership that, as legislative forums, they were unwieldy and inefficient. It was indeed appropriate that one of the first problems discussed by the Rio Piedras Senate was the proposed fusion of four existing colleges into a new single Faculty of Liberal Arts, for hitherto the growth of a general university *esprit de corps* has been frustrated by a sort of college empire system with college faculties generally ignorant of affairs and trends of thought in colleges other than their own. It is therefore sad to have to report that the inability of the Senate to reach any accord on that vexed issue has been followed by the inevitable invitation to an outside authority to write the inevitable outside report.

The introduction of the senatorial form, as a matter of fact, is reform only; it is not basic reconstruction. The weaknesses of the present innovation are obvious enough when the Faculty Representative can report that the four to six issues resolved in the Rio Piedras Senate during its first eighteen months of life have been in a form pleasing to the administration and that the really urgent problems facing the University have been avoided.[23] It is clear that changes looking towards academic self-government will have to be far more radical before they completely satisfy. The measures for University reform put forward by *claustro* papers and reports during the last three years or so certainly look far beyond the present regime. They would set up a body which, popularly elected but also including the Chancellor and the college deans, would take over the strictly academic functions presently exercised by the University Boards. The latter would remain as advisory bodies to the Chancellor in the strictly administrative field. The democratic principle would be further strengthened by the requirement that all deans would henceforward be named by the Chancellor in consultation with, and with the approval of, the individual faculties, and that they would serve for a maximum period of four years, with re-eligibility for appointment allowed. Even more: the Chancellor himself would be appointed, as is now the case, by the Superior Educational Council, but with the advice and consent of the Academic Senate; he would be named for an initial term of six years, but would be eligible for reappointment, again by the Council with senatorial approval. It would be worth adding to these proposals a body somewhat comparable to the Guild of Graduates in the governing structure of the neighboring university in Jamaica, thereby granting the alumni a responsible and continuing interest in the alma mater. The whole aggravating problem of relationships with the subordinate Mayagüez campus again can perhaps be solved only by converting that campus into a separate university in its own right, following the worldwide general trend, from California to Wales, towards the defederalization of modern universities. It might be going too far to say, with one of the more eager *claustro* critics of the present rectorial regime, that the general University atmosphere has become one of cynicism, with too many faculty members being preoccupied solely with making more money or obtaining a position of authority within the ruling hierarchy. It would be a brave person, even so, who would claim that the general morale of the University is that of a Puerto Rican Platonic academy. There is too much poisonous gossip, too much character assassination, too much altogether of a spirit of intellectual impotence. To say that this is the inescapable result of the nature of Puerto Ricans is to embrace the illusion of "national character." It is far more likely to flow from a social and intellectual energy that is at present not receiving adequate expression through fully representative institutions in the governance of the University.[24] The particular reforms here cited, of course, are open to debate; a fixed term for the Chancellor, for example, is a doubtful device of direct democracy which could arbitrarily interfere with the work of a first-class incumbent. At the same time, the narrow vote in the University faculty debate of 1963 shows that there is widespread sentiment in favor of basic reform. It is certainly libellous to seek to imply that the reformers are nothing more than *independentistas* or disappointed candidates for high office.

There is finally the question of the place of the Superior Educational Council. The original purpose in creating that body seems to have been to eliminate the excessive interference in the University's internal affairs that had been the chief vice of its predecessor, the old Board of Trustees, set up by the University Law of 1925. But the unhappy tussle between the government and the University during the last few years, although momentarily in respite, has demonstrated only too vividly that the 1942 reorganization has merely served to pour new wine into old bottles. Caught in the middle of that tussle, the Council has shown a readiness to invade areas—curriculum content, the reorganization of colleges and departments, internal operating costs—that ought to be the preserve of the University authorities. Paradoxically the tendency towards interference has been accompanied by a regrettable tardiness in arriving at vital decisions in other matters—the ratification, for example, of rectorial nominations to leading University posts, action on reports like those of Dr. Bowles in 1954 and of Floyd Reeves in 1955, the question of appointing a University Controller in order to help rationalize the University's fiscal structure—of some urgency. Or in turn the Council undertook to commission, in collaboration with the House Committee on Education, a series of reports on the University, usually by American consultants, without proper consultation with the University authorities; and the angry exchange of charges and countercharges precipitated by that fact undoubtedly constitutes one of the most undignified episodes in the history of Puerto Rican education. The general consequence of all this was that, for a prolonged period, there occurred a gradual slowing down of University activities. For if, generally speaking, the Council fails to act on its statutory powers, stagnation sets in, since no other body—the Rector, the University faculty, the administrative Boards—can usurp those powers. It may be exaggeration to see in all this a conscious war of attrition on the part of an unfriendly Council majority against the Chancellor. Yet the fact is that, to many people, it appeared to be so; and the suspicion only made a meeting of minds between the two sides all the more difficult to arrange.

The Council as it now stands has become, beyond power of contradiction, an archaic piece of machinery. Executive nomination of its members makes them seem to be, even if they are not, the creatures of the Governor. The triple role of the Secretary of Education being at once the President of the Council, the head of his department, and a member of the political cabinet seriously inhibits his usefulness, for his very impartiality is immediately called into question once the Governor adopts a public attitude of "no confidence" in the University leadership. He serves thus to subject education to politics. He is obliged to two masters; inevitably he must become either the ally of one or the suspect of both. The Council's membership of seven is far too small, commensurate to its duties; and if it is decided to mend it and not end it, it will be necessary, as Dr. Bowles has suggested, to increase its membership to no less than fifteen and no more than thirty, so that it may set up a proper system of subcommittees. The Secretary of Education should go, so that he could concentrate on his proper job of controlling primary and secondary education, and for which, of course, he should possess exclusive responsibility. If reconstituted thus, the Council ought to ponder whether it ought not to open its meetings to the press, for not the least of its present failings is that its habit of the secret session—an evil habit anywhere —ensures that the public shall only get the sort of information about its deliberations a Council member or the Chancellor is willing to divulge to insisting pressmen. Mention must also be made of the fact that (until 1961) at least two of the Council members have always been continental Americans, under a narrow interpretation of the statutory requirement that the Council shall include "two eminent educators identified by their history with the cause of democratic culture." This has produced an element of absentee government, for it has not been unusual for the continental members to arrive at Council meetings post-haste from the airport, trailing clouds of baggage behind them, or, even worse, for Council business to be held up while, because of their commitments elsewhere, the American members must be reached for their views by transoceanic telephone communication. The requirement, as it has thus been interpreted, is thoroughly colonialist in its assumption that Puerto Rico is not capable of producing at least seven persons of academic competence and democratic sympathies. Its usefulness in any case has in large part been nullified at the present moment by the remarkable achievement of one of the continental nominees in alienating practically all shades of insular opinion by the irresponsible arrogance of his behavior during his island visits. The place for the outsider in any case is on the consultative level, not on the level of permanent membership of a local governing body.

The Council, as a lay, part-time body, has without doubt outlived its original usefulness. Its responsibility for the supervision of the total insular educational system is too wide, with the growing complexity and specialization of education. What is now needed, as Alfredo Nazario has suggested, is a new University Law that would dismantle the Council and replace it with (1) the academic Senate (now in existence) to take over the general powers of higher educational supervision presently exercised by the Council and (2) an Insular Board of Education, to include the Secretary of Education and the University Chancellor in its membership and to be responsible for planning the general education of the society as a whole. The recommendations, if carried out, would make for enormous improvement. The Senate promises to relieve the titular head of the University of some of his own overcrowded duties; for it is no slight upon the Chancellor to say that, as with most American state university presidencies, the office has become under pressure less and less concerned with internal affairs and more and more concerned with external public relations and assiduous fund gathering. A reconstructed board of education in its turn would maximize the possibility of mutual trust between both sides as they worked together on the common educational problems of the society. In the long run the board, or some similar body, could become something akin to the

University Grants Committee in the United Kingdom, an institution that successfully performs the dual function of being at once the guardian of academic freedom and the watchdog of governmental interests, especially financial. Such a role requires of course both parity of representation and the presence of a sense of mutual confidence between both sides. The Governor has already agreed in principle to the changes in machinery that this would necessitate. For while it is true that the appointment in 1960 of a Secretary of Education more friendly to the University promised a more cooperative period between both sides, it would be dangerous to assume that institutional changes may therefore once again be shelved, for that would encourage the habit, already too prevalent in insular affairs, of leaving everything to the private interchanges of eminent personalities.

Once the decks were thus cleared, the way would be open for a frontal onslaught upon the educational ills of the society. At the lower levels there is the need to eliminate the evils of the *doble matrícula*— the double matriculation system whereby some 29 percent of schoolchildren can attend congested schools for only half a day—and the mass production of students with too little attention paid to individual idiosyncrasies. There is the failure to provide enough new schools to keep up with the pressing educational demands of the new communities spawned by the mass housing projects; the result is the kind of frightening chaos that takes place daily in a school like the elementary school of the *Hermanas Dávila* urbanization, where classes run full-blast from 7 A.M. to 5:30 P.M. seeking to "educate" 872 children in seven classrooms on three different shifts; or the madness of the Bayamon Central High School where some 2,900 students crowd into a thirty-year-old building to take "classes" in the cafeteria, the gymnasium, and even a part of the Principal's office space.[25] There is the problem, gigantic in itself, of the proper training of the teacher force, for there is an alarmingly high percentage of provisionally trained teachers in the total number, more than 6,000 as against 7,356 fully trained permanent staff. And even when fully trained the school system cannot be certain of keeping the teacher, for poor pay and a heavy student-teacher ratio—the average classroom in the system as a whole soars to an enrollment of sixty children—combine to produce a heavy loss through resignation: many teachers abandon the task for jobs apparently regarded as being more congenial. In such conditions, clearly enough, the professional ethic finds it hard to survive.

There are, again, all the problems concerned with the general principle of equality of educational opportunity. The general Puerto Rican view of education as a social escalator has already been noted. Yet that view becomes more and more of a social myth as facts belie its claim, as new realities overtake it. Recent sociological investigation suggests that whatever may have been the case earlier on there is, today, a growing failure to provide for the higher education of the children of the industrial and agricultural working classes as those classes increase in both absolute and relative numbers in the total population. Those children, as a group, are obtaining a declining share of university enrollments as against the children of the professional and white-collar classes. There is, even more, an increasing discrimination against the rural schoolchild in favor of his urban and suburban counterpart; when 49.9 percent of urban dwellers speak English as against only 28 percent of rural residents it is evident enough that the "new" Puerto Rico has not really solved the problem, so endemic in the "old" Puerto Rico, of the neglect of the rural masses and their children. The new regional colleges scheme may help here. But that is at best a long-term solution. The infant status of the scheme —the first regional college at Humacao has recruited only 250 students—suggests that it may achieve nothing more than simply provide new local educational opportunities for the same middle-class groups of the leading townships outside the metropolitan area.[26]

There are other problems equally pressing. The teaching of English as a second language (as distinct from the wholly different question of English as the vehicle of school instruction) is, it is generally conceded, in a bad way. Compared with the remarkable success in this field in neighboring multilingual Aruba, the Puerto Rican effort fails dismally, although it must be added, in all fairness, that much of the failure is directly attributable to the fact that, copying so closely the United States educational system, that of Puerto Rico has been victimized by the American failure to establish an effective second language program in its own schools. Even more: the Puerto Rican schoolchild, by virtue of living within the Caribbean, ought to have the chance to learn the other Caribbean languages apart from English, especially French and Portuguese. Educational materials suffer from the same copying habit, for some 80 percent of all textbooks used in the schools are ordered from outside publishers, despite the fact that the printing plant of the local Department of Education is capable of producing all that are needed.[27] The almost total neglect of the mentally retarded child must be remedied. Above all else, however, the public school system needs a massive improvement in its general quality at almost every level. That there is something fundamentally wrong can be seen from the growing strength of the private school, threatening, as it does, the rise of a dual educational system, with one education for the children of the middle class and one for the children of the poorer groups; there have even been physical skirmishes in Rio Piedras between private and public students. For there is a clear connection between the emergence of the flourishing private schools within the last decade and the growth of the new urban and suburban middle-class groups; with the single exception, perhaps, of the San Antonio Abad school in the Humacao region, none of those schools have made their appearance in the rural areas. Both a vague feeling in parents about the need for a religious education and the appeal of social snobbishness feed this drift towards the private foundation. The 1959 report of European educators is nothing so much as a pro-longed warning that if the Commonwealth government does not adopt a vigorous policy of bettering the public school, its facilities, its teaching force, and its standards of instruction, the tendency will continue, with its inevitable intensification of social stratification and class sentiment.[28] For in the long run, as the Caribbean Union of Teachers urged in its 1957 Conference Report, Caribbean society must have a system of free and universal primary and secondary school education for all children capable of benefiting from it. Nor should sight be lost of the fact, in the Puerto Rican case, that the private schools, especially the Catholic, have become at the same time vehicles of deculturalization, widely using textbooks in the English language and inculcating pro-American civic sentiments quite alien to the life of the Puerto Rican child, as the titles of such books—*This is Our Land, This is Our Heritage, This is Our Town*—reveal-ingly suggest. That fact makes all the more dangerous the persistent campaign of those schools, waged under the specious slogan of parental choice, to obtain exemption from governmental norms and standards. There is much to be said, altogether, for the demand of the *Tesis Política* of the *Movimiento Pro Independencia* that a free Puerto Rico should abolish the private school as being an instrument of social, economic, racial, and religious discrimination.

At the collegiate level, the *desiderata* have already been mapped out in a legion of reports. The University must go ahead to make of itself a center of higher education in the fullest sense. That means the creation of graduate study programs in all leading fields of knowledge. There must be a heavier emphasis upon graduate and post-graduate work. There must be a more imaginative treatment of the *patrimonio cultural*, the scientific analysis of Puerto Rican language forms, for example, suggested as far back as 1915 by José de Diego in his still-born scheme for an Antillean Union uniting the three universities of Puerto Rico, Cuba, and the Dominican Republic. There must be a better academic preparation for much of the faculty, for one does not have to condone the debasing of the academic coinage that the pitiably low quality of much of American doctoral work illustrates to be perturbed at the fact that only 20 percent of the University of Puerto Rico faculty possess the doctoral degree.[29] The whole field of the natural sciences, in particular, suffers from that fact, for only one out of the ten physics teachers at the Rio Piedras campus has the degree and only three of the twenty-eight mathematicians; and so intense indeed is the competition both from local private industry and continental universities that the Dean of Natural Sciences has been driven to the expedient, among others, of offering an expense-paid trip to a stateside physicist who he had heard suffered from an allergy requiring residence in a tropical climate.[30] That particular situation is all the more ironic when it is recalled that nineteenth-century Puerto Rico made no small contribution to the natural sciences field with names like Carbonell, Bello y Espinosa, and Agustín Stahl, the latter, indeed, enjoying an international reputation. The general situation is in no way aided, either, by the high degree of inbreeding that occurs in faculty recruitment: in the 1954 academic year, 81 percent of the faculty were native-born islanders, just over 14 percent were continental Americans, and 4 percent of foreign nationality. The result, as Dr. Bowles has pointed out, is that the University, more so than stateside colleges, draws its faculty too heavily from its own students and thereby artificially limits its area of selection.[31] Granted the size, again, of the total faculty, there ought to be a much larger production in the field of research. A number of faculty members are prolific composers of newspaper articles; one of them is even a regular newspaper columnist. But that is hardly research. A learned journal like the *Social and Economic Studies* of the University College of the West Indies has already made an international reputation for itself, while the Puerto Rican *Revista de Ciencias Sociales,* possibly because of a series of part-time, interrupted editorships, has yet to do that. When the University moves forward to this task, it will at least be carrying on the remarkable precedent already established by its scholars in the field of Caribbean studies, and especially by those—Margot Arce, Luis Díaz Soler, Eugenio Fernández-Méndez, Thomas Mathews, Arturo Morales-Carrión, Lidio Cruz Monclova, Arturo Santana—who have specialized in the area of Caribbean historical studies.

Some means, again, must be found for the more generous compensation of the teacher at all levels. For while a university ought never to place major emphasis upon the financial reward that it offers, at the same time there is something unsatisfactory about a situation in which combined salaries of faculty members are some 20 percent lower than the stateside equivalents, despite the fact that living costs in the island economy are some 12 percent higher, if the rate of bonus paid to federal employees in the island offices of the federal agencies as a means of offsetting the higher living costs is taken as a yardstick.[32] Far too many faculty members live by the skin of their teeth, so that time and energy that should go into creative work are perforce expended in earning extra pittances through adding extra classes to an already heavy teaching load. The loss thereby sustained is further exacerbated by the still constant exodus of faculty members to government appointments and, more latterly, to appointments in private industry and its modern offshoots of mass communications, consultation, and public relations enterprises. The University, bluntly, is raided for talent by the very institutions of society that it has helped to create. The situation here is so grave that one day, perhaps, there ought to be a commission of inquiry to examine its scope and consequences. The business society rewards the acquisitive spirit that keeps an eye on the "main chance." But it is not the function of an academic center to echo the prejudice; nor should it be required to suffer thereby.

Reform, patently, is for the future. In the meanwhile the University, like most other Puerto Rican institutions, suffers from its environment of a neo-colonial society. It reflects, when it does not actually encourage, all the moral emptiness and the ennui of such a society. That can be seen, as much as anywhere else, in the lamentations of the patriotic critics over the last generation, for there is a remarkable continuity about those utterances. "The truth is," stated Vicente Géigel Polanco in 1940, "that the University of Puerto Rico has been putting out a young people quite colorless, without courage, lacking enterprise or faith, devoid of any quality of superiority or spirit. Young people who have gone into the fields of the various professions in order to assure themselves a handsome economic position rather than to ennoble their lives, contribute something to the general cultural estate, stimulate the general welfare or serve the vital interests of the community. If lawyers, they are more concerned with petty disputes than the defense of causes; if engineers, more preoccupied with contracts than with the style of urban growth; if accountants, looking more to the fees of private industry than to the grave problems of public finance; if teachers, watching the clock or dispensing the routine textbook rather than being concerned with the moral and intellectual formation of the rising generation. . . . Set hours, strict regulations, tough discipline, the required textbook, the mechanical assignment: such are the characteristics of our leading academic institution, incapable of implanting in its students any ideal save that of getting good grades. . . . Nowhere is there any sense of community between faculty and students. They live in different worlds: the students, in search of good grades or devising schemes of getting through courses with the least possible effort; the faculty members, save for some exceptions who ought never to be forgotten, in the officious discharge of their duties, lacking enthusiasm or spirit, without any real faith in their work and lacking any zeal for research or investigation."[33]

Twenty years later, however, it is possible for another critic to make much the same sort of indictment. "Where is the youthfulness of our young people?" José Emilio González asks. "The best of them study, and in doing so fulfil a task worthy of de Hostos, who always loved the truth. But these are few, very few. The rest perambulate the corridors and the grounds of the University campus, interminably chattering. A small number in the library. Many more in the University student center where they amuse themselves behind the barrier of cups of coffee. They kill time before time kills them. And so life passes by for them, moving from one piece of fun to another. And, beyond that, there are the social occasions, ROTC, the Pershing Rifles, the fraternities, the sororities and the last Broadway hit. Where are the great ideals whereby one is wont to measure a young generation? Where is the conscience of that generation? Ask any one of these youngsters what he wants to do or to be. A good job in government or in a flourishing commercial enterprise. Money. A house in an exclusive urbanization. A wife. Television. Icebox. Hi-fi. . . . It is a docile youth, worshiping everything, accepting everything as long as it carries with it the stamp of approval of established political and economic authority. . . . All the emptiness of a colonial life, of a people bereft of any sense of destiny spreads out into the streets and the *plazas,* permeates the home, poisons the spirit, breaks it down, destroys it. It reduces men to bundles of rags, dragging out an existence devoid of spirit, prisoners of a time-killing ennui, of the mechanical turn of the hours, in which each day they die every hour, going around endlessly in the same place, possessed of neither hope nor promise. . . ."[34]

That all this is not *independentista* rhetoric is evident enough from the sociological evidence that the picture it draws is based on empirical data. The researches of Dr. Richard Trent on the confusion prevailing in University of Puerto Rico students about the subject of their cultural identity speak volumes about University life, for they show that the average student oscillates unhappily between the self-image of the traditional Hispanic *caballero* and the North American business entrepreneur, between the concept of the Spanish wife-mother figure and that of the American career girl.[35] It is, as one reads it, a grave indictment of the failure of the University to attack in any way the one single cardinal fact that governs the lives of its members. If it is said that it is not the business of a university to involve itself in such a controversial political issue it is surely proper to retort that the function of the university in a colonial society is, and ought to be, fundamentally different to that of the university in an independent society. Much is heard in Puerto Rico, following the famous argument of Ortego y Gasset, of the "mission of the university." But on analysis it turns out to be an endless rhetorical re-iteration of the classical European doctrine of the academic life, carefully avoiding the issue as to whether centers of higher learning in a colonialist culture can even begin successfully to practice the European academic functions. It is not too much to say, altogether, that however adequately the academic centers in Puerto Rico reform their institutional frames they will not give themselves a new birth of freedom until they address themselves boldly to the large political issue that presently cramps their potential.

The Character of Public Opinion

A DEMOCRATIC society, in theory, is ruled by its public opinion. As Puerto Rico has taken over American democratic theory it has taken over likewise American democratic assumptions about the nature of opinion. Similarly, however, American qualms about the general validity of these assumptions have also begun to plague Puerto Ricans as it becomes evident that there is little to justify the utopian expectations of the democratic thinkers of the eighteenth and early nineteenth centuries that popular opinion, an informed electorate, and a free press would act as effective defendants of liberty against arbitrary government. Popular education in its turn, as it has gone about organizing the degradation of the democratic dogma, has sacrificed the earlier liberal idea of free intellectual growth to the pseudo-Deweyite ideology of "life adjustment" education, and contemporary psychological concepts have been increasingly utilized to reinforce this anti-intellectual bias; so that tension between individual and society is now not so much seen as one possible source of intellectual or artistic creativity as it is regarded as an index of personal maladjustment. Public opinion, then, is less something that is born than it is made, and made increasingly by the forces of the modern mass communications revolution. What people think becomes less their own spontaneous reaction to events than the final product of a vast semi-coercive process of mass suggestiveness and indoctrination controlled by the "hidden persuaders" and the "image merchants." The press is less what Jeffersonian liberalism dreamed of it as being, the palladium of popular liberties, than it is a vehicle of propaganda appealing normally to the lowest common denominator of the popular audience. The process of vulgarization has been strengthened with the advent of radio, film, and television programs devoting themselves, in Gilbert Seldes's phrase, to the business of exploiting personality rather than to that of developing character, programs which are in general guilty not so much of setting out deliberately to debase the public taste as of failing to possess any desire to improve it.[1]

If all this is evidence of a modern "developed" society then Puerto

Rico cannot in any way be defined as an "underdeveloped" society. The ravages of the "communications revolution" have blighted the island scene as elsewhere. It is occasionally suggested, usually by the transient visitor, that Hispanic "individualism" or the "small society" will save Puerto Ricans from the phenomenon and its effects. But these are jejune judgments with little of either historical or sociological justification. The supplementary argument is sometimes heard that the "small society" offers a more positive sense of "belonging" to its members. Again this is doubtful. For the gulf that divides social classes in small societies like Trinidad or Jamaica is certainly wider than is the case in American life; indeed it is still possible for the middle classes of these island societies to see classes beneath them through the mirror of Victorian gentility, even to the point of still using the Victorian class phraseology, the "lower orders" and so on; nothing but class fear, for example, could explain the vituperative language used by "respectable" people in reaction against the Rastafari "uprising" of 1959 in Jamaica. Puerto Ricans, it is true, experience a passionate attachment to their island home. Yet they are plagued with the question "Who are We?" to a degree that must seem paranoiac to one who is unaware of the emotional disturbance that colonialism works upon its victims. The *criollo* public opinion, even the *criollo* personality, has been shaped by that fact. Nor must it be forgotten that, colonialism apart, clashes of interest and opinion within a territorially small society rapidly become elaborate interpersonal vendettas, since their protagonists are physically pushed up against each other, cannot avoid each other as is the case in the larger anonymity of the big community, are altogether more conspicuous in the public eye. The climate of opinion is thus in a manner not unlike the Guelph-Ghibelline atmosphere of the medieval city state. To the burden of modern technology, then, there is added the burden of small-town *ambiente*. No discussion of Puerto Rican public opinion can ignore that quality of environment.

As elsewhere, the main agencies helping to shape public opinion are the press, radio, television, and the movies. (It is worth noting that, insofar as some of these have been carriers of the English language, their influence upon Puerto Rican Spanish has been one of vocabulary rather than of syntax or pronunciation.) As elsewhere too there has been a steady decline in the degree of real competition as ownership has become more concentrated. Of the island newspapers, *El Día* of Ponce remains about the only surviving newspaper outside of the capital metropolitan area. Of the two leading metropolitan dailies, *El Mundo* is a conservative, rather staid, journal that devotes appreciable space to the reporting of world events, while *El Imparcial* concentrates heavily upon a coverage of crime, sex, and politics at once exaggerated and sensationalist, although it is amusing to see the mixture accompanied at times by the serialization of novelists like Alexandre Dumas. Both papers are persistent critics of government although (just as in the case of the pro-Republican sympathies of the majority of the American press) the fact seems to have had so far little influence upon voting habits. Neither journal is in any way first class. There is in both of them too little space devoted to readers' opinions, grossly insufficient coverage of legislative debates, a distinct prejudice in favor of the Catholic Church in the limited coverage of religious news, and a generally unpleasing format. *El Mundo* devotes a great deal of attention to the recording of the activities of the upper-class social world of San Juan and very little, by comparison, to important matters like industrial relations, art, music, and literature. Both newspapers repeat in Spanish some of the syndicated columns of the Anglo-American press—Drew Pearson, the Alsop brothers, Cassandra of the London *Daily Mirror*—as well as the Hollywood gossip columnists like Louella Parsons; it can hardly be said that the fare as a whole makes edifying reading. *El Imparcial* adds to this an exaggerated portrait of crime and juvenile delinquency as its most characteristic feature. Nor must the point be omitted that, in that paper's reporting of sex crimes and especially rape, the cruel and unethical practice of publishing the names of victims is habitually resorted to; while in the matter of the reportage of court cases the deficient law of libel is taken advantage of to exercise what is in substance "trial by newspaper." Both newspapers carry lively local political columnists; and both of them are certainly more catholic in their appeal than either *El Día*, the Ferré-sponsored Ponce paper or *El Debate*, the unofficial organ of the Catholic Church. But neither of them manages to produce good book reviewing or music criticism; there has been an unhappy decline in the use of the *crónica*, the lively commentary on local life and manners once ably practiced by older journalists such as Mariano Abril and Pérez Losada; while *El Mundo* is occasionally guilty of gross irresponsibility, its recent unfounded attack, for example, upon the government station WIPR as being full of Communist and Nationalist subversive elements.[2]

Of the two English-language papers, *The Island Times* and *The San Juan Star*, it would not be too much to say that while both make a gallant attempt to be open-minded they generally reflect—like most English-language efforts in the history of insular journalism—the North American *colon* outlook. The first is a pro-government public relations sheet only enlivened by the weekly serialization of the Earl

Parker Hanson life-story, in which that irrepressible spirit answers, to its own undisguised satisfaction, the large rhetorical questions that it propounds to itself. The second does better, for it makes a real effort to cover the Puerto Rican scene, even including politics and government in the neighboring Virgin Islands. The award of the Pulitzer Prize testifies to its liberalism. Yet it is a liberalism on continental rather than insular lines, for while it will battle for church-state separatism or administrative honesty in government it is generally hostile to the *Popular* welfare state, not surprising when its ownership by the American Gardner Cowles interests is called to mind. It goes without saying, of course, that anything that either newspaper says on matters touching Puerto Rican independence will be utterly untrustworthy.

Clearly enough, the island press as a whole leaves much to be desired: a situation all the more unhealthy when it is remembered that the press wields a more than usual influence in small island societies like the Puerto Rican, as the frequent practice of writing letters of rebuttal or of explanation to newspaper editors on the part of Puerto Rican government departmental heads shows.

The state of the entertainment arts—radio, television, the movies—is, if possible, even more parlous. The 1953 report of the insular Senate Education Committee on the quality of local radio programs is a damning indictment of the managements of the thirty-two radio stations operating throughout the island, the government station WIPR excepted. Completely lacking any apparent guiding principles, the programs are an astonishing amalgam of low-quality imported serials and *novelas*, macabre representations of "real life" drama usually centered around the commission of the more offensive type of crime, comedy items of grotesque buffoonery, and strident commercial advertising, and all monitored by generally ill-educated and unskilled announcers. It is a depressing record, and all the more of a threat to the growth of a cultured democracy on account of the fact that the radio constitutes the most common vehicle of mass communications throughout the island with practically no competition from the newspapers or television in the rural and mountain population centers.[3] The six television stations provide somewhat better fare, but not much better, for all rely heavily on the canned network programs. There are seriously minded newscasters; but even the best of them do little more than demonstrate that they read the *New York Times* meticulously. The government station WIPR-TV has proved, once more, that public enterprise can do better, for the private stations have done little to match, for example, its coverage of the annual Casals Festival or its series of forums on public affairs issues. Much of the credit for that achievement goes to the imaginative directorship of Jack Delano. For the rest, there is the usual dreary round of Westerns, low comedies, and incessant commercial advertising. It is all incredibly dull, and made all the duller by the equally incredible passivity with which the Puerto Rican audience, with individual exceptions, accepts it.

The world of local theater is perhaps better. There are theatrical offerings in both English and Spanish; there are interesting experimental workshops in both Santurce and Caguas; and the University theater group takes classical and light drama to the island small town audiences with its traveling theater. Imaginative directors do new things with old material in the tropics, the presentation, for example, of Lope de Vega and Shakespeare classics in the open air courtyard of the Spanish San Cristóbal fort. As for the movies, the Puerto Rican audience has to take what it can get through the filter of a double censorship. The first is the self-imposed censorship of the Hollywood studios, reinforced by the organized black-listing of actors and writers regarded as "subversives." The second is the strict censorship addressed by the Federal Collector of Customs in San Juan to the importation of non-United States films into the island circuit, over which the local interests have no control and against the decisions of which they have no power of appeal. As a consequence the local movie audience suffers from the Hollywoodian degradation of the film art in which the movies have replaced religion as the opiate of the people, and only the members of the perennial private-membership clubs are saved from it. The films with any distinctively Puerto Rican flavor, suggestively enough, are made under the auspices of the local Division of Community Education and not by the Puerto Rican actors and actresses—José Ferrer, Juano Hernández, Rita Moreno—who are popularly regarded as Puerto Rican members of the Hollywood jungle society. And to all this, finally, there must be added the fact that, according to a 1956 legislative committee report, there is a dangerous condition of oligopoly in the field of local film distribution and exhibition unrelieved so far by any vigorous enforcement of the local price-control and anti-monopoly legislation.[4]

The case for positive remedial action could hardly require more ample documentation. There are far too many social groups, far too many points of view, that are effectively denied a chance to be heard over the mass communications media. The well-to-do professional groups, like the doctors or the mill owners, can pay for full-page advertisements in the press in a way that more indigent groups cannot. The exchange of correspondence in 1957 between the Governor and the Director in Puerto Rico of the AFL-CIO on the question of the ability of the trade unions to obtain the use of government radio and television stations suggests that organized labor might even be deliberately discriminated against in this matter. It suggests further that remedial action will have perforce to accept a struggle with the federal controlling agency, the Federal Communications Commission, for the Governor cited, as part of his argument justifying inaction, the presence of the federal jurisdiction.[5] Yet the truth is, of course, that the recent policy of the federal body, as the Van Doren and payola scandals of 1959-1960 showed, has been one of caution so excessive that it has had the general result of handing over the radio-television audience to the mercy of station owners, sponsors, and producers, with the public interest left almost entirely in the hands of the licensee's sense of public obligation. A local Puerto Rican jurisdiction could hardly be worse, and could indeed be a lot better. What is needed is, in part, a public ownership policy and, in part, a genuine competitive system, either within that framework or outside of it, which would permit a variety of civic and professional groups to contribute their quota to an imaginative entertainment fare. Mere public supervision, on the record, is hardly enough. The dismal record alone of the present Public Service Commission of the Commonwealth government, operating under a law passed in 1917, is enough to disillusion the champion of the regulatory device; the Commission, for example, has failed to protect the Puerto Rican telephone consumer from the worst vagaries of the local subsidiary of the International Telephone and Telegraph Corporation. A former Secretary of Justice has suggested that a citizens' committee might be set up to act as a moderator of the press, by means, in part, of an annual report on performance rendered to the public.[6] But the achievement of the Press Council in the United Kingdom is hardly an encouragement to this line of thought. Nor is self-regulation a more successful principle of policy, since experience has shown that the czars of the information media move to put their house in order only when a national scandal involving their malpractices forces their hand. The argument is heard in Puerto Rico, as elsewhere, that the media only give the public what it wants. It would be truer to say that the public does not so much get what it wants as wants what it gets. The abdication of any kind of leadership in shaping mature public taste is thus falsely justified in terms of a "democratic" acquiescence to "popular" demand which quite evades the question as to whether the demand has not itself been shaped in large measure by the forces that invoke it as an alibi. Mass conformity and passivity are cited as their own cause instead of being recognized as consequences that flow from the persistent abuse of the mass media by the network executive and the advertising sponsor.

It can be argued of course that government control, maybe public ownership, is out of the question because it would be too "radical." Perhaps. But one element of Puerto Rican public opinion, already noted, is worth emphasizing once again in this respect. The businessman has rarely enjoyed in the island the prestige with which the "folklore of capitalism" has endowed him and his type in American life. One of the first popular American books on the island after 1898 could say that "With an income, a comfortable home, and nothing to do, Porto Rico is on the borders of Lotus Land."[7] This of course is exaggerated journalistic comment. It is true nevertheless that the victory of the Calvinistic economic virtues is far from complete in contemporary Puerto Rican life. An educator like Chancellor Benítez or an actor like José Ferrer or a baseball player like Rubén Gómez are household names in a way that no business leader is. Luis Ferré is known widely more in his capacity as a political leader than in that of a millionaire. A "get-rich-quick" mentality is certainly widespread, as the statistics on insular gambling habits show.[8] Yet, surprisingly enough, the pre-industrial arts of the *trovador* and the *declamadora* remain still as popular entertainments. Mere wealth as such certainly brings deference in rural and small town life. But real popular respect is reserved for the wealthy man who combines with his wealth the catalogue of virtues that make up the popular image of the *patrón* or, in the narrower world of *compadragismo*, of the ideal *compadre*. And even when Puerto Ricans themselves embrace the American race for money, they still feel obliged to deride the American "hustler" who sacrifices everything in order to win; just as in neighboring Trinidad a fiercely competitive Creole society in its own right finds it possible to caricature the more self-seeking of its members "working for the Yankee dollar." Much the same attitude explains why Puerto Ricans proudly refer the visitor to the fact that the Governor is one of the rare politicians in Latin American and Caribbean life who has not used his office as a means of self-enrichment. Whether all this is enough in itself to counteract the rapaciously acquisitive instincts let loose by rapid economic development along capitalist lines is, of course, problematical. It is there nonetheless, and could provide a foundation of sentiment for a radical public policy standing up against the forces that presently control too many of the information media of the society.

For a fair discussion, however, the Puerto Rican communal psychology must be examined in its completeness; and not all of it is as attractive as its attitude to the ethos of the profit motive. Much of it has been shaped by inherited attitudes to authority, many of them boding ill, to be frank, for the ideal of personal liberty within the free society. The island radical literature—Géigel Polanco's *Despertar de un Pueblo* and Enrique Calderon's *El Dolor de Un Pueblo Esclavo* are examples—has been full of a bitter upbraiding against the passivity of the Puerto Rican spirit in the presence of its colonial masters, and it is possible that many of contemporary island attitudes can be traced to an uneasy sense of guilt on that score. Be that as it may, it is certain that there is a strong whiff of neo-authoritarianism in much of the Puerto Rican make-up. The individual person tends to accept strong leadership without resentment provided it is wielded paternalistically. Equally, if he himself exercises authority he tends to adopt a habit of command of sometimes unpleasant brusqueness. The delegation of authority is embarked upon only reluctantly, and few moves will be made, in office or shop or factory, that do not have the certain approbation of the man in charge. There is more than a fair share of the usual secretiveness that marks all government bureaucracies. Newspapermen suspect, for example, that the public relations officers of the government departments act not so much as a channel of communication between government and press as censors who only permit the transmission of facts that are favorable to their departments. The story of the prolonged campaign of *The San Juan Star* to force the publication of reports long held secret by the Governor is symptomatic; while the suspicion is not alleviated by the alarming infrequency with which the Governor holds press conferences.

The general temper of administration in Puerto Rico has already been discussed. But it is worth emphasizing once again the limits of the liberty that it permits to its employees. At least one government official has frankly declared that at the operational level of government business there is no way in which an employee can freely discuss work problems with his superior officers.[9] In some governmental services there is even open hostility between management and workers, with worker loyalty going exclusively to the union; that is especially the case in the notorious example of the metropolitan bus service. Little of this is surprising when it is remembered, to illustrate further, that the entire schoolteaching group is debarred by law from any sort of participation in political activities, a policy that goes back to the repressive atmosphere of colonial government in the earlier period. For while it is true, as has already been argued, that the civil servant in the Puerto Rican situation ought not to be permitted full freedom of political activities the principle ought, after all, to apply in the main to the top echelons only and there is little reason why it should be used, as it is in Puerto Rico, to debar all levels of staff from participation in civic affairs of a political character. A similar negative attitude tends to characterize official responses to outside criticism, and there is a temptation to insist upon "constructive" criticism, which really means criticism that is friendly to government. Attention to the substance of criticism is thereby too easily subordinated to furious speculation upon the motives of the author. Something of that must explain why both the Secretary of Health and the Chairman of the Planning Board have had a bad press, although of course there is also the consideration, in both of these cases, that the press has been more or less the mouthpiece of economic vested interests threatened by departmental policies. The general result is that criticism is quietly repressed or seeks refuge in the guise of anonymity. Even more, freedom to express critical opinions uninhibitedly comes to be restricted to small groups; thus, in the pre-plebiscite hearings of 1962 most witnesses came, significantly, from the ranks of lawyers, businessmen, university teachers, and retired public figures, and hardly anything was seen of the "people" whose name was so loudly invoked.

It would be unfair, of course, and grossly erroneous to put all this in terms of government bureaucracy stifling the freedom of an intellectually vigorous people. For the truth of the matter is that official attitudes here have a strong foundation in popular attitudes. If Lord Acton's dictum is correct, that the real test of any society is how much liberty it allows to minorities, then the Puerto Rican society does not show at all handsomely. Possibly the most suggestive piece of evidence on this score is Professor Edwin Seda's report on the spectrum of public attitudes in the field of local civil liberties, despite its tendency, perhaps, to a sort of professional sociological pessimism. In an elaborate cross sample of group and class attitudes to various hypothetical questions relating to civil-liberties issues, Seda and his associates discovered an alarming degree of apathy, even outright intolerance, to most of the issues presented. If the calculations involved are correct, some 64 percent of the population would deny free speech to persons with anti-religious viewpoints and some 72 percent would purge public library shelves of any book advocating such viewpoints. An even higher percentage, 76 percent, would deny the right of an avowed atheist to teach in a university, while almost a third of the population would be willing to imprison members of a Communist group. Even more: there is a marked tendency in the public mind, according to this report, to accept with indifference any repressive action against minority civil rights that might be undertaken by the police authorities. Some 37 percent of those questioned would elect to remain silent (in the example presented to them) in the presence of the known rifling of public funds by a dishonest mayor, and the reasons offered in justification of their silence appear to indicate a real fear in a large section of the public that any sort of protest against delinquent authority would bring down rapid reprisals upon the heads of the complainants. There tends apparently to be a higher degree of tolerance towards the unpopular minority groups among Protestants than among Catholics, and among educated groups as against those who have only had a brief schooling. The sole exception to this correlation between education and liberal attitude appears, interestingly enough, in the area of attitudes to color: for on the question of the whole range of social intercourse between colored and non-colored persons, including the possibility of interracial marriage, proletarian individuals are distinctly more liberal than college-educated individuals. At the point, this is to say, where a liberal response could conflict with deep-seated feeling, as in the matter of color, the power of a formal educational experience to override feeling rapidly wanes—a warning to those Puerto Rican liberals who are tempted to eulogize education as the universal solvent of the social ills.[10]

Altogether this is a grim picture, if true, of a majoritarian illiberalism; the deference to authority which is its base is certainly a far cry from the irreverent defiance of authority so characteristic of the Trinidadian personality. In part it is the result of tropical childhood, for the middle-class child only too often is a spoiled spirit rarely inured to the habit of self-denial. In part it is the terror of ridicule that makes the Puerto Rican adult so conscious of respect; it is perhaps significant that there is little wit in Puerto Rican politics, for the existence of one skilled cartoon satirist, Joaquín of the *Island Times*, does not make a *Canard Enchaîné*. Above all perhaps it is the sheer pressure of the struggle for survival in a still poverty-stricken society. The manifestations of the social frustrations that thereby ensue are characteristic: the passivity in the face of crisis, the suspicion of others, the conviction that collective action of any sort against the difficulties of life is useless. The very idiom that the poor Puerto Rican employs—the language of *ay bendito*, for example—reflects the defense mechanisms he has thrown up in order to escape the direct confrontation of the difficulties. It is easy to see how all this becomes a distrust of the stranger, familiar in all village life; but how too when the individual migrates to the town or, further afield, to the American city, it becomes translated into a group hostility to all ideas or forces that seem to threaten the precarious balance of the "new life." Professor Herbert Marty's study of the behavior patterns of Puerto Rican working-class migrants to Chicago would appear to bear out the argument and to help explain the cultural isolation of the American urban Puerto Rican populations that follows from these patterns. It is a personality structure which, faced with new situations, turns inward to repressed feeling, not outward to remedial action. This is perhaps why, as

Adolfo de Hostos has noted, the Puerto Rican who stays at home tends to accept cultural adaptation more willingly than his compatriot who moves to New York, for the latter is compelled to live in tightly packed slum ghettoes, as if enclosed in a social cyst, sullenly hostile to the American environment and often morally sustained only by the traditional influences of the old culture.[11] This is also perhaps why there is a temptation, under strain, for the individual Puerto Rican to resort to savage and unpremeditated acts of violence against those who offend him and sometimes, as the suicide rate of the island unhappily indicates, against his own person. The people of Puerto Rico, as Herbert Marty and Carlos Albizu conclude in their analysis of their countrymen's conduct under strain, "have learned to cast larger numbers of clean votes and possess a stronger critical faculty, but it is no less certain that *personalismo* and the habit of yielding up authority into the hands of the leader—from the lowest up to the highest levels of collective social effort—remain still to testify to a general incapacity or inertia that belies the high ideals that are accepted as the norms."[12] A readiness to defend the civil liberties of the dissenter or the nonconformist is hardly likely to flourish within such a socio-psychological environment.

This is perhaps the challenge above all others that Puerto Rico faces, whether it be as a state of the Union or an independent republic or, as now, the no man's land of the associated Commonwealth. For any show of eccentricity is liable to receive short shrift and at times indeed rough handling. Tourists who visit the University campus in sports wear are liable to be molested, albeit by a perhaps unrepresentative minority of students. The bachelor-girl is still almost an unknown phenomenon. The University faculty member who gets drunk in public may perhaps be excused, for this after all is a social life of *fiestas*; but any sexual irregularity will be frowned upon, possibly even punished, as vigorously as on an American small town campus. There is at least one case in which the Board of Directors of the Faculty Club has been perhaps vindictive in its sanctions against a member guilty, at the most, of an act of momentary indiscretion on the premises. It may be possible that the newly formed Association of University Professors will come to act as a watchdog of faculty civil liberties in this particular field of professional life in the society.

The outsider who takes a partisan stand on local political issues, especially that of status, is likely to find himself vehemently attacked, by those whose political shibboleths he queries, as an imported and irresponsible intellectual bent on mischief.[13] There is a widespread feeling among Protestants that they are badly treated by agents of public authority. There is at least one authenticated case of a large town newspaper attempting a crude and vicious boycott against a local Jewish refugee merchant, thus showing that anti-Semitism is not entirely absent.[14] A real free-thought element seems not to be present; at least it is suggestive that of all the critical comment invoked by the Catholic hierarchy's Pastoral Letters in 1960 most of it seemed content to rest upon a mild separation of church and state position and little of it seemed disposed to go beyond the immediate symptoms and see, in agnostic fashion, that in all logic the Church must adopt an anti-libertarian attitude once its dogma of authoritative truth is accepted. The ideal of the amateur, again, always so hospitable to creative effort, remains powerful still in the field of insular *belles lettres* but is rapidly being pushed aside in most other fields by a narrowing professionalism; the view recently expressed by the former Secretary of Education, that the Dean of the University's College of Education should be a "professional educator," is a typical example of the trend. Nor is it a satisfactory explanation of all this to say, with the head of the government's Personnel Office in a letter to the press, that the "climate of fear" the Puerto Rican citizen lives in, especially with reference to his attitudes to government, must be seen as a consequence of the authoritarianism of the Spanish colonial past.[15] For those ancestral roots are over sixty years old, and the generation that knew the *año terrible* of 1887 has long since passed away. The argument is similar to the rationalization that is frequently advanced in the other Caribbean islands excusing present attitudes as a legacy of slavery. Sociologically both arguments are unsound. But they are interesting because they reveal a temptation to excuse present failings in terms of past injustice.

It would be more exact to say that the problem here being discussed is somewhat more understandable if it is referred back to the Puerto Rican pathology of *dignidad*. It is true of course that in its obsessive pride and its overweening sensitivity to even the mildest of criticism that factor has colonial roots. For its ravages afflict all the Caribbean peoples; they are perhaps only more noticeable in a people like the Puerto Ricans because of the Roman quality of Spanish imperial manners of which they are a vulgarized modern survival, just as, in the British islands, the trait is colored by the more subdued arrogance, the quality of deliberate understatement, of the British governing class manner and, in the French islands, it is colored by the pose of the *boulevardier parisien*. But it survives in the present because present conditions feed it. Social inequality means that it is now used, not by Spaniard against Puerto Rican, but by Puerto Rican against Puerto Rican. The mediocre person, at all occupational levels, is only too easily tempted to convert notice of his mediocrity into an insult to his "dignity" and to meet criticism, however legitimate, with a show of injured pride. The consequences are indeed far-reaching. It feeds resistance to the impartial examination of individual claims. It leads to excessive praise for modest accomplishments. It inhibits free speech; one local critic has noted, humorously, that with some of its sufferers the disease tends to view even the mildest of criticisms as an insult not only to themselves but also to Christopher Columbus, to whose discovery of America they owe their existence.[16] It helps to explain why, as one of the ablest young theater directors of the island has frankly hinted, there is no real criticism in the area of the arts, and why what there is of it amounts to not much more than innocuous commentaries by friends of authors; while much real criticism gets stifled because of the reluctance of its potential authors to get themselves into embarrassing rows.[17] It is hardly surprising that a great deal of humorless pedantry and solemn self-esteem go unchallenged. There grows up a debased concept of what constitutes true intellectual authority, so that even the slightest of opinions may get itself acclaimed as a serious *ponencia*, while snobbishness ordains that the pompous titles of *seminario* and *simposio* shall be reserved to gatherings presided over by at least a person who can boast a doctoral degree, preferably invited from outside the island and generally at great expense.[18] This protocol of manners must at times, of course, overstep the mark, and becomes patently silly when it subjects a resident as eminent as Don Pablo Casals to its processes, arising comically as that episode did out of the story of a telegraph employee in the French village of Prades who had allegedly never heard of Puerto Rico.[19] Charles Emerson noted this facet of the islanders' character more than a century ago when comparing the cordiality of their social manners with the Puritan frigidity of New England manners. "They are," he wrote, "a people of beautiful manners. They are constitutionally social. Their courtesy seems to be a constituent part of their language, so that one is sometimes puzzled to determine whether there is any merit due to the individuals for those expressions of politeness which they learned in their very grammars and dictionaries."[20] For many American residents today the puzzle probably still remains.

In some measure much of this is the contrast between outward neighborliness and subterranean conflict characteristic of most small societies: the village, the small township, the tight little island. There are the hallmarks of the close-ranked, inward-turned society: the petty malice, the poison of gossip, the daily murder of personal reputations. The very physical propinquity of Puerto Ricans, living, as they do, mostly on top of each other, aggravates it all, for there is little of the formal detachment from neighbors which the English, also living in crowded conditions, have developed as a means of ensuring the inner privacy of their homes and lives. To some degree, it is the feeling of the colonialist inferiority complex that must come from having seen second-rate continentals preferred to better-rate Puerto Ricans in public appointments. But that period is now substantially over. The able Puerto Rican is no longer under the felt need to invoke the social psychology and tactics of *dignidad* as a means of disguising incompetence. He can stand confidently on his own feet; and he does. The danger now is, however, that, to the detriment of local standards, the refuge will be invoked by the ungifted or the merely lazy. It becomes the outward pose of the insecure, the rapid resentment of imagined insult, the strutting in the pseudo-epic manner, the verbal turbulence that disguises weak argument, the search for prestige through the deployment of personal flamboyance, the manner in which in interpersonal intercourse self-importance seems to be more powerful than compassion for others. There is something of all this in the loud defence of the teachers of English in the public schools when, in fact, the generally unsatisfactory nature of the teaching of the second language has been attested to in numerous official reports.[21] There are intimations of it when college students memorialize the Superior Educational Council on the alleged deficiencies of individual faculty members. It helps to explain altogether the strong taste of melodrama that there is in much of the island life. For the Puerto Rican (or at least this kind of Puerto Rican), in the phrase of one observer, is a lion who walks alone in the streets. That sort of self-image is bound to lead to a combative view of life.

This exploitative use of *dignidad*, in itself one of the worst scars of cultural destitution, can indeed become a serious obstacle to the growth of democratic equality in Puerto Rican life. Social egalitarianism makes of it a laughable anachronism. "A man," writes Governor Tugwell in his perceptive discussion on this point, "who had to pretend that he was made of special stuff so that he could walk safely among primitive folk and even command their labor and their wealth, had use for the feelings, the sense, of inherent superiority. A man, however, who must walk among equals, giving and taking in daily exchange, depending on the goodwill and the cooperation which are the essence of the democratic way of life, simply cannot carry the weight of imperial manners. It will ruin him because its maintenance requires that its pretension shall never be examined or contested."[22] Although the democratic dogma may be accepted by this type of Puerto Rican, it is accepted as a set of theoretical convictions only, in potential conflict, always, with a set of habits and assumptions with which it is profoundly incompatible. It is of some interest to note that the passage from Governor Tugwell's account, published originally in the immediate post-war period, has recently been selected by a Puerto Rican scholar as an appropriate item for inclusion in an edited series of readings on the nature of the local society.[23] It will be interesting to see how all this turns out as the idea of equality takes firmer hold on the communal psychology.

The challenge of social egalitarianism is certain in any case to emerge sooner or later. For Puerto Rico cannot expect to escape the ethical problems that arise out of the new inequalities created by the modern industrial society founded on the profit motive. The eruption of the church-state issue in 1960 and of the absentee-capital issue in 1961 proves only too well how wrong those Puerto Ricans can be who believe that the leading controversial questions cannot arise in the "new" Puerto Rican society. Yet where the discussion of such questions is not inhibited by the posture of *dignidad* it is frequently characterized by the paternalism of groups who see themselves as the new élite of the new society. The paternalism, deeply undemocratic as it is, has been noted in the political field. But it is there in other fields as well. There is probably no single group, for example, that is so self-less in its devotion to community welfare as that of the social workers. They have done wonders in their work, especially when it is remembered that they have to work frequently in physical facilities often shoddy and depressing, such as the building used by the Juvenile and Family Relations courts in San Juan, or when it is remembered again that they have to work with understaffed resources against appalling difficulties: thus, to take a single instance only, there were only some 13 probation officers in 1961 in the San Juan Court Administration's Social Services Division to meet the influx of dope addicts and habitual narcotics traffickers paroled or "deported" to the island by New York authorities.[24] The profession, as a whole, has given some famous figures to the Puerto Rican field of selfless public service, the now aged Señorita Beatriz Lasalle, for example, who can surely lay claim to being the Jane Addams of insular history. Even so, the leading assumption of much of the professional outlook is that of a directive guardianship leading the society into more fruitful channels of activity. There is a presumption that the "community leaders" can counterbalance the disorganization of social life and structure worked by incipient industrialization by offering against it, especially to the new middle-class groups, a "life model" of higher values, and that the "leaders" will come mainly from the ranks of the social workers themselves.[25] Descriptively, the assumption is in error because it fails to see that social leadership emerges from within social classes as an expression of felt class needs, and is not imposed upon them by elements that supposedly transcend class experience. Morally, it is in error because it has an unpleasant smell of elitism about it. For good government here as elsewhere is rarely better than self-government. The lesson is none the less true because the professional social worker, like the professional educator, manages to clothe the elitism with an avalanche of rhetoric about democracy.

But it is only natural that in a society so educationally conscious the most characteristic expression of elitism should appear in the educational field. It would be churlish to belittle the splendid contribution that has been made to Puerto Rican thought by the younger generation of intellectuals trained mostly in the Chicago school under the Hutchins influence. They have openly challenged the older generation. They have seen that a great university must promote the adventure of ideas or stagnate. They have nurtured the strict intellectual discipline so fatally compromised by the "progressive" canon; and the influence, truly revitalizing, of the outlook can be seen in the General Studies program of the University. Yet the skeptic (who is, after all, the hero figure of the Socratic dialogue) may perhaps be pardoned for feeling that if, on the one hand, the devil of Columbia Teachers College has thus been exorcised, it has been replaced by the deep blue sea of Chicago neo-Aquinan idealism. There has been the redolent atmosphere of the "Great Books" enthusiasm, with its questionable assumption that all the great books are born free and equal and with little appreciation of the truth of Emerson's remark that in the final test each age must write its own books. The revision of the University curricula, especially in the undergraduate General Studies program, has been refreshing. But, as in the original Chicago dispensation, it has had the unfortunate result of drenching students with Freudian theory before they have had the chance to take a solid foundation course in psychology, or with advanced historical interpretations (Tawney, Toynbee, Max Weber) before they have a good grounding in history. Hence a widespread intellectual indigestion. Hence the snobbishness that comes from the conviction that metaphysics can save the world. Hence, finally, the bright undergraduate whose mind is an eloquent confusion of theories which, properly speaking, should be the meat of advanced graduate studies. Nor does the separation of the advanced from the mediocre student that much of this means in the way of teaching arrangements (the best students are frequently placed by themselves in experimental classes) augur well for the democratic idea of a commonly shared educational experience as the seed ground of adult citizenship. Not least of all, the student under this regimen ceases to see his own society in any concreteness. Thus for all of their philosophic persuasiveness a series of articles such as that of Professor José Arsenio Torres on the problems of Puerto Rican education are couched in such general intellectual terms that they could almost apply to any school system in any liberal society.[26] It is a mode of education which, for all of its value in combating the limitations of the specialist or vocationalist mind, could produce its own peculiar hazards. Not least of all, it could build up, in Dixon Wecter's phrase, the storm troopers of some yet new and undefined totalitarianism.

In all of this the masses play as yet a subservient role. They remain still the wards rather than the social equals of the elite groups. Their world of life and thought is still a *terra incognita*, for the middle and upper classes hardly share the interest of the sociologist in that world; and even then the sociological interest may do no more than garner lessons for the better social control of the masses in the fashion of a recent project on interpersonal violence at the Social Sciences Research Center of the University which seeks, among other ends, to improve the police patrolling system. The astonishing truth about Puerto Rican society, indeed, is that underneath the fragile surface of modernization there are submerged layers of thought and experience that find no reflection in the mass media. That can be seen in the way in which working class life and opinion are expressed through media like the popular religious meeting, or the *velorio*, or wake, celebrating the recently dead, or the drinking bouts in the small bars that proliferate everywhere, and very little of which reaches the press unless it results in violence. It can be seen in the pathology of social fear in which the proletarian lives and which only gets public notice when, for example, slum dwellers refuse to move to new housing projects because of their fears of a new economic regimentation that the compulsory payment of rent brings to their mind. It is there, again, in the ease with which escaped criminals obtain widespread public protection against their police pursuers—as the history of the outlaw Correa Cotto reveals—thereby indicating a popular disrespect for the police of no mean dimension and on which very little is ever said. Or, again, there are the *hojas sueltas*, the cheaply printed broadsheets, that are basically social narratives expressing the reaction of the popular spirit to events of the day: they may annotate a crime, or caricature the morals of the clergy, or attack a member of the university faculties from the viewpoint of *separatista* students, or take the Director of the Institute of Puerto Rican Culture to task because he has dared to suggest the pagan origins of the patron saint of the Loiza Aldea festival. Finally, of course, there is the cultural penumbra of Puerto Rican Catholicism, the parasitic growth of popular spiritualistic beliefs, best seen, perhaps, in the enormous variety of *oraciones* by means of which the working class Puerto Rican seeks semi-orthodox, semi-occult aid in love, sickness, family affairs, struggles with evil neighbors, business affairs, and even the turn of the lottery; they have been carefully gathered together in Pablo Garrido's *Esoteria y Fervor Populares de Puerto Rico*. Altogether, there is an underground social life and struggle quite separate from the leading institutions and dominant groups of the Puerto Rican social establishment that gives the lie to the popular myth that the insular society is held together by a common sense of loyalty to the principle of *puertorriqueñidad*.

The conquest of the liberal idea, patently enough, is yet far from complete in the Puerto Rican society. The tradition of individualism is young still. Democratic institutions of government are hardly a generation old. The power of the family remains an anti-progressive force, as both Plato and Marx recognized it, *sui generis*, to be; and in the Puerto Rican case the power is reinforced by the American pseudo-religion of "togetherness," stifling individual oddity in the name of "democratic" unanimity. The masses remain, still, a quiescent force taking their cue from middle-class leaderships. The Catholic Church, despite the inglorious defeat of the Catholic Action Party in 1960, remains a force on the anti-liberal side. To read the occasional productions of a Catholic publicist like Ana María O'Neill is to be reminded of the instinct to repress "heretical" thought that is never far from the Catholic hierarchical mind, while to read Father Connell's McManus Lectures at the Catholic University on *The Purpose and Nature of a Catholic University* is to perceive once again how the great example of Newman works still to persuade his Roman coreligionists to sacrifice reason on the altar of authority.[27] Nor—despite the fact that there are outstanding liberal Catholic minds at the University— has any Catholic-liberal movement emerged to challenge that traditionalist orthodoxy that is in any way comparable to the modernist movement associated, in the European Catholic congregations, with the names of Loisy and Tyrrell around the turn of the century. Puerto Rican liberals who are Catholics have yet to work out their own answer, their own *via crucis*, to the tragic dilemma that confronts them.

Puerto Rican liberalism, even so, is far from being dormant. Muñoz, as always, is a tower of strength. The record of the national University on academic freedom is relatively unblemished. Certainly it was one of the very few state universities that resisted the poison of McCarthyism. There were few university presidents, even in 1963, ready to go on record, as did Chancellor Benítez in that year, as supporting in principle the academic employment of a known Communist; by comparison there is the question-begging formula of the Catholic University enshrined in Father Connell's dictum that "if a professor will not conform his teaching to what every sensible person knows to be the truth, his resignation can be demanded."[28] It is odd that the record on this score tends to be overlooked in the reports on the national University of bodies like the Middle States Association of Colleges and Secondary Schools. It is true that the University of Puerto Rico has a long way to go before it is a consciously Puerto Rican center; thus, it was suggestive that, in the 1963 debate, both the reformist and the anti-reformist side tended to exhibit an unfortunate mental dependency upon American standards, the one appealing to the norms of the American Association of University Professors, the other to the norms of the body of the Middle States Association of Colleges. But this, perhaps, is a habit that will pass away with time.

The Puerto Rican play and novel, again, have been on the side of social realism and humanism as their creators, encouraged by inno-vating magazines like *Asomante,* have shifted emphasis from the older theme of the *ambiente jíbaro,* the romantic eulogy of rural Puerto Rico, to more contemporary and more pressing topics. The older theatrical tradition of the bourgeois family drama, borrowed from the classical Spanish school, has given way to more urgent moral prob-lems, especially with the innovating work of Emilio Belaval and his colleagues in the *Club Artístico del Casino de Puerto Rico* after 1933. The moral issues posed by colonialism, indeed, for the Puerto Rican with any sense of justice about him have provided fare for the local writer for more than a generation, from Belaval's own *La Hacienda de los Cuatro Vientos* of 1940, dealing with the struggle of conscience set loose in the heart and mind of a Spanish gentleman planter who has come to nineteenth-century Puerto Rico to take over his legacy of a plantation estate and is caught up in the local agitation for slavery abolition, to a play like Gerard Paul Marín's *Al Final de la Calle* that deals with a similar struggle unleashed in Puerto Rican minds by the abortive Nationalist uprising of 1950. Emphasis has moved away from the habit of looking back nostalgically to the past, exemplified best, perhaps, in the work of Miguel Melendez Muñoz, to the newer themes of urbanized slum life, social class conflict, and the Puerto Rican abroad. The tradition of genteel dilettantism is still there of course, as a reading of the literary pages of *El Mundo* will readily show, and it will certainly take more than the catastrophic decline of the old-time newspapers and weeklies to kill the habit of poetizing and pamphleteering by the amateur writer. But there are new notes and new themes. Books like *El hombre en la calle* of José Luis González have turned attention to the brutalization of life un-leashed by urban uprootedness and industrial change, while it would be difficult to find a more touching account of the anguished home-sickness that must assail many Puerto Rican exiles in New York than Pedro Juan Soto's collection of short tales entitled *Spiks,* derived, as that title is, from the derogatory term that the New York Italian com-munity applies to the Puerto Rican *barrio* in East Harlem. That

theme, indeed, of the Pureto Rican *diáspora* has become one of the
major themes of the new Puerto Rican literature, along with the other
theme of the psychology of the Puerto Rican nationalist rebel. For
that first theme there are Manuel Mendez Ballester's *Encrucijada* and
Fernando Sierra Berdecía's *Esta Noche Juega el Joker*; for the second,
there are Enrique Laguerre's *El Laberinto, Los Derrotados* of César
Andreu Iglesias and the splendid allegorical tale, *La Víspera del
Hombre*, of René Marqués. All of this renaissance has given birth in
its turn to new reading publics. The recently formed Book Club of
Puerto Rico promises to carry further the work, initiated by organizations like the *Biblioteca de Autores Puertorriqueños* and the *Instituto de la Literatura Puertorriqueña*, of bringing the literary talent
of the society into closer touch with the popular audience. The new
readers, naturally, have been bred by the popular educational program
of the society, so that it is encouraging to note that the new generation
of University students, or at least one element of it, looks like becoming another force for good; it is something at least that its members can assail the illiberalism of a "campus queen" election system
that crowns the winning candidate in swank tourist hotels inaccessible,
for financial reasons, to the bulk of the student population.[29]

All these are constructive elements as far as they help to get Puerto
Rico away from the stage—in which most underdeveloped economies
begin—where the cultural apparatus is confined to small middle- or
upper-class circles that have hitherto formed the only public available
for cultural activities; and in Puerto Rico itself a body like the *Casino
de Puerto Rico* testifies still to that earlier tradition. As the educated
and professional classes become more diversified the sources of opinion making within the society will become wider and therefore more
representative of all social groups. The original monopoly that the
older élite has enjoyed in the colonial political and cultural movements will thus tend to be replaced with these more recent élites recruited, through mass education, from wider social sources. They will
bring with them of course their own prides and prejudices. Their demand for respect in Puerto Rican life, as the phrase goes, can only
too easily involve mental orthodoxy. Their pride in their social elevation can only too easily become a cult of strident thankfulness to the
system that promotes the elevation, with a consequent denigration of
social criticism as a legitimate enterprise in a democratic society. They
may be tempted to equate citizenship with national self-congratulation. If, however, they can manage to resist those temptations they
may yet become the vanguard of new currents that could carry the
island society forward from its present stage of political democracy
to the next stage of social democracy.

THE FUTURE

21

Puerto Rico and the Caribbean

ON ANY showing, Puerto Rico is a Caribbean society whose future must be connected, for all of its continuing Americanization, with the future of the Caribbean as a whole. Culturally it was, to begin with, a section of the Taino division of the Arawak group in the islands before the time of historic contact; and for four centuries after its discovery by Columbus on his second voyage it remained a part of the Spanish Antillean culture. It is in this sense that San Juan, like Havana and Port-au-Prince and even New Orleans, has throughout belonged, and belongs still, to a Hellenistic world formed by the Caribbean Sea and the Gulf of Mexico as those two land-water areas were colonized by the Mediterranean conquerors crossing the oceanic bridge between Puerto Rico and the Azores. The Americanization of the island society must therefore be seen as a quite recent phenomenon, antedated historically by the reverse process of cultural diffusion stretching northwards from the Caribbean-Gulf of Mexico region into the southern littoral of the United States. The twin seminal forces of race and religion left their mark upon the entire area. This is why the history of post-Emancipation Antillean society was not unlike the history of the *post bellum* American South and why even today the cultural Catholicism of the area means that, other things being equal, it is easier for a politician who is also Catholic in religious affiliation to succeed in Caracas or San Juan or New Orleans than it is for other political types. If a novelist like Faulkner has annotated the sociology of the decayed white gentleman class in the American South, a Carribbean novelist like Edgar Mittelholtzer has composed, in a not dissimilar fashion, the saga of the decline of the Dutch planter class in his Kaywana series. The similarities to be noted in these semi-fictional, semi-historical accounts are suggestive, and they bring out vividly how so many of the problems that presently beset both the American South and the Pan-Caribbean basin go back, albeit in different manifestations, to the one transcending fact of race admixture carried on between resident ethnic stocks over a period of centuries. The mixture indeed has been so widespread that it is almost

491

as impossible to use anthropological criteria to distinguish one ethnic group from another in modern Caribbean society as it is in the mainland societies of Central America and the old Spanish Main.

By geographical location alone Puerto Rico belongs to all of this. And the final charge to be levelled against both the Spanish and the current American suzerainties is that, by insisting upon a neo-mercantilist exclusivism, both of them prevented Puerto Ricans from developing the intimate Caribbean relations, and therefore a Caribbean consciousness, to which geographical location entitles them. The isolationism has in some ways been perhaps even worse since 1898. For under Spain there was at least the liaison, clandestine much of the time, between the Puerto Rican and the Cuban insurrectionary movements, which gave rise to the well-known poetic fancy that the two Caribbean colonies were the two wings of the same dove. The Puerto Rican Julio Vizcarrondo and the Cuban-born Rafael María de Labra formed the Spanish Abolitionist Society in 1865, thereby giving an internal reinforcement to the foreign abolitionist pressures which were responsible, much more than Spanish home opinion, for the Moret law of 1870 and the final reluctant abolition of 1873. Puerto Rican educators like de Hostos enjoyed a reputation throughout Latin America, with the perambulations of de Hostos finally leading him to a residence in the Dominican Republic and the attempted reconstruction of its educational system. For a time, earlier in the nineteenth century, there had been close relations with Bolívar and the mainland liberationist leaderships, while Bolívar's *Letter to a Gentleman in Jamaica* is well-known evidence of that famous statesman's lifelong interest in the future of the two island territories. Yet for all that there is today, even in the educated Puerto Rican, at best only a casual knowledge of the larger Caribbean, of the anti-colonial struggles in the other islands, of Caribbean history in general. The University library in Rio Piedras possesses hardly a few dozen volumes, oddly assorted, on the area to compare with its fine Puerto Rican collection. There is a legend, of the old colonial days, that the Puerto Rican would not put out to sea lest he meet the Dutch marauders; and insularist psychology still works today to prevent any but the adventuresome few from undertaking anything more than a weekend in St. Thomas or Santo Domingo. The Institute of Caribbean Studies, designed to bring local scholars and students into closer association with the area, had to wait until 1958 for its establishment at the leading university in conjunction with the Pan-American Union. Tariff economics, the unilateral direction of air and sea communications, migration patterns, educational opportunities—all have conspired to make the average Puerto Rican far more familiar with

Miami or New York than with Fort-de-France or Cartagena. He will think of himself as a Puerto Rican or an American, but rarely as a Caribbean citizen. And this indifference to the other islands is reinforced at times by a suspicion that their inhabitants are "black" people with whom he would not care to associate. This sentiment was sufficiently expressed a century ago in the advice of Ramón de la Sagra that "The European or white element being at present predominant in Porto Rico, and nearly so in Cuba, these two Spanish colonies will take the lead in the transformation which is now preparing. . . . We advise the inhabitants of Cuba to increase, by all possible means, the industrious white population; for such may be, some day to come, the commercial and political preponderance of the most important of the Antilles—lying at the entrance to the Gulf of Mexico—that it will change the future destinies of the other islands, by exercising over all a favorable reaction by the combined influence of a well-cultivated soil, and the superiority of intelligence of its population of European origin."[1]

This ethnocentrism is common to the whole area. The Caribbean peoples, it is well known, have always been congenitally migratory. But whereas before 1940 the migration was of an intra-Caribbean character—West Indians, for example, in Costa Rica and the Panama Canal Zone—since the war it has been more extra-Caribbean in character, with the two great streams of Puerto Rican migration to the United States and West Indian migration to Britain. Inter-island communication is still, by comparison, on a minor scale. One reason for the collapse of the West Indies Federation was perhaps the fact that federalist sentiment was frustrated by the very narrow limits of inter-island intercourse, this intercourse having in fact been very largely restricted, as the British Guianese observer to the Montego Bay Conference of 1947 observed, to the two groups of members of visiting cricket teams and civil service officials. The avenues of travel and communication remain in substance avenues between each territory and its present or former metropolitan controlling power, not between the individual territories themselves. The subordination of Caribbean to metropolitan interests remains still to plague the region; thus the Puerto Rican Commonwealth government has only recently succeeded in its struggle to obtain charters from the Civil Aeronautics Board for direct air flights between San Juan and Western Europe (the vacation trip to Spain has always been popular with those Puerto Ricans who can afford it), while the development of a national air carrier for the West Indies as a whole is still a dream only because Washington and London have been unable to reconcile their competing world interests and revise the outmoded 1946 Bermuda Air Agreement which currently places an artificial limitation upon the further growth of Caribbean air services. Yet a revolution which brought air fares within the reach of the pocket of the Caribbean common man would not be of much use to him so long as a genuine freedom of movement is made impossible by the existence of a vast mosaic of customs and migration barriers within the area. Even the short-lived West Indies Federation could not agree upon a federal customs union between the constituent units of the federal enterprise, and it is painfully clear that a regional freedom of movement covering the larger Pan-Caribbean region remains as yet a hope beyond the shadow of a dream. The consequences of this fact are various. It creates the peculiar problem of Caribbean illegal migrant traffic, as with the illicit entry of Haitians into the Bahamas. It stimulates the age-old smuggling of contraband goods, such as takes place between Trinidad and Venezuela across the poorly policed Gulf of Paria. It puts the Caribbean reader at the mercy of inadequate and inefficient news services when he seeks knowledge about other islands; there are no Puerto Rican news correspondents, for example, in the other Caribbean and Latin American capitals which means that the Puerto Rican reader is driven to rely almost exclusively upon the strongly prejudiced syndicated column of Jules Dubois of the *Chicago Tribune* when he looks for other than United States news.

This is not accident: it is rooted in the history of the Caribbean and its prolonged period of metropolitan domination. The islands of the archipelago have been distributed and redistributed in accordance with the changing fortunes of the European and American powers; thus Puerto Rico changed hands from Spain to the United States in 1898 in pretty much the same way as Jamaica had been transferred from Spain to England in 1655. The prime loyalty demanded from the local colony has always been towards the power owning it at any given time, and the individual West Indian has been expected to switch this loyalty as frequently as the ownership changed. The Puerto Rican was expected to transform himself overnight from being a good Spaniard to becoming a good American, just as in 1802 Trinidadians had been expected to redirect their allegiance from Spain to England. The impact of all this upon the general Caribbean psychology has been tremendous. It explains why there is as yet little of a real Pan-Caribbean consciousness. It explains the continuing Balkanization, both political and economic, of the area. And this is why the area is characterized by colonial variants of the respective metropolitan national patriotisms. So, there are the absurdities, in the past, of the court of the Haitian black Napoleons; the "little England" temper today of Barbados—Cheltenham, as it were, with tropical overtones; the overseas *citoyen français* in Martinique and Guadeloupe; the American *pitiyanqui* in Puerto Rico; what Ansell Hart has aptly styled the social religion of Anglolatry in Jamaica; while in the Dominican Republic there has been an official effort to keep up the cultural connections with Spain and to discourage those with the neighboring Caribbean Negro peoples lest a new sense of Africanism help to promote once again the earlier racial unity of Hispaniola.

This absence of a Caribbean *civismo* has been accompanied by the absence of a real Caribbean culture which might have become its foundation. There has been little of an indigenous character which might have been opposed to cultural imperialism. Language, family structure, education, the basic values of life itself, have been transplanted from outside and so completely assimilated by the Caribbean peoples, out of a false sense of what is proper, that one of the most deeply felt of their present discontents is a sense of cultural loss, an absence of cultural identity. The original aboriginal civilization left little behind it, except for a few scattered Indian artifacts, so that the Caribbean individual, unlike his African counterpart, has nothing like the great medieval African kingdoms that he can look back to as a national past. He is, in the Martiniquan saying, *peau noir, masque blanc,* the uneasy possessor of a pseudo-European culture in an Afro-Asian environment. Nor is there any general indigenous language to hold the various peoples of the region together. Creole, like "talky-talky" in Surinam or *papiamento* in Curaçao, is the *lingua franca* of each of the individual territories, but there is no general unifying Creole language that could be made into the linguistic foundation of a Pan-Caribbean national sense. Hence the peculiar language problems of the area; to take an example only, politics in St. Croix are distorted out of their natural development by the presence of a vocal Puerto Rican minority which, despite its common American citizenship with the native Crucian majority, is divided artificially from the majority because it lacks English. The most urgent task facing the region, it follows from all this, is the organization of a Caribbean revolution which will give to the Caribbean native not only political independence but also, first, real economic rehabilitation and, second, final release from cultural dependency. It has to bring in a new world in order to redress the inheritance of the old.

Everything suggests that the Caribbean is in fact on the threshold of this revolution. The fall of the Batista and Trujillo dictatorships heralds a new era in which Cuba and the Dominican Republic will take their places of leadership within the area along new lines of development. Jamaica and Trinidad have become independent nations within the Commonwealth. There is a growing dissatisfaction with the various forms of constitutional association whereby the metro-politan powers have attempted to maintain their control while re-linquishing the more offensive techniques of domination. This explains the collapse of the British-type West Indies Federation; the general recognition in the French Antilles that the departmentalization policy of 1946 has turned out to be a pathetic failure; the dissatisfaction of the new radical intelligentsia in Surinam and the Netherlands Antilles with the arrangements, extremely liberal as they are, of the Dutch Kingdom Statute of 1954; and, in Puerto Rico itself, an expanding frustration as the realities of the system of Congressional government within the island give the lie to the grandiose theories of the Common-wealth legalists and politicians. This new note, in turn, replacing gradualist reformism with belligerent nationalism, is the product of the new style of nationalist political party emerging in the region, like the rejuvenated Socialist and Communist parties in the French Antilles, the Peoples' National Movement in Trinidad, the Peoples' Progressive Party in British Guiana, and the more radical groups in the new political ferment of the post-Trujillo Dominican Republic. The old style of flamboyant political independent—summed up in the fictional figure of David Boyeur in Alec Waugh's novel, *Island in the Sun*—has been as a type an adept in street violence, usually a trade union "little Caesar" with little understanding of democratic organization, usually devoid, even more, of constructive ideas, whose "program" consists mainly of sterile agitation against the metropolitan colonial office. He is now being replaced by the university-educated leader and the fully organized mass party based on constitutional methods and following nationalist purposes. The amateur, who came usually from the ranks of the legal or medical professions, is thus yielding to the professional trained in economics and political science.

The old type of leader of course reflected the old type of colonial-ism. "Powerless to mold policy," the Dominica Conference report of 1932 noted of the type, "still more powerless to act independently, paralyzed by the subconscious fear of impending repression and therefore bereft of constructive thought, the West Indian politician has hitherto been inclined to dissipate his energies in acute and penetrating but embittered and essentially destructive criticism of the government on which, nevertheless, he has waited for the initiation of all policies intended to benefit his people, and which he has ex-pected to assume the full responsibility for all necessary decisions. His political life has been overshadowed by a government too om-nipotent and too omnipresent, and has had little opportunity for independent growth."[2] This generally has been the definition, in the British Caribbean, of men like Gairy, Joshua, Butler, Sir Alexander Bustamante, the Creole Beau Brummels, the Indian "Bengal Leopards," and the calypsonian politicians. With the advent of national independence their day, for most of them, is clearly at an end—although the colonial period has left behind it sufficient psychological debris to enable them to carry on a prolonged rearguard action as oppositions to the new nationalist leaderships. The issue is clearly drawn between the politics of the old colonial world and the politics of the new nationalist world. "It is a conflict," Dr. Eric Williams of Trinidad has said of the Trinidadian situation, "between those who take to the sword and who will perish by the pen, a conflict between obscene language and university analysis, a conflict between *patois* and Latin, between the *mauvaise langue* whispered from house to house and the intelligent mass meeting of the age of political education dispensed by the Peoples' National Movement."[3] The advance of the new style had certainly proceeded far enough in the early 1960's to invalidate the misguided suggestion of an American liberal commentator in 1947 that a literacy voting test should be imposed on the Caribbean "mobocracy" as universal suffrage became a fact, lest the emergence of local legislatures based on mass electorates encourage still further the victory of the Bustamante political type.[4] On the contrary, the new democratic constitutions have given rise to a quality of leadership that compares more than favorably with Anglo-American leadership; certainly Caribbean leaders like Cheddi Jagan and Eric Williams, Norman Manley and Governor Muñoz Marín, José Figueres and Juan Bosch, embody in their persons gifts of genius and statesmanship equal to anything that the more "mature" great nations can show.

The Caribbean revolution, of course, is only just beginning. It still lacks a Pan-Caribbean sense and remains still a disconnected series of separate movements within the various islands. There is an inequality of development resulting from the fact that reforms have been imposed piecemeal upon the region by varying and different imperial policies—political independence being the goal in the British Caribbean, constitutional assimilationism the goal in the French Caribbean, and so on. There exists an astonishing hodgepodge of constitutional and political devices throughout the region—single-chamber legislatures, bicameral legislatures, general councils, nominated memberships, departmental commissions, nominated governors, elected officials—possessed of no rational guiding principle save that of particular colonial policies which have their genesis in the changing domestic political fortunes of the metropolitan society.

Progress throughout has been intermittent, occasional, uncoordinated. Puerto Rico was granted its elective governorship in 1947; British West Indians had to wait until 1959 before obtaining the lesser advance of the first nominated governor drawn from Creole ranks in the appointment of Sir Solomon Hochoy to the Trinidad governorship. Even then, there has been no assurance that reforms granted would not be rescinded; thus in 1953 the Prefect of Guadeloupe suspended the local *Conseil Général* (for the first time since 1874) and instituted arbitrary rule, while the British government in the same year suspended the British Guiana constitution on the ground (never satisfactorily proved) that the popularly elected government of Dr. Jagan had plotted to institute a Communist regime in the territory. Puerto Rico, again, has a Resident Commissioner in Washington, but the neighboring American Virgin Islands have so far failed—as the dismal history of the 1962 Kennedy administration-backed bill demonstrates—to obtain either minor concessions or the larger gift of a locally elected governorship and enfranchisement in Presidential elections. The Bahamas have been ruled, right into the middle of the twentieth century, by a white mercantile aristocracy operating a fantastic eighteenth-century constitution, and the appointment of the exiled Duke of Windsor to its governorship a generation ago aptly demonstrated how that sinecure could be used to rid the official British establishment of an embarrassing figure whom it wished to punish for the abdication of 1936. Even now, late in the colonial day as it is, the British West Indies can still be viewed as a seat for comfortable appointments for "home" personnel: the first and only Governor General of the short-lived West Indies Federation was, in the figure of Lord Hailes, a retired Tory whip from the House of Commons; and the upper echelons of the French Antillean civil service bureaucracy remain, as the Martiniquan riots of 1959 and the infamous "Letter of the Eighteen" that accompanied them show, the preserve of a narrow-minded group of French expatriates. As for the formally independent republics of the region, their present plight of economic feudalism and political authoritarianism goes back in large measure to their abandonment by their former colonial masters and their continued exclusion from the influence of the liberal ideology of the outside world. Their economic life on the whole is that of a rural peasantry living on the margins of subsistence, and their political life an opéra bouffe politics punctuated by perennial palace revolutions. Trollope, a century ago, described the arrival of a deposed Haitian President in Kingston, Jamaica; and the practice still persists, based as it has been, historically, upon a revolutionary ritual in which a revolting general leads an army of *cacos,* the typical Haitian peasant *condottiere,* south from Cap Haitien to the capital to "overthrow" the incumbent President who usually decamps, often with a load of treasure, to the Jamaican refuge. The present condition of the island republics is indeed eloquent warning that in an interdependent world national independence, if viewed as merely an end in itself, can lead to stagnation and decay.

To be complete, in other words, the nationalist democratic principle will have to stretch out its hands to embrace the idea, cherished by one mainstream of Caribbean political thought in Betances and Schoelcher, Martí and de Hostos, of a unified Caribbean political and economic system, federal or confederationist, which will help the region to throw off the artificial boundaries and insular psychologies imposed by imperialism. Such a system, to begin with, will have to take on a loose federal form, for the record of previous attempts at closer regional association—the old Leeward Islands Confederation, the short-lived Pan-American Federation of Labor after 1918, the various attempts at Central American unity, the more recent West Indies Federation—shows that even a limited federalist sense of citizenship will be the long-term consequence rather than an immediate cause of such federalizing enterprises. The chief business of the political form, after that, will be the establishment of plans for the rational economic planning of the area on a positive regionalist basis, following the lines tentatively laid out in the Trinidad Government's tract, *The Economics of Nationhood.* For one of the great hazards of independence will be (and this includes Puerto Rico) the loss of economic protection from the former imperial mercantilist systems; West Indian leaders are already aware of the fact that the probable entry of the United Kingdom into the European Common Market will mean the erosion of imperial tariff margins and therefore of the protected status of West Indian bananas and citrus fruits in the British economy. This calls for nothing less than the establishment of a Caribbean Economic Community (to which an independent Puerto Rico would be able to adhere) capable internally of offsetting the uneconomic costs of competitive industrialization by means of a real customs union, and externally of giving new protective strength, as a single bargaining unit, to the Caribbean economic interest in the world outside. Alongside this economic program there would go a concerted effort, on the cultural level, to rid the region's peoples of their continuing servile mentality, shown, for example, in their continuing dependence upon European ideas and American popular amusements. This means, frankly, a nationalist dynamic founded on the concept of a national culture making its own unique contribution to world civilization. It also means a developing relationship between culture, government, and politics in ways and means perhaps radically different from those traditionally prevailing in the liberal Western societies.

No student of Caribbean life is likely to take lightly the massive difficulties confronting all this. The idea of an independent Caribbean is strange even to many Caribbean groups and leaders. For many of them "independence" means merely creating societies that resemble as closely as possible the "home" societies. They speak of West Indian culture, but in practice—particularly in Jamaica and Puerto Rico—they have permitted an inundation of their societies by the cultural nihilism of American popular amusements. Their very concept of culture is frequently pedestrian; Leopold Senghor's remark that "African politicians have a tendency to neglect culture and to make it a dependency of politics" applies as much to many Caribbean leaders as it does to West Africa.[5] There is much ado about the multi-racial virtues of Caribbean life. In practice, however, there is a color-class classificatory principle which could easily ossify into a permanent caste system if the passion for light color is allowed to prevail in social attitudes. The very pluralism of the society still means that there are many subgroups which have not yet been brought together, as equals, under the umbrella of an overall nationalism; the Javanese and Hindustani minorities in Surinam, for example, or the Amerindian tribal groups in the Guianas. Nor has the new gospel of nationalism always succeeded in forging a new alliance between the masses and the classes; on the Caribbean circumference the tragic *violencia* in the Colombian interior perpetuates still the old Latin American story of murderous civil war between peasants and soldiers, and in the Caribbean center the stubborn sociocultural conservatism of ruling Creole white groups like the burgher aristocracy, both Dutch Protestant and Sephardic Jew, of Curaçao has stood in the way of effective inter-group fluidity in that overseas Dutch society. All this in turn inhibits the growth of national self-respect, for it perpetuates Caribbean society as a house divided against itself. The history of the Haitian war of independence, in which the rural masses closed ranks with the new Negro generals against the mulatto and white colonist groups, would be in itself enough to indicate the tremendous power of inter-group animosity, based mainly on racial separatism, in the regional life; and even today, after a century and a half, the schizoid culture of Haiti continues to belie the promise of the earlier magnificent conquest of liberty in that society. In the British islands national self-respect has been inhibited by the habit of political atheism in the Creole middle-class group: instead of being a free leisured class or the leaders of peasants and workers in the national cause, its members are only too often prone to retreat into an elaborate social ballet of trivial prestige seeking, the final goal of which is conceived as a citation in the Royal Birthday Honors List. The average Caribbean citizen, afflicted by all this, has only too frequently sought to run away from it all, so that geographical migration has been accompanied by a habit of psychological migration. Marcus Garvey has described how, when he arrived in New York in 1916, the members of the West Indian colony which he found in Harlem were in the habit of passing themselves off to American Negroes as Indians, not as Negroes, a palpable myth which succeeded only because of the American Negro's ignorance of the geography and history of his own race.[6] A similar sense of ethnic shame has driven many Puerto Ricans today to disguise themselves as "Latins" in order to escape the stigma of Negro or even "lousy Puerto Rican" in the same Harlem jungle society. So long as these phobias remain they will constitute formidable obstacles to the growth in the Caribbean of what one of its local journalist writers has aptly termed the "assimilative state."

"Every society," wrote Burke, "must have some compensation for its slavery." The reconstruction of Caribbean society today is all the more difficult because it has had so very few compensations. It cannot build, as can the emergent African states, upon a rich pre-European historical past; it would be difficult to compose a book on the area which would match Basil Davidson's *Old Africa Rediscovered.* Even so, there is enough to start building on. There are Carnival and the remarkable growth of the steelband in Trinidad. There is the tremendous renaissance of the Port-au-Prince school of painters. There is the contribution of the Cuban Negro to the dance, music techniques, and folklore in general, annotated in the pioneering scholarship of Ortiz. There is the magico-religious system of Voudoun which, in its magnificent poetic vision and artistic expression constitutes the revolt of the Haitian rural masses against the religious imperialism of the French Catholic church. In Puerto Rico itself there are the older folk-music forms of the *décima* and the *aguinaldo,* still very much alive despite the avalanche of American entertainment styles. At the more consciously intellectual level, the work of collecting, editing, and interpreting the history of the region, so splendidly begun by the earlier nineteenth-century Puerto Rican scholars like Acosta, Salvador Brau, Tapia y Rivera, remains now to be completed as the archival treasures of the metropolitan centers of London, Paris, Washington, and Seville, for so long inaccessible to Caribbean scholars, are opened up. This in itself will do much to shed light on dark passages; it is not too much to say, for example, that the economic history of Spanish Puerto Rico resides, still essentially untouched, in the massive documentation of the *Archivo General de Indias* in Seville. The new group of sociologists and anthropologists at the University of the West Indies has already undertaken the analysis of the region with the tools of the modern social sciences; the politics and government of the region now await similar attention, for, despite the political transformation going on, no competent book has been written on the British area, for example, since Hume Wrong's book of 1923.

Above all, there is the upsurge of the West Indian literary genius that has taken place in the post-war period. A whole new picaresque school of novelists has flowered in the figures of Lamming, Naipaul, Selvon, Vic Reid, John Hearne. Some of its work of course goes back to an earlier literary tradition of resurgent pride in the Negro past, in the hitherto repressed history of the slave society, in the beauty of the *belle négresse,* the Caribbean woman, reflected in novels like Jean Brière's *Le Drapeau de Demain* and essays like the *Ainsi Parle l'Oncle* of Price-Mars. Some of it carries on the tradition of social protest embodied, in Puerto Rico, in the *La Charca* of Zeno Gandía which described the moral and physical debilitation of the Puerto Rican highland *campesino* class in the last decade of the Spanish suzerainty. Some of it again is a healthy reaction against the sort of romantic distortion worked by earlier writers who exploited the temptation to see the Caribbean as merely a picturesque scene; the various novels of the Jamaican Herbert de Lisser are perhaps only the most unfortunate example of this genre. And not the least interesting aspect of this movement is the fact that it has been set in motion in large part by young writers who have been forced to seek the centers of the outside world that could provide them with the amenities— publishing houses, paying assignments, established reading audiences —denied to them by Creole societies that have been intellectually depressed and capable only of offering its bright spirits struggling and frustrating existences as schoolteachers or civil servants. As the new national consciousness grows, this inequality of opportunity will no doubt be redressed. Less will be heard of the "pleasures of exile," more of the responsibilities of return. The literature of the Caribbean exile itself—Selvon's *The Lonely Londoners,* Zobel's *Fête à Paris,* Cotto-Thorner's *Trópico en Manhattan*—will give way to a new literature set on native grounds. As this takes place, the region will begin to recover its lost identity, find its place in the sun—"make its play," in the phrase of the calypsonian, for the international recognition of itself as a birthplace of new nations in its own right.

Yet the heart and center of the Caribbean revolution, for good or ill, is the new Cuba of Fidel Castro. Since its inception after the tremendous guerrilla campaign of the high *sierra,* the victorious 26th of July movement has launched a real revolution in Cuban society, as distinct from the merely ameliorative reforms of the Puerto Rican *Populares* over the last two decades. The pre-eminence that Puerto Rico enjoyed for so long is thus being rapidly eclipsed: in the politico-constitutional field, her leader position is being eclipsed as other Caribbean territories obtain full national independence while she remains tied to the United States; in the socio-economic field it is being eclipsed as the Cuban method, basically socialist, offers a new alternative to the Caribbean "condition of the people" question. This truth, moreover, applies not only to the Caribbean area but to Latin America as a whole. For despite things like the Figueres-Betancourt-Muñoz Marín liberal alliance, Puerto Ricans have not been signally successful in their effort to persuade their Latin brothers that they are not still colonial wards of the American power. On that wider canvas, Cuba has clearly stepped into the leadership role of the Mexican Revolution a generation ago, a role made all the easier since the leading left-wing Latin American parties, most famously the *Aprista* movement in Peru, have lost something of their initial radicalism. It is not too much to claim, then, that within the next generation Cuba will make the same emotional appeal to the Western Hemisphere that Soviet Russia did to the European after 1917. The war of words has already reached gigantic proportions in the form of a vast body of literature, some apocalyptically eulogistic, some frenziedly hostile. The mere size of this output, compared with the mere handful of books that Puerto Rico has been able to generate during the last twenty years, points to the truth that it is Havana, not San Juan, that has finally and explosively brought the Caribbean, hitherto a neglected backwater, to the forefront of international attention.

There can be no proper understanding of revolutionary Cuba without an understanding of the pre-revolutionary Batista regime. What Carleton Beals termed "the crime of Cuba," just before the first Batista *coup d'état,* was a typical Latin-American police state ruling over a colonialist economy wherein the labor of the landless rural masses and the enormously rich agricultural potential of the island were deployed in the service of an export crop system, sugar, tobacco, and coffee, of which an alliance of local planters and expatriate business corporations was the chief beneficiary. Politically the regime was not the sort of amazing feudal patrimony such as that of the Trujillo family described in Jesús de Galíndez's *Era de Trujillo*; but it was, under Batista as under Gómez and Machado before him, the pawn of the typical Caribbean dictator who used his power, in Roman dreams of grandeur, for personal aggrandizement and social brutalization. Basically traditionalist in ideology, it did not seek (like Nazi Germany) to rearrange the internal power balance between social classes; both the Havana aristocracy and the middle class were able to retain their social positions so long as they supported the regime. The army, in simliar fashion, remained the Praetorian guard of the dictator, rather than producing, in the form of a rising educated young officer class, the nucleus of a new, modernizing power bloc within the society. The external pillar of support for the regime was, of course, an American foreign policy using its power, under the Platt Amendment, to intervene in Cuban politics on the side of despotic governments which guaranteed to protect American business corporate interests. The record of this policy, studiously documented in Professor Robert Smith's book, *The United States and Cuba: Business and Diplomacy 1917-1960,* makes the United States quite directly responsible for the rise of the socialist Cuba that now confronts it south of the Florida Keys. For Batista's ascendancy—starting in 1933, the year of Franklin Roosevelt's accession to the presidency—could not have perpetuated itself without the continuing approval of the United States government.[7] The New Deal here made little difference to traditional State Department attitudes; and these attitudes remained posited, to the very last, on the cynicism of the remark of a Louisiana Congressman early in 1902: "After the war, it was 'Root, hog or die.' And we rooted. Let Cuba root awhile."[8] To many Latin eyes today— even those which themselves dislike the revolution's official relations with the Communist bloc—the Caribbean drama looks like a Cuban David challenging an American Goliath; and the major responsibility for this fact lies at the door of American foreign policy.

Like all revolutions, the Cuban has had to deploy much of its energy in survival against counter-revolution. The 1961 fiasco of the Bay of Pigs CIA-sponsored invasion showed the reality of the danger of American armed intervention, even under a supposedly liberal Democratic administration. The possibility of a second attempt—a belief in its certainty is an article of faith in Havana—would be enough in itself to deter the revolutionary leadership from any interventionist adventures of its own in the Caribbean. Those who see the new Havana as a possible plotting ground for such adventures overlook the fact that, Mexico apart, no country in the area has the power and resources to undertake such a policy. Castro has indeed spoken in favor of Puerto Rican independence and has castigated the Trujillo dictatorship, but no overt action has followed; and the Dominican regime fell by agencies other than Castro's. One consequence of the environment of international hostility has been, of course, the organized arming of the Cuban masses into a citizen army: this in itself proves that the regime exists on a solid base of popular support, for no government can for long impose itself upon a people in arms. Preoccupation with the Communist issue, combined with the gross inadequacy of American press reporting on the Revolution and the State Department ban on travel to the republic, has thus prevented the American people from arriving at any real understanding of the ideology and program of the new regime. Yet the overall achievement has been remarkable. Educational and welfare programs have concentrated on the mass literacy scheme, with a major emphasis upon the rehabilitation of the individual Cuban family rather than upon collectivist living after the modern Israeli manner. A vast housing program, undertaken by cooperative labor and financed, in the urban sector, by the national lottery (a prime source of corruption in the old days), has begun to tackle the primitivism of the old housing conditions. A frontal onslaught on racial discrimination has been launched, a tremendously significant item in the light of the traditional isolation of the Cuban Negro from the mainstream of the national life; it is not for nothing that Cuba's greatest novel, Villaverde's *Cecilia Valdés* of 1833, deals with the tragic love of a beautiful octaroon for a white youth from the Havana family elite. National economic policy, above all, has concentrated upon the elimination of the twin afflictions of the old regime: the feudal maldistribution of wealth, with all of its consequent social repercussions, and the draining off of the national wealth to overseas sources in the form of sugar profits, in its turn the consequence of the phenomenon of absentee ownership of the rich latifundia. The major weapon here has been the agrarian land reform operated by the famous Agrarian Reform Institute. Of its confiscatory aspect it is enough to point out that, far from being new, it has a well-known precedent in the earlier Mexican expropriation of the foreign oil companies and that, although the nature of the compensation agreements may be regrettable, it is in part justified in view of the generally unsatisfactory service record of United States companies operating public utility franchises in Latin American countries. Its distributive aspect, with the tripartite arrangement of individual smallholdings, state farms, and cooperatives, is also in line with most Latin American sentiment. Its administrative techniques have yet to be fully matured, as the admittedly widespread degree of managerial incompetency in the new state machinery shows. But of the technical efficiency in terms of increased production and of a new social efficiency stemming from the new elevation in the social status of the peasant in the national life there can be little doubt. Mexican scholarly studies have testified to the productivity increase, despite the conversion of the island into a veritable siege economy as a consequence of the United States trade embargo, reinforced by the naval embargo during the crisis of October 1962; while even commentators generally critical of the new regime have agreed in testifying to the tremendous rehabilitation of the Cuban countryside.[9] And, finally, the basically moralistic tone of the revolution is perhaps best illustrated in the moral cleansing by the regime of a Havana which, ever since the economic consequences of the American Prohibition experiment, had degenerated into little more than a gigantic saloon and brothel for American liquor and crime syndicates; the mere conversion of the sumptuous villas built by the gambling interests in the exclusive Miramar district of the capital into a new university center would be enough in itself to testify to the new scale of national values.

Like Soviet Russia before it, the Cuban Revolution has of course provoked a veritable barrage of calumny and misrepresentation, especially from the United States press. Some critics, like Theodore Draper, have talked of the "betrayal" of the "middle class," thus failing to comprehend the truth that the movement from the beginning was overwhelmingly a peasant *jacquerie,* with the more liberal section of the national middle-class groups, like the university students, playing at best an ancillary role. The soured bourgeois refugee, indeed, is merely testimony to the genuine austerity of the socialist regime; although a student of the Puerto Rican scene must regret that one outcome of the refugee stream is the congregation of some 15,000 refugees, mostly middle-class professional people, in San Juan, and the consequent reinforcement of the more reactionary elements of the insular life and politics they have brought about. On a larger Latin American scale, critics like Adolf Berle and Arthur Schlesinger Jr. have argued that the United States must ally itself with the "middle groups" in the Hemisphere, thereby fatally overlooking the fact that the general consequence of American policy and influence over the years has been to stunt the growth of such "middle groups" in favor of the feudal and *comprador* elements in the hemispheric societies, Cuba included; not to mention the general sociological fact that the "middle groups" in question, far from being Latin variants of the North American middle-class image, continue in fact to be ideological adherents of the traditional ruling classes.

By the more irresponsible critics the whole Cuban matter has been reduced to the simple-minded moral drama—so dear to the more credulous elements of the American public mind—of an evil Communism intruding itself illegitimately into the Hemisphere in order to destroy the American "way of life." It must be said immediately that if there is indeed a Communist element in the Revolution, as the inclusion of the Cuban Communists into the national leadership would appear to show is the case, this merely serves to prove, in one way, the emptiness of the thesis of American exceptionability to European social ideas; for the thesis has validity only if the particular social experience of the United States is identified with the general social experience of the Hemisphere as a whole. The idea of the Soviet presence in the Caribbean is itself not new; a generation ago Paul Morand wrote an amusing farce, *Magie Noire,* around the figure of a Port-au-Prince political adventurer who, incited by the official visit of a Soviet flotilla to that port, successfully engineered a *coup d'état* and then proceeded to convert the Palais National into the Haitian Kremlin and to revive—a typically Caribbean touch—the ancient black communism of the old African kingdoms through the medium of the Port-au-Prince soviets. There is real truth in the fancy; for if the Cuban Revolution is Marxist-Leninist, as in truth its leader has officially declared, everything about its environmental framework —the deep power of Cuban nationalism, the age-old Creole struggle against an expatriate Catholic Church, the Latin touch of political romanticism, the peculiar importance of the peasantry in Latin life— conspires to give the doctrine a Cuban stamp. The emerging canon of the revolution, in fact, challenges one of the basic tenets of traditional Marxism—the industrial bias against the rural world—by its own emphasis, so much a part of Major Guevara's book, upon the thesis that a disaffected peasantry can in itself provide the directive force for violent social change; and there is evidence to suggest that this in itself will be sufficient to deter Havana from alienating the peasant masses by a forced collectivization program and thereby emulating the most tragic mistake of the Russian commissars. Even the doctrine of "revolutionary unity" can be seen not as a piece of orthodox Marxist theory so much as the insistence, common to all new revolutionary orders, monarchist, bourgeois or proletarian, that acceptance of the basic principle of the new national order must be made the starting point of all domestic political activity. Nationalism, rather than Communism, thus remains still the driving force of the revolution. That this has not as yet been appreciated by the American public is due, in large part, to the irresponsible portrayal by the American communications media of Castro as a hysterical Latin demagogue, when in reality what are viewed as his oratorical intemperance and physical contortions are in fact Latin American culture traits not readily understood by the American puritan mind.

None of this, of course, is to deny the less pleasing aspects of the Cuban drama. For a century or more the brutalizing violence of civil war—something Puerto Rico has never really known—has scarred the national life and spirit, and it would be surprising if the new regime did not exhibit something of that legacy. Its summary execution of political prisoners, however much justified by the record of the Batista dictatorship, was enough in itself to alienate the best of the American liberal conscience; and no socialist can forget that one of the greatest chapters in the history of socialist martyrology is the mass murder of the Paris Communards by the Thiers regime in 1871. Nor was the method made any less ugly by the regime's employment of the disreputable American ex-convict Herman Marks as its chief executioner. The crass intransigence and stupidity of American policy may help to explain these features of the regime, but they do not excuse them. Nor does the fact that the regime is more generally a popular tyranny make it any the less a tyranny from the viewpoint of the maintenance of classic political liberties. It may be urged, with much persuasiveness, that to apply this yardstick to the revolution is arbitrarily to apply Anglo-Saxon norms to Latin experience; the cry for "free elections" becomes meaningless when it is recalled that for some sixty years before Castro Cuban elections were simply the facade of a rampant spoils system run by an ignoble class of professional politicians allied to the dictator of the day. The fact remains nonetheless that the comparison has been invoked by the Revolution itself; for to read the moving oration of Fidel Castro at the 1953 Moncada courthouse trial is to be made aware of the fact that not only is he steeped in the history of Western political thought, the liberal current of which has to this very day scarcely penetrated the Iberian peninsula and its Latin American colonial derivatives, but also that he and his colleagues consciously sought to make the liberal ethic of political liberty the moral foundation of the new society they were struggling to bring into being. It is true, concededly, that a social revolution cannot be conducted along the lines of a university seminar, even more true that so long as the Miami refugee world remains a potential source of counter-revolutionary invasion the internal liberalization of the regime must inevitably be deferred. Yet the ability and the willingness to promote that liberalization, as the political counterpart to social justice, will surely remain the supreme test for a Revolution that has so enthusiastically identified itself with the romantic liberalism of Martí.

Meanwhile the Revolution's greatest source of strength remains its international significance, the contagious quality of its message for the Caribbean and Latin American masses. That message is a source of disturbance throughout the whole area, not so much in the old sense of being a vehicle of filibustering adventures as in a new sense of constituting a basic ideological force capable of attracting real intellectual adherence. It promises action where there has hitherto merely been romantic theorizing; Che Guevara's dictum that "the time is past for café discussions" expresses a fundamental truth, for up until now Latin American intellectuals and politicians have been reduced to frustrated talk while the privilege of action has been restricted to the soldiers and the landlords. With its real strength in the lowlier white and *mestizo* cultivators of rural Cuba, the Revolution seeks to re-dress the balance between city and country rather than follow the general pattern, as in Puerto Rico, of concentrating so much on in-dustrialization that the traditional neglect of the rural sector is exacerbated; while its socialist base promises a new departure from the orthodox policies of mere government encouragement of small farming enterprise, the failure of which is obvious enough in the neighboring Jamaican agricultural development program. Above all else, perhaps, by its open defiance of the United States, its implicit challenge to the Monroe Doctrine, its public taunting of the *gringos,* the Revolution has skillfully identified itself with the resentment against the *Yanqui* civilization that is latent throughout all Latin America and much of the Caribbean. The Cuban affair, in sum, has done for twentieth-century Caribbean society what the Haitian revolt did for its nineteenth-century predecessor: it has struck a new note so urgent and compelling that henceforward all progress and develop-ment will be judged in terms of the challenge that it has thrown down.

It is therefore of some interest to note the response of the Puerto Rican independent-minded forces to that challenge. The official re-sponse of San Juan, of course, hardly merits notice, for it invariably follows the lines laid down in Washington. One of the most considered declarations of pro-Cuban policy is to be found in the authorita-tive utterances of the General Secretary, Juan Mari Bras, of the *Movimiento Pro Independencia*. The Puerto Rican struggle, the argu-ment runs, is one that seeks not only formal political independence but also the final release of the national patrimony, both economic and cultural, from the control of American imperialism. That being so, it must support the Cuban Revolution, since it is in Cuba that imperialism has suffered its first major setback in Latin America. At the same time, however, since the MPI is neither a socialist organiza-tion nor based, theoretically, upon Marxism-Leninism, it cannot support the socialist aspect of the Revolution. Theoretically, indeed, the MPI must be viewed as a Christian movement; rejecting the death penalty, it must oppose the Cuban *paredón* as much as the American electric chair; and the ethical basis of Puerto Rican life being Catholic Christianity, a natural incompatibility arises with the Marxism of the Cuban Revolution. Puerto Rico must therefore support the Revolution to the degree that it is a nationalist liberationist movement, but must remain aloof from its socialism.[10]

The argument is persuasive enough, as far as it goes. Its weakness is that it does not go very far. The social policy of a "Christian" Puerto Rican republic could mean anything, from Christian Socialism to a Catholic-backed reformist capitalism. It is doubtful, again, if the unique essence of the Cuban Revolution is, as Mari Bras argues, its character as a champion of the national patrimony against foreign control, and not its socialism, for Mexico yesterday and Venezuela today constitute Latin American nationalist forces counteracting against North American economic penetration; and the fact that the United States has found it possible to make its peace with its critics in both cases suggests that it is the socialist aspect of the Cuban development that makes reconciliation impossible between Havana and Washington. It is worth noting, too, that elsewhere in his argument Mari Bras criticizes the traditional independent forces in Puerto Rico for operating on the premise that the United States is a friendly and benevolent democracy whose institutions can be copied by a free Puerto Rico once independence has been achieved. Yet it is surely because those traditionalist forces have lacked the analytical tools of a socialist attitude towards the American economy that they have been enabled to be so uncritical; anything less than a socialist analysis too easily declines into an amiable liberalism assuming that American imperial behavior is the result of a regrettable forgetfulness of national liberal principles and not, as it surely is, the consequence of the basic root principle of the American business civilization. The new Cuba, being socialist, quarrels with the essence of that civilization, not with its accidents of behavior and character; and American policy architects have instinctively realized that therein lies a radical challenge to the very basis of their way of life not postulated by the mere reformism of the later stages of the Mexican revolution. A Puerto Rican liberating movement that fails to identify itself with that challenge must inescapably find itself aligned with the pro-United States forces in the Hemisphere. To the degree that it thus aligns itself it will embrace more and more the "legend of the Yankee democracy" that Mari Bras finds so distasteful in so many present-day *independentistas*.

Where then does Puerto Rico fit into all this? The cardinal fact to be considered is the American connection. For just as the peculiar nature of that connection has created a debilitating ambivalence in insular domestic politics so it creates a similar ambivalence in the island's international relations. Puerto Ricans cannot cut themselves off from the outer Caribbean, and the local press coverage of Cuban and Santo Dominican news testifies to their keen interest in the destinies of their Spanish-speaking neighbors. At the same time the continuing Congressional monopoly over their foreign relations in all fields, commercial, military, diplomatic, prevents them from following any independent line of their own. The Kennedy appointment of Teodoro Moscoso to the directorship of the Alliance for Progress scheme is felt as a real honor by most islanders, but it is far from being anything like real self-determination in foreign affairs. Even the island's ability to criticize the Washington policies that affect them is limited, for it is only natural prudence that men who must look continually to the Congress for all sorts of favors and privileges—Governor Muñoz Marín's arduous private lobbying in early 1962 to obtain Puerto Rican exemption from the dreaded Administration tax bill covering the earnings of American subsidiary business companies abroad revealed pretty grimly the terrible vulnerability of the island economy—will move cautiously in expressing their opinions on what Congress does in foreign relations. The Governor has been a vigorous champion of what he calls "the Democratic Left" in the Hemisphere and therefore a critic of the Washington tendency to support conservative forces in the area. But the Governor, in any case, is a somewhat privileged voice. Apart from him, there are few Puerto Rican public figures who would care to utter in public the kind of radical skepticism about the Alliance for Progress voiced by Arnold Toynbee in his recent Weatherhead Lectures at their leading university. When, too, the American national supremacy is challenged by any crisis the Puerto Rican ranks automatically close; and few things were more distressing about the American-Soviet *détente* of October 1962 over the Cuban missiles issue than the spectacle of Puerto Rican leaders vying with each other to echo the moral indignation of Washington when, in harsh fact, that indignation could hardly have been altogether genuine in the light of the fact that, since 1949, the American power had itself ringed the Soviet Union with potentially offensive missile sites. There is a tendency to excuse all this by arguing that Puerto Rico is compensated on account of the private influence that its friendly advice carries in Washington policy-making circles. Yet it is doubtful if such an influence really exists. Certainly it was powerless to prevent the Cuban invasion fiasco of 1961, and it was not consulted on the 1962 blockade move. Dinner with the President does not make Governor Muñoz into a Harry Hopkins, any more than Don Pablo Casals in the White House makes of that supreme cellist a Puerto Rican ambassador.

There are two important corollaries of this. The first is that Puerto Rico's capacity to become a real leader in the area is cramped, cabined, and confined by the suspicion on the part of other peoples and governments that it is not so much a free agent as a pawn of Washington. Technical and economic missions from San Juan have helped in the rehabilitation of the new Dominican Republic, but it is arguable that they are not so much proof of a genuine Caribbean mutual aid program as they are elements of a United States drive to include the republic in the pro-American fold within the region; and Rafael Picó, in any case, has visited Santo Domingo not as the representative of Governor Muñoz but of President Kennedy. The Commonwealth government can do nothing when the federal Naturalization and Immigration Service permits Dominican refugees like General Echevarría Rodríguez and Dr. Balaguer to remain in the island for some time, and the fact only serves to compromise it in Latin American eyes. There is much bold talk about the "international personality" of Puerto Rico. But the truth is that whatever degree of such a personality exists begins and continues at the sufferance of Congress. This was sufficiently illustrated by the Congressional debate of May 1961 on the entry of Puerto Rico into the new Caribbean Organization, for Congressional opinion there was unanimous in its belief that, notwithstanding the fact that Puerto Rico had become the host country of the new body and has assumed responsibility for membership fees hitherto paid by Congress, the Congress could pull the island unilaterally out of the organization, presumably with an eye to the possibility that policies unpalatable to the United States might some day materialize.[11] Real leadership does not easily emerge from such a humiliating dependency. Nor is it likely to emerge when the political genius with whose name Puerto Rico is axiomatically associated—Governor Muñoz Marín—tries to establish before a Harvard audience the dubious thesis that nationalism must be discarded because it is aggressive and reactionary. To speak of the "political emotions of nationalism" as if they were a form of psychological infantilism and to assert the theme of "the darkly hidden obsolescence of nationalism" is hardly calculated to help Puerto Rico to win friends and influence people in the Caribbean and Latin American countries where nationalism, as in Europe four centuries ago, is the revolutionary gospel of the day.[12]

The second corollary of the general argument being pursued here is that this very ambivalence of the Puerto Rican status makes the island itself vulnerable to the hostile attentions of the hemispheric nationalist forces. The history of the *proyectos emancipadores* goes back to the period of the 1820's and '30s when the Latin American patriot liberators schemed to launch invasions against the Antillean colonies of Spain, frequently with an eye to using up the potentially dangerous feelings of the unemployed liberationist army generals in sporting adventures overseas.[13] For Puerto Rico the day for invasion has passed long ago. Yet there are other more respectable methods that are sufficiently embarrassing. Some domestic *independentista* groups are turning to the United Nations, and it may only be a matter of time before they persuade a UN majority of ex-colonial African and Asian states to undertake an examination of the Puerto Rican question under the terms of the 1960 Resolution 1514 of the General Assembly. It would be unjust, certainly, to say, in the ungracious vocabulary of those groups, that the *Popular* leadership has become the "tool of the Yankee imperialists." But it would not be unfair to say that the position that that leadership has taken on general American affairs, undoubtedly from sincere motives, has put it in a situation where its members seem always to be defending the United States. The general consequence is that leadership in the Caribbean *Kulturkampf* is taken up by others; on the radical Left by Cuba and in the liberal center by parties like the Costa Rican *Liberación Nacional* and the *Venezuelan Acción Democrática,* whose educational arm is the lively *Instituto de Educación Política* in San José.

This makes it difficult for the territory to play a genuinely Caribbean role. Its status is of such a character that, like Joseph in Egypt, it brings many privileges but nonetheless stands in the way of a natural relationship with its possessor's Caribbean brothers. There is, after all, a long tradition of Puerto Rican sympathy with its Caribbean neighbors, and in Enrique Laguerre's *El Laberinto* the theme of Puerto Rican participation in the overthrow of a Caribbean dictatorship has been made the leading element of an outstanding contemporary Puerto Rican novel. It is not then surprising that for many islanders a truly Caribbean role requires full-blown national independence. For them, the remark of Morales Lemus to Betances—"without an independent Puerto Rico no confederation is possible"—remains the key to the successful organization of the "providential confederation" of which de Hostos had dreamed. The present Caribbean Organization is for them a bogus rather than a real collectivity. Not only does it retain the colonialist device of metropolitan representation of subordinate units, as in the case of France and the French Antillean colonies, but to the degree that its membership does not include Cuba, Haiti, the Dominican Republic, Venezuela, Colombia, or any of the Central American republics it is, obviously, a hopelessly truncated and thoroughly unrepresentative body. A real federal alliance, founded on the membership of really independent units, would gradually create an Antillean community capable of asserting the Caribbean presence against the intruding outside presences, Soviet, American, or otherwise. It would look in towards itself, not outwards to others. It would replace inter-island competition with cooperation: the undignified struggles between each other for a share of the United States sugar quota are a distressing example of how the outside influence helps to pit neighbor against neighbor. It would help create a Caribbean public policy founded on positive and not negative considerations: it is well known, for example, that Aimé Césaire reluctantly accepted the French assimilationist law in 1946 mainly because he feared that an independent Martinique within a weak regional confederation would be too powerless to stand against the possibility of American expansionism and control. For Puerto Rico, membership in a new Caribbean community would revive the Antillean relationships that were broken up in 1898. Those relationships form an important chapter in insular history and it is only necessary to recall one of its episodes— the author of one of the most famous of all *indianista* novels, Manuel de Jesús Galván's *Enriquillo,* was a Dominican writer who conceived the theme of his work while witnessing, as an exile, the ceremony of the reading of the proclamation of slavery abolition in San Juan in 1873—to feel the rich quality of the tradition. For a set of multilateral relationships, by any measure, is always to be preferred to an exclusively bilateral relationship which of necessity narrows the mental horizons of a people.

With or without Puerto Rico there is much unfinished business for Caribbean statesmanship to undertake, much of it the consequence of the debris left behind by colonialism. The health and happiness of the Caribbean common man are crippled by poverty, malnutrition, illiteracy, illegitimacy, evil housing, and bad education. Governments and peoples, cities and countryside are dangerously divorced from each other. Racial and religious tensions, although easily melodramatized by the sensation-seeking Caribbean novel, are real enough to inhibit the growth of effective community or of common enjoyment. Social classes live only too often in a mid-Victorian climate of fear and envy. Science and technology have hardly begun to affect the region as liberating forces; to illustrate only, the region, alone in the Western Hemisphere, continues as host to the yellow fever carrying *aedes aegypti* variant of mosquito. Constitutional government scarcely exists except in those territories that have benefited from the Anglo-American political tradition, Puerto Rico here included. A dictatorial politics still prevails elsewhere, giving rise to the Caribbean "playboys of the Western world" of whom Ramfis Trujillo was perhaps the best-known example. The twin forces of nationalism and democracy still have before them the task of creating a Caribbean nationhood accepted as an equal in the comity of nations. The old one-way-street relationship, in which Puerto Ricans know more of the United States than Americans know of Puerto Rico, will have to give way to a more mutual relationship. If it is right to speak of the "Caribbean danger zone," it must be remembered that much of the danger springs from the tensions created by the strategy diplomacy of the great powers: Panamanian dissatisfaction with the terms of the United States occupation of the Canal Zone, for example, or the British-Guatemalan dispute, or the continuing churlish treatment of the American Virgin Islands by the United States Congress, or Russian Cold War strategy in Cuba. The region clearly needs a collective security system whereby the problems of those danger spots can be made susceptible to consultation and arbitration. All this, and more, needs to be done. Puerto Rico has a role to play in the task. But the character of that role will be determined in the long run by the island's domestic development, for the problems of external sovereignty cannot logically or practically be separated from those of internal sovereignty.

Puerto Rico and the Americas

ROUGHLY equidistant from both continents of the Western Hemisphere, Puerto Rico, like the Caribbean itself, occupies a geographical location of no mean importance. It is on the edge of both of the major hemispheric civilizations, the North American world of modern industrial capitalism, the South American world of semi-agrarian feudalism; the one Protestant and Anglo-Saxon in its cultural mold, the other Hispanic and Catholic, with its twenty-one republics sharing, in their various ways, the common Spanish background that they inherited as the successor states to the Spanish Empire of the Indies; Portuguese Brazil, of course, excepted.

What gives the Caribbean location its peculiar significance today is that for the first time since the Discovery those two twin civilizations have arrived at a point where, instead of continuing to develop along separate lines with only occasional encounters to engender conflict between them, they now confront the massive problem of meeting each other head on, of organizing their hitherto scattered and disparate mutual relations into a closer and more permanent framework, of developing a spirit of mutual understanding and a system of mutual aid in the name of a common hemispheric destiny. Various forces, only half-consciously perceived, have conspired to bring about this historic turning point: the termination of North American expansionism with the closure of the Western frontier; the awakening of the South American sleeping giants like Brazil, Argentina, and Venezuela as they seek to join the modern world; the challenge to Pan-Americanism thrown down by the intrusion of Communism into the region; the assertion by the United States of the position and the responsibilities of world leadership, of the status of the new Rome of the modern Hellenistic world, and for which a century of isolationism has hardly prepared either the American people or the American government; the growth, above all else, of a thermonuclear technology so utterly global in its power to destroy that the very idea itself of a common Western hemispheric defense system has become obsolete even before hemispheric statesmen have been able to give the idea any adequate institutional garb. The future of the entire Caribbean depends upon the ultimate outcome of this seminal confrontation of the two continental-size hemispheric culture systems. If the outcome is the birth of a genuine Pan-American system based upon the old idea of Pan-American unity, the Caribbean Sea, along with the old Spanish Main, could become its common meeting ground, serving both because fully dependent upon neither. If the result is not cooperation but conflict—assuming, for example, the emergence of more Cubas south of the Rio Grande—then the Middle American sea could quite rapidly become a sort of no man's land over which both protagonists waged their war, whether psychological or physical. In that event Puerto Rico, with the other Caribbean and Central American states, would degenerate into a pawn of rival state systems, like Poland caught between Russia and Germany in the eighteenth and nineteenth centuries, or like the new states of the Middle East caught between the Soviet Union and the United States at the present time. Merely to state this possibility is to emphasize the great stake which Puerto Rico has in the growth of peace and prosperity within the hemisphere.

The island's American future, then, becomes a question of its future relationships with the United States and with the Latin American world to the south. And the cardinal fact to be considered in any discussion of that matter is the connection of the island with the North American power. For just as the connection circumscribes Puerto Rican relationships with the Caribbean neighbors, so it likewise limits relationships with the Latin American societies. Logically, if a genuinely Caribbean life for the island requires independence, so does a genuinely hemispheric life. A Puerto Rican historian has remarked that the modern Puerto Rican is the result of a "Mediterranean streak that runs from southern Greece to southern Italy and the Balearic Islands, and from there to southern Spain and the Azores and the Canaries, and on to Puerto Rico and the Spanish Antilles."[1] This fact puts him, culturally, in the Latin American fold rather than in a North American milieu the main traits of which have been shaped by the northern European element. Since 1898, however, education, economic interest, political affiliation have all conspired to blur this truth. Even open debate on the truth is itself discouraged, not so much by a brutal American repression (which, to be fair, does not exist) as by the workings of the Puerto Rican colonial mentality itself, adept as it has become in pushing unpleasant or disturbing facts into its subterranean subconscious or at best disguising their unpleasant flavor by elaborate sophistry. This explains why colonial isolationism is only indirectly discussed by means of a genteel debate on "cultural identity"; or why the growth of an atomic arsenal in the island, largely because of the refusal of the Atlantic seaboard states to accept such a hazardous role in the national defence system, is only talked about in discreet whispers; or why the official *Popular* answer to the *independentista* propagandist groups is to assert the gratuitous libel that independence would isolate the island from the rest of the world. The price that the Puerto Rican pays for all this is heavy indeed. He is still treated as a second-class citizen within the United States, both in economic and legal senses, and he is also denied fraternal recognition by Latin Americans who dismiss him, frequently unjustly, as a political salesman for American interests. He is caught between the devil and the deep blue sea. To extricate himself from this cruel dilemma is the necessary prelude to the growth of his Pan-American self in the fullest sense.

The politico-constitutional status of the island as a continuing neo-colonial society and the sociocultural consequences of that fact have already been discussed. There are certain points, however, that merit additional emphasis. To begin with, one of the most astonishing things about the insular subordinate status is that the legislative vehicle of the subordination is a system of American federal Congressional government that has hardly changed in its basic characteristics since the American flag came to the island. The incisive criticism of that system penned in Alpheus Snow's imperially minded volume of 1902, *The Administration of Dependencies*, can be reiterated, sixty years later, without any serious alteration as a valid portrait of a federal legislative structure completely ill adapted, now as then, to the governance of overseas dependencies. "Considering, first," Snow summed up his argument, "the question of the propriety of attempting to administer the dependencies wholly through the instrumentality of the Congress, it is to be noticed that, if such were the habitual and constant method of administration, it would amount, when viewed from the standpoint of the dependencies, to habitual and constant administration by an oligarchy of foreigners. If the oligarchy were composed of a small body of men, having a unity of view and interest, and familiar with the local circumstances and conditions of the dependencies as well as with those of the Union, such a body might be, perhaps, a very proper and effective instrumentality for the performance of the national trust. As a matter of fact, however, the Congress is not a small but a large body; it has not a unity of view and interest, but is always divided into at least two great parties, and always represents local interests, many of which are opposed not only to the interests of the dependencies, but to the interests of each other; its members are elected primarily for the protection of local interests, secondarily for the protection of the interests of the whole Union, and lastly, when these interests have been protected, to protect the interests of the dependencies. With the best and most honest intentions in the world, a man elected to the Senate or House of Representatives is under a pressure to protect the local interests and the interests of the whole Union, which makes it impossible for him to place the interests of the dependencies on anything like an equality with the other interests."[2]

Congressional-Puerto Rican relations today still revolve around that fatal truth. Puerto Ricans have suffered from the ingrained conservatism of Congressional policy; more, they have suffered from the deep-set conservatism of the very structure of American national government. The very modernism for which Puerto Ricans adulate Americans has been signally absent in the growth—or rather the absence of growth—of the national political institutions. That temper of political feudalism has certain been strong enough to prevent even minor reforms, let alone the major reforms of a centralized federal colonial office, manned by a class of colonial service officials, which Snow borrowed from the writings of Paul Leroy-Bealieu on colonial administration. Thus today as in 1902 Puerto Ricans are governed in innumerable ways by an "oligarchy of foreigners" in the rooms of Congressional committees. A chosen few, it is true, will seriously attempt to educate themselves on dependency problems, and men like Representatives Homer Bone and Charles Porter and the late Fred Crawford have done yeoman service fighting for the rights of the territories and commonwealths of the nation. Once in a while there is the Congressman like Representative Donald Irwin of Connecticut whose mastery of Spanish (in his case, springing out of a boyhood spent in Argentina) makes him peculiarly fitted to defend Puerto Rican interests. But the majority of members are necessarily subject to the political laws that Snow described, which go back to the pervasive influence of the "locality rule" in the theory and practice of American electoral representation. Only too often, too, there is real Congressional hostility to Puerto Rican claims, or, if not hostility, an ignorance of Puerto Rican matters that produces similar results. The petulant remark of the Chairman of the House Armed Services Committee, made in connection with discussion in the committee of appropriations for the naval radio station at Sabaña Seca in the island—"all these foreign countries, with such outlandish names"[3]—is not unrepresentative of the general attitude. Congress has been traditionally slow in changes in colonial administration, as Puerto Ricans know to their cost. And a President is always apt to wait for Congress to move in this field, unless driven by irresistible necessities, for otherwise he runs the risk of humiliating defeat. The inability of the Kennedy administration to

persuade Congress to pass the executive-sponsored 1962 legislation
that would have abolished the discriminatory literacy tests that effectively disenfranchise so many non-English-speaking Puerto Rican
citizens in New York provides only the most recent proof of that fact.
Even more proof has been provided by the long, embittered struggle
of United States Virgin Islanders to obtain Congressional assent to
the grant of local home rule and thereby final release from the joint
control of the Interior Department and the House Interior and Insular
Affairs Committee, a struggle that has driven the island forces to
inventing innumerable techniques—advisory reports from academic
scholars, paid lobbyists in Washington, memorials to the federally appointed Governor—designed to circumvent Congressional inertia. The
general Congressional attitude to the problem of the Virgin Islands,
indeed, has been summed up in the book written by the Chief Assistant Librarian to the Library of Congress in 1945—Luther Evans'
The Virgin Islands: From Naval Base to New Deal—which, after
a lengthy apologetic for American rule and a vicious attack upon the
moral character of the islanders, ends with the callous suggestion that
since "work in Harlem is far better than federal charity in Santa Cruz"
the federal government should logically "not object if the population
of the Virgin Islands should dwindle until a caretaker had to be sent
over from Puerto Rico, although local businessmen and federal as well
as local job-holders would see degeneracy and barbarism in such a
development."[4]

And if the United States–Puerto Rican political relations are unsatisfactory, the cultural relations are even more so. The economic
base of the relations is unequal, for on the whole Americans come to
the island to fill well-paid white collar jobs while Puerto Ricans go to
the States to fill low-paid proletarian occupations. The Commonwealth's Office of Migration has done much to protect the island
worker on the mainland. Even so, it has been relatively powerless to
prevent the exploitation of rural migrant workers in the fruit-picking
areas and the failure of the organized labor movement to prevent the
exploitation of Negro and Puerto Rican workers by racket unions in
the New York City area. Nor has the political protection of the exiles
been any better. Despite the occasional colorful incursions of the
Mayor of San Juan into New York politics, the Puerto Rican *barrio*
there remains a ghetto of cultural aliens who have yet to prove that
they can hold their own against the Tammany Hall chieftains or even
that they can exact their reward from the Wagner reform elements for
the Puerto Rican support of those elements in the dramatic mayoralty
struggle of 1961. They become, indeed, the hapless victims of moral
preachments to the effect that they must "Americanize" themselves in

order to win as a group in what has always been, in New York politics, an ugly pattern of ethnic separatism. There is little evidence that, conversely, New Yorkers are prepared to accept the utopian advice of Puerto Rican social workers that they in turn have much to learn from their Puerto Rican neighbors in the way of pleasing customs, good moral principles, and a strong family sense.[5] The pressures and tensions of American city life are indeed working to divide Puerto Rican against Puerto Rican rather than to unite them into a single voting bloc; the furious argument within the New York island community unleashed by the unfortunate remarks of the Director of the Commonwealth's city Migration Office in 1958 points to a serious group conflict, characteristic of the history of all migrant peoples in American life, between the first generation group and the second generation group, many of the latter being college-educated persons uprooted from the ghetto life, knowing little Spanish, and whose knowledge of Puerto Rico itself comes solely from what they have heard about it.[6]

Nor are matters much better in the cultural milieu of the island life itself. The official picture is that of American–Puerto Rican amity. The reality, however, is less pleasing. Many of the "continentals" make real and successful efforts to reach across to the Puerto Rican neighbor. Many of them even manage to submerge themselves so well that they become completely Puerto Rican. Americans have a fine record of public service in the island, from the very beginning; to name only two examples, agricultural research owes much to the early work of David W. May, while the basis of the fine Puerto Rican collection in the University library in Rio Piedras comes from the private collection of the curious German-American Robert Junghanns who came to the island about 1898. But these do not constitute a general rule. They were isolated, perhaps eccentric, Americans in the older, pre-industrial Puerto Rico, while the American resident community today lives a thoroughly American life in the urbanized sector of a rapidly Americanizing industrial society. Its members may take a real interest in Puerto Rican folkways, but they rarely see them as an alternative to the "American way." At the strategic points of intercourse the real concessions have to be made by the Puerto Ricans; thus, in the language question, the social imposition of English has gone so far that the typical businessmen's clubs like the Lions and the Elks conduct their proceedings in English despite the fact that the majority of their memberships are Puerto Rican. The assumption throughout is that Puerto Ricans are at school with the United States, not American residents at school with Puerto Rico. Nor is this simply a matter of the American business-commercial community, where the sentiment is frequently that of a crude contempt for the islander. It also infects the educated *norteamericano*, who ought to know better but whose learning is quaintly culture-bound when the basic moral superiority of the American way, as he sees it, is called into question. The Puerto Ricans become, every so often, the captive audience of the visiting stateside academic or writer who chides them for their "provincialism" at the same time as he unwittingly reveals his own. For if the Puerto Rican intellectual is imprisoned within his own narrow framework of ideas, it is equally true that his American critic, who judges him so condescendingly, is likewise imprisoned within his own framework of American liberal assumptions. One of the latest essays of gratuitous advice admonishes the local intellectual that his future lies in making a place for himself in the "new, materialistic, mobile society" that is being fashioned by Operation Bootstrap, without any recognition of the fact that there may be other concepts of the sociology of the intelligentsia, English, European, Latin American, which the Puerto Rican intellectual might prefer.[7] At this point, too, we might note Dr. Asher Tropp's contention that much of this sort of thing comes from that type of American Jewish intellectual who is peculiarly unfitted, emotionally, to appreciate objectively the Puerto Rican thesis of cultural nationalism because he himself has been shaped by his attempt to escape from Jewish culture and the ghetto world of scholarship into the American mainstream. And not the least consequence of that fact is that the pro-American article will find it easy to get itself published in the American journal like *Commentary* and *The Yale Review*, while the article critical of the American connection must go to a more hospitable review like *Cuadernos Americanos*.

The Puerto Rican response to all this has been the creation of a psychology, both individual and collective, characterized by the complicated repression of frustrations and resentments behind a mask of docility. René Marqués has nicely analyzed the features of that psychology: inferiority disguised as "hospitality" and "courtesy"; the lingering belief, against all known facts, in the eventuality of independence, because otherwise the present situation would be too intolerable to bear; the atrophy of reason which persuades too many Puerto Ricans, most absurdly in the case of the Negro annexationist, that full incorporation into the American system is the only road to freedom; the ultimate despair which, losing hope in any real release from political subordination, deliberately seeks self-immolation in the suicidal violence of terroristic nationalism.[8] It is clear enough that most Puerto Ricans harbor a strong anti-American sentiment, perhaps even true that most of them are emotionally if not overtly *independentista*. The consequent tension between appearance and reality is only belied by the exterior of placidity that they carry; and the inability to rebel is the outcome, not alone of an imperialist America keeping its Puerto Rican fief by force, but of a servile mentality whereby the Puerto Rican has become his own oppressor, rationalizing his own imprisonment. The guilt complex, in truth, works both ways. The liberal American knows that there can be no reconciliation between Puerto Rican subordination and the American creed, so he rationalizes the patent contradiction by becoming the most ardent supporter of the *estado libre asociado*. The Puerto Rican with any moral integrity feels the abrasive humiliation of his condition, so he assuages the feeling by the occasional outburst; this is why Puerto Ricans were every so often given an angry speech by Ernesto Ramos Antonini in which that eminent *Popular* denounced with great sound and fury some aspect of the Americanizing process which he and his party had done so much to promote. He wielded his lance with vigor. But a closer look soon persuaded his audience that it was the misdirected vigor of a Puerto Rican Don Quixote tilting at imaginary windmills while the real battle took place elsewhere.

What has gone wrong, in one sense, is that Puerto Rican ardor has been damped by American realities. From the beginning the Puerto Rican view of America was colored by the image of an egalitarian popular democracy, made doubly appealing by contrast with the reactionary and authoritarian character of the Spanish yoke. The inaugural address of the Puerto Rican scholar de Hostos at the 1877 meeting of the Venezuelan Institute of Social Sciences in Caracas reveals how idyllic America must have seemed to men subject to the Spanish rule, for it constitutes a lyrical hymn of praise in which the American social system is held up as at once an embodiment of laws of rational social biology and a model for emulation by Latin America.[9] The Puerto Rican generation of 1898 took over the image and filled its literature with it. "We are Americans," declared a *Unionista* leader in 1929 in a typical expression of the credo, "in the highest sense of the word. Admirers of the great institution of that fine people, enthusiastic readers of Whitman, followers of Emerson, believers in the mission of salvation that they are undertaking in America and throughout the world."[10] It was a generous enthusiasm and it infected the leading Puerto Rican writers of the period: Roberto Todd, Juan B. Huyke, Samuel Quiñones, José Padin. Yet it was grievously misplaced, for already by 1898 the United States had passed from a democratic rural republic to an industrial capitalism, with all the consequences for the dogma of equality that the transformation involved. It took time for the change to make itself felt in the tropical dependencies. But what today has been eulogized as the "transformation" of Puerto Rico is in fact the final transference to the island of the maturated industrial capitalism of the mainland society and its myriad consequences: the sacrifice of the rural world to the urban jungle, the creation of an uprooted people and an uprooted communal psychology to accompany it, the degradation of the democratic dogma, the growth of a coercive social conformity. In turn, the earlier literary optimism has been replaced by an aggressive literary pessimism in which practically all Puerto Rican writers, irrespective of their individual ideologies, have shared. The wheel has come full circle. It would be difficult to discover any island writer today who would be ready to echo the hymn of praise to the American society sent up by de Hostos. This literary disillusionment only awaits now a new alignment of local political forces to give it appropriate political clothing.

In the meanwhile a new temper of sharp criticism about the American connection makes itself felt. There is a growing resentment that the island is used increasingly for American convenience without any real consultation with Puerto Ricans. The United States Joint Chiefs of Staff convene top secret meetings at the Ramey Air Force Base. The Peace Corps sets up camps in the island interior and places fresh burdens upon an already overworked university teaching system. American family planning associations use Puerto Rican housewives in a preliminary test of the new oral contraceptive pill before attempting the experiment with the more pampered housewives of Hollywood. Too many individual Puerto Ricans get caught up in official and semi-official American schemes; many islanders, for example, regret that, by consenting to perform in the United States, Pablo Casals has been persuaded to break his vow never to play in any country recognizing the Franco Spanish regime. Inter-governmental relations, both executive and legislative, still await even a rudimentary machinery of consultation and remain the preserve of private channels between politicians over which the electorate has little real control. The University of Puerto Rico may offer aid to the newly liberated University of Santo Domingo, but it will do so as a tropical replica of American educational ideology and practice. And all of this is invariably couched in terms of the American "know-all" bringing his American "know-how" to solve the insular problems. "It is so rare to hear or read," a Puerto Rican playwright-*independentista* has declared in a moving *cri de coeur*, "a personal report on Puerto Ricans coming from an American visitor who is neither a public relations official on Government payroll, a smiling Congressman, a New York politician, a 'goodwill' visitor on a well paid tropical vacation, or a 'generous friend of Puerto Rico' with thousands of dollars at stake on the island. Honest Puerto Ricans are simply fed up with so much praise and flattery, so much sugar and honey, so much superficiality, so much outrageous demagogy coming from so many patronizing *amigos*."[11]

However utopian it may appear, and in spite of the massive political and economic dislocations that its application would involve, only
a full and unconditional grant of national independence seems to be
the appropriate prescription for cure of this malaise. The terms of
separation would naturally require careful study and elaborate preparation. Politically, there is no reason why the United States should not
continue to enjoy the facilities of the island as the linchpin of the
Caribbean sea frontier—but as a partner in a bilateral agreement and
not unilaterally as an occupying power. Joint control and operation
of bases—along the lines, for example, of the United States–Brazil
agreement—would do much to meet Puerto Rican wishes. Economically, the enforced dependency upon the American economy obligates
Washington to underwrite, by means of economic treaty, the insular
economy for at least a prolonged transitional period. "The United
States," wrote two critics a generation ago, "is morally obligated not
to give Puerto Rico her independence unless she is prepared either to
give her special tariff preference in the American sugar market or to
underwrite her economic existence by the guarantee of relief grants
for a number of years."[12] The methods may have to be different, but
the principle remains as sound as ever. For in the period since that
observation was made the American state has accepted the basic principles of economic aid to independent nations and moral obligation
to aid underdeveloped economies by its acceptance of the Act of
Bogotá of 1960 and its launching of the Alliance for Progress in
1961; Puerto Rico, as an independent state, could be accommodated
under the developing arrangements of these schemes.

It can be argued that the American strategic investment in the
island, as distinct from considerations of "dollar diplomacy," might
effectively deter Congress from this line of policy. Perhaps so. There
is a well-known passage in the *Wealth of Nations* in which Adam
Smith argues that a dominant power will never voluntarily relinquish
its control over a dependency.[13] The later history of the Commonwealth, and especially the British retreat from India, proved Smith
wrong. But there is, for the modern period, Aimé Césaire's pessimistic
remark that the American domination is the only one from which
there is no escape.[14] Yet it would be tragic if the American people and
government sought in their future Caribbean policies merely to prove
that the French-Antillean poet-deputy was right. That way lies continuing Puerto Rican anguish and possibly, as the chauvinistic nationalism of the newly born Asian-African nations becomes more
powerful in international affairs, a growing source of embarrassment
to the United States. Magnanimity, on the other hand, could lay the

foundations for lasting friendship between Puerto Ricans and Americans, for it would end all those things that presently succor anti-American sentiment in the island population. Puerto Ricans, after all, are a profoundly humanist people. The colonial tie once broken, the affront to national self-respect removed, they would embrace a new relationship of friendship with Americans as surely as Indians did with the English after 1947. "The solution of the problems of Puerto Rico," wrote a Spanish observer in 1951, "ought to come by way of agreement between Washington and San Juan. More generosity in Washington and more patience in San Juan."[15] Americans could hardly complain if less generosity on their part were to evoke less patience on the part of Puerto Ricans.

The running sore of American overlordship thus healed, Puerto Ricans could address themselves more directly and more energetically to finding their appropriate place and their proper contribution within the Latin American family. They could more easily avoid the temptation, currently so widespread, simply to follow United States opinion on Latin American affairs. By refusing to lend themselves to the United States—in one Puerto Rican's phrase—as the Pocahontas who would make it easier for Americans to gain the Latin peoples' friendships they would the better establish their letters of credential with those Latin nations—Mexico and Brazil, for example—who feel that the American-Russian power struggle has little relevance to their own peculiar problems. Their political parties would be enabled to affiliate and cooperate more fully with the myriad political groupings of the contemporary Latin political panorama which are centered ideologically around the radical social-democratic nationalism which has grown out of the dual influence, over the last fifty years, of the Mexican Revolution of 1910 and the Peruvian *Aprista* movement since its foundation in 1924. Above all, they would perhaps be able, in their collective intellectual and artistic life, to re-establish fruitful contact with the rich and varied Indo-American cultures. For, apart from the very occasional inter-American conference, the Puerto Rican artist and intellectual have grievously little contact with the exciting circles of the Latin intelligentsia in Caracas, Buenos Aires, and Mexico City, by comparison with which the world of the United States intelligentsia can seem woefully provincial. The unpardonable dearth of any kind of Latin American courses or studies in the curricula of the Puerto Rican universities is in fact unhappy evidence of the way in which Puerto Ricans repeat the profound ignorance about South America that prevails even among educated Americans.

This can no longer continue. For, simply put, the southern continent is in revolutionary ferment. The various elements of the ferment are at once dramatic and explosive. There is the concerted drive to foment an industrial revolution which will offset the historic and precarious role of the Latin economies as the producers of tropical primary products for the advanced industrial nations, particularly the United States, with little or no control over world prices or world economic fluctuations. Internally in each country that condition has led to the characteristic evils of monoculture, with a single-commodity economy generating basic structural imbalances: sugar in Cuba, oil in Venezuela, coffee in Brazil. Externally it has given rise to a dangerous vulnerability on the world market, as the terrible effects of the economic blizzard of the 1930's upon the Latin economies showed, with the total exports of the twenty-one republics declining by 65 percent within a brief period of three years. Hence, too, the savage alternations of extravagant prosperity and overwhelming depression, in turn precipitating political and social revolution, against the impact of which no Latin country, not even the wealthiest like Mexico and Venezuela, has yet been able to build up the Keynesian defense mechanisms of the Western-style welfare state. There are the social problems that arise not only out of the drive towards industrialization but even more out of the fact that the drive has to take place within the pre-revolutionary, at times pre-Columbian structure of Latin American society. Thus there is the appalling problem of urbanization, with the squalor of the new suburban slums that fester around every growing South American city and in whose incredible cantonments there is a stark poverty the like of which the United States, even during the period of the "shame of the cities" in the Gilded Age, has never known. Not only does this illuminate the gross inequality between city and rural and mountain hinterland—demographically the Latin American population clusters around the coastline—but it also depicts the cultural deracination of the Latin American peasant as he has responded to the illusive promise of the city lights. Reinforcing all this, the inflationary policies of the Latin dictatorships have sought to assuage mass discontent by huge city public works programs which pampered the metropolis and neglected the countryside; the Pérez Jiménez regime in Venezuela thus converted Caracas, in the phrase of José Bernal, into a millionaire city based on a mechanized tropical dictatorship operating on the horse power from oil. Culturally, there is the depressed status of the alien Indian communities living on the margins of a social system that is predominantly European in stamp. Brazil, indeed, is the only country that so far has managed a successful hybridization of the South American ethnic components, white, Indian, Negro, into a harmonious national society.

Finally, in terms of social structure, there is an intensifying class struggle taking place as the older traditionalist groups—the Creole agrarian magnates, the finance capitalists, the warrior politicians, the clerical princes of the Catholic Church—are being challenged by the new social formations of the intellectuals, the new industrial and commercial wings of the middle class, and the new class of industrial workers. This new alignment of social forces constitutes the key to the changing politics of the continent. The rising groups are no longer prepared to accept a traditional way of life which, for all its old world charm, assumed that poverty, ignorance, and disease were the consequences of natural law rather than of social arrangement; and their insurgent rebelliousness explains why the old-style *caudillo* regimes are giving way, first to conservative-constitutionalist regimes offering a limited degree of political democracy, as in Peru and Chile, and, second, to newly formed liberal regimes led, as with Frondizi in Argentina and Lleras Camargo in Colombia, by a new type of Westernizing liberal statesman. An old world is moving out and a new world is clamoring for existence.

Certain aspects of this continental revolution deserve special emphasis, lest its proper character be misinterpreted. It would be profoundly erroneous to see it, as too much American opinion tends to see it, as a transition, in the classic European sense, from a feudal to a liberal society. The element of political liberalism is of course there, as the history of Latin American political thought from Bolívar to Martí shows, and there is hardly a revolutionary movement in the continent, of whatever ideological color, even Castroism, which has not shared the liberal hatred of Latin American tryanny, of which Sarmiento's famous denunciation of the Rosas regime in Venezuela is perhaps the most moving expression. The liberal critic must still face the danger of political murder, as the de Galíndez case showed, from an outraged *caciquismo*, and a Puerto Rican newspaper has recently described in detail for its readers the barbarous mob murder of the famous liberal leader Eloy Alfaro in the streets of Quito in 1912 at the instigation of the Ecuadorian clerical-conservative forces.[16] At the same time, the contemporary movement is primarily a social revolution, stemming from the twin currents of social justice and land hunger. The demand for social justice, made keener by the traditional Latin American sensitive feeling for the dignity of human personality, seeks to end, or at least seriously amend, the division of Latin American society into the "two nations" of the multitudinous poor and the few rich, the modern legacy of the older master-slave society. It seeks to clothe the empty rodomontade of innumerable high-minded constitutions with the flesh and blood of social change.

It has behind it an important socialist tradition which, in its intellectual foundations, goes back at least to the famous essay of Bilbao in 1845 in which that fiery free thinker demanded the complete renovation of Chilean society on the basis of social equality and mental rationalism. It demands action, not legalist-constitutionalist theory. It seeks thus to emphasize the truth that Alberdi underwrote in his observation, a century ago, that "Today we seek the practical reality of that which in other days we were content to proclaim in writing. This is the end of constitutions today; they must organize and bring into being the great practical measures which will lift an already emancipated America from its present obscure and secondary position."[17]

The issue of agrarian reform is even more demanding. In the days of Bilbao and Alberdi the social force propelling change was that of a tiny intelligentsia, frequently operating in hapless exile. Today the social propellant is the alliance of unemployed slum dwellers and landless farm workers, both victims of the agrarian question. And that question, in modern Latin America as in sixteenth-century England, dominates all else. With the exception of Haiti, which is a special case in itself, all over the continent the rational exploitation of the land is prevented by the phenomenon of the latifundia, concentrating ownership within a tiny class of privileged *hacendados*, still living in that halo of romanticized barbarity with which Sarmiento clothed their predecessors of the old Argentinian gaucho cowboys in his most famous book. The system perpetuates a rigid neo-feudal stratification of social classes and a politics dominated by the agrarian chieftain and the gentleman farmer. It is the chief factor behind the vast movements of internal migration that create rural depopulation and exaggerated urbanization, movements nonetheless real because there is a distressing absence of adequate statistical data about them and therefore a fatal drag upon the formation of proper public policies to control them.[18] Its stranglehold is amply proved by the grim fact that although land reform has been the central issue of all Latin American political permutations for years the resistance of the *latifundarios* and their allies has been astonishingly successful. On the continental level as a whole, some ninety percent of the land still belongs to ten percent of the landowners. For a politically backward country like Bolivia, where land reform only goes back to 1952, this may not be surprising. But the land picture is not very different even in those countries, like Uruguay and Costa Rica, where comparatively stable political institutions provide at least the framework for progressive economic reforms. Most revealing of all, there is the admitted breakdown of the agrarian reform in the Mexican "permanent revolution," for since the termination of the Cárdenas presidency national economic policy has moved away from redistributive reform to state-sponsored industrialization of the Puerto Rican Operation Bootstrap type. So in rural Mexico, as elsewhere, the peasant lives a depressed existence outside of the national community, and the "pulverization of the *ejidos*" awaits a genuine Tiberius Gracchus to rise in new revolutionary anger against it. This kind of leadership is already emerging in figures like the Francisco Julião who has been largely responsible for the rise of the peasant leagues of the Brazilian Northeast and the struggle against the encroachments of the big coffee barons spreading out from the half-exhausted lands of São Paulo; and the student of Brazilian social history is not likely to forget that the greatest of all Brazilian works of fiction, da Cunha's *Os sertões,* treats monumentally of the effort of the Brazilian state power to crush the agrarian insurrection that exploded in the northeast region of Canudos at the turn of the century, and that the life conditions of the region have not substantially improved since that time. The land, all this is to say, is the key issue in all Latin American change, despite the European tendency to think of the continent as a romantic setting for magnificent cities. This, much more than its political tone of Communism, is the secret of the Cuban Revolution's appeal. That Revolution, like all others that may follow it, will be tested above all else on the land issue.

This then constitutes the stage background for the entry of the United States into the hemispheric drama, announced by the promulgation of President Kennedy's "Alliance for Progress" program in 1961. No one can read the sum total of the various Presidential addresses on that program without being moved by its vibrant social idealism, its readiness to break away from the characteristic timidity of American public opinion by its open invitation to "transform the American continents into a vast crucible of revolutionary ideas and efforts," its bold invocation of the authentic voice of the American Revolution of 1776, above all, perhaps, its frank confession that Americans in their ignorance know little of the great civilization to the south of them. It promises, if carried out, to commit the United States to a full partnership with the other hemispheric republics in a concerted attack upon the hemispheric social and economic ills, and to conceive the enterprise, in the President's words to Congress, not as negatively fighting Communism but as an historical demonstration that economic growth and political democracy can develop hand in hand. Above all, by the very magnitude of the aid it offers it demonstrates that American leadership is now prepared to treat Latin Americans fully as equals, an attitude which seemed before to have been reserved, as reflected through schemes like the postwar Marshall Plan, for its European allies.

Clearly enough, the very future of the hemisphere rests upon the final practical outcome of this noble vision. Puerto Rican opinion, like liberal opinion everywhere, has been aroused by the seeming revolution in American attitudes: the contrast between Latin American reaction to Vice-President Nixon's ill-fated tour of 1958 and the response to President Kennedy's statesmanlike program has been remarkable. And Puerto Ricans have noted the new spirit implicit in the Administration's readiness to employ Puerto Rican economic and administrative talent—Moscoso, Picó, Morales-Carrión—in the program's top echelon. What, then, are the prospects for success? To begin with, the basic working concept of the Alliance assumes the development, within each recipient nation, of a national planning program undertaking efforts of resource mobilization, self-help, and internal reforms covering land reform, fiscal and administrative reorganization, and improved educational and social services. This indeed does not constitute anything more revolutionary than the introduction of the liberal social welfare state. But within Latin American eighteenth-century political and administrative conditions it does in effect constitute revolution. The conditions undoubtedly are necessary. For the failure of the older aid programs has been that in leaving their local administration to the traditionalist governmental bureaucracies in the receiving countries they have merely succeeded in giving a new lease of life, by means of United States funds, to the existing semi-feudal social structures. Yet apart from the vexed question as to whether such conditions do not constitute—as of course they do—American intervention in Latin American domestic affairs, they raise the even more vexed question as to whether the Latin American ruling classes are prepared to yield up the massive privileges which accepting the conditions would surely involve. Granted their political power, their opposition could destroy the Alliance; their cooperation could ensure its success. They constitute, much more than their European aristocratic counterparts, what Teodoro Moscoso has called a "leader class." As such they can determine whether the Alliance will inaugurate a peaceful revolution or, by its failure, promote a violent one.

No student of Latin American government and politics is entitled even to a cautious optimism on this aspect of the problem. True, the Roman Catholic hierarchy has supported reforms in some countries, Chile and Colombia among others, and in general the Church is moving away from its old reactionary position to closer identification with liberal opinion. There are also pockets of strategic liberal opinion within the armed forces; the universities are changing; and gallant efforts are being made, usually with United Nations expert help, to modernize public administration. But not much more than this can be said. Politics throughout the continent are much more "French" than American in that they are the professional sport of a myriad of groupings, parties, and movements out of which it is almost impossible to organize a majority government after the Anglo-American fashion. Positive public policy thus becomes the victim of maneuver and compromise, as the Frondizi experiment in Argentina showed. Even worse, there may be such an utter absence of mutual trust between rival parties—the *sine qua non* of constitutionalist politics—that actual civil war can only be prevented by peculiar methods, such as the National Union system which alternates the Colombian Presidency in Bogotá between the leading Liberal and Conservative parties. The old type of "strong man" dictatorship is indeed rapidly disappearing, but it is being replaced not so much by an Anglo-Saxon democratic system as by a sort of quasi-democratic authoritarian regime, led by the demagogic *caudillo* and finding its electoral strength in a new alliance with the organized labor movements, for whom the regime provides a bogus radicalism. This has been the nature of Argentinian *peronismo* and Brazilian *getulismo*; and although those movements are out at the moment they are by no means permanently out. "Free elections," with which the American political mind at times seems to identify the democratic process in a narrow political sense, remain an ideal in most countries. José Figueres' observation, speaking for the Latin American liberals, that "we are convinced that a bad government is to be preferred to a good revolution, so long as the electoral path remains open," is possibly a noble sentiment, but the grim fact remains that, for the overwhelming majority of Latin American countries, the electoral path is closed. The ousters of Frondizi in Argentina and Quadros in Brazil demonstrate how readily constitutional legality can be violated by strategic groups acting extra-constitutionally. They demonstrate, even more, how much the spirit of Latin American political struggle is different from that of American politics. "The Americans," noted Ramiro de Maeztu, "fight for the power of money, the Hispano-Americans for the money of power."

All this emphasizes the gross naiveté of American expectations about Latin American change. A political system reflects a social structure. The "immature" politics south of the Rio Grande thus mirrors the moral "backwardness" of the South American ruling classes. There is no more reason to believe that these classes will voluntarily undertake fundamental reform of the system whereby they live than did the French aristocrat of 1789 or the Southern slave-owner of 1861. A ruling class, wrote Bagehot, will prefer to fight a losing battle rather than to fight no battle at all. The glacial pace of domestic reforms to match the Alliance funds from Washington would appear to suggest that the battle has already been joined. In that event, Washington must either completely retreat or openly take sides. Everything now indeed points to an American determination to take sides, and in favor of the Latin American middle classes— what are euphemistically termed the "middle sectors." Yet the evidence suggests that the nouveaux riches groups will be as ineffective in bringing about fundamental reform as have the traditional privileged classes. The decline of the Mexican Revolution stems from the fact that the vast increase in the national income since 1940 has been accompanied by fiscal and social policies that have arrogated the profits to the new middle classes created by industrialization and the austerity to the industrial workers—not unlike what has occurred in Puerto Rico. From the viewpoint of the majority, they have simply been taken out of the bondage of a landlord oligarchy in order to perish in the wilderness of a middle-class oligarchy. The Alliance planners have been unable, or unwilling, to see all this because, at bottom, they have made the mistake of seeing Latin America through American eyes and of therefore grossly distorting the realities. Just as in the political realm it is profoundly misleading to see Latin American parties in terms of the American ideological spectrum of liberalism, so in the social realm it is erroneous to apply the yardstick of the American middle-class spread and its *embourgeoisement* of the national life style.

Nor is this all. The Latin American critic is entitled to ask whether the conversion of a liberal President to a new hemispheric partnership bespeaks also the conversion of Congress and, behind Congress, the conversion of national public opinion. The congenital conservatism of the Congressional temper, as well as the obsolescence of Congress as an institution in modern life, have had their full meaning for Puerto Rico. Their meaning for Latin America is no less real. A President can only go as far as Congress will allow him. Congress in turn always works on the thesis that its business is to follow public opinion, not to reshape it. And although the national public opinion is no longer classically isolationist, neither is it notorious for its continent-wide sympathies. "Frankly," a Puerto Rican political commentator has written, with justifiable heat, "I think that a real sampling of such opinion might reveal that the great American public is scared to death of Castro and all he stands for; that otherwise it doesn't care a damn about our neighbors south of the Rio Grande; that it looks askance at foreign 'give-away' programs; that it is lured by such senseless slogans as 'soft on Communism'; that it still believes, in the age of imminent atomic destruction, that we can afford to wield the big stick and that we lose face and honor when we don't."[19]

If this analysis is correct, the Alliance may easily degenerate into simply a new device in the Cold War, notwithstanding its supposedly liberal intentions. At the best, Americans will see it as an insurance policy against world Communism in an "underdeveloped" area, thus offending Latin American sensibilities on the double count of using the Latin American "neighbors" as pawns in the game of world politics and discounting their continental society as a "primitive" region when in reality it is not so much an underdeveloped system as an enormously rich and sophisticated structure that has been badly developed. And, at the worst, Latin Americans, except the Quisling elements, will contract out of the experiment once they feel that the United States seeks, through its means, to take out a proprietorial custodianship of the Latin American revolution in order to direct it into "safe" channels.

A wall of mutual suspicion thus exists to imperil the flowering of the Alliance into a full-fledged system of hemispheric mutual aid which could break down the economic barriers that divide the continent against itself. This will not yield to American utterances of selfless virtue, since it stems in large part from the unenviable record of American policies in Latin America during the recent past. The earlier conversion of the Caribbean into the American Mediterranean has already been discussed. And, although the Rooseveltian good neighbor policy interrupted it for a while, the gathering storm of the Second World War brought back an American strategic-security concern with the area and a fresh emphasis upon the paramountcy of American interests both there and in the Hemisphere as a whole. Thus not even traditional Anglo-American friendship could deter President Roosevelt from driving a hard "Yankee" bargain with Prime Minister Churchill over the destroyers-bases agreement of 1941, and the documents describing the prolonged transactions show with embarrassing clarity how not even the Churchillian romantic concept of the Anglo-Saxon "Atlantic Community" could deter the Americans from overriding all British pleas to place the agreement on a higher moral level, despite the fact that, as the Prime Minister himself noted, there was "no comparison between the intrinsic value of these antiquated and inefficient craft and the immense permanent strategic security offered to the United States by the enjoyment of the Island bases."[20] If Washington could thus be harsh with its friends, it has been even harsher with its neighbors. There has been the notorious friendship with the region's dictators, gratuitously publicized by the open embraces of local resident ambassadors or of touring United States Congressmen. There was the United States fomenting —now generally attested to—of the internal revolt against the Guate-

malan government in 1954.[21] The flagrant violation of international
law perpetrated by the attempted Cuban invasion shocked the world,
and one consequence of that venture is the unpleasant aroma left by
the subsequent claim of the Guatemalan President that the United
States had secretly agreed to diplomatic aid in pressing the Guatemalan claims to British Honduras in return for the use of Guatemalan
territory in training the Cuban invading force.[22] In addition to all
this, there has been the needless display of American armed force to
command "respect" for its interests—the dispatch in 1958, for example, of marines and paratroopers into Caribbean bases in order
to safeguard Vice-President Nixon against the hostile Caracas crowds,
without consultation with the Venezuelan government. The United
States has also practiced the old type of police operation, the protection of unstable governments in Nicaragua and Guatemala against
hostile invasion by the deployment of United States navy patrols in
the area, for example, or, later, the dispatch of a naval flotilla to
Dominican waters in order to buttress the Balaguer regime against
counter-revolution. Such measures are only removed by a step or
two from the more audacious usage of the "big stick," from the kind
of policy summed up in the editorial advice of one of the more
jingoist New York newspapers that any United States State Department official who goes to Panama to discuss the recent anti-American
demonstrations there should be accompanied by "a large detachment
of Marines—purely as an honor guard on a good will mission, of
course, but with all battle equipment, without which no Marine ever
feels confortable as such."[23] Very little of this sounds like—in a
favorite phrase of Governor Muñoz Marín's which has more poetry
than truth in it—a United States so forgetful of its bigness that it
fully reveals its greatness. Even less does it justify the claim of the
Governor's cabinet colleague, Hiram Cancio, that the "big stick"
policy has long become a myth. Indeed, not the least ironic aspect
of that claim, made before the Navy League Convention in San Juan,
is that it provoked angry comment among its listeners because it
presumed to mix its large praise of the United States with some tiny
and hesitant criticisms, thereby demonstrating that for many Americans there can be no halfway house between undiluted adulation of
their country and subversive hostility.[24]

The United States of course has a real and legitimate interest in the
region, both by weight of its geographical location and its politico-
economic power. The gravamen of Latin American criticism is not
that this interest exists, and naturally seeks expression in American
policies, but that the expression has taken the form of unilateral
American action rather than real multilateral action through organiza-

tions like the Organization of American States. The United States is legally committed to multilateral action, including consultation and, if possible, joint action, on hemispheric affairs by means of its adherence to the Rio Treaty, the Bogotá Charter, and the Declaration of San José. Yet the post-war record has shown that though Washington has been prepared to invoke, and share in, the regional arbitration procedures in cases where it has not felt its interests to be in jeopardy —the 1948 Costa Rica–Nicaragua dispute, for instance—it has been more than ready to bypass them in what it has regarded as more dangerous situations, especially where it has suspected that Latin American nationalism would oppose its policies. The doctrine of "non-intervention" has been used to justify refusal to move against the region's dictatorships, but it was violated by the episode of the Cuban invasion. The OAS Council has been ignored in favor of unilateral action, even when the action, as in the case of the United States support for the Balaguer regime against the danger of the returning Trujillo brothers in 1961, would surely have gained the approval of the Council. On the other hand, American foreign-policy planners have turned eagerly to the Council when convenience has prompted, the most noteworthy occasion, of course, being the 1962 Punta del Este Conference which excluded Cuba from the inter-American system. Yet this was at best a pyrrhic victory for Secretary Rusk, for the United States delegation only obtained a bare majority vote for its policy after anguished diplomatic parleying, and it was humiliatingly obliged to rely upon the morally questionable vote of the ugly Duvalier regime in Haiti for success. That conference, indeed, marked the decisive emergence within the Hemisphere of a solid independent bloc of important leader nations, including the "big three" of Mexico, Brazil, and Argentina, determined to resist the American tendency to convert the inter-American system into the police arm of the Monroe Doctrine. For no other interpretation can be placed upon a system which, in 1960, imposes mild economic and diplomatic sanctions against the Trujillo regime in the Dominican Republic and by contrast, in 1962, isolates Cuba and thus reinforces the punitive measures of economic warfare let loose by the United States.

Developments of this character obviously bring into question the present status of the Monroe Doctrine in hemispheric affairs. As a protection for vested interests, that famous utterance is clearly ineffective, for Cuba demonstrates that ideas do not respect national frontiers or hemispheric barriers. Under the so-called Kennedy Doctrine it has become in reality an instrument for affirming the supremacy of American national interests over the moral and legal restraints imposed by international law. It thus works to exaggerate the police aspects of bodies like the OAS and to minimize their economic aspects. It denies to Latin American governments the right to submit their disputes to the United Nations for discussion and determination. It is obsolete in terms of the logistics of modern warfare, for Pearl Harbor showed, even before the advent of nuclear intercontinental weaponry, that the sanctity of the Hemisphere could be violated without the kind of outside imperialist intrusion that the Doctrine originally anticipated. Above all, it places the United States upon a privileged pedestal in inter-regional relationships. And one consequence of that fact, among others, is that the "Inter-American System," as it now stands, constitutes, in the courteous language of the now historic letter of the Chilean university students to President Eisenhower, the most complete of the many hemispheric international arrangements in which the United States takes part, and the one in which the United States obtains most advantages, while acquiring fewest obligations in respect to its associates.[25]

In the meanwhile both of the Americas continue to exist in an astonishing ignorance of each other. Cultural exchange remains minimal. Only a trickle of *norteamericano* students attends the Latin American university centers. At the extreme poles of feeling, absolute hatred blinds the opponents. Thus the American hatred of the Cuban Revolution engenders an almost universal press distortion, including a syndicated comic-strip which grotesquely caricatures Fidel Castro as a cigar-smoking animal. On the other hand, Latin American ignorance of the sheer complexity of the North American civilization becomes, in a book like Dr. Arévalo's *The Shark and the Sardines*, a tirade of ill-mannered abuse against all things American and a distorted portraiture of United States relations with Latin America as merely a shameful record of "money, gunpowder, and hypocrisy." A game of mutual sensationalist exposure grows up, amusingly illustrated by the Brazilian retort to the account of slum conditions in Rio de Janeiro published in *Life* magazine, which took the form of an account of the wretched struggle of Negroes and Puerto Ricans to survive in New York City published in the Brazilian review *O Cruzeiro Internacional*—and reproduced in a Puerto Rican newspaper for the Caribbean reader.[26] What good will is created by the American scholar specializing in Latin America—Russell Fitzgibbon, for example, or Oscar Lewis—is only too frequently set aside by the crass mistakes of the politicians and ambassadors. The pathogical obsession of Americans with Communism gains little response from Latin Americans to whom Communism seems irrelevant to the problems they confront; so, simply by reaction, American policy breeds enemies needlessly. And there is much ironic truth in the bitter observation of a Costa Rican parliamentary deputy that "There are two classes of Communists, the supporters of historical materialism, who daily make communion with the ABC of the prostituted socialism dictated by the bosses of the Kremlin, and the Communists who are manufactured by the crawlers, the idolators and the servile followers of the White House."[27] This situation is in no way helped, either, by the "exchange" that takes place between American tourists visiting Mexico and Mexican "wetback" laborers entering the southwestern United States.

Both civilizations, north and south, clearly must come increasingly together. A set of common tasks awaits their combined energies: the establishment of a hemispheric common market, the engineering of profound social change, the creation of a genuine collective security system. Puerto Rico's role could obviously be that of broker between the two. But the role patently demands that she be able to present herself to both as a genuinely independent "third force," in however small a way. The grant of independence, moreover, would do much to enhance American prestige in the Hemisphere. It would create a fund of permanent good will throughout the region comparable to that created for Britain in Asia by the evacuation of India in 1947. Done with generosity, it would kill two birds with one stone. It would alleviate the Puerto Rican fears about the economic consequences of independence, thereby releasing the island psychology from a morbid psychosis. And it would steal the thunder of those Latin American elements which presently cite Puerto Rico as evidence of a continuing American imperialism. Should the United States refuse to be statesmanlike, however, a different prospect looms ahead. For then, to say the least, Puerto Ricans would be increasingly driven to give some concrete expression to the nobly defiant sentence of Muñoz Rivera that Puerto Rico, the martyr of a Caesar, would perish in the circus, but it would perish without saluting Caesar.[28]

Puerto Rico and the World Society

PUERTO RICO exists within a triple membership: of the Caribbean, of Latin America, and of the world at large. This truism bears repeating because its practical implementation has been blocked by the parochialism imposed by the colonial mentality. There has been until only recently a geographical isolation of the entire region from the rest of the world. There still remains a psychological isolation; not even a common language could stay the fragmentalization of the West Indies Federation. Even when the insular "small island mind" has been decried by the liberal publicist, he himself has only too often concluded that the region as a whole can do no better than to reconcile itself to being an American sphere of influence, as books like Adolphe Roberts' *The Caribbean* or Professor Fred Rippy's *The Caribbean Danger Zone* (both published in the fateful year 1940) show. The attitude of the colonial masters has of course been one of undisguised contempt. A former French Minister of the Colonies could compose a book on the French colonial kingdom with only a brief mention of the Antilles, and even that was a few pages nostalgically describing the "old empire" before 1789. And Puerto Ricans themselves have had to put up with American complacency, nicely summed up in the remark of an early American author on the island that "there is no reason to think that there will be any discontent in the future under the liberal and beneficent government of the United States."[1] The ability of Caribbean society to make a positive contribution to world civilization as a whole has thus been effectively frustrated. It has in fact only belonged to that larger civilization in an indirect sense as the appendage of various world powers and not in a direct sense in its own right.

With the breakdown of colonialism, the stage is set for that positive and direct role. A new international personality promises to grow up as the newly independent states take up active membership in international organizations. There is a steady proliferation of shared common services among the units of the intra-Caribbean area. For the long haul there are new and fascinating problems to meet and solve:

the function of the small nation state within an internationalist technology; the changing relationship between nationalism and world
order; the cultural contribution that the plastic, composite Afro-
Antillean society can make to a "one world" in which variety ought
to be the spice of life; the new importance of race in the modern
world; the urgent necessity of shaping grand policies to meet the
problems of world population and world poverty, hitherto neglected
by the "have" nations to the detriment of the "have-not" nations;
and many more. For, in more general terms, the old world is breaking up, not only in the immediately dramatic sense of being caught up
in the nuclear age but in the less dramatic sense of having arrived at
one of the great divides of world history. Whether that historical
moment is defined as the final rush of industrialization over the world
as a whole, or the displacement of Atlantic capitalism by Eurasian
socialism, or the revolt of hitherto docile masses, it opens up a new
world for the Caribbean peoples—as new as the world opened up by
the original Discovery itself or as that unleashed by the historic
emancipation of slavery. One way of putting this is to say that those
peoples finally have a chance to influence, rather than merely being
influenced by, the outside world. For four centuries their weakness
has meant that America and Europe have been able to extend the
conflicts of the big colonial powers to their Caribbean possessions,
thus adding new germs of social disorder to those already at work. In
that way the social truce of the early Barbadian plantocracy was
destroyed by the intrusion of the English Royalist-Roundhead civil
war in the 1650's; each successive stage of the great French Revolution was exported to the new arena of black Haiti, ending with the
absurd aping of Napoleonic Caesarism in the great fortress of King
Henri Christophe's *Citadelle*; and today the new political alignments
of the region seem to be drawing themselves up in response to the
commanding dictates of the Cold War. It may be too early to say
that the new forces at work will now enable the Caribbean to terminate that sort of interventionism. But at least they will be able to
offer it some kind of new resistance. The rest waits upon the outcome
of world-wide generative principles and powers over which these
tiny, weak societies can never hope to exercise any real control.

Foremost of all of the integral elements of this "new look" in the
former colonial areas is the growth of a new nationalism at the very
moment when, in the advanced Western societies, it has been fashionable to speak of the "end of nationalism." Ironically, indeed, is that
so; for the leading friend of the colonial freedom movements was the
radical socialist ideology of the metropolitan left-wing parties which

anticipated the replacement of nationalism with an internationalist socialism. Like Marxian Communism, that ideology undoubtedly underestimated the emotional power of nationalism; it tended to see it only as a socially reactionary force; and since nationalism, for the leading architects of the First and Second Internationals, meant in effect European nationalism, it was identified with the retrogressive political fragmentation of the Baltic and Balkan states. The "new nationalism," however, has given patriotism a new lease of life since it has appeared as the chief antagonist of imperialism and colonialism; it has socialized nationalism insofar as it seeks to lead peasant and worker into a reconstructed society; it is peculiarly galvanized by its identification with the new religion of racial pride; and, finally, it emphasizes the cultural dimension of the nationalist creed in societies where European or American cultural imperialism have denigrated local culture and enshrined metropolitan culture. Fifty years of Europe are no longer equal to a cycle of Cathay for the new canon. In Sékou Touré's phrase, speaking for all the new nationalists in Asia, Africa, and Latin America, for them nationalism is psychologically inevitable. Civic pride, personal and collective cultural identification, real love of country, all go into the mixture. "He has to seek for a capital within him," a local writer has said of the Caribbean citizen, "where the color of his skin will provide him with the same assurance, the same dignity, the same pride as that which the Englishman and Canadian have enjoyed over the years. *Civis Antillia,* or *Civis Caribbeanus*—whatever the national designation—must have the same force as *Civis Romanus* of long ago or the *Civis Britannicus* of yesterday."[2]

Certain aspects of all this raise serious questions of both practical politics and social ideology. To begin with, there is a traditionalist element within the new patriotism in the sense that it works as a catalyzing agent in the construction of the new national unity—a social cement, as it were, to hold together the diverse racial and religious subgroups of pluralist societies hitherto held together by the imperial power alone. This can be done, for the case of the Belgian Congo does not in itself substantiate the pessimistic prophecies of the Furnivall school in its analysis of the "plural society." Froude in a way anticipated that pessimism in his infamous book, *The English in the West Indies*, though his prophecy that, with independence under a Negro majority, the white groups in the West Indian society would migrate *en masse* has not been borne out. Yet the problem of building up a new civic nationalism, of course, remains, for the tragedy of incertitude and discontinuity in the national life haunts the thoughtful Antillean citizen. "We are uncertain of ourselves," in the words of a Puerto Rican, "so we cling to the memory of past grandeur. We are still unassimilated, and think of ourselves as Spaniards or Negroes, as grandees or *jíbaros,* masters or rebellious slaves. Few of us have been able to put the threads of our culture together and see the possibility of bright new designs."[3]

How the new nationalism goes about meeting this social legacy of its past is one fascinating aspect of the "new worlds," the Caribbean included. Once in charge of the state power, it throws up political parties which not only govern but also enshrine in themselves the new national principle; correspondingly, opposition groups, to be effective, must place that principle beyond the boundaries of partisan debate. The machinery of the new state is then deployed in the task of "decolonization," the reconversion, in the sentence of the policy statement of the Guinea Democratic Party, of colonial habits into national habits. A new mass education naturally plays a leading part in this task, with the emphasis on education not as abstract culture or merely personal intellectual refinement but as the moral and intellectual culture of the people as a whole. It insists upon what the African scholar Alioune Diop has called the natural bond between politics and culture, thus reviving for the new Afro-Asian societies the classical politics of the ancient Greco-Roman world. The political leader is neither, on the one hand, the type of the American professional machine politician with his usual anti-intellectual prejudices nor, on the other, the type of the English gentleman politician whose gifts of manners and learning express themselves within the narrow framework of the English national Establishment. The ideal, naturally, is frequently more honored in the breach than in the observance; and it can lead easily to the "cult of personality." Yet the Caribbean, lacking at once an African tradition of social communalism and an African historical past of lost civilizations, has itself been remarkably successful in breeding the new style of leadership: whether it is the poet politician like Muñoz Marín, or the Oxford scholar turned mass educator like Eric Williams, or the Queen's Counsel finding a new charisma in politics like Norman Manley, or the Aimé Césaire whose poem *Cahier d'un retour au pays natal* is the confession of faith, in the tradition of Rousseau, of the new Caribbean humanism. Not least of all, Jean Paul Sartre's impressionistic pen portrait of Fidel Castro suggests that the Cuban leader belongs to that same august company.

The new nationalism erects its own new Pantheons of national fame. Pride replaces shame as the dominant attitude towards the native past. A new hero worship replaces the old borrowed from the annals of the past of the imperial power. The process has already gone far in Mexico, even to the point where the pre-Spanish Mexican tyrants have illogically become transformed into the great protagonists of the national democratic revolution. The process is getting under way in the Caribbean proper, and it will only be a matter of time before the forgotten heroes of the Creole past, now only occasionally noted in brief newspaper articles or scholarly journals—Gordon and Richard Hill in Jamaica, Arizmendi and Betances in Puerto Rico, Falconer in Dominica, Thorne and Webber in British Guiana—will replace the gallery of "mother country" heroes in the school textbook and the civic address. A new scholarship makes itself felt, concentrating upon the social history of the West Indian underprivileged classes and emphasizing a new interpretation of events—as in C.L.R. James's *The Black Jacobins,* for example, or Dr. Williams' *Capitalism and Slavery*—which have hitherto been looked at only from the viewpoint of metropolitan scholarship. There is much still to be done in this field. The heroic epics of Caribbean history still await their modern Thucydides to immortalize them: the Haitian war of liberation, the long-drawn-out struggle of the Jamaican Maroons, the Cuban Ten Years War, and innumerable slave revolts. And not the least important aspect of it all that the future historian will have to emphasize is the significant fact that, in the effort of the Caribbean to protect its indigenous culture against erosion and neglect, the most spirited defense has come from the region's lower classes. The middle and upper classes on the whole have aped the metropolitan culture models; there is profound truth in Mahatma Gandhi's charge that "It is we, the English-knowing Indians, that have enslaved India," and it applies as much to Caribbean society as to Indian society. It was the Trinidadian *jamette* class which kept alive the tradition of Carnival at a time when the Creole respectability rejected it, and later the steelband came out of the lower-class social recesses of the Laventille hills in the years after the war. The Afro-Cuban musical tradition found its staunchest supporters in the Cuban Negro proletariat; it has been a similar case with the Jamaican Maroon legends and the oral tradition of the *décima* in Puerto Rico; and Gilberto Freyre has pointed out in his monumental study of Brazil that it was the African slave, not the European master, who kept alive the real tradition of Brazilian agriculture in the form of maintaining the home crops of indigenous foods. The nationalist credo here obviously joins hands with a tradition of social radicalism. It would be fatal if it were to lose that connection in the future.

There is something in this of the civic religion of the Greek city state. There is even more in it of early European nationalism, something like the fierce English patriotism of the Shakespearean historical plays. What is perhaps new is the additional component of race and race feeling. For the emergence of the colonial peoples since 1939 has been, at bottom, the emergence of the colored peoples. Their new

gospel is, basically, an alliance of racial pride and nationalist sentiment. Much of it goes back to Garveyism, the "return to Africa"
ideology, the appeal of black Zionism; much of it is a new variation
on the old theme of separate national sovereignty. "We will give up,"
declaimed Garvey in a typical expression of the ideology, "the vain
desire of having a seat in the White House in America, of having a
seat in the House of Lords in England, of being President of France,
for the chance and opportunity of filling these positions in a country
of our own."[4] The dream has become reality in the years since the
"black prophet" died in obscurity and poverty in the London of 1940.
In the Caribbean the dream has had a peculiar virulency, since it
has been fed by the sordid history of race relations in the area.
Napoleon's contempt for the Negro is well known. And there was a
host of Parisian detractors who, smarting from the loss of Haiti to
the Empire, ridiculed the new Negro monarchy of Henri Christophe
in the years after the defeat of the LeClerc expedition—critics answered by the remarkable series of books defending the Negro culture
tradition, composed by the curious Baron de Vastey and published at
the Haitian court itself.[5] The Americans carried on, however, where
the French left off. The dominant American attitude towards the
Caribbean colored peoples was summed up in John Adams' uncouth
dismissal of Hamilton: "born on a Speck more obscure than Corsica,
from an Original not only contemptible but infamous." The racist
prejudice became more dangerous in the present century as the
Americans carried it with them in setting up their sphere of influence
within the region. All the public institutions of the Panama Canal
Zone were based on "Jim Crow" policies, a practice supported by the
AFL "lily-white" unions until the CIO organizers moved into the
reservation after 1947. Much of present-day Haitian attitude to
Americans, to take another example, goes back to the period of the
United States occupation after 1915, when Marine Corps officers and
NCO's were permitted to become veritable potentates in their administrative districts; one of them later composed a book on his
experiences with the offensive title of *The White King of La Gonave.*[6]
The deep wound left behind by this general record of "white supremacy" still scars the Caribbean consciousness, both personal and
collective. Its healing is one of the first calls upon the non-white
statesmanship of the region. It is wholly appropriate, then, that the
new nationalist politics is filled with a moving appeal to a new racial
pride, a new sense of self-respect:

> Soon, in the West Indies
> It will be Please, Mr. Nigger, please.

Puerto Rico is both inside and outside all of this. Inside, because the official policy of the Commonwealth government is that of a cultural nationalism even when it ignores the nationalist ethic in its political and economic policies. In half a dozen fields of activity—theater, education, the encouragement of the arts, the planned preservation of historic San Juan, small industry fiscal policy—the influence of Pedreira's doctrine of "cultural affirmation" is plainly discernible. Beyond official boundaries the artist and writer are almost unanimously on the side of a vital and creative *puertorriqueñidad*—René Marqués has pointed to the significant fact that, almost without exception, no Puerto Rican novelist has been found to write favorably on the idea of annexation to the United States. Puerto Ricans as a mass may behave like Americans, but they feel intensely that they are Puerto Ricans. The distinction is not always logically sound. But its sentimental foundation is unmistakably present. It is reinforced in turn by other culture traits—the respect for old age, for example, or a widespread sense of history—not generally regarded as being strong points in the superordinate American culture. This perhaps explains why there is a real popular respect for the aged warriors of the clan, now retired, like the Don Florencio Cabello who as an old-time socialist was active after 1920 in the creation of the new working-class housing projects now known as the slums of *Barrio Obrero,* or like Doña María de Pérez Almiroty, in the years after 1936 the first woman Senator at a time when politics were jealously guarded as a masculine prerogative. It also explains, to take another random example, why there is a real pride in the famous Puerto Rican mothers: the Pilar Defilló whose memories of the island home were instrumental in shaping the life and art of her son, Pablo Casals, or the Raquel Rose Hoheb who not only defied Spanish convention by leaving her sheltered Mayagüez home to study art in Paris in the 1870's but went on to marry an Englishman reared in St. Thomas and to give her son, William Carlos Williams, to the world of American poetry. Puerto Ricans are proud of their contribution, however small, to the larger world society. If, then, Garvey could write with pride of the contribution that the African civilizations of Carthage and Alexandria had made to the life of the ancient world, Muñoz Rivera, writing as a Hispano-Caribbean citizen, could justifiably remind Americans that Las Casas had undertaken the task of bringing Christianity to the aboriginal inhabitants of America long before William Penn began his work with the North American Indians.[7]

Puerto Rico is thus within the new nationalist tradition. But it is also in many ways outside it. The American political connection, once again, here as elsewhere, seriously inhibits any sort of fructifying alliance with new nations for whom "independence" is an almost magical word. By seeing nationalism (as in his Harvard lectures) as

an artificial barrier instead of a natural boundary, Governor Muñoz
makes it difficult, if not impossible, to establish any kind of empathy
with the rising tide of nationalism all around him. Freedom without
independence appears to nationalist sentiment as Hamlet without the
Prince of Denmark; and no amount of Muñoz-like logic chopping is
likely to undermine that conviction. In addition, two particular factors
conspire to reinforce this isolationism away from the main stream. In
the first place, *puertorriqueñidad* lacks the tremendous stimulant of
Negro nationalist sentiment, both pride and prejudice. The peculiar
ethnic history of the island and the psychological ambivalence to the
whole question of race relations that pervades the island outlook have
already been discussed. A latent race prejudice, as a matter of fact,
sets the Puerto Rican, as he sees himself, as a people apart in the
predominantly Negro Caribbean. The theme has indeed been quite
frankly and fully explored by the Puerto Rican writer, perhaps going
back to Tapia y Rivera's *Leyenda de los Veinte Años* of 1874. There
are Afro-Negroid elements in the popular culture as well as in the
popular speech, but only too often a sense of shame drives people to
the rationalizing argument that they are of Spanish or at least "Moorish" origin. So long as this feeling prevails, Puerto Ricans will stand
in their own way when the question of Caribbean identification raises
itself. They will become their own best enemies.

The second contributing factor is related to this first one. For racial
snobbery is not far removed from social snobbery. Much of Puerto
Rican cultural nationalism, like much of Latin American sentiment,
has been motivated by the natural urge of local ruling classes, along
with professional groups, to protect their semi-feudal way of life
against the democratic idea; and it has been easy to disguise the motives under the shelter of a rationalizing ideology in which Spanish
or Latin manners and taste are opposed to American vulgarity. The
Platonic dislike of the democratic man is obviously present here, particularly in the light of the emphatic stamp of traditional European
learning and philosophy upon Latin American higher education. The
picture of an idealized Spain of austerity and chivalry is set over
against that of a sensual and materialist America, as in Manuel
Gálvez' essay on *El Solar de la Raza*. Even more, the Caliban-Ariel
allegory is employed, as in Rodó, to defend the aristocratic society
against the democratic. These intellectual influences undoubtedly
helped to shape the Puerto Rican variant of the theme in Pedreira's
Insularismo, and any account of contemporary Puerto Rican attitudes
to the outside world must recognize the genesis they have in that book.
The tone of the argument is one of social conservatism, which perhaps
explains why the movements it has inspired seem so far to have a petit

bourgeois rather than a working-class note about them. It is suggestive, at least, that very little of their literature contains much of a forthright socialist criticism of the American civilization. Paradoxically, this is in itself an outcome of the nature of that civilization, for in the anatomy of colonial nationalism there is a very real sense in which the colonial freedom movements themselves are shaped by the spirit of the progressive movements of the "mother country." The influence of the British Labor Party upon the nationalist movements in the former British colonial territories is well known, as is the influence of French humanistic socialism upon the educated intelligentsia whose members today are the rulers of the new states like Guinea, Senegal, and the Ivory Coast. In a similar fashion the basic assumptions of the reformist movements both in Puerto Rico and the Virgin Islands have been those of American liberalism, which has rarely been socialist and has in fact been concerned not so much to remove the profit motive from American life as merely to exorcise its more unpleasing and anti-social manifestations. All the leading elements of the American liberal creed have thus been exported to the dependencies: the idea of a basic social consensus which dispenses with the need for really radical ideology, the trust in reason as a means of resolving conflict, the sometimes arid constitutionalism, the "do-good" passion, the emphasis on personality; and they have fatally circumscribed the intellectual horizons of the Caribbean liberal as much as they have those of the American liberal.

This important point merits additional emphasis. American intellectual empiricism, by its distrust of theory, encourages a politics of opportunism, since it leaves a political leadership with nothing else to do except respond intelligibly to the pressures of the day. Maneuver replaces principle; theoretical analysis gives way to organization and the "organization man." As a result, it cripples the organ of dialectics. Copied by the overseas territorial progressive elements, it ostracizes every idea or program that goes beyond the immediately practical as "utopian" or "doctrinaire" or "rigid"—all adjectives, interestingly enough, that flourish as the green bay tree in Puerto Rican political discussions. Thus the New Deal program in Puerto Rico never went beyond the assumption of the larger American New Deal program that the collapse of the economic order merely required piecemeal reform measures along "practical" lines. The assumption was aptly summed up in the remark of an American official in the island at that time that "we must use scientific men, impersonally scientific, in every element of the island problem, with a visionary, a practical sentimentalist, in chief authority over them."[8] The influence of Rexford Tugwell on local political thinking has only aggravated that element, for it speaks, mysteriously, of an "art of politics" the business of which is to "plan" the business society rather than to replace it with an entirely new society operating on fundamentally new assumptions. Puerto Ricans and Virgin Islanders have of course received much from the stateside liberal tradition—the work of the American Civil Liberties Union, for example, in promoting and protecting their civil liberties. But they have received little in the way of pure theory, while the post-war intellectual climate of liberal America, with its social conformism and its comforting conviction that all the great questions of social theory have now been effectively foreclosed with the advent of economic prosperity, has turned speculation on first principles almost into an "un-American" activity. So, just as the Monroe Doctrine worked in the previous century to isolate Latin America from the intellectual influence of liberal Europe, in a similar way the American connection has worked in this century to isolate Puerto Ricans from the intellectual influence of nationalist and Marxist circles in the Latin American centers of thought. The discipline of sociology perhaps best illustrates this truth. As the new American orthodoxy it has deeply infected the Puerto Rican scholar educated in the northern universities. For it is a sociology of statics, emphasizing the moral worth of stability in social institutions, apprehensive of change—which is almost always seen as a threat to those institutions. Yet nothing could be more fantastically inappropriate to the analysis of those societies, like Latin America, where all institutions are in dynamic flux and where, even more, the desirability of change is accepted as a fixed notion in all groups except those of the ruling classes. In such societies the tools of intellectual analysis should be as varied and as flexible as possible, including especially those of Marxism. For the main analytical concepts of Marxism, as Schumpeter has pointed out, are legitimate instruments of continuing social analysis, and would most certainly have been developed by later sociology after Marx if there had been an atmosphere of unbiased research.[9] The intellectual tragedy of Puerto Rico is that, in the throes of a social dynamics, she has been made the prisoner of a social statics. She will not be able to rejoin the world universe of discourse until that condition is rectified.

The rise of the new nationalism has of course provoked criticism. In Puerto Rico, as elsewhere, it has been assailed as a new provincialism hopelessly archaic in an internationalist world. Nationalism is a heady wine, warn the critics; it engenders nationalist self-righteousness, ethnocentrism, arrogance, the worst features of *raison d'état* in international politics. There is little reason to assume that Negro nationalism will be any more pleasing, in these respects, than European nationalism. To the degree that the world listens once more to the nationalist call, it will reopen all of the phobias that have thus far stood so stubbornly in the way of world government and world community.

There is indubitably some sense in the critical view. For apart from the theoretical considerations pertinent to the place of sovereignty in a transnational world, there are enough unattractive features in the general face of the new nationalism to give pause to both the liberal and the internationalist sentiments. It invokes concepts of race and racial purity which are as unscientific when applied to Afro-American as to Caucasian. Garvey's admonition to the Negro populations that "you have become the most corrupted people of the world, the generally abused people of the world, the mixed people of the world"[10] is symptomatic. It helps to explain the elements of black fascism in his program, as well as his readiness to work with the "white supremacists" of the Deep South in promoting a racial separatism both wanted for different reasons. The appeal to art and literature to be loyal to the new tradition can give rise to a "nationalist realism" as absurd in its more excessive manifestations as "socialist realism." Some of the more comic examples from the Puerto Rican scene have been cited earlier. Policies of nationalist economic self-sufficiency are self-defeating in a world market. National sovereignty in itself will solve few of the harsh problems facing the underdeveloped countries, as the sickness of Haitian society proves in the Caribbean. And from the viewpoint of national security, Caribbean history surely proves—it is urged—that the Caribbean islands have been able to preserve their territorial integrity only when they have been shielded by some strong power willing to maintain their autonomy.

Yet to put the problem in these terms is almost certainly to misstate it. The choice before the leadership of any new nation is not one between nationalism and internationalism but between a nationalism *à outrance* and a nationalism willing to modify itself within a framework of closer association with others. This is why the debate between *insularismo* and *occidentalismo* in Puerto Rico is so false and farcical, for it uses polarized concepts which have little to do with the pungent realities. There is in fact nothing incompatible between national loyalty and a world civic sense, for the one is, psychologically speaking, the precondition of the other. Men do, in fact, belong to the army of world humanity; but they are, before this, members of their small platoon, in their experience of which they learn to apprehend the larger membership. The emotional intensity of patriotism in Ghana or Indonesia or Trinidad may seem alarming to the European or the

Englishman. But this is largely because the Western observer is unconsciously making a comparison with his own rather vapid national
sense. Historically speaking, the only fair comparison is with the nationalism of the Western societies in their own "moment of truth," as
it were—their own earlier periods of nascent national growth. It is
the England of the Tudor monarchs or the France of the age of Louis
XIV, seeking to instill a new national patriotism against the forces of
medieval feudalism and fraticidal civil war, with which contemporary
Trinidad or Guinea must be compared. Similarly the modern American critic should understand that the proper yardstick by which to
judge the nationalist "affirmation" in present-day Puerto Rican art and
letters is not America as a world power in the twentieth century, but
the younger republic in the century after 1787 and the struggle of its
native genius, from Freneau and Barlow to Whitman and Hamlin
Garland, to emancipate the American creative spirit from the reign
of the genteel imposed upon it by the Anglophilist prejudices of the
New England mind. For just as that mind produced, in its typical
poetry, a moralistic sentimental genre of work utterly divorced from
the harsh American realities of the Gilded Age, so the artless copying
of the Romantic schools has produced a typical Puerto Rican poetry—
in Gautier Benítez, for example—of mellow private moods in which
nihil novum sub sole except perhaps the Afro-Negroid work of Luis
Palés Matos. The Pauline doctrine of the diversity of gifts applies no
less to peoples than it does to individuals and in its division of labor
it is a leading characteristic of the arts of civilization. Each people, as
Pedreira saw, makes its own unique contribution. Each people, too,
goes through its various periods of production, sometimes placid,
sometimes in exciting ferment. A sympathetic understanding of this
truth ought to check impatient criticism—although regrettably it has
never been a virtue of Americans, any more than of Englishmen, to
look with complacency upon manners or philosophies which appear
strange to them.

A similar reply is appropriate to the criticisms made of the economic and political, as distinct from the cultural, dimensions of the
new nationalism. Political sovereignty and international economic
planning do not, it is true, easily go hand in hand. The obsolescence
of the nation state from the viewpoint of the rational organization
of world resources is by now a well-recognized truth; indeed when a
British Conservative Prime Minister can say that he can no longer feel
bound by the United Nations Charter clause which prohibits interference in the domestic affairs of nations it is evident that the conviction has acquired the status of a respectable idea. The future of
nationalism, then, lies in the gradual surrender of its sovereignty to

interregional and international bodies, probably of a functional character, which imperceptibly take over policy and administration responsibilities in one area of common concern after another; for in a unified world the world itself is the only viable economic unit. The ways and means whereby this transcendence of the nation state will take place will probably revolve around two concepts: one, that of functional federalism, whereby governments join together in the joint organization of services and, two, that of commodity multilateralism, whereby governments cooperate in the joint planning of specialized production and distribution of various commodities. This, it is argued, is the road on which the leading Western nations have already commenced to walk, as the development of the European Common Market shows. It would be catastrophic if that work were now put in jeopardy by the sudden rise of a rejuvenated nationalism from the former colonial regions of the world.

How much are the new nations bound by this line of argument? They are of course bound by it to the degree that it summarizes all of those various considerations that have rendered obsolete the nation state of the age set by the political thought of which Grotius provided the first magistral summary. No man can add one cubit to his stature; similarly no nation can co-opt out of membership of the general world society and the general laws that propel it. Lectures on the morality of internationalism, then, are superfluous. And they are superfluous because the new nations have themselves already shown themselves adept at organizing regional cooperative schemes for common purposes. They have become the most ardent supporters of the United Nations, if only because they see in that structure the only possible vehicle existing at present for making their contribution to world peace—a contribution which must be on the moral plane only, where size and power cease to be the main determinants. It is Paris, not Tunis, Washington, not Havana, which have allowed delusive notions of national dignity to stand in the way of consenting to international arbitration of their various differences. It is Nkrumah, not the leaders in London or Capetown or Salisbury, who has dreamed of a United States of Africa and has seen that such a federalist scheme is possible only on the basis of Negro-majoritarian rule on the continent rather than on the basis of a "white supremacy" disguised in the language of "partnership." Similarly in the Caribbean the real answer to the problems of economic vulnerability and political instability that plague the area has been provided not by the bogus West Indies federal scheme propounded by British colonial policymakers who have known nothing at first hand of the problems of federalism but by Eric Williams who, as a West Indian economic historian, has long ago perceived the absolute necessity for a viable Caribbean Economic Community that would undertake, through its unified political and administrative services, the regional economic planning of the area's resources as a whole. Some of this internationalist sentiment on the part of the new nations springs from dogma —the new socialism, for example, of the Afro-Asian peoples. Some of it springs from interracial unity. Some of it comes from a hard recognition of economic facts and of the truth that mutual aid is the only salvation for colonial economies which—in the apt language of the 1928 Program of the Communist International—have been compelled to represent the world rural district in relation to the industrial countries, which have represented the world city.

This indeed explains why the new states are less ready than they might otherwise be to extend their internationalism further afield, and especially in alliance with the already developed industrial nations. It is one thing to ask them to join a genuine system of world planning or even of world government. It is quite another to ask them to yield up their new-found sovereignty to regional defense organizations like the Warsaw Pact group or the North Atlantic Treaty Organization which are essentially Cold War instruments adopting, in Hobbes's phrase, the posture of armed gladiators one towards the other. There are both sense and virtue in joining organizations like the World Health Organization and the General Agreement on Tariffs and Trade; the first has done much to eradicate major tropical diseases in the Caribbean, while the Jamaican decision to end her long-standing aloofness from membership in GATT is testimony to the genuine effort of its organizers to accommodate its major task of tariff elimination to the special problems of infant industries within the less developed countries that might still feel the need for a neo-protectionist policy. But there is a justifiable suspicion of other economic and commercial regional schemes which, like the European Common Market, seem primarily to be concerned with building up a new European economic order and protecting it, by means of a continental tariff wall, against competition from both the established rival capitalist systems like that of the United States and the new industrial products of the modernizing backward economies. The West Indian food and citrus producers quite rightly suspect that a British entry into the European scheme, by ending the imperial tariff preferences, will have the effect of terminating their privileged status within the British market; and they face a hazardous position when the attainment of any concession—such as the grant of Associated Overseas Territories status—which would help lessen the blow would depend upon the willingness and ability of a British government to undertake a campaign on behalf of its former colonial wards with its new European colleagues. Any West Indian leader, contemplating the possibilities, is bound to reflect upon the British tendency— brutally apparent in the 1962 Immigration Control bill—to follow the American policy of restricted immigration, and upon what it means for the glittering phraseology of Commonwealth unity and amity.[11]

In a world, in other words, where the interests of the advanced industrial countries frequently masquerade as internationalism, it is only prudent for the new nation economies to seek to hold what they have rather than sacrifice all upon any doctrinal altar of world unity or world government. They will welcome foreign aid. But they will point out, at the same time, the risks that accompany it, the political control that frequently attempts to accompany economic assistance, and which could only be eliminated by the channeling of such aid through international agencies. As primarily food and raw-materials producers they will insist that so long as the major industrial economies protect their own large-scale ranching enterprises by dis-criminatory tariff legislation, as is more notoriously the case with the United States, they themselves must retaliate by means of their own tariff walls, regional customs unions, and so on. For all the fanfare that has accompanied the foreign aid programs of the developed societies, the terrible inequalities in international living standards not only remain but in fact are worsening. These inequalities will not be eradicated by the growth of an international welfare state, or by the generosity of even left-wing governments in European capitals, but by the growing political power of the former colonial world. The leadership of the new nations knows that the outstanding fact of world politics during the last two decades is that the revolutionary initiative has passed to the colonial world. For the European socialist movements have aided and abetted modern industrialism to destroy native economic systems over Asia and Africa with little attempt either to prevent or alleviate the misery and degradation which overcame them. By virtue of their very character as national move-ments, neither American liberalism nor a socialism like that of the British Fabians has been able to emancipate itself from national as-sumptions; and the aid that can come from such sources is therefore at once limited and parochial.

The real internationalism that the new nations confront, indeed, is not the internationalism of the socialist utopias but the bogus inter-nationalism of the "NATO intellectuals," on the political level, and of the banking and loan houses of the American-European capitals on the economic level. Their response to their political dilemma is to be seen in the rise of neutralism as their characteristic foreign policy. Their response to the economic dilemma centers around the general attempt to build up their own resources by regional cooperative effort and to lessen, as best as they can, their necessary dependence upon foreign investment capital. The extravagant dimensions of that dependence in Puerto Rico are well known. But it is a problem by no means restricted to the underdeveloped economies. It afflicts the developed economies as well. Thus, to take instances only, a royal commission has recommended stringent measures to regulate the acquisition of Norwegian natural resources, especially water power, by foreign persons; various royal commissions in Canada have warned against increasing United States economic control of the federal economy, including the dangers arising from the deluge of American journals and newspapers that threaten to convert the Dominion into an American cultural satellite; while it is enough to read the British House of Commons debates of November 1960 on the Treasury decision to permit the transfer of a majority of the shares of the British Ford Motor Company to the American Detroit automobile interests to appreciate how, for many Englishmen, this threatens the possibility of a serious alienation of important industrial resources, entailing serious consequences not only for employment policies in British industry but also for foreign policy; for should a future British Labor government move to nationalize the automobile industry it would find itself confronted with a foreign relations crisis not unlike the one flowing out of the Mexican nationalization of the United States oil companies after 1937. A democratic domestic policy is thus placed in grave jeopardy by the extraterritorial location of economic power. This is perhaps the real reason for the need to retain local political sovereignty; and a Puerto Rican opposition group has insisted that political authority is in fact a prerequisite of economic liberty, for without it there cannot take place that decision making between various alternative policies which in essence constitutes the economic problem.[12] It is regrettable that much of the eulogistic literature on the industrialization program in the Caribbean island is so preoccupied with the complacent recital of gains and benefits that it almost utterly ignores this basic aspect of the problem. This is perhaps why the extensive pamphlet of the National Planning Association in 1958, William H. Stead's *Fomento: The Economic Development of Puerto Rico,* could catalogue, without any critical comment, the apprehensions of American business investors arising from the growth of union power in the economy and from the development of domestic minimum wage legislation and manage to say nothing at all about the problems arising out of absentee economic and fiscal ownership. This is perhaps why, too, Werner Baer's monograph of 1962, *The Puerto Rican Economy and United States Economic Fluctuations,* could weakly conclude, after a rather inconclusive study of the local effects of continental industrial fluctuations, that the local economy could only hope to protect itself to a limited degree by a program of public works projects and by increased tax exemption benefits, the absence of a Puerto Rican independent banking system meaning that in a drastic depression the burden of countercyclical policies would fall on the Federal government and therefore outside the control of the local power.[13]

Most liberal-minded people would perhaps agree that the ultimate solution for all this is some sort of world government that can offer to the smaller and weaker nations some assurance of protection against the ills which presently so grievously beset them. Small states located, like those of the Caribbean, in a vital zone of commercial and military strategy are of necessity insecure so long as such a world order does not exist. But it would surely be utopia-mongering to imagine that such an order will have either a swift or an easy birth. It can come about only stage by stage, as shown by the glacial pace whereby the federal political institutions that are the logical counterpart of the present regional economic agreements in the European economy are emerging. The path for the small nations to follow, then, is the organization of regional groupings with their like-minded fellows. But that agreement to join together must be the result of full consultation with all concerned, with slices of sovereignty, as it were, surrendered voluntarily and on a basis of equality. And this has not been the case with Puerto Rico. As the Indian delegate in the UN discussion of 1953 on Puerto Rico pointed out, there can be a genuine compact between two countries only on a basis of equality, and Puerto Rico was by no means independent of external pressure when the "compact" of 1952 was ratified. Any association between states under any form characterized by such pressure is not a grant of real independence but rather a method of camouflaging the relics of a colonial past.[14] To request the surrender of national sovereignty when the sovereignty is there to be surrendered is fair enough. To request it when the sovereignty does not exist is to add insult to injury. "There can be no internationalism without nations," a Puerto Rican critic of Governor Muñoz Marín has succinctly put it, "for internationalism is relations between nations, either proper or improper. Muñoz Marín is not a partisan of a proper relationship. He is the partisan of the improper relationship between subjugated nations, like Puerto Rico, and subjugating nations, like the United States. The partisans of a true and proper internationalism are we adherents of independence in Puerto Rico, for we seek to incorporate Puerto Rico into the proper life of international relationships between all nations throughout the world."[15]

For the new nationalism has grown up, of course, as a response to the old colonialism. If it is a disease it is not a disease *sui generis,* but a brave effort of the native peoples to create the self-respect and national pride undermined by the servile colonial mentality. The contempt of the Victorian educated European for the learning and wisdom of the older Oriental and African civilizations is well known; it is enough to remember Macaulay's scornful assertion that "all the historical information which has been collected from all the books written in the Sanskrit language is less valuable than what may be found in the most paltry abridgments used at preparatory schools in England," or Lord Acton's imperial dictum that "The Persians, the Greeks, the Romans, and the Teutons are the only makers of history, the only authors of advancement. Other races . . . are a negative element in the world; sometimes the barrier, sometimes the instrument, sometimes the materials of those races to whom it is given to originate and to advance."[16] No educated Westerner would perhaps speak so unguardedly today. Yet the attitude here expressed has changed little in any real sense so far as the general middle groups of Western society are concerned. A cursory examination of the British press will reveal the widespread ignorance of, and racially tinged contempt for, the West Indian person. It is still possible for a prominent Canadian newspaper to opine, editorially, that the Jamaican future is jeopardized by the phenomenon of "the number of semi-literate civil servants who are replacing experienced English officials and clerical help"—a gross misrepresentation swiftly corrected by the newspaper's Canadian West Indian readers.[17] Puerto Rico itself has long suffered from the still popular belief on the part of the average American that Latins are emotionally different, an opinion aptly expressed in a 1927 book on the island that "These islanders, like the rest of their race, are fundamentally emotional while the continental is unemotional."[18] Alfred Kazin's article on the island, finally, startlingly shows that even a supposedly sensitive literary critic can be goaded into composing an essay of virulent and coarse contempt for a tropical *ambiente* that seems to have deeply disturbed his comfort, both physical and mental.[19]

This persistence of colonial attitudes helps to explain why some form of nationalism is one of the strongest social emotions in the newly independent or emergent countries. The decline of the attitudes would probably encourage the decline of at least the more xenophobic nationalisms, although the history of the emotion in its earlier European forms suggests that, once established, it is likely to run a long course. But in its latter-day manifestations it has its positive as well as its merely negative elements. It is humanistic. The grace and warmth of much Latin American life are the end result of a percolating process from the original spring of classic Spanish humanism, and when Puerto Rican officials petition Governor Rockefeller to spare the life of a New York–Puerto Rican juvenile killer like Salvador Agrón they testify to the continuing power of the tradition in the island life. There is a new attitude to art and education; both Mexico and Haiti exemplify it in art; and the cornerstone of the new contemporary nationalism beyond Europe is state education. It seeks to eradicate the poison of racialism from the world, which likewise implies the search for a new partnership of equality between the white and the non-white peoples. For it knows, only too keenly, that both for American liberal and European socialist the ideal of international solidarity has too often ended at the boundaries of color. It does not seek so much to reject European learning and knowledge as to give it new directions, apply it to new problems. That seems to be the tenor of the moving *Lettre à Maurice Thorez* in which Aimé Césaire, announcing his resignation from the French Communist Party, demanded a thoroughgoing moral reorientation of traditional Marxism and Communism to ensure that those doctrines should now be put at the service of the colored peoples, not the colored peoples at the service of the doctrines. Their anti-colonialism, the Antillean leader tells the Parisian commissars, carries within itself the stigmata of the very colonialism against which it struggles: it bears the same assimilationist bias, the same unconscious chauvinism, the same conviction of the superiority of Western society which stamp the European bourgeois attitude to the rest of the world. The colonial peoples have thus been the victims, he concludes, of a veritable Copernican revolution in which European leadership, from extreme Right to extreme Left, has taken on the habit of doing things for us, of arranging matters for us, of thinking for us, in brief, of denying to us that right of initiative which is the ultimate right of personality.[20]

What will all this mean for old world–new world relationships? Some things are already apparent. Diplomatically it means a foreign policy of neutrality, probably of varying nuances, with its roots in (1) a reluctance to become embroiled in big-power machinations and (2) a natural anxiety to save as much energy and spirit as possible for the domestic problems of economic growth and social change. Americans, it might be noted, as a people with their own long tradition of isolation, ought surely to be tolerant of countries currently experiencing a similar evolution and demonstrating similar symptoms on the international scene. Strategically, this logically leads to a reluctance to be parties to the new strategic imperialism of the age. Immediate withdrawal from present commitments would of course be difficult; thus an independent Puerto Rico might start with proposals—following the recent Trinidadian recommendations concerning the Chaguaramas base—for a joint administration of the American bases on the island, and move on later to an agreement that would safeguard the Puerto Rican right to consultation before the establishment of long-range missile sites, provide for a shortened leasehold period and possibly look forward to the eventual termination of bases after the manner of the 1959 United States–Philippines accord. Some such agreement will surely have to be made on the future of the Guantánamo base in Cuba, and negotiation ought to be made easier in the light of the fact, well known to the United States Navy chiefs, that the strategic-operational usefulness of the base has practically disappeared with the modern revolution in naval technology, so much so that, today, it serves merely as a training base for the Atlantic fleet and as a recreation center for aged Navy hands on their last tour of duty before retirement.

Yet this, after all, is political neutrality, nothing more. The more seminal contribution of the new nationalism is certain to take place in the realm of twentieth-century ideas. For some three centuries political theory has been largely a European preserve of thought, and its theories of liberty, society, and the state have inevitably been recapitulations of a narrow and selective historical experience restricted to the leading European and North American societies, rather than universal precepts; even Marxism has been part of the classical economics, in its economic presuppositions, and in its moral ideas what has been aptly styled the last great heresy of Christianity. These theories are consequently questionable guides for societies profoundly non-Western in their history, psychology, and general character. Liberty, for the Western liberal mind, has thus meant an absence of social restraint upon the individual will, while taking for granted the comforts of the social order; its theory of the state has not meant much more than T. H. Green's remover of obstacles to the good life: certainly, despite the Anglo-American welfare state, the popularity of phrases such as "the affluent society" and "the irresponsible society" reflects the basic truth that neither the American liberal nor the European socialist has yet done much to curb the social dominion of the profit motive in the modern industrial octopus, let alone replace it with the collectivist commonwealth. The rise of nationalism in its European form, moreover, coincided with the rise of capitalism, while the new nationalism comes at a time when capitalism in its basic forms is on the decline. Even the Russian Revolution of 1917 did not escape the assumption, pre-eminently capitalistic, that machine technology is destined to destroy all pre-industrial culture, so that the achievement of its leaders was largely the fulfillment of Peter the Great's dream of a Westernized Russia, imposed upon the Russian masses with a relentless swiftness and thoroughness far beyond anything attempted by the czarist monarchs. By comparison the new nationalisms, African, Asian, Latin American, seek a synthesis of civilizations in which the passion for the new does not involve, as it has done in the growth of the American civilization, a contempt for the past.

What form all this will take time alone will tell. It will certainly be shaped by the new political theory that is bound to come out of Accra and New Delhi, Cairo and Jakarta, Port-of-Spain and Havana within the next generation. It will certainly revolve, substantively, around an intellectual attempt to rewrite the terms of relationship between socialism, nationalism, and internationalism. In part, it will go back to the socialist humanism of the younger Marx. In part, it will build upon the communal sentiment of its own pre-industrial social orders—for there is much truth in Leopold Senghor's boast that Africans had already achieved socialism before the advent of the European. It will attempt to get away from the vulgarized materialism of Westernized life. In that respect there is a real warning for Puerto Ricans in the observation of the recent Church of Scotland report on the Central African Federation that it is essentially a leaf out of the Communist, and not the Christian, notebook to harp on economic advantages as the primary and almost the sufficient justification for constitutional constructions. New theoretical concepts of both the political party and the trade union may be expected to appear. The study of internationalism, both in functional and ethical terms, is certain to receive a new and tremendous impetus. A prophetic anticipation of the sort of moral imperative which that study is likely to yield may perhaps be seen in the admonition given to a Puerto Rican audience by the Mexican intellectual José Gaos that the way out of the present global struggle between the two big powers may lie in a gradual process of transformation whereby the so-called "free world" becomes more socialized and the Communist world liberalized, both benefiting from the unconscious and mutual assimilation of their respective creeds.[21]

Much of this could be interpreted as a total rejection of Western culture and society in Spenglerian terms. And the influence of Spengler's neo-fascism is, in fact, very real in the *negrismo integral* of certain African and Caribbean intellectuals. But the mainstream of the new nationalism seeks less to overthrow Europe than to insist that the dominion of the European age, not to mention the "American century," must now admit, on a basis of equality, the claim of other continental societies to make their new contributions to world life and culture. This is likely to express itself most fully in a new and radical exchange of art and culture between the new and the old worlds. Hitherto the new worlds have been relegated to the role of silent background to the "Atlantic community"—a phrase in itself little more than a Churchillian euphemism for "white supremacy" in international affairs. There is likely to occur a "colonialism in reverse" as the former colonial areas begin to give and the former imperialist societies begin to receive. Such a process was envisaged some seventy-five years ago by Charles Kingsley in his book on the West Indies. "Great and worthy exertions," he wrote, "are made, every London Season, for the conversion of the Negro and the Heathen, and the abolition of their barbarous customs and dances. It is to be hoped that the Negro and the Heathen will some day show their gratitude to us, by sending missionaries hither to convert the London Season, dances and all; and assist it to take the beam out of its own eye, in return for having taken the mote out of theirs."[22]

This process is indeed already under way. For Puerto Rico, in particular, it promises a new day. Once granted political independence, her cultural function as a crossroads of the Americas would immediately become clarified. For it would separate that function from the politicization which presently surrounds discussion on the point. Much rhetorical nonsense is at present declaimed about the whole issue, while the real issue—whether a politically subordinate society, in Puerto Rico a ceded territory, can in reality play an independent cultural role—is carefully evaded. This can be seen plainly enough in the scheme for setting up an inter-American scholastic center in the island—a topic of intermittent discussion ever since 1899. The assumption behind the discussion has always been that such a center of higher education would be an instrument for the furtherance of North American influence throughout the Hemisphere. This can be seen in the revealingly candid passage of the Report of the Commissioner for Education for the territory written in 1904. "The machinery for a great Central American university," the American official argued, "located on American soil, in the midst of a people of the Latin race, thoroughly American in spirit and desire, and being rapidly transformed into a thorough understanding of American life and institutions, awaits the endowment which must come in a large measure from the private wealth of the citizens of the United States. Such an institution, adequately endowed, giving advanced instruction in both the English and Spanish languages, and uniting the best elements of

American and Spanish-American scholarship, would exert a mighty influence for good upon the whole of Central and South America. It would draw students from all of these countries, and it would spread American institutions, interpret and enforce the Monroe Doctrine, train public servants for service in Spanish-American countries, mould the professional men and leaders of society, and do more to extend the sphere of American influence legitimately and promote friendly relations with the countries south of us than five American battle ships, and its complete endowment would not cost more than one battle ship."[23] It is possible that these political purposes—put perhaps less coarsely—may be the driving motivations still of the present-day universities in Puerto Rico when they speak about their hemispheric function. So long as such a situation prevails, Puerto Rico will find it difficult to take her proper place in the councils of the Americas and of the world at large.

Conclusion

IT IS painfully apparent that any "conclusion" on the Puerto Rican matter must be in the way of being inconclusive. This is not a classic case of colonial oppression, as with Dutch Indonesia or French Algeria. In fiscal and economic terms indeed the territory has had what really amounts to a privileged status. Yet this has been in a way a drawback in disguise, for it has had the effect of frustrating the rise of a colonial war of independence and of conferring upon the Puerto Rican spirit a subtle yet real guilt complex. Other peoples fight for independence; Puerto Ricans, it seems, when it comes, will have independence thrust upon them. Politically the territory retains the anomalous status, in essence unchanged, imposed upon it in 1900, and even the faith of the ruling *Popular* group in the doctrine of "associated status" begins to wear an apologetic look. For Americans the embarrassing contrast between the American creed of equality and the denial of full equality to Puerto Rico remains, perhaps, assuaged by the fact that the basic rationalizing argument in defense of the situation has recently become not so much that Americans do not want changes as that Puerto Ricans do not seek them. And so long as American rule means affluence for the dominant social groups while independence would entail for them a nationalist program of some grim austerity those groups will continue to prefer social privilege to nationalist faith.

In the meanwhile the American connection, even in those areas of Puerto Rican life where it seems most beneficent, continues to work its distorting influence upon the local life. It has brought much wealth and progress. But it has brought with those gifts the rules of the American national capitalism that make them, on close analysis, far less pleasing than they appear at first sight. For just as in the continental economy neither New Deal nor "New Frontier" has been capable of preventing the fundamental inequity between the relative developments of the private and public sectors, this has been equally the case with the Puerto Rican copy of those public policies. There is a similar contrast between private affluence and public squalor, between economic development and social welfare, between government philosophy and business behavior. And in the Caribbean economy those contrasts are heightened by the fact that the local police power can exercise very little real control over an economic development which has its main investment sources owned and controlled overseas. In San Juan as in Washington, government—so the liberal guide lines decree—may intervene but not operate, regulate but not control. Hence problems of public policy in San Juan take on more and more the character of their larger federal counterparts. There is the absence of effective control over location of industry; some 57 percent of all Fomento industries are concentrated in the three leading island cities, and the larger part of the rest in the neighboring municipal districts.[1] There is the imbalance of incentive which gives to the schoolteacher much praise and little reward and to others, especially in the economic development bureaus, economic returns far more attractive.[2] There is the disastrous condition of most public welfare programs, in part due to the low economic status of the social welfare worker, in part due to the almost complete absence of a body of voluntary workers to help out; with the general consequence that in the face of the terrible social disorganization worked by colonialism and industrialization, in fields ranging from juvenile delinquency and alcoholism to narcotics addiction and illegitimacy, there is hardly anything in the way of an aggressive counterattack by a fully fledged social service system.[3] There is a growing fundamental maladjustment in the national organization and development of the country's resources, with the single vital difference that the massive prodigality of the federal economy may make the waste tolerable while the limited resources of the insular economy make it at once intolerable and inexcusable. The American system, with its hold upon the Puerto Rican mind, has the effect of thus reproducing in the lesser economy the gross contrast between private affluence and public squalor of the major economy; with two-thirds of the island population medically indigent, for example, it is beyond justification that the same vested interests that stand in the way of a federal program of medical insurance should also operate, so far successfully, on the island. And so long as public policy in San Juan is set, by and large, by public policy in Washington, there can be little hope of Puerto Rican leadership striking out along fundamentally different avenues of experimentation.

The socio-cultural consequences of the continuing American connection have already been documented. It is enough to add, here, that phenomena that are merely amusing in the life of the superordinate society frequently become ludicrous, even tragicomic, when copied in the life of the subordinate society. Some day, perhaps, someone will have to write the history of the colonial society as a comic institution. In the meanwhile there is much rich data awaiting excavation. There is the exaggerated and morbid commercialization of Mother's Day injected into a Caribbean society so matriarchal in its familial mores that the very last charge that could be brought against the average Puerto Rican is neglect of his mother. There is the new waste that follows the neglect of the old taste, exhibited in the Puerto Rican exchange of the older European-style open-air café for the American-style soda fountain: a sad lapse of aesthetic judgment not inaptly anticipated by the spectacle of Ponce de León deserting sixteenth-century Puerto Rico in search of the *fons juventutis* in inhospitable Florida when he might have found something like it in the medicinal sulphur waters of the local Coamo Springs. There is even a process of cultural osmosis whereby the phenomena of cultural imperialism are given a new dress and acclaimed as *criollo*, attested to in Puerto Rico by the popular belief that dance steps like the mambo, the merengue, and the cha-cha-cha are indigenous popular styles whereas in reality they are imported Afro-Yanqui forms whose popularity works to the detriment of the genuinely Puerto Rican dances such as the *danzas*, the *seis*, the *aguinaldos*, and the *plenas*. A separate wealth of material, again, awaits the chronicler of the more laughable aspects of Puerto Rican—American interpersonal relationships. The ribald encounter between the young American lady of Rio Piedras and the Puerto Rican serenader from Quebradillas whose incapacity in English led him into a fatal *faux pas* is only one of many stories. Few things, again, are more entertaining, and yet at the same time more distressing, than the spectacle of the individual Puerto Rican seeking to impress an American acquaintance; and only an Englishman who knows how frequently the American sounds apologetic in the presence of English acquaintances is likely to appreciate the full piquant irony of the spectacle. There is much material, too, for the analyst of social snobbery in the colonial setting. The new middle classes seek their new forms of status here as elsewhere, and American humorous comment on the phenomenon is likely to evoke Puerto Rican anger; thus the editor of the *Island Times* has been taken to task because, seeking to satirize the introduction of a Social Register, he spoke jestingly of the island population being "just a bunch of Puerto Ricans of mixed Spanish, Indian, and African ancestry."[4] Yet it is a Puerto Rican observer who has described the *raquetero social* in which society matrons, anxious to find suitable partners for their daughters in the San Juan social whirligig, become the victims of extortionate demands from prospective candidates from "good families" and justify their behavior on the mistaken ground that it is an American custom.[5]

Independence of course would not terminate continental-insular relationships. But it would release them from their present framework of inequality. From that viewpoint the present status of the *estado libre asociado* is clearly unsatisfactory. The point has already been sufficiently labored. But it is worth adding a footnote at this stage of the argument. More than a century ago the English Benthamite critic Sir George Cornewall Lewis noted in his minor classic work *On the Government of Dependencies* (1841) the inherent difficulties of a scheme of imperial government which permits a large degree of internal self-government within its colonies and yet at the same time retains ultimate sovereignty in the hands of the metropolitan government. The scheme he discussed along those lines constituted in fact a remarkable anticipation of the present-day "associated status" of Puerto Rico. Yet Lewis was driven to admit its long-term impossibility. "There is a constant tendency, from inevitable causes," he noted, "to a misconception of the character and powers of a subordinate government. The relation of a subordinate to a supreme government is a complicated relation, which the people both of the dominant country and the dependency are likely to misunderstand, and the incorrect notions entertained by either party are likely to give rise to unfounded expectations and to practical errors in their political conduct. It is the duty of the dominant country to do everything in its power to diffuse correct opinions and to dispel errors respecting its political relations with the dependency, and still more to avoid creating an error on this subject; since, in case of any collision between the dominant country and the dependency, which an error on this subject is likely to produce, the weaker party, that is the dependency, can scarcely fail to be the chief sufferer."

The passage is an admirable summation of what has happened in United States-Puerto Rican relations since 1950. Lewis went even further; for he saw that the logic of his criticism led to the final solution of independence. "Unless," he continued, "the dominant country should be prepared to concede virtual independence, it ought carefully to avoid encouraging the people of the dependency to advance pretensions which nothing short of independence can satisfy. If a dominant country grants to a dependency popular institutions, and professes to allow it to exercise self-government, without being prepared to treat it as virtually independent, the dominant country by such conduct only mocks its dependency with the semblance of political institutions without their reality. It is no genuine concession to grant to a dependency the names and forms and machinery of popular institutions, unless the dominant country will permit those institutions to bear the meaning which they possess in an independent community; nor do such apparent concessions produce any benefit to the dependency, but, on the contrary, they sow the seeds of political dissensions, and perhaps of insurrections and wars, which would not otherwise arise."[6] Analysis of this kind cuts through the maze of rhetoric and constitutionalist mumbo-jumbo that has bedeviled discussion of the Puerto Rican case since 1950—indeed since 1900—and pinpoints the essential issue. That issue will be satisfactorily resolved only when both Washington and San Juan begin to see that it is the only analysis consonant with the facts.

The advantages and disadvantages of a grant of independence for the island territory have already been discussed. There would also be advantages and disadvantages for the United States as a consequence of such a grant. But the advantages would beyond doubt far outweigh the disadvantages. It would put American-Puerto Rican relations on an entirely new and better footing. It would enable Puerto Rico to identify itself with the Latin American hemispheric market, a market which, as Raul Prebisch forecast at the 1957 meeting of the United Nations Economic Committee for Latin America, is certain soon to expand in capital goods production and intra-regional trade. This identification would not necessarily mean cutting economic ties with the United States; such ties, perhaps somewhat altered, could continue as part of a joint United States–Puerto Rico participation in the Alliance for Progress. Americans would find a more wholesome reception for the genuine American creed, a reception currently soiled in Puerto Rico by the colonialist relationship. That creed is at its best liberal, utilitarian, egalitarian; it rejects, in the approving phrase of a Puerto Rican *independentista* novelist, an effete romanticism which gives more importance to the perfumed wig of Louis XVI than to the fall of the Bastille.[7] But at present the best of the creed gets little chance to be heard among the strident praise of the economic benefits of the American connection that floods the literature on insular-continental relations, the sort of thing sentimentalized in *West Side Story:*

> Pink Oldsmobile in America,
> Chromium steel in America,
> Wire-spoke wheel in America,
> Very big deal in America.

Future relations necessarily depend upon future United States policies. The debate therefore tends to be set in terms of American generosity. Yet this is gravely misleading. For it thus tends to overlook the fact that the United States-Caribbean relationship, historically, has been a two-way street much of the time, with very real advantages accruing to the Northern partner. Indeed, the American debt to the Caribbean island societies has been deep and lasting. Historical research has catalogued, as in the volumes of Chinard and Geoffrey Atkinson, how the sixteenth and seventeenth-century literature of political Utopias from which the American colonists drew so much of the concepts used to justify their rebellion against England— the law of nature, the evil of too much government, primitive democracy in society, the life of reason—was itself stimulated in large part by the accounts of the exploratory voyages to the Caribbean during the years after 1600 in writers like Biet, Clodore, Boyer, and du Têrtre.[8] Wylie Sypher has described in *Guinea's Captive Kings* how the romantic concept of the "noble savage" was popularized by the eighteenth-century discussion on the theme of Africa and the African slave in the Americas. The small island of Nevis gave Alexander Hamilton to the United States; Jamaica gave Marcus Garvey. The large holdings of the colonial American bourgeoisie in the West Indies did much to finance the Revolutionary War; the success of the Haitian revolt against French colonialism facilitated the Louisiana Purchase; and the refusal of the Caribbean populations to instigate any anti-American subversive movements during the Second World War, even in the Vichy-controlled French West Indies, left the Allied navies free to concentrate on the war in the Atlantic approaches. Perhaps most important of all, the American debate on slavery before 1860 was vastly influenced by the earlier debate within the Caribbean slave societies. The West Indian Emancipation of 1834 gave an enormous fillip to the Northern abolitionist cause. The American Quaker movement sent two of its members to analyze the consequences of the Emancipation; the result was Thome and Kimball's *Emancipation in the West Indies* (1838). There was also the remarkable book of the American observer William Sewell, *The Ordeal of Free Labor in the British West Indies,* published originally as a series of articles in the *New York Times* on the eve of the Civil War and containing, among other things, an exhaustive rebuttal, based upon statistical observations, of the myth that the decline of the West Indian sugar industry had been the direct consequence of the lowered productivity of the freed slave.

This is an impressive record. It suggests that the Caribbean peoples are deeply committed to the culture tradition of the American hemisphere and that the United States has little to lose in seeking their fraternal alliance. At bottom they admire the American tradition of the United States and are more than ready to forge chains of friendship with it. The friendship must not be mistaken, of course, for something more; it is the weakness of books like Robert Hill's *Cuba and*

Puerto Rico with the Other Islands of the West Indies that they have mistaken British West Indian discontent with Crown Colony rule for a desire for annexation to the United States. But granted their natural passion for independence, American indebtedness to the Caribbean area has a chance now of being repaid with interest. And Americans can give much in return. There is the lesson of constitutional government, something that Britain, too, has given to her former Caribbean possessions; for, as regards France, there is much justice in the observation of a Caribbean writer that if Haiti's political instability since Toussaint's original legacy of freedom has been cited by hostile observers as proof of the incapacity of the black man to govern himself, the notorious instability of France itself, especially since 1940, makes it difficult here for Europeans to be self-righteous.[9] There is the ready warmth of the individual American, his concern with "getting on" with people. For all its comic and awkward moments, it is perhaps to be preferred to the icy aloofness of the English colonial enclaves. Beyond all, the fine elements of American liberalism await their full flowering in a region which has long been an American Mediterranean insulated against their full impact. Given a chance to reshape the American–Puerto Rican relationship, they would emancipate both sides; for magnanimous generosity blesses both him who gives and him who receives.

Such an experiment in friendship could not wish for a more pleasing environment than the Caribbean region. Its necklace of islands, from Cuba to Trinidad, running through the Greater and the Lesser Antilles, along with its pendant strings of the Saints and the Grenadines, encompasses a beauty basically semitropical but immeasurably enhanced by its juxtaposition to the tropic waters of the Caribbean Sea and the Gulf of Mexico. Its fronded landscapes, the terraced heights of its *mornes,* the gracious amplitude of its *plazas* and *savannahs,* the green and purple richness of its vegetation, the splendid sweep of its sugar cane fields make up altogether a veritable Garden of Eden portrait, and all of them fixed within the sun-drenched luminosity of the Caribbean atmosphere. It is not for nothing that from the very beginning its European conquerors found it difficult to resist its tremendous power to charm and to hold. Columbus himself believed that he had discovered the site of the Terrestrial Paradise in the region of the vast Orinoco gulf. Cortes and his handful of Spanish warriors, who started their famous expedition from Cuba, could think of nothing but the legends of Amadis when the splendid magnificence of the great Valley of Mexico unfolded before their astonished gaze. Men of entirely different character succumbed to the spell of this New World: from the Las Casas who began his great history in defense of the New World peoples in his tiny Dominican monastery in the island of Hispaniola to the Père Labat whose *vagabunda loquacitas* and exhaustive curiosity combined to produce one of the most Rabelaisian *nouveaux voyages* on the Caribbean society of the last period of the seventeenth century. The romantic elements of the new literature so fascinated Pope Leo X that he reportedly sat up all night to read the *Decades* of Peter Martyr. For the social fascination of the Caribbean is no less real than its natural appeal. To visit even today—when so many of the outside influences have toned down much of the region's quaint eccentricity— the more isolated island societies such as Montserrat or Bequia or the curious rock of Saba is to feel something of the pleasures of exploration. There is a happy congruity between the small town societies and the small islands that form their natural setting; and to stay in any of them for any length of time is to begin to realize what the Thucydidean Pericles meant by his eulogy of the civic friendliness of Athens and to understand the sad nostalgia for his beloved Geneva that tortured Rousseau throughout his lonely wanderings.

Puerto Rico has its own special variation on this general theme. It shares with the rest of the Caribbean an almost idyllic climate; more than three hundred years ago Peter Heylin's *Cosmographie* remarked that it was "not scorched with furious heats in Summer, nor made offensive by the fall of continual rains." The division of the island by the mountain range of the *cordillera central* has created a remarkable variety of geographic districts, from the moist tropical rain forest of *El Yunque* through the river alluvial plains of the north coast to the various limestone outcroppings of the western central mountains, and yet again to the semi-arid open spaces of the southern littoral. The stratigraphy and paleontology of the island, exhaustively mapped by American scholarship, provide an attractive setting for the narrow roads that spiral their tortuous way through the central and western mountain sections. To travel the old *Camino Real* from Coamo to Barranquitas, the deep gorge-like valleys of the Manatí and Usabón river basins, the high sierra road from Guayama to Cayey is to feel the peculiar exhilaration that comes from all mountain travel. Those areas do not possess the gigantic scale of the great divides of the American Rockies or the Peruvian Andes, but they nonetheless have a compact charm all of their own; in the apt phrase of Julián Marias, they seem like an Asturias of the tropics. And there is, finally, the blaze of glory of Puerto Rican trees: the ceiba, the calabash tree, the Indian laurel, the royal palm, the elegant flamboyán. It is assuredly not for nothing that all of this, each generation, evokes the praise of a romantically extravagant verse on the part of the insular poets.

Nor is the conventional topography of the island, as distinct from the natural, any less pleasing. The architectural treasures of San Juan, saved from the usual blight of city commercialization by the zeal of the Institute of Puerto Rican Culture, are well known: the *Casa Blanca,* San José church, *La Fortaleza,* the Cathedral, the military complexes, still really unexplored in any scientific way, of the *El Morro* and *San Cristóbal* forts. There are the many colonial towns of the Spanish municipal charters, fully written up by the Puerto Rican antiquarians: Bayamón, Vega Alta, Manatí, Camuy, Juana Díaz, Guayanilla. Small townships like Naranjito and San Sebastián still retain their native simplicity; and to look upon the uplands summer resort of colonial Barranquitas from the massive volcanic rocks that cradle it is to gain the sharp impression of a Spanish medieval print. There is a distinct Mediterranean air about an old colonial center like San Germán, with its elongated *plaza* overlooked by the early sixteenth-century Porta Coeli church which probably antedates even the church missions of Spanish California; a charming legend even insists that the famous swallows of San Juan Capistrano winter in that Puerto Rican center. Further north there is the mountain fastness of Lares, still the heart of a flourishing coffee culture, well known for the *plaza* monument that commemorates the heroes of the nationalist Lares revolt of 1868. All of this testifies to a spirit of municipal pride which, although weakening under modern pressures, is evidence of the older Puerto Rican devotion to the "home town." Humacao is the *Cenicienta del Este,* Ponce the *Perla del Sur,* Mayagüez the *Sultana del Oeste*—proud titles suggesting that even in a tiny island society local attachment may coexist with national sentiment.

It would of course be easy to exaggerate the general picture of Caribbean charm. The Antillean literature, from the very beginning when Las Casas penned his chapter describing, as he saw it, the social innocence of the aboriginal inhabitants in the island of Columbus' first call somewhere in the Bahama cays, has frequently fallen into the trap of glamorizing the regional scene. Behind the legend, even so, there has been some real measure of truth. The special Caribbean mixture of man, society, and nature makes for a way of life in which the human spirit does not so much struggle against as cooperate with the principles of the natural order. Climate, in the temperate zones, presses down on man; in the semitropic zones its very benevolence releases him from a constant fight against its hostile elements, except of course for the dread terror of the hurricane. New dimensions are given to the sensual side of life, for all senses are assaulted by sights and sounds and fragrances absent in more northern latitudes. Even a different sense of time is felt; the distinction in

Puerto Rican conversation between "American time" and "Puerto Rican time" is a distinction between a business culture in which punctuality, like thrift, is one of the honorific economic virtues and an older culture in which time is made for man and not man for time. Even love, the first "industry" of the Caribbean economy, is touched by this environment. Many an American has thus discovered that much of the appeal that Puerto Rico finally holds for him has come from the special Indo-Spanish beauty of its women and from the nice order of its amorous arrangements: the bold flirtatiousness of girls that hides a real innocence, the deep patience that awaits results, so different from the furious rush of the American battle of the sexes, and finally the capacity of the more mature Puerto Rican woman to develop a pattern of relationships with men, even in the professional fields where the thing is the most difficult because she is still a newcomer, that is not spoiled by the attitudes of aggressive competitiveness and exploitative sex so much affected by her North American counterpart. All this does not of course make of Puerto Rico the Celestial City. But it could be the threshold, as it were, of that final destination, offering from its Delectable Mountains a view of the noble end of the journey.

Notes

References carry full data of author, title, publisher, and place and date of publication only when first cited within each chapter. Subsequent references give author's surname and "short title" of the work cited. Full data are again furnished with each new chapter. (See below, Chapter 1, notes 14 and 16, Tumin and Feldman; Chapter 3, notes 1 and 3, Cruz Monclova; and Chapter 5, note 1, Cruz Monclova.)

CHAPTER 1

1. Editorial, "El *Mirror* y los Boricuas," *El Mundo,* August 13, 1959. For the general failure of metropolitan services to meet Puerto Rican immigrant needs, see Martin B. Dworkis, ed., *The Impact of Puerto Rican Migration on Governmental Services in New York City* (New York University Press, 1957); and relevant sections in William Ferree, Joseph P. Fitzpatrick, and John D. Illich, eds., *Report on the First Conference on the Spiritual Care of Puerto Rican Migrants* (New York, Office of the Coordinator of Spanish-American Catholic Action, 1955).

2. House of Representatives, 64th Congress, 1st Session, *A Civil Government for Porto Rico,* Hearings Before the Committee on Insular Affairs on HR 8501 (Washington, U.S. Government Printing Office, 1916), pp. 33-34. From the beginning the American attitude to Puerto Ricans reflected the assumption that Puerto Rico, like the Deep South, was poor and Negro. An early picture book of the new possessions subtitled one picture of rural Puerto Rico as follows: "The farming class is about on a par with the poor darkies down South, and varies much even in race and color, ranging from Spanish white trash to full-blooded Ethiopians." *Neely's Panorama Of Our New Possessions* (New York, F. Tennyson Neely, 1899).

3. Luis M. Díaz Soler, *Rosendo Matienzo Cintrón: Recopilación de su Obra Escrita* (Rio Piedras, Ediciones de la Literatura Puertorriqueña, Universidad de Puerto Rico, 1960), 2 vols., Vol. I, p. 463.

4. John P. Augelli, "San Lorenzo: A Case Study of Recent Migrations in Interior Puerto Rico," *American Journal of Economics and Sociology* (January 1952); and Robert O. Carleton, *New Aspects of Puerto Rican Migration,* Puerto Rico Planning Board, presented at 19th Annual Meeting, American Statistical Association (Washington, mimeographed, 1959).

5. Commonwealth Government of Puerto Rico, Economic Development Administration, Office of Economic Research, *Selected Statistics on the Visitors and Hotel Industry in Puerto Rico* (San Juan, mimeographed, 1960).

6. Governor Luis Muñoz Marín, *Breakthrough from Nationalism: A Small Island Looks at a Big Trouble,* The Godkin Lectures, Harvard University (San Juan, Office of the Governor, mimeographed, April 1959).

7. United States Tariff Commission, *The Economy of Puerto Rico with Special Reference to the Economic Implications of Independence and Other Proposals to Change Its Political Status* (Washington, U.S. Government Printing Office, 1946), pp. 11-13.

8. Clarence W. Hall, "Samoa: America's Shame in the South Seas," *Readers Digest* (July 1961).

9. Harry A. Franck, *Roaming Through the West Indies* (New York, Century, 1920), p. 485.

10. Paul Blanshard, *Democracy and Empire in the Caribbean* (New York, Macmillan, 1947), pp. 339-340.

11. A. D. Hall, *Porto Rico: Its History, Products and Possibilities* (New York, Street & Smith, 1898), p. 57.

12. University of Puerto Rico, *Notes on a Proposal for the Establishment in Puerto Rico of a Hemispheric Center for Cultural and Technical Interchange* (Rio Piedras, mimeographed, 1960), p. 1.

13. Earl Parker Hanson, *Puerto Rico: Land of Wonders* (New York, Knopf, 1960).

14. Melvin M. Tumin and Arnold Feldman, *Social Class and Social Change in Puerto Rico* (Princeton University Press, 1961).

15. Middle States Association of Colleges and Secondary Schools, Commission on Institutions of Higher Education, *A Report on the University of Puerto Rico* (Rio Piedras, University of Puerto Rico, November 1959), pp. 7, 10.

16. Tumin and Feldman, *Social Class and Social Change in Puerto Rico,* p. 466.

CHAPTER 2

1. Bryan Edwards, *The History, Civil and Commercial, of the British West Indies* (London, 1802), 5 vols., Vol. 4, p. 36.

2. Anonymous, *Antigua and the Antiguans* (London, 1844), 2 vols., Vol. 2, p. 141.

3. Fernando Ortiz, *Hampa Afrocubana: Los Negros Esclavos* (Havana, 1916), Chapter 20; Luis M. Díaz Soler, *Historia de la Esclavitud Negra en Puerto Rico, 1493-1890* (Rio Piedras, Ediciones de la Universidad de Puerto Rico, 1953), pp. 192-194. For an up-to-date history of the slave trade, see Daniel P. Mannix and Malcolm Cowley, *Black Cargoes: A History of the Atlantic Slave Trade* (New York, Viking, 1962).

4. Adam Smith, *The Wealth of Nations* (London, Everyman Library edition, 1917), Book IV, Chapter 7, Part ii, 84-85.

5. Abbé Raynal, *Histoire Philosophique et Politique des Establissements et du Commerce des Européens dans les Deux Indes* (London, English translation, 1788), 8 vols., Vol. 5, p. 309.

6. *El Mundo,* December 31, 1959.

7. Rexford G. Tugwell, *The Stricken Land* (New York, Doubleday, 1947).

8. J. J. Thomas, *Froudacity: West Indian Fables Explained* (London, Unwin, 1889), pp. 6-7.

9. Thomas G. Mathews, *Puerto Rican Politics and the New Deal* (Gainesville, University of Florida Press, 1960), p. 159.

10. Benjamin Kidd, *The Control of the Tropics* (London, Macmillan, 1898), pp. 52-53.

11. W. R. Brownlow, *Lectures on Slavery and Serfdom in Europe* (London, Burns & Oates, 1892), pp. xxvii-xlviii.

12. H. A. Wyndham, *The Atlantic and Emancipation* (London, Oxford University Press, 1937), p. 117.

13. W. P. Livingstone, *Black Jamaica: A Study in Evolution* (London, Sampson Low, 1899), p. 233.

CHAPTER 3

1. Adolfo de Hostos, *Temas Cubanos,* p. 10, quoted in Lidio Cruz Monclova, *Historia de Puerto Rico (Siglo XIX)* (Rio Piedras, Universidad de Puerto Rico, 1958), 3 vols., Vol. 1, pp. 323-324.

2. Alexander Humboldt, *The Island of Cuba*, translated from the Spanish (New York, Derby & Jackson, 1856), pp. 328-349.

3. Diego A. Martínez, in *Diario de las Sesiones de Cortes, Congreso de los Diputados*, Legislatura de 1879-1880, Vol. 10, p. 4828, quoted in Cruz Monclova, *Historia de Puerto Rico*, Vol. 2, pp. 566-567.

4. Arturo Morales-Carrión, *Puerto Rico and the Non-Hispanic Caribbean: A Study in the Decline of Spanish Exclusivism* (Rio Piedras, University of Puerto Rico, 1952).

5. Calixto Bernal, *Apuntes sobre la Cuestión de la Reforma Política y de la Introducción de los Africanos en Cuba y Puerto Rico*, p. 288, quoted in Cruz Monclova, *Historia de Puerto Rico*, Vol. 1, p. 302.

6. Salvador Brau, "Cartas al Ministerio de Ultramar," in Eugenio Fernández-Méndez, ed., *Salvador Brau: Disquisiciones Sociológicas y Otros Ensayos* (Rio Piedras, Universidad de Puerto Rico, 1956), p. 290.

7. J. J. Gurney, *A Winter in the West Indies* (London, John Murray, 1840), pp. 206-221.

8. Rafael María de Labra, *Política y Sistemas Coloniales*, p. 35, quoted in Cruz Monclova, *Historia de Puerto Rico*, Vol. 1, p. 634.

9. José Julián Acosta, *Notas*, p. 262, quoted in Cruz Monclova, *Historia de Puerto Rico*, Vol. 1, p. 613.

10. Alejandro Tapia y Rivera, *Mis Memorias, o Puerto Rico como lo Encontré y como lo Dejo* (New York, De Laisne & Rossboro, 1928), pp. 113-114.

11. *Ibid.*, pp. 88-89

12. Fernando Miyares González, *Noticias Particulares de la Isla y Playa de San Juan Bautista de Puerto Rico*, ed. Eugenio Fernández-Méndez (Rio Piedras, University of Puerto Rico Press, 1957).

13. Rafael María de Labra, *Porto Rico en 1885*, quoted in Antonio S. Pedreira, *El Año Terrible del 1887* (San Juan, Biblioteca de Autores Puertorriqueños, 1948), pp. 30-31.

14. Henry K. Carroll, *Report on the Island of Porto Rico* (Washington, U.S. Government Printing Office, 1899).

15. Marshal O'Reylly, *Memoria sobre la Isla de Puerto Rico* (1785), in Alejandro Tapia y Rivera, ed., *Biblioteca Histórica de Puerto Rico* (San Juan, Instituto de Literatura Puertorriqueña, 1945), p. 528.

16. Colonel George Flinter, *An Account of the Present State of the Island of Porto Rico* (London, Longman, 1834).

17. Fray Iñigo Abbad y Lasierra, *Historia Geográfica, Civil y Natural de la Isla de San Juan Bautista de Puerto Rico*, ed. Isabel Gutiérrez del Arroyo (Rio Piedras, Ediciones de la Universidad de Puerto Rico, 1959), pp. 183-184.

18. *Ibid.*, pp. 182-183.

19. Luis M. Díaz Soler, *Historia de la Esclavitud Negra en Puerto Rico, 1493-1890* (Rio Piedras, Ediciones de la Universidad de Puerto Rico, 1953), Chapter 9.

20. "Informe de la Junta Informativa sobre la Abolición de la Esclavitud" (1867), in Cruz Monclova, *Historia de Puerto Rico*, Vol. 1, pp. 508-512. See also Luis M. Díaz Soler, ed., *Proyecto para la Abolición de la Esclavitud en Puerto Rico* (San Juan, Instituto de Cultura Puertorriqueña, 1959).

21. Diego de Torres Varga, *Descripción de la Isla y Ciudad de Puerto Rico*, in Eugenio Fernández-Méndez, ed., *Crónicas de Puerto Rico, 1493-1797* (San Juan, Ediciones del Gobierno Estado Libre Asociado de Puerto Rico, 1957), pp. 208-209.

22. Salvador Brau, "Las Clases Jornaleras de Puerto Rico," in Fernández-Méndez, ed., *Salvador Brau: Disquisiciones Sociológicas y Otros Ensayos*, p. 150.

23. William Dinwiddie, *Porto Rico and Its Possibilities* (New York and London, Harpers, 1899), p. 205.

24. Eugenio Fernández-Méndez, ed., *Crónicas de Puerto Rico, 1493-1797*, p. 188.

25. Manuel Alonso, *El Gíbaro* (Rio Piedras, Edición Colegio Hostos, 1949), pp. 34-39.

26. Salvador Brau, "Las Clases Jornaleras de Puerto Rico," in Fernández-Méndez, ed., *Salvador Brau: Disquisiciones Sociológicas y Otros Ensayos*, pp. 143-155.

27. *Ibid.*, p. 289.

28. Adolfo de Hostos, quoted in Cruz Monclova, *Historia de Puerto Rico*, Vol. 2, p. 10, n. 15.

29. "Informe de la Junta Informativa sobre la Abolición de la Esclavitud," in Cruz Monclova, *Historia de Puerto Rico*, Vol. 1, p. 544.

30. Pilar Barbosa de Rosario, *La Obra de José Celso Barbosa* (San Juan, Imprenta Venezuela, 1957), 6 vols., Vol. 6, *La Comisión Autonomista de 1896*, p. 52.

31. *Ibid.*, p. 311.

32. Tapia y Rivera, ed., *Biblioteca Histórica de Puerto Rico*, pp. 123-124, 202-206, 555-557. For the juridical theory of the Spanish state generally in the Indies, as opposed to the realities, see José María Ots Capdequi, *El Estado Español en las Indias* (Colegio de Mexico, 1941).

33. Lidio Cruz Monclova, "Cómo Puerto Rico Estuvo a Punto a Convertirse en Colonia de Francia," *Puerto Rico Ilustrado* (June 26, 1941). Spanish rule of this sort naturally evoked a strong patriotism among all Puerto Rican social classes. For this see the contemporary account of the local reaction to the repression of 1887 in Francisco Mariano Quinoñes, *Apuntes para la Historia de Puerto Rico* (San Juan, Instituto de Literatura Puertorriqueña, (1957); and the contemporary account of the later period 1885-1899 in René Jimenez Malaret, ed., *Epistolario Historico del Dr. Felix Tio y Malaret* (San Juan, Imprenta Soltero, 1953). The latter volume bears testimony to the widespread secret separatist sentiment among all social classes (pp. 19-21).

34. Pilar Barbosa de Rosario, *La Obra de José Celso Barbosa*, Vol. 6, p. 66. It is worth adding to this discussion of the Puerto Rican political strategy under Spain the observations of a later critic, himself Puerto Rican, Roberto H. Todd in his *Estampas Coloniales* (San Juan, Biblioteca de Autores Puertorriqueños, 1954). Noting that the ideology of provincial autonomy, best stated in the Ponce Plan of 1886, was a harebrained enterprise from the beginning, he quotes the significant remark of the Spanish minister Antonio Canovas del Castillo to the Spanish parliament that no one had as yet offered a satisfactory definition of the word autonomy; and he adds his own remark that even now, sixty-three years later (1949), Spain has not yet learned the meaning of the word (pp. 71-78).

CHAPTER 4

1. Albert K. Weinberg, *Manifest Destiny: A Study of Nationalist Expansionism in American History* (Baltimore, Johns Hopkins Press, 1935), p. 65.

2. Walter Millis, *The Martial Spirit: A Study of Our War with Spain* (Boston, Houghton Mifflin, 1931).

3. Melvin M. Knight, *The Americans in Santo Domingo* (New York, Vanguard, 1928), p. 139.

4. A. D. Gayer, P. T. Homan and E. K. James, *The Sugar Economy of Porto Rico* (New York, Columbia University Press, 1938), pp. 105-110.

5. Rómulo Betancourt, *Venezuela: Factoría Petrolera* (Mexico, Editores Beatriz

de Silva, 1954). See also Arturo Uzlar-Pietri, *De Una a Otra Venezuela* (Caracas, Ediciones Mesa Redonda, 1949).

6. Benjamin Kidd, *The Control of the Tropics* (London, Macmillan, 1898), pp. 42-43.

7. Quoted in Adolphe Roberts, *The Caribbean: The Story of Our Sea of Destiny* (Philadelphia, Bobbs-Merrill, 1940), p. 263.

8. Weinberg, *Manifest Destiny*, p. 324.

9. P. T. Moon, in C. L. Jones, H. K. Norton and P. T. Moon, *The United States and the Caribbean* (University of Chicago Press, 1929), p. 203.

10. James McGregor Burns, *Roosevelt: The Lion and the Fox* (New York, Harcourt Brace, 1956), pp. 387-388.

11. F. E. Chadwick, *Relations of the United States and Spain* (New York, Scribner, 1909), p. 500.

12. Weinberg, *Manifest Destiny*.

13. *Ibid.*, p. 327.

14. *Ibid.*, p. 432.

15. Quoted in Burton J. Hendrick, *Life and Letters of Walter Hines Page* (New York, Doubleday Page, 1922-1925), 3 vols., Vol. 1, p. 205.

16. Quoted in Philip C. Jessup, *Elihu Root* (New York, Dodd Mead, 1938), 2 vols., Vol. 2, p. 513.

17. Weinberg, *Manifest Destiny*, p. 446.

18. Harry A. Franck, *Roaming Through the West Indies* (New York, Century, 1920), p. 245.

19. Knight, *The Americans in Santo Domingo,* Chapter 10. For Santo Domingo in general, and its relations with the United States, see Sumner Gardner Welles, *Naboth's Vineyard: The Dominican Republic 1844-1924* (New York, Payson & Clarke, 1928), 2 vols.

20. Weinberg, *Manifest Destiny*, p. 429.

CHAPTER 5

1. Quoted in Lidio Cruz Monclova, *Historia de Puerto Rico (Siglo XIX)* (Rio Piedras, Universidad de Puerto Rico, 1958), 3 vols., Vol. I, pp. 669-670.

2. Report of the British Vice-Consul, Fernando M. Toro, in *The World Journal* (San Juan), December 29, 1956.

3. Paul Morand, *Hiver Caraïbe* (Paris, Flammarion, 1929), pp. 146-148.

4. Eugenio Fernández-Méndez, "Reflexiones sobre 50 Años de Cambio Cultural en Puerto Rico," *Historia* (Rio Piedras, October 1955), pp. 274-279.

5. Albert Gardner Robinson, *The Porto Rico of Today* (New York, Scribner, 1899), p. v.

6. Henry K. Carroll, *Report on the Island of Porto Rico* (Washington, Department of War, Government Printing Office, 1899), p. 51.

7. *Annual Report of the Governor of Porto Rico to the Secretary of War* (Washington, U.S. Government Printing Office, 1900), p. 30.

8. *Annual Report of the Governor of Porto Rico to the Secretary of War* (Washington, U.S. Government Printing Office, 1901), p. 99.

9. House of Representatives, *Congressional Record* (57th Congress, April 1900, Vol. 33, Part 8, Appendix), p. 219, quoted in Eugenio Fernández-Méndez, ed., *Portrait of a Society: A Book of Readings on Puerto Rican Society* (Rio Piedras, University of Puerto Rico, 1956), pp. 154-155.

10. Thomas Childs Cochran, *The Puerto Rican Businessman: A Study in Cultural Change* (Philadelphia, University of Pennsylvania Press, 1958).

11. Armando Torres Vega, *Penumbras en la Vida de mi Pueblo* (San Juan, Imprenta Soltero, 1952), pp. 139-141. For the plight of Puerto Rican coffee after 1898, see also *El Porvenir de Nuestro Café: La Conquista del Mercado Americano* (La Comisión Organizadora de la Asociación Nacional de Productores de Café, Ponce, 1916).

12. Victor S. Clark and associates, *Porto Rico and Its Problems* (Washington, Brookings Institution, 1930), pp. 562-564.

13. *Ibid.*, p. 490.

14. Santiago Iglesias Pantín, quoted in Harry A. Franck, *Roaming Through the West Indies* (New York, Century, 1920), p. 277.

15. Quoted in Gaston Martin, *Histoire de l'Esclavage dans les Colonies Françaises* (Paris, Presses Universitaires de France, 1948), p. 105.

16. Miguel Guerra-Mondragón, "The Legal Background of Agrarian Reform in Puerto Rico," in Fernández-Méndez, ed., *Portrait of a Society*, pp. 159-160. For a more extended treatment of the agrarian reform, see Mathew D. Edel, "Land Reform in Puerto Rico, 1941-1959," *Caribbean Studies* (Rio Piedras, October 1962, January 1963).

17. Miguel Guerra-Mondragón, "The Legal Background of Agrarian Reform in Puerto Rico," in Fernández-Méndez, ed., *Portrait of a Society*, p. 162.

18. Letter from Harold Ickes to Senator Duncan N. Fletcher, January 15, 1935, in Thomas Mathews, *Puerto Rican Politics and the New Deal* (Gainesville, University of Florida Press, 1960), p. 215.

19. Sidney W. Mintz, "The Cultural History of a Puerto Rican Sugar Cane Plantation, 1876-1949," *Hispanic American Historical Review* (May 1953), pp. 224-251. Mintz has elaborated much of this in his later *Worker in the Cane: A Puerto Rican Life History* (New Haven, Yale University Press, 1960).

20. Statement of the Comité Territorial del Partido Socialista de Puerto Rico, quoted in *La Democracia* (San Juan), August 18, 1927. For early fictional accounts of the social costs of the Americanization of the post-1898 economy, see the two novels of Ramon Julia Marín, *Tierra Adentro* (1911) and *La Gleba* (1912), recently reissued by La Asociación de Jóvenes Emiliano Nazario (Utuado, Puerto Rico, 1962). For an early American account, see Randolph Long, "The Passing of the Plantation Life," *The Island Times,* February 17, 1961.

21. Quoted in Victor Clark and associates, *Porto Rico and Its Problems,* p. 40, n. 25.

22. Quoted in Dean Fleagle, *Social Problems of Porto Rico* (Boston, Heath, 1917), pp. 10-15.

23. José Colombán Rosario, "The Porto Rican Peasant and His Historical Antecedents," in Victor Clark and associates, *Porto Rico and Its Problems,* Appendix A.

24. *Ibid.,* p. 418.

25. Bailey W. and Justine Whitfield Diffie, *Porto Rico: A Broken Pledge* (New York, Vanguard, 1931), pp. 55-56.

26. *Ibid.,* p. 85.

27. Clark and associates, *Porto Rico and Its Problems,* pp. 216-218.

28. Whitelaw Reid, *Problems of Expansion* (New York, Century, 1900), p. 158.

29. Franck, *Roaming Through the West Indies,* pp. 277-278.

30. A. Hyatt Verrill, *Porto Rico Past and Present and San Domingo of Today* (New York, Dodd Mead, 1914), pp. 139-140.

31. F. M. Zeno, *Concurso Científico del Ateneo Puertorriqueño* (San Juan, Imprenta La Correspondencia, 1922), pp. 87, 125-129; also F. M. Zeno, "El Obrero Agrícola como Factor de Progreso," in E. Fernández García, ed., *El Libro de Porto Rico* (San Juan, El Libro Azul, 1923), pp. 737-743.

CHAPTER 6

1. Bolívar Pagán, *Historia de los Partidos Políticos Puertorriqueños* (San Juan, Librería Campos, 1959), 2 vols., Vol. I, p. 46.

2. Whitelaw Reid, *Problems of Expansion* (New York, Century, 1900), pp. 186-187.

3. Quoted in Pedro Muñoz-Amato, "Major Trends in the Constitutional History of Puerto Rico, 1493-1917," *Revista de Derecho, Ley y Jurisprudencia del Colegio de Abogados de Puerto Rico* (July-September 1949), p. 296. For the Charter of Autonomy of 1897 see Reece B. Bothwell and Lidio Cruz Monclova, eds., *Los Documentos: Que Dicen?* (San Juan, Ediciones de la Universidad de Puerto Rico, 1960), pp. 185-200, and for an English translation, Division of Customs and Insular Affairs, War Department, *Constitution Establishing Self-Government in the Islands of Cuba and Porto Rico* (Washington, U.S. Government Printing Office, 1899).

4. Muñoz-Amato, "Major Trends in the Constitutional History of Puerto Rico, 1493-1917," p. 289.

5. *Ibid.,* p. 266.

6. *Downes v. Bidwell*, 21 S.Ct. 770, 182 U.S. 244, 45 L.Ed. 1088 (1901).

7. *Dorr v. United States*, 24 S.Ct. 808, 195 U.S. 138, 49 L.Ed. 128 (1904).

8. *Downes v. Bidwell*, 21 S.Ct. 770, 182 U.S. 244, 45 L.Ed. 1088 (1901).

9. *Ibid.,* 280. For more discussion of these Insular cases see Marcos A. Ramírez, "Los Casos Insulares: Un Estudio sobre el Proceso Judicial," *Revista Juridica de la Universidad de Puerto Rico* (November-December 1946). The cases have been conveniently brought together in *Documents on the Constitutional History of Puerto Rico* (Washington, Office of Puerto Rico, N.D.), pp. 117-151.

10. *Balzac v. Porto Rico*, 42 S.Ct. 343, 258 U.S. 298, 66 L.Ed. 627 (1922). For a general view of the governmental system of the territory developed along the lines of the Insular cases see William F. Willoughby, *Territories and Dependencies of the United States: Their Government and Administration* (New York, Century, 1905).

11. Pagán, *Historia de los Partidos Políticos Puertorriqueños,* Vol. 1, p. 74.

12. F. M. Zeno, *Concurso Científico del Ateneo Puertorriqueño* (San Juan, Imprenta La Correspondencia, 1922), pp. 77-79.

13. Henry K. Carroll, *Report on the Island of Porto Rico* (Washington, U.S. Government Printing Office, 1899), pp. 56-58.

14. Reid, *Problems of Expansion,* p. 117.

15. *Congressional Record,* 61st Congress, 1st Session, 1910, Vol. 44, p. 1866, quoted in Muñoz-Amato, "Major Trends in the Constitutional History of Puerto Rico," p. 282.

16. Walter Scott, *Life of Napoleon* (in *Prose Works,* London, 1819), Vol. 13, p. 332.

17. Quoted in Muñoz-Amato, "Major Trends in the Constitutional History of Puerto Rico," p. 288.

18. Quoted in Pagán, *Historia de los Partidos Políticos Puertorriqueños,* Vol. 1, pp. 90-94.

19. Quoted *Ibid.,* p. 171.

20. Santiago Iglesias Pantín, *Luchas Emancipadoras* (San Juan, Cantero Fernández, 1929), pp. 90-91.

21. *The Dominica Dial* (Roseau, Dominica, British West Indies), November 13, 1886.

22. James Farley, *Jim Farley's Story: The Roosevelt Years* (New York, Whittlesey House, 1948), pp. 240-243.

23. Rexford G. Tugwell, *The Stricken Land* (New York, Doubleday, 1947), p. 80.

24. Theodore Roosevelt Jr., *Colonial Policies of the United States* (New York, Doubleday Doran, 1937), p. 100.

25. William D. Boyce, *United States Colonies and Dependencies* (New York, Rand McNally, 1914), pp. 415, 459.

26. Theodore Roosevelt Jr., *Colonial Policies of the United States,* pp. 118-119.

CHAPTER 7

1. Luis Muñoz Rivera, *Obras Completas* (Madrid, Ediciones Puerto Rico, 1920), 3 vols., Vol. 2, p. 82.

2. William Dinwiddie, *Porto Rico and Its Possibilities* (New York and London, Harpers, 1899), p. 247.

3. Victor S. Clark and associates, *Porto Rico and Its Problems* (Washington, Brookings Institution, 1930), pp. xxvii-xxviii.

4. Earl Parker Hanson, *Transformation: The Story of Modern Puerto Rico* (New York, Simon & Schuster, 1955).

5. Harold L. Ickes, *The Secret Diary of Harold L. Ickes* (New York, Simon & Schuster, 1954), 3 vols., Vol. 1, pp. 502-506.

6. Thomas Mathews, *Puerto Rican Politics and the New Deal* (Gainesville, University of Florida Press, 1960), pp. 154-158.

7. *Ibid.,* p. 151.

8. Hanson, *Transformation: The Story of Modern Puerto Rico,* pp. 207-208.

9. *Ibid.,* pp. 54-56.

10. Mathews, *Puerto Rican Politics and the New Deal,* p. 324.

11. Earl S. Garver and Ernest B. Fincher, *Puerto Rico: Unsolved Problem* (Elgin, Illinois, Brethren Publishing House, 1945), pp. 105-106.

12. Mathews, *Puerto Rican Politics and the New Deal,* p. 146.

13. *Ibid.,* p. 162.

14. *Ibid.,* p. 161.

15. Bailey W. and Justine Whitfield Diffie, *Porto Rico: A Broken Pledge.*

16. Ickes, *Secret Diary,* Vol. 1, p. 228.

17. Mathews, *Puerto Rican Politics and the New Deal,* p. 231.

18. *Ibid.,* pp. 74-76.

19. Quoted in Clark and associates, *Porto Rico and Its Problems,* p. 524.

20. Mathews, *Puerto Rican Politics and the New Deal,* pp. 188-189.

21. Wenzell Brown, *Dynamite on Our Doorstep* (New York, Greenberg, 1945), p. 287. This book has to be read with extreme caution due to its violent-tempered preoccupation with everything that seems to its author to be "anti-American"; a responsible American scholar on things Puerto Rican has aptly observed that the book is no more balanced than *Tobacco Road* would be if it were presented as a description of life in the United States, Clarence Senior, *Self-Determination for Puerto Rico* (New York, Post War Council, 1946), p. 29. A similar warning must be issued against Brown's later book on the Caribbean as a whole, *Angry Men, Laughing Men: The Caribbean Cauldron* (New York, Greenberg, 1947).

22. Ickes, *Secret Diary,* Vol. 1, p. 547.

23. *Ibid.*

24. Quoted in Mathews, *Puerto Rican Politics and the New Deal,* pp. 257-258.

25. Ickes, *Secret Diary,* Vol. 2, p. 6.

26. Quoted in Mathews, *Puerto Rican Politics and the New Deal,* p. 313. For the attitude of the Puerto Rican colonial government to what it termed these "several unfortunate occurrences," see Government of Puerto Rico, Bureau of

Supplies, Printing, and Transportation, *37th Annual Report of the Governor of Puerto Rico* (San Juan, 1937), p. 12.

27. Juan José Osuna, *A History of Education in Puerto Rico* (Rio Piedras, Ediciones de la Universidad de Puerto Rico, 1949), pp. 376-377.

28. Carlos E. Chardón, *Viajes y Naturaleza* (Caracas, Ediciones Sucre, 1941).

29. Dr. E. W. Brandes, quoted in Mathews, *Puerto Rican Politics and the New Deal,* p. 181.

30. Quoted, *Ibid.,* pp. 263-264.

31. Trumbull White, *Puerto Rico and Its People* (New York, Stokes, 1938), pp. 278-279.

32. Osuna, *A History of Education in Puerto Rico,* pp. 387-392.

33. Mathews, *Puerto Rican Politics and the New Deal,* p. 325.

34. Alpheus H. Snow, *The Administration of Dependencies* (New York and London, Putnam, 1902), p. 593.

35. *Ibid.,* pp. 587-590.

36. Ickes, *Secret Diary,* Vol. 1, p. 151.

CHAPTER 8

1. Thomas Mathews, *Puerto Rican Politics and the New Deal* (Gainesville, University of Florida Press, 1960), p. 295.

2. Quoted in Rexford G. Tugwell, *The Stricken Land* (New York, Doubleday, 1947), p. 39.

3. Olivo de Liebán Córdova, *Siete Años con Muñoz-Marín* (San Juan, Editorial Esther, 1945), pp. 46-50.

4. Domingo Targa, *El Modus Operandi de las Artes Electorales* (San Juan, Imprenta La Correspondencia, 1940), quoted in Mathews, *Puerto Rican Politics and the New Deal,* p. 303 and n. 46.

5. Victor S. Clark and associates, *Porto Rico and Its Problems* (Washington, Brookings Institution, 1930), p. 37.

6. For a full description of this early political campaign of 1938 see Liebán Córdova, *Siete Años con Muñoz-Marín,* pp. 39-96.

7. Wenzell Brown, *Dynamite on Our Doorstep,* p. 144.

8. Sidney W. Mintz, "Cañamelar: The Subculture of a Rural Sugar Plantation Proletariat," in Julian Steward, ed., *The People of Puerto Rico* (University of Illinois Press and Social Sciences Research Center, University of Puerto Rico, 1949), p. 397.

9. Theodore Roosevelt Jr., *Colonial Policies of the United States* (New York, Doubleday Doran, 1937), pp. 105-106.

10. Earl Parker Hanson, *Transformation: The Story of Modern Puerto Rico* (New York, Simon & Schuster, 1955), pp. 196-197.

11. Enrique Lugo-Silva, *The Tugwell Administration in Puerto Rico, 1941-46* (Rio Piedras, University of Puerto Rico, 1955). Apart from his autobiographical volume, *The Stricken Land,* Governor Tugwell's own account of his administration is reflected in his *Puerto Rican Public Papers* (San Juan, Government of Puerto Rico, 1945).

12. Government of Puerto Rico, Office of Information for Puerto Rico, *Three Fourths Ill-Fed, Ill-Clothed, Ill-Housed* (San Juan, 1943), p. 19.

13. Tugwell, *The Stricken Land,* pp. 252-253.

14. *Ibid.,* p. 148.

15. *Ibid.,* pp. 382-384.

16. Frank Torres Lopéz, *The Governor Goes Professor, A Glaring Story of Rexford Guy Tugwell: Puerto Rico's Reign of Expert Regimentation* (Ponce, Frank Torres Lopéz, 1946).

17. Tugwell, *The Stricken Land,* p. 469.

18. United States Senate, Committee on Territories and Insular Affairs, *Report of the Committee on Territories and Insular Affairs Pursuant to Senate Resolution No. 26,* 78th Congress, 1st Session (Washington, U.S. Government Printing Office, 1944), pp. 54-55.

19. United States Senate, *Congressional Record,* 78th Congress, 1st Session (Washington, U.S. Government Printing Office, February 25, 1943), pp. 1291-1293.

20. Tugwell, *The Stricken Land,* pp. 640-643.

21. C. L. R. James, *The Life of Captain Cipriani* (Nelson, Lancashire, England, Coulton & Co., 1932), p. 6.

22. Tugwell, *The Stricken Land,* p. 172.

23. *Ibid.,* pp. 143-148.

24. Harold L. Ickes, *The Secret Diary of Harold L. Ickes* (New York, Simon & Schuster, 1954), 3 vols., Vol. 3, p. 548.

25. Tugwell, *The Stricken Land,* pp. 545-547.

26. Marion Blythe, *An American Bride in Porto Rico* (New York, Fleming H. Revell, 1911).

27. House of Representatives, *Congressional Record,* 78th Congress, 1st Session (Washington, U.S. Government Printing Office, January 11, 1943), pp. 111-112.

28. Letter of Rafael Picó to the Secretary of the Interior, November 1945, printed in Hanson, *Transformation: The Story of Modern Puerto Rico,* pp. 58-59.

CHAPTER 9

1. Frederic P. Bartlett and associates, *A Development Plan for Puerto Rico* (San Juan, Puerto Rico Planning, Urbanizing and Zoning Board, Technical Paper No. 1, January 1944), p. 21.

2. Harvey S. Perloff, *Puerto Rico's Economic Future: A Study in Planned Development* (University of Chicago Press, 1949), p. 137.

3. Daniel Creamer, *The Net Income of the Puerto Rican Economy 1940-1944* (Rio Piedras, University of Puerto Rico, Social Sciences Research Center, 1947), p. 33.

4. Perloff, *Puerto Rico's Economic Future,* p. 165.

5. Manuel Márquez Sterling, *Las Conferencias de Shoreham: El Cesarismo en Cuba* (Mexico, 1933), p. 26.

6. Earl Parker Hanson, *Transformation: The Story of Modern Puerto Rico* (New York, Simon & Schuster, 1955); Stuart Chase, *"Operation Bootstrap" in Puerto Rico: Report of Progress* (Washington, National Planning Association, Public Pamphlet 75, 1951); Government of Puerto Rico, Government Development Bank, *The Progress of Puerto Rico, USA* (San Juan, 1950); American Academy of Political and Social Science, "Puerto Rico: A Study in Democratic Development," *Annals* (January 1953); David F. Ross, "The Costs and Benefits of Puerto Rico's Fomento Programmes," University College of the West Indies, *Social and Economic Studies* (September 1957); William H. Stead, *Fomento: The Economic Development of Puerto Rico* (Washington, National Planning Association, Public Pamphlet 103, 1958); and William Dorvillier, *Workshop U.S.A.: The Challenge of Puerto Rico* (New York, Coward-McCann, 1962).

7. Victor S. Clark and associates, *Porto Rico and Its Problems* (Washington, Brookings Institution, 1930), p. xxv.

8. Erich W. Zimmermann, *Staff Report to the Interdepartmental Committee on Puerto Rico* (Washington, mimeographed, September 9, 1940), p. 32.

9. Bartlett and associates, *A Development Plan for Puerto Rico,* p. 34.

10. W. Arthur Lewis, "The Industrialization of the British West Indies," *Caribbean Economic Review* (May 1950); and Caribbean Commission, British Section, Development and Welfare in the West Indies, *The Development of Primary and Secondary Industries in the Caribbean Area* (Bridgetown, Barbados, Bulletin No. 27, 1949).

11. Perloff, *Puerto Rico's Economic Future,* p. 53.

12. Teodoro Moscoso, *Logros y Metas de la Industrialización en Puerto Rico* (San Juan, Administración de Fomento Económico, 1955).

13. Lewis, "The Industrialization of the British West Indies," pp. 37-38.

14. Puerto Rico Planning Board, Bureau of Economics and Statistics, *Net Income and Gross Product, Puerto Rico: 1940 and 1947-1955* (San Juan, 1956), pp. 3-4.

15. Economic Development Administration, Office of Economic Research, *Social Directions in Industrial Development* (San Juan, mimeographed, January 3, 1957), p. 5.

16. José M. García Calderón, in *El Imparcial,* November 14, 1954.

17. Hearings of Special Committee of the Legislature on the Sugar Industry, in *El Mundo,* October 9, 1957; also remarks of Orestes Ramos, *El Mundo,* July 7, November 12, 1962.

18. Speech of Governor Luis Muñoz Marín on agriculture, in *El Mundo,* April 24, 1959.

19. For all this see Nathan Koenig and associates, *A Comprehensive Agricultural Program for Puerto Rico* (Washington, Department of Agriculture, 1953); Donald J. O'Connor, *The Developmental Potential of the Sugar Industry of Puerto Rico* (Rio Piedras, University of Puerto Rico, June 1959); Commonwealth Government of Puerto Rico, House of Representatives, *Report on Measures to Develop a Sound Permanent Economic Structure for the Coffee Region of Puerto Rico* (San Juan, March 1948); Walter E. Packard, "The Land Authority and Democratic Processes in Puerto Rico," *Inter-American Economic Affairs* (Summer 1948); Report on Agriculture of Juan B. Gaztambide Associates, in *El Mundo,* December 18, 1959; Report of the President of the Puerto Rico Farmers Association, *El Mundo,* July 7, 1962; and Mathew D. Edel, "Land Reform in Puerto Rico, 1941-1959," *Caribbean Studies* (Rio Piedras, October 1962, January 1963).

20. Puerto Rico Planning Board, *Net Income and Gross Product, Puerto Rico: 1940 and 1947-1955,* p. 23.

21. *Ibid.,* pp. 25-27.

22. *San Juan Star,* August 31, 1960; and article by Patrick McMahon in *San Juan Star,* October 27, 1961. For a more favorable discussion of the transferability of the Puerto Rican industrialization program to other underdeveloped economies, see Stead, *Fomento: The Economic Development of Puerto Rico,* pp. 107-124, and James C. Ingram, *Regional Payments Mechanisms: The Case of Puerto Rico* (Chapel Hill, University of North Carolina Press, 1962), pp. 134-143.

23. Henry K. Carroll, *Report on the Industrial and Commercial Condition of Porto Rico* (Washington, U.S. Government Printing Office, 1899), pp. 22-23. It should be noted that this report cited here is quite distinct from the other report of Carroll made around the same time, *Report on the Island of Porto Rico,* and quoted elsewhere in the text.

NOTES TO PAGES 190–198

CHAPTER 10

1. British West Indies, Barbados, *House of Assembly Debates* (Bridgetown, Barbados, July 19, 1954), pp. 1124-1125.

2. Puerto Rico Planning Board, Bureau of Economics and Statistics, *Net Income and Gross Product, Puerto Rico: 1940 and 1947-1955* (San Juan, 1956), p. 27 and Table 10.

3. Quoted in *El Mundo*, May 17, 1957.

4. David F. Ross, "The Costs and Benefits of Puerto Rico's Fomento Programmes," in University College of the West Indies, *Social and Economic Studies* (September 1957), p. 343.

5. *New York Times*, August 18, 1956.

6. *New York Times*, February 11, 1957, and *San Juan Star*, October 20, 1961.

7. Milton C. Taylor, "Tax Exemption and New Industry in Puerto Rico," University College of the West Indies, *Social and Economic Studies* (June 1955), p. 121; also by the same author, *Industrial Tax Exemption in Puerto Rico: A Case Study in the Use of Tax Subsidies for Industrializing Underdeveloped Areas* (Madison, University of Wisconsin Press, 1957).

8. For selected examples in the case of American economic federalism, see Arthur W. MacMahon, ed., *Federalism Mature and Emergent* (Garden City, New York, Doubleday, 1955), pp. 300, 322, 345, 354-360.

9. Editorial "A Punta de Pistola," *El Mundo*, January 20, 1962.

10. Hugh Barton, *Puerto Rico's Industrial Future* (San Juan, Puerto Rico Economic Association, mimeographed, 1957), p. 2.

11. Robert R. Nathan Associates, *An Evaluation of Minimum Wage Policy in Puerto Rico*, Prepared for the Joint Committee on Labor of the Legislature of the Commonwealth of Puerto Rico (Washington, mimeographed, November 1955), pp. 13-17.

12. Luis Muñoz Marín, "Our Progress in Puerto Rico," AFL-CIO *The American Federationist* (July 1959), pp. 8-9.

13. *Wall Street Journal*, quoted in *The Island Times*, April 5, 1957.

14. *El Mundo*, March 11, 1958.

15. *El Mundo*, January 29, 1960.

16. Harvey S. Perloff, *Puerto Rico's Economic Future: A Study in Planned Development* (University of Chicago Press, 1949), p. 128.

17. Economic Development Administration, Office of Economic Research, *An Appraisal of Fomento Programs* (San Juan, mimeographed, October 24, 1955), pp. 22-23.

18. *El Mundo*, July 16, 1957.

19. Statement of the Planning Board, quoted in *El Mundo*, October 23, 1956.

20. Barton, *Puerto Rico's Industrial Future*, pp. 1-2.

21. Gunnar Myrdal, *Economic Theory and Underdeveloped Regions* (London, Duckworth, 1957), pp. 58-62. For a discussion of the advantages and disadvantages of "enforced bilateralism" in the special field of balance of payments problems, see James C. Ingram, *Regional Payments Mechanisms: The Case of Puerto Rico* (Chapel Hill, University of North Carolina Press, 1962). The Commonwealth Government, through its Department of Commerce, has recently spearheaded a drive to expand its Caribbean commercial and trading activities. But it remains yet to be seen whether (1) this is anything more than an exercise in Puerto Rican economic imperialism, under the protection of the United States tariff wall and (2) the existing restrictions upon Puerto Rico's freedom of trade will permit Puerto Rican participation in, for example, a Caribbean customs union venture.

22. Teodoro Moscoso, "Industrial Development in Puerto Rico," in American Academy of Political and Social Science, *Annals* (January 1953), p. 67.

23. *El Mundo*, March 29, 1957.

24. Perloff, *Puerto Rico's Economic Future*, pp. 266-277.

25. For all this see *El Mundo*, August 11, 1961; *El Imparcial*, January 6, 1962; *Annual Report of the Governor of Porto Rico to the Secretary of War* (Washington, U.S. Government Printing Office, 1925), p. 55; and Collett and Clapp Associates, *Estudio sobre la Organización Necessaria para el Desarrollo de Servicios de Transportación y Comunicaciones en Puerto Rico* (San Juan, mimeographed, N.D.).

26. Charles Gore, article on Puerto Rico, *Daily Gleaner* (Kingston, Jamaica), June 12, 1960.

27. Editorial, "Transportación en Masa," *El Mundo*, October 28, 1958.

28. Harvey S. Perloff, *Education for Planning, City, State and Regional* (Baltimore, Johns Hopkins Press, 1957), pp. 141-142.

29. Antonio Kayanan, "On Certain Misconceptions," *San Juan Star*, July 14, 1961.

30. Santiago Iglesias hijo, "La Perla de Jane Drew," *El Mundo*, June 22, 1961.

31. Quoted in *El Mundo*, October 8, 1956.

32. *El Mundo*, September 12, October 27, 1958.

33. The Puerto Rican press carries continuing references to this problem of the discriminating effects of the United States shipping legislation and the struggle to develop a Puerto Rican independent maritime service. See also the report on *Puerto Rico's Problem with the United States Maritime Laws* issued by the Commonwealth Government of Puerto Rico, Ports Authority (San Juan, 1961). See also the testimony of Puerto Rican witnesses in the hearings of the Federal Maritime Commission in San Juan, December 1962, especially the testimony of the Director of the Fomento Office of Economic Research, in *San Juan Star*, December 15, 1962.

34. Samuel Eastman and Daniel Marx, *Ships and Sugar: An Evaluation of Puerto Rican Offshore Shipping* (Rio Piedras, University of Puerto Rico Press, 1953), p. 215.

35. Economic Development Administration, *An Appraisal of Fomento Programs*, p. 33.

36. Statement of Movimiento Pro-Independencia, "Control Federal de la Vida Puertorriqueña," reprinted in *El Mundo*, March 30, 1959. See also Movimiento Pro-Independencia, *La Hora de la Independencia: Tesis Política MPI* (San Juan, Movimiento Pro-Independencia, 1963), Chapter 1.

37. Everett V. Reimer, *A Reply to "The Predictive Process"* (San Juan, mimeographed, 1961), p. 34.

38. Government of Puerto Rico, *Brief of the Government of Puerto Rico Presented to the Committee for Reciprocity Information* (Washington, Office of Puerto Rico, January 1947), pp. 60-61.

39. Robert E. Cushman, *The Independent Regulatory Commissions* (New York, Oxford University Press, 1941), pp. 730-733.

40. Marver H. Bernstein, *Regulating Business by Independent Commission* (Princeton University Press, 1955), pp. 294-296; C. Wilcox, *Public Policies Toward Business* (Homewood, Illinios, Irwin, 1955); Walter Adams and Horace M. Gray, *Monopoly in America: The Government as Promotor* (New York, Macmillan, 1955).

41. James M. Landis, *Report on Regulatory Agencies to the President-Elect* (Ad Press, New York, December 1960), pp. 41, 65.

42. Quoted by Ernesto Ramos Antonini in *El Mundo*, July 24, 1961.

43. Political and Economic Planning, *Management and Underdeveloped Territories* (London, 1959).

44. *El Mundo*, August 10, 1961.

45. *El Mundo,* October 12, 1961.

46. Joseph Airov, *The Location of the Synthetic-Fiber Industry* (New York, Technical Press of the Massachusetts Institute of Technology and John Wiley & Sons, 1959), pp. 148-149.

47. Cándido Oliveras and Alvin Mayne, *The Puerto Rican Economy and Social Scene and Trends for the Future* (San Juan, Puerto Rico Planning Board, mimeographed, 1958), pp. 37-38.

48. *El Mundo,* August 22, 1961.

CHAPTER 11

1. Peter Gregory, "El Desarrollo de la Fuerza Obrera Industrial en Puerto Rico," *Revista de Ciencias Sociales* (University of Puerto Rico, December 1958), pp. 447-468.

2. Robert R. Nathan Associates, *An Evaluation of Minimum Wage Policy in Puerto Rico,* Prepared for the Joint Committee on Labor of the Legislature of the Commonwealth of Puerto Rico (Washington, mimeographed, November 1955), p. 12.

3. *Ibid.,* p. 96.

4. Quoted in *El Mundo,* March 8, 1957.

5. *El Mundo,* February 20, 1959.

6. *El Mundo,* February 10, 1958.

7. *El Mundo,* August 3, 1959.

8. *El Mundo,* February 5, 1957.

9. Luis Muñoz Marín, *El Estado Libre Asociado: Casa de Buena Voluntad* (San Juan, Editorial del Departamento de Instrucción Pública, 1956).

10. Nathan Associates, *An Evaluation of Minimum Wage Policy in Puerto Rico,* p. 112.

11. See, for example, House of Representatives, Committee on Education and Labor, *Hearings . . . on Bills relating to Minimum Wages in Certain Territories, Possessions and Overseas Areas of the United States,* 84th Congress, 2nd Session (Washington, U.S. Government Printing Office, 1956), Part 1, pp. 92-95.

12. *El Mundo,* December 14, 1957, and February 20, 1959.

13. See the testimony of Walter J. Mason, Legislative Representative AFL-CIO, House of Representatives, Committee on Education and Labor, *Hearings &c,* Part 1, pp. 149-152, and the testimony of the President of the Central Labor Union-Metal Trades Council of the Panama Canal Zone, *Ibid.,* Part 2, pp. 435-437.

14. Nathan Associates, *An Evaluation of Minimum Wage Policy in Puerto Rico,* p. 101.

15. *Ibid.,* pp. 35-36.

16. *El Mundo,* May 20, 1958.

17. Puerto Rico Planning Board, *Informe Económico,* quoted in *El Mundo,* May 16, 1959; and Cámara de Representantes, *Informe de la Comisión Especial sobre la Industria de Aguja,* quoted in *El Mundo,* May 20, 1958.

18. Santiago Iglesias Pantín, *Luchas Emancipadoras* (San Juan, Cantero Fernández, 1929), pp. 90-94.

19. David F. Ross, "Gordon Lewis on Puerto Rico's Development Program," *Journal of Politics* (February 1957).

20. *El Mundo,* December 31, 1958.

21. Antonio J. Colorado and Fernando M. Torres, "La Automatización y el Hombre," *El Mundo,* March 15, 1958.

22. Nathan Associates, *An Evaluation of Minimum Wage Policy in Puerto Rico,* p. 56.

23. Joseph E. Finley, *The National Labor Relations Board: The Record Under the Eisenhower Administration* (Washington, Public Affairs Institute, 1957).

24. *El Mundo,* March 21, 1960.

25. *El Mundo,* November 13, 25, 1958.

26. *El Imparcial,* September 19, 1959.

27. Elena Padilla, "Nocorá: The Subculture of Workers in a Government-owned Sugar Plantation," in Julian Steward, ed., *The People of Puerto Rico* (University of Illinois Press and Social Sciences Research Center, University of Puerto Rico, 1949), pp. 265-313.

28. Escuela de Salud Pública y Medicina Administrativa de la Universidad de Columbia y el Departamento de Salud de Puerto Rico, *Estudio sobre Servicios Médico-Hospitalarios* (San Juan, December 1960), p. 93; and the fuller report in English, Columbia University, School of Public Health and Administrative Medicine, and Department of Health of Puerto Rico, *Medical and Hospital Care in Puerto Rico* (San Juan, February 1962).

29. *El Mundo,* June 11, 1958. For this same matter of the state of the insular prisons see the series of revealing articles by Ralph Carazo, *The Island Times,* April 19, 26 and May 3, 1963.

30. *El Mundo,* July 15, 1958, and August 13, 1959.

31. United States Senate, Committee on Labor and Public Welfare, *Puerto Rico's Elders: A Factual Report to the White House Conference on Aging,* in *A Report by the Subcommittee on Problems of the Aged and Aging* (Washington, U.S. Government Printing Office, 1960), Part XI.

32. Charles Rosario, *Cambios en Algunas Instituciones y Estructuras Sociales* (Rio Piedras, Universidad de Puerto Rico, mimeographed, March 1957), pp. 16-17.

33. Simon Rottenberg, "Labor's Role in Industrialization," in American Academy of Political and Social Science, "Puerto Rico: A Study in Democratic Development," *Annals* (January 1953), pp. 85-90.

34. Roy G. Francis, *The Predictive Process* (Rio Piedras, Social Sciences Research Center, University of Puerto Rico, 1960), pp. 126-130.

35. Everett V. Reimer, *A Reply to "The Predictive Process"* (San Juan, mimeographed, 1961), pp. 32-33.

36. Quoted in Julian Steward, ed., *The People of Puerto Rico,* p. 398.

37. American Federation of Labor, Annual Convention, *Proceedings* (1900), pp. 115-116, quoted in Antonio J. González, "Apuntes para la Historia del Movimiento Sindical de Puerto Rico," *Revista de Ciencias Sociales* (September 1957), pp. 453-455. See also Julio Rivera Rivera, "Orígenes de la Organización Obrera en Puerto Rico, 1838-1898," *Historia* (April 1955), pp. 91-112.

38. *El Mundo,* December 31, 1958.

39. Remarks of Hipólito Marcano, in *El Mundo,* June 14, 1958.

40. Statement of Hipólito Marcano and Alberto E. Sánchez, in *El Mundo,* August 4, 1961.

41. Luis Silva Recio, *Effects of Public Wage-Fixing on Labor and Collective Bargaining in Puerto Rico* (unpublished Ph.D thesis, University of Puerto Rico, Institute of Labor Relations, 1960), especially Chapter 4, "Labor's Participation in the Minimum-Wage Process."

42. *Ibid.,* p. 166.

43. Quoted in González, "Apuntes para la Historia del Movimiento Sindical," p. 466.

44. *Ibid.*

45. See, for example, *Informe del Comité de Muelles,* quoted in *El Mundo,* December 18, 1956. The attitude, elsewhere in the Caribbean, of a progressive trade union like the Barbados Workers' Union in Barbados, to the problems created by necessary technical advances in traditional Caribbean industries is of much interest as a comparison to the Puerto Rican case. See Barbados Workers' Union, *Seventeenth Annual Report* (Bridgetown, Barbados, 1958).

46. Santiago Iglesias Pantín, *Luchas Emancipadoras,* p. 52.

47. *Ibid.,* p. 55.

48. *Ibid.,* pp. 118-119.

CHAPTER 12

1. Kurt W. Back, Reuben Hill and J. Mayone Stycos, "The Puerto Rican Field Experiment in Population Control," *Human Relations* (November 1957), pp. 315-334. For a general criticism of American sociological work on Puerto Rico from a Puerto Rican sociologist, see Luis Nieves Falcón, "La Investigación Sociológica en Puerto Rico: Possibilidades y Limitaciones," in Congreso Latinoamericano de Sociología, *Memoria* (Caracas, 1961), Vol. 1, pp. 167-173.

2. Raymond Scheele, "The Prominent Families of Puerto Rico," in Julian Steward, ed., *The People of Puerto Rico* (University of Illinois Press and Social Sciences Research Center, University of Puerto Rico, 1949), p. 440.

3. Economic Development Administration, Department of Industrial Services, *Puerto Rican General Managers in Fomento Plants* (San Juan, mimeographed, November 26, 1958).

4. Puerto Rico Planning Board, Bureau of Economic Statistics, *Net Income and Gross Product, Puerto Rico: 1940 and 1947-1955* (San Juan, 1956), Table 21 and pp. 180-183.

5. *El Mundo,* October 27, 1958.

6. H. Ramírez, "A Socio-Economic Study of South-Western Puerto Rico," *Journal of Agriculture of the University of Puerto Rico* (August 1947); Felix Mejías, *Condiciones de la Vida de las Clases Jornaleras de Puerto Rico* (Río Piedras, Junta Editora de la Universidad de Puerto Rico, 1946). For general conditions a decade earlier, see P. Morales Otero, Manuel Pérez and others, "Health and Socio-Economic Conditions in the Tobacco, Coffee and Fruit Regions," *Puerto Rican Journal of Public Health and Tropical Medicine* (October 1938); and, by the same authors, "Health and Socio-Economic Conditions on a Sugar Cane Plantation," *Puerto Rican Journal of Public Health and Tropical Medicine* (June 1937).

7. Steward, ed., *The People of Puerto Rico,* p. 487.

8. Arthur Vidich, *Material on the Class Structure of Trujillo Alto* (Río Piedras, University of Puerto Rico, mimeographed, 1959), pp. 67-69. This type of material must be read with caution, for despite its very proper emphasis upon the peculiar tensions of Puerto Rican life, at all class levels, its basic premises in the sociological concepts of conflict and competition debar it from a full appreciation of the countervailing elements present, especially in Puerto Rican working class life. The individual Puerto Rican proletarian *barrio* has much of a popular collectivism about it: its sense of mutual aid in crisis, its social tolerance of illegitimacy, its widespread kinship family form which acts as a rude method of social insurance, and its social friendliness so much absent in the new life-style of the modernizing urbanizations. An American sociology concerned more with social structure than with social spirit is bound to miss much of this. For a more sympathetic view of the life of the Puerto Rican hill towns, see Norman Thomas di Giovanni, "A Farm in the Hills,"

Atlantic Monthly (December 1962). The life of the rural interior has also been annotated with perceptive affection throughout the last few years by John Hawes in his weekly column, "The Islander," in *The Island Times.*

9. Enrique Laguerre, *Pulso de Puerto Rico* (San Juan, Biblioteca de Autores Puertorriqueños, 1954), p. 67.

10. Charles F. Cannell, Fred G. Wale and Stephen B. Withey, eds., "Community Change: An Action Program in Puerto Rico," *Journal of Social Issues* (June 1953), pp. 1-57.

11. Lidio Cruz Monclova, *Historia de Puerto Rico (Siglo XIX)* (Rio Piedras, Editorial Universitaria, Universidad de Puerto Rico, 1958), 3 vols., Vol. 1, p. 666.

12. Napoleon Hill, "Ciencia del Exito," *El Mundo,* September 8, 13, 24, 28, 1957.

13. Harold W. Brown and Bion R. East, *A Study of Puerto Rico's Physician and Dentist Needs* (Rio Piedras, University of Puerto Rico, mimeographed, January 1955), pp. 21-22.

14. Columbia University, School of Public Health and Administrative Medicine, and Department of Health of Puerto Rico, *Medical and Hospital Care in Puerto Rico* (San Juan, February 1962), pp. 31-32; and *El Mundo,* August 16, 18, 1961.

15. Brown and East, *A Study of Puerto Rico's Physician and Dentist Needs,* p. 38.

16. *El Mundo,* August 4, 1961.

17. For all this see *El Mundo,* September 5, December 2, 1961; and *Revista de Ciencias Sociales* (March 1960), p. 176.

18. Richard M. Morse, *The Higher Learning in Puerto Rico* (Rio Piedras, Faculty of General Studies, University of Puerto Rico, mimeographed, 1959), p. 19.

19. Steward, ed., *The People of Puerto Rico,* p. 498.

20. José Colombán Rosario, *Problemas Sociales: La Prostitución en Puerto Rico* (Rio Piedras, University of Puerto Rico, 1951), pp. 91-93. See also the series of articles by Helen V. Tooker in *The Island Times,* June 7, 14, 1963. The anomalies of Puerto Rican law are illustrated by the curious fact that abortion is illegal, whereas prostitution is not. For the abortion racket in Puerto Rico, see *El Mundo,* May 9, 1963, and *San Juan Star,* May 8, 9, 10, 1963.

21. *Informe de la Junta de Planificación,* quoted in *El Mundo,* March 29, 1957.

22. Letter quoted by Frank Otto Gatell, "San Juan Under Spain in the 1830's," *The Island Times,* August 28, 1959.

23. See correspondence on this point, *The Island Times,* July 10, 1959.

24. Stuart Chase, *"Operation Bootstrap" in Puerto Rico: Report of Progress* (Washington, National Planning Association, Public Pamphlet 75, 1951), p. 45.

25. Eleanor Maccoby and Francis Fielder, *Savings Among Upper-Income Families in Puerto Rico* (Rio Piedras, University of Puerto Rico Press, 1953), pp. 69-70. See also Lydia J. Roberts and Rosa Luisa Stefani, *Patterns of Living in Puerto Rican Families* (Rio Piedras, University of Puerto Rico, 1949). For the continuing income inequalities of the Puerto Rican economy, see Euladio Rodríquez Otero, "Lo Que No Se Dice Sobre Nuestro Desarrollo Económico," *Boricua* (December 1962). For a more optimistic view, much of it based upon questionable statistical exercises, see Commonwealth Government of Puerto Rico, Committee on Human Resources, *Unemployment, Family Income and Level of Living in Puerto Rico* (San Juan, November 1959).

26. From the report of a New York psychiatrist (not named) on San Juan middle class patterns of work and living, in *El Mundo,* September 1, 1959. For the general anti-cultural bias of these middle class patterns see the acid remarks of Ricardo Alegría, in *El Mundo,* December 1, 1962.

27. Peter Gregory, "Worker Attitudes Toward Authority and Supervision," Economic Development Administration, *Management Information Bulletin* (San Juan, March 12, 1959).

28. Walter E. Weyl, "Labor Conditions in Porto Rico," *Bulletin of the Bureau of Labor,* United States Department of Commerce and Labor (November 1905), p. 776.

29. Letter of Charles Emerson, January 19, 1833, quoted by Frank Otto Gatell, "San Juan Under Spain in the 1830's," *The Island Times,* September 4, 1959.

30. Steward, ed., *The People of Puerto Rico,* p. 488.

31. Melvin M. Tumin and Arnold Feldman, *Social Class and Social Change in Puerto Rico* (Princeton University Press, 1961), p. 477.

32. *Ibid.,* p. 458.

33. M. G. Smith, "Social and Cultural Pluralism," in *Social and Cultural Pluralism in the Caribbean,* Annals of the New York Academy of Sciences (January 1960), pp. 763-785.

34. Charles Wagley, "Recent Studies of Caribbean Local Societies," in A. Curtis Wilgus, ed., *The Caribbean: Natural Resources* (Gainesville, University of Florida Press, 1959), p. 203.

CHAPTER 13

1. J. Mayone Stycos, *Family and Fertility in Puerto Rico* (New York, Columbia University Press, 1955), p. 248.

2. *Ibid.,* Chapters 4, 6.

3. Kathleen L. Wolf, "Growing Up and Its Price in Three Puerto Rican Subcultures," in Eugenio Fernández-Méndez, ed., *Portrait of a Society: A Book of Readings on Puerto Rican Society* (Rio Piedras, University of Puerto Rico, 1956), p. 238.

4. *El Mundo,* February 4, 1960.

5. Stycos, *Family and Fertility in Puerto Rico,* p. 122.

6. Charles Rosario, "Dos Tipos del Amor Romántico," *Revista de Ciencias Sociales* (September 1958), pp. 349-360.

7. Efrain Sanchez Hidalgo, "Posibles Efectos de la Industrialización Rapida sobre la Familia Puertorriqueña," in Convención de Orientacion Social de Puerto Rico, *Octava Convención de Orientación Social de Puerto Rico* (San Juan, 1955), pp. 104-105.

8. Puerto Rico Planning Board, Bureau of Economics and Statistics, *Anuario Estadístico 1956* (San Juan, 1957), Tables 63-68.

9. Commonwealth Government of Puerto Rico, Civil Liberties Committee, *Informe sobre Discrímenes por Motivo de Raza, Color, Sexo, Nacimiento y Condición Social* (San Juan, mimeographed, November 10, 1958), p. 25; in printed form in *Revista del Colegio de Abogados de Puerto Rico* (May 1962).

10. Tomás Blanco, *El Prejucio Racial en Puerto Rico* (San Juan, Biblioteca de Autores Puertorriqueños, 1942), pp. 89-90.

11. Alejandro Tapia y Rivera, *Mis Memorias, o Puerto Rico como lo Encontré y como lo Dejo* (New York, De Laisne & Rossboro, 1928), p. 122.

12. Stycos, *Family and Fertility in Puerto Rico,* p. 160.

13. Felix S. Cohen, "Science and Politics in Plans for Puerto Rico," *Journal of Social Issues* (Fall 1947).

14. Quoted in Fernández-Méndez, ed., *Portrait of a Society,* pp. 133-134.

15. University College of the West Indies, Institute of Social and Economic Research, *The Rastafari Movement in Kingston, Jamaica* (Mona, Jamaica, 1960).

16. Arthur James, *Thirty Years in Porto Rico* (San Juan, Porto Rico Progress, 1927), p. 37.

17. *Ibid.,* p. 34.

18. J. Merle Davis, *The Church in Puerto Rico's Dilemma* (New York, International Missionary Council, 1942), p. 63.

19. *Ibid.,* pp. 68-69.

20. J. Mayone Stycos, Kurt Back and Reuben Hill, "Contraception and Catholicism in Puerto Rico," *Millbank Memorial Fund Quarterly* (April 1956), p. 158.

21. Melvin J. Tumin and Arnold S. Feldman, "The Miracle at Sabana Grande," *Public Opinion Quarterly* (Summer 1955). For the continuing problems of Catholic organizational work in the island parishes see the various articles in William Ferree, Joseph P. Fitzpatrick and John D. Illich, eds., *Report on the First Conference on the Spiritual Care of Puerto Rican Migrants* (New York, Office of Coordinator of Spanish-American Catholic Action, 1955), especially Rev. Gregory Loebach, "Problems of Religious Practice on the Island."

22. Luis Díaz Soler, *Rosendo Matienzo Cintrón: Recopilación de su Obra Escrita* (Rio Piedras, Ediciones de la Literatura Puertorriqueña, Universidad de Puerto Rico, 1960), 2 vols., Vol. 1, pp. 621-634, Vol. 2, pp. 423-504.

23. *El Debate,* San Juan and Ponce, August 12, 1962.

24. For all this see "Open Letter to Their Excellencies . . . ," *San Juan Star,* July 4, 1962; Movimiento Pro-Independencia, *Carta Semanal,* June 20, 1962; *El Mundo,* August 6, 1962; and *El Imparcial,* July 13, 1962. For a more extensive criticism of the official Catholic leadership by another lay Catholic group, see *Carta a Monseñor Manuel Clarizio, Nuncio Papal en Santo Domingo y Delegado Apostólico para Puerto Rico,* signed by Euladio Rodriquez Otero, José M. Lazaro and others, in *El Mundo,* November 7, 1962.

25. *El Mundo,* April 17, May 7, 12, September 27, October 18, 29, November 3, 6, 1956.

26. Remarks of Senator Cruz Ortiz Stella, in *El Mundo,* December 7, 1956.

27. United States Senate, Report of the Committee on Interior and Insular Affairs, quoted in *El Mundo,* June 11, 1952.

28. Commonwealth Government of Puerto Rico, Civil Liberties Committee, *La Libertad de Religión* (San Juan, mimeographed, 1959), p. 15.

29. *Ibid.,* pp. 14-15.

30. Rafael de Jesús Toro, "Obispos no Deben Endosar Inscripción PAC," *El Mundo,* August 23, 1960.

31. Henry Wells, "Administrative Reorganization in Puerto Rico," *Western Political Quarterly* (June 1956), p. 486. For a more judicious estimate of Puerto Rican social problems, including that of racial prejudice, see Pablo Morales Otero, *Nuestros Problemas* (San Juan, Biblioteca de Autores Puertorriqueños, 1947), especially pp. 191-196. An additional rationalization sometimes advanced by Puerto Rican patriotic sources is that racial prejudice, if it exists, is of American origin. See, for example, Movimiento Pro-Independencia, *Tesis Política: La Hora de la Independencia* (San Juan, Movimiento Pro-Independencia, 1963), pp. 87-88.

32. Cayetano Coll y Toste, ed., *Boletín Histórico de Puerto Rico* (San Juan, Cantero Fernández, 1923), Vol. 10, p. 72.

33. Henry K. Carroll, *Report on the Island of Porto Rico,* p. 51. This liberal tradition in racial matters has been a part of the Puerto Rican radical spirit, as, for example, in the figure of Ramon Betances. For Betances, see Maria Luisa de Angelís, *Ramon E. Betances: Su Vida y Su Labor Política* (San German, Maria Luisa de Angelís, 1913), pp. 15-17.

34. José Colombán Rosario and Justina Carrión, *Problemas Sociales: El Negro* (Rio Piedras, Universidad de Puerto Rico, 1940), pp. 125-126.

35. Trumbull White, *Porto Rico and Its People* (New York, Stokes, 1938), p. 258.

36. Exchange of correspondence between Mary Weld Coates and Charles W. St. John, *Current History* (April-September 1922), pp. 650-651.

37. *Puerto Rico Libre* (San Juan), February 26, 1944.

38. Raymond Scheele, "The Prominent Families of Puerto Rico," in Julian Steward, ed., *The People of Puerto Rico* (University of Illinois Press and Social Sciences Research Center, University of Puerto Rico, 1949), pp. 424-425.

39. Salvador Arana Soto, "Refutando a Luis Palés Matos," *El Mundo,* May 25, 1959. For a more sympathetic treatment of Palés Matos, see Tomás Blanco, *Sobre Palés Matos* (San Juan, Biblioteca de Autores Puertorriqueños, 1950). Yet even such a humanist spirit as Tomás Blanco is still obviously puzzled by his compatriot's identification, as a white Puerto Rican artist, with the Caribbean Afro-Negroid cultural tradition. The Puerto Rican Negro, in his uniquely Hispanized milieu, as distinct from the Haitian or the Martiniquan Negro, has been later treated by the poet Cesáreo Rosa-Nieves, *Diapasón Negro* (San Juan, Editorial Campos, 1960). For the leading present-day Negro poet, Victorio Llanes Allende, see Juan Díaz de Andino, *El Mundo, Suplemento Sabatino,* December 1, 1962.

40. José Colombán Rosario and Justina Carrión, *Problemas Sociales: El Negro,* pp. 144-158.

41. Commonwealth Government of Puerto Rico, Civil Liberties Committee, *Informe sobre Discrímenes por Motivo de Raza . . .,* pp. 1-18.

42. Melvin M. Tumin and Arnold Feldman, *Social Class and Social Change in Puerto Rico* (Princeton University Press, 1961), p. 233.

43. Commonwealth Government of Puerto Rico, Civil Liberties Committee, *Informe sobre Discrímenes por Motivo de Raza . . .,* p. 8.

44. Tumin and Feldman, *Social Class and Social Change in Puerto Rico,* p. 233.

45. *Brown v. Board of Education,* 349 U.S. 294, 300 (1954); and the text of the brief of the National Association for the Advancement of Colored People to the United States Supreme Court in the *New York Times,* September 11, 1958.

46. *El Mundo,* November 6, 1961.

CHAPTER 14

1. Marion Blythe, *An American Bride in Porto Rico* (New York, Fleming H. Revell, 1911), pp. 158-159. For a volume of pleasing reminiscence about life in old San Juan and Ponce under the Spanish and early American regimes, see Albert E. Lee, *An Island Grows,* ed. Earl Parker Hanson (San Juan, Albert E. Lee & Son, 1963).

2. *Current History* (April-September 1922), pp. 650-651.

3. Vicente Balbás Capó, *Porto Rico a los Diez Años de Americanización* (San Juan, Tipografía Heraldo Español, 1910), pp. 13-15. For a general comparative discussion of the Spanish and American colonial regimes, heavily in favor of the American, see Rafael López Landron, *Cartas Abiertas a el Pueblo de Puerto Rico* (San Juan, Imprenta Venezuela, 1928).

4. William Dinwiddie, *Porto Rico and Its Possibilities* (New York and London, Harpers, 1899), p. 166.

5. Juan B. Soto, *Causas y Consecuencias: Antecedentes Diplomáticos y Efectos de la Guerra Hispanoamericana* (San Juan, La Correspondencia, 1922), p. 248. For a typical example of the abject adulation of the new American masters after 1898, see Néstor I. Vincenty, *La Civilización Americana y el Porvenir de Puerto Rico* (San Juan, Negociado de Materiales, Imprenta y Transporte, 1928), a high school

address distributed to the schools by the Department of Education as an apt expression of the official American educational policy.

6. Roy Schuckman, *Puerto Rican Neighbor* (Pendle Hill, Pennsylvania, 1954).

7. Antonio S. Pedreira, *Insularismo: Ensayos de Interpretación Puertorriqueña* (San Juan, Biblioteca de Autores Puertorriqueños, 1934), p. 99.

8. *Ibid.,* p. 200.

9. *Ibid.,* p. 104.

10. Thomas Hayes, in *El Mundo,* December 14, 1954.

11. Antonio J. Colorado, in *El Imparcial,* December 19, 1954.

12. Pedreira, *Insularismo,* pp. 97-101. For Pedreira generally, see Fernando Sierra Berdecía, *Antonio S. Pedreira: Buceador de la Personalidad Puertorriqueña* (San Juan, Biblioteca de Autores Puertorriqueños, 1942). For critical estimates by sympathetic *independentista* writers, see Margot Arce de Vázquez, *Impresiones: Notas Puertorriqueñas* (San Juan, Editorial Yaurel, 1950), and Manuel Maldonado Denis, "Visión y Revisión de Insularismo," *Asomante* (San Juan, January-March, 1963). The more radical of the friendly critics note the socially conservative emphasis of Pedreira; thus Margot Arce aptly comments that Pedreira "does not identify the real essence of democracy, nor does he perceive the falsification of democracy worked by colonialism. . . . The evils he attributes to the democratic system are not the evils of democracy as such but of a particular interpretation of democracy" (*Impresiones,* pp. 117-119).

13. Eugenio Fernández-Méndez, *Filiación y Sentido de una Isla* (San Juan, Departamento de Instrucción Pública, 1955), pp. 6-8.

14. *El Imparcial,* May 17, 1957.

15. Ismael Rodríguez Bou, "Los Medios de Comunicación y la Opinión Pública," *El Mundo,* September 19, 1957.

16. Ernesto J. Ruiz de la Mata, "Teatro, Vejigante y Cultura," *El Mundo,* November 3, 1958.

17. Miguel Angel Yumet, in *El Imparcial,* August 31, 1957.

18. Francisco M. Zeno, quoted in Julian H. Steward, ed., *The People of Puerto Rico* (University of Illinois Press and Social Sciences Research Center, University of Puerto Rico, 1949), p. 172.

19. Julio Soto Ramos, *Un Panorama Cultural en Cueros* (Barcelona, Imprenta Suñol, 1960). The sort of xenophobia here referred to reflects, in one way, the confusion in the Puerto Rican mind as to what constitutes Puerto Rican "culture." One report on the cultural values that the Puerto Rican school is seen as defending thus includes the astonishing list of hospitality, friendship, generosity, Christian charity, personal dignity, love of order, respect for old age, love of children, devotion to work, and faith in education as a means of resolving individual and national problems. See Consejo Superior de Enseñanza, División de Investigaciones Pedagógicas, "Hacia Una Filosofia Educativa para Puerto Rico," *Estudio del Sistema Educativo de Puerto Rico* (San Juan, Camara de Representantes, 1962), 3 vols., Vol. 1.

20. Armando Torres Vega, *Penumbras en la Vida de mi Pueblo* (San Juan, Imprenta Soltero, 1952), p. 51.

21. Mariano Picón-Salas, *Apología de la Pequeña Nación* (Rio Piedras, Junta Editora de la Universidad de Puerto Rico, 1946).

22. René Marqués, "Reply to Alfred Kazin," *San Juan Star,* March 8, 1960.

23. Dean Fleagle, *Social Problems of Porto Rico* (Boston, Heath, 1917), p. 35. See also Knowlton Mixer, *Porto Rico: History and Conditions—Social, Economic and Political* (New York, Macmillan, 1926), p. 181.

24. Victor S. Clark and associates, *Porto Rico and Its Problems* (Washington,

Brookings Institution, 1930), p. 11; and Richard M. Morse, "La Transformación Ilusoria de Puerto Rico," *Revista de Ciencias Sociales* (June 1960), p. 375.

25. Daniel Boorstin, "Self-Discovery in Puerto Rico," *Yale Review* (December 1955).

26. *Ibid.*, p. 237.

27. Nilita Vientós Gastón, "Comentarios a un Ensayo sobre Puerto Rico," *El Mundo*, March 1, 1956. See also the comments of other Puerto Rican critics collected in Adolfo de Hostos, *Polémica sobre Boorstin* (Hato Rey, Editorial del Departamento de Instrucción Pública, 1956).

28. *El Mundo*, February 28, 1957.

29. José Luis Sert, in *El Mundo*, February 9, 1959.

30. Leonard Bernstein, in *El Mundo*, April 18, 1956.

31. Canario, in *El Mundo*, September 15, 1956. For the general Puerto Rican tradition of dance and song see, among much else, Ramón Marín, *Las Fiestas Populares de Ponce* (Ponce, Tipográfico El Vapor, 1875); Manuel Fernández Juncos, *Costumbres y Tradiciones* (San Juan, El Buscapié 1883); Richard A. Waterman, *Folk Music of Puerto Rico* (Washington, Library of Congress, Music Division, Folk Music of the Americas, U.S. Government Printing Office, 1947); Pablo Garrido, *Esotería y Fervor Popular de Puerto Rico* (Madrid, Editorial Cultura Hispánica, 1952); and José Luis Vivas Maldonado, "La Décima Popular en Puerto Rico," *Revista* (Rio Piedras, Facultad de Estudios Generales, Universidad de Puerto Rico, 1960).

32. Editorial, "Y Nuestra Tradición?" *El Imparcial*, December 11, 1956. For a beautifully rendered tribute in bilingual form to the Puerto Rican *aguinaldo* tradition, see Tomás Blanco, *Los Aguinaldos del Infante: Glosa de Epifanía; The Child's Gifts: A Twelfth Night Tale*, translated by Harriet de Onis, musical ornaments by Jack Delano and illustrations by Irene Delano (San Juan, Pava Prints, 1962). For its historical interest, see also Junta Editora de la Universidad de Puerto Rico, *Aguinaldo Puertorriqueño de 1843*, Edición Conmemorativa del Centenario (Mexico, Editorial Orión, 1946). For the *aguinaldo* as sung in present-day Puerto Rico see María Luisa Muñoz, *Canciones de Navidad* (San Juan, Festival de la Navidad, 1950); and Francisco López Cruz, *El Aguinaldo y el Villancico en el Folklore Puertorriqueño* (San Juan, Instituto de Cultura Puertorriqueña, 1956).

33. A. Hyatt Verrill, *Porto Rico Past and Present and San Domingo of Today* (New York, Dodd Mead, 1914), pp. 105-106.

34. *The Island Times*, June 27, 1958. It is symptomatic of the colonial character of Puerto Rican life that there is a plethora of reports and studies on Puerto Rican adjustments to North American ways but hardly anything on the adjustments of the local continental American residents to Puerto Rican ways. An exception, virtually a pioneer study, albeit brief, is Virginia M. Seplowin, *A Study of Integration: The United States Continental in Puerto Rico* (San Juan, mimeographed, August 30, 1961). The study's conclusions are hardly encouraging: "The participants were under pressure to appear friendly and liberal. They wished also to live up to the national self-image of 'the good guy,' but praise came harder than criticism. Feelings of superiority were often ill-concealed. Making friends with Puerto Ricans seemed a chore to some. It was notable that in keeping with other sociological studies, although friendships had been formed with Puerto Ricans of the same social-economic level, contact did not lessen the stereotype of a Puerto Rican as poor, dark and ignorant" (p. 10).

35. *The Island Times*, June 13, 1958.

36. Nilita Vientós Gastón, "Indice Cultural," *El Mundo*, March 21, 1959.

37. Quoted by Earl Parker Hanson, *The Island Times*, May 31, 1957.

38. Thomas Hayes, in *El Mundo,* January 23, 1957.

39. José Padín, quoted in Juan José Osuna, *A History of Education in Puerto Rico* (Rio Piedras, Ediciones de la Universidad de Puerto Rico, 1949), pp. 200-201.

40. Ateneo Puertorriqueño, *Catálogo . . . de las Obras Existentes en la Biblioteca del Ateneo Puertorriqueño* (San Juan, Tipografía de "El Pais," 1897). In this matter the influence of the resident foreign community must have been important. See Estela Cifre de Loubriel, *Catálogo de Extranjeros Residentes en Puerto Rico en el Siglo XIX* (Rio Piedras, Ediciones de la Universidad de Puerto Rico, 1962).

CHAPTER 15

1. Henry K. Wells, *The Office of the Governor of Puerto Rico* (Rio Piedras, mimeographed, April 1956), p. 5.

2. University of Puerto Rico, School of Public Administration, *Report on the Reorganization of the Executive Branch* (Rio Piedras, University of Puerto Rico, 1949), pp. 13-14.

3. Fred L. Crawford, *Operation Bootstrap: A Report on the Activities of Puerto Rico in Its Effort to Provide Fuller Employment for Members of Its Manpower Task Force* (Washington, U.S. Government Printing Office, 1951).

4. *Constitution of the Commonwealth of Puerto Rico,* Art. IV, Sec. 4, para. 6 (Washington, U.S. Government Printing Office, 1952).

5. Gobierno de Puerto Rico, Convención Constituyente, *Diario de Sesiones: Procidimientos y Debates de la Convención Constituyente de Puerto Rico* (San Juan, December 5, 1951), pp. 246-261.

6. *Constitution,* Art. IV, Secs. 7-8.

7. *Ibid.,* Art. III, Sec. 21.

8. Henry K. Wells, "Administrative Reorganization in Puerto Rico," *Western Political Quarterly* (June 1956), p. 486.

9. José Trías Monge, in *El Mundo,* February 25, 1956.

10. *El Mundo,* October 7-11, 1955.

11. *El Mundo,* November 29, 1958.

12. Marshall Dimock, *Los Objetivos de la Reorganización Gubernamental* (Rio Piedras, Universidad de Puerto Rico, Escuela de Administración Pública, 1951), pp. 11-18.

13. Universidad de Puerto Rico, Escuela de Administración Pública, *La Nueva Constitución: Informes a la Convención Constituyente* (Rio Piedras, Ediciones de la Universidad de Puerto Rico, 1954), pp. 511-512.

14. *Ibid.*

15. University of Puerto Rico, School of Public Administration, *Report on the Reorganization of the Executive Branch,* pp. 10-11.

16. For all this see John C. Honey, *Public Personnel Administration in Puerto Rico* (unpublished Ph.D thesis, University of Puerto Rico, Social Sciences Library, mimeographed, 1949).

17. *Ibid.,* p. 90.

18. *Ibid.,* pp. 107-108, 165-166.

19. Antonio Cuevas Viret, "Filosofía y Objetivos de Un Sistema de Mérito," in American Society of Public Administration, Puerto Rican Chapter, *Qué es un Buen Sistema de Mérito para el Servicio Público?* (San Juan, June 1959).

20. Pedro Muñoz-Amato, *Informe sobre Problemas de Derechos Civiles en la Administración de Personal de Servicio* (San Juan, Commonwealth Government of Puerto Rico, Civil Liberties Committee, mimeographed, September 25, 1958), p. 32. Later reprinted as *Problemas de Derechos Civiles en la Administración de Personal*

del Estado Libre Asociado de Puerto Rico (Rio Piedras, Universidad de Puerto Rico, Escuela de Administración Pública, 1961).

21. *Gil A. Suarez v. Secretario de Hacienda y Junta de Personal de Puerto Rico*, Tribunal Superior, Sala de San Juan. Num. 54,705, May 13, 1958; and Estado Libre Asociado, Junta de Personal de Puerto Rico, *Resolución de la Junta de Personal de Puerto Rico del 13 Septiembre 1951 en el caso de destitución de Fernando Fuentes Jiménez.*

22. Estado Libre Asociado, Junta de Personal de Puerto Rico, *Resolución de la Junta de Personal de Puerto Rico del 23 Diciembre 1957 en el caso de destitución de Deusdedit Marrero.* The general work of the Personnel Board, especially in matters not dealing with political offenses, may be conveniently observed in Irma García de Serrano and Mercedes Portillo de Negrón, *Selección de Casos de la Junta de Personal de Puerto Rico* (Rio Piedras, Escuela de Administración Pública, mimeographed, 1963).

23. Estado Libre Asociado de Puerto Rico, Comité del Gobernador para el Estudio de los Derechos Civiles en Puerto Rico, *Informe al Honorable Gobernador del Estado Libre Asociado de Puerto Rico* (San Juan, Editorial Colegio de Abogados de Puerto Rico, 1959), p. 38.

24. Letter quoted in Eliseo Combas Guerra, "En Torno a la Fortaleza," *El Mundo*, September 26, 1959. See also Henry K. Wells, *Government Financing of Political Parties in Puerto Rico* (Princeton, Citizen Research Foundation, 1961), pp. 29-30.

25. Estado Libre Asociado de Puerto Rico, Comité del Gobernador &c, *Informe al Honorable Gobernador*, pp. 56-57.

26. Pedro Muñoz-Amato, *Informe sobre Problemas de Derechos Civiles*, pp. 45-50.

27. *Constitution*, Art. II, Secs. 7, 10-12.

28. *Ibid.*, Sec. 20.

29. Santos P. Amadeo and Víctor Vargas Negrón, *Informe sobre los Derechos Civiles en la Fase Criminal de la Justicia* (San Juan, Commonwealth Government of Puerto Rico, Civil Liberties Committee, mimeographed, November 11, 1958), pp. 191-192.

30. *El Pueblo de Puerto Rico v. Confesor Meléndez Santos*, Tribunal Superior de Puerto Rico, Sala de San Juan, Num. 16,208. San Juan, October 24, 1958.

31. Amadeo and Vargas Negrón, *Informe sobre los Derechos Civiles*, p. 67. One of the worst blots on the judicial record of the Commonwealth Government is the prolonged and continuing incarceration of political prisoners, of whom the Nationalist Party leader Pedro Albizu Campos is only the most famous. For the protest of one *independentista* group, Acción Patriótica Unitaria, see *El Mundo*, June 21, 1963.

32. David M. Helfeld, with the assistance of Guillermo Bobonis, *Discrimination for Political Beliefs and Associations* (San Juan, Commonwealth Government of Puerto Rico, Civil Liberties Committee, mimeographed, December 29, 1958), p. 39.

33. *Ibid.*, p. 113.

34. Amadeo and Vargas Negrón, *Informe sobre los Derechos Civiles*, p. 36.

35. *El Mundo*, June 21, 1961.

36. American Society of Public Administration, Puerto Rican Chapter, *Boletín de Gerencia Administrativa* (June 1957), pp. 6-7.

37. Estado Libre Asociado de Puerto Rico, Comité del Gobernador, *Informe al Honorable Gobernador*, Chapter 13.

38. Honey, *Public Personnel Administration in Puerto Rico*, p. 411. An im-

portant preliminary study of the public administration process in Puerto Rico, drawing frank attention to its more serious weaknesses, is Miguel A. Velázquez Rivera, "El Debido Procidimiento de Ley en el Sector Administrativo del Gobierno," *Revista del Colegio de Abogados de Puerto Rico* (August 1962). See also Rafael Morales Couvertier, "The Trend Toward a Centralized Administration in Puerto Rico," in Sociedad Puertorriqueña de Administración Pública, *Ensayos Premiados en los Certámenes Auspiciados por la Sociedad Durante los Años 1959-1960 y 1960-1961* (San Juan, 1962).

CHAPTER 16

1. Universidad de Puerto Rico, Escuela de Administración Pública, *La Nueva Constitucion: Informes a la Convención Constituyente* (Rio Piedras, Ediciones de la Universidad de Puerto Rico, 1954), pp. 287-299.

2. *Constitution of the Commonwealth of Puerto Rico,* Art. III, Sec. 7 (Washington, U.S. Government Printing Office, 1952).

3. Federico Cordero, letter of resignation from legislative seat, in *El Mundo,* January 16, 1962.

4. Milton Pabón, Robert W. Anderson and Víctor J. Rivera Rodríguez, *Informe sobre los Derechos Civiles y los Partidos Políticos* (San Juan, Commonwealth Government of Puerto Rico, Civil Liberties Committee, mimeographed, November 18, 1958), p. 127. See also Robert W. Anderson, *Party Politics in Puerto Rico* (Rio Piedras, unpublished Ph.D. thesis, mimeographed, 1962), pp. 200-205.

5. *El Mundo,* August 10, 17, 19, 1957; *El Imparcial,* August 15, 1957.

6. Estado Libre Asociado, Asamblea Legislativa, *Diario de Sesiones: Procidimientos y Debates* (San Juan, January 30, 1953), p. 182.

7. Universidad de Puerto Rico, Escuela de Administración Pública, *La Nueva Constitución,* p. 511.

8. Pabón, Anderson, and Rivera Rodríguez, *Informe sobre los Derechos Civiles y los Partidos Políticos,* p. 142. See also Anderson, *Party Politics in Puerto Rico,* pp. 333-336.

9. Estado Libre Asociado, Asamblea Legislativa, Comisión Investigadora del Negociado de Industrias Pecuarias, *Informe a la Asamblea Legislativa* (San Juan, February 11, 1958), pp. 5-6.

10. *Ibid.*

11. *Ibid.,* p. 150.

12. *El Mundo,* November 29, 1958. See also the complaints of a group of *Popular* party Senators, *El Mundo,* January 11, 1962.

13. Estado Libre Asociado, Asamblea Legislativa, *Diario de Sesiones* (San Juan, January 30, February 2, 1953).

14. *Ibid.,* January 30, 1953, pp. 187-188.

15. *Ibid.,* pp. 177-178.

16. *Ibid.,* May 25, 1957.

17. *Ibid.,* January 30, 1953, pp. 148-152.

18. *Ibid.,* p. 176.

19. *Ibid.,* pp. 182-185.

20. *Ibid.,* p. 178.

21. *El Mundo,* May 24, July 2, 1962. See also Anderson, *Party Politics in Puerto Rico,* pp. 338-340.

22. *Constitution,* Art. I, Sec. 2.

23. Estado Libre Asociado, Asamblea Legislativa, *Diario de Sesiones,* February 2, 1955. See the full text also printed in *El Imparcial,* February 7, 1955.

24. *Constitution,* Art. III, Secs. 1-2.

25. Estado Libre Asociado, Asamblea Legislativa, *Diario de Sesiones,* January 30, 1953, p. 176.

26. Néstor Rigual, *El Poder Legislativo de Puerto Rico* (Rio Piedras, Ediciones de la Universidad de Puerto Rico, 1961), pp. 40-41.

27. Letter reprinted in *San Juan Star,* May 29, 1961.

28. Willis Sweet, *Self-Government for Porto Rico* (San Juan, Tipografía la Republica Española, 1906), pp. 31, 60-61.

29. Gobierno de Puerto Rico, Asamblea Legislativa, *En Defensa de Puerto Rico: Carta Dirigida al Comisionado Residente de Puerto Rico en Washington, April 2, 1928* (San Juan, 1928).

30. Gobierno de Puerto Rico, Senado, Oficina del Secretario, *Libertad de Prensa: Etica Parlementaria, Etica Periodista* (San Juan, 1951).

31. *San Juan Star,* May 24-26, 28, 1962. For the report of the Controller of Puerto Rico largely substantiating these charges, see *San Juan Star,* June 20, 1963. It is typical of the status of the Legislature as one of the sanctified institutions of Puerto Rican life that a report on a matter so much of public concern as charges of legislative-political corruption should have taken more than a year to prepare and publish.

32. Quoted in *El Mundo,* February 28, 1957.

33. *El Mundo,* September 8, 1959.

34. Henry K. Wells, *Office of the Controller* (Rio Piedras, mimeographed, 1956), pp. 26-27. See also Jaime A. Santiago Meléndez, *La Oficina del Contralor del Estado Libre Asociado de Puerto Rico* (Rio Piedras, mimeographed, N.D.), which also includes a discussion of the predecessor of the Office of the Controller, the Office of the Auditor of Porto Rico, 1898-1952.

35. Robert W. Anderson, "Partidos Políticos en Puerto Rico: El Contenido Legal," *Revista de Ciencias Sociales* (September 1961), p. 364.

36. Rigual, *El Poder Legislativo,* p. 205. This legislative somnolence may in fact finally be shaken by the growing pressure of organized interest groups in the changing Puerto Rican society upon an old-fashioned legislative system. Both manufacturing and medical groups have latterly become active along those lines. For the lobbying activities of a group of public employees in defense of their proposed legislation favoring a medical insurance plan for public servants, see Asociación de Empleados del Gobierno de Puerto Rico, *Boletín Informativo* (March 1963).

CHAPTER 17

1. Exchange of correspondence between Benjamín Ortiz and Miguel García Méndez, in *El Mundo,* December 3, 8, 1956.

2. Quoted in Thomas Mathews, *Puerto Rican Politics and the New Deal* (Gainesville, University of Florida Press, 1960), p. 235.

3. Federico Degetau y González, quoted in Pilar Barbosa de Rosario, *La Obra de José Celso Barbosa* (San Juan, Imprenta Venezuela, 1957), 6 vols., Vol. 6, Apendice D, p. 199. For Degetau y González, see Angel Mergal, *Federico Degetau: Un Orientador de su Pueblo* (New York, Hispanic Institute in the United States, 1944).

4. Pilar Barbosa de Rosario, *La Obra de José Celso Barbosa,* Vol. 6, p. 200.

5. Milton Pabón, Robert W. Anderson, and Víctor J. Rivera Rodríguez, *Informe sobre los Derechos Civiles y los Partidos Políticos* (San Juan, Commonwealth Gov-

ernment of Puerto Rico, Civil Liberties Committee, mimeographed, November 18, 1958), pp. 109-110.

6. Raúl Serrano Geyls and Roberto F. Rexach Benítez, *Un Sistema de Elecciones Primarias en Puerto Rico* (Rio Piedras, Universidad de Puerto Rico, Escuela de Administración Pública, 1955), pp. 122-123.

7. Pabón, Anderson and Rivera Rodríguez, *Informe sobre los Derechos Civiles y los Partidos Políticos,* pp. 111-113.

8. Estado Libre Asociado, Asamblea Legislativa, *Diario de Sesiones: Procidimientos y Debates,* November 13, 1958, p. 409.

9. Pabón, Anderson and Rivera Rodríguez, *Informe sobre los Derechos Civiles y los Partidos Políticos,* pp. 67-68.

10. Estado Libre Asociado, Asamblea Legislativa, *Diario de Sesiones,* May 17, 1958, pp. 1795-1796.

11. *Ibid.,* pp. 1794-1797.

12. Commonwealth Government of Puerto Rico, Office of the Controller, *Informe Fondo Electoral* (San Juan, March 24, 1959), Anexo I.

13. Harry Kantor, "Public Finances Parties," *National Municipal Review* (March 1958).

14. Partido Independentista Puertorriqueño, *Los Subsidios Gubernamentales a los Partidos Políticos* (San Juan, mimeographed, 1957).

15. Estado Libre Asociado, Asamblea Legislativa, *Diario de Sesiones,* May 25, 1957, pp. 1924-1925.

16. Statement by Executive Committee of Popular Democratic Party, in *El Mundo,* September 19, 1959.

17. *El Mundo,* August 24, 1960.

18. Robert W. Anderson, *Party Politics in Puerto Rico* (Rio Piedras, unpublished Ph.D. thesis, mimeographed, 1962), pp. 363-364. The discussion of the similar problem of the institutionalization of party rule, in order to offset the hazards of unipersonal leadership and the "cult of personality," in Fidel Castro's important speech of December 1, 1961, is of vast interest as a Cuban parallel to the Puerto Rican problem. See the speech reprinted in Universidad de Venezuela, Instituto de Estudios Políticos, *Documentos* (Caracas, October-December 1961), pp. 194-210.

19. *The Island Times,* June 29, 1962. See also the series of articles on the state of the San Juan municipal government in the *San Juan Star* throughout June 1962.

20. Quoted in E. Fernández García, ed., *El Libro de Porto Rico* (San Juan, El Libro Azul, 1923), pp. 205-207. For a later statement of the Statehood ideal from the pen of a self-styled Socialist see Bolívar Pagán, *Puerto Rico: The Next State* (Washington, Dwyer Press, 1942). See also Emilio del Toro Cuebas, *Puerto Rico: Nuevo Estado de la Unión* (San Juan, Asociación Puertorriqueña pro Estadidad, N.D.). The great name of the Statehood ideology, of course, is that of Barbosa. For Barbosa see Antonio S. Pedreira, *Un Hombre del Pueblo: José Celso Barbosa* (San Juan, Imprenta Venezuela, 1937).

21. Inés María Mendoza de Muñoz Marín, "Un Recordatorio sobre lo que Significa 'Dictadura'," *El Mundo,* November 2, 1956.

22. Theodore Brameld, *The Remaking of a Culture: Life and Education in Puerto Rico* (New York, Harpers, 1959), p. 328.

23. Benjamín Ortiz, "El Conservadorismo de Ferré," *El Mundo,* November 26, 1956.

24. Remarks of Luis Ferré, in *El Mundo,* March 4, 1957.

25. Teófilo Maldonado, *Hombres de Primera Plana* (San Juan, Editorial Campos, 1958), p. 128.

26. Commonwealth Government of Puerto Rico, State Board of Elections, *Estadísticas de los Votos Integros por Distritos Senatoriales y Barrios de las Elecciones Generales Celebradas en Noviembre 6 de 1956* (San Juan, 1957).

27. Arnold G. Dana, *Porto Rico's Case: Outcome of American Sovereignty* (New Haven, Arnold G. Dana, 1928), pp. 32-33.

28. Remarks of Gilberto Concepción de Gracia, quoted in *El Mundo,* October 12, 1956; and Economic Development Administration, Office of Economic Research, *An Analysis of the Costs and Benefits of Fomento Programs* (San Juan, mimeographed, September 1956).

29. Partido Independentista Puertorriqueño, *Programa Económico, Social y Político del Partido Independentista Puertorriqueño* (San Juan, 1956); and Movimiento Pro-Independencia, *Programa y Declaración de Principios,* in *El Mundo,* March 3, 1959.

30. Remarks of Gilberto Concepción de Gracia, quoted in *El Mundo,* November 22, 1956. See also Movimiento Pro-Independencia, *La Hora de la Independencia: Tesis Política MPI* (San Juan, 1963), pp. 109-113.

31. Asociación de Socialistas de Puerto Rico, "Un Mensaje al Pueblo," in *El Mundo,* December 14, 1956.

32. Statement of leaders of the new political grouping seceding from the Partido Independentista Puertorriqueño, in *El Mundo,* November 27, 1957.

33. Movimiento Pro-Independencia, *Programa,* in *El Mundo,* March 3, 1959. For a friendly criticism of the Movimiento Pro-Independencia as a radical nationalist movement which, although not fully socialist, has proceeded significantly in a socialist direction, as distinct from the traditional romantic nationalism of *independentista* groups in Puerto Rico, see Manuel Bruckman, "From Independence to National Liberation: Puerto Rican Nationalism Today," *Marxist Leninist Quarterly* (December 1962).

34. Manifesto of the new political grouping led by Jorge Luis Landing and others, in *El Mundo,* October 7, 1958.

35. Harold J. Lidin, in *San Juan Star,* November 16, 1959. See also William H. Hackett, *The Nationalist Party: A Report Prepared for the Committee on Interior and Insular Affairs,* House of Representatives (Washington, U.S. Government Printing Office, 1951), for a hostile Congressional report on Nationalist and Communist Party activities in Puerto Rico. There are megalomaniac elements, of course, in the Nationalist groups. For the violent hatred of Governor Muñoz Marín entertained by some of them see the volume of slanderous verse by Pablo Neruda, *Canta a Puerto Rico* (San Juan, Juventud Acción Patriótica Unitaria, 1963).

36. Robert J. Hunter, *Puerto Rico: A Survey of Historical, Economic and Political Affairs,* House of Representatives, Committee on Interior and Insular Affairs (Washington, U.S. Government Printing Office, 1959), p. 43.

37. Raúl Serrano Geyls, *Executive-Legislative Relationships in the Government of Puerto Rico* (Rio Piedras, University of Puerto Rico, mimeographed, 1954), pp. 45-50.

38. Gilberto Concepción de Gracia, in Estado Libre Asociado, Senado de Puerto Rico, *Diario de Sesiones,* February 24, 1958, p. 294.

39. Vincenzo Petrullo, *Puerto Rican Paradox* (Philadelphia, University of Pennsylvania Press, 1947), p. 180.

40. Mary Weld Coates, "What's the Matter in Porto Rico?" *Current History* (April-September 1922), p. 110.

41. *El Mundo,* March 3, 1958.

42. *El Mundo,* December 7, 1957.

43. *El Mundo,* April 15, 1958.

44. Ursula von Eckardt, in *San Juan Star,* September 24, 1962. Miss von Eckardt, in her shriller moments as a newspaper columnist in the *San Juan Star,* is a good example of what frequently happens to American liberalism when relocated in an alien Caribbean environment.

45. *El Mundo,* September 30, 1961.

CHAPTER 18

1. Nilita Vientós Gastón, "Indice Cultural: Comentarios a un Ensayo sobre Puerto Rico," in *El Mundo,* February 25, 1956.

2. Editorial, *The Washington Post,* quoted in *El Mundo,* February 20, 1957.

3. Robert J. Hunter, *Puerto Rico: A Survey of Historical, Economic and Political Affairs,* House of Representatives, Committee on Interior and Insular Affairs (Washington, U.S. Government Printing Office, 1959), p. 24.

4. Juan M. García Passalacqua, "The Alternative: A Federal Solution to the Colonial Problem" (San Juan, mimeographed, 1959). See also, by the same author, "Notas para una Teoría de la Asociación Federalista," *Revista de Ciencias Sociales* (June 1959).

5. Antonio Fernós-Isern, *Puerto Rico Libre y Federado* (San Juan, Biblioteca de Autores Puertorriqueños, 1948), pp. 91-92. See also, by the same author, *The Significance of the Reform* (Washington, Office of Puerto Rico, 1948). The atmosphere of naive optimism dominating the Puerto Rican legislative reception of the Congressional passage of Public Law 600 is well expressed in the pamphlet of collected speeches, *Constitution: Act to Implement It Approved* (San Juan, Government of Puerto Rico, Department of Finance, 1950).

6. Quoted in *The Island Times,* June 19, 1959.

7. José Angel Poventud, "La Ley 600 y la Propuesta Constitución en Relación con el Status Político de Puerto Rico," incorporated in remarks of Celestino Iriarte, Gobierno de Puerto Rico, Convención Constituyente, *Diario de Sesiones: Procidimientos y Debates de la Convención Constituyente de Puerto Rico* (November 23, 1951), pp. 148-149.

8. Remarks of Mario Orsini Martínez, in Gobierno de Puerto Rico, Convención Constituyente, *Diario de Sesiones: Procidimientos y Debates de la Convención Constituyente de Puerto Rico* (San Juan, December 10, 1951), pp. 277-282; and remarks of Reyes Delgado, *ibid.* (November 30, 1951), pp. 164-168. For an earlier discussion of Puerto Rican constitutional status after 1900, see Pedro Capó Rodríquez, "The Relations Between the United States and Porto Rico," *American Journal of International Law* (July 1919), and, by the same author, "Colonial Representation in the American Empire," *American Journal of International Law* (October 1921).

9. Statement of H. Silverman, in United States Senate, Committee on Interior and Insular Affairs, *Hearings . . . on the S.J. Res. 151,* 82nd Congress, 2nd Session (Washington, U.S. Government Printing Office, 1952), pp. 43-44.

10. David M. Helfeld, "Congressional Intent and Attitude Toward Public Law 600 and the Constitution of the Commonwealth of Puerto Rico," *Revista Jurídica de la Universidad de Puerto Rico* (May-June 1952), p. 293.

11. *Ibid.,* p. 304.

12. Hunter, *Puerto Rico: A Survey of Historical, Economic and Political Affairs,* pp. 69-71.

13. *Ibid.,* pp. 71-74.

14. *Ibid.,* p. 75.

15. *Ibid.,* p. 70.

16. *Memorandum,* Assistant Attorney General, Office of Legal Counsel, to the Chairman, Committee on Interior and Insular Affairs, House of Representatives, United States Congress, 1960, quoted in Gordon K. Lewis, *Puerto Rico: A Case Study in the Problems of Contemporary American Federalism* (Port of Spain, Trinidad, 1960), p. 41.

17. *Ibid.*

18. Exchange of views between Senator Henry Jackson and Governor Luis Muñoz Marín, *Hearings,* Committee on Interior and Insular Affairs, United States Senate, June 1959, reprinted in Lewis, *Puerto Rico: A Case Study,* pp. 96-99.

19. Puerto Rican Resident Commissioner in Washington, quoted in *El Mundo,* October 8, 1956.

20. *El Mundo,* March 13, 1957.

21. Text of Statement by the American Civil Liberties Union, quoted in *El Mundo,* November 11, 1959.

22. Commonwealth of Puerto Rico, Puerto Rico Labor Relations Board, *Hilton Hotels International Inc. v. Unión de Trabajadores de la Industria Gastronómica,* Cases No. P-958 and P-959, D-141, November 9, 1955.

23. *El Mundo,* September 8, 1958.

24. Carl J. Friedrich, *Puerto Rico: Middle Road to Freedom* (New York, Rinehart, 1959).

25. F. R. Scott, "The End of Dominion Status," *American Journal of International Law* (January 1944).

26. Text of brief of group of San Juan attorneys, quoted in *San Juan Star,* November 19, 1959.

27. Henry K. Wells and Víctor Gutiérrez-Franqui, "The Commonwealth Constitution," American Academy of Political and Social Sciences, *Annals* (January 1953), p. 40.

28. A. B. Keith, ed., *Speeches and Documents on the British Dominions (1918-1931)* (London and New York, Oxford University Press, World's Classics, 1948), pp. 149-160.

29. Remarks of Senator Miguel García-Méndez, quoted in *El Mundo,* March 3, 1958; and remarks of Gilberto Concepción de Gracia in Asamblea Legislativa, *Diario de Sesiones: Procidimientos y Debates* (San Juan, January 27, 1958).

30. The Republicans of Porto Rico, *Address to the Congress* (San Juan, Times Publishing Company, 1919), p. 6.

31. United States Bureau of the Budget, *Flow of Federal Funds into, and Receipts from, the Commonwealth of Puerto Rico* (Washington, U.S. Government Printing Office, October 1959). For a more optimistic estimate of the Puerto Rican ability to absorb the fiscal obligations of statehood, see Arthur E. Burns, *Fiscal Report on Puerto Rico as a State,* reprinted in the *San Juan Star,* May 27, 1963.

32. *El Mundo,* December 24, 1959.

33. *El Mundo,* September 19, 1958.

34. Remarks of Senator Miguel García-Méndez, quoted in *El Mundo,* June 11, 1959.

35. Governor Luis Muñoz Marín, Declaration of Cidra, September 1959, reprinted in Lewis, *Puerto Rico: A Case Study,* pp. 100-102.

36. The Republicans of Porto Rico, *Address to the Congress,* p. 15.

37. *Ibid.*

38. Statement of Luis Ferré to Committee on Interior and Insular Affairs (O'Brien Committee), House of Representatives, quoted in *El Mundo,* December 24, 1959.

39. Luis Ferré, quoted in *The Island Times,* June 12, 1959.

40. Government of Trinidad and Tobago, Office of the Premier and Ministry of Finance, *Economic Development of the Independent West Indies Federation* (Port of Spain, October 1960), *The Economics of Nationhood* (Port of Spain, September 1959), and *European Integration and West Indian Trade* (Port of Spain, September 1960).

41. Governor Luis Muñoz Marín, "Development Through Democracy," American Academy of Political and Social Sciences, *Annals* (January 1953), pp. 2-5.

42. Text of letters exchanged on the status issue, reprinted in the *San Juan Star,* October 19, 1962.

43. For all this, see the local San Juan press, especially in the period August 22- September 20, 1962. The plebiscite scheme was finally abandoned summarily by the Puerto Rican governmental leadership in November 1962 in favor of a return to the older strategy of direct negotiation with Congress. For criticisms of the change in policy see, for example, statement of leaders of the Partido Independentista Puertorriqueño, in *El Mundo,* November 24, 1962. For text of House of Representatives resolution setting up a joint legislative-executive commission to inquire into the Puerto Rican status problem, see *San Juan Star,* May 1, 1963. For text of report of Bureau of the Budget to the House of Representatives Subcommittee on Territories and Insular Affairs, see *San Juan Star,* May 21, 1963. For transcript of testimony on the House Resolution in the House Subcommittee on Territories and Insular Affairs, see *San Juan Star,* May 17, 18, 1963.

44. Antonio Fernós-Isern, "El Plebiscito es Fiambre," *El Imparcial,* January 9, 1955.

45. Samuel R. Quiñones, in *El Mundo,* April 4, 1959.

46. Commonwealth of Puerto Rico, Department of Justice, *Memorandum of Law,* prepared by Hiram R. Cancio, Attorney General of the Commonwealth of Puerto Rico (San Juan, June 1959), p. 26; Statement of Hiram R. Cancio before the Committee on Interior and Insular Affairs, House of Representatives (San Juan, mimeographed, December 5, 1959); and House of Representatives, Committee on Interior and Insular Affairs, *Memorandum from the Assistant Attorney General, Office of Legal Counsel* (Washington, U.S. Government Printing Office, 1960), p. 9. See also *Revista del Colegio de Abogados de Puerto Rico* (May 1962), p. 343.

CHAPTER 19

1. Juan José Osuna, *A History of Education in Puerto Rico* (Rio Piedras, Ediciones de la Universidad de Puerto Rico, 1949), Appendix VI, "Tax Collections and School Costs in Puerto Rico, 1899-1947," pp. 620-621.

2. *Ibid.,* p. 282.

3. *Ibid.,* p. 342.

4. *Ibid.,* p. 370. See also the remarks of Charles F. Reid, in Columbia University, Teachers College, *Education in the Territories and Outlying Possessions of the United States* (New York, Bureau of Publications, Teachers College, 1941), p. 297. And see Robert Morss Lovett, *Observations on the Teaching of English in Puerto Rico* (Rio Piedras, University of Puerto Rico Bulletin, 1946).

5. *El Imparcial,* July 11, 1962.

6. Ismael Rodríguez Bou, Director of Office of Educational Research, Superior Educational Council, *Report to the Education Committee,* House of Representatives, Commonwealth of Puerto Rico, quoted in *El Mundo,* March 18, 1959.

7. Report of National Education Association, quoted in *Daily Gleaner* (Kingston, Jamaica), June 2, 1960.

8. Quoted in Eliseo Combas Guerra, "En Torno a la Fortaleza," *El Mundo,* March 30, 1959.

9. *El Mundo,* March 8, 1957.

10. Quoted in Theodore Brameld, *The Remaking of a Culture: Life and Education in Puerto Rico* (New York, Harpers, 1959), pp. 72, 80. For a local Catholic criticism of this volume, see the review by Edmund J. Baumeister, "Remaking or Unmaking of Puerto Rican Culture?" in *Horizontes* (Ponce, April 1960).

11. Dean Fleagle, *Social Problems of Porto Rico* (Boston, Heath, 1917), Chapter 15.

12. Brameld, *The Remaking of a Culture,* pp. 81, 407.

13. *Ibid.,* pp. 74-77.

14. *Ibid.,* pp. 319-326.

15. Enrique Laguerre, in *El Mundo,* March 7, 1958; and Ismael Rodríguez Bou, in *El Mundo,* January 11, 1960.

16. University of Puerto Rico, Office of the Chancellor, *Informe del Rector al Consejo Superior de Enseñanza* (Rio Piedras, June 1957), pp. 25-26.

17. Jaime Benítez, *Education for Democracy on a Cultural Frontier* (University of Puerto Rico Bulletin, N.D.), p. 26. The Chancellor's full-length account of his stewardship as leader of the University during the post-1940 generation is to be found in his volume of collected addresses and speeches, *Junto a La Torre: Jornadas de un Programa Universitario (1942-1962)* (Rio Piedras, Universidad de Puerto Rico, 1962).

18. Quoted in *El Mundo,* March 18, 1959.

19. Quoted in Pedro Muñoz-Amato, *Informe Preliminar sobre el Derecho a la Educación y la Libertad Académica* (San Juan, mimeographed, 1958), pp. 50-51.

20. Burton Dean Friedman, *Administrative Reorganization of the University of Puerto Rico* (Rio Piedras, University of Puerto Rico, Department of Finance, 1959) pp. 40-41.

21. *El Mundo,* May 8, 1959.

22. Rubén del Rosario, *Report to the Faculty,* quoted in *El Mundo,* May 8, 1959.

23. Rubén del Rosario, *Report to the Faculty* (Rio Piedras, mimeographed, September 25, 1961), p. 3.

24. For the rash of eager constitution-making provoked by the University reform discussion of 1958-1963 see, among much else, Comité del Claustro, Universidad de Puerto Rico, *Anteproyecto de la Ley Universitaria* (Rio Piedras, mimeographed, March 3, 1958); Claustro de los Colegios de Rio Piedras, *Proyecto de Constitución del Senado Académico* (Rio Piedras, mimeographed, May 5, 1959); Rubén del Rosario, *Historia del Senado Académico* (Rio Piedras, mimeographed, January 1960); Asociación Puertorriqueña de Profesores Universitarios, Capítulo de Rio Piedras, *Propuestas de Reforma al Estatuto Universitario Aprobados por la Junta de Directores* (Rio Piedras, mimeographed, 1962); *Anteproyecto de Ley Universitaria,* Comité de Ley y Reglamento del Senado Académico de Rio Piedras (Rio Piedras, Oficina del Rector, Universidad de Puerto Rico, March 1963); series of amendments to Senate Committee Report in *Circular Num. 40* (Rio Piedras, Oficina del Rector, Universidad de Puerto Rico, March 1963); and successive issues during 1962-1963 of *El Espectador Universitario,* monthly organ of the Puerto Rican Association of University Professors.

25. *San Juan Star,* October 16, 1961.

26. For all this, see Luis Nieves Falcón, *Algunas Consideraciones Sociales en Torno a la Educación Universitaria en Puerto Rico* (Rio Piedras, University of Puerto Rico, mimeographed, March 1962); United States Census Bureau, *General Social and Economic Characteristics of Puerto Rico,* quoted in *San Juan Star,* July

28, 1962; and Universidad de Puerto Rico y Departamento de Instrucción Pública, *Informe a la Asamblea Legislativa de Puerto Rico sobre Colegios Regionales* (Rio Piedras, 1962).

27. Report by Leonard Shatzkin on Department of Education, quoted in *San Juan Star,* February 22, 1960.

28. *Report on Education in Puerto Rico,* Advisory Committee of European Educators, Chapter 7, reprinted in *El Mundo,* June 16, 1960. The private school and the "language problem" are obviously interrelated. It is worth quoting as still largely true the comment of a 1936 advisory committee report that "the only bilingual problem in Puerto Rico exists among the American residents." Michael West, *The Language Problem and the Teaching of English in Puerto Rico,* in Ismael Rodríguez Bou, ed., *Problemas de Lectura y Lengua en Puerto Rico* (Rio Piedras, Universidad de Puerto Rico, 1948), p. 107.

29. Universidad de Puerto Rico, *Informe del Rector al Consejo Superior de Enseñanza* (Rio Piedras, June 1957), p. 33.

30. *San Juan Star,* July 15, 1961.

31. W. Bowles, *Preliminary Report to the Superior Educational Council and Chancellor of the University of Puerto Rico Relative to the Development of the Graduate Program at the University* (Rio Piedras, University of Puerto Rico, April 1954).

32. Rubén del Rosario, *Promedio de Sueldos de Personal Docente en los Estados Unidos y en Puerto Rico* (Rio Piedras, mimeographed, July 10, 1959); Statement of Director of Department of English, University of Puerto Rico, in *El Mundo,* May 26, 1959; and Asociación Puertorriqueña de Profesores Universitarios, *Memorial a la Legislatura de Puerto Rico,* printed in *El Mundo,* May 11, 1962.

33. Vicente Géigel Polanco, 1940 address on the University, reprinted in César Andreu Iglesias, "Cosas de Aquí," *El Imparcial,* October 13, 15, 1962.

34. José Emilio González, "Hostos, el Olvidado," in *El Mundo,* March 3, 1962.

35. Report of Richard D. Trent on university students, quoted in *San Juan Star,* October 13, 1962.

CHAPTER 20

1. Gilbert Seldes, *The Public Arts* (New York, Simon & Schuster, 1956), pp. 84, 294.

2. For most of this see Commonwealth Government of Puerto Rico, Civil Liberties Committee, *Informe sobre la Libertad de Prensa* (San Juan, mimeographed, 1959), pp. 1-22.

3. Estado Libre Asociado, *Comisión de Instrucción del Senado sobre la Radio-difusión en Puerto Rico,* quoted in Commonwealth Government of Puerto Rico, Civil Liberties Committee, *Informe sobre la Libertad de Prensa,* pp. 38-41.

4. Informe del Comité de Técnicos a la Comisión Especial de la Cámara de Representantes, *El Negocio de Exhibición de Películas Cinematográficos en Puerto Rico* (March 1956), quoted in Commonwealth Government of Puerto Rico, Civil Liberties Committee, *Informe sobre la Libertad de Prensa,* pp. 46-47.

5. Correspondence between Hipólito Marcano and Governor Muñoz Marín, in Commonwealth Government of Puerto Rico, Civil Liberties Committee, *Informe sobre la Libertad de Prensa,* pp. 34-36.

6. José Trías Monge, in *El Mundo,* March 13, 1957.

7. Albert Gardner Robinson, *The Porto Rico of Today* (New York, Scribner, 1899), p. 162. Yet the American influence, being throughout always more commercial than aesthetic, has done little to enliven this intellectually depressed con-

dition of the Puerto Rican society. A note on "collective forces" in Puerto Rican life in 1925 listed the majority of American-sponsored organizations as being business groups or "moral uplift" groups: the Knights of Columbus, the Elks, the Oddfellows, the YMCA, the Red Cross, and the Chamber of Commerce. Claudio Capó, *The Island of Porto Rico* (San Juan, Globe Publishing Company, 1925), pp. 76-78. Things are not much different today.

8. Richard V. Gilbert, *Report of San Juan Racing Association on Games of Chance,* quoted in *El Mundo,* January 16, 1960.

9. Sixto Toro Cintrón, testimony in Hearings of Civil Liberties Committee, quoted in Commonwealth Government of Puerto Rico, Civil Liberties Committee, *Informe sobre Libertad de Pensamiento y Expresión en el Clima Cultural de Puerto Rico* (San Juan, mimeographed, 1959), p. 15, n. 16.

10. For all this see Edwin Seda Bonilla, *Actitud, Conocimiento y Apercepción de los Derechos Civiles en el Pueblo Puertorriqueño* (Rio Piedras, Facultad de Ciencias Sociales, Centro de Investigaciones Sociales, mimeographed, 1959). The social docility of the Puerto Rican people here noted is reinforced by the cultural homogeneity of the society. The sense of a common Puerto Ricanness, the absence of internal racial divisions on a Haitian or British Guianese model, of anything comparable to the cultural gulf that divides the Latin American Indian from the *mestizo* or the Trinidadian East Indian from the Negro majority, makes straight-forward class control much easier in Puerto Rican life. This is obviously related to the fact that Puerto Rico is not a plural society. See the earlier discussion on this point in Chapter 12.

11. Adolfo de Hostos, in *The World Journal* (San Juan), October 15, 1956.

12. Carlos Albizu Miranda and Herbert Marty Torres, "Atisbos de la Personalidad Puertorriqueña," *Revista de Ciencias Sociales* (September 1958), p. 400.

13. For examples of this, see the leaflet of protest against the visit of Professor Carl Friedrich, Federación de Universitarios Pro-Independencia, *Otra Faena Política* (Rio Piedras, 1958), and the remarks on Professor Ursula von Eckardt in *Información Estudiantil* (Rio Piedras, June 27, 1962).

14. See the reports in *The Island Times,* August 7, 14, 1959.

15. Letter of Antonio Cuevas Viret, in *El Mundo,* September 25, 1959.

16. Analio Vega, "El Nuevo Concepto del Insulto," *El Mundo,* November 4, 1957.

17. Nilda González, "Problemática del Teatro Puertorriqueño," *Presente* (Publicación de la Fraternidad Cultural Universitaria Mu Epsilon Kappa, Rio Piedras, April-May, 1959).

18. E. Fernández Vanga, "Los Cipieis," *El Mundo,* January 2, 1960.

19. Letter of Pablo Casals, in *El Mundo,* April 30, 1959. Pablo Casals, of course, is only the latest name in the list of outsiders who throughout Puerto Rican history have contributed with their genius to island life and thought. Medical men have been particularly outstanding. For Dr. Bailey K. Ashford see Helen V. Tooker, "Puerto Rico's Debt to Dr. Ashford," *Island Times,* November 23, 1962; for Dr. Agustín Stahl see Carlos E. Chardon, "Semblanza del Dr. Agustín Stahl," *El Mundo, Suplemento Sabatino,* March 26, 1960; and for Dr. Juan Gundlach see Juan Bauzá Rullán, "El doctor Juan Gundlach: Su Aportación al Conocimiento de la Fauna de Puerto Rico," *El Mundo, Suplemento Sabatino,* October 7, 1961. The record has an ironic note about it in the light of the opposition of the Puerto Rican Medical Association to legislation permitting foreign doctors to accept government medical appointments in the island, *San Juan Star,* July 1, 1963.

20. Letter of Charles Emerson, January 19, 1833, quoted by Frank Otto Gatell, "San Juan Under Spain in the 1830's" *The Island Times,* September 4, 1959.

21. For an example of this see John M. Iagrossi in *El Mundo,* April 21, 1959.

22. Rexford G. Tugwell, *The Stricken Land* (New York, Doubleday, 1947), pp. 488-489.

23. Eugenio Fernández-Méndez, ed., *Portrait of a Society: A Book of Readings on Puerto Rican Society* (Rio Piedras, University of Puerto Rico, 1956), pp. 259-262.

24. *San Juan Star,* July 7, 1961.

25. Jaime Toro Calder, "Posibles Efectos de una Industrialización Rápida en la Estructura Social de Puerto Rico," Convención de Orientación Social de Puerto Rico, *Octava Convención* (San Juan, 1955), pp. 85-87.

26. José Arsenio Torres, "La Educación Pública en Puerto Rico," *El Mundo,* September 26, 27, 30, October 5, 7, 1957. José Arsenio Torres has been the talented leading figure in the University reform movement. But his writings on the subject suggest that the reform, if achieved, would be a change in university administrative structure and policies and not of philosophic direction.

27. Ana María O'Neill, *Communismo, Capitalismo y Cooperación* (San Juan, Estado Libre Asociado, Liga de Cooperativas de Puerto Rico, Editorial de Instrucción Pública, 1956); and Very Rev. Francis J. Connell, C.SS.R., *On the Purpose and Nature of a Catholic University,* McManus Lectures (Catholic University of Puerto Rico, 1960). For the socially and culturally conservative position of some Catholic lay elements, see "Carta a Monseñor Manuel Clarizio . . ." in *El Mundo,* November 7, 1962. The list of recommendations of an almost theocratic nature includes the recognition of Catholicism as the official state religion, with the Irish precedent specifically cited, religious teaching in the state schools, the abolition, apparently, of the right of divorce, diplomatic relations to be established between San Juan and the Vatican City, and official control of "pornographic" literature. Under such a program an independent Puerto Rico could easily decline into the condition of a tropical Irish Free State. It is worth noting that the American Catholic influence in the island has been that of the Irish-American element, probably the most illiberal section of the American Catholic Church.

28. Commonwealth Government of Puerto Rico, Civil Liberties Committee, *Informe Preliminar sobre el Derecho a la Educación y la Libertad Académica* (San Juan, mimeographed, 1958), pp. 38-39. But for the view of Puerto Rican Communist Party leaders on the place of their party in insular life see David M. Helfeld, with the assistance of Guillermo Bobonis, *Discrimination for Political Beliefs and Associations* (San Juan, Commonwealth Government of Puerto Rico, Civil Liberties Committee, mimeographed, December 29, 1958), Appendix 7, "Statement of the Communist Party of Puerto Rico," and Appendix 8, "Letter of J. Enamorado Cuesta, May 29, 1958."

29. *Universidad,* Organo del Estudiantado de la Universidad de Puerto Rico, March 12, 1959.

CHAPTER 21

1. Ramón de la Sagra, quoted in L. de Verteuil, *Trinidad* (London, Cassell, 2d. edition, 1884), p. 59.

2. The West Indian Conference, convened by the Dominica Taxpayers Reform Association, *Proceedings,* Dominica, British West Indies (Castries, St. Lucia, Voice Printery, October-November 1932), pp. 1-2.

3. Eric Williams, quoted in *The Trinidad Guardian* (Port of Spain), July 11, 1956.

4. Paul Blanshard, *Democracy and Empire in the Caribbean* (New York, Macmillan, 1947), p. 341. The various books on the Caribbean by an earlier American

publicist, Chester Lloyd Jones, reveal an equally powerful bias in favor of American interests in the region. See, for example, his *Caribbean Interests of the United States* (New York, Appleton, 1916), Chapter 21.

5. Leopold Senghor, Constituent Congress of the Parti Fédération Africaine, *Report on the Principles and Programme of the Party* (Paris, Présence Africaine), p. 67.

6. Len S. Nembhard, *Trials and Triumphs of Marcus Garvey* (Kingston, Jamaica, The Gleaner Company, 1940), p. 118. The growth of an anti-white, anti-European Caribbean literature of *negrismo integral* is fully described in G.R. Coulthard, *Raza y Color en la Literatura Antillana* (Sevilla, Escuela de Estudios Hispano-Americanos, 1958).

7. Robert Smith, *The United States and Cuba: Business and Diplomacy, 1917-1960* (New York, Bookman Associates, 1961).

8. Quoted in Carleton Beals, *The Crime of Cuba* (Philadelphia, Lippincott, 1933), p. 405.

9. Ramón Ramírez Gomez, in *Investigación Económica,* Organo de la Escuela Nacional Autónoma de Mexico (Mexico, July 1961); report of George Lafaurie in *L'Express* (Paris), September 20, 1962, reprinted in English in *The Militant* (New York, Socialist Workers Party), October 8, 1962.

10. Juan Mari Bras, in Movimiento Pro-Independencia, *Carta Semanal* (September 28, October 5, 1962). For a Marxist critique of this position on Cuba and socialism see Manuel Bruckman, "From Independence to National Liberation: Puerto Rican Nationalism Today," *Marxist Leninist Quarterly* (December 1962).

11. United States Senate, Committee on Foreign Relations, *Hearing . . . Caribbean Organization,* 87th Congress, 1st Session (Washington, U.S. Government Printing Office, 1961).

12. Luis Muñoz Marín, The Godkin Lectures, *Breakthrough from Nationalism: A Small Island Looks at a Big Trouble* (San Juan, mimeographed, April 1959).

13. Jorge Quintana, "Proyectos Emancipadores," *El Mundo,* April 21, 1962. It should be noted that as one result of the Cuban Revolution and the counter-revolutionary response the old Caribbean art of the filibuster has come in for a vigorous revival. The Caribbean progressive movements have sought to meet the danger by supporting a growing demand for the denuclearization of the area as part of the general denuclearization of Latin America. This of course would entail the dismantling of the nuclear aspects of American naval and military installations in Puerto Rico. See Movimiento Pro-Independencia, *Carta Semanal,* November 8, 23, 1962; and René Marqués, "Carta a Gobernador Muñoz Marín sobre Desnuclearización de America Latina," *Claridad* (December 1962).

CHAPTER 22

1. Arturo Morales-Carrión, "What Is a Puerto Rican?" speech delivered to New York Instituto de Puerto Rico at Columbia University, reprinted in *The Island Times,* November 24, 1961.

2. Alpheus H. Snow, *The Administration of Dependencies* (New York and London, Putnam, 1902), pp. 528-529.

3. House of Representatives, Committee on Armed Services, *Hearings,* 86th Congress, 1st Session (Washington, U.S. Government Printing Office, March 2, 1959), p. 1109. See also report of the rough treatment meted out to Puerto Rican sugar industry representatives by the Agriculture Committee of the House of Representatives in *El Imparcial,* June 12, 1962. The hostile reception of Governor Muñoz Marín by the Republican members of the May 1963 hearings of the Territories Subcommittee of the House of Representatives is also symptomatic of the precarious hold that

Puerto Rico has on the Congress; see report of the transcript of the testimony in *San Juan Star,* May 17, 18, 1963. There are interesting accounts of the Puerto Rican lobbying struggle of the earlier pre-war period in the memoirs of the then Puerto Rican Resident Commissioner in Washington, Bolívar Pagán, *Crónicas de Washington* (San Juan, Biblioteca de Autores Puertorriqueños, 1949), especially pp. 61-77.

4. Luther H. Evans, *The Virgin Islands: From Naval Base to New Deal* (Ann Arbor, Michigan, J. W. Edwards, 1945), p. 316.

5. Trina Rivera de Ríos, "Yo me Quito el Sombrero antes los Puertorriqueños de Nueva York," *El Imparcial,* July 25, 1959.

6. *El Mundo,* December 24, 1958.

7. John Bennett, *The Puerto Rican Intellectuals* (Rio Piedras, mimeographed, 1961), p. 11.

8. René Marqués, "El Puertorriqueño Dócil," *Cuadernos Americanos* (Mexico, January-February 1962).

9. Eugenio María de Hostos, "Influencia de la Sociología en la Dirección Política de Nuevas Sociedades," in Luis Villalba Villalba, ed., *El Primer Instituto Venezolano de Ciencias Sociales* (Caracas, Asociación Venezolana de Sociología, 1961).

10. Quoted by Juan B. Huyke, "Un Discurso de Hace 30 Años," *El Mundo: Suplemento Sabatino,* August 29, 1959.

11. René Marqués, "Reply to Alfred Kazin," *San Juan Star,* March 8, 1960.

12. Earl S. Garver and Ernest B. Fincher, *Puerto Rico: Unsolved Problem* (Elgin, Illinois, Brethren Publishing House, 1945), p. 104. A later American liberal writer supported the recommendation of a possible Puerto Rican-United States treaty that would contain favorable economic and trade provisions enabling an independent Puerto Rico to pass through a transition period of adjustment. Clarence Senior, *Self-Determination for Puerto Rico* (New York, Post War World Council, 1946), pp. 26-27.

13. Adam Smith, *The Wealth of Nations* (London, Everyman Library edition, 1917), Book IV, Chapter 7, Part iii.

14. Aimé Césaire, quoted in Daniel Guérin, *Les Antilles Décolonisées* (Paris, Présence Africaine, 1956), p. 155.

15. Carlos Sentis, *Tragedia Política en el Caribe: Puerto Rico o Puerto Pobre?* (Madrid, Colección ABC, 1951), p. 96.

16. *El Mundo: Suplemento Sabatino,* February 17, 1962.

17. Juan Bautista Alberdi, *Bases y Puntos de Partida para la Organización de la Confederación Argentina* (1812), quoted in William R. Crawford, *A Century of Latin American Thought* (Cambridge, Harvard University Press, 1944), p. 22.

18. Estanislau Fischlowitz, "Exodo Rural en Latinoamérica en 1960," *Combate* (San José, Costa Rica, April-May 1961). For the general political condition of Latin America as a whole, see Mario Monteforte Toledo, *Partidos Políticos de Ibero-américa* (Universidad Nacional Autónoma de Mexico, Instituto de Investigaciones Sociales, 1961). For the general social condition of Latin America as a whole, see Centro Latino Americano de Pesquisas Em Ciencias Sociais, *Situacao Social da America* (Rio de Janeiro, December 1961); Orlando Fals Borda, *La Transformación de la America Latina y sus Implicaciones Sociales y Económicas* (Bogota, Universidad Nacional de Colombia, 1961); and Ediciones Combate, *Latinoamérica mas allá de sus Fronteras* (San José, Costa Rica, 1960).

19. Earl Parker Hanson, in *The Island Times,* February 9, 1962.

20. Eric Williams, *The History of Chaguaramas* (Port of Spain, Trinidad, PNM Publishing Company, N.D.); and *The Trinidad Guardian* (Port of Spain), June 29, 1958.

21. Guillermo Toriello, *La Batalla de Guatemala* (Buenos Aires, Ediciones Pueblos de América, 1956).

22. *New York Times,* January 2, 3, 1962.

23. New York *Daily News,* November 18, 1959, quoted in *San Juan Star,* November 19, 1959.

24. Secretary of Justice Hiram R. Cancio, speech delivered before Navy League Convention, San Juan (San Juan, mimeographed, November 6, 1959).

25. "Cartas Cruzadas entre los Estudiantes Chilenos y el Presidente Eisenhower," *Combate* (San José, Costa Rica, July-August 1960), pp. 58-69.

26. *El Imparcial,* February 17, 1962.

27. Enrique Obregón, quoted by Halcro Ferguson in *Public Opinion* (Kingston, Jamaica), September 12, 1959.

28. Luis Muñoz Rivera, *Obras Completas* (Madrid, Ediciones Puerto Rico, 1920), 3 vols., Vol. 1, p. 143.

CHAPTER 23

1. Jacques Stern, *The French Colonies Past and Present* (New York, Didier, 1944); and A. D. Hall, *Porto Rico: Its History, Products and Possibilities* (New York, Street & Smith, 1898), p. 26.

2. Reginald Clyne, in *The Torchlight* (St. Georges, Grenada, British West Indies), January 25, 1957.

3. Wenzell Brown, *Dynamite on Our Doorstep* (New York, Greenberg, 1945), p. 221.

4. Amy Jacques-Garvey, ed., *Philosophy and Opinions of Marcus Garvey* (New York, Universal Publishing House, 1926), 2 vols., Vol. 2, p. 107.

5. Baron de Vastey, *Le Système Colonial Dévoilé* (Cap Henri, Haiti, 1814); *Réflexions sur une Lettre de Mazères, Ex-Colon Français, sur les Noirs et les Blancs, la Civilisation de l'Afrique et le Royaume d'Haiti* (Cap Henri, 1816); and *Réflexions Politiques sur Quelques Ouvrages et Journaux Français Concernant Haiti* (Imprimerie Royale à Sans Souci, Haiti, 1817).

6. Faustin Wilkins and Tanay Dudley, *The White King of La Gonave* (New York, Doubleday Doran, 1931).

7. Luis Muñoz Rivera, in *La Democracia* (San Juan), October 28, 1911.

8. Quoted in Trumbull White, *Porto Rico and Its People* (New York, Stokes, 1938), p. 374.

9. Joseph Schumpeter, *History of Economic Analysis* (New York, Oxford University Press, 1955), p. 440.

10. Quoted in *The Torchlight* (St. Georges, Grenada), March 20, 1957.

11. For all this, see Government of Trinidad and Tobago, Office of the Premier, *European Integration and West Indian Trade* (Port of Spain, 1960); Political and Economic Planning, *Commonwealth Preference in the United Kingdom* (London, 1960); and The West India Committee, London, *Britain in ECM: How It May Affect the West Indies,* reprinted in *Daily Gleaner* (Kingston, Jamaica), February 11, 1962.

12. For criticism of "Operation Bootstrap" from the radical nationalist viewpoint, see Paquita Pesquera de Mari in *El Mundo,* July 19, 1961; and Movimiento Pro-Independencia, *La Hora de la Independencia: Tésis Política MPI* (San Juan, Movimiento Pro-Independencia, 1963), pp. 16-23.

13. William H. Stead, *Fomento: The Economic Development of Puerto Rico* (Washington, National Planning Association, Public Pamphlet 103, 1958), pp. 101-103; and Werner Baer, *The Puerto Rican Economy and United States Economic Fluctuations* (Rio Piedras, University of Puerto Rico, Social Sciences Research Center, 1962), pp. 148-149.

14. United Nations, General Assembly, 8th Session, A/PV. 459, November 27, 1953, pp. 1193-1194.

15. Juan Antonio Corretjer, *La Lucha por la Independencia de Puerto Rico* (San Juan, Unión del Pueblo Pro-Constituyente, 1949), p. 101. Corretjer has written extensively on the general theme of Pan-Antillean unity and federation. See his *Futuro Sin Falla: Mito Realidad Antillana* (Guaynabo, Cooperativa de Artes Gráficas Romualdo Real, 1963).

16. Quoted in Eric Williams, *History of the People of Trinidad and Tobago* (Port of Spain, PNM Publishing Company, 1962), p. 111.

17. *Globe and Mail*, Toronto, May 7, 1958, quoted in *Public Opinion* (Kingston, Jamaica), May 24, 1958.

18. Arthur James, *Thirty Years in Porto Rico* (San Juan, Porto Rico Progress, 1927), p. 20.

19. Alfred Kazin, "In Puerto Rico," *Commentary* (February 1960); see also correspondence, "Kazin and His Critics," *Commentary* (May 1960).

20. Aimé Césaire, *Lettre à Maurice Thorez* (Paris, Présence Africaine, 1956), pp. 12-13.

21. *El Mundo*, February 12, 1962.

22. Charles Kingsley, *At Last: A Christmas in the West Indies* (London, Macmillan, 1887), p. 308.

23. Department of the Interior, *Report of the Commissioner of Education for Porto Rico, 1904*, in *Annual Report of the Department, 1904* (Washington, U.S. Government Printing Office, 1904), pp. 444-445.

CHAPTER 24

1. Report of Administración de Fomento Económico, quoted in *El Mundo*, April 6, 1962.

2. See, for example, Report of Puerto Rican Association of University Professors, *Memorial a la Legislatura de Puerto Rico*, in *El Mundo*, May 11, 1962.

3. Pedro Hernández hijo in *El Mundo*, March 27, 1962, especially the remarks of the Director of the Office of Public Assistance in the Department of Public Welfare. The welfare of entire communities can be shattered by the sale of industries to foreign investors. See, for example, the social and economic consequences of the sale and closure of the Plazuela sugar mill in the Barceloneta district, *San Juan Star*, July 4, 1963. The general burden upon the insular government's public welfare programs can be gauged from the attempt in 1962 to obtain federal recognition of the entire island economy as a high unemployment area eligible for federal relief funds.

4. *The Island Times*, October 5, 12, 1962.

5. Luis Santullano, *Mirada al Caribe: Fricción de Culturas en Puerto Rico*, in *Jornadas 54* (Mexico, El Colegio de Mexico, 1945), p. 58.

6. Sir George Cornewall Lewis, *On the Government of Dependencies* (1841), reprinted C.P. Lucas, ed. (London, Oxford University Press, 1891), p. 306-307.

7. Enrique Laguerre, *Pulso de Puerto Rico* (San Juan, Biblioteca de Autores Puertorriqueños, 1954), p. 71.

8. Gilbert Chinard, *L'Amérique et le Rêve Exotique dans la Littérature Française au xviie et au xviiie Siècles* (Paris, E. Droz, 1934); and Geoffrey Atkinson, *Les Relations de Voyages du xviie Siècle et l'Evolution des Idées* (Paris, Librairie Ancienne Edouard Champion, N.D.).

9. Reginald Clyne, in *The Torchlight* (St. Georges, Grenada, British West Indies), October 25, 1957.

Index

NOTE: This index does not cover the Notes, nor does it include some names and titles to which the text makes only passing reference.